Solutions Manual for

Advanced Mathematics

An Incremental Development

John H. Saxon, Jr.

SAXON PUBLISHERS, INC.
Norman, Oklahoma

Advanced Mathematics
An Incremental Development
Solutions Manual

Printed in the United States of America

ISBN: 0-939798-57-3

Second Printing: October 1992

This manual contains solutions to every problem in the 1989 edition of *Advanced Mathematics, An Incremental Development* by Saxon. Early solutions of a problem of a particular type contain every step. Later solutions omit steps considered unnecessary.

With appreciation to Diana Stolfus who provided the initial manuscript. We also thank David Pond, Chad Threet, John Chitwood, and Scott Kirby for typing this manual, creating art and the many revisions which went into it. We thank Joan Coleman for overseeing the production of the manual.

Saxon Publishers, Inc.
1320 W. Lindsey, Suite 100
Norman, OK 73069

REVIEW LESSON A

1. $\dfrac{6 + \frac{3}{4}}{2 - \frac{5}{4}} = \dfrac{\frac{27}{4}}{\frac{3}{4}} = \dfrac{27}{4} \cdot \dfrac{4}{3} = 9$

which equals 3^2; therefore C

2. $\dfrac{x + y}{y} = \dfrac{x}{y} + \dfrac{y}{y} = \dfrac{x}{y} + 1$; therefore C

3. $\sqrt{\dfrac{1}{4}} + \sqrt{\dfrac{1}{25}} = \dfrac{1}{2} + \dfrac{1}{5}$

$\dfrac{5}{10} + \dfrac{2}{10} = \dfrac{7}{10}$

$\sqrt{\dfrac{1}{4} + \dfrac{1}{25}} = \sqrt{\dfrac{25}{100} + \dfrac{4}{100}}$

$\sqrt{\dfrac{29}{100}} \approx \dfrac{\mathbf{5.4}}{\mathbf{10}}$

Therefore A

4. Since $x < 0$ and $y < 0$, x and y are both negative; therefore $x + y < x - y$.
B

5. $\dfrac{80}{100} = \dfrac{1420}{M}$

$4M = 5(1420)$

$M = \dfrac{5(1420)}{4} = \mathbf{1775\ grams}$

6. $P = 17, O = 2, T = 342$

$\dfrac{O}{P + O} = \dfrac{O}{T}$

$\dfrac{2}{17 + 2} = \dfrac{O}{342}$

$\dfrac{2}{19} = \dfrac{O}{342}$

$19(O) = 2(342)$

$O = \dfrac{2(342)}{19} = \mathbf{36}$

7. $\dfrac{4}{7} + \dfrac{3}{x + 3} = \dfrac{5}{3}$

$x \neq -3$

Multiply by $21(x + 3)$

$3(x + 3)(4) + 7(3)(3) = 7(x + 3)(5)$

$12x + 36 + 63 = 35x + 105$

$-6 = 23x$

$x = -\dfrac{\mathbf{6}}{\mathbf{23}}$

8. $\dfrac{5}{3} - \dfrac{2}{x - 4} = \dfrac{1}{2}$

$x \neq 4$

Multiply by $6(x - 4)$

$2(x - 4)(5) - 3(2)(2) = 3(x - 4)$

$10x - 40 - 12 = 3x - 12$

$10x - 52 = 3x - 12$

$7x = 40$

$x = \dfrac{\mathbf{40}}{\mathbf{7}}$

9. $\dfrac{1}{x - 7} + \dfrac{1}{4} = \dfrac{1}{3}$

$x \neq 7$

Multiply by $12(x - 7)$

$12 + (x - 7)3 = 4(x - 7)$

$12 + 3x - 21 = 4x - 28$

$3x - 9 = 4x - 28$

$-9 + 28 = 4x - 3x$

$x = \mathbf{19}$

10. $\dfrac{3}{7}x + \dfrac{2}{5}y = 11$

$0.03x - 0.2y = -0.37$

$15x + 14y = 385$

$3x - 20y = -37$

$\begin{array}{r} 15x + 14y = 385 \\ (-)\ 15x - 100y = -185 \\ \hline 114y = 570 \\ y = 5 \end{array}$

$3x - 20(5) = -37$

$3x = 63$

$x = 21$

(21, 5)

11. $\dfrac{2}{3}x + \dfrac{3}{5}y = 12$

$0.1x + 0.02y = 1.1$

$\begin{array}{r} 10x + 9y = 180 \\ (-)\ 10x + 2y = 110 \\ \hline 7y = 70 \\ y = 10 \end{array}$

$10x + 20 = 10$

$10x = 90$

$x = 9$

(9, 10)

12. $\sqrt[3]{x-5}-1=2$

$\sqrt[3]{x-5}=3$

$x-5=27$

$x=\mathbf{32}$

13. $\sqrt{s-27}+\sqrt{s}=9$

$\sqrt{s-27}=9-\sqrt{s}$

$s-27=81-18\sqrt{s}+s$

$18\sqrt{s}=108$

$\sqrt{s}=6$

$s=\mathbf{36}$

14. $\sqrt{s-7}+\sqrt{s}=7$

$\sqrt{s-7}=7-\sqrt{s}$

$s-7=49-14\sqrt{s}+s$

$14\sqrt{s}=56$

$\sqrt{s}=4$

$s=\mathbf{16}$

15.
$$\begin{array}{r} 2x+2y-z=9 \\ (+)\,3x+3y+z=16 \\ \hline 5x+5y\phantom{{}+z}=25 \end{array}$$

$$\begin{array}{r} x+y=5 \\ (-)\,x-2y=-1 \\ \hline 3y=6 \\ y=2 \end{array}$$

$x+2=5$

$x=3$

$2(3)+2(2)-z=9$

$z=1$

$(\mathbf{3,2,1})$

16. A: $x-2y+z=-2$

B: $2x-2y-z=-3$

C: $x+y-2z=1$

$$\begin{array}{r} 2A+C:\;3x-3y=-3 \\ 2B-C:\;3x-5y=-7 \\ \hline 2y=4 \\ y=2 \end{array}$$

$x-y=-1$

$x-2=-1$

$x=1$

$1+2-2z=1$

$z=1$

$(\mathbf{1,2,1})$

17. A: $2x-y+z=0$

B: $4x+2y+z=2$

C: $2x-y-2z=-4$

$$\begin{array}{r} \tfrac{1}{2}(A+C):\;2x-y=-2 \\ B+C:\;6x+y=-2 \\ \hline 8x\phantom{{}+y}=-4 \\ x\phantom{{}+y}=-\tfrac{1}{2} \end{array}$$

$2\left(-\tfrac{1}{2}\right)-y=-2$

$-1-y=-2$

$y=1$

$2\left(-\tfrac{1}{2}\right)-1-2z=-2$

$z=2$

$\left(-\dfrac{1}{2},1,2\right)$

18. A: $2x+3y=-1$

B: $x-2z=-3$

C: $2y-z=-4$

$$\begin{array}{r} A-2B:\;3y+4z=5 \\ 4C:\;8y-4z=-16 \\ \hline 11y\phantom{{}+4z}=-11 \\ y\phantom{{}+4z}=-1 \end{array}$$

$2(-1)-z=-4$

$z=2$

$x-2(2)=-3$

$x=1$

$(\mathbf{1,-1,2})$

19. $\dfrac{x}{2}+\dfrac{y}{4}=2$ multiply by 8

$x-\dfrac{z}{3}=1$ multiply by 3

$\dfrac{y}{2}+z=5$ multiply by 2

A: $2x+y=8$

B: $3x-z=3$

C: $y+2z=10$

$3(2)-z=3$

$z=3$

$y+2(3)=10$

$y=4$

$(\mathbf{2,4,3})$

20. A: $x - y = 1$
B: $y - 2z = 1$
C: $3x - 4z = 7$

$$2(A + B):\ 2x - 4z = 4$$
$$C:\ 3x - 4z = 7$$
$$\overline{}$$
$$-x \quad\ = -3$$
$$x \quad\ = 3$$

$1 - y = 1$
$y = 2$
$2 - 2z = 1$
$z = 3$

$$\left(3, 2, \frac{1}{2}\right)$$

21. $\sqrt{x^3 y^2}\ \sqrt[4]{xy^3} = x^{3/2} y x^{1/4} y^{3/4}$
$= x^{6/4} y x^{1/4} y^{3/4} = x^{7/4} y^{7/4}$

22. $x^{3/4} x^{1/2} y^{1/2} x^{1/2} x^{4/3}$
$= x^{9/12} x^{6/12} y^{1/2} x^{6/12} x^{16/12} = x^{37/12} y^{1/2}$

23. $a^{x/2} y^{1-x/2} a^{-4x} y^{2x}$
$= a^{x/2} a^{-8x/2} y^{1-x/2} y^{4x/2}$
$= a^{-7x/2} y^{1+3x/2}$

24. $y^{x+3} y^{x/2-1} z^a y^{-x/2+a/2} z^{-x/3+a/3}$
$= y^{x+2+a/2} z^{4a/3-x/3}$

25. $\dfrac{2\sqrt{3}}{\sqrt{2}} - \dfrac{3\sqrt{2}}{\sqrt{3}} + 4\sqrt{6}$
$= \sqrt{6} - \sqrt{6} + 4\sqrt{6} = 4\sqrt{6}$

26. $\dfrac{2\sqrt{7}}{\sqrt{3}} - \dfrac{\sqrt{3}}{\sqrt{7}} - 4\sqrt{21}$

$= \dfrac{2\sqrt{21}}{3} - \dfrac{\sqrt{21}}{7} - 4\sqrt{21}$

$= \dfrac{14\sqrt{21}}{21} - \dfrac{3\sqrt{21}}{21} - \dfrac{84\sqrt{21}}{21}$

$= \dfrac{-73\sqrt{21}}{21}$

27. $\left(\sqrt{2} - \sqrt{x}\right)\left(1 - \sqrt{x}\right)$
$= \sqrt{2} - \sqrt{2x} - \sqrt{x} + x$
$= \sqrt{2} - \sqrt{x}\left(\sqrt{2} + 1\right) + x$

28. $\left(\sqrt{3} + \sqrt{x}\right)\left(\sqrt{3} + \sqrt{x}\right)$
$= 3 + \sqrt{3x} + \sqrt{3x} + x$
$= 3 + 2\sqrt{3x} + x$

29. $\sqrt{2x}\left(\sqrt{3x} + \sqrt{x}\right) = x\sqrt{6} + x\sqrt{2}$
$= x\left(\sqrt{6} + \sqrt{2}\right)$

30. $\dfrac{x^{-2} + y^{-2}}{(xy)^{-1}} \cdot \dfrac{\dfrac{1}{x^2} + \dfrac{1}{y^2}}{\dfrac{1}{xy}}$

$= \dfrac{\dfrac{y^2 + x^2}{x^2 y^2}}{\dfrac{1}{xy}} = \dfrac{y^2 + x^2}{x^2 y^2} \cdot \dfrac{xy}{1}$

$= \dfrac{x^2 + y^2}{xy}$

REVIEW LESSON B

1. $\dfrac{60}{100} = \dfrac{1800}{A}$
$3A = 5(1800)$
$A = 3000$
$\underline{\ -\ 1800\ }$
1200

2. $B = 2, D = 5,\ A = 7$
$\dfrac{D}{A} = \dfrac{D}{A}$
$\dfrac{5}{7} = \dfrac{85}{A}$
$5A = 7(85)$
$A = 119$

3. $3i^4 + 2i^5 + 3i^3 + 2i^2$
$= 3 + 2i - 3i - 2 = 1 - i$

4. $\sqrt{-3}\ \sqrt{4} + 3\sqrt{-2}\ \sqrt{-9} + \sqrt{-16}\ \sqrt{-16}$
$= 2i\sqrt{3} - 9\sqrt{2} + 4i + 4$
$= 4 - 9\sqrt{2} + 4i + 2\sqrt{3}\,i$
$= \left(4 - 9\sqrt{2}\right) + \left(4 + 2\sqrt{3}\right)i$

5. $2i^3 + 3i^2 + 2i - 2\sqrt{2}i$
$= -2i - 3 + 2i - 2\sqrt{2}\,i = -3 - 2\sqrt{2}\,i$

6. $2\sqrt{-2}\sqrt{2} + 3i\sqrt{2} - \sqrt{-2}\sqrt{2}$

$= 4i + 3\sqrt{2}\,i - 2i = 2i + 3\sqrt{2}\,i$

$= \left(2 + 3\sqrt{2}\,i\right)$

7. $\dfrac{2 + i - 2i^3}{2i^3 + 4} = \dfrac{2 + i + 2i}{-2i + 4}$

$= \dfrac{2 + 3i}{4 - 2i}$

$= \dfrac{(2 + 3i)(4 + 2i)}{(4 - 2i)(4 + 2i)}$

$= \dfrac{8 + 16i - 6}{16 + 4}$

$= \dfrac{2 + 16i}{20} = \dfrac{1}{10} + \dfrac{4}{5}\,i$

8. $\left(\dfrac{4 + \sqrt{3}}{2 - 3\sqrt{3}}\right)\left(\dfrac{2 + 3\sqrt{3}}{2 + 3\sqrt{3}}\right)$

$= \dfrac{8 + 14\sqrt{3} + 9}{4 - 27}$

$= \dfrac{17 + 14\sqrt{3}}{-23}$

9. $\dfrac{3 - i^2 + 2i^5 - 2}{2i^3 + 3i}$

$= \dfrac{3 + 1 + 2i - 2}{2i + 3i}$

$= \left(\dfrac{2 + 2i}{5i}\right)\dfrac{5i}{5i}$

$= \dfrac{10i - 10}{-25} = \dfrac{5(-2 + 2i)}{25}$

$= \dfrac{-2 + 2i}{-5} = \dfrac{2}{5} - \dfrac{2}{5}\,i$

10. $x + 3x^2 = -5$

$3x^2 + x + 5 = 0$

$x^2 + \dfrac{1}{3}x + \dfrac{5}{3} = 0$

$x^2 + \dfrac{1}{3}x = -\dfrac{5}{3}$

$x^2 + \dfrac{1}{3}x + \dfrac{1}{36} = -\dfrac{5}{3} + \dfrac{1}{36}$

$\left(x + \dfrac{1}{6}\right)^2 = -\dfrac{59}{36}$

$x + \dfrac{1}{6} = \pm\sqrt{-\dfrac{59}{36}}$

$x = -\dfrac{1}{6} \pm \dfrac{\sqrt{59}}{6}\,i$

11. $-2x - 2x^2 = 5$

$2x^2 + 2x + 5 = 0$

$x^2 + x + \dfrac{5}{2} = 0$

$x^2 + x = -\dfrac{5}{2}$

$x^2 + x + \dfrac{1}{4} = -\dfrac{5}{2} + \dfrac{1}{4}$

$\left(x + \dfrac{1}{2}\right)^2 = -\dfrac{9}{4}$

$x + \dfrac{1}{2} = \pm\sqrt{-\dfrac{9}{4}}$

$x = -\dfrac{1}{2} \pm \dfrac{3}{2}\,i$

12. $ax^2 + bx + c = 0$

$x^2 + \dfrac{b}{a}x + \dfrac{c}{a} = 0$

$x^2 + \dfrac{b}{a}x = -\dfrac{c}{a}$

$x^2 + \dfrac{b}{a}x + \dfrac{b^2}{4a^2} = \dfrac{b^2}{4a^2} - \dfrac{c}{a}$

$\left(x + \dfrac{b}{2a}\right)^2 = \dfrac{b^2 - 4ac}{4a^2}$

$x + \dfrac{b}{2a} = \pm\sqrt{\dfrac{b^2 - 4ac}{4a^2}}$

$x = -\dfrac{b}{2a} \pm \dfrac{\sqrt{b^2 - 4ac}}{2a}$

$x = \dfrac{-b \pm \sqrt{b^2 - 4ac}}{2a}$

13. $3x^2 + 2x + 5 = 0$

$x = \dfrac{-2 \pm \sqrt{4 - 4(3)(5)}}{6}$

$x = \dfrac{-2 \pm \sqrt{4 - 60}}{6}$

$x = \dfrac{-2 \pm \sqrt{-56}}{6}$

$x = -\dfrac{1}{3} \pm \dfrac{\sqrt{14}}{3}\,i$

14. $-x = -3x^2 + 4$

$3x^2 - x - 4 = 0$

$x = \dfrac{1 \pm \sqrt{1 - 4(3)(-4)}}{6}$

$x = \dfrac{1 \pm \sqrt{1 + 48}}{6} = \dfrac{1 \pm \sqrt{49}}{6}$

$x = \dfrac{1 \pm 7}{6} = \dfrac{4}{3}, -1$

15. $-3x = 2x^2 + 7$

$2x^2 + 3x + 7 = 0$

$x = \dfrac{-3 \pm \sqrt{9 - 4(2)(7)}}{4}$

$x = \dfrac{-3 \pm \sqrt{9 - 56}}{4}$

$x = \dfrac{-3 \pm \sqrt{-47}}{4}$

$x = -\dfrac{3}{4} \pm \dfrac{\sqrt{47}}{4}i$

16. $2y(x + z) = 2y(z)$ since $x = 0$; and since y and z are both positive $2yz$ must be positive. $x(y + z) = 0$ since $x = 0$; therefore **A**.

17. $2A - 18B = 2(3) - 18\left(\dfrac{1}{6}\right) = 6 - 3 = 3$

$3A - 36B = 3(3) - 36\left(\dfrac{1}{6}\right) = 9 - 6 = 3$

Therefore **C**

18. $\dfrac{2}{x + 4} - \dfrac{1}{5} = \dfrac{2}{3}$

Multiply by $15(x + 4)$

$2(15) - 3(x + 4) = 2(5)(x + 4)$

$30 - 3x - 12 = 10x + 40$

$-3x + 18 = 10x + 40$

$-22 = 13x$

$x = -\dfrac{22}{13}$

19. $\dfrac{2}{3}x - \dfrac{4}{5}y = 0$

$0.02x - 0.1y = -0.76$

$5x - 6y = 0$

$x - 5y = -38$

$$
\begin{array}{r}
5x - 6y = 0 \\
(-)\,5x - 25y = -190 \\
\hline
19y = 190 \\
y = 10
\end{array}
$$

$x - 5(10) = -38$

$x = -38 + 50 = 12$

(12, 10)

20. $\sqrt{2s - 7} + \sqrt{25} = 7$

$\sqrt{2s - 7} = 7 - \sqrt{25}$

$2s - 7 = 4$

$2s = 11$

$s = \dfrac{11}{2}$

21. A: $x + 2y - z = 9$

B: $x + 3y = 9$

C: $2x - z = 8$

$$
\begin{array}{rr}
A - C: & -x + 2y = 1 \\
B: & x + 3y = 9 \\
\hline
& 5y = 10 \\
& y = 2
\end{array}
$$

$x + 3(2) = 9$

$x = 9 - 6 = 3$

$2(3) - z = 8$

$z = 6 - 8 = -2$

(3, 2, –2)

22. A: $x - y + 2z = 7$

B: $2x + y - z = 0$

C: $x + 2y + z = 9$

$$
\begin{array}{rr}
A + B: & 3x + z = 7 \\
2A + C: (-)\, & 3x + 5z = 23 \\
\hline
& -4z = -16 \\
& z = 4
\end{array}
$$

$3x + 4 = 7$

$x = 1$

$2(1) + y - 4 = 0$

$y = -2 + 4 = 2$

(1, 2, 4)

23. $\dfrac{x}{2} - \dfrac{y}{3} = \dfrac{5}{6}$

$\dfrac{2}{3}x + \dfrac{z}{5} = \dfrac{11}{5}$

$0.1y + 0.02z = 0.22$

A: $3x - 2y = 5$

B: $10x + 3z = 33$

C: $10y + 2z = 22$

$$
\begin{array}{rr}
3(5A + C): & 45x + 6z = 141 \\
2B: (-)\, & 20x + 6z = 66 \\
\hline
& 25x = 75 \\
& x = 3
\end{array}
$$

$3(3) - 2y = 5$

$y = 2$

$10(2) + 2z = 22$

$z = 1$

(3, 2, 1)

24. A: $x + y - z = 2$
B: $2x - y + z = 4$
C: $3x + 2y - z = 5$

$(A + B)$: $3x \quad = 6$
$B + C$: $5x + y = 9$

$x = \dfrac{6}{3} = 2$

$5(2) + y = 9$
$y = -1$
$2 + (-1) - z = 2$
$z = 2 - 2 + 1 = 1$
$(2, -1, 1)$

25. $x^{2/3}x^{2/3}yx^{2/5}y^{1/5}$
$= x^{10/15}x^{10/15}yx^{6/15}y^{1/5} = x^{26/15}y^{6/5}$

26. $y^{x/2+1}y^{a/2}2y^{2a+3} = 2y^{5a/2+x/2+4}$

27. $\dfrac{2\sqrt{3}}{\sqrt{2}} - \dfrac{4\sqrt{2}}{\sqrt{3}} + 3\sqrt{24}$

$= \dfrac{2\sqrt{6}}{2} - \dfrac{4\sqrt{6}}{3} + 6\sqrt{6}$

$= 7\sqrt{6} - \dfrac{4\sqrt{6}}{3} = \dfrac{17\sqrt{6}}{3}$

28. $\left(\sqrt{2} + \sqrt{x}\right)\left(\sqrt{2} + \sqrt{x}\right)$
$= 2 + 2\sqrt{2x} + x$

29. $(x^{1/2} + y^{1/2})^2 = x + 2x^{1/2}y^{1/2} + y$

30. $\dfrac{a^{-2} + b^{-1}}{a^{-1}b} = \dfrac{\dfrac{1}{a^2} + \dfrac{1}{b}}{\dfrac{b}{a}} = \dfrac{\dfrac{b + a^2}{a^2b}}{\dfrac{b}{a}}$

$= \dfrac{b + a^2}{a^2b} \cdot \dfrac{a}{b} = \dfrac{b + a^2}{ab^2}$

REVIEW LESSON C

1. $\dfrac{N_G}{N_B} = \dfrac{2}{5}$
$5N_G = 2N_B$
$N_B - 40 = 2N_G$

$N_B = 2N_G + 40$
$5N_G = 2(2N_G + 40)$

$5N_G = 4N_G + 80$
$N_G = \mathbf{80}$
$N_B = \mathbf{200}$

2. $0.1R + 0.2B = 24$
$3R - 20 = B$

$R + 2B = 240$
$R + 2(3R - 20) = 240$
$7R - 40 = 240$
$7R = 280$
$R = \mathbf{40}$
$B = 120 - 20 = \mathbf{100}$

3.
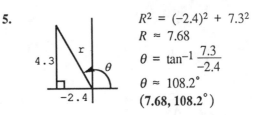

$\cos 62° = \dfrac{5000}{s}$

$0.4695 \approx \dfrac{5000}{s}$

$s \approx \mathbf{10{,}649.6\ ft}$

4. $R^2 = 3.06^2 + (-2.75)^2$
$R \approx 4.11$
$\theta = \tan^{-1}\dfrac{-2.75}{3.06}$
$\theta \approx -41.95°$
$\mathbf{(4.11, 318.05°)}$

5. $R^2 = (-2.4)^2 + 7.3^2$
$R \approx 7.68$
$\theta = \tan^{-1}\dfrac{7.3}{-2.4}$
$\theta \approx 108.2°$
$\mathbf{(7.68, 108.2°)}$

6. $x = R\cos\theta$
$x = 0.75$
$y = R\sin\theta$
$y \approx 8.57$
$\mathbf{(0.75, 8.57)}$

7. $x = -5.93$
$y = -4.47$
$\mathbf{(-5.93, -4.47)}$

8. $\sqrt{-3}\sqrt{3} - \sqrt{2}\,i - \sqrt{-3}\sqrt{-2} - 2$
$= 3i - \sqrt{2}\,i + \sqrt{6} - 2$
$= \left(\sqrt{6} - 2\right) + \left(3 - \sqrt{2}\right)i$

9. $\left(\dfrac{2 + 2\sqrt{3}}{1 - \sqrt{3}}\right)\left(\dfrac{1 + \sqrt{3}}{1 + \sqrt{3}}\right)$

$= \dfrac{2 + 4\sqrt{3} + 6}{1 - 3} = \dfrac{8 + 4\sqrt{3}}{-2}$

$= \mathbf{-4 - 2\sqrt{3}}$

10. $\dfrac{2i^3 - 2i^2 - 1}{i^3 - 2i^4 + 2} = \dfrac{-2i + 2 - 1}{i - 2 + 2}$

$= \dfrac{1 - 2i}{-i}\left(\dfrac{-i}{-i}\right) = \dfrac{-i - 2}{-1} = \mathbf{2 + i}$

11. $\dfrac{3i + 2 - 2i^3}{2i - 3i^5 + 2} = \dfrac{3i + 2 + 2i}{2i - 3i + 2}$

$= \dfrac{2 + 5i}{2 - i}\left(\dfrac{2 + i}{2 + i}\right)$

$= \dfrac{4 + 12i - 5}{4 + 1}$

$= \dfrac{-1 + 12i}{5} = \mathbf{-\dfrac{1}{5} + \dfrac{12}{5}i}$

12. $2x^2 + x + 5 = 0$

$x^2 + \dfrac{1}{2}x + \dfrac{5}{2} = 0$

$x^2 + \dfrac{1}{2}x + \dfrac{1}{16} = \dfrac{1}{16} - \dfrac{5}{2}$

$\left(x + \dfrac{1}{4}\right)^2 = \dfrac{-39}{16}$

$x + \dfrac{1}{4} = \pm\sqrt{\dfrac{-39}{16}}$

$x = \mathbf{-\dfrac{1}{4} \pm \dfrac{\sqrt{39}}{4}i}$

13. $3x^2 - 2x - 7 = 0$

$x^2 - \dfrac{2}{3}x - \dfrac{7}{3} = 0$

$x^2 - \dfrac{2}{3}x + \dfrac{1}{9} = \dfrac{1}{9} + \dfrac{7}{3}$

$\left(x - \dfrac{1}{3}\right)^2 = \dfrac{22}{9}$

$x - \dfrac{1}{3} = \pm\sqrt{\dfrac{22}{9}}$

$x = \mathbf{\dfrac{1}{3} \pm \dfrac{\sqrt{22}}{3}}$

14. $ax^2 + bx + c = 0$

$x^2 + \dfrac{b}{a}x + \dfrac{c}{a} = 0$

$x^2 + \dfrac{b}{a}x = -\dfrac{c}{a}$

$x^2 + \dfrac{b}{a}x + \dfrac{b^2}{4a^2} = -\dfrac{b^2}{4a^2} - \dfrac{c}{a}$

$\left(x + \dfrac{b}{2a}\right)^2 = \dfrac{b^2 - 4ac}{4a^2}$

$x + \dfrac{b}{2a} = \pm\sqrt{\dfrac{b^2 - 4ac}{4a^2}}$

$x = -\dfrac{b}{2a} \pm \dfrac{\sqrt{b^2 - 4ac}}{2a}$

$x = \mathbf{\dfrac{-b \pm \sqrt{b^2 - 4ac}}{2a}}$

15. $2x^2 - x + 5 = 0$

$x = \dfrac{1 \pm \sqrt{1 - 4(2)(5)}}{4}$

$x = \dfrac{1 \pm \sqrt{-39}}{4}$

$x = \mathbf{\dfrac{1}{4} \pm \dfrac{39}{4}}$

16. $3x^2 + 2x + 4 = 0$

$x = \dfrac{-2 \pm \sqrt{4 - 4(3)(4)}}{6}$

$x = \dfrac{-2 \pm \sqrt{-44}}{6}$

$x = -\dfrac{1}{3} \pm \dfrac{2\sqrt{11}}{6}i$

$x = \mathbf{-\dfrac{1}{3} \pm \dfrac{\sqrt{11}}{3}i}$

17. Since $0 < y < 12$

$-2 < y - 2 < 10$

$0 < x < 10$; therefore **D**

18. If $x > y$ then $x - y$ is positive and $y - x$ is negative.

If $x < y$ then $x - y$ is negative and $y - x$ is positive.

If $x = y$ then $x - y = 0$ and $y - x = 0$.

D

19. $24x - 20y = 7$

$x + 10y = 3$

$\begin{aligned} 24x - 20y &= 7 \\ 2x + 20y &= 6 \\ \hline 26x \quad\quad &= 13 \\ x \quad\quad &= \dfrac{1}{2} \end{aligned}$

$\dfrac{1}{2} + 10y = 3$

$10y = \dfrac{5}{2}$

$y = \dfrac{1}{4}$ $\quad\quad \left(\dfrac{1}{2}, \dfrac{1}{4}\right)$

20. $\sqrt{3x-5} = 5 - \sqrt{3x}$

$3x - 5 = 25 - 10\sqrt{3x} + 3x$

$10\sqrt{3x} = 30$

$\sqrt{3x} = 3$

$3x = 9$

$x = 3$

21. A: $x + 2y + z = -1$
B: $x + z = 3$
C: $3x + y = 4$

A − B: $2y = -4$
   $y = -2$

$3x - 2 = 4$

$x = 2$

$2 + z = 3$

$z = 1$

$(2, -2, 1)$

22. A: $2x - y + z = 5$
B: $x + y - z = 4$
C: $-x + 2y + z = 5$

B + C: $3y = 9$
   $y = 3$
A + B: $3x = 9$
   $x = 3$

$3 + 3 - z = 4$

$-z = -2$

$z = 2$

$(3, 3, 2)$

23. A: $3x - 2y = 1$
B: $5x + 6z = 39$
C: $y + 2z = 12$

A + 2C: $9x + 4z = 25$
   C: $5x + 6z = 39$
   $9x + 12z = 75$
(−) $10x + 12z = 78$
   $-x = -3$
   $x = 3$

$9 - 2y = 1$

$y = 4$

$4 + 2z = 12$

$z = 4$

$(3, 4, 4)$

24. A: $x + 2y - z = 7$
B: $x - 2z = 2$
C: $y + 3z = 5$

A − B: $2y + z = 5$
   C: $y + 3z = 5$

$2y + z = 5$
(−) $2y + 6z = 10$
   $-5z = -5$
   $z = 1$

$x - 2 = 2$

$x = 4$

$y + 3 = 5$

$y = 2$

$(4, 2, 1)$

25. $a^2 a^{3/5} b^{1/5} a^{2/3} b^{4/3}$

$= a^{30/15} a^{9/15} b^{3/15} a^{10/15} b^{20/15}$

$= a^{49/13} b^{23/15}$

26. $x^{a/2-4} y^{b/2-3/2} x^{-2a} y^{-a/2}$

$= x^{-3a/2-4} y^{(b-a-3)/2}$

27. $\dfrac{3\sqrt{7}}{\sqrt{2}} - \dfrac{2\sqrt{2}}{\sqrt{7}} + 3\sqrt{56}$

$= \dfrac{3\sqrt{14}}{2} - \dfrac{2\sqrt{14}}{7} + 6\sqrt{14}$

$= \dfrac{21\sqrt{14}}{14} - \dfrac{4\sqrt{14}}{14} + \dfrac{84\sqrt{14}}{14} = \dfrac{101\sqrt{14}}{14}$

28. $(x^{1/2} + y^{1/2})(x^{1/2} - y^{-1/2})$

$= x - x^{1/2} y^{-1/2} + x^{1/2} y^{1/2} - 1$

29. $\left(\sqrt{2} - x\right)\left(2 - \sqrt{x}\right)$

$= 2\sqrt{2} - \sqrt{2x} - 2x + x\sqrt{x}$

30. $\dfrac{x^{-1} + y^{-1}}{x^{-1}y} = \dfrac{\dfrac{1}{x} + \dfrac{1}{y}}{\dfrac{y}{x}} = \dfrac{\dfrac{y+x}{xy}}{\dfrac{y}{x}}$

$= \dfrac{y+x}{xy} \cdot \dfrac{x}{y} = \dfrac{y+x}{y^2}$

REVIEW LESSON D

1. $\dfrac{W}{H} = \dfrac{7}{3}$

$3W = 7H$

$3H + 40 = 2W$

$6W = 14H$

$9H + 120 = 6W$

$9H + 120 = 14H$

$120 = 5H$

$H = \mathbf{24}$

$3W = 168$

$W = \mathbf{56}$

2. $0.14B + 0.2G = 54$

$5B - 100 = 2G$

$\begin{array}{r} 14B + 20G = 5400 \\ 50B - 20G = 1000 \\ \hline 64B \phantom{{}+20G} = 6400 \\ B \phantom{{}+20G} = \mathbf{100} \end{array}$

$500 - 2G = 100$

$2G = 400$

$G = \mathbf{200}$

3.

$\sin 20° = \dfrac{2000}{D}$

$0.3420 \approx \dfrac{2000}{D}$

$D \approx \mathbf{5847.6 \ ft}$

4. $m = \dfrac{5 - 3}{-4 + 6} = \dfrac{2}{2} = 1$

$y = mx + b$

$5 = 1(-4) + b$

$b = 8$

$y = x + 9$

5. $2x + 3y = 5$

$3y = -2x + 5$

$y = -\dfrac{2}{3}x + \dfrac{5}{3}$

$m_\perp = \dfrac{3}{2}$

$5 = \dfrac{3}{2}(-2) + b = -3 + b$

$b = 8$

$y = \dfrac{3}{2}x + 8$

6. $\dfrac{\dfrac{x + ba}{a^2}}{\dfrac{c - ak}{a^2c}} = \dfrac{x + ba}{a^2} \cdot \dfrac{a^2c}{c - ak} = \dfrac{cx - abc}{c - ak}$

7. $\dfrac{p}{m + \dfrac{m}{\dfrac{c + b}{c}}} = \dfrac{p}{m + \dfrac{cm}{c + b}}$

$= \dfrac{p}{\dfrac{cm + bm + cm}{c + b}} = \dfrac{cp + bp}{2cm + bm}$

$= \dfrac{p(c + b)}{m(2c + b)}$

8. $\dfrac{a}{x + \dfrac{y}{\dfrac{pc + m}{c}}} = \dfrac{a}{x + \dfrac{cy}{pc + m}}$

$= \dfrac{a}{\dfrac{cpx + xm + cy}{pc + m}} = \dfrac{a(cp + m)}{cpx + mx + cy}$

9. $y = \dfrac{ma}{x} + \dfrac{b}{c}$

$cxy = acm + bx$

$c(xy - am) = bx$

$c = \dfrac{bx}{xy - am}$

10. $x = \dfrac{pm}{y} + \dfrac{amp}{bd}$

$bdxy = bdmp + ampy$

$d(bxy - bmp) = ampy$

$d = \dfrac{ampy}{b(xy - mp)}$

11.

$$\begin{array}{r} x^2 + 2x + 4 + 7/(x-2) \\ x - 2 \enclose{longdiv}{x^3 + 0x^2 + 0x - 1} \\ \underline{x^3 - 2x^2} \\ 2x^2 + 0x \\ \underline{2x^2 - 4x} \\ 4x - 1 \\ \underline{4x - 8} \\ 7 \end{array}$$

12. $R^2 = (-7.08)^2 + 4.2^2$
$R = 8.23$
$\theta = \tan^{-1}\left(\dfrac{4.2}{-7.08}\right) = 149.32°$
(8.23, 149.32°)

13. $R^2 = 4.2^2 + 3^2$
$R = 5.16$
$\theta = \tan^{-1}\left(\dfrac{-3}{4.2}\right) = -35.54°$
(5.16, -35.54°)

14. $x = R\cos\theta = -15\cos -135° = -13.59$
$y = R\sin\theta = -15\sin -135° = -6.34$
(-13.59, -6.34)

15. $x = R\cos\theta = -42\cos 138° = 31.21$
$y = R\cos\theta = -42\sin 138° = -28.10$
(31.21, -28.1)

16. $2i - \sqrt{2}\,i - 2i + i = \left(-\sqrt{2} + 1\right)i$

17. $\left(\dfrac{3 + 2\sqrt{3}}{4 - 12\sqrt{3}}\right)\left(\dfrac{4 + 12\sqrt{3}}{4 + 12\sqrt{3}}\right)$

$= \dfrac{12 + 44\sqrt{3} + 72}{16 - 432}$

$= \dfrac{84 + 44\sqrt{3}}{-416} = \dfrac{-21 - 11\sqrt{3}}{104}$

18. $\dfrac{-2 - 3i - 4i}{2i - 3i + 2} = \left(\dfrac{-2 - 7i}{2 - i}\right)\left(\dfrac{2 + i}{2 + i}\right)$

$= \dfrac{-4 - 16i + 7}{4 + 1} = \dfrac{3 - 16i}{5} = \dfrac{3}{5} - \dfrac{16}{5}i$

19. $3x^2 + x + 6 = 0$

$x^2 + \dfrac{1}{3}x + 2 = 0$

$x^2 + \dfrac{1}{3}x \qquad = -2$

$x^2 + \dfrac{1}{3}x + \dfrac{1}{36} = \dfrac{1}{36} - 2$

$\left(x + \dfrac{1}{6}\right)^2 = -\dfrac{71}{36}$

$x + \dfrac{1}{6} = \pm\sqrt{-\dfrac{71}{36}}$

$x = -\dfrac{1}{6} \pm \dfrac{\sqrt{71}}{6}i$

20. $2x^2 - 4x - 7 = 0$

$x^2 - 2x - \dfrac{7}{2} = 0$

$x^2 - 2x + 1 = 1 + \dfrac{7}{2}$

$(x - 1)^2 = \dfrac{9}{2}$

$x - 1 = \pm\sqrt{\dfrac{9}{2}}$

$x = 1 \pm \dfrac{3\sqrt{2}}{2}$

21. $ax^2 + bx + c = 0$

$x^2 + \dfrac{b}{a}x + \dfrac{c}{a} = 0$

$x^2 + \dfrac{b}{a}x \qquad = -\dfrac{c}{a}$

$x^2 + \dfrac{b}{a}x + \dfrac{b^2}{4a^2} = -\dfrac{b^2}{4a^2} - \dfrac{c}{a}$

$\left(x + \dfrac{b}{2a}\right)^2 = \dfrac{b^2 - 4ac}{4a^2}$

$x + \dfrac{b}{2a} = \pm\sqrt{\dfrac{b^2 - 4ac}{4a^2}}$

$x = -\dfrac{b}{2a} \pm \dfrac{\sqrt{b^2 - 4ac}}{2a}$

$x = \dfrac{-b \pm \sqrt{b^2 - 4ac}}{2a}$

22. $3x^2 - \dfrac{2}{5}x + 3 = 0$

$15x^2 - 2x + 15 = 0$

$x = \dfrac{2 \pm \sqrt{4 - 4(15)(15)}}{30}$

$x = \dfrac{2 \pm \sqrt{-896}}{30} = \dfrac{2 \pm 8\sqrt{-14}}{30}$

$x = \dfrac{1}{15} \pm \dfrac{4\sqrt{14}}{15}i$

23. $x = \dfrac{1}{y + z}$

$\dfrac{5}{x} = \dfrac{5}{\dfrac{1}{y + z}} = 5(y + z)$

therefore C

24. z is negative; thus $\dfrac{1}{z^5}$ is negative

and $\dfrac{1}{z^4}$ is positive. Therefore B.

25. A: $x + 2y - z = -5$
B: $2x - y + z = 11$
C: $x + y - z = -2$

A + B: $3x + y = 6$
B + C: $(-)3x = 9$

$y = -3$

$3x - 3 = 6$
$3x = 9$
$x = 3$
$3 - 3 - z = -2$
$z = 2$
$(3, -3, 2)$

26. A: $2x - z = 5$
B: $3x + 2y = 13$
C: $y - 2z = 0$
Substitute $y = 2z$ into B to get
$3x + 4z = 13$
4A: $8x - 4z = 20$
B: $3x + 4z = 13$

$11x = 33$
$x = 3$
$z = 2(3) - 5$
$z = 1$
$y = 2(1) = 2$
$(3, 2, 1)$

27. A: $2x - 3y = 10$
B: $5x - 6z = -8$
Divide $40y - 5z = -95$ by 5 to get
C: $8y - z = -19$

$(B - 6C):$ $5x - 48y = 106$
$-16A: -32x + 48y = -160$

$-27x = -54$
$x = 2$

$-3y = 6$
$y = -2$
$10 - 6z = -8$
$-6z = -18$
$z = 3$
$(2, -2, 3)$

28. $b^2 a^{1/3} b^{4/3} a^{1/5} b^{3/5} = a^{8/15} b^{59/15}$

29. $x^{(4/3)-2} y^{b/3-2/3} x^{-2a} y^{2a/3} = x^{(-5a/3)-2} y^{(b-2-2a)/3}$

30. $(2x^{3/4} + y^{-1/2})(2x^{3/4} - y^{-1/2})$
$4x^{3/2} - y^{-1} = 4x^{3/2} - \dfrac{1}{y}$

REVIEW LESSON E

1. $N_B + 7 = N_W + N_G$
$N_G - 1 = N_B + N_W$
$3N_B = N_G$

$N_B + 7 = N_W + 3N_B$
$3N_B - 1 = N_B + N_W$

$7 = N_W + 2N_B$
$1 = -N_W + 2N_B$

$8 = 4N_B$
$N_B = 2$
$N_G = 3(2)$
$N_G = 6$
$7 = N_W + 4$
$N_W = 3$

2. $N_N + N_D + N_Q = 20$
$5N_N + 10N_D + 25N_Q = 205$

$N_N + 4N_Q = 20$
$5N_N + 55N_Q = 205$

$-5N_N - 20N_Q = -100$
$5N_N + 55N_Q = 205$

$35N_Q = 105$
$N_Q = 3$
$3N_Q = N_D$
$N_D = 9$
$N_N = 8$

3. $\left(\dfrac{RG^2}{B}\right)_1 = \left(\dfrac{RG^2}{B}\right)_2$

$\dfrac{5(16)}{2} = \dfrac{R(16)}{4}$

$R(2)(16) = 4(5)(16)$
$2R = 20$
$R = 10$

4.
T = tens' digit
U = units' digit
$10T + U$ = original number
$10U + T$ = reversed number
$T + U = 13$
$10T + U + 45 = 10U + T$
$9T - 9U = 45$

$$T + U = 13$$
$$\underline{T - U = -5}$$
$$2T \quad = 8$$
$$T \quad = 4$$

$U = 9$
$N = \mathbf{49}$

5.
$0.14(P_N) + 89(0.47) = 0.29(P_N + 89)$
$0.14P_N + 41.83 = 0.29P_N + 25.81$
$16.02 = 0.15P_N$
$P_N = \mathbf{106.8\ oz}$

6.
$$
\begin{array}{rcl}
C_3 & = & 36 \\
H_7 & = & 7 \\
\underline{Cl} & = & \underline{35} \\
C_3H_7Cl & = & 78
\end{array}
$$
$\dfrac{35}{78} = \dfrac{400}{G}$
$35G = 78(400)$
$G = \mathbf{891.43}$

7.
$5x - 2y + 4 = 0$
$2y = 5x + 4$
$y = \dfrac{5}{2}x + 2$
$m_\perp = -\dfrac{2}{5}$
$3 = -\dfrac{2}{5}(-2) + b$
$3 = \dfrac{4}{5} + b$
$b = \dfrac{11}{5}$
$y = -\dfrac{2}{5}x + \dfrac{11}{5}$

8.
$$\dfrac{\dfrac{m^2}{a^2} + \dfrac{7y}{x}}{\dfrac{p^2}{ax} - \dfrac{3}{a^2}} = \dfrac{\dfrac{m^2x + 7ya^2}{a^2x}}{\dfrac{p^2a - 3x}{a^2x}}$$
$$= \dfrac{m^2x + 7a^2y}{a^2x} \cdot \dfrac{a^2x}{p^2a - 3x}$$
$$= \dfrac{m^2x + 7a^2y}{ap^2 - 3x}$$

9.
$$\dfrac{m}{a + \dfrac{b}{\dfrac{d+c}{d}}} = \dfrac{m}{a + \dfrac{bd}{d+c}}$$
$$= \dfrac{m}{\dfrac{ad + ac + bd}{d+c}} = \dfrac{m(d+c)}{ad + ac + bd}$$

10.
$$\dfrac{k}{a + \dfrac{b}{\dfrac{xd+c}{d}}} = \dfrac{k}{a + \dfrac{bd}{xd+c}}$$
$$= \dfrac{k}{\dfrac{adx + ac + bd}{xd+c}} = \dfrac{k(xd+c)}{adx + ac + bd}$$

11.
$x = \dfrac{kb}{c} - \dfrac{abk}{x}$
$cx^2 = bkx - abck$
$cx^2 + abck = bkx$
$c = \dfrac{bkx}{x^2 + abk}$

12.
$mc = \dfrac{ap}{cm} + \dfrac{2p}{ck}$
$c^2m^2k = akp + 2mp$
$c^2m^2k - akp = 2mp$
$k = \dfrac{2mp}{c^2m^2 - ap}$

13.
$$
\require{enclose}
\begin{array}{r}
x^2 + \quad 1 - 1/(x^2-1) \\[-2pt]
x^2-1\,\overline{\smash{\big)}\,x^4 + 0x^3 + 0x^2 + 0x - 2} \\
\underline{x^4 \quad - \quad x^2} \\
x^2 \quad - 2 \\
\underline{x^2 \quad - 1} \\
-1
\end{array}
$$

14.
$x_1 = -6.58$
$x_2 = \underline{\ \ 0.52\ }$
$x_T = -6.06$

$y_1 = \ \ 2.39$
$y_2 = \underline{-4.97}$
$y_T = -2.58$

$\mathbf{-6.06i - 2.58j}$

15. $x_1 = 9.0$

$x_2 = \underline{6.06}$

$x_T = 15.06$

$y_1 = -10.72$

$y_2 = \underline{-3.5}$

$y_T = -14.22$

$-15.06i - 14.22j$

16. $2i + -3 + 2i - i = -3 + 3i$

17. $\dfrac{4 + 4\sqrt{3}}{6 - 4\sqrt{3}} = \dfrac{2\left(2 + 2\sqrt{3}\right)}{2\left(3 - 2\sqrt{3}\right)} \dfrac{\left(3 + 2\sqrt{3}\right)}{\left(3 + 2\sqrt{3}\right)}$

$= \dfrac{6 + 4\sqrt{3} + 6\sqrt{3} + 12}{9 + 6\sqrt{3} - 6\sqrt{3} - 12}$

$= \dfrac{18 + 10\sqrt{3}}{-3}$

18. $\dfrac{-3i - 2i - 1}{1 + 4i}$

$= \left(\dfrac{-1 - 5i}{1 + 4i}\right)\left(\dfrac{1 - 4i}{1 - 4i}\right)$

$= \dfrac{-1 - i - 20}{1 + 16} = \dfrac{-21 - i}{17} = -\dfrac{21}{17} - \dfrac{1}{17}i$

19. $4x^2 + 2x + 5 = 0$

$x^2 + \dfrac{1}{2}x + \dfrac{5}{4} = 0$

$x^2 + \dfrac{1}{2}x + \dfrac{1}{16} = \dfrac{1}{16} - \dfrac{5}{4}$

$\left(x + \dfrac{1}{4}\right)^2 = -\dfrac{19}{16}$

$x + \dfrac{1}{4} = \pm\dfrac{\sqrt{19}}{4}i$

$x = -\dfrac{1}{4} \pm \dfrac{\sqrt{19}}{4}i$

20. $4x^2 - 3x - 7 = 0$

$x^2 - \dfrac{3}{4}x - \dfrac{7}{4} = 0$

$x^2 - \dfrac{3}{4}x + \dfrac{9}{64} = \dfrac{9}{64} + \dfrac{7}{4}$

$\left(x - \dfrac{3}{8}\right)^2 = \dfrac{121}{64}$

$x - \dfrac{3}{8} = \pm\dfrac{11}{8}$

$x = \dfrac{3}{8} \pm \dfrac{11}{8}$

$x = \dfrac{7}{4}, -1$

21. $ax^2 + bx + c = 0$

$x^2 + \dfrac{b}{a}x + \dfrac{c}{a} = 0$

$x^2 + \dfrac{b}{a}x = -\dfrac{c}{a}$

$x^2 + \dfrac{b}{a}x + \dfrac{b^2}{4a^2} = -\dfrac{b^2}{4a^2} - \dfrac{c}{a}$

$\left(x + \dfrac{b}{2a}\right)^2 = \dfrac{b^2 - 4ac}{4a^2}$

$x + \dfrac{b}{2a} = \pm\sqrt{\dfrac{b^2 - 4ac}{4a^2}}$

$x = -\dfrac{b}{2a} \pm \dfrac{\sqrt{b^2 - 4ac}}{2a}$

$x = \dfrac{-b \pm \sqrt{b^2 - 4ac}}{2a}$

22. $3x^2 - 2x + 4 = 0$

$x = \dfrac{2 \pm \sqrt{4 - 4(3)(4)}}{6}$

$x = \dfrac{2 \pm \sqrt{-44}}{6}$

$x = \dfrac{2 \pm 2\sqrt{11}\,i}{6}$

$x = \dfrac{1}{3} \pm \dfrac{\sqrt{11}}{3}i$

23. A: 5

B: $\sqrt{9} + \sqrt{16} = 3 + 4 = 7$

Therefore **B**

24. A: 5

B: $\sqrt{3^2 + 2^2} = \sqrt{9 + 4}$

$\sqrt{13} \approx 3.6$

Therefore **A**

25. A: $2x + 2y - z = -1$

B: $x + y - 3z = -8$

C: $2x - y + z = 8$

$\begin{aligned} \text{B} + \text{C}: \quad & 3x - 2z = 0 \\ \underline{2(\text{A} + 2\text{C}):} \quad & \underline{12x + 2z = 30} \\ & 15x = 30 \\ & x = 2 \end{aligned}$

$z = \dfrac{3}{2}(2) = 3$

$y = -8 + 3(3) - 2$

$y = -1$

$(2, -1, 3)$

26.   A: $2x - z = 10$
       B: $y + 2z = -2$
       C: $3x - 2y = 8$

$2(2A + B):$ $8x + 2y = 36$
        $C:$ $3x - 2y = 8$
              $11x$ $= 44$
                x $= 4$
$3(4) - 2y = 8$
$-2y = 8 - 12 = -4$
$y = 2$
$z = 2(2) - 10 = -2$
(4, 2, –2)

27.   A: $9x + 8y = 3$
       B: $-2x + z = -4$
       C: $20y - 4z = -68$

$9\left(B + \frac{1}{4}C\right):\ -18x + 45y = -189$
           $2A:$ $18x + 16y =$ 6
                      $61y = -183$
                        $y =$ -3
$9x = 3 - 8(-3)$
$x = \frac{27}{9} = 3$
$z = -4 + 2(3) = 2$
(3, –3, 2)

28. $x^3 x^{3/2} y^{1/2} a^2 b^{2/3} = a^2 b^{2/3} x^{9/2} y^{1/2}$

29. $x^{a/2-3} y^{b/2-3/2} x^{-3a} y^{-2a/3}$
      $= x^{-5a/2-3} y^{b/2-2a/3-3/2}$
      $= x^{(-5a/2)-3} y^{(b-3)/2-2a/3}$

30. $(2x^{a/2} + y^{b/2})(2x^{a/2} - y^{b/2})$
      $= 4x^a - y^b$

REVIEW LESSON F

1. $N_R + 11 = N_B + N_W$
    $N_W + 3 = N_R + N_B$
    Substitute $N_W - 1 = N_B$ to get
    $N_R + 11 = 2N_W - 1$
    $N_W + 3 = N_R + N_W - 1$

    $N_R - 2N_W = -12$
    $-N_R = -4$
    $N_R = \mathbf{4}$
    $-2N_W = -16$
    $N_W = \mathbf{8}$
    $N_B = 8 - 1$
    $N_B = \mathbf{7}$

2. $P + N + D = 30$
    $P + 5N + 10D = 135$
    $2D = P$

    $N + 3D = 30$
    $5N + 12D = 135$

    $-4N - 12D = -120$
    $\underline{5N + 12D = 135}$
    $N = \mathbf{15}$
    $3D = 30 - 15$

$D = \mathbf{5}$
$P = 30 - 5 - 15$
$P = \mathbf{10}$

3. $B = \dfrac{kG^2}{T}$

    $200 = \dfrac{k(10)^2}{20}$

    $k = 20$
    $B = \dfrac{40G^2}{T} = \dfrac{40(8)^2}{2}$
    $B = \mathbf{1280\ boys}$

4. T = tens' digit
    U = units' digit
    $10T + U$ = original number
    $10U + T$ = reversed number
    $T + U = 5$
    $10U + T - 27 = 10T + U$
    $-9T + 9U = 27$

    $T + \ U = 5$
    $\underline{-T + \ U = 3}$
          $2U = 8$
           $U = 4$
    $T = 5 - 4 = 1$
    14, 41

5. $W + S = 20$
   $W = 20 - S$

   $0.9S + 0.58W = 0.78(20)$
   $0.9S + 0.58(20 - S) = 0.78(20)$
   $0.32S = 4$
   $S = \textbf{12.5 liters 90\%}$
   $W = \textbf{7.5 liters 58\%}$

6. $0.135(M) + 0.06(370) = 0.1(370 + M)$
   $0.135M + 22.2 = 37 + 0.1M$
   $0.035M = 14.8$
   $M = \textbf{422.86 ml}$

7. $3x + 2y - 4 = 0$
   $2y = -3x + 4$
   $y = -\dfrac{3}{2}x + 2$
   $m = -\dfrac{3}{2}$
   $y = mx + b$
   $4 = -\dfrac{3}{2}(-2) + b$
   $4 = 3 + b$
   $b = 1$
   $y = -\dfrac{3}{2}x + 1$

8. $y = x + 1$
   $x = \dfrac{-1 + \sqrt{17}}{2}$
   $y = \dfrac{-1 + \sqrt{17}}{2} + 1$
   $y = \dfrac{-1 + \sqrt{17} + 2}{2}$
   $y = \dfrac{1 + \sqrt{17}}{2}$
   $\left(\dfrac{-1 + \sqrt{17}}{2}, \dfrac{1 + \sqrt{17}}{2}\right)$
   $x = \dfrac{-1 - \sqrt{17}}{2}$
   $y = \dfrac{-1 - \sqrt{17}}{2} + 1$
   $y = \dfrac{-1 - \sqrt{17} + 2}{2}$
   $y = \dfrac{1 - \sqrt{17}}{2}$
   $\left(\dfrac{-1 - \sqrt{17}}{2}, \dfrac{1 - \sqrt{17}}{2}\right)$

9. $y^2 = 9 - x^2$
   $x = 1$
   $y^2 = 9 - (1)^2$
   $y^2 = 8$
   $y = \pm 2\sqrt{2}$
   $\left(1, 2\sqrt{2}\right)\left(1, -2\sqrt{2}\right)$
   $x = -1$
   $y^2 = 9 - (-1)^2$
   $y^2 = 8$
   $y = \pm 2\sqrt{2}$
   $\left(-1, 2\sqrt{2}\right)\left(-1, -2\sqrt{2}\right)$

10. $xy = -4$
    $y = -x - 2$
    $x(-x - 2) = -4$
    $-x^2 - 2x = -4$
    $x^2 + 2x - 4 = 0$
    $x = \dfrac{-2 \pm \sqrt{4 + 16}}{2}$
    $x = -1 \pm \sqrt{5}$
    $y = -x - 2$
    $x = -1 + \sqrt{5}$
    $y = -\left(-1 + \sqrt{5}\right) - 2$
    $y = 1 - \sqrt{5} - 2$
    $y = -1 - \sqrt{5}$
    $\left(-1 + \sqrt{5}, -1 - \sqrt{5}\right)$
    $y = -x - 2$
    $x = -1 - \sqrt{5}$
    $y = -\left(-1 - \sqrt{5}\right) - 2$
    $y = 1 + \sqrt{5} - 2$
    $y = -1 + \sqrt{5}$
    $\left(-1 - \sqrt{5}, -1 + \sqrt{5}\right)$

11. $8x^6y^3 + p^3 = (2x^2y)^3 + (p)^3 = $
    $(2x^2y + p)(4x^4y^2 - 2px^2y + p^2)$

12. $27x^{12}y^6 - z^9 = (3x^4y^2)^3 - (z^3)^3 = $
    $(3x^4y^2 - z^3)(9x^8y^4 + 3x^4y^2z^3 + z^6)$

13. $\dfrac{\dfrac{n^2}{b^3} + \dfrac{7p}{a}}{\dfrac{r^2}{ba} - \dfrac{4}{b^3}} = \dfrac{\dfrac{an^2 + 7b^3p}{b^3a}}{\dfrac{b^2r^2 - 4a}{b^3a}}$

    $= \dfrac{an^2 + 7b^3p}{b^3a} \cdot \dfrac{b^3a}{b^2r^2 - 4a}$

    $= \dfrac{an^2 + 7b^3p}{b^2r^2 - 4a}$

14.

$$\frac{m}{c + \dfrac{f}{\dfrac{2h + g}{h}}} = \frac{m}{c + \dfrac{fh}{2h + g}}$$

$$= \frac{m}{\dfrac{2ch + cg + fh}{2h + g}} = \frac{m(2h + g)}{2ch + cg + fh}$$

15. $k^2 = \dfrac{x}{3bc} - \dfrac{6y^3}{bcd}$

$3bcdk^2 = dx - 18y^3$

$3bcdk^2 + 18y^3 = dx$

$x = \dfrac{3(bcdk^2 + 6y^3)}{d} = 3k^2bc + \dfrac{18y^3}{d}$

16.

$$\begin{array}{r} x^2 - x - 2 - 7/(x-2) \\ x - 2 \overline{\smash{\big)}\, x^3 - 3x^2 + 0x - 3} \\ \underline{x^3 - 2x^2} \\ -x^2 + 0x \\ \underline{-x^2 + 2x} \\ -2x - 3 \\ \underline{-2x - 8} \\ -7 \end{array}$$

17. $x_1 = \quad 3$

$x_2 = \quad -2.121$

$x_T = \quad \underline{0.879}$

$y_1 = \quad 5.196$

$y_2 = \quad \underline{2.121}$

$x_T = \quad 7.317$

$-0.88i - 7.32j$

18. $3i + 2 + 2i + 5i + \sqrt{3}\,i$

$= 2 + 10i + \sqrt{3}\,i$

$= 2 + \left(10 + \sqrt{3}\right)i$

19. $\left(\dfrac{3 + 4\sqrt{3}}{2 - 16\sqrt{3}}\right)\left(\dfrac{2 + 16\sqrt{3}}{2 + 16\sqrt{3}}\right)$

$= \dfrac{6 + 56\sqrt{3} + 192}{4 - 768} = \dfrac{198 + 56\sqrt{3}}{-764}$

$= \dfrac{2\left(99 + 28\sqrt{3}\right)}{2(-382)} = \dfrac{-99 - 28\sqrt{3}}{382}$

20. $\dfrac{3 + 2 - i}{1 + 3 + 3i} = \left(\dfrac{5 - i}{4 + 3i}\right)\left(\dfrac{4 - 3i}{4 - 3i}\right)$

$= \dfrac{20 - 19i - 3}{16 + 9} = \dfrac{17 - 19i}{25} = \dfrac{17}{25} - \dfrac{19}{25}i$

21. $3x^2 - 3x + 4 = 0$

$x^2 - x + \dfrac{1}{4} = \dfrac{1}{4} - \dfrac{4}{3}$

$\left(x - \dfrac{1}{2}\right)^2 = -\dfrac{13}{12}$

$x - \dfrac{1}{2} = \pm\dfrac{\sqrt{13}}{2\sqrt{3}}\,i$

$x = \dfrac{1}{2} \pm \dfrac{\sqrt{39}}{6}\,i$

22. $2x^2 + 6x + 9 = 0$

$x^2 + 3x + \dfrac{9}{4} = \dfrac{9}{4} - \dfrac{9}{2}$

$\left(x + \dfrac{3}{2}\right)^2 = -\dfrac{9}{4}$

$x + \dfrac{3}{2} = \pm\dfrac{3i}{2}$

$x = -\dfrac{3}{2} \pm \dfrac{3}{2}i$

23. If x is large (19) and y is small (1)

$\dfrac{y}{x} + 5 = 23$

$\dfrac{y}{x} + 10 = 10.05$

then A.

If x is small (1) and y is large (23)

$\dfrac{y}{x} + 5 = 5.04$

$\dfrac{y}{x} + 10 = 33$

then B.

Therefore D.

24. Regardless of the values of x and y,

$\dfrac{x}{y} = \dfrac{x}{y}$ so $\dfrac{x}{y} < \dfrac{x}{y} + 1$

Therefore B.

25. A: $2x + 3y - z = 6$

B: $3x - y + z = 1$

C: $x + y + z = 1$

$$\begin{array}{r} -2(A + B): \quad -10x - 4y = -14 \\ B + C: \quad \underline{3x + 4y = \quad 7} \\ -7x \quad = -7 \\ x \quad = \quad 1 \end{array}$$

$3(1) + 4y = 7$

$y = 1$

$z = 1 - 1 - 1$

$z = -1$

$(1, 1, -1)$

26. A: $2x - z = 1$
B: $y + 2z = 7$
C: $3x - y = 5$

B + C: $3x + 2z = 12$
2A: $4x - 2z = 2$
$\overline{7x = 14}$
$x = 2$
$z = 2(2) - 1 = 3$
$y = 7 - 2(3) = 1$
(2, 1, 3)

27. A: $3x + 10y = 32$
B: $-x - z = -5$
C: $25y - 40z = 10$

A + 3B: $-10y - 3z = 17$
$-2C: -10y + 16z = -4$
$\overline{13z = 13}$
$z = 1$
$x = -(1) + 5 = 4$
$3(4) + 10y = 32$
$y = 2$
(4, 2, 1)

28. $x^3 x^2 y^{3/2} x y^{1/3} = x^6 y^{11/6}$

29. $x^{a/3-2} y^{b/3-2/3} x^{-2a} y^{-2a/3}$
$= x^{-5a/3-2} y^{(-2a+b-2)/3}$

30. $(3x^{a/2} + 2y^{b/3})(2x^{a/2} - 2y^{b/3})$
$= 6x^a - 6x^{a/2}y^{b/3} + 4x^{a/2}y^{b/3} - 4y^{2b/3}$
$= 6x^a - 2x^{a/2}y^{b/3} - 4y^{2b/3}$

PROBLEM SET 1

1. T = tens' digit, U = units' digit
$10T + U$ = original number
$10U + T$ = reversed number
$T + U = 12$
$T = 12 - U$
$\dfrac{U}{T} = \dfrac{1}{2}$
$T = 2U$
$12 - U = 2U$
$12 = 3U$
$4 = U$
$T = 8$
Original number = **84**

2. $N_N + N_D + N_Q = 12$
$5N_N + 10N_D + 25N_Q = 155$
Substitute $N_N = N_Q + 1$

$N_Q + 1 + N_D + N_Q = 12$
$5(N_Q + 1) + 10N_D + 25N_Q = 155$

$-20N_Q - 10N_D = -110$
$\dfrac{30N_Q + 10N_D = 150}{10N_Q = 40}$
N_Q = **4 quarters**
N_D = **3 dimes**
N_N = **5 nickels**

3. $0.40R + 0.60G = 56$
$\dfrac{R}{G} = \dfrac{1}{4}$
$4R + 6G = 560$
$4R = G$ (substitute)

$2R + 3G = 280$
$2R + 3(4R) = 280$
$14R = 280$
$R = \mathbf{20}$
$G = \mathbf{80}$

4.

Amt	x		20		$x + 20$
% Copper	100%	+	20%	=	100%

$100x + 20(20) = 50(x + 2)$
$100x + 400 = 50x + 1000$
$50x = 600$
$x = 12$
Pure copper = **12 lb**

5. $2R = 3B + 8$
$\dfrac{R}{R + B} = \dfrac{5}{7}$

$2R - 3B = 8$
$7R = 5R + 5B$
$2R = 5B$

Substitute $2R = 5B$ into
$2R = 3B + 8$ to get
$5B = 3B + 8$
$2B = 8$
$B = \mathbf{4}$
$R = \mathbf{10}$

6.

Amt	x		100		$x + 100$
% Alcohol	100%	+	96.5%	=	98.5%

$100x + 96.5(100) = 98.5(x + 100)$
$1000x + 965(100) = 985(x + 100)$
$1000x + 96{,}500 = 985x + 98{,}500$
$15x = 2000$
$x = \mathbf{133.3\ ounces}$

7.　$y = \dfrac{3}{5}x + b$

$0 = \dfrac{3}{5}(-2) + b$

$0 = -\dfrac{6}{5} + b$

$b = \dfrac{6}{5}$

$y = \dfrac{3}{5}x + \dfrac{6}{5}$

Use these triangles for problems 8–10.

8.　$\tan 60° = \dfrac{\sqrt{3}}{1}$

$4 \tan 60° = 4\left(\sqrt{3}\right) = 4\sqrt{3}$

9.　$\cos 30° = \dfrac{\sqrt{3}}{2}$

$6\sqrt{3}\cos 30° = 6\sqrt{2}\left(\dfrac{\sqrt{3}}{2}\right) = 3\sqrt{6}$

10.　$\sin 45° = \dfrac{1}{\sqrt{2}} = \dfrac{\sqrt{2}}{2}$

$6\sqrt{3}\sin 45° = 6\sqrt{3}\left(\dfrac{\sqrt{2}}{2}\right) = 3\sqrt{6}$

11.　$x^2 + y^2 = 9$
$y = 2x + 1$

$x^2 + (2x + 1)^2 = 9$
$x^2 + 4x^2 + 4x + 1 = 9$
$5x^2 + 4x - 8 = 0$

$x = \dfrac{-4 \pm \sqrt{16 - 4(5)(-8)}}{2(5)}$

$x = \dfrac{-4 \pm 4\sqrt{11}}{10} = \dfrac{-2 \pm 2\sqrt{11}}{5}$

$x = \dfrac{-2 + 2\sqrt{11}}{5}$ or $x = \dfrac{-2 - 2\sqrt{11}}{5}$

Substitute into $y = 2x + 1$

$y = 2\left(\dfrac{-2 \pm 2\sqrt{11}}{5}\right) + 1$

$y = \dfrac{1 + 4\sqrt{11}}{5}$ or

$y = \dfrac{1 - 4\sqrt{11}}{5}$

$\left(-\dfrac{2}{5} + \dfrac{2\sqrt{11}}{5}, \dfrac{1}{5} + \dfrac{4\sqrt{11}}{5}\right)$

$\left(-\dfrac{2}{5} - \dfrac{2\sqrt{11}}{5}, \dfrac{1}{5} - \dfrac{4\sqrt{11}}{5}\right)$

12.　$(3xy^2 + 2p)(9x^2y^4 - 6xy^2p + 4p^2)$

13.　$(2xy^4 - 3z^3)(4x^2y^8 + 6xy^4z^3 + 9z^6)$

14.　$\dfrac{\dfrac{n^3a - 7p^2b^3}{b^3a}}{\dfrac{s^3b - 5t}{b^3a}} = \dfrac{n^3a - 7p^2b^3}{b^3a} \cdot \dfrac{b^3a}{s^3b - 5t}$

$= \dfrac{n^3a - 7p^2b^3}{s^3b - 5t}$

15.　$\dfrac{x}{2y - \dfrac{6z}{\dfrac{3t + s}{t}}} = \dfrac{x}{2y - \dfrac{6zt}{3t + s}}$

$= \dfrac{x}{\dfrac{6yt + 2ys - 6zt}{3t + s}} = \dfrac{3tx + xs}{6yt + 2ys - 6zt}$

16.　$s^2 = \dfrac{4y}{3df} - \dfrac{7x^3}{gdf}$

Multiply by $(3dfg)$
$3dfs^2g = 4yg - 7x^3(3)$
$3dfs^2g + 21x^3 = 4gy$
$y = \dfrac{3dfs^2g + 21x^3}{4g}$

17.

$$
\begin{array}{r}
x^2 + 1 \\
x^2 - 1\overline{\smash)\,x^4 + 0x^3 + 0x^2 - 0x - 6} \\
\underline{x^4 - x^2} \\
x^2 - 6 \\
\underline{x^2 - 1} \\
- 5
\end{array}
$$

$$x^2 + 1 - \frac{5}{x^2 - 1}$$

18. $x = r \cos A$ $\qquad$ $y = r \sin A$

$x = 8 \cos(-250°)$ $\qquad$ $y = 8 \sin(-250°)$

$x = -3 \cos(125°)$ $\qquad$ $y = -3 \sin(125°)$

$(-2.74i + 7.52j) + (1.72i - 2.46j)$

$(-2.74 + 1.72)i + (7.52 - 2.46)j$

Resultant: $-1.02i + 5.06j$

Equilibrant: $1.02i - 5.06j$

19. $\sqrt{3}\sqrt{3}\sqrt{3}\,i - \sqrt{2}\,i\sqrt{2}\,i\sqrt{2}\,i - 5(3i) + 3i$

$3\sqrt{3}\,i - 2\sqrt{2}\,i^3 - 15i + 3i$

$3\sqrt{3}\,i + 2\sqrt{2}\,i - 15i + 3i$

$\left(3\sqrt{3} + 2\sqrt{2} - 12\right)i$

20. $\dfrac{2 - 3\sqrt{24}}{3 - 2\sqrt{54}} = \dfrac{2 - 6\sqrt{6}}{3 - 6\sqrt{6}} \cdot \dfrac{3 + 6\sqrt{6}}{3 + 6\sqrt{6}}$

$= \dfrac{6 + 12\sqrt{6} - 18\sqrt{6} - 216}{9 + 18\sqrt{6} - 18\sqrt{6} - 216}$

$= \dfrac{-210 - 6\sqrt{6}}{-207} = \dfrac{70 + 2\sqrt{6}}{69}$

21. $\dfrac{-3i + 2 - i}{2 + 4 + 2i} = \dfrac{2 - 4i}{6 + 2i} \cdot \dfrac{6 - 2i}{6 - 2i}$

$= \dfrac{12 - 4i - 24i + 8i^2}{36 - 4i^2} = \dfrac{4 - 28i}{40}$

$= \dfrac{1 - 7i}{10} = \dfrac{1}{10} - \dfrac{7}{10}i$

22. $2x^2 - 4x = -3$

$x^2 - 2x + 1 = -\dfrac{3}{2} + 1$

$(x - 1)^2 = -\dfrac{1}{2}$

$x - 1 = \pm\sqrt{-\dfrac{1}{2}}$

$x - 1 = \pm\dfrac{\sqrt{2}\,i}{2}$

$x = 1 \pm \dfrac{\sqrt{2}}{2}i$

23. $3x^2 + 5x = -8$

$x^2 + \dfrac{5}{3}x + \dfrac{25}{36} = -\dfrac{8}{3} + \dfrac{25}{36}$

$\left(x + \dfrac{5}{6}\right)^2 = -\dfrac{71}{36}$

$x + \dfrac{5}{6} = \pm\dfrac{\sqrt{71}}{6}i$

$x = -\dfrac{5}{6} \pm \dfrac{\sqrt{71}}{6}i$

24.   For all values, $x - y$ is positive.
For all values, $y - x$ is negative. **A**

25.   If x is positive, then y is positive.
The denominator of B is larger; therefore the fraction is smaller. **A**

26.
$$
\begin{array}{rcr}
2x - 3y + z &=& -1 \\
x + 3y - z &=& 4 \\
\hline
3x &=& 3 \\
x &=& 1
\end{array}
$$

Multiply $x + 3y - z = 4$ by 2
$$
\begin{array}{rcr}
2x + 6y - 2z &=& 8 \\
x - 2y + 2z &=& 3 \\
\hline
3x + 4y &=& 11 \\
3(1) + 4y &=& 11 \\
4y &=& 8
\end{array}
$$

$y = 2$

$(1) - 2(2) + 2z = 3$

$2z = 6$

$z = 3$

(1, 2, 3)

27.   Substitute $y = -3z + 9$
into $2x - y = -1$ to get
$2x - (-3z + 9) = -1$
$2x + 3z - 9 = -1$
$2x + 3z = 8$

$$
\begin{array}{rcr}
2x + 3z &=& 8 \\
9x - 3z &=& 3 \\
\hline
11x &=& 11 \\
x &=& 1
\end{array}
$$

$3(1) - z = 1$

$z = 2$

$y = -3(2) + 9$

$y = 3$

(1, 3, 2)

28. A: $3x - 10z = -8$ $3y = 9$
   B: $-x + 3y = 5$ $y = 3$
   C: $4x + 3z = 22$ $(4, 3, 2)$

   3A: $9x - 30z = -24$
   10B: $\underline{40x + 30z = 220}$
   $49x \qquad\quad = 196$
   $x \qquad\quad = 4$
   $3(4) - 10z = -8$
   $-10z = -20$
   $z = 2$
   $-4 + 3y = 5$

29. $x^3 x^{3/2} y^{a/3} x^{2a/3} x^{-a} y^{-2a}$
   $= x^{3+3/2+2a/3-a} y^{a/3-2a}$
   $= x^{(18+9+4a-6a)/6} y^{(a-6a)/3}$
   $= x^{(27-2a)/6} y^{-5a/3} = x^{9/2-a/3} y^{-5a/3}$

30. $6x^{9/3+9/2} - 8x^{a/3}z^{b/3} - 9x^{a/2}z^{2b/3} + 12z^{3b/3}$
   $= 6x^{(2a+3a)/6} - 8x^{a/3}z^{b/3} - 9x^{a/2}z^{2b/3} + 12z^b$
   $= 6x^{5a/6} - 8x^{a/3}z^{b/3} - 9x^{a/2}z^{2b/3} + 12z^b$

PROBLEM SET 2

1. T = tens' digit $175N = 875$
   U = units' digit $N = \mathbf{5}$
   $10T + U$ = original number $D = \mathbf{20}$
   $10U + T$ = reversed number $S = \mathbf{10}$
   $T + U = 9$
   $T = 9 - U$
   $10U + T = 10T + U + 9$
   $9U - 9T = 9$
   $U - T = 1$
   $T = U - 1$
   $T = 9 - U$ and $T = U - 1$
   Therefore $9 - U = U - 1$
   $10 = 2U$
   $U = 5$
   $T = 4$
   Original number = **45**
   Reversed number = **54**

2. A: $N + D + S = 35$
   B: $5N + 10D + 100S = 1225$

   Substitute $S = 2N$ into A to get
   $N + D + 2N = 35$
   $3N + D = 35$

   C: $D = 35 - N$
   Substitute $S = 2N$ into B to get
   $5N + 10D + 100(2N) = 1225$

   D: $205N + 10D = 1225$
   Substitute C into D to get
   $205N + 10D(35 - 3N) = 1225$

3.
   $$\boxed{\begin{array}{c} P_N \\ 37\% \end{array}} + \boxed{\begin{array}{c} 143 \\ 73\% \end{array}} = \boxed{\begin{array}{c} P_N + 143 \\ 51\% \end{array}}$$
   $37P_N + 73(143) = 51(P_N + 143)$
   $37P_N + 10439 = 51P_N + 7293$
   $14P_N = 3146$
   $P_N = \mathbf{224.7\ liters}$

4. $G = R + B + 9$
   $B + G = 4R + 1$
   Substitute $R = 2B$ to get
   $G = 2B + B + 9$
   $B + G = 4(2B) + 1$

   $\qquad G - 3B = 9$
   $\qquad \underline{(-)G - 7B = 1}$
   $\qquad\qquad 4B = 8$
   $\qquad\qquad\ B = 2$
   $R = 2(2)$
   $R = \mathbf{4}$
   $G = 9 + 3(2)$
   $G = \mathbf{15}$

5. $\dfrac{2}{7}W = 7\dfrac{1}{8}$
   $W = \dfrac{57}{8} \cdot \dfrac{7}{2} = \dfrac{399}{16} = 24\dfrac{15}{16}$

6. $(-4, -2), (5, 7)$

$m = \dfrac{7 - (-2)}{5 - (-4)} = \dfrac{9}{9} = 1$

$m_\perp = -1$

$y = -x + b$

$5 = -1(-2) + b$

$5 = 2 + b$

$b = 3$

$y = -x + 3$

7. (*a*) **0.0168**

(*b*) **2.441 × 10⁸**

8. $y = 4^x$

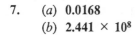

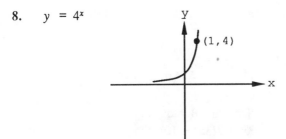

9. $y = \left(\dfrac{1}{3}\right)^x$

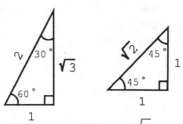

Use these triangles for problems 10 and 11.

10. $4\sqrt{3}\cos 60° = 4\sqrt{3}\left(\dfrac{1}{2}\right) = \dfrac{4\sqrt{3}}{2} = 2\sqrt{3}$

11. $8\tan 45° = 8(1) = 8$

12. A: $xy = 6$

B: $y = x - 3$

Substituting A into B gives

$x(x - 3) = 6$

$x^2 - 3x - 6 = 0$

$x = \dfrac{3 \pm \sqrt{9 - 4(1)(-6)}}{2} = \dfrac{3 \pm \sqrt{33}}{2}$

Substitute $x = \dfrac{3 + \sqrt{33}}{2}$ into $y = x - 3$

$y = \dfrac{3 + \sqrt{33}}{2} - 3 = \dfrac{3 + \sqrt{33} - 6}{2}$

$y = \dfrac{-3 + \sqrt{33}}{2}$

Substitute $x = \dfrac{3 - \sqrt{33}}{2}$ into $y = x - 3$

$y = \dfrac{3 - \sqrt{33}}{2} - 3 = \dfrac{3 - \sqrt{33} - 6}{2}$

$y = \dfrac{-3 - \sqrt{33}}{2}$

$\left(\dfrac{3 + \sqrt{33}}{2}, \dfrac{-3 + \sqrt{33}}{2}\right)$

$\left(\dfrac{3 - \sqrt{33}}{2}, \dfrac{-3 - \sqrt{33}}{2}\right)$

13. $(4ab^3 - 2p)(16a^2b^6 + 8ab^3p + 4p^2)$

14. $(3b^3a^2 - 4c)(9b^6a^4 + 12b^3a^2c + 16c^2)$

15. $\dfrac{\dfrac{a^3y - 6m^2x}{x^2y^2}}{\dfrac{l^2x^2 - 6ty^2}{x^2y^2}} = \dfrac{a^3y - 6m^2x}{x^2y^2} \cdot \dfrac{x^2y^2}{l^2x^2 - 6ty^2}$

$= \dfrac{a^3y - 6m^2x}{l^2x^2 - 6ty^2}$

16. $\dfrac{3x}{4y - \dfrac{6z}{\dfrac{8l + k}{2l}}} = \dfrac{3x}{4y - \dfrac{12zl}{8l + k}}$

$= \dfrac{3x}{\dfrac{32ly + 4ky - 12zl}{8l + k}}$

$= \dfrac{3x(8l + k)}{32ly + 4ky - 12zl}$

$= \dfrac{24xl + 3xk}{32ly + 4ky - 12zl}$

17. $2t = \dfrac{5z}{18s^2} - \dfrac{4m}{3s^2n}$

Multiply by $18s^2$

$36s^2nt = 5zn - 24m$

$5zn = 36s^2nt + 24m$

$z = \dfrac{36s^2nt + 24m}{5n} = \dfrac{36s^2t}{5} + \dfrac{24m}{5n}$

18.

$$x^3 + 2x^2 + 4x + 6 + 13/(x-2)$$

$$x - 2 \overline{)\; x^4 + 0x^3 + 0x^2 - 3x + 1}$$

$$\underline{x^4 - 2x^3}$$

$$2x^3 + 0x^2$$
$$\underline{2x^3 - 4x^2}$$

$$4x^2 - 2x$$
$$\underline{4x^2 - 8x}$$

$$6x + 1$$
$$\underline{6x - 12}$$

$$13$$

19.

$$6 \;\underline{/135°} = -4.24i + (-4.24)j$$
$$4 \;\underline{/-130°} = \underline{-2.57i + 3.06j}$$
$$ -6.81i - 1.18j$$

or $\tan H = \dfrac{1.18}{6.8}$

$H = 9.8°$

$r = \sqrt{1.18^2 + 6.8^2}$

$r = \sqrt{1.39 + 46.2}$

$r = \sqrt{47.63} = 6.9$

$A = 180° + 9.8° = 189.8°$

$$6.9 \;\underline{/189°}$$

20.

$$\sqrt{3}\sqrt{2}\sqrt{3}i\sqrt{2}i + \sqrt{3}\,(3i) + 5(4i) - 3i$$
$$= 6i^2 + 3\sqrt{3}\,i + 20i - 3i$$
$$= -6 + 17i + 3\sqrt{3}i$$
$$= -6 + \left(17 + 3\sqrt{3}\right)i$$

21.

$$\frac{3 - 4\sqrt{3}}{1 - 3\sqrt{3}} \cdot \frac{1 + 3\sqrt{3}}{1 + 3\sqrt{3}}$$

$$= \frac{3 - 4\sqrt{3} + 9\sqrt{3} - 36}{1 - 27} = \frac{-33 + 5\sqrt{3}}{-26}$$

$$= \frac{33 - 5\sqrt{3}}{26}$$

22.

$$\frac{5(-1) - 2(-i) + 1}{-2(-i) + 4i - 4i} = \frac{-4 + 2i}{+2i}$$

$$= \frac{-2 + i}{i}\frac{(-i)}{(-i)} = \frac{2i + 1}{-i^2} = 1 + 2i$$

23.

$$3x^2 - 5x + 4 = 0$$

$$x^2 - \frac{5}{3}x + \frac{25}{36} = -\frac{4}{3} + \frac{25}{36}$$

$$\left(x - \frac{5}{6}\right)^2 = -\frac{23}{36}$$

$$x - \frac{5}{6} = \pm\frac{\sqrt{23}\,i}{6} = \frac{5}{6} \pm \frac{\sqrt{23}}{6}i$$

24.

$$4x^2 + 6x - 9 = 0$$

$$x^2 + \frac{3}{2}x + \frac{9}{16} = \frac{9}{4} + \frac{9}{16}$$

$$\left(x + \frac{3}{4}\right)^2 = \frac{45}{16}$$

$$x + \frac{3}{4} = \pm\frac{3\sqrt{5}}{4}$$

$$x = -\frac{3}{4} \pm \frac{3\sqrt{5}}{4}$$

25. $n + 1 > n - 1$; therefore A

26. a and b are equal if $\dfrac{a}{b} = 1$; therefore C

27. A: $3x - 2y = 5$
B: $y = 3z - 10$
C: $2x - z = -1$
Substitute B into A to get
$3x - 2(3z - 10) = 5$
$3x - 6z = -15$
$3x - 6(2x + 1) = -15$
$3x - 12x - 6 = -15$
$-9x = -9$
$x = 1$
$z = 2(1) + 1 = 3$
$y = 3(3) - 10 = -1$
(1, -1, 3)

28. A: $4x - 5y = 10$
B: $-6y + z = -8$
C: $x - 5z = -15$
Substitute $z = 6y - 8$ into C to get
$x - 5(6y - 8) = -15$
$x - 30y = -55$
$x = 30y - 55$ (substitute into A)
$4(30y - 5) - 5y = 10$
$120y - 220 - 5y = 10$
$115y = 230$
$y = 2$
$x = 30(2) - 55 = 5$
$z = 6(2) - 8 = 4$
(5, 2, 4)

29. $a^{2x}b^{3x}a^{3x/2}b^{-x+y}a^{-1} = a^{2x+3x/2-1}b^{3x-x+y}$
$= a^{7x/2-1}b^{2x+y}$

30. $6x^{3a}y^{2a} - 4y^{5a/2} - 3x^{5a} + 2x^{2a}y^{a/2}$

PROBLEM SET 3

1. T = tens' digit
U = units' digit
$10T + U$ = original number
$10U + T$ = reversed number
$T + U = 8$
$T = 8 - U$
$10U + T = 10T + U - 36$
$9U - 9T = -36$
$T - U = 4$
$T = U + 4 = 8 - U$
$2U = 4$
$U = 2$
$T = 8 - 2 = 6$
Original number = **62**
Reversed number = **26**

2. $N_P + N_N + N_Q = 24$
$N_P + 5N_N + 25N_Q = 160$
$N_N = N_P$ (substitute into the above equations)

$N_N + N_N + N_Q = 24$
$N_N + 5N_N + 25N_Q = 160$

$2N_N + N_Q = 24$
$6N_N + 25N_Q = 160$

$N_Q = 24 - 2N_N$
(substitute into second equation)

$6N_N + 25(24 - 2N_N) = 160$
$6N_N + 600 - 50N_N = 160$
$-44N_N = -440$
$N_N = \mathbf{10}$
$N_P = \mathbf{10}$
$N_Q = \mathbf{4}$

3.

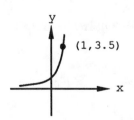

$33\frac{1}{3}(27) + 0x = 25(27 + x)$

$x = \frac{1}{25}(900 - 675)$

$x = \mathbf{9\ gal}$

4. $2(B + G) = R + 4$
$R + B = G + 7$
$R = 2G$ (substitute)

$2B + 2G - R = 4$
$R + B - G = 7$

$2B + 2G - 2G = 4$
$2G + B - G = 7$

$2B = 4$
$B = \mathbf{2}$
$G = \mathbf{5}$
$R = \mathbf{10}$

5. $4\frac{1}{2}x = 2\frac{1}{5}$

$\frac{9}{2}x = \frac{11}{5}$

$x = \frac{11}{5} \cdot \frac{2}{9} = \mathbf{\frac{22}{45}}$

6. $m = \frac{-2 - 7}{-8 + 5} = \frac{-9}{-3} = 3$

$m_\perp = -\frac{1}{3}$

$y = -\frac{1}{3}x + b$

$-2 = -\frac{1}{3}(5) + b$

$-2 = -\frac{5}{3} + b$

$-\frac{1}{3} = b$

$y = -\frac{1}{3}x - \frac{1}{3}$

7. (a) **0.3121**
(b) **0.3872**

8. $y = 3.5^x$

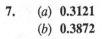

9. $y = \left(\frac{1}{2}\right)^x$

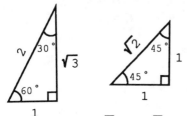

Use these triangles for problems 10 and 11.

10. $2\sqrt{2}\sin 60° = 2\sqrt{2}\left(\dfrac{\sqrt{3}}{2}\right) = \dfrac{2\sqrt{6}}{2} = \sqrt{6}$

11. $4\sqrt{3}\cos 45° = 4\sqrt{3}\left(\dfrac{\sqrt{2}}{2}\right) = \dfrac{4\sqrt{6}}{2} = 2\sqrt{6}$

12. The line segments have the same length.

13. An angle whose measure is between $0°$ and $90°$.

14.

$$x^2 - 2y^2 = -9$$
$$\underline{-x^2 - \;\;y^2 = -18}$$
$$-3y^2 = -27$$
$$y = 9$$
$$y = \pm 3$$

If $y = 3$	If $y = -3$
$x^2 = 18 - (3)^2$	$x^2 = 18 - (-3)^2$
$x^2 = 18 - 9$	$x^2 = 19 = 8 - 9$
$x^2 = 9$	$x^2 = 9$
$x = \pm 3$	$x = \pm 3$

$(3, 3), (3, -3), (-3, 3), (-3, -3)$

15. $(2xb^2 - 3p)(4x^2b^4 + 6xb^2p + 9p^2)$

16. $\dfrac{\dfrac{b^3c - 6m^2a}{a^2c^2}}{\dfrac{x^3c - 6ya^2}{a^2c^2}} = \dfrac{b^3c - 6m^2a}{a^2c^2} \cdot \dfrac{a^2c^2}{x^3c - 6ya^2}$

$= \dfrac{b^3c - 6m^2a}{x^3c - 65ya^2}$

17. $\dfrac{3s}{2m - \dfrac{z}{1 + \dfrac{k}{l}}} = \dfrac{3s}{2m - \dfrac{z}{\dfrac{l+k}{l}}} = \dfrac{3s}{2m - \dfrac{zl}{l+k}}$

$= \dfrac{3s}{\dfrac{2ml + 2mk - zl}{l+k}} = \dfrac{3sl + 3sk}{2ml + 2mk - zl}$

18. $3z = \dfrac{12ms}{nt} - \dfrac{8ml}{nk}$

Multiply by ntk

$3ntkz = 12msk - 8mlt$

$3nkzt + 8mlt = 12msk$

$t(3nkz + 8ml) = 12msk$

$t = \dfrac{12msk}{3nkz + 8ml}$

19.

$$
\begin{array}{r}
x^2 - 4x - 11 - 21/(x-2) \\
x - 2 \;\overline{)\; x^3 - 6x^2 - 3x + 1} \\
\underline{x^3 - 2x^2} \\
-4x^2 - 3x \\
\underline{4x^2 + 8x} \\
-11x + 1 \\
\underline{-11x + 22} \\
-21
\end{array}
$$

20. $-4 \;\underline{/-140°} = 3.06i + 2.57j$

$-6 \;\underline{/150°} = \underline{5.20i - 3j}$

Resultant: $\qquad 8.26i - 0.43j$

Equilibrant: $\qquad \mathbf{-8.26i + 0.43j}$

21. $\sqrt{5}\sqrt{2}\sqrt{5}\,i\sqrt{2}\,i + \sqrt{3}(3i) + 5 \cdot 2\sqrt{2}\,i\sqrt{2} + 6i$

$= 10i^2 + 3\sqrt{3}\,i + 20i + 6i$

$= \mathbf{-10 + \left(3\sqrt{3} + 26\right)i}$

22. $\dfrac{2 - 6\sqrt{6}}{3 + 2\sqrt{6}} \cdot \dfrac{3 - 2\sqrt{6}}{3 - 2\sqrt{6}}$

$= \dfrac{6 - 4\sqrt{6} - 18\sqrt{6} + 72}{9 - 24}$

$= \dfrac{78 - 22\sqrt{6}}{15} = \dfrac{-78 + 22\sqrt{6}}{15}$

23. $\dfrac{-6i - 4 - 6i}{-3 - 5i + 5i} = \dfrac{-4 - 12i}{-3}$

$= \dfrac{4 + 12i}{3} = \dfrac{4}{3} + 4i$

24. $4x^2 - 6x + 5 = 0$

$x^2 - \dfrac{3}{2}x + \dfrac{9}{16} = -\dfrac{5}{4} + \dfrac{9}{16}$

$\left(x - \dfrac{3}{4}\right)^2 = -\dfrac{11}{16}$

$x = \dfrac{3}{4} \pm \dfrac{\sqrt{11}\,i}{4}$

25. a is positive and b is positive

$\dfrac{a}{b} = \dfrac{2}{1}$

$a > b$; therefore A

26. **D**

27.
$3x - 2y + z = -1$
$\underline{x + 2y - z = 9}$
$4x = 8$
$x = 2$

$x + 2y - z = 9$
$\underline{4x - 2y + 4z = 4}$
$5x + 3z = 13$
$5(2) + 3z = 13$
$3z = 13 - 10 = 3$
$z = 1$
$2 + 2y - 1 = 9$
$y = 4$
(2, 4, 1)

28. A: $2x - y = 2$
B: $-x + 2z = -2$
C: $2y - 2z = 10$

B: $-x + 2z = -2$
$\underline{\text{C: } 2y - 2z = 10}$
$-x + 2y = 8$
$\underline{\text{2A: } 4x - 2y = 4}$
$3x = 12$
$x = 4$

$2(4) - y = 2$
$y = 6$
$-4 + 2z = -2$
$2z = 2$
$z = 1$
(4, 6, 1)

29. $\dfrac{x^{3a+2}\left(x^{3/2}\right)^{2a}}{y^{2a-4}\left(x^{1/2}\right)^{2a+1}} = \dfrac{x^{3a+2}x^{3a}}{y^{2a-4}x^{a+1/2}}$

$= x^{3a+2}x^{3a}y^{-2a+4}x^{-a-1/2} = x^{3a+2+3a-a-1/2}y^{-2a+4}$

$= x^{5a+3/2}y^{-2a+4}$

30. $36x^3 + 12x^{3/2}y^{1/2} - 12x^{3/2}y^{1/2} - 4y$

$= \mathbf{36x^3 - 4y}$

PROBLEM SET 4

1.
$N_D + N_Q + H = 14$
$10N_D + 25N_Q + 50H = 250$
$N_Q = H \text{ (substitute)}$

$N_D + H + H = 14$
$10N_D + 25H + 50H = 250$

$N_D + 2H = 14$
$10N_D + 75H = 250$

$N_D = 14 - 2H \text{ (substitute)}$
$10(14 - 2H) + 75H = 250$
$140 - 20H + 75H = 250$
$55H = 110$
$H = \mathbf{2}$
$N_Q = \mathbf{2}$
$N_D = \mathbf{10}$

2. $T = \text{tens' digit}$
$U = \text{units' digit}$

$10T + U = \text{original number}$
$10U + T = \text{reversed number}$

$T + U = 10$
$U = 10 - T$
$10U + T = 10T + U - 36$
$9U - 9T = -36$
$9(10 - T) - 9T = -36$
$90 - 9T - 9T = -36$
$-18T = -126$
$T = 7$
$U = 10 - 7 = 3$
Original number $= \mathbf{73}$
Reversed number $= \mathbf{37}$

3.

$$\boxed{\begin{array}{c}P_N \\ 3.5\%\end{array}} + \boxed{\begin{array}{c}176 \\ 4.75\%\end{array}} = \boxed{\begin{array}{c}P_N + 176 \\ 4\%\end{array}}$$

$$3.5P_N + 4.75(176) = 4(P_N + 176)$$
$$350P_N + 475(176) = 400(P_N + 176)$$
$$50P_N = 13200$$
$$P_N = \textbf{264 ml}$$

4.
$$N_R + N_B = 1 + N_G$$
$$3N_R + 2N_B = N_G + 9$$
$$3N_B = N_G + 2$$

$$N_R + N_B - N_G = 1$$
$$3N_R + 2N_B - N_G = 9$$
$$N_G = 3N_B - 2 \text{ (substitute)}$$

$$N_R + N_B - 3N_B + 2 = 1$$
$$3N_R + 2N_B - 3N_B + 2 = 9$$

$$N_R - 2N_B = -1$$
$$3N_R - N_B = 7$$
Substitute $N_R = 2N_B - 1$
$$3(2N_B - 1) - N_B = 7$$
$$6N_B - 3 - N_B = 7$$
$$5N_B = 10$$
$$N_B = \textbf{2}$$
$$N_R = \textbf{3}$$
$$N_G = \textbf{4}$$

5.
$$3\frac{1}{8}M = 8\frac{1}{4}$$
$$\frac{25}{8}M = \frac{33}{4}$$
$$M = \frac{33}{4} \cdot \frac{8}{25}$$
$$M = \frac{\textbf{66}}{\textbf{25}}$$

6.
$$m = \frac{-3 - 2}{8 - 5} = \frac{-5}{3}$$
$$m_\perp = \frac{3}{5}$$
$$y = \frac{3}{5}x + b$$
$$-3 = \frac{3}{5}(-2) + b$$
$$-3 = -\frac{6}{5} + b$$
$$b = -\frac{9}{5}$$
$$y = \frac{3}{5}x - \frac{9}{5}$$

7. (a) **1733.5**
(b) **0.62**

8. $y = 4.3^x$

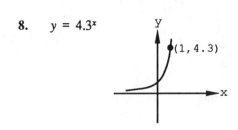

9. $y = \left(\frac{1}{10}\right)^x$

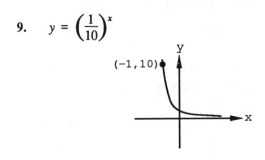

Use these triangles for problems 10–13.

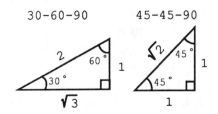

10. $\dfrac{1}{2} + \dfrac{\sqrt{2}}{2} = \dfrac{1 + \sqrt{2}}{2}$

11. $1 + 2\left(\dfrac{\sqrt{3}}{3}\right) = 1 + \dfrac{2\sqrt{3}}{3} = \dfrac{3 + 2\sqrt{3}}{3}$

12. $\dfrac{\sqrt{3}}{2}\left(\dfrac{\sqrt{3}}{3}\right) + \sqrt{2}\left(\dfrac{1}{2}\right) = \dfrac{1 + \sqrt{2}}{2}$

13. $\sqrt{2}\left(\dfrac{1}{2}\right) + 2(1) = \dfrac{\sqrt{2} + 4}{2}$

14. $x^2 + y^2 = 4$
$y = 1 - 2x$ (substitute)

$$x^2 + (1 - 2x)^2 = 4$$
$$x^2 + 1 - 4x + 4x^2 = 4$$
$$5x^2 - 4x - 3 = 0$$
$$x = \frac{4 \pm \sqrt{16 - 4(5)(-3)}}{2(5)}$$

$$x = \frac{4 \pm \sqrt{76}}{10} = \frac{4 \pm 2\sqrt{19}}{10} = \frac{2 \pm \sqrt{19}}{5}$$

$$y = 1 - 2x$$

$$y = 1 - 2\left(\frac{2 \pm \sqrt{19}}{5}\right)$$

$$y = \frac{5}{5} - \frac{4 \pm 2\sqrt{19}}{5}$$

$$y = \frac{1 \pm 2\sqrt{19}}{5}$$

$$\left(\frac{2 + \sqrt{19}}{5}, \frac{1 - 2\sqrt{19}}{5}\right)$$

$$\left(\frac{2 - \sqrt{19}}{5}, \frac{1 + 2\sqrt{19}}{5}\right)$$

15. $(3a^2b^3 - 2p)(9a^4b^6 + 6a^2b^3p + 4p^2)$

16.
$$\frac{\dfrac{ac^3 - 6m^3xy}{x^3y^2}}{\dfrac{d^2fy - gx^2f}{x^2fy}}$$

$$= \frac{ac^3 - 6m^3xy}{x^3y^2} \cdot \frac{x^2fy}{d^2fy - gx^2f}$$

$$= \frac{ac^3 - 6m^3xy}{d^2xy^2 - gx^3y}$$

17.
$$\frac{2z}{1 - \dfrac{\dfrac{3k}{mt - s}}{t}} = \frac{2z}{1 - \dfrac{3kt}{mt - s}}$$

$$= \frac{2z}{\dfrac{mt - s - 3kt}{mt - s}} = \frac{2zmt - 2zs}{mt - s - 3kt}$$

18. $4s = \dfrac{3zat^2}{2m} - \dfrac{18mz}{mh}$

Multiply by $2mh$

$8mhs = 3zat^2h - 36mz$

$8mhs - 3zat^2h = -36mz$

$h(8ms - 3zat^2) = -36mz$

$$h = \frac{36mz}{3zat^2 - 8ms}$$

19.

$$
\begin{array}{r}
x^3 - x + \quad (x - 3)/(x^2 + 1) \\
x^2 + 1\ \overline{)\ x^5 + 0x^3 + 0x - 3} \\
\underline{x^5 + x^3} \\
-x^3 + 0x \\
\underline{-x^3 - x} \\
x - 3
\end{array}
$$

20. $-6\ \underline{/30°}\ = \quad -5.2i - 3j$

$8\ \underline{/-140°}\ = \ \underline{-6.13i - 5.14j}$

Resultant: $\quad -11.32i - 8.14j$

Equilibrant: $\quad 11.32i + 8.14j$

21. $\sqrt{6}\sqrt{3}\sqrt{2}\,i\sqrt{4}\,i + \sqrt{2}\sqrt{2}\,i - 6 \cdot 2\sqrt{2}\,i\sqrt{2}$

$= 24i^2 + 2i - 24i = -24 - 22i$

22. $\dfrac{3 - 6\sqrt{2}}{4 + 6\sqrt{2}} \cdot \dfrac{\left(4 - 6\sqrt{2}\right)}{\left(4 - 6\sqrt{2}\right)}$

$$= \frac{12 - 18\sqrt{2} - 24\sqrt{2} + 72}{16 - 72}$$

$$= \frac{84 - 42\sqrt{2}}{-56} = \frac{-6 + 3\sqrt{2}}{4}$$

23. $\dfrac{8(1) - 4(-i) - 6i}{-3(-i) + 5i - 4i} = \dfrac{8 - 2i}{4i}$

$$= \frac{4 - i}{2i} \cdot \frac{-2i}{-2i} = \frac{-8i + 2i^2}{-4i^2}$$

$$= \frac{-2 - 8i}{4} = -\frac{1}{2} - 2i$$

24. $5x^2 + 2x - 6 = 0$

$$x^2 + \frac{2}{5}x + \frac{1}{25} = \frac{6}{5} + \frac{1}{25}$$

$$\left(x + \frac{1}{5}\right)^2 = \frac{31}{25}$$

$$x + \frac{1}{5} = \pm\frac{\sqrt{31}}{5}$$

$$x = -\frac{1}{5} \pm \frac{\sqrt{31}}{5}$$

25. If $\dfrac{a}{b} = \dfrac{c}{d}$ then $ad = bc$.

Therefore $ad > bc - 1$.

A

26. If $a > b$ then $-a < -b$.

B

27.
A: $2x - 3y + z = -6$

B: $\underline{\ x + 2y - z = 1\ }$

D: $3x - y \quad = -5$

2A: $4x - 6y + z = -12$

C: $\underline{\ 3x + y - 2z = -5\ }$

E: $7x - 5y = -17$

-5D: $-15x + 5y = 25$

E: $\underline{7x - 5y = -17}$

$\qquad -8x = 8$

$\qquad\quad x = -1$

$z = 2$

$y = 2$

$(-1, 2, 2)$

$x + 2(2) = 14$

$x = 10$

$y - 8(2) = -12$

$y = 4$

$(10, 4, 2)$

29. $a^{3z+6}\left(b^{3/4}\right)^{3z+2}b^{-3z+2}a^{-4z+3}$

$= a^{3z+6}b^{9z/4+3/2}b^{-3z+2}a^{-4z+3}$

$= a^{3z+6-4z+3}b^{9z/4+3/2-3z+2}$

$= a^{-z+9}b^{-3z/4+7/2}$

28. A: $4x + 5z = 50$

B: $y - 8z = -12$

C: $x + 2z = 14$

A: $4x + 5z = 50$

$\underline{-4\text{C}: 4x - 8z = -56}$

$\qquad\quad -3z = -6$

$\qquad\qquad z = 2$

30. $12x^0 + 4x^{1/2}z^{1/4} - 6x^{-1/2}z^{-3/4} - 2z^{-1/2}$

$12 + 4x^{1/2}z^{1/4} - 6x^{-1/2}z^{-3/4} - 2z^{-1/2}$

PROBLEM SET 5

1.

	Now	−5 years	+5 years
Orville:	O_N	$O_N - 5$	$O_N + 5$
Wilbur:	W_N	$W_N - 5$	$W_N + 5$

$O_N - 5 = 2\left(W_N - 5\right)$

$O_N - 5 = 2W_N - 10$

$O_N + 5 = \dfrac{3}{2}\left(W_N + 5\right)$

$2O_N + 10 = 3W_N + 15$

$O_N - 2W_N = -5$

$2O_N - 3W_N = 5$

$2O_N - 4W_N = -10$

$\underline{-2O_N + 3W_N = 5}$

$\qquad\quad -W_N = -15$

$W_N = 15$

$O_N = 25$

$R_P T_P + R_T T_T = 6$

$\dfrac{2}{3}(T + 1) + \dfrac{3}{2}T = 6$

$\dfrac{2}{3}T + \dfrac{3}{2}T = \dfrac{16}{3}$

$T = \dfrac{32}{13}\,\text{hr}$

3.

	Rate
Sandra:	$\dfrac{3}{5}$
Fred:	R_F

Time together $= 3$

$R_S T_S + R_F T_F = 3$

$\dfrac{3}{5}(3) + R_F(3) = 3$

$R_F = \dfrac{2}{5}\,\dfrac{\text{sandcastles}}{\text{hr}}$

4. Rate $\cdot$ time $\cdot$ cows $=$ jobs

Rate $\cdot\ 9\ \cdot\ 6 = 1$

Rate $= \dfrac{1}{54}$

$\dfrac{1}{54}\cdot\ 5\ \cdot$ cows $= 3$

Cows $= 32\dfrac{2}{5}$

2.

	Rate
Peter:	$\dfrac{2}{3}\dfrac{\text{holes}}{\text{hr}}$
Thomas:	$\dfrac{3}{2}\dfrac{\text{holes}}{\text{hr}}$

$T = $ time worked together

5.
$$T + U = 14$$
$$0.75U + U = 14$$
$$1.75U = 14$$
$$U = 8$$
$$\frac{T}{U} = 0.75$$
$$0.75U = T$$
$$T = 6$$
Number = **68**

6.
$$m = \frac{4 - 2}{3 + 1} = \frac{2}{4} = \frac{1}{2}$$
$$y = mx + b$$
$$1 = \frac{1}{2}(3) + b$$
$$1 = \frac{3}{2} + b$$
$$b = 1 - \frac{3}{2} = -\frac{1}{2}$$
$$y = \frac{1}{2}x - \frac{1}{2}$$

7.   (a) $2.61^{5.1} \approx \mathbf{133.31}$
  (b) $2.4^{-2.1} \approx \mathbf{0.16}$

8. $y = 2.5^x$

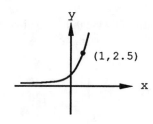

(1, 2.5)

9. $y = \left(\frac{1}{3}\right)^x$

(−1, 3)

Use 30–60–90 and 45–45–90 triangles for problems 10–13. (Refer to Problem Set 1, problem 8.)

10. $\dfrac{\sqrt{2}}{2}\cos 45° - 2\sin 60° = \dfrac{\sqrt{2}}{2}\left(\dfrac{\sqrt{2}}{2}\right) - 2\dfrac{\sqrt{3}}{2}$

$= \dfrac{1}{2} - \sqrt{3} = \dfrac{1 - 2\sqrt{3}}{2}$

11. $\sin 60° - \cos 30° = \dfrac{\sqrt{3}}{2} - \dfrac{\sqrt{3}}{2} = 0$

12. $\dfrac{\sqrt{3}}{2}\cos 30° + \dfrac{1}{2}\sin 30°$

$= \dfrac{\sqrt{3}}{2}\left(\dfrac{\sqrt{3}}{2}\right) + \dfrac{1}{2}\left(\dfrac{1}{2}\right) = \dfrac{3}{4} + \dfrac{1}{4} = 1$

13. $\sqrt{2}\sin 30° - 2\tan 30° = \sqrt{2}\left(\dfrac{1}{2}\right) - 2\left(\dfrac{\sqrt{3}}{3}\right)$

$= \dfrac{\sqrt{2}}{2} - \dfrac{2\sqrt{3}}{3} = \dfrac{3\sqrt{2} - 4\sqrt{3}}{6}$

14.
$$\begin{array}{rcl} x^2 + y^2 & = & 9 \\ 2x^2 - y^2 & = & 6 \\ \hline 3x^2 & = & 15 \\ x^2 & = & 5 \\ x & = & \pm\sqrt{5} \end{array}$$
$$5 + y^2 = 9$$
$$y^2 = 4$$
$$y = \pm 2$$
$$\left(\sqrt{5}, -2\right), \left(\sqrt{5}, 2\right), \left(-\sqrt{5}, -2\right), \left(-\sqrt{5}, 2\right)$$

15. $8x^3y^6 - 27a^6b9 = (2xy^2)^3 - (3a^2b^3)^3$
$= (2xy^2 - 3a^2b^3)(4x^2y^4 + 6a^2b^3xy^2 + 9a^4b^6)$

16. $\dfrac{\dfrac{b^2c}{x^3y} - \dfrac{6m^2}{x^2y^2}}{\dfrac{mf}{x^3} + \dfrac{h}{y^2}} = \dfrac{\dfrac{b^2cy - 6m^2x}{x^3y^2}}{\dfrac{mfy^2 + hx^3}{x^3y^2}} = \dfrac{b^2cy - 6m^2x}{mfy^2 + hx^3}$

17. $\dfrac{3s}{2 - \dfrac{6l}{m - \dfrac{q}{r}}} = \dfrac{3s}{2 - \dfrac{6l}{\dfrac{mr - q}{r}}}$

$= \dfrac{3s}{2 - \dfrac{6lr}{mr - q}} = \dfrac{3s}{\dfrac{2mr - 2q - 6lr}{mr - q}}$

$= \dfrac{3mrs - 3qs}{2mr - 2q - 6lr}$

18. $5s = \dfrac{18kt}{mz} - \dfrac{12k^2}{m^2}$

Multiply by m^2z.
$$5m^2sz = 18kmt - 12k^2z$$
$$z(5m^2s + 12k^2) = 18kmt$$
$$z = \dfrac{18kmt}{5m^2s + 12k^2}$$

19.

$$x - 2 \overline{)\, x^4 - 6x^3 + 7x^2 + 0x - 5\,} \quad x^3 - 4x^2 - x - 2 - 9/(x{-}2)$$

$$\underline{x^4 - 2x^3}$$
$$-4x^3 + 7x^2$$
$$\underline{-4x^3 + 8x^2}$$
$$-x^2 + 0x$$
$$\underline{-x^2 + 2x}$$
$$-2x - 5$$
$$\underline{-2x + 4}$$
$$-9$$

20. $-5 \;\underline{/60°} \;+\; 10 \;\underline{/220°}$

$x_1 = -2.50$	$y_1 = -4.33$
$x_2 = \underline{-7.66}$	$y_2 = \underline{-6.43}$
$x_T = -10.16$	$y_T = -10.76$

Equilibrant $= \mathbf{10.16}i + \mathbf{10.76}j$

21. $-6 + 3i - 28i = \mathbf{-6 - 25i}$

22. $\dfrac{3 - 4\sqrt{3}}{4 + 3\sqrt{3}} \dfrac{\left(4 - 3\sqrt{3}\right)}{\left(4 - 3\sqrt{3}\right)}$

$$= \dfrac{12 - 25\sqrt{3} + 36}{16 - 27} = \dfrac{48 - 25\sqrt{3}}{-11}$$

$$= \dfrac{48 + 25\sqrt{3}}{11}$$

23. $\dfrac{6i - 4i - 6i}{3i + 6i - 3i} = \dfrac{-4i}{6i} = -\dfrac{2}{3}$

24. $6x^2 + 3x = 8$

$$x^2 + \dfrac{1}{2}x + \dfrac{1}{16} = \dfrac{4}{3} + \dfrac{1}{16}$$

$$\left(x + \dfrac{1}{4}\right)^2 = \dfrac{16}{48}$$

$$x = -\dfrac{1}{4} + \dfrac{\sqrt{67}}{4\sqrt{3}} = -\dfrac{1}{4} + \dfrac{\sqrt{201}}{12}$$

25. $AB > CB$; therefore

$A > C$ if B is positive

$A < C$ if B is negative

Thus the answer is D

26. $A + B > C + B$

$A > C$; therefore the answer is A

27.
$$2x + 2y - z = 8$$
$$\underline{x - 2y + z = -2}$$
$$3x \qquad\qquad = 6$$
$$x \qquad\qquad = 2$$

Substitute x back into the second equation.

$-2y + z = -2 - 2 = -4$

Multiply by -3 and add the last equation.

$$6y - 3z = 12$$
$$\underline{y + 3z = -5}$$
$$7y \qquad = 7$$
$$y \qquad = 1$$

$z = -2 - 2 + 2(1) = -2$

$(2, 1, -2)$

28. $4x - 3y = 24$

$x + 3z = 15$

$4y + 2z = 20$

Multiply the third equation by 6.

$$4x - 3y = 24$$
$$\underline{-4x - 12z = -60}$$
$$-3y - 12z = -36$$
$$\underline{24y + 12z = 120}$$
$$24y \qquad = 84$$
$$y \qquad = 4$$

$$z = \dfrac{120 - 24(4)}{12} = \dfrac{24}{12} = 2$$

$x = 15 - 3(2) = 9$

$(9, 4, 2)$

29. $a^{2z-3}b^{4z+8}a^{-4z-2}b^{-2z+3} = a^{-2z-5}b^{2z+11}$

30. $(3x^{1/2} - 2z^{1/4})(3x^{1/2} + 2z^{1/4}) = 9x - 4z^{1/2}$

1.

	Now	+5 years	−5 years
Charlotte:	C_N	$C_N + 10$	$C_N - 5$
Emily:	E_N	$E_N + 10$	$C_N - 5$

$(C_N + 10) = 2(E_N + 10)$
$C_N + 10 = 2E_N + 20$
$C_N = 2E_N + 10$
$(C_N - 5) = 5(E_N - 5)$
$C_N - 5 = 5E_N - 25$
$C_N = 5E_N - 20$
$2E_N + 10 = 5E_N - 20$
$30 = 3E_N$
$E_N = \mathbf{10}$
$C_N = \mathbf{30}$

2.

	Rate
Father:	$\dfrac{1}{30}\dfrac{\text{lawn}}{\text{min}}$
Daughter:	$\dfrac{1}{40}\dfrac{\text{lawn}}{\text{min}}$

T = time working together
$R_F T_F + R_D T_D = 1$
$\dfrac{1}{30}(T + 10) + \dfrac{1}{40}T = 1$
$T = \dfrac{80}{7}$ **min**

3. Rate · time · men = food
Rate · 10 · 20 = 360
Rate = $\dfrac{9}{5}$

$\dfrac{9}{5}$ · time · 25 = 360
Time = **8 days**

4. $R_S T_S = 450$
$R_R T_R = 325$
$R_S + 20 = R_R$
$R_S = R_R - 20$
$2T_R = T_S$
$(R_R - 20)(2T_R) = 450$
$2R_R T_R - 40T_R = 450$
$2(325) - 40T_R = 450$
$200 = 40T_R$
$T_R = \mathbf{5\ hr}$
$R_S = \mathbf{45\ mph}$
$R_R = \mathbf{65\ mph}$
$T_S = \mathbf{10\ hr}$

5. $\dfrac{V_1}{T_1} = \dfrac{V_2}{T_2}$

$\dfrac{400}{1000} = \dfrac{V_2}{2000}$

$V_2 = \mathbf{800\ liters}$

6. $y = 3.5^x$

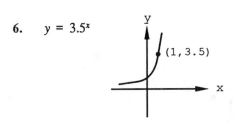

(1, 3.5)

Use the 30–60–90 and 45–45–90 triangles for problems 7–10. (Refer to Problem Set 1, problem 8.)

7. $\dfrac{\sqrt{3}}{2}\cos 45° - \dfrac{\sqrt{2}}{2}\sin 60°$

$= \dfrac{\sqrt{3}}{2}\left(\dfrac{\sqrt{2}}{2}\right) - \dfrac{\sqrt{2}}{2}\left(\dfrac{\sqrt{3}}{2}\right)$

$= \dfrac{\sqrt{6}}{4} - \dfrac{\sqrt{6}}{4} = \mathbf{0}$

8. $\dfrac{\sqrt{2}}{2}\tan 45° - \sqrt{3}\tan 30°$

$= \dfrac{\sqrt{2}}{2}(1) - \sqrt{3}\left(\dfrac{\sqrt{3}}{3}\right)$

$= \dfrac{\sqrt{2}}{2} - 1 = \dfrac{\sqrt{2} - 2}{2}$

9. $\dfrac{\sin 60°}{\cos 60°} - \tan 60°$

$= \dfrac{\dfrac{\sqrt{3}}{2}}{\dfrac{1}{2}} - \sqrt{3} = \sqrt{3} - \sqrt{3} = \mathbf{0}$

10. $2\sin 30° \cos 30° - \sin 60°$

$= 2\left(\dfrac{1}{2}\right)\left(\dfrac{\sqrt{3}}{2}\right) - \dfrac{\sqrt{3}}{2} = \dfrac{\sqrt{3}}{2} - \dfrac{\sqrt{3}}{2} = \mathbf{0}$

11. $\log^k 7 = p$
$k^p = \mathbf{7}$

12. $k^p = 7$
$\log_k 7 = \mathbf{p}$

13. $\log_b 27 = 3$

$b^3 = 27$

$b^3 = 3^3$

$b = 3$

14. $\log_2 \dfrac{1}{8} = m$

$2^m = \dfrac{1}{8}$

$2^m = 2^{-3}$

$m = -3$

15. $\log_{1/2} x = -4$

$\left(\dfrac{1}{2}\right)^{-4} = x$

$x = 16$

16. $2x^2 - y^2 = 1$

$y + 2x = 1$

$y = 1 - 2x$

$y^2 = 1 - 4x + 4x^2$

$2x^2 - 1 + 4x - 4x^2 = 1$

$2x^2 - 4x + 2 = 0$

$x^2 - 2x + 1 = 0$

$(x - 1)(x - 1) = 0$

$x = 1$

$y = -1$

$(1, -1)$

17. $64x^{12}y^6 - 27a^6b^9 = (4x^4y^2)^3 - (3a^2b^3)^3$

$= (4x^4y^2 - 3a^2b^3)(16x^8y^4 + 12a^2b^3x^4y^2 + 9a^4b^6)$

18. $\dfrac{\dfrac{cd^2}{x^2y^3} - \dfrac{6m^2}{x^2y}}{\dfrac{mf}{xy^2} + \dfrac{h}{y^3}} = \dfrac{\dfrac{cd^2 - 6m^2y^2}{x^2y^3}}{\dfrac{mfy + hx}{xy^3}}$

$= \dfrac{cd^2 - 6m^2y^2}{x^2y^3} \cdot \dfrac{xy^3}{mfy + hx} = \dfrac{cd^2 - 6m^2y^2}{fmxy - hx^2}$

19. $3s = \dfrac{6z}{3pt} - \dfrac{6q}{3pr}$

Multiply by $3prt$.

$9prst = 6rz - 6qt$

$t(9prs + 6q) = 6rz$

$t = \dfrac{6rz}{9prs + 6q} = \dfrac{2rz}{3prs + 2q}$

20. $-4 \underline{\big/ 130°} - 6 \underline{\big/ {-220°}}$

$x_1 = 2.57$	$y_1 = -3.06$
$x_2 = \underline{4.60}$	$y_2 = \underline{-3.86}$
$x_T = 7.17$	$y_T = -6.92$

Equalibrant: $-7.17i + 6.92j$

21. $\sqrt{3}\sqrt{-3}\sqrt{-6}\sqrt{2} + \sqrt{2}\sqrt{3}\sqrt{-2}\sqrt{-3} - 4i$

$= -6\sqrt{3} + 6(i)(i) - 4i$

$= -6\sqrt{3} - 6 - 4i$

22. $\left(\dfrac{4 - 6\sqrt{3}}{2 + 3\sqrt{3}}\right)\left(\dfrac{2 - 3\sqrt{3}}{2 - 3\sqrt{3}}\right) = \dfrac{8 - 24\sqrt{3} + 54}{4 - 27}$

$= \dfrac{62 - 24\sqrt{3}}{-23} = \dfrac{-62 + 24\sqrt{3}}{23}$

23. $\dfrac{6 + 4i + 6i}{4i + 6i - 2i} = \dfrac{6 + 10i}{8i} = \dfrac{3 + 5i}{4i}\left(\dfrac{i}{i}\right)$

$= \dfrac{3i + 5i^2}{4i^2} = \dfrac{-5 + 3i}{-4} = \dfrac{5}{4} - \dfrac{3}{4}i$

24. $2x^2 - 3x = 8$

$x^2 - \dfrac{3}{2}x = 4$

$x^2 - \dfrac{3}{2}x + \dfrac{9}{16} = 4 + \dfrac{9}{16}$

$\left(x - \dfrac{3}{4}\right)^2 = \dfrac{73}{16}$

$x = \dfrac{3}{4} \pm \dfrac{\sqrt{73}}{4}$

25. $\dfrac{A}{B} > \dfrac{C}{B}$

If $B > 0$ then $\dfrac{A}{B}B > \dfrac{C}{B}C$; thus $A > C$

If $B < 0$ then $\dfrac{A}{B}B < \dfrac{C}{B}B$; thus $A < C$

Therefore **D**

26. $A - B = A + B$

Thus, $-B = B$

$B = 0$; therefore **B**

27. A: $x - 2y + 2z = 4$

B: $2x - y - 2z = 8$

C: $x - 2y + z = 3$

Add A + B to get

$3x - 3y = 12$

$x - y = 4$

$x = 4 + y$ (substitute into the equation given

by B + 2C: $4x - 5y = 14$)

$4(4 + y) - 5y = 14$

$16 - y = 14$

$y = 2$

$x = 4 + 2 = 6$

$z = 3 - 6 + 2(2) = 1$

$(6, 2, 1)$

28. A: $4x + 3y = 24$
B: $x + 4z = 11$
C: $4y - 2z = 12$
B + 2C: $x + 8y = 35$
$\quad\quad\quad x = 35 - 8y$
Substitute into equation A to get
$4(35 - 8y) + 3y = 24$
$140 - 29y = 24$
$29y = 116$
$y = 4$
$x = 35 - 8(4) = 3$

$4z = 11 - 3$
$z = \dfrac{8}{4} = 2$
$(3, 4, 2)$

29. $x^{2a+3}(b^a)^{2a+2}x^{-3a+2}b^{-6a} = x^{2a+3}x^{-3a+2}b^{2a^2+2a}b^{-6a}$
$= x^{-a+5}b^{2a^2-4a}$

30. $(2x^{1/3} - 3z^{1/2})(2x^{2/3} + 3z^{1/2})$
$= 4x + 6x^{1/3}z^{1/2} - 6x^{2/3}z^{1/2} - 9z$

PROBLEM SET 7

1.

	Now	−5 years	+1 year
George:	G_N	$G_N - 5$	$G_N + 1$
Marshall:	M_N	$M_N - 5$	$M_N + 1$

$(G_N + 1) = 2(M_N + 1)$
$C_N = 2M_N + 1$
$(G_N - 5) = 8(M_N - 5)$
$G_N = 8M_N - 35$
$2M_N + 1 = 8M_N - 35$
$36 = 6M_N$
$M_N = \mathbf{6}$
$G_N = \mathbf{13}$

2.

	Rate
Marie:	$\dfrac{1}{10} \dfrac{\text{cake}}{\text{min}}$
Antoinette:	R_A

Time working together $= 4$
$R_N T_N + R_A T_A = 1$
$\dfrac{1}{10}(3 + 4) + R_A(4) = 1$
$R_A = \dfrac{3}{40} \dfrac{\text{cakes}}{\text{min}}$
$R_A T_A = 1$
$\dfrac{3}{40} T_A = 1$
$T_A = \dfrac{40}{3} \text{ min}$

3. $(B + W)T_D = D_D$
$(B + W)3 = 30$
$B + W = 10$
$(B - W)T_U = D_U$
$(B - W)5 = 30$
$B - W = 6$

$2B = 16$
$B = \mathbf{8 \text{ mph}}$
$W = \mathbf{2 \text{ mph}}$

4. $A = \dfrac{kw}{s^2}$
$28 = \dfrac{k(7)}{3^2}$
$k = 36$
$A = \dfrac{36w}{s^2} = \dfrac{36(4)}{2^2} = \mathbf{36 \text{ acorns}}$

5. Rate $\cdot$ time $\cdot$ men $=$ jobs
Rate $\cdot\ 3 \cdot 2 = 6$
Rate $= 1$
$1 \cdot$ time $\cdot\ 6 = 6$
Time $= \mathbf{1 \text{ day}}$

6. $y = \left(\dfrac{1}{3}\right)^x$

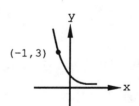

7. $2 \sin 135° = 2 \sin 45° = 2\left(\dfrac{\sqrt{2}}{2}\right) = \sqrt{2}$

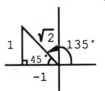

8. $-2 \cos(-300°) = -2 \cos 60° = -2\left(\frac{1}{2}\right) = \mathbf{-1}$

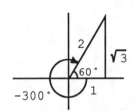

9. $3 \cos 300° - \cos 60° = 3 \cos 60° - \cos 60°$

$= 3\left(\frac{1}{2}\right) - \frac{1}{2} = \frac{3}{2} - \frac{1}{2} = \mathbf{1}$

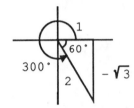

10. $\sin(-150°) + \dfrac{\sqrt{3}}{2} \sin 30°$

$= -\sin 30° + \dfrac{\sqrt{3}}{2} \sin 30° = -\dfrac{1}{2} + \dfrac{\sqrt{3}}{2}\left(\dfrac{1}{2}\right)$

$= -\dfrac{1}{2} + \dfrac{\sqrt{3}}{4} = \mathbf{\dfrac{-2 + \sqrt{3}}{4}}$

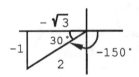

11. $\log_m 8 = n$

$\mathbf{m^n = 8}$

12. $7 = 3^k$

$\mathbf{\log_3 7 = k}$

13. $\log_B 64 = 3$

$B^3 = 64$

$B^3 = 4^3$

$\mathbf{B = 4}$

14. $\log_3 \dfrac{1}{27} = N$

$3^N = \dfrac{1}{27}$

$3^N = 3^{-3}$

$\mathbf{N = -3}$

15. $\log_{1/2} y = -2$

$\left(\dfrac{1}{2}\right)^{-2} = y$

$y = \mathbf{4}$

16. A: $x^2 + y^2 = 16$

B: $y - 3x = 4$

$y = 3x + 4$

$y^2 = 9x^2 + 24x + 16$

Substitute into equation A to get

$x^2 + 9x^2 + 24x + 16 = 16$

$10x^2 + 24x = 0$

$2x(5x + 12) = 0$

$x = 0, \ -\dfrac{12}{5}$

If $x = 0$

$y = 3(0) + 4 = 4$

$\mathbf{(0, 4)}$

If $x = -\dfrac{12}{5}$

$y = 3\left(-\dfrac{12}{5}\right) + 4 = -\dfrac{36}{5} + \dfrac{20}{5} = -\dfrac{16}{5}$

$\mathbf{\left(-\dfrac{12}{5}, -\dfrac{16}{5}\right)}$

17. $3y^{2n+1} + 12y^{3n+2} = \mathbf{3y^{2n+1}(1 + 4y^{n+1})}$

18. $\dfrac{\dfrac{ac^2}{bd^3} - \dfrac{c^3a}{b^2d}}{\dfrac{mn}{b^2d^2} - \dfrac{n}{d^3}} = \dfrac{\dfrac{abc^2 - ac^3d^2}{b^2d^3}}{\dfrac{dmn - b^2n}{b^2d^3}}$

$= \dfrac{abc^2 - ac^3d^2}{b^2d^3} \cdot \dfrac{b^2d^3}{dmn - b^2n}$

$= \mathbf{\dfrac{abc^2 - ac^3d^2}{dmn - b^2n}}$

19. $2t = \dfrac{3z}{25a} - \dfrac{k}{25p}$

Multiply by $25ap$

$50apt = 3pZ - ak$

$a(5050pt + k) = 3pz$

$\mathbf{a = \dfrac{3pz}{50pt + k}}$

20. $-2 \ \underline{/120°} + 5 \ \underline{/-130°}$

$x_1 = 1.00$	$y_1 = -1.73$
$x_2 = \underline{-3.21}$	$y_2 = \underline{-3.83}$
$x_T = -2.21$	$y_T = -5.56$

Equilibrant: $\mathbf{2.21i + 5.56j}$

21. $\sqrt{2}\sqrt{3}\sqrt{-3}\sqrt{-2} - \sqrt{2}\sqrt{6}\sqrt{-6}\sqrt{3} + 13i$

$= (2)(3)i^2 - 6i\sqrt{6} + 13i$

$= -6 - 6i\sqrt{6} + 13i$

$= -6 + \left(13 - 6\sqrt{6}\right)i$

22. $\dfrac{3 - 3\sqrt{2}}{1 + 4\sqrt{2}} \cdot \dfrac{1 - 4\sqrt{2}}{1 - 4\sqrt{2}}$

$= \dfrac{3 - 15\sqrt{2} + 24}{1 - 32} = \dfrac{27 - 15\sqrt{2}}{-31}$

$= \dfrac{-27 + 15\sqrt{2}}{31}$

23. $\dfrac{4 + 4}{1 - 2i} = \dfrac{8}{1 - 2i} \cdot \dfrac{1 + 2i}{1 + 2i}$

$= \dfrac{8 + 16i}{1 + 4} = \dfrac{8}{5} + \dfrac{16}{5}i$

24. $4x^2 - 2x = -2$

$x^2 - \dfrac{1}{2}x + \dfrac{1}{16} = -\dfrac{1}{2} + \dfrac{1}{16}$

$\left(x - \dfrac{1}{4}\right)^2 = -\dfrac{7}{16}$

$x = \dfrac{1}{4} \pm \dfrac{\sqrt{7}}{4}i$

25. $x^2 = 9 \qquad\qquad y^2 = 16$

$x = \pm 3 \qquad\qquad y = \pm 4$

Therefore **D**

26. $x^3 = -8 \qquad\qquad y^3 = -16$

$x = -2 \qquad\qquad y = \sqrt[3]{16}$

Therefore **A**

27. A: $2x - 5y = -40$

B: $x + 2z = 13$

C: $y - 2z = 2$

$$\begin{array}{rrrr} \text{A:} & 2x - & 5y & = -40 \\ 2(\text{B} + \text{C}): & -2x - & 2y & = -30 \\ \hline & & -7y & = -70 \\ & & y & = \ \ 10 \end{array}$$

$x + y = 15$

$x = 15 - 10 = 5$

$z = \dfrac{13 - 5}{2} = 4$

(5, 10, 4)

28. $x^{a+3}\left(x^{3/2}\right)^{a+1}x^{-3a+2} = x^{a+3}x^{3a/2+3/2}x^{-3a+2}$

$= x^{-a/2+13/2} = x^{(-a+13)/2}$

29. $9x^0 + 18x^{1/3}z^{-1/2} - 18x^{-1/3}z^{1/2} - 36z^0$

$= 9 + 18x^{1/3}z^{-1/2} - 18x^{-1/3}z^{1/2} - 36$

$= -27 + 18x^{1/3}z^{-1/2} - 18x^{-1/3}z^{1/2}$

30. $3y - 2x + 1 = 0$

$3y = 2x - 1$

$y = \dfrac{2}{3}x - \dfrac{1}{3}$

$m = \dfrac{2}{3}$ and passes through $(2, -1)$

$-1 = \dfrac{2}{3}(2) + b$

$-1 = \dfrac{4}{3} + b$

$b = -\dfrac{7}{3}$

$y = \dfrac{2}{3}x - \dfrac{7}{3}$

PROBLEM SET 8

1.

	Now	+7 years
Dylan:	D_N	$D_N + 7$
Thomas:	T_N	$T_N + 7$

$(D_N + 7) = 3D_N$

$D_N = 3T_N - 7$

$2T_N = D_N$

$3T_N - 7 = 2T_N$

$T_N =$ **7 years**

$D_N =$ **14 years**

2.

	Rate
James:	$\dfrac{1}{20}\dfrac{\text{mission}}{\text{hr}}$
Irwin:	R_I

Time together $= 4$

$R_S T_S + R_I T_I = 1$

$\dfrac{1}{20}(4 + 3) + R_I(4) = \dfrac{7}{20} + 4R_I(4) = 1$

$R_I = \dfrac{13}{80}$

$R_I T_I = \dfrac{13}{80}T_I = 1$ thus $T = \dfrac{80}{13}$ hr

3.

	Old	New
Distance:	x	x
Rate:	p	?
Time:	$\dfrac{x}{p}$	$\dfrac{x}{p} - 2$

$$\text{Rate} = \frac{x}{\dfrac{x}{p} - 2} = \frac{x}{\dfrac{x - 2p}{p}}$$

$$= \frac{xp}{x - 2p}\ \text{mph}$$

4.

	Old	New
Distance:	RT	$RT + 20$
Rate:	R	$R + 5$
Time:	T	?

$$\text{Time} = \frac{RT + 20}{R + 5}\ \text{hr}$$

5. Rate $\cdot$ time $\cdot$ men = jobs

Rate $\cdot$ 5 $\cdot$ 7 = 3

$$\text{Rate} = \frac{3}{35}$$

$$\frac{3}{35} \cdot \text{time} \cdot 10 = 4$$

$$\text{Time} = \frac{14}{3}\ \text{days}$$

6. $y = 2.5^x$

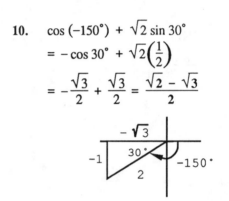

(1, 2.5)

7. $3 \sin 210° = 3(-\sin 30°) = 3\left(-\dfrac{1}{2}\right) = -\dfrac{3}{2}$

210°
$-\sqrt{3}$
30°
-1
2

8. $-2 \sin(-300°) = -2(\sin 60°) = -2\left(\dfrac{\sqrt{3}}{2}\right)$

$$= -\sqrt{3}$$

$-300°$
2
$\sqrt{3}$
60°
1

9. $2 \cos(-330°) + \sin 60°$

$= 2 \cos 30° + \sin 60°$

$$= 2\left(\frac{\sqrt{3}}{2}\right) + \frac{\sqrt{3}}{2} = \sqrt{3} + \frac{\sqrt{3}}{2} = \frac{3\sqrt{3}}{2}$$

$-330°$
2
1
30°
$\sqrt{3}$

10. $\cos(-150°) + \sqrt{2} \sin 30°$

$= -\cos 30° + \sqrt{2}\left(\dfrac{1}{2}\right)$

$$= -\frac{\sqrt{3}}{2} + \frac{\sqrt{3}}{2} = \frac{\sqrt{2} - \sqrt{3}}{2}$$

$-\sqrt{3}$
30°
-1
2
$-150°$

11. $9 = 2^k$

$\log_2 9 = k$

12. $\log_c 27 = 3$

$c^3 = 27$

$c^3 = 3^3$

$c = 3$

13. $\log_2 \dfrac{1}{16} = m$

$2^m = \dfrac{1}{16}$

$2^m = 2^{-4}$

$m = -4$

14. $\log_{1/4} z = -2$

$\left(\dfrac{1}{4}\right)^{-2} = z$

$z = 16$

15. $\dfrac{8!}{2!\,4!} = \dfrac{8 \cdot 7 \cdot 6 \cdot 5}{2 \cdot 1} = 40 \cdot 21 = 840$

16. $\dfrac{9!}{3!\,3!} = \dfrac{9 \cdot 8 \cdot 7 \cdot 6 \cdot 5 \cdot 4}{3 \cdot 2 \cdot 1}$

$= 9 \cdot 8 \cdot 7 \cdot 5 \cdot 4$

$= 9 \cdot 56 \cdot 20 = 10,080$

17. $x^2 + y^2 = 4$
$x^2 - y^2 = 4$
Adding the two equations together gives
$2x^2 = 8$
$x^2 = 4$
$x = \pm 2$; substitute into $y^2 = 4 - x^2$
$y^2 = 4 - (\pm 2)^2$
$y^2 = 0$
$y = 0$
$(2, 0), (-2, 0)$

18. $4a^{3m+2} - 16a^{3m} = 4a^{3m}(a^2 - 4)$
$= 4a^{3m}(a + 2)(a - 2)$

19. $\dfrac{\dfrac{x^2y}{ca^3} - \dfrac{y^3z}{a^2}}{\dfrac{s^2t}{a^2} - \dfrac{r^2z}{a^3c}} = \dfrac{\dfrac{x^2y - acy^3z}{a^3c}}{\dfrac{acs^2t - r^2z}{a^3c}} = \dfrac{x^2y - acy^3z}{acs^2t - r^2z}$

20. $3z = -\dfrac{10d}{ch} + \dfrac{4k}{c}$
Multiply by ch
$3chz = -10d + 4hk$
$h(3cZ - 4k) = -10d$
$h = \dfrac{-10d}{3cz - 4k} = \dfrac{10d}{4k - 3cz}$

21. $-3 \ \underline{/\ 200°} \ + -6 \ \underline{/\ -140°}$
$x_1 = 2.82 \qquad\qquad y_1 = 1.03$
$x_2 = \underline{4.60} \qquad\qquad y_2 = \underline{3.86}$
$x_T = 7.42 \qquad\qquad y_T = 4.89$
Equilibrant: $-7.42i - 4.88j$

22. $\dfrac{6i + 4i + 5i}{1 + 2i} = \dfrac{15i}{1 + 2i}\left(\dfrac{1 - 2i}{1 - 2i}\right)$
$= \dfrac{30 + 15i}{1 + 4} = 6 + 3i$

23. $\dfrac{4 - 3\sqrt{2}}{2 - 2\sqrt{2}}\left(\dfrac{2 + 2\sqrt{2}}{2 + 2\sqrt{2}}\right) = \dfrac{8 + 2\sqrt{2} - 12}{4 - 8}$
$= \dfrac{-4 + 2\sqrt{2}}{-4} = 1 - \dfrac{\sqrt{2}}{2}$

24. $5x^2 + 3x = -6$
$x^2 + \dfrac{3}{5}x + \dfrac{9}{100} = -\dfrac{6}{5} + \dfrac{9}{100}$
$\left(x + \dfrac{3}{10}\right)^2 = -\dfrac{111}{100}$
$x = -\dfrac{3}{10} \pm \dfrac{\sqrt{111}}{10}i$

25. $x + y = 7$
$x + y - 2 = 5$
$x - y = 5$
Substituting gives
$x + y - 2 = x - y$
$2y = 2$
$y = 1$
$x = 6$; therefore A

26. $x^2 + y^2 = 25$
$x = 3$; substituting gives
$9 + y^2 = 25$
$y^2 = 16$
$y = \pm 4$; therefore D

27. A: $5x - 3z = 15$
B: $x + 2y = 10$
C: $2y - z = -1$

$\begin{aligned} \text{A:} \quad & 5x - 3z = 15 \\ 3(\text{B}-\text{C}): \quad & 3x + 3z = 33 \\ \hline & 8x \qquad = 48 \\ & x \qquad = 6 \end{aligned}$

$z = 11 - 6 = 5$
$y = \dfrac{-1 + 5}{2} = 2$

$(6, 2, 5)$

28. $y^{a+2}(y^2)^{2a-1}y^{-3a-2} = y^{a+2}y^{4a-2}y^{-3a-2} = y^{2a-2}$

29. $(2a^{3/2} - 3b^{-1/2})(4a^{-3/2} + 2b^{3/2})$
$= 8a^0 + 4a^{3/2}b^{3/2} - 12a^{-3/2}b^{-1/2} - 6b$
$= 8 + 4a^{3/2}b^{3/2} - 12a^{-3/2}b^{-1/2} - 6b$

30.
$$\begin{array}{r} x^3 - 2x^2 - 2x - 6/(x-1) \\ x - 2\overline{\smash{)}\ x^4 - 3x^3 + 0x^2 + 2x - 6} \\ \underline{x^4 - x^3} \\ -2x^3 + 0x^2 \\ \underline{-2x^3 + 2x^2} \\ -2x^2 + 2x \\ \underline{-2x^2 + 2x} \\ 0x - 6 \end{array}$$

1.

	Now	−10 years	+20 years
Ophelia:	O_N	$O_N - 10$	$O_N + 20$
Laertes:	L_N	$L_N - 10$	$L_N + 20$

$$O_N = \frac{4}{5}L_N$$

$$O_N - 10 = \frac{3}{5}\left(L_N - 10\right)$$

$$5O_N = 4L_N$$
$$5O_N - 50 = 3L_N - 30$$

$$\begin{aligned}5O_N - 4L_N &= 0\\ (-)\,5O_N - 3L_N &= 20\\ \hline L_N &= 20\end{aligned}$$

$$O_N = 16$$
$$O_N + 20 = 16 + 20 = \mathbf{36}$$
$$L_N + 20 = 20 + 20 = \mathbf{40}$$

2.

	Rate
Taskmaster:	$\dfrac{1}{40}\dfrac{\text{task}}{\text{min}}$
Apprentice:	$\dfrac{1}{60}\dfrac{\text{task}}{\text{min}}$

T = time working together

$$\frac{1}{40}(60) + \frac{1}{40}(T) + \frac{1}{60}(T) = 5$$

Multiply by 120

$$180 + 3T + 2T = 600$$
$$5T = 420$$
$$T = \frac{420}{5} = \mathbf{84\ minutes}$$

3.

	Old	New
Rate:	p	?
Time:	$\dfrac{x}{p}$	$\dfrac{x}{p} - 2$
Distance:	x	$x + 10$

$$\text{Rate} = \frac{\text{distance}}{\text{time}} = \frac{x + 10}{\dfrac{x - 2p}{p}}$$

$$= \frac{xp + 10p}{x - 2p}\ \frac{\text{mi}}{\text{hr}}$$

4.   Rate · time · men = jobs
Rate · 4 · 30 = 6
$$\text{Rate} = \frac{6}{120} = \frac{1}{20}$$
$$\frac{1}{20}\cdot \text{time} \cdot 20 = 4$$
Time = **4 days**

5.   Since the only multiple of 2 between 6 and 24 that is evenly divisible by $5\frac{1}{2}$ is 22, the builder should order 22-ft lengths to avoid throwing away short pieces of board.

6. $y = \left(\dfrac{1}{4}\right)^x$

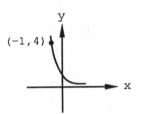

7. $\text{Arcsin}\,\dfrac{\sqrt{3}}{2} = \mathbf{60°}$

8. $\dfrac{\sqrt{3}}{2}$

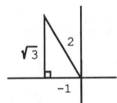

9. $\dfrac{5\sqrt{41}}{41}$

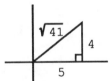

10.

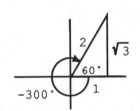

$$2\left(\frac{\sqrt{3}}{2}\right) + \left(-\frac{\sqrt{2}}{2}\right) = \sqrt{3} - \frac{\sqrt{2}}{2}$$

$$= \frac{2\sqrt{3} - \sqrt{2}}{2}$$

Advanced Mathematics

11.

$$-2\sqrt{2}\,(1) - \left(\frac{\sqrt{2}}{2}\right)\left(\frac{\sqrt{2}}{2}\right) = -2\sqrt{2} - \frac{2}{4}$$

$$= -2\sqrt{2} - \frac{1}{2} = \frac{-4\sqrt{2} - 1}{2} = -2\sqrt{2} - \frac{1}{2}$$

12. $a^2 = 36$

$a = 6$

13. $3^n = \dfrac{1}{81}$

$3^n = \dfrac{1}{3^4}$

$3^n = 3^{-4}$

$n = -4$

14. $\left(\dfrac{1}{3}\right)^{-4} = p$

$3^4 = p$

$p = 81$

15. $\dfrac{9 \cdot 8 \cdot 7 \cdot 6 \cdot 5!}{4 \cdot 3 \cdot 2 \cdot 1 \cdot 5!} = 126$

16. $\dfrac{10 \cdot 9 \cdot 8 \cdot 7 \cdot 6!}{4 \cdot 3 \cdot 2 \cdot 1 \cdot 6!} = 210$

17. $y^2 - x^2 = 4$

$y = 2 - 3x$ (substitute)

$(2 - 3x)^2 - x^2 = 4$

$4 - 12x + 9x^2 - x^2 = 4$

$8x^2 - 12x = 0$

$4x(2x - 3) = 0$

$4x = 0$	$2x - 3 = 0$
$x = 0$	$x = \dfrac{3}{2}$
$y = 2 - 3(0)$	$y = 2 - 3\left(\dfrac{3}{2}\right)$
$y = 2$	$y = -\dfrac{5}{2}$
$(0, 2)$	$\left(\dfrac{3}{2}, -\dfrac{5}{2}\right)$

18. $16b^{4n} \cdot b^3 + 6b^{4n} \cdot b^2$

$= 2b^{4n}b^2(8b + 3) = 2b^{4n+2}(8b + 3)$

19. $\dfrac{2}{6b + \dfrac{3t}{1 + \dfrac{3}{x}}} = \dfrac{2}{6b + \dfrac{3t}{\dfrac{x + 3}{x}}}$

$= \dfrac{2}{6b + \dfrac{3tx}{x + 3}} = \dfrac{2}{\dfrac{6bx + 18b + 3tx}{x + 3}}$

$= \dfrac{2(x + 3)}{6bx + 18b + 3tx}$

20. $s = \dfrac{5dag^2}{2h} - \dfrac{10d}{h}$

$2hs = 5dag^2 - 20d$

$5dag^2 = 2hs + 20d$

$g^2 = \dfrac{2hs + 20d}{5ad}$

$g = \pm\sqrt{\dfrac{2hs + 20d}{5ad}}$

$g = \pm\sqrt{\dfrac{2hs}{5ad} + \dfrac{4}{a}}$

21.

-2	$\angle\,120°\;=$	$1i - 1.73j$
6	$\angle\,-130°\;=$	$-3.86i - 4.60j$
Resultant $=$		$-2.86i - 6.33j$
Equilibrant $=$		$2.86i + 6.33j$

22. $\dfrac{\sqrt{3}\sqrt{3}\,i\sqrt{2}\sqrt{2}\,i - 4i + \sqrt{5}\,i\sqrt{5}}{1 - 4i \cdot i^2}$

$= \dfrac{6i^2 - 4i + 5i}{1 + 4i} = \dfrac{-4i + 5i}{1 + 4i}$

$= \dfrac{-6 + i}{1 + 4i} \cdot \dfrac{(1 - 4i)}{(1 - 4i)}$

$= \dfrac{-6 + 24i + i + 4}{1 + 16} = \dfrac{-2 + 25i}{17}$

23. $\dfrac{6 - 4\sqrt{3}}{12 - \sqrt{3}} \cdot \dfrac{(12 + \sqrt{3})}{(12 + \sqrt{3})}$

$= \dfrac{72 + 6\sqrt{3} - 48\sqrt{3} - 12}{144 - 3}$

$= \dfrac{60 - 42\sqrt{3}}{141} = \dfrac{20 - 14\sqrt{3}}{47}$

24. $x^2 - \dfrac{1}{3}x + \dfrac{1}{36} = -\dfrac{1}{6} + \dfrac{1}{36}$

$= \left(x - \dfrac{1}{6}\right)^2 = -\dfrac{5}{36}$

$x - \dfrac{1}{6} = \pm\dfrac{\sqrt{5}\,i}{6}$

$x = \dfrac{1}{6} \pm \dfrac{\sqrt{5}\,i}{6}$

25. **D**

26. **A**

27. A: $2a - b = 4$
    B: $a + 2c = 10$
    C: $b - 3c = 2$
    Substitute $a = -2c + 10$ into A to get
    $2(-2c + 10) - b = 4$
    D: $-4c - b = -16$
    C: $\underline{-3c + b = 2}$
    $-7c = -14$
    $c = 2$
    $b = 3(2) + 2$
    $b = 8$
    $a = -2(2) + 10$
    $a = 6$

28. $\dfrac{z^{3+b}\left(z^{3/2}\right)^{b+1}}{z^b} = z^{3+b}z^{3b/2+3/2}z^{-b} = z^{3b+9/2}$

29. $(2xy^2 - 3ab^3)(4x^2y^4 + 6xy^2ab^3 + 9a^2b^2)$

30. $2y = 4x + 6$
    $y = 2x + 3$
    $m = 2$
    $m_\perp = -\dfrac{1}{2}$
    $y = mx + b$
    $2 = -\dfrac{1}{2}(1) + b$
    $b = \dfrac{5}{2}$
    $y = -\dfrac{1}{2}x + \dfrac{5}{2}$

PROBLEM SET 10

1.
Now	-10 years	$+10$ years
O_N	$O_N - 10$	$O_N + 10$
J_N	$J_N - 10$	$J_N + 10$

$O_N - 10 = 2\left(J_N - 10\right)$
$O_N - 2J_N = -10$
$2(O_N + 10) = 3(J_N + 10)$
$2O_N - 3J_N = 0$
$O_N = 30$
$J_N = 20$
$O_{45} = 30 + 45$
$O_{45} = 75$
$J_{45} = 20 + 45$
$J_{45} = 65$

2.
	Rate
Dennis:	$\dfrac{1}{4}$
Loretta:	R_L

Time together $= 13$ days
$R_DT_D + R_LT_L = 10$
$\dfrac{1}{4}(1) + \dfrac{1}{4}(13) + R_L(13) = 10$
$13R_L = 10 - \dfrac{14}{4} = \dfrac{13}{2}$
$R_L = \dfrac{1}{2}\dfrac{\text{henway}}{\text{day}}$

3. Down: $(B + W)T_D = D_D$
   Up: $(B - W)T_U = D_U$
   $(B + W)3 = 30$
   $(B - W)5 = 30$

   $3B + 3W = 30$
   $5B - 5W = 30$

   $B + W = 10$
   $B - W = 6$
   $B = 8\text{ mph}, W = 2\text{ mph}$

4. Rate $\cdot$ time $\cdot$ women = jobs
   Rate $\cdot$ 6 $\cdot$ 20 = 10
   Rate $= \dfrac{1}{12}$
   $\dfrac{1}{12} \cdot$ time $\cdot$ 30 = 20
   Time $= 20 \cdot \dfrac{12}{30} = 8$ **days**

5.
	Old	New
Rate:	$\dfrac{g}{x}$	$\dfrac{g}{x} + p$
Time:	x	ax
Distance:	g	?

Distance = rate $\cdot$ time $= \dfrac{g + px}{x}(ax)$

$= ag + apx$ **miles**

6. $y = (3.2)^x$

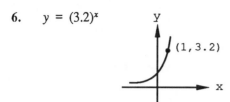

Use the 30–60–90 and 45–45–90 triangles for problems 7 and 9–11. (Refer to Problem Set 1, problem 8.)

7. $60°$

8. $\dfrac{\sqrt{7}}{4}$

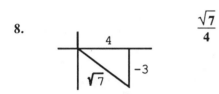

9. $\dfrac{\sqrt{2}}{2}$

10. $3\left(\dfrac{1}{2}\right) + 0 = \dfrac{3}{2}$

11. $2\left(\dfrac{1}{2}\right)\left(\dfrac{\sqrt{3}}{2}\right) - \left(\dfrac{\sqrt{3}}{2}\right) + 0 = 0$

12. $2(0) - 3(0) + 0 = 0$

13. $b^2 = 49$
$(b^2)^{1/2} = (49)^{1/2}$
$b = 7$

14. $5^c = \dfrac{1}{125}$
$5^c = \dfrac{1}{5^3} = 5^{-3}$
$c = -3$

15. $\left(\dfrac{1}{4}\right)^{-3} = k$
$4^3 = k$
$k = 64$

16. $\dfrac{8 \cdot 7 \cdot 6 \cdot 5 \cdot 4 \cdot 3 \cdot 2!}{2 \cdot 1 \cdot 2!} = 10{,}080$

17. $\dfrac{15 \cdot 14 \cdot 13 \cdot 12 \cdot 10 \cdot 9 \cdot 8!}{5 \cdot 4 \cdot 3 \cdot 2 \cdot 1 \cdot 8!} = 270{,}270$

18.
$x^2 - y^2 = 8$
$\underline{2x^2 + y^2 = 19}$
$3x^2 = 27$
$x^2 = 9$
$x = \pm 3$

$x = 3$	$x = -3$
$y^2 = x^2 - 8$	$y^2 = x^2 - 8$
$y^2 = 9 - 8$	$y^2 = (-3)^2 - 8$
$y^2 = 1$	$y^2 = 1$
$y = \pm 1$	$y = \pm 1$
$(3, 1), (3, -1)$	$(-3, 1), (-3, -1)$

19. $(2ab - 3c^2d^2)(4a^2b^2 + 6abc^2d^2 + 9c^4d^4)$

20. $\dfrac{3}{2c + \dfrac{t}{\dfrac{z+4}{z}}} = \dfrac{3}{2c + \dfrac{tz}{z+4}}$

$= \dfrac{3}{\dfrac{2cz + 8c + tz}{z+4}} = \dfrac{3z + 12}{2cz + 8c + tz}$

21. $d = \dfrac{24gt}{kh} - \dfrac{18gs}{kr}$
Multiply by khr
$dkhr = 24gtr - 18gsh$
$dkhr + 18gsh = 24gtr$
$h(dkr + 18gs) = 24gtr$
$h = \dfrac{24gtr}{dkr + 18gs}$

22. $-3 \ \angle\ 135° = 2.12i - 2.12j$
$7 \ \angle -140° = -5.36i - 4.5j$
Resultant $= -3.24i - 6.62j$
Equilibrant $= 3.24i + 6.62j$

23. $\dfrac{\sqrt{5}\sqrt{5}\,i\sqrt{6}\sqrt{6}\,i + 5i - 4i}{-3(-1) - 3i(i)} = \dfrac{-30 + i}{6}$
$= -5 + \dfrac{1}{6}i$

24. $x^2 + \dfrac{3}{4}x + \dfrac{9}{64} = \dfrac{2}{4} + \dfrac{9}{64}$
$\left(x + \dfrac{3}{8}\right)^2 = \dfrac{41}{64}$
$x + \dfrac{3}{8} = \pm\dfrac{\sqrt{41}}{8}$
$x = -\dfrac{3}{8} \pm \dfrac{\sqrt{41}}{8}$

25. If $-x > -y$ then $x < y$
D

26. **D** since a and b could be negative.

27. A: $x - 2y = 6$
B: $x - 4y = 6$
C: $y + 3z = 5$
Substitute $x = 2y + 6$ into B to get
  $(2y + 6) - 4z = 6$
  $2y - 4z = 0$
D: $y - 2z = 0$
Subtract D from C to get
$5z = 5$

$z = 1$
$y = 2(1) = 2$
$x - 2(2) = 6$
$x = 10$
(10, 2, 1)

28. $\dfrac{x^{2a+2}(x^{3/2})^{a+2}}{x^{a-2}} = x^{2a+2}x^{3a/2+3}x^{-a+2}$
$= x^{2a+2+3a/2+3-a+2} = x^{5a/2+7}$

29. $a^0 + a^{2a}b^{1/2} - a^{-2a}b^{1/2} - b^1$
$= 1 + a^{2a}b^{1/2} - a^{-2a}b^{1/2} - b$

30. **4.27**

PROBLEM SET 11

1. Down: $(B + W)T_D = D_D$
Up: $(B - W)T_U = D_U$

$(B + W)3 = 45$
$(B - W)5 = 45$

$3B + 3W = 45$
$5B - 5W = 45$

$B + W = 15$
$B - W = 9$
$2B = 24$

$B = \textbf{12 mph}$
$W = \textbf{3 mph}$

2.

	Old	New
Rate:	m	?
Time:	$\dfrac{100}{m}$	$\dfrac{100}{m} - 1$
Distance:	100	100

$\text{Rate} = \dfrac{\text{distance}}{\text{time}} = \dfrac{100}{\dfrac{100 - m}{m}}$

$= \dfrac{\textbf{100}\textit{m}}{\textbf{100} - \textit{m}}$ **mph**

3. $\dfrac{\text{part}}{\text{whole}}(100) = \text{percentage}$

$\dfrac{V}{V + W}(100) = \dfrac{\textbf{100}\textit{V}}{\textit{V} + \textit{W}}$

4.

	Rate
Jeff:	$\dfrac{1}{5}$
Peeto:	R_P

Time together = 15
$R_J T_J + R_P T_P = 22$
$\dfrac{4}{5}(15) + R_P(15) = 22$
$R_P = \dfrac{2}{3}$
$R_P T_P = 1$
$\dfrac{2}{3}T_P = 1$
$T_P = \dfrac{\textbf{3}}{\textbf{2}}$ **hr**

5. Rate $\cdot$ time $\cdot$ men = food in pounds
Rate $\cdot$ 2 $\cdot$ 15 = 45
Rate $= \dfrac{45}{30} = \dfrac{3}{2}$

$\dfrac{3}{2} \cdot 10 \cdot 25 = $ food in pounds

Food = **375 lb**

6. $y = \left(\dfrac{1}{3}\right)^x$

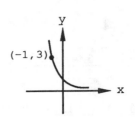

$(-1, 3)$

Use the 30–60–90 and 45–45–90 triangles for problems 7, 8, 10 and 11. (Refer to Problem Set 1, problem 8.)

7. $60°$

8. $\dfrac{\sqrt{3}}{2}$

9. $-\dfrac{3}{4}$

10. $2\left(-\dfrac{\sqrt{2}}{2}\right) + 0 = -\sqrt{2}$

11. $\dfrac{\frac{1}{2}}{\frac{\sqrt{3}}{2}} - (-1) + 1 = \dfrac{1}{\sqrt{3}} + 2 = \dfrac{\sqrt{3}}{3} + 2$

12. $2(1)(-1) - (0) = -2$

13. $\displaystyle\sum_{i=1}^{6} 2i^0 = 2(1)^0 + 2(2)^0 + 2(3)^0$
    $+ 2(4)^0 + 2(5)^0 + 2(6)^0 = 12$

14. $\displaystyle\sum_{i=2}^{4} \dfrac{2j}{1-j} = \dfrac{2^2}{1-2} + \dfrac{2^3}{1-3} + \dfrac{2^4}{1-4}$
    $= \dfrac{4}{-1} + \dfrac{8}{-2} + \dfrac{16}{-3} = -\dfrac{40}{3}$

15. $d^3 = 64$
    $(d^3)^{1/3} = (64)^{1/3} = \sqrt[3]{64} = 4$

16. $2f = \dfrac{1}{64}$
    $2f = \dfrac{1}{2^6} = 2^{-6}$
    $f = -6$

17. $\left(\dfrac{1}{2}\right)^{-3} = p$
    $p = 2^3 = 8$

18. $\dfrac{9 \cdot 8 \cdot 7 \cdot 6 \cdot 5 \cdot 4 \cdot 3!}{2 \cdot 1 \cdot 3!}$
    $= 9 \cdot 8 \cdot 7 \cdot 6 \cdot 5 \cdot 2 = \mathbf{30,240}$

19. $x^2 - y^2 = 4$
    $y = 2 - x$ (substitute into above equation)
    $x^2 - (2-x)^2 = 4$
    $x^2 - (4 - 4x + x^2) = 4$
    $x^2 - 4 + 4x - x^2 = 4$
    $4x = 8$
    $x = 2$
    $y = 2 - x$
    $y = 2 - 2 = 0$
    $(2, 0)$

20. $\dfrac{\frac{a^2b - cfg^2}{c^2d^3}}{\frac{x^2yd^2 + z^3c}{c^2d^3}} = \dfrac{a^2b - cfg^2}{c^2d^3} \cdot \dfrac{c^2d^3}{x^2yd^2 + z^3c}$
    $= \dfrac{a^2b - cfg^2}{x^2yd^2 + z^3c}$

21. $h = \dfrac{8ds}{fg} + \dfrac{4ds}{fr}$
    Multiply by fgr
    $hfgr = 8dsr + 4dsg$
    $hfgr - 4dsg = 8dsr$
    $g(hfr - 4ds) = 8dsr$
    $g = \dfrac{8dsr}{hfr - 4ds}$

22. $-2 \; \underline{/\,140°} = 1.53i - 1.29j$
    $3 \; \underline{/\,-120°} = \underline{-1.5i - 2.6j}$
    Resultant $= 0.03i - 3.89j$
    Equilibrant $= -0.03i + 3.89j$

23. $\dfrac{\sqrt{2}\sqrt{3}\,i\sqrt{2}\,i\sqrt{3} - 4i}{-4(-i) - 4i \cdot i} = \dfrac{-6 - 4i}{4i + 4}$
    $= \dfrac{-3 - 2i}{2 + 2i} \cdot \dfrac{(2 - 2i)}{(2 - 2i)}$
    $= \dfrac{-6 + 6i - 4i + 4i}{4 - 4i^2}$
    $= \dfrac{-10 + 2i}{8} = \dfrac{-5 + i}{4}$

24. $3x^2 + 2x = 6$
    $x^2 + \dfrac{2}{3}x + \dfrac{1}{9} = 2 + \dfrac{1}{9}$
    $\left(x + \dfrac{1}{3}\right)^2 = \dfrac{19}{9}$
    $x + \dfrac{1}{3} = \pm\dfrac{\sqrt{19}}{3}$
    $x = -\dfrac{1}{3} \pm \dfrac{\sqrt{19}}{3}$

25. $\dfrac{a}{b} = \dfrac{c}{d}$

Therefore, $\dfrac{a}{c} = \dfrac{b}{d}$. Thus the answer is C.

26. $\dfrac{a}{b} = 4$

Therefore, $a = 4b$. Thus the answer is C.

27. A: $2x + y - z = 1$
B: $x - 2y + z = 0$
C: $3x + y - 2z = -1$
A + B gives
D: $3x - y = 1$

2B: $2x - 4y + 2z = 0$
C: $\underline{3x + y - 2z = -1}$
E: $5x - 3y = -1$

3D: $-9x + 3y = -3$
E: $\underline{5x - 3y = -1}$
  $-4x = -4$
  $x = 1$

$5(1) - 3y = -1$
$y = 2$
$z = -1 + 2 + 2(1) = 3$
(1, 2, 3)

28. $\dfrac{a^{3b+1}\left(a^{3/2}\right)^{b-1}}{a^{2b+1}} = a^{3b+1}a^{3b/2-3/2}a^{-2b-1}$

$= a^{3b+1+3b/2-3/2-2b-1} = a^{5b/2-3/2}$

29. $4a^x a^2 - 12a^x a^3 = 4a^x a^2(1 - 3a)$
$= \mathbf{4a^{x+2}(1 - 3a)}$

30. $-2y = -4x - 3$

$y = 2x + \dfrac{3}{2}$

$m_\perp = -\dfrac{1}{2}$ and passes through $(2, 2)$

$y = mx + b$

$2 = -\dfrac{1}{2}(2) + b$

$b = 1$

$y = -\dfrac{1}{2}x + 3$

PROBLEM SET 12

1. $\dfrac{R}{B} = \dfrac{4}{1}$ $\qquad R = 4B$

$\dfrac{B}{G} = \dfrac{2}{1}$ $\qquad B = 2G$

$R + B + G = 55$

Substitute $R = 4B$ and $G = \dfrac{B}{2}$ to get

$4B + B + \dfrac{B}{2} = 55$

$8B + 2B + B = 110$

$11B = 110$

$B = \mathbf{10}$

$R = \mathbf{40}$

$G = \mathbf{5}$

2. Rate $\cdot$ time $\cdot$ men = concoctions
Rate $\cdot$ 5 $\cdot$ 3 = 20

Rate $= \dfrac{20}{15} = \dfrac{4}{3}$

$\dfrac{4}{3} \cdot$ time $\cdot$ 5 = 14

$\dfrac{20}{3} \cdot$ time = 14

Time $= 14 \cdot \dfrac{3}{20} = \mathbf{2.1\ hr}$

3.

	Old	New
Rate:	z	?
Time:	$\dfrac{m}{z}$	$\dfrac{m}{z} - 3$
Distance:	m	m

Rate $= \dfrac{\text{distance}}{\text{time}} = \dfrac{m}{\dfrac{m - 3z}{z}}$

$= \dfrac{mz}{m - 3z}$ **mph**

4.

	Rate
Greg:	$\dfrac{2}{5}$
Jackie:	$\dfrac{1}{6}$

$\dfrac{2}{5}T + \dfrac{1}{6}T = 10$

Multiply by 30

$12T + 5T = 17T = 300$

$T = \dfrac{\mathbf{300}}{\mathbf{17}}$ **hr**

5.　R_B = rate B charged
　　R_A = rate A charged
　　$R_B \cdot 16 = 120$
　　$R_B = \dfrac{120}{16} = \dfrac{15}{2}$
　　$R_A = \dfrac{3}{2} R_B$
　　$R_A = \dfrac{3}{2}\left(\dfrac{15}{2}\right) = \dfrac{45}{4}$
　　12 calls $= 12\left(\dfrac{45}{4}\right) = \$135$

6.　$C_1 + F\left(C_2 - C_1\right)$
　　$= -2 + \dfrac{2}{5}(6 - (-2)) = -2 + \dfrac{2}{5}(8)$
　　$= -2 + \dfrac{16}{5} = \dfrac{6}{5}$

7.　$C_1 + F\left(C_2 - C_1\right)$
　　$= 4\dfrac{3}{8} + \dfrac{5}{6}\left(-2\dfrac{5}{8} - 4\dfrac{3}{8}\right)$
　　$= \dfrac{35}{8} + \dfrac{5}{6}\left(-\dfrac{21}{8} - \dfrac{35}{8}\right)$
　　$= \dfrac{35}{8} + \dfrac{5}{6}\left(-\dfrac{56}{8}\right) = \dfrac{35}{8} + \dfrac{5}{6}(-7)$
　　$= \dfrac{35}{8} - \dfrac{35}{6} = \dfrac{105}{24} - \dfrac{140}{24} = -\dfrac{35}{24}$

8.　$\sqrt{(x - 2)^2 + (y + 1)^2}$

9.　**45°**

10.
$\dfrac{3}{4}$

11.
$\dfrac{1}{\sqrt{10}} = \dfrac{\sqrt{10}}{10}$

12.　$2\left(-\dfrac{\sqrt{2}}{2}\right) - 0 = -\sqrt{2}$

13.　$3\left(\dfrac{1}{2}\right)\left(\dfrac{1}{2}\right) - (1)(0) = \dfrac{3}{4}$

14.　$6\left(\dfrac{1}{2}\right)(1) - (0)(1) = 3$

15.　$\displaystyle\sum_{i=1}^{7} 3i^0 = 3(1)^0 + 3(2)^0 + 3(3)^0$
　　$+ 3(4)^0 + 3(5)^0 + 3(6)^0 + 3(7)^0$
　　$= 3 + 3 + 3 + 3 + 3 + 3 + 3 = \mathbf{21}$

16.　$\displaystyle\sum_{j=0}^{2} \dfrac{3j}{1 - 2j}$
　　$= \dfrac{3^0}{1 - 2(0)} + \dfrac{3^1}{1 - 2(1)} + \dfrac{3^2}{1 - 2(2)}$
　　$= 1 + (-3) + (-3) = \mathbf{-5}$

17.　$f^3 = 125$
　　$(f^3)^{1/3} = (125)^{1/3}$
　　$f = \mathbf{5}$

18.　$2^g = \dfrac{1}{32}$
　　$2^g = \dfrac{1}{2^5} = 2^{-5}$
　　$g = \mathbf{-5}$

19.　$\left(\dfrac{1}{2}\right)^{-2} = p$
　　$p = 2^2$
　　$p = \mathbf{4}$

20.　$\dfrac{10 \cdot 9 \cdot 8 \cdot 7 \cdot 6 \cdot 5 \cdot 4!}{2 \cdot 1 \cdot 4!} = \mathbf{75{,}600}$

21.　$\begin{aligned}
x^2 + y^2 &= 10 \\
2x^2 - y^2 &= 17 \\
\hline
3x^2 &= 27 \\
x^2 &= 9 \\
x &= \pm 3
\end{aligned}$

　　$x = 3$ 　　　　　　　$x = -3$
　　$y^2 = 10 - 3^2$ 　　$y^2 = 10 - (-3)^2$
　　$y^2 = 10 - 9$ 　　　$y^2 = 10 - 9$
　　$y^2 = 1$ 　　　　　　$y^2 = 1$
　　$y = \pm 1$ 　　　　　$y = \pm 1$
　　(3, 1), (3, –1) 　　**(–3, 1), (–3, –1)**

22. $\dfrac{\dfrac{x^2yd - z^2c}{cd^3}}{\dfrac{gh^2d^2 - fc^3}{c^3d^3}} = \dfrac{x^2yd - z^2c}{cd^3} \cdot \dfrac{c^3d^3}{gh^2d^2 - fc^3}$

$= \dfrac{c^2(x^2yd - z^2c)}{gh^2d^2 - fc^3}$

23. $\dfrac{y^2}{z} = \dfrac{12st}{rx} - \dfrac{9sz}{rk}$

Multiply by $rxzk$

$rxky^2 = 12stzk - 9sz^2x$

$rxky^2 + 9sz^2x = 12stzk$

$x(rky^2 + 9sz^2) = 12stzk$

$x = \dfrac{12stzk}{rky^2 + 9sz^2}$

24. $-3\ \underline{/-135°}\ =$ $2.12i + 2.12j$

$-2\ \underline{/-140°}\ =$ $1.53i + 1.29j$

Resultant = $\mathbf{3.65i + 3.41j}$

Equilibrant = $\mathbf{-3.65i - 3.41j}$

25. $\dfrac{2i\sqrt{5}\sqrt{5}\,i - 5i}{-2(-i) + 2i} = \dfrac{-10 - 5i}{4i}\dfrac{(-4i)}{(-4i)}$

$= \dfrac{40i + 20i^2}{-16i^2} = \dfrac{-20 + 40i}{16} = \dfrac{-5 + 10i}{4}$

26. $\dfrac{x + 2y}{x} = \dfrac{x}{x} + \dfrac{2y}{x} = 1 + \dfrac{2y}{x}$; therefore C

27. $\dfrac{a}{b} = \dfrac{c}{d}$

try $\dfrac{3}{6} = \dfrac{2}{4}$

$\dfrac{3 + 2}{6 + 4} = \dfrac{5}{10}$; therefore C

28. A: $5x - y = 7$

B: $2y - 3z = -6$

C: $x + z = 6$

Substitute $y = 5x - 7$ into B to get

$2(5x - 7) - 3z = -6$

D: $10x - 3z = 8$

Substitute $x = 6 - z$ into D to get

$10(6 - z) - 3z = 8$

$-13z = -52$

$z = 4$

$x = 6 - 4 = 2$

$y = 5(2) - 7 = 3$

$(2, 3, 4)$

29. $2x^2 - 3x = 6$

$x^2 - \dfrac{3}{2}x + \dfrac{9}{16} = 3 + \dfrac{9}{16}$

$\left(x - \dfrac{3}{4}\right)^2 = \dfrac{57}{16}$

$x - \dfrac{3}{4} = \pm\dfrac{\sqrt{57}}{4}$

$x = \dfrac{3}{4} \pm \dfrac{\sqrt{57}}{4}$

30. $(2xy^2 - 3a^3b^2)(4x^2y^4 + 6xy^2a^3b^2 + 9a^6b^4)$

PROBLEM SET 13

1. A: $4N_W = 9N_R + 10$

$\dfrac{N_B}{N_R} = \dfrac{3}{1}$

B: $N_B = 3N_R$

C: $N_R + N_B + N_W = 65$

Substitute $N_B = 3N_R$ into C to get

$N_R + 3N_R + N_W = 65$

D: $4N_R + N_W = 65$

    A: $-9N_R + 4N_W = 10$

$\underline{-4\text{D}: -16N_R - 4N_W = 260}$

      $-25N_R = -250$

          $N_R = 10$

$N_B = 3(10)$

$N_B = \mathbf{30}$

$N_W = \mathbf{25}$

2. Downwind: $(5W + W)\left(T_U + \dfrac{1}{2}\right) = 369$

$6WT_U + 3W = 396$

Upwind: $(5W - W)T_U = 132$

$4WT_U = 132$

$WT_U = 33$

$6WT_U + 3W = 396$

$6(33) + 3W = 396$

$W = \mathbf{66\ mph}$

$A = \mathbf{330\ mph}$

3. $S = \dfrac{kWD^2}{L}$

   $2000 = \dfrac{k(2)(8)^2}{16}$

   $k = \dfrac{2000(16)}{128} = 25$

   $S = \dfrac{25(8)(2)^2}{16} = \mathbf{500\ lb}$

4.
	Rate
Sally's:	$\dfrac{3}{8}$
Jack's:	R_J

   Time working together $= 4$

   $R_S T_S + R_J T_J = 6$

   $\dfrac{3}{8}(4) + R_S(4) = 6$

   $R_S = \mathbf{\dfrac{9}{8}\ \dfrac{jobs}{hr}}$

5. $T = \sqrt{\dfrac{L}{4}}$

   $3T = 3\sqrt{\dfrac{L}{4}} = \sqrt{\dfrac{9L}{4}}$

   Multiply by 9

6. $C_1 + F\left(C_2 - C_1\right)$

   $= -3 + \dfrac{3}{5}[9 - (-3)] = -3 + \dfrac{3}{5}(12)$

   $= -3 + \dfrac{36}{5} = -\dfrac{15}{5} + \dfrac{36}{5} = \mathbf{\dfrac{21}{5}}$

7. $C_1 + F\left(C_2 - C_1\right)$

   $= -3\dfrac{5}{6} + \dfrac{7}{8}\left[2\dfrac{1}{6} - \left(-3\dfrac{5}{6}\right)\right]$

   $= -\dfrac{23}{6} + \dfrac{7}{8}\left(\dfrac{13}{6} + \dfrac{23}{6}\right) = -\dfrac{23}{6} + \dfrac{7}{8}(6)$

   $= -\dfrac{23}{6} + \dfrac{21}{4} = -\dfrac{92}{24} + \dfrac{126}{24} = \dfrac{34}{24} = \mathbf{\dfrac{17}{12}}$

8. $\sqrt{(x-3)^2 + (y+2)^2}$

   or $\sqrt{(3-x)^2 + (-2-y)^2}$

Use the 30–60–90 and 45–45–90 triangles for problems 7 and 9–11. (Refer to Problem Set 1, problem 8.)

9. $\mathbf{30°}$

10. $-\dfrac{4}{5}$

11.
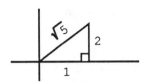
$\dfrac{2}{\sqrt{5}} = \dfrac{2\sqrt{5}}{5}$

12. $(0) - \dfrac{\sqrt{3}}{3} = -\dfrac{\sqrt{3}}{3}$

13. $\left(-\dfrac{\sqrt{3}}{2}\right) + \dfrac{1}{2} = \dfrac{-\sqrt{3}+1}{2}$

14. $\tan 210° + \cos(-45°) = \dfrac{\sqrt{3}}{3} + \dfrac{\sqrt{2}}{2}$

    $= \dfrac{2\sqrt{3} + 3\sqrt{2}}{6}$

15. $\displaystyle\sum_{j=5}^{6} \dfrac{2}{j} = \dfrac{2}{5} + \dfrac{2}{6} = \dfrac{12 + 10}{30} = \dfrac{22}{30} = \mathbf{\dfrac{11}{15}}$

16. $\displaystyle\sum_{n=0}^{3} \dfrac{3^n}{n+1} = \dfrac{3^0}{0+1} + \dfrac{3^1}{1+1}$

    $+ \dfrac{3^2}{2+1} + \dfrac{3^3}{3+1}$

    $= 1 + \dfrac{3}{2} + 3 + \dfrac{27}{4} = \mathbf{\dfrac{49}{4}}$

17. $x^3 = 64$

    $(x^3)^{1/3} = (64)^{1/3}$

    $x = \mathbf{4}$

18. $3^y = \dfrac{1}{27}$

    $3^y = \dfrac{1}{3^3} = 3^{-3}$

    $y = \mathbf{-3}$

19. $\left(\dfrac{1}{3}\right)^{-3} = K$

    $3^3 = K$

    $K = \mathbf{27}$

20. $\dfrac{11 \cdot 10 \cdot 9 \cdot 8 \cdot 7 \cdot 6 \cdot 5 \cdot 4!}{3 \cdot 2 \cdot 4!} = \mathbf{277{,}200}$

21. $x^2 + y^2 = 16$
$y = 4 - 3x$
$x^2 + (4 - 3x)^2 = 16$
$x^2 + 16 - 24x + 9x^2 = 16$
$10x^2 - 24x = 0$
$2x(5x - 12) = 0$

$2x = 0 \qquad\qquad 5x - 12 = 0$
$x = 0 \qquad\qquad x = \dfrac{12}{5}$

$y = 4 - 3(0) \qquad y = 4 - 3\left(\dfrac{12}{5}\right)$

$y = 4 \qquad\qquad y = 4 - \dfrac{36}{5}$

$y = 4 \qquad\qquad y = -\dfrac{16}{5}$

$(0, 4), \left(\dfrac{12}{5}, -\dfrac{16}{5}\right)$

22. $\dfrac{2}{1 + \dfrac{3s}{\dfrac{m + x}{m}}} = \dfrac{2}{1 + \dfrac{3ms}{m + x}}$

$= \dfrac{2}{\dfrac{m + x + 3ms}{m + x}} = \dfrac{2(m + x)}{m + x + 3ms}$

23. $\dfrac{t^2}{z} = \dfrac{12ms}{nx} + \dfrac{9m}{4nk}$
Multiply by $4nkxz$
$4nxkt^2 - 9mxz = 48mskz$
$x(4nkt^2 - 9mz) = 48mskz$

$x = \dfrac{48mskz}{4nkt^2 - 9mz}$

24. $-2 \;\underline{/\,120°} \;= \; 1i - 1.73j$
$-3 \;\underline{/\,135°} \;= \; 2.12i - 2.12j$
Resultant $= \quad \mathbf{3.12i - 3.85j}$

25. $\dfrac{-\sqrt{3}\,i\sqrt{3} - \sqrt{2}\sqrt{3}\,i\sqrt{6}\,i}{3 - 2i}$

$= \dfrac{-3i + 6}{3 - 2i} = \dfrac{6 - 3i(3 + 2i)}{3 - 2i(3 + 2i)}$

$= \dfrac{18 + 12i - 9i + 6}{9 + 4} = \dfrac{24 + 3i}{13}$

26. a is negative
b is negative
$a - b > a + B$
A

27. $\dfrac{1}{a^3} > \dfrac{1}{a^4}$
A

28. A: $2x - y + z = 5$
B: $x + 2y - z = -1$
C: $x + y + 2z = 10$

$\begin{array}{l} \text{A: } 2x - \;\;y + z = \;\;5 \\ \underline{\text{B: } \;\;x + 2y - z = -1} \\ \text{D: } 3x + \;\;y \qquad\;\; = \;\;4 \end{array}$

$\begin{array}{l} \text{2B: } 2x + 4y - 2z = -2 \\ \underline{\text{C: } \;\;x + \;\;y + 2z = 10} \\ \text{E: } 3x + 5y \qquad\quad = \;\;8 \end{array}$

$\begin{array}{l} \text{-D: } -3x - \;\;y = -4 \\ \underline{\text{E: } \;\;3x + 5y = \;\;8} \\ \qquad\qquad 4y = \;\;4 \\ \qquad\qquad\;\; y = \;\;1 \end{array}$

$3x + 5(1) = 8$
$x = 1$
$2(1) + z = 5$
$z = 1$
(1, 1, 4)

29. $\sqrt{2s - 7} = 7 - \sqrt{2s}$
$2s - 7 = 49 - 14\sqrt{2s} + 2s$
$14\sqrt{2s} = 56$
$\sqrt{2s} = 4$
$2s = 16$
$s = \mathbf{8}$

30.

$$x - 2\,\overline{\big)\, x^4 - 2x^3 + 0x^2 + 3x + 1}$$

quotient: $x^3 \qquad + 3 + 7/(x-2)$

$\underline{x^4 - 2x^3}$

$0x^2 + 3x + 1$

$\underline{3x - 6}$

$+7$

$x^3 + 3 + \dfrac{7}{x - 2}$

PROBLEM SET 14

1. $P = 4W$
    $T_D + 1 = T_U$
    Down: $(4W + W)T_D = 400$
    Up: $(4W - W)T_U = 300$
    $5WT_D = 400$
    $\quad\quad WT_D = 80$
    $3WT_D + 3W = 300$
    $3(80) + 3W = 300$
    $3W = 60$
    $W = \textbf{20 mph}, P = \textbf{80 mph}$

2. A: $0.20W = R + 10$
    B: $\frac{3}{5}B = 3R$
    C: $0.10(R + B) = W - 94$

    A: $2W = 10R + 100$
    B: $3B = 15R$
    C: $R + B = 10W - 940$

    A: $W = 5R + 50$
    B: $B = 5R$
    C: $R + B - 10W = -940$
    Substitute $B = 5R$ into C to get
    $\quad R + 5R - 10W = -940$
    $\quad 6R - 10W = -940$
    D: $3R - 5W = -470$
    Substitute $W = 5R + 50$ into D to get
    $3R - 5(5R + 50) = -470$
    $3R - 25R - 250 = -470$
    $R = \textbf{10}$
    $B = \textbf{50}$
    $W = \textbf{100}$

3. $\frac{2}{\sqrt{6}} \cdot N = 3\sqrt{2}$

    $N = 3\sqrt{2} \cdot \frac{\sqrt{6}}{2} = \frac{3\sqrt{12}}{2} = \frac{6\sqrt{3}}{2} = \textbf{3}\sqrt{\textbf{3}}$

4. $x^4 - y^4 = (x^2 + y^2)(x^2 - y^2)$
    $= (2)(4) = \textbf{8}$

5. $A = (1.2l)(0.8w) = 0.96wl$
    decreased 4%

6. $\sqrt{(x - 3)^2 + (y - 4)^2}$
    $= \sqrt{(x + 2)^2 + (y + 1)^2}$

$x^2 - 6x + 9 \pm y^2 - 8y + 16$
$= x^2 + 4x + 4 + y^2 + 2y + 1$
$-10x - 10y + 20 = 0$
$x + y - 2 = 0$
$\textbf{\textit{y} = --\textit{x} + 2}$

7. $\sqrt{(x - 0)^2 + (y - 2)^2}$
    $= \sqrt{(x - 5)^2 + (y - 3)^2}$
    $x^2 + y^2 - 4y + 4$
    $= x^2 - 10x + 25 + y^2 - 6y + 9$
    $10x + 2y - 30 = 0$
    $5x + y - 15 = 0$
    $\textbf{\textit{y} = --5\textit{x} + 15}$

8. $\left(\dfrac{-3 + 4}{2}, \dfrac{6 + 8}{2}\right) = \left(\dfrac{1}{2}, 7\right)$

9. $-3\dfrac{3}{7} + \dfrac{2}{9}\left(4\dfrac{2}{7} + 3\dfrac{3}{7}\right)$

    $= -\dfrac{24}{7} + \dfrac{2}{9}\left(\dfrac{30}{7} + \dfrac{24}{7}\right)$

    $= -\dfrac{24}{7} + \dfrac{2}{9}\left(\dfrac{54}{7}\right) = -\dfrac{24}{7} + \dfrac{108}{63}$

    $= \dfrac{-216 + 108}{63} = -\dfrac{108}{63} = -\dfrac{\textbf{12}}{\textbf{7}}$

10. **--30°**

11. $\dfrac{2\sqrt{10}}{7}$

    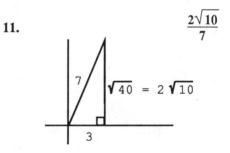

12. $\dfrac{3}{\sqrt{10}} = \dfrac{3\sqrt{10}}{10}$

    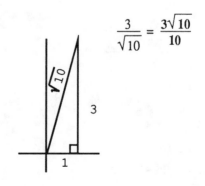

13. $0 - \tan 60° = -\sqrt{3}$

14. $\sin 30° - \cos 135°$

$\dfrac{1}{2} - \left(-\dfrac{\sqrt{2}}{2}\right) = \dfrac{1 + \sqrt{2}}{2}$

15. $(+1) + \left(\dfrac{1}{2}\right)\left(\dfrac{1}{2}\right) = 1 + \dfrac{1}{4} = \dfrac{5}{4}$

16. $\displaystyle\sum_{x=3}^{5} \dfrac{3}{x+1} = \dfrac{3}{3+1} + \dfrac{3}{4+1} + \dfrac{3}{5+1}$

$= \dfrac{3}{4} + \dfrac{3}{5} + \dfrac{1}{2} = \dfrac{15 + 12 + 10}{20} = \dfrac{37}{20}$

17. $\displaystyle\sum_{y=-3}^{3} 2y^2 = 2(-3)^2 + 2(-2)^2 + 2(-1)^2$

$+ \ 2(0)^2 + 2(1)^2 + 2(2)^2 + 2(3)^2$

$= 18 + 8 + 2 + 0 + 2 + 8 + 18 = \mathbf{56}$

18. $y^3 = 27$

$\left(y^3\right)^{1/3} = (27)^{1/3}$

$y = \mathbf{3}$

19. $2^t = \dfrac{1}{64}$

$2^t = \dfrac{1}{2^6} = 2^{-6}$

$t = \mathbf{-6}$

20. $3^{-2} = k$

$k = \dfrac{1}{9}$

21. $\dfrac{10 \cdot 9 \cdot 8 \cdot 7 \cdot 6!}{4 \cdot 3 \cdot 2 \cdot 6!} = \mathbf{210}$

22.

$\begin{aligned} x^2 - 2y^2 &= 6 \\ -x^2 + 3y^2 &= 3 \\ \hline y^2 &= 9 \\ y &= \pm 3 \end{aligned}$

$y = 3$ $y = -3$

$x^2 = 2(3)^2 + 6$ $x^2 = 2(-3)^2 + 6$

$x^2 = 24$ $x^2 = 24$

$x = \pm 2\sqrt{6}$ $x = \pm 2\sqrt{6}$

$\left(2\sqrt{6}, 3\right), \left(-2\sqrt{6}, 3\right)$

$\left(2\sqrt{6}, -3\right), \left(-2\sqrt{6}, -3\right)$

23. $\dfrac{\dfrac{3a^2bc - d^4}{c^2d}}{\dfrac{4s^2t - lc^2}{c^2d}} = \dfrac{3a^2bc - d^4}{c^2d} \cdot \dfrac{c^2d}{4s^2t - lc^2}$

$= \dfrac{3a^2bc - d^4}{4s^2t - lc^2}$

24. $2s = \sqrt{h^2 + 3t}$

$4s^2 = h^2 + 3t$

$3t = 4s^2 - h^2$

$t = \dfrac{4s^2 - h^2}{3}$

25. $-3 \ \angle{-135°} = 2.12i + 2.12j$

$4 \ \angle{140°} = \underline{-3.06i + 2.57j}$

Resultant $= -0.94i + 4.69j$

Equilibrant $= 0.94i - 4.69j$

26. $\dfrac{-\sqrt{2}\,i\sqrt{2} + \sqrt{3}\sqrt{3}\,i3i}{3(-i) + 3(i)i^3} = \dfrac{-2i + 9i^2}{-3i + 3i^4}$

$= \dfrac{-9 - 2i}{3 - 3i} = \dfrac{-9 - 2i}{3 - 3i} \cdot \dfrac{(3 + 3i)}{(3 + 3i)}$

$= \dfrac{-27 - 27i - 6i + 6}{9 + 9}$

$= \dfrac{-21 - 33i}{18} = \dfrac{-7 - 11i}{6}$

27. a is positive

b is positive

Therefore **D**

28. A: $2x - y = 8$

B: $3x - 2z = 12$

C: $y - z = 1$

A: $2x - y = 8$

C: $\underline{y - z = 1}$

D: $2x - z = 9$

2D: $-4x + 2z = -18$

B: $\underline{3x - 2z = 12}$

$x = 6$

$y = 2(6) - 8 = 4$

$z = (4) - 1 = 3$

$\mathbf{(6, 4, 3)}$

29. $(2xy^2 - 3ab^3)(4x^2y^4 + 6xy^2ab^3 + 9a^2b^6)$

30. $18a^1 + 6a^{1/2}b^{1/2} - 3a^{1/2}b^{-1/2} - b^0$

$= 18a + 6a^{1/2}b^{1/2} - 3a^{1/2}b^{-1/2} - 1$

PROBLEM SET 15

1. $P = 6W$
    Downwind: $(6W + W)T_D = 560$
    $\qquad\qquad 7WT_D = 560$
    $\qquad\qquad WT_D = 80$
    $T_U = T_D + 3$
    Upwind: $\quad (6W - W)\left(T_D + 3\right) = 700$
    $\qquad\qquad 5WT_D + 15W = 700$
    $\qquad\qquad 5(80) + 15W = 700$
    $W = \mathbf{20\ mph}$
    $P = \mathbf{120\ mph}$

2. $\dfrac{2000}{10{,}000} = \dfrac{x}{1920}$
    $10{,}000x = 3{,}840{,}000$
    $x = \mathbf{\$384}$

3. $50\% = 0.50 = \dfrac{1}{2}$
    $\dfrac{1}{2}\left(\dfrac{3}{4}\right) = \dfrac{3}{8}$

4. Rate · time · men = dollars
    Rate · 15 · 10 = 6000
    Rate = 40
    40 · 5 · 20 = **$4000**

5.
	Old	New
Rate:	m	?
Time:	$\dfrac{k}{m}$	$\dfrac{k}{m} - 2$
Distance:	k	$k + 10$

    Rate $= \dfrac{\text{distance}}{\text{time}} = \dfrac{k + 10}{\dfrac{k}{m} - 2} = \dfrac{k + 10}{\dfrac{k - 2m}{m}}$

    $= \dfrac{m(k + 10)}{k - 2m}\ \mathbf{mph}$

6. $\boxed{5\ \ 5\ \ 5\ \ 5} = \mathbf{625}$

7. $\boxed{2\ \ 2\ \ 2\ \ 2\ \ 2\ \ 2\ \ 2\ \ 2\ \ 2\ \ 2}$
    $= 2^{10} = \mathbf{1024}$

8. $\boxed{4\ \ 3\ \ 2\ \ 1} = \mathbf{24}$

9. $\sqrt{(x - 3)^2 + (y - 2)^2}$
    $= \sqrt{(x + 4)^2 + (y + 3)^2}$
    $x^2 - 6x + 9 + y^2 - 4y + 4$

    $= x^2 + 8x + 16 + y^2 + 6y + 9$
    $-14x - 10y - 12 = 0$
    $\mathbf{7x + 5y + 6 = 0}$

10. $\left(\dfrac{-4 + 3}{2}, \dfrac{7 + 2}{2}\right) = \left(-\dfrac{1}{2}, \dfrac{9}{2}\right)$

11. $C_1 + F\left(C_2 - C_1\right)$
    $= -2\dfrac{2}{5} + \dfrac{3}{7}\left(3\dfrac{1}{5} + 2\dfrac{2}{5}\right)$
    $= -\dfrac{12}{5} + \dfrac{3}{7}\left(\dfrac{16}{5} + \dfrac{12}{5}\right)$
    $= -\dfrac{12}{5} + \dfrac{3}{7}\left(\dfrac{28}{5}\right) = -\dfrac{12}{5} + \dfrac{85}{35}$
    $= -\dfrac{84}{35} + \dfrac{84}{35} = \mathbf{0}$

12. **60°**

13.
    $\dfrac{3}{5}$

14.
    $\dfrac{1}{\sqrt{5}} = \dfrac{\sqrt{5}}{5}$

15. $\sin(-30°) + \cos 135° = -\dfrac{1}{2} - \dfrac{\sqrt{2}}{2}$
    $= \dfrac{\mathbf{-1 - \sqrt{2}}}{\mathbf{2}}$

16. $\tan(-135°) - \sin 225° = (+1) - \left(-\dfrac{\sqrt{2}}{2}\right)$
    $= \dfrac{\mathbf{2 + \sqrt{2}}}{\mathbf{2}}$

17. $\left(\dfrac{\sqrt{3}}{2}\right)\left(-\dfrac{\sqrt{2}}{2}\right) - 0 = -\dfrac{\sqrt{6}}{4}$

18. $\displaystyle\sum_{k=2}^{5} (k^2 - 2) = (2^2 - 2)$
$+ (3^2 - 2) + (4^2 - 2) + (5^2 - 2)$
$= 2 + 7 + 14 + 23 = \mathbf{46}$

19. $x^5 = 32$
$(x^5)^{1/5} = (32)^{1/5}$
$x = \mathbf{2}$

20. $3^x = \dfrac{1}{81}$
$3^x = \dfrac{1}{3^4} = 3^{-4}$
$x = \mathbf{-4}$

21. $\left(\dfrac{1}{2}\right)^{-4} = t$
$(2)^4 = t$
$t = \mathbf{16}$

22. $\dfrac{10 \cdot 9 \cdot 8 \cdot 7 \cdot 6!}{3 \cdot 2 \cdot 6!} = \mathbf{840}$

23. $x^2 + y^2 = 4$
$y = 2 - 2x$; substitute to get
$x^2 + (2 - 2x)^2 = 4$
$x^2 + 4 - 8x + 4x^2 = 4$
$5x^2 - 8x = 0$
$x(5x - 8) = 0$

$x = 0 \qquad\qquad 5x - 8 = 0$
$\qquad\qquad\qquad x = \dfrac{8}{5}$

$y = 2 - 2(0) \qquad y = 2 - 2\left(\dfrac{8}{5}\right)$

$y = 2 \qquad\qquad y = -\dfrac{6}{5}$

$(0, 2), \left(\dfrac{8}{5}, -\dfrac{6}{5}\right)$

24. $\dfrac{2}{1 + \dfrac{t}{\dfrac{sl - z}{l}}} = \dfrac{2}{1 + \dfrac{tl}{sl - z}}$

$= \dfrac{2}{\dfrac{sl - z + tl}{sl - z}} = \dfrac{2(sl - z)}{sl - z + tl}$

25. $\sqrt{5zt} = 3t + 10k$
$5zt = 9t^2 + 60t + 100k^2$
$z = \dfrac{9t^2 + 60tk + 100k^2}{5t}$

26. $-2 \ \underline{/-130°} = 1.29i + 1.53j$
$6 \ \underline{/180°} = i + 0j$
Resultant $= -4.71i + 1.53j$
Equilibrant $= \mathbf{4.71i - 1.53j}$

27. $\dfrac{-\sqrt{3}\sqrt{3}\,i\sqrt{2}\sqrt{2}\,i \ -\sqrt{6}\,i\sqrt{6}}{4(-i) + 4i \cdot i}$

$= \dfrac{+6 - 6i}{-4 - 4i} \cdot \dfrac{(-4 + 4i)}{(-4 + 4i)}$

$= \dfrac{-24 + 24i + 24i + 24}{16 + 16} = \dfrac{48i}{32} = \dfrac{3i}{2}$

28. $\mathbf{B}$

29. A: $x - 2y + z = -2$
B: $2x - y + z = 3$
C: $x + y + 2z = 3$

$\begin{array}{l} -2\text{A: } -2x + 4y - 2z = 4 \\ \text{B: } 2x - y + z = 3 \\ \hline 3y - z = 7 \end{array}$

$\begin{array}{l} \text{A: } x - 2y + z = -2 \\ -\text{C: } -x - y - 2z = -3 \\ \hline -3y - z = -5 \end{array}$

$\begin{array}{l} 3y - z = 7 \\ -3y - z = -5 \\ \hline -2z = 2 \\ z = -1 \end{array}$

$-3y - (-1) = -5$
$-3y = -6$
$y = 2$
$x - 2(2) - 1 = -2$
$x = 3$
$\mathbf{(3, 2, -1)}$

30.

$$\begin{array}{r} x^3 + x + 1 \\ x - 1 \overline{\smash{\big)}\, x^4 - x^3 + x^2 + 0x - 1} \\ \underline{x^4 - x^3} \\ x^2 + 0x \\ \underline{x^2 - x} \\ x - 1 \\ \underline{x - 1} \\ 0 \end{array}$$

$\boldsymbol{x^3 + x + 1}$

1. Boat = $4W$
$T_U = T_D - 1$

   Downstream: $(4W + W)T_D = 60$
   $5WT_D = 60$
   $WT_D = 12$

   Upstream: $(4W - W)(T_D - 1) = 27$
   $3WT_D - 3W = 27$
   $3(12) - 3W = 27$
   $W = 3$ **mph**
   $B = 12$ **mph**

2.

	1st leg	2nd leg
Distance:	RT	$RT + 100$
Rate:	R	?
Time:	T	$T + P$

   Rate $= \dfrac{RT + 100}{T + P}$ mph

3. Total distance = 1000 mi
   Overall rate = 40 mph
   Total time $= \dfrac{\text{distance}}{\text{rate}} - \dfrac{1000}{40} = 25$ hr
   Time first leg = 5 hr
   Time second leg = 10 hr
   Therefore, time third leg = 10 hr
   Rate $= \dfrac{\text{distance}}{\text{time}} = \dfrac{500}{10} = 50$ **mph**

4. $W + S = 20$
   $W = 20 - S$
   $0.9S + 0.75W = 0.78(20)$
   $0.9S + 0.75(20 - S) = 0.78(20)$
   $0.9S + 15 - 0.75S = 15.6$
   $0.15S = 0.6$
   $S = $ **4 liters 90%**
   $W = $ **16 liters 75%**

5.

	Rate
Oscar:	$\dfrac{1}{10}$
Sally:	R_S

   Time working together = 2 hr
   $R_D T_D + R_S T_S = 1$
   $\dfrac{1}{10}(4 + 2) + R_S(2) = 1$

   $\dfrac{6}{10} + 2R_S = 1$
   $R_S = \dfrac{1}{5}$
   $R_S T_S = 1$
   $\left(\dfrac{1}{5}\right)T_S = 1$
   $T_S = $ **5 hr**

6. $5 \cdot 5 \cdot 5 \cdot 5 \cdot 5 = 5^5 = $ **3125**

7. $6 \cdot 5 \cdot 4 = $ **120**

8. $3 \cdot 3 \cdot 3 \cdot 3 \cdot 3 = 3^5 = $ **243**

9. $\sqrt{(x - 4)^2 + (y - 2)^2}$
   $= \sqrt{(x + 4)^2 + (y + 3)^2}$
   $x^2 - 8x + 16 + y^2 - 4y + 4$
   $= x^2 + 8x + 16 + y^2 + 6y + 9$
   $-10y = 16x + 5$
   $y = -\dfrac{8}{5}x - \dfrac{1}{2}$

10. $x = \dfrac{1 + 6}{2}$
    $y = \dfrac{3 + 5}{2}$
    $\left(\dfrac{7}{2}, 4\right)$

11. $C_1 + F(C_2 - C_1)$
    $= -\dfrac{32}{5} + \dfrac{2}{27}\left(\dfrac{22}{5} + \dfrac{32}{5}\right)$
    $= -\dfrac{32}{5} + \dfrac{2}{27}\left(\dfrac{54}{5}\right)$
    $= -\dfrac{32}{5} + \dfrac{4}{5} = -\dfrac{28}{5}$

12.

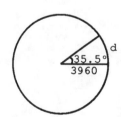

    $35.5° = 0.6196$ rad
    Distance $= 0.6916(3960) = $ **2453.6 mi**

13. Arctan $(-1) = $ **−45°**

14. $\sin\left(\text{Arctan}\dfrac{2}{5}\right) = \dfrac{2}{\sqrt{29}} = \dfrac{2\sqrt{2}}{29}$

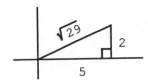

15. $\cos\left(\text{Arcsin}\dfrac{3}{4}\right) = \dfrac{\sqrt{7}}{4}$

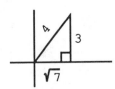

16. $\sin\left(-\dfrac{13\pi}{6}\right) - \tan\left(\dfrac{11\pi}{4}\right)$

$= \sin(-30°) - \tan(135°) = -\dfrac{1}{2} - (-1) = \dfrac{1}{2}$

17. $\sin\dfrac{\pi}{2}\cos\dfrac{3\pi}{4} - \tan\dfrac{\pi}{6}$

$= \sin 90° \cos 135° - \tan 30°$

$= 1\left(-\dfrac{\sqrt{2}}{2}\right) - \dfrac{\sqrt{3}}{3} = -\dfrac{\sqrt{2}}{2} - \dfrac{\sqrt{3}}{3}$

$= -\dfrac{3\sqrt{2}}{6} - \dfrac{2\sqrt{3}}{6} = \dfrac{-3\sqrt{2} - 2\sqrt{3}}{6}$

18. $\sin 90° \cos 270° - \sin 60°$

$= 1(0) - \dfrac{\sqrt{3}}{2} = -\dfrac{\sqrt{3}}{2}$

19. $\left(\dfrac{1}{4} + 1\right) + 0 + \left(\dfrac{1}{4} - 1\right)$

$+ (1 - 2) + \left(\dfrac{9}{4} - 3\right) = \dfrac{1}{2} - 4 + \dfrac{9}{4}$

$= \dfrac{2}{4} - \dfrac{16}{4} + \dfrac{9}{4} = -\dfrac{5}{4}$

20. $x^{-1/3} = \dfrac{1}{8}$

$x = \left(\dfrac{1}{8}\right)^{-1/3}$

$x = (2^{-3})^{-1/3}$

$x = 2$

21. $2^s = \dfrac{1}{16}$

$2^s = 2^{-4}$

$s = -4$

22. $\left(\dfrac{1}{3}\right)^{-2} = R$

$R = \dfrac{1}{\left(\dfrac{1}{3}\right)^2} = \dfrac{1}{\dfrac{1}{9}}$

$R = 9$

23. $\dfrac{11 \cdot 10 \cdot 9 \cdot 8 \cdot 7 \cdot 6 \cdot 5!}{4 \cdot 3 \cdot 2 \cdot 1 \cdot 5!}$

$= 11 \cdot 10 \cdot 3 \cdot 7 \cdot 6 = 13{,}860$

24.
$$\begin{array}{rcl} 2y^2 - x^2 &=& 5 \\ 2y^2 + y^2 &=& 11 \\ \hline 4y^2 &=& 16 \\ y^2 &=& 4 \end{array}$$

$y = \pm 2$

$2y^2 + x^2 = 11$

$8 + x^2 = 11$

$x^2 = 3$

$x = \pm\sqrt{3}$

$\left(\sqrt{3}, 2\right), \left(\sqrt{3}, -2\right),$

$\left(-\sqrt{3}, 2\right), \left(-\sqrt{3}, -2\right)$

25. $z^{2a-3}(z^{3/2})^{a+2}z^{-2a}z^{-1} = z^{2a-3}z^{3a/2+3}z^{-2a}z^{-1}$

$= z^{3a/2-1}$

26. $s = x_0 + v_0 t + \dfrac{1}{2}gt^2$

$s - x_0 - v_0 t = \dfrac{1}{2}gt^2$

$g = \dfrac{2(s - x_0 - v_0 t)}{t^2}$

27. $-4\ \angle{-120°}\ -\ 8\ \angle{90°}$

$x_1 = 2.29$	$y_1 = 3.28$
$x_2 = 0$	$y_2 = -8$
$x_T = 2.29$	$y_T = -4.72$

Equilibrant: $-2.29i + 4.72j$

28. If $A < 0$ then $\dfrac{1}{A}$ is negative

and $\dfrac{1}{A^2}$ is positive; therefore $B > A$.

Thus the answer is B.

29.

A: $2x - 4y = 2$
B: $2x - z = 9$
C: $2y - z = 3$

$\begin{array}{r} \text{A:} \quad 2x - 4y = 2 \\ \underline{-\text{B:} \quad 2x - z = 9} \\ -4y + z = -4 \\ 2y - z = 3 \\ y = 2 \end{array}$

$2(2) - z = 3$

$z = 1$
$2x - 1 = 9$
$2x = 10$
$x = 5$
(5, 2, 1)

30. $8a^3b^6 - 27x^6y^9 = (3x^2y^3)^3$
$= (2ab^2 - 3x^2y^3)(4a^2b^4 + 6ab^2x^2y^3 + 9x^4y^6)$

PROBLEM SET 17

1.

A: $G + F + M = 90$
B: $3(G - 5 + F - S) = 2(M - 5) + 50$
C: $(F + 5) + (M + 5) = G + 5 + 55$
A: $F + M + G = 90$
B: $3F - 2M + 3G = 70$
C: $F + M - G = 50$

$\begin{array}{r} \text{A:} \quad F + M + G = 90 \\ \underline{\text{B:} \quad F + M - G = 50} \\ \text{D:} \quad 2F + 2M \phantom{{}- G} = 140 \end{array}$

$\begin{array}{r} \text{B:} \quad 3F - 2M + 3G = 70 \\ \underline{\text{C:} \quad 3F + 3M - 3G = 150} \\ \text{E:} \quad 6F + M \phantom{{}- 3G} = 220 \end{array}$

$\begin{array}{r} \text{D:} \quad 2F + 2M = 140 \\ \underline{\text{E:} \quad -12F - 2M = -440} \\ \text{D:} \quad -10F \phantom{{}- 2M} = -300 \\ F = 30 \end{array}$

$2(30) + 2M = 140$
$2M = 80$
$M = 40$
$F = 30 + 175 = \mathbf{205}$
$M = 40 + 175 = \mathbf{215}$
$G = 20 + 175 = \mathbf{195}$

2.

	Rate
Gadansk:	$\frac{1}{4}$
Krakow:	R_K

Time working together = 40
$R_G T_G + R_K T_K = 18$
$\frac{1}{40}(40) + R_K(40) = 18$
$R_K = \dfrac{\mathbf{1}}{\mathbf{5}}$

$R_K T_K = 1$
$\frac{1}{5}T_K = 1$
$T_K = \mathbf{5\ hr}$

3.

$\begin{array}{r} x + y = 22 \\ \underline{x - y = 6} \\ 2x \phantom{{}+ y} = 28 \\ x \phantom{{}+ y} = 14 \end{array}$

$y = 22 - 14 = 8$
$14 \cdot 8 = \mathbf{112}$

4. $z = \dfrac{3y}{x}$

If $\dfrac{3(3y)}{2x}$ then $\dfrac{3}{2}z$

Multiplied by $\dfrac{3}{2}$

5. Mean $= \dfrac{2 + 5 + 7 + 11 + 20}{6}$

$= \dfrac{60}{6} = 10$

Median = halfway between 7 and 11 = **9**

6. $7 \cdot 6 \cdot 5 \cdot 4 \cdot 3 = \mathbf{2520}$

7. $6 \cdot 6 \cdot 6 = \mathbf{216}$

8. $7 \cdot 6 \cdot 5 \cdot 4 = \mathbf{840}$

9. $2(SF) = 3$
$SF = \dfrac{3}{2}$
$3\left(\dfrac{3}{2}\right) = b = \dfrac{\mathbf{9}}{\mathbf{2}}$
$4\left(\dfrac{3}{2}\right) = a = \mathbf{6}$

10. $\dfrac{a}{e} = \dfrac{b}{a}$

$\dfrac{a}{e} = \dfrac{c}{f}$

$\dfrac{b}{a} = \dfrac{c}{f}$

11. $\sqrt{(x-6)^2 + (y-4)^2}$
$= \sqrt{(x+4)^2 + (y+2)^2}$
$x^2 - 12x + 36 + y^2 - 8y + 16$
$= x^2 + 8x + 16 + y^2 + 4y + 4$
$-20x - 12y = -32$
$-5x - 3y = -8$
$y = -\dfrac{5}{3}x + \dfrac{8}{3}$

12. $\left(\dfrac{-3+6}{2}, \dfrac{4-2}{2}\right) = \left(\dfrac{3}{2}, 1\right)$

13. $C_1 + F\left(C_2 - C_1\right)$

$= -4\dfrac{1}{7} + \dfrac{7}{13}\left(3\dfrac{2}{7} + 4\dfrac{1}{7}\right)$

$= -\dfrac{29}{7} + \dfrac{7}{13}\left(\dfrac{23}{7} + \dfrac{29}{7}\right)$

$= -\dfrac{29}{7} + \dfrac{7}{13}\left(\dfrac{52}{7}\right)$

$= -\dfrac{29}{7} + 4 = -\dfrac{29}{7} + \dfrac{28}{7}$

$= -\dfrac{1}{7}$

14.

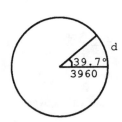

$39.7° = 0.693$ radians
Distance $= 3960(0.693) \approx$ **2742 mi**

15. $-30°$

16. $\dfrac{\sqrt{21}}{5}$

17. $\dfrac{-2}{\sqrt{13}} = \dfrac{-2\sqrt{13}}{13}$

18. $\sin(-60°)\cos 450° - \tan(-390°)$
$\sin(-60°)\cos 90° - \tan(-30°)$
$\left(-\dfrac{\sqrt{3}}{2}\right)(0) - \left(-\dfrac{\sqrt{3}}{3}\right) = \dfrac{\sqrt{3}}{3}$

19. $\sin 90° \cos 0° - \sin 210° = (1)(1) - \left(-\dfrac{1}{2}\right)$

$= \dfrac{3}{2}$

20. $\tan 390° - \sin 90° = \tan 30° - \sin 90°$

$= \dfrac{\sqrt{3}}{3} - 1$

21. $\dfrac{(-2-2^2)}{3} + \dfrac{(-1-2)^2}{3}$

$+ \dfrac{(0-2)^2}{3} + \dfrac{(1-2)^2}{3} = 10$

22. $(a^{-2})^{-1/2} = \left(\dfrac{1}{9}\right)^{-1/2} = 9^{1/2} = 3$

23. $3^k = \dfrac{1}{27}$

$3^k = 3^{-3}$

$k = -3$

24. $\left(\dfrac{1}{4}\right)^{-3} = x$

$x = 4^3 = 64$

25. $\dfrac{12 \cdot 11 \cdot 10 \cdot 9!}{3 \cdot 2 \cdot 9!} = 220$

26. $x^2 + y^2 = 9$
$y = x - 3$
$x^2 + (x-3)^2 = 9$
$x^2 + x^2 - 6x + 9 = 9$
$2x^2 - 6x = 0$
$2x(x-3) = 0$
$x = 0 \qquad\qquad x = 3$
$y = 0 - 3 = -3 \qquad y = 3 - 3 = 0$
$(0, -3), (3, 0)$

27.
$$r^2s^2 = qt - \frac{1}{3}h$$
$$qt = r^2s^2 + \frac{1}{3}h$$
$$t = \frac{3r^2s^2 + h}{3q}$$

28.
$$-5\ \underline{/-135°} = 3.54i + 3.54j$$
$$6\ \underline{/140°} = \quad -4.60i + 3.86j$$

Resultant $= \quad -1.06i + 7.40j$

Equilibrant $= \quad 1.06i - 7.40j$

29.
$$A:\ 2x - y + z = 7$$
$$\underline{B:\ x + 2y - z = 0}$$
$$D:\ 3x + y \quad\ = 7$$

$$B:\ 2x + 4y - 2z = 0$$
$$\underline{C:\ x - y + 2z = 9}$$
$$E:\ 3x + 3y \quad\ = 9$$
$$x + y \quad\ = 3$$

$$D:\ 3x + y = 7$$
$$\underline{E:\ \ x + y = 3}$$
$$2x \quad\quad = 4$$
$$x \quad\quad = 2$$
$$y = -2 + 3 = 1$$
$$z = 2 + 2(1) = 4$$
(2, 1, 4)

30.

$$x - 2\overline{)\,x^3 - 3x^2 + 3x - 4\,}^{\,x^2\quad + 3 + 10/(x-2)}$$
$$\underline{x^3 - 2x^2}$$
$$3x + 4$$
$$\underline{3x - 6}$$
$$10$$

$$x^2 + 3 + \frac{10}{x - 2}$$

PROBLEM SET 18

1. A = angle
$90 - A$ = complement
$4(90 - A) = 200$
$360 - 4A = 200$
$A = 40°$

2. A = angle
$180 - A$ = supplement
$3(180 - A) = 450$
$540 - 3A = 450$
$A = 30°$

3.

	1st	2nd	3rd
Rate:	30	10	?
Time:	2	2	T
Distance:	60	20	20

Average time $= \dfrac{\text{total distance}}{\text{total time}}$

$$20 = \frac{60 + 20 + 20}{2 + 2 + T}$$
$$20 = \frac{100}{4 + T}$$
$$T = 1\ \text{hr}$$
$$\text{Rate} = \frac{20}{1} = \mathbf{20\ mph}$$

4.

	Old	New
Rate:	$\dfrac{y}{s}$	?
Time:	s	$s + 10$
Distance:	y	$2y$

$$\text{Rate} = \frac{2y}{s + 10}\ \frac{\text{yd}}{\text{sec}}$$

5. Rate $\cdot$ time $\cdot$ men = jobs
Rate $\cdot$ 10 $\cdot$ 5 = 1
Rate $= \dfrac{1}{50}$

$\left(\dfrac{1}{50}\right)$ time (2) = 1

Time = **25 days**

6. $\boxed{7\ |\ 6\ |\ 5} = \mathbf{210}$

7. $\angle x$ and $\angle y$ are vertical $\angle$'s.
$\angle x + \angle p = 180°$ and
$\angle p + \angle y = 180°$ because
each pair of angles forms a straight line.
Thus, $\angle x + \angle p = \angle p + \angle y$.
Subtracting $\angle p$ from each side gives
$\angle x = \angle y$. The vertical angles are equal.

8. A: $3x - 2y = 40$
    B: $2x + 4y + 40 + 60 = 180$

    A: $3x - 2y = 40$
    B: $2x + 4y = 80$

    Substituting $x = 40 - 2y$ into A gives
    $3(40 - 2y) - 2y = 40$
    $-8y = -80$
    $y = 10$
    $x = 40 - 2(10)$
    $x = 20$

9. $y - y_1 = m(x - x_1)$

    $y - 3 = \frac{1}{2}(x + 2)$

    $2y - 6 = x + 2$

    $x - 2y + 8 = 0$

10. $3x - 2y + 6$

    $\frac{3x}{-6} - \frac{2y}{-6} = \frac{-6}{-6}$

    $\frac{x}{-2} + \frac{y}{3} = 1$

11. $1(SF) = 3$

    $SF = \frac{1}{3}$

    $q = \frac{1}{3}(4) = \frac{4}{3}$

    $p = \frac{1}{3}(4) = \frac{4}{3}$

12. $\triangle ABC \sim \triangle EBD$

    $\frac{AB}{EB} = \frac{BC}{BD}$

    $\frac{AB}{EB} = \frac{AC}{BD}$

    $\frac{BC}{BD} = \frac{AC}{BD}$

13. $\sqrt{(x - 3)^2 + (y - 2)^2}$
    $= \sqrt{(x + 4)^2 + (y + 3)^2}$
    $x^2 - 6x + 9 + y^2 - 4y + 4$
    $= x^2 + 8x + 16 + y^2 + 6y + 9$
    $-14x - 10y - 12 = 0$
    $7x + 5y - 6 = 0$

14. $\left(\frac{-2 + 6}{2}, \frac{6 + 3}{2}\right) = \left(2, \frac{9}{2}\right)$

15. $C_1 + F(C_2 - C_1)$

    $= -3\frac{2}{3} + \frac{5}{6}\left(6\frac{1}{3} + 3\frac{2}{3}\right)$

    $= -\frac{11}{3} + \frac{5}{6}\left(\frac{19}{3} + \frac{11}{3}\right)$

    $= -\frac{11}{3} + \frac{5}{6}\left(\frac{30}{3}\right) = -\frac{11}{3} + \frac{25}{3}$

    $= \frac{14}{3}$

16. Arc = radius $\times$ radian angle
    $= (4)(0.5233) = 2.093 = $ **2.1 in**

17. **$-45°$**

18.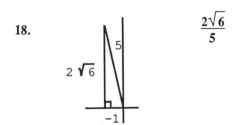

    $\dfrac{2\sqrt{6}}{5}$

19.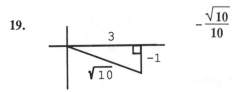

    $-\dfrac{\sqrt{10}}{10}$

20. $\sin 60° \cos 60° - \sin 60°$

    $= \left(\frac{\sqrt{3}}{2}\right)\left(\frac{1}{2}\right) - \frac{\sqrt{3}}{2} = \frac{\sqrt{3} - 2\sqrt{3}}{4} = \frac{-\sqrt{3}}{4}$

21. $\tan(-45°)\cos 90° + \sin 0°$
    $= (-1)(0) + 0 = $ **0**

22. $\cos(-390°) + \sin 390°$
    $= \cos(-30°) + \sin 30°$
    $= \frac{\sqrt{3}}{2} + \frac{1}{2} = \frac{\sqrt{3} + 1}{2}$

23. $\frac{(-1)^2 - 2}{4} + \frac{0^2 - 2}{4} + \frac{1^2 - 2}{4}$

    $+ \frac{2^2 - 2}{4} + \frac{3^2 - 2}{4}$

    $= -\frac{1}{4} - \frac{1}{2} - \frac{1}{4} + \frac{1}{2} + \frac{7}{4} = \frac{5}{4}$

24. $(b^{-3})^{-1/3} = \left(\frac{1}{27}\right)^{-1/3}$

    $b = 27^{1/3} = $ **3**

25. $4^k = \dfrac{1}{64}$

   $4^k = 4^{-3}$

   $k = -3$

26. $\left(\dfrac{1}{3}\right)^{-2} = y$

   $y = 3^2 = 9$

27. $\dfrac{11 \cdot 10 \cdot 9 \cdot 8 \cdot 7 \cdot 6!}{3 \cdot 2 \cdot 6!} = 9240$

28. $\begin{aligned} x^2 + y^2 &= 13 \\ \underline{2x^2 - y^2} &= \underline{14} \\ 3x^2 &= 27 \\ x^2 &= 9 \\ x &= \pm 3 \end{aligned}$

$\begin{aligned} x &= 3 & x &= -3 \\ y^2 &= 13 - 3^2 & y^2 &= 13 - (-3)^2 \\ y^2 &= 4 & y^2 &= 4 \\ y &= \pm 2 & y &= \pm 2 \end{aligned}$

$(3, 2), (3, -2) \qquad\quad (-3, 2), (-3, -2)$

29. $x^{3a-2}\left(x^{3/4}\right)^{a-2} x^{-3} = x^{3a-2+3a/4-3/2-3} = x^{15a/4-13/2}$

30. $-3 \ \underline{/\,35^\circ} = -2.46i - 1.72j$

   $6 \ \underline{/\,-40^\circ} = \underline{4.60i - 3.86j}$

   Resultant $= \ \ 2.14i - 5.58j$

   Equilibrant $= -2.14i + 5.58j$

PROBLEM SET 19

1. A = angle

   $90 - A$ = complement

   $180 - A$ = supplement

   $4(90 - A) = 180 - A + 60$

   $360 - 4A = 240 - A$

   $A = 40^\circ$

2. $P = 6W$

   $T_U = T_D + 1$

   Down: $(6W + W)T_D = 700$

   $\qquad\quad 7WT_D = 700$

   $\qquad\quad WT_D = 100$

   Up: $\quad (6W - W)\left(T_D + 1\right) = 600$

   $\qquad\quad 5WT_D + 5W = 600$

   $\qquad\quad 5(100) + 5W = 600$

   $\qquad\quad 5W = 100$

   $W = 20$ mph

   $P = 120$ mph

3.

	1st	2nd	3rd
Rate:	15	25	R
Time:	3	2	$\dfrac{85}{R}$
Distance:	45	50	85

   Average rate $= \dfrac{\text{total distance}}{\text{total time}}$

   $18 = \dfrac{45 + 50 + 85}{5 + \dfrac{85}{R}}$

   $18 = \dfrac{180}{\dfrac{5R + 85}{R}} = \dfrac{180R}{5R + 85}$

   $18(5R + 85) = 180R$

   $90R + 1530 = 180R$

   $90R = 1530$

   $R = 17$ mph

4.

Amt	410		x		410 + x
% Tin	16%	+	100%	=	18%

   $16(410) + 100x = 18(410 + x)$

   $6560 + 100x = 7380 + 18x$

   $82x = 820$

   $x = 10$ lb

5. If you remove the outside layers of a 4" cube the result is a 2" cube.

   $2 \times 2 \times 2 = 8$ one-inch cubes

6. $\boxed{20}\,\boxed{19}\,\boxed{18}\,\boxed{17}\,\boxed{16} = 1{,}860{,}480$

7. $\angle x$ and $\angle y$ are vertical $\angle$'s.

   $\angle x + \angle p = 180^\circ$ and

   $\angle p + \angle y = 180^\circ$ because

   each pair of angles forms a straight line.

   Thus, $\angle x + \angle p = \angle p + \angle y$.

   Subtracting $\angle p$ from each side gives

   $\angle x = \angle y$. The vertical angles are equal.

8.   A: $3x + 4y = 100$
B: $2x + y + 130 = 180$
Rearranging B gives $y = -2x + 50$
and substituting back into A gives
$3x + 4(-2x + 50) = 100$
$3x - 8x + 200 = 100$
$-5x = -100$
$x = \mathbf{20}$
$y = -2(20) + 50$
$y = \mathbf{10}$

9. $y - y_1 = m\left(x_2 - x_1\right)$

$y - 4 = -\dfrac{1}{3}(x - 3)$

$3y - 12 = -x - 3$
$x + 3y - 9 = 0$

10. $\dfrac{2x}{-5} \dfrac{-4y}{-5} = \dfrac{-5}{-5}$

$\dfrac{x}{-5/2} + \dfrac{y}{5/4} = 1$

11. $2(SF) = \dfrac{3}{2}$

$SF = \dfrac{3}{4}$

$4\left(\dfrac{3}{4}\right) = a = 3$

$3\left(\dfrac{3}{4}\right) = b = \dfrac{9}{4}$

12. $\cos 48° = \dfrac{7000}{x}$

$x = \dfrac{7000}{\cos 48°} = \mathbf{10{,}461\ ft}$

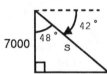

13. $\sqrt{(z + 4)^2 + (y - 2)^2}$
$= \sqrt{(x - 5)^2 + (y - 3)^2}$
$x^2 + 8x + 16 + y^2 - 4y + 4$
$= x^2 - 10x + 25 + y^2 - 6y + 9$
$18x + 2y - 14 = 0$
$9x + y - 7 = 0$

14. $\left(\dfrac{-3 + 6}{2}, \dfrac{4 + 2}{2}\right) = \left(\dfrac{3}{2}, 3\right)$

15. $C_1 + F\left(C_2 - C_1\right)$

$= 2\dfrac{1}{4} + \dfrac{2}{3}\left(6\dfrac{3}{4} - 2\dfrac{1}{4}\right)$

$= \dfrac{9}{4} + \dfrac{2}{3}\left(\dfrac{27}{4} - \dfrac{9}{4}\right) = \dfrac{9}{4} + \dfrac{2}{3}\left(\dfrac{18}{4}\right)$

$= \dfrac{9}{4} + 3 = \dfrac{21}{4}$

16.   Arc $=$ radius $\times$ radian angle
$= (30)(0.6106) = \mathbf{18.32\ ft}$

17. $\mathbf{-45°}$

18. $\dfrac{\mathbf{1}}{\mathbf{2}}$

19. $\dfrac{3\sqrt{3}}{13}$

20. $\sin 120° \cos 120° - \sin 240°$

$= \left(\dfrac{\sqrt{3}}{2}\right)\left(-\dfrac{1}{2}\right) - \left(-\dfrac{\sqrt{3}}{2}\right) = -\dfrac{\sqrt{3}}{4} + \dfrac{\sqrt{3}}{2}$

$= \dfrac{-\sqrt{3} + 2\sqrt{3}}{4} = \dfrac{\sqrt{3}}{4}$

21. $\tan(-135°) \cos 90° - \sin 90°$
$= (+1)(0) - 1 = \mathbf{-1}$

22. $\sin(-570°) + \sin 390°$

$= \sin(-210°) + \sin 30° = \dfrac{1}{2} + \dfrac{1}{2} = \mathbf{1}$

23. $\dfrac{2(-2) - 3}{3} + \dfrac{2(-1) - 3}{3} + \dfrac{2(0) - 3}{3}$

$+ \dfrac{2(1) - 3}{3} = -\dfrac{7}{3} - \dfrac{5}{3} - 1 - \dfrac{1}{3} = -\dfrac{16}{3}$

24. $\log_a (3.4) = \log_a (x - 2)$
$12 = x - 2$
$x = \mathbf{14}$

25. $\log_3 \left(\dfrac{x + 2}{x - 1}\right) = \log_3 4$

$\dfrac{x + 2}{x - 1} = 4$

$x + 2 = 4x - 4$
$3x = 6$
$x = \mathbf{2}$

26. $\log_c x^3 = \log_c 27$
$x^3 = 27$
$x = 3$

27. $\log_{12} x = \log_{12} 27^{2/3}$
$x = 27^{2/3}$
$x = 9$

28. $(2xy^2 - 3ay^3)(4x^2y^4 + 6xy^2ay^3 + 9ay^6)$
$= (2xy^2 - 3ay^3)(4x^2y^4 + 6xay^5 + 9a^2y^6)$

29. $2k + 2p = \sqrt{3z}$
$4k^2 + 8kp + 4p^2 = 3z$
$z = \dfrac{4k^2 + 8kp + 4p^2}{3} = \dfrac{1}{3}(2k + 2p)^2$

30. $\sqrt{x + 16} = 8 - \sqrt{x}$
$x + 16 = 64 - 16\sqrt{x} + x$
$16\sqrt{x} = 48$
$\sqrt{x} = 3$
$x = 9$

PROBLEM SET 20

1. A = angle
$90 - A$ = complement
$180 - A$ = supplement
$5(90 - A) - 30 = 2(180 - A)$
$450 - 5A - 30 = 360 - 2A$
$60 = 3A$
$A = 20°$

2.

	1st	2nd	3rd
Distance:	36	45	54
Rate:	12	15	R
Time:	3	3	T

Total time $= \dfrac{\text{distance}}{\text{rate}} = \dfrac{135}{15} = 9$
$3 + 3 + T = 9$
$T = 3$
$R = \dfrac{54}{3} = 18$ mph

3. Rate $\cdot$ time $\cdot$ men = jobs
Rate $\cdot 5 \cdot 600 = \dfrac{3}{4}$ jobs completed
$\dfrac{1}{4000} \cdot 5 \cdot m = \dfrac{1}{4}$ jobs to be finished
$m = 200$ men

4.

	Old	New
Distance:	m	m
Rate:	$\dfrac{m}{h}$	?
Time:	h	$h - 3$

Rate $= \dfrac{\text{distance}}{\text{time}} = \dfrac{m}{h - 3}$ mph

5.

	Rate
Bubber:	$\dfrac{1 \text{ job}}{3 \text{ hr}}$
Dougan:	$\dfrac{1 \text{ job}}{6 \text{ hr}}$

T = time together
$R_B T_B + R_D T_D = 4$
$\dfrac{1}{3}(3 + T) + \dfrac{1}{6}T = 4$
$T = 6$; therefore 9:00 p.m.

6. $_{12}P_4 = \dfrac{12 \cdot 11 \cdot 10 \cdot 9 \cdot 8!}{8!} = 11{,}880$

7. $_{13}P_5 = \dfrac{13!}{8!} = 154{,}400$

8. $\angle x$ and $\angle y$ are vertical $\angle$'s.
$\angle x + \angle p = 180°$ and
$\angle p + \angle y = 180°$ because
each pair of angles forms a straight line.
Thus, $\angle x + \angle p = \angle p + \angle y$.
Subtracting $\angle p$ from each side gives
$\angle x = \angle y$. The vertical angles are equal.

9. A: $4x - 3y = 30$
B: $6x - y = 80$
Substitute $y = 6x - 80$ into A to get
$4x - 3(6x - 80) = 30$
$4x - 18x + 240 = 30$
$-14x = -210$
$x = 15$
$y = 90 - 80$
$y = 10$

10. $y - 3 = -\dfrac{1}{3}(x + 2)$

$y = -\dfrac{1}{3}x + \dfrac{7}{3}$

$3y = -x + 7$

$x + 3y - 7 = 0$

11. $5x - 3y = -6$

$-\dfrac{5}{6}x + \dfrac{1}{2}y = 1$

$\dfrac{x}{-6/5} + \dfrac{y}{2} = 1$

12. $3(s) = 6$

$s = 2$

$x = 5(2) = \mathbf{10}$

$y = 6(2) = \mathbf{12}$

13. $\dfrac{AB}{HG} = \dfrac{AC}{HF}$

$\dfrac{AB}{HG} = \dfrac{BC}{GF}$

$\dfrac{AC}{HF} = \dfrac{BC}{GF}$

14. $\sqrt{(x - 2)^2 + (y - 4)^2}$

$= \sqrt{(x + 4)^2 + (y - 6)^2}$

$x^2 - 4x + 4 + y^2 - 8y + 16$

$= x^2 + 8x + 16 + y^2 - 12y + 36$

$-32 = 12x - 4y$

$3x - y + 8 = 0$

15. $\left(\dfrac{-3 + 6}{2}, \dfrac{4 - 2}{2}\right) = \left(\dfrac{3}{2}, 1\right)$

16. $50° = 0.8727$ rad

Distance = radius × radians

Distance = $35(0.8727) = \mathbf{30.54}$ ft

17. $C_1 + F\left(C_2 - C_1\right)$

$= -\dfrac{15}{4} + \dfrac{4}{13}\left(\dfrac{24}{4} + \dfrac{15}{4}\right)$

$= -\dfrac{15}{4} + \dfrac{4}{13}\left(\dfrac{39}{4}\right)$

$= -\dfrac{15}{4} + \dfrac{12}{4} = -\dfrac{3}{4}$

18. $\text{Arccos}\left(-\dfrac{\sqrt{3}}{2}\right) = \mathbf{150°}$

19.

$\sin\left[\text{Arctan}\left(-\dfrac{3}{4}\right)\right] = -\dfrac{3}{5}$

20.

$\cos\left[\text{Arcsin}\left(-\dfrac{2}{3}\right)\right] = \dfrac{\sqrt{5}}{3}$

21. $\sec\left(-\dfrac{\pi}{3}\right) + \cot\left(-\dfrac{13\pi}{6}\right)$

$= \sec(-60°) + \cot(-30°)$

$= 2 + -\sqrt{3} = \mathbf{2 - \sqrt{3}}$

22. $\csc(-330°) - \sec 390°$

$= 2 - \dfrac{2\sqrt{3}}{3} = \dfrac{\mathbf{6 - 2\sqrt{3}}}{\mathbf{3}}$

23. $\displaystyle\sum_{z=-2}^{1} \dfrac{z^3 - 1}{3} = -3 - \dfrac{2}{3} - \dfrac{1}{3} + 0 = \mathbf{-4}$

24. $\log_4 2 + \log_4 8 = \log_4 (x + 3)$

$\log_4 16 = \log_4 (x + 3)$

$16 = x + 3$

$x = \mathbf{13}$

25. $\log_3 (x - 2) - \log_3 (x + 1) = \log_3 5$

$\log_3\left(\dfrac{x - 2}{x + 1}\right) = \log_3 5$

$x - 2 = 5(x + 1)$

$-7 = 4x$

$x = -\dfrac{7}{4}, \textbf{No solution}$

26. $4 \log_c x = \log_c 81$

$\log_c x^4 = \log_c 81$

$x^4 = 81$

$x = \mathbf{3}$

27. $\log_{13} 13 = \dfrac{3}{4} \log_{13} 16$

$x = 16^{3/4} = \mathbf{8}$

28. $g^2z^2 = 4h - ts^3$

$4h = g^2z^2 + ts^3$

$h = \dfrac{g^2z^2 + ts^3}{4}$

29. $-2\ \underline{/140°}\ +\ 8\ \underline{/150°}$

$x_1 = 1.532 \qquad\qquad y_1 = -1.28$

$x_2 = \underline{-6.298} \qquad\quad y_2 = \underline{4.00}$

$x_T = -5.396 \qquad\quad y_T = 2.714$

Resultant = **$-5.40i + 2.71j$**

30. $\dfrac{-\sqrt{3}\sqrt{-3}\sqrt{2}\sqrt{-2} - \sqrt{8}\sqrt{2}}{\sqrt{-16} + \sqrt{3}}$

$= \dfrac{6 - 4}{4i + 3} = \dfrac{2}{3 + 4i}\ \dfrac{(3 - 4i)}{(3 - 4i)}$

$= \dfrac{6 - 8i}{9 - 16i^2} = \dfrac{6 - 8i}{25} = \dfrac{6}{25} - \dfrac{8}{25}i$

PROBLEM SET 21

1. Rate · time · men = jobs

Rate · 3 · 5 = 7

Rate $= \dfrac{7}{15}$

$\dfrac{7}{15}$ · time · 10 = 14

Time = **3 days**

2. Normal play $= \dfrac{160}{4} = \$4.00$ per hour

New pay = \$4.00 + 0.25(\$4.00) = \$5.00

Weekly pay = 60(\$5.00) = **\$300**

3. Downstream: $(B + W)3 = 75$

Upstream: $(B - W)5 = 75$

$3B + 3W = 75$

$5B - 5W = 75$

$B + W = 25$

$B - W = 15$

$B = $ **20 mph**

$W = $ **5 mph**

4.

	1st	2nd
Rate:	$\dfrac{100}{9.8}$	$\dfrac{440}{49}$
Time:	9.8	49
Distance:	100	440

Ratio $= \dfrac{\frac{440}{49}}{\frac{100}{9.8}} = \dfrac{440}{49} \cdot \dfrac{9.8}{100} = \dfrac{4.4}{5} = \dfrac{22}{25}$

5.

	Rate
Petal:	$\dfrac{1 \text{ job}}{12 \text{ hr}}$
Petunia:	R_P

Time working together = 5

$\dfrac{1}{12}(5) + R_P(5) = \dfrac{25}{24}$

$R_P = \dfrac{1}{8}$

$R_P T_P = 2$

$\dfrac{1}{8}T_P = 2$

$T_P = $ **16 hr to do 2 jobs**

6. $\dfrac{10!}{5!} = \dfrac{10 \cdot 9 \cdot 8 \cdot 7 \cdot 6 \cdot 5!}{5!} = 30{,}240$

7. $\dfrac{10 \cdot 9 \cdot 8 \cdot 7 \cdot 6 \cdot 5 \cdot 4!}{3 \cdot 2 \cdot 4!} = 25{,}200$

8. $(x - 3)^2 + (y - 4)^2 = r^2$

9. $y = \left(\dfrac{1}{4}\right)^x$

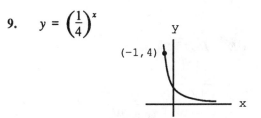

10. $y = 4\left(\dfrac{1}{2}\right)^x$

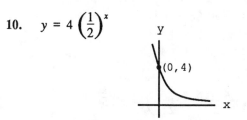

11. Refer to Solution Set 18, problem 7.

12.
$$\begin{array}{rcl} x + 2y &=& 37 \\ -3x - 2y &=& -51 \\ \hline -2x &=& -14 \\ x &=& 7 \end{array}$$

$7 + 2y = 37$

$2y = 30$

$y = 15$

$x = 7$

13. $y - 3 = -\dfrac{2}{5}(x + 1)$

$5y - 15 = -2x - 2$

$2x + 5y - 13 = 0$

14. $\dfrac{6x}{3} - \dfrac{5y}{3} = \dfrac{3}{3}$

$\dfrac{x}{1/2} - \dfrac{y}{3/5} = 1$

15. $\dfrac{3}{2}(SF) = 4$

$SF = \dfrac{8}{3}$

$4\left(\dfrac{8}{3}\right) = a = \dfrac{32}{3}$

$\dfrac{7}{2}\left(\dfrac{8}{3}\right) = b = \dfrac{28}{3}$

16. $\dfrac{AB}{DE} = \dfrac{AC}{CE}$

$\dfrac{AB}{DE} = \dfrac{BC}{DC}$

$\dfrac{AC}{CE} = \dfrac{BC}{DC}$

17. $\sqrt{(x - 1)^2 + (y - 4)^2}$

$= \sqrt{(x + 3)^2 + (y - 2)^2}$

$x^2 - 2x + 1 + y^2 - 8y + 16$

$= x^2 + 6x + 9 + y^2 - 4y + 4$

$-8x - 4y + 4 = 0$

$2x + y - 1 = 0$

18. $\left(\dfrac{-4 + 8}{2}, \dfrac{6 + 4}{2}\right) = (2, 5)$

19. $C_1 + F\left(C_2 - C_1\right)$

$= 3\dfrac{1}{2} + \dfrac{6}{7}\left(6\dfrac{2}{3} - 3\dfrac{1}{2}\right) = \dfrac{7}{2} + \dfrac{6}{7}\left(\dfrac{20}{8} - \dfrac{7}{2}\right)$

$= \dfrac{7}{2} + \dfrac{6}{7}\left(\dfrac{40}{6} - \dfrac{21}{6}\right) = \dfrac{7}{2} + \dfrac{6}{7}\left(\dfrac{19}{6}\right)$

$= \dfrac{7}{2} + \dfrac{19}{7} = \dfrac{49}{14} + \dfrac{38}{14} = \dfrac{87}{14}$

20. Arc = radius × angle in radians

Arc = $1500\,(0.698) = $ **1047 ft**

21. $-60°$

22. $\dfrac{\sqrt{7}}{4}$

23. $\dfrac{3}{5}$

24. $\sec 45° - \sin 30° = \sqrt{2} - \dfrac{1}{2} = \dfrac{2\sqrt{2} - 1}{2}$

25. $\csc(-30°) - \cot(-390°)$

$= -2 - \left(-\sqrt{3}\right) = -2 + \sqrt{3}$

26. $\log_7 x^2 = 4$

$(7^4)^{1/2} = (x^2)^{1/2}$

$x = 7^2 = $ **49**

27. $\log_2 \dfrac{(x + 4)}{(x + 4)} = \log_2 5$

$\dfrac{x + 4}{x + 4} = 5$

$x + 4 = 5x - 20$

$x = 6$

28. $\log_6 x^4 = \log_6 81$

$(x^4)^{1/4} = 81^{1/4}$

$x = 3$

29. $\log_{14} x = \log_{14} 16^{3/2}$
$x = 16^{3/2}$
$x = \mathbf{64}$

30.

$$
\begin{array}{r}
x^2 \quad\ -\ 2 \\
x - 3\ \overline{\big)\ x^3 - 3x^2 - 2x - 5} \\
\underline{x^3 - 3x^2} \\
-2x + 5 \\
\underline{-2x + 6} \\
-1
\end{array}
$$

$$x^2 - 2 - \dfrac{1}{x - 3}$$

PROBLEM SET 22

1. Rate · time · men = jobs
Rate · 12 · 10 = 1
Rate $= \dfrac{1}{120}$

$\left(\dfrac{1}{120}\right)(5)(8) + \dfrac{1}{120}$ (time)(4) $= 1$

$\dfrac{40}{120} + \dfrac{4}{120}t = 1$

$\dfrac{1}{30}t = \dfrac{2}{3}$

$t = \mathbf{20\ days}$

2.

	Now	+10 years
Sally:	S_N	$S_N + 10$
John:	J_N	$J_N + 10$

$5S_N = 3J_N + 30$
$5S_N - 3J_N = 30$
$2\big(S_N + 10\big) = J_N + 10 + 26$
$2S_N - J_N = 16$
$J_N = 2S_N - 16$
$5S_N - 3\big(2S_N - 16\big) = 30$
$S_N = 18$
$J_N = 20$
In 13 years:
Sally = **31**, John = **33**

3.

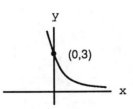

$\dfrac{F}{S} = \dfrac{X}{S_x}$
$FS_x = XS$
$S_x = \dfrac{XS}{F}$ **ft**

4. $\dfrac{56}{35} = \$1.60$ per hour

$1\dfrac{1}{2}$ times $\$1.60 = \$2.40$ new rate

$40(1.60) + H(2.40) = 88$
$2.4H = 24$
$H = 10$
$40 + 10 = \mathbf{50\ hr}$

5. $\dfrac{\text{total price}}{\text{price/gallon}} = \text{gallons} = G$

$G = \dfrac{2000}{130 + f + s}$ **gal**

6. $_9P_6 = \dfrac{8!}{2!} = 20160$

$_8P_5 = \dfrac{8!}{3!} = 6720$

$20160 - 6720 = \mathbf{13{,}440}$

7. $y = \mathbf{5 \sin x}$

8. $y = \mathbf{10 - 6 \cos \theta}$

9. $[(-1)^2 - 3] + [(0)^2 - 3]$
$+\ [1^2 - 3] + [2^2 - 3] + [3^2 - 3]$
$= -2 + (-3) + (-2) + 1 + 6 = \mathbf{0}$

10. $(x + 2)^2 + (y - 3)^2 = r^2$

11. $y = 3\left(\dfrac{1}{3}\right)^x$

12. Refer to Solution Set 18, problem 7.

13. $4a - b = 40$

$6a - \dfrac{1}{2}b = 80$

$b = 4a - 40$
$12a - b = 160$

$12a - (4a - 40) = 160$
$8a + 40 = 160$
$a = \mathbf{15}$
$b = \mathbf{20}$

14. $y - 3 = -\dfrac{1}{4}(x + 2)$

$4y - 12 = -x - 2$
$\mathbf{x + 4y - 10 = 0}$

15. $1(SF) = \dfrac{5}{2}$

$SF = \dfrac{5}{2}$

$\dfrac{5}{2}\left(\dfrac{5}{2}\right) = q = \dfrac{25}{4}$

$3\left(\dfrac{5}{2}\right) = p = \dfrac{15}{2}$

16. $0 + 1 = 1$
$5 - 1 = 4$
$\mathbf{B}$

17. $\sqrt{(x + 3)^2 + (y + 2)^2}$
$= \sqrt{(x - 2)^2 + (y - 3)^2}$
$x^2 + 6x + 9 + y^2 + 4y + 4$
$= x^2 - 4x + 4 + y^2 - 6y + 9$
$10x - 10y = 0$
$\mathbf{x + y = 0}$

18. $\left(\dfrac{-3 + 8}{2}, \dfrac{4 - 3}{2}\right) = \left(\dfrac{5}{2}, \dfrac{1}{2}\right)$

19. $C_1 + F\left(C_2 - C_1\right) = 1\dfrac{1}{4} + \dfrac{4}{5}\left(-6\dfrac{2}{3} - 1\dfrac{1}{4}\right)$

$= \dfrac{5}{4} + \dfrac{4}{5}\left(-\dfrac{20}{3} - \dfrac{5}{4}\right) = \dfrac{5}{4} + \dfrac{4}{5}\left(-\dfrac{80}{12} - \dfrac{15}{12}\right)$

$= \dfrac{5}{4} + \dfrac{4}{5}\left(-\dfrac{95}{12}\right) = \dfrac{5}{4} - \dfrac{19}{3}$

$= \dfrac{15 - 76}{12} = -\dfrac{\mathbf{61}}{\mathbf{12}}$

20. Arc = radius × angle in radians

Arc $= 300\left(60° \times \dfrac{\pi}{180°}\right) = \mathbf{314 \ yd}$

21. $\mathbf{45°}$

22.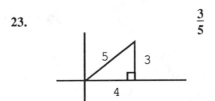
$\dfrac{3}{5}$

23.
$\dfrac{3}{5}$

24. $\csc(-135°) + \cos(-35°) = -\sqrt{2} + \dfrac{\sqrt{3}}{2}$

$= \dfrac{-2\sqrt{2} + \sqrt{3}}{2}$

25. $\sec(-570°) + \csc(-60°)$
$= \sec(-210°) + \csc(-60°)$

$= \dfrac{1}{\cos(-210°)} + \dfrac{1}{\sin(-60°)} = \dfrac{1}{-\dfrac{\sqrt{3}}{2}} + \dfrac{1}{-\dfrac{\sqrt{3}}{2}}$

$= \dfrac{2}{-\dfrac{\sqrt{3}}{2}} = \dfrac{-4\sqrt{3}}{3}$

26. $\log_4(8)(6) = \log_4(3x + 2)$
$48 = 3x + 2$
$3x = 46$
$x = \dfrac{46}{3}$

27. $\log_3 \dfrac{(x - 3)}{(x + 1)} = \log_3 12$

$\dfrac{(x - 3)}{(x + 1)} = 12$

$x - 3 = 12(x + 1)$
$x - 3 = 12x + 12$
$-11x = 15$
$x = -\dfrac{15}{11}$

$(x + 1) = \left(-\dfrac{15}{11} + 1\right) = $ negative

No solution

28. $x^4 = 16$
$(x^4)^{1/4} = (16)^{1/4}$
$x = 2$

29. $\log_{15} x = \log_{15} 8^{2/3}$
$x = 8^{2/3} = 4$

30. $25q^2r^2 = 3t^2 - 4s$
$3t^2 = 25q^2r^2 + 4s$
$t^2 = \dfrac{25q^2r^2 + 4s}{3}$
$t = \pm\sqrt{\dfrac{25q^2r^2 + 4s}{3}}$

PROBLEM SET 23

1. $R(1) + 3R(10) = 3100$
$31R = 3100$
$R = 100\,\dfrac{\text{m}}{\text{year}}$
100 miles

2. Rate $\cdot$ time $\cdot$ men = cookies
Rate $\cdot$ h $\cdot$ w = c
Rate $= \dfrac{c}{hw}$
$\dfrac{c}{hw} \cdot$ time $\cdot (w + m) = c$
$\dfrac{c(w + m)}{hw} \cdot$ time $= c$
Time $= \dfrac{chw}{c(w + m)} = \dfrac{hw}{w + m}$ **hours**

3. Rate $\cdot$ time $\cdot$ men = cookies
Rate $\cdot$ m $\cdot$ c = p
Rate $= \dfrac{p}{mc}$
$\dfrac{p}{mc} \cdot$ time $\cdot c + n = p$
Time $= \dfrac{pmc}{p(c + n)} = \dfrac{mc}{c + n}$ **min**

4. Cost of each drum $= \dfrac{x}{d}$
New cost $= \left(\dfrac{x}{d} - 5\right) = \dfrac{x - 5d}{d}$
Rate $\cdot$ drums = cost
$\left(\dfrac{x - 5d}{d}\right) \cdot$ drums $= 100$
Drums $= \dfrac{100d}{x - 5d}$

5. $\dfrac{\frac{6}{2}}{y + z} = \dfrac{6}{1} \cdot \dfrac{y + z}{2} = 3(y + z)$

6. $\boxed{5\ 4\ 3\ 2} = 120$

7. $\boxed{6\ 5\ 4\ 3} = 360$

8. $y = 7 - 3\cos x$

9. $y = 4 + 7\sin x$

10. $(1^2 - 2) + (2^2 - 2) + (3^2 - 2)$
$= (-1) + 2 + 7 = 8$

11. $(x - h)^2 + (y - k)^2 = 25$

12. $y = \left(\dfrac{1}{4}\right)\left(\dfrac{1}{2}\right)^x$

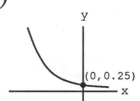

(0,0.25)

13. Refer to Solution Set 18, problem 7.

14. $4x + \dfrac{6}{5}y = 60$
$4y = 40$
$y = 10$
$4x + \dfrac{6}{5}(10) = 60$
$4x + 12 = 60$
$4x = 48$
$x = 12$
$y = 10$

15. $10(SF) = 25$
$SF = \dfrac{5}{2}$
$22\left(\dfrac{5}{2}\right) = a = 55$
$19\left(\dfrac{5}{2}\right) = b = \dfrac{95}{2}$

16. $\dfrac{a}{d} = \dfrac{c}{e}, \dfrac{a}{d} = \dfrac{b}{f}, \dfrac{c}{e} = \dfrac{b}{f}$

17. $\sqrt{(x + 6)^2 + (y - 4)^2}$
$= \sqrt{(x - 0)^2 + (y - 8)^2}$
$= x^2 + 12x + 36 + y^2 - 8y + 16$
$= x^2 + y^2 - 16y + 64$
$12x + 8y - 12 = 0$
$3x + 2y - 3 = 0$
$y = -\dfrac{3}{2}x + \dfrac{3}{2}$

18. $\left(\dfrac{-6 + 7}{2}, \dfrac{2 + 4}{2}\right) = \left(\dfrac{1}{2}, 3\right)$

19. $C_1 + F\left(C_2 - C_1\right)$
$= 2\dfrac{2}{3} + \dfrac{1}{3}\left(6\dfrac{1}{3} - 2\dfrac{2}{3}\right) = \dfrac{8}{3} + \dfrac{1}{3}\left(\dfrac{19}{3} - \dfrac{8}{3}\right)$
$= \dfrac{8}{3} + \dfrac{1}{3}\left(\dfrac{11}{3}\right) = \dfrac{8}{3} + \dfrac{11}{9} = \dfrac{24}{9} + \dfrac{11}{9} = \dfrac{35}{9}$

20. Arc = radius × angle in radians
Arc $= 1000\left(\dfrac{\pi}{6}\right) = \dfrac{500\pi}{3}$ or **520 ft**

21. $-30°$

22. $-\dfrac{3}{5}$

23.

$\dfrac{3}{5}$

24. $\sec(-210°) + \csc 60° = -\dfrac{2\sqrt{3}}{3} + \dfrac{2\sqrt{3}}{3} = 0$

25. $\sec(-135°) - \cot 90° = -\sqrt{2} - 0 = -\sqrt{2}$

26. $\log_3 (6)(3) \ \log_3 (4x + 2)$
$18 = 4x + 2$
$x = \mathbf{4}$

27. $\log_7 \dfrac{x + 2}{x - 4} = \log_7 2$
$\dfrac{x + 2}{x - 4} = 2$
$x + 2 = 2x - 8$
$x = \mathbf{10}$

28. $\log_x 4^2 = 2$
$x^2 = 4^2$
$x = \mathbf{4}$

29. $\log_5 (2x + 1) - \log_5 2^2 = \log_5 3$
$\log_5 \dfrac{2x + 1}{4} = \log_5 3$
$\dfrac{2x + 1}{4} = 3$
$2x + 1 = 12$
$x = \dfrac{\mathbf{11}}{\mathbf{2}}$

30. $\sqrt{x + 9} = 9 - \sqrt{x}$
$x + 9 = 81 - 18\sqrt{x} + x$
$18\sqrt{x} = 72$
$\sqrt{x} = 4$
$x = \mathbf{16}$

PROBLEM SET 24

1. $R_1T_1 = 24$
$R_2T_2 = 24$
$2R_1 = R_2$
$T_1 + T_2 = 9$

$R_1\left(9 - T_2\right) = 24$
$2R_1T_2 = 24$
$T_1 = 9 - T_2$

$9R_1 - R_1T_1 = 24$
$R_1T_1 = 12$

$9R_1 - 12 = 24$
$9R_1 = 36$
$R_1 = \mathbf{4\ mph\ going}$
$R_2 = \mathbf{8\ mph\ returning}$
$T_2 = \mathbf{3\ hr\ returning}$
$T_1 = \mathbf{6\ hr\ going}$

2. $0.92(4000) - 1(L) = 0.8(4000 - L)$
$3680 - L = 3200 - 0.8L$
$480 = 0.2L$
$L = \mathbf{2400\ liters}$

3. Rate · time · men = jobs

    Rate · f · k = c

    Rate = $\dfrac{c}{fk}$

    $\dfrac{c}{fk}$ · time · $(k - x)$ = $c + 10$

    Time = $\dfrac{kf(c + 10)}{c(k - x)}$ hours

4. $G = 2B$

    $2(B + W) - 10 = G$

    $W + B + G = 35$

    $2B + 2W - 2B = 10$

    $\;B + G = 30$

    $(-)\,\dfrac{-2B + G = 0}{}$

    $3B = 30$

    $B = 10$

    $2W = 10$

    $W = \mathbf{5}$

    $G = 2(10)$

    $G = \mathbf{20}$

    $B = \mathbf{10}$

5. $k = \dfrac{1}{m + n}$

    $\dfrac{5}{k} = \dfrac{5}{\dfrac{1}{m + n}} = 5(m + n)$

6. $\boxed{1\;|\;5\;|\;5}$ = 25

7. $\boxed{6\;|\;5\;|\;4\;|\;3\;|\;2\;|\;1\;|\;3\;|\;2\;|\;1}$ = 4320

    Then put English first = 4320

    4320 + 4320 = **8640**

8. $y = -10 \sin x$

9. $y = 3 + 5 \cos x$

10. $_6P_3 = \dfrac{6!}{3!} = 6 \cdot 5 \cdot 4 = \mathbf{120}$

11. $(x - h)^2 + (y - k)^2 = 25$

12. $y = \left(\dfrac{1}{2}\right)^{-x+1} = \left(\dfrac{1}{2}\right)^{-x} \cdot \left(\dfrac{1}{2}\right)^{1}$

    $= \dfrac{1}{2}\left[\left(\dfrac{1}{2}\right)^{-1}\right]^{x} = \dfrac{1}{2}(2^x)$

    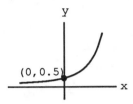

13. Refer to Solution Set 18, problem 7.

14.
    $\begin{aligned} x + y &= 50 \\ 3x - y &= 70 \\ \hline 4x &= 120 \\ x &= 30 \end{aligned}$

    $30 + y = 50$

    $y = \mathbf{20}$

    $x = \mathbf{30}$

15. $SF = \dfrac{5}{2}$

    $m = \dfrac{4}{5}\left(\dfrac{5}{2}\right)$

    $n = \dfrac{3}{2}\left(\dfrac{5}{2}\right)$

    $m = \mathbf{2}$

    $n = \dfrac{\mathbf{15}}{\mathbf{4}}$

16. $x < -1$ $\qquad\qquad$ $y > 4$

    $x + 5 < 4$ $\qquad\quad$ $y - 1 > 3$

    Therefore the answer is D

17. $6x - 5y = -7$

    $-\dfrac{6}{7}x + \dfrac{5}{7}y = 1$

    $\dfrac{x}{-7/6} + \dfrac{y}{7/5} = 1$

18. $\sqrt{(x + 4)^2 + (y + 3)^2}$

    $= \sqrt{(x - 4)^2 + (y - 6)^2}$

    $x^2 + 8x + 16 + y^2 + 6y + 9$

    $= x^2 - 8x + 16 + y^2 - 12y + 36$

    $16x + 18y = 27$

    $18y = -16x + 27$

    $y = -\dfrac{8}{9}x + \dfrac{3}{2}$

19. $x^2 + y^2 = 5$
    $x + y = 2$

    $x = 2 - y$
    $x^2 = 4 - 4y + y^2$
    Substitute into $x^2 + y^2 = 5$ to get
    $2y^2 - 4y + 4 = 5$
    $2y^2 - 4y - 1 = 0$
    $y = \dfrac{4 \pm \sqrt{16 - 4(2)(-1)}}{4}$
    $y = \dfrac{4 \pm \sqrt{16 + 8}}{4}$
    $y = \dfrac{4 \pm 2\sqrt{6}}{4} = 1 \pm \dfrac{\sqrt{6}}{2}$
    $x = 2 - \left(1 \pm \dfrac{\sqrt{6}}{2}\right)$
    $\left(1 - \dfrac{\sqrt{6}}{2}, 1 + \dfrac{\sqrt{6}}{2}\right)$
    $\left(1 + \dfrac{\sqrt{6}}{2}, 1 - \dfrac{\sqrt{6}}{2}\right)$

20. $(xy^2)^3 + (p^2z^3)^3$
    $= (xy^2 + p^2z^3)(x^2y^4 - p^2xy^2z^3 + p^4z^6)$

21. $R = 3960$
    $40.5° \times \dfrac{\pi\,\text{rad}}{180°} = 0.7069\text{ rad}$
    $(3960)(0.7069) = \mathbf{2799.2\text{ mi}}$

22. $\dfrac{\sqrt{7}}{4}$

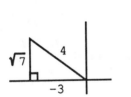

23. $\dfrac{-2}{\sqrt{13}} = \dfrac{-2\sqrt{13}}{13}$

24. $\sec(150°) + \cos 270° = \dfrac{-2\sqrt{3}}{3} + 0 = -\dfrac{2\sqrt{3}}{3}$

25. $\csc(135°) - \sec(210°)$
    $= \sqrt{2} + \dfrac{2\sqrt{3}}{3} = \dfrac{3\sqrt{2} + 2\sqrt{3}}{3}$

26. $\log_5 56 = \log_5 (2x - 4)$
    $2x - 4 = 56$
    $2x = 60$
    $x = \mathbf{30}$

27. $\log_3 \dfrac{x - 1}{x} = \log_3 15$
    $x - 1 = 15x$
    $-1 = 14x$
    $x = -\dfrac{1}{14}$
    No solution

28. $\log_c x^3 = \log_c 64$
    $x^3 = 64$
    $x = \mathbf{4}$

29. $\log_{10} 10000^{3/4} = x$
    $10^x = 10^3$
    $x = \mathbf{3}$

30. A: $3x - 2y = 4$
    B: $5x - z = 6$
    C: $y - z = -3$

    $$\begin{array}{rrcr}
    \text{A:} & 3x - 2y & = & 4 \\
    -2(\text{B}-\text{C}): & -10x + 2y & = & -18 \\
    \hline
    & -7x & = & -14 \\
    & x & = & 2
    \end{array}$$

    $3(2) - 2y = 4$
    $-2y = -2$
    $y = 1$
    $1 - z = -3$
    $-z = -4$
    $z = 4$
    (2, 1, 4)

PROBLEM SET 25

1. $R_G T_G = 36$
$R_R T_R = 36$
$R_R = 2R_G$
$T_G + T_R = 6$
$T_R = 6 - T_G$

$2R_G(6 - T_G) = 36$
$12R_G - 2R_G T_G = 36$
$12R_G - 2(36) = 36$
$12R_G = 108$
$R_G = \textbf{9 mph}$
$R_R = \textbf{18 mph}$

2. $\boxed{\dfrac{1000}{90\%}} - \boxed{\dfrac{x}{100\%}} = \boxed{\dfrac{1000 - x}{80\%}}$

$90(1000) - 100x = 80(1000 - x)$
$90{,}000 - 100x = 80{,}000 - 80x$
$-20x = -10000$
$x = \textbf{500 liters}$

3. Rate · time · men = food
Rate · d · $y = x$
Rate $= \dfrac{x}{dy} \dfrac{\text{food}}{\text{man} \cdot \text{days}}$

$\dfrac{x}{dy} \cdot \text{time} \cdot (y + 50) = x$

Time $= \dfrac{x\,dy}{x(y + 50)} = \dfrac{dy}{y + 50}$ days

4. $\dfrac{R}{E} = \dfrac{3}{1}$ $R = 3E$
$\dfrac{E}{D} = \dfrac{2}{1}$ $E = 2D$
$R + E + D = 18$

$R = 3(2D)$
$R = 6D$
$R + (2D) + D = 18$
$R = 18 - 3D$
$6D = 18 - 3D$
$9D = 18$
$D = \textbf{2}$
$R = \textbf{12}$
$E = \textbf{4}$

5. $\dfrac{3}{\dfrac{1}{b + c}} = 3(b + c) = 3b + 3c$

6. $\boxed{1}\,\boxed{5}\,\boxed{5} = \textbf{25}$

7. $\underbrace{\boxed{4}\,\boxed{3}\,\boxed{2}\,\boxed{1}}_{\text{Math}} \cdot \underbrace{\boxed{6}\,\boxed{5}\,\boxed{4}\,\boxed{3}\,\boxed{2}\,\boxed{1}}_{\text{Literature}}$
$= 17{,}280$
$\underbrace{\boxed{6}\,\boxed{5}\,\boxed{4}\,\boxed{3}\,\boxed{2}\,\boxed{1}}_{\text{Literature}} \cdot \underbrace{\boxed{4}\,\boxed{3}\,\boxed{2}\,\boxed{1}}_{\text{Math}}$
$= 17{,}280$
$17{,}280 + 17{,}280 = \textbf{34,560}$

8. $[x - (2 - 3i)][x - (2 + 3i)] = 0$
$(x - 2 + 3i)(x - 2 - 3i) = x^2 - 2x$
$\quad - 3xi - 2x + 4 + 6i + 3xi - 6i + 9$
$\boldsymbol{x^2 - 4x + 13 = 0}$

9. $x^2 + 3x + 6 = 0$
$x = \dfrac{-3 \pm \sqrt{9 - 4(1)(6)}}{2(1)}$
$x = \dfrac{-3 \pm \sqrt{-15}}{2} = \dfrac{-3 \pm \sqrt{15}\,i}{2}$
$x = \dfrac{-3 + \sqrt{15}\,i}{2}, \dfrac{-3 - \sqrt{15}\,i}{2}$
$\left[x - \left(\dfrac{-3 + \sqrt{15}\,i}{2}\right)\right]$
$\left[x - \left(\dfrac{-3 - \sqrt{15}\,i}{2}\right)\right]$

10. $y = 1 - 11\cos\theta$

11. $y = 3 - 7\sin x$

12. $\dfrac{8!}{4!} = \textbf{1680}$

13. $(x - h)^2 + (y - k)^2 = 36$

14. $y = \left(\dfrac{1}{3}\right)^{-x}\left(\dfrac{1}{3}\right)^2 = \dfrac{1}{9} \cdot 3^x$

15. Refer to Solution Set 18, problem 7.

16. $4x + y = 50$
$7x + 3y = 90$

$y = 50 - 4x$ (substitute)
$7x + 3(50 - 4x) = 90$
$-5x = -60$
$x = \mathbf{12}$
$y = \mathbf{2}$

17. $1(SF) = \dfrac{3}{4}$

$SF = \dfrac{3}{4}$

$2\left(\dfrac{3}{4}\right) = n = \dfrac{3}{2}$

$\dfrac{3}{2}\left(\dfrac{3}{4}\right) = m = \dfrac{9}{8}$

18. $2x - 6y = 3$
$\dfrac{2x}{3} - \dfrac{6y}{3} = 1$

$\dfrac{x}{3/2} + \dfrac{y}{-1/2} = \mathbf{1}$

19. $(x, y)\,(3, 4) = (x, y)\,(6, 8)$
$\sqrt{(x + 3)^2 + (y - 4)^2}$
$= \sqrt{(x - 6)^2 + (y - 8)^2}$
$x^2 + 6x + 9 + y^2 - 8y + 16$
$= x^2 - 12x + 36 + y^2 - 16y + 64$
$18x + 8y - 75 = 0$
$8y = -18y + 75$
$y = -\dfrac{9}{4}x + \dfrac{75}{8}$

20. $C_1 + F\left(C_2 - C_1\right)$

$= 2\dfrac{1}{3} + \dfrac{2}{3}\left(4\dfrac{2}{3} - 2\dfrac{1}{3}\right) = \dfrac{7}{3} + \dfrac{2}{3}\left(\dfrac{14}{3} - \dfrac{7}{3}\right)$

$= \dfrac{7}{3} + \dfrac{2}{3}\left(\dfrac{7}{3}\right) = \dfrac{7}{3} + \dfrac{14}{9} = \dfrac{21 + 14}{9} = \dfrac{35}{9}$

21. Arc = radius × angle in radians
Arc $= (600)\left(60° \cdot \dfrac{\pi}{180°}\right) = \mathbf{628\ meters}$

22.

$\dfrac{\sqrt{119}}{12}$

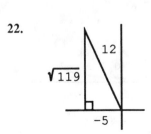

23.

$\dfrac{-5\sqrt{194}}{194}$

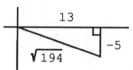

24. $\cos(-45°) + \sin 45° = \dfrac{\sqrt{2}}{2} + \dfrac{\sqrt{2}}{2} = \sqrt{2}$

25. $\csc 45° - \sec(-45°) = \sqrt{2} - \sqrt{2} = 0$

26. $\log_4 4^{5/2} = \log_4 (2x - 3)$
$4^{5/2} = 2x - 3$
$32 = 2x - 3$
$x = \dfrac{35}{2}$

27. $\log_3 \dfrac{x + 2}{x} = \log_3 10$
$\dfrac{x + 2}{x} = 10$
$x + 2 = 10x$
$x = \dfrac{2}{9}$

28. $\log_c x^2 = \log_c 64$
$x^2 = 64$
$x = \mathbf{8}$

29. $\log_8 x = \log_8 16^{3/4}$
$x = 16^{3/4} = \mathbf{8}$

30. A: $2x - y = 6$
B: $y - 2z = -12$
C: $2x - z = -4$
A: $y = 2x - 6$
B: $y = 2z - 12$

$2x - 6 = 2z - 12$
$2x - 2z = -6$
$x - z = 3$
$x = z - 3$; substitute into C to get
$2(z - 3) - z = -4$
$2z - 6 - z = -4$
$y = 2(2) - 12 = -8$
$z = 2$
$y = -8$
$x = -1$
$(\mathbf{-1, -8, 2})$

PROBLEM SET 26

1. $F = 4C$
   $T_D = T_U + 1$
   Upstream: $(4C - C)T_U = 30$
              $3CT_U = 30$
              $CT_U = 10$
   Downstream: $(4C - C)(T_U + 1) = 100$
              $5CT_U + 5C = 100$
              $5(10) + 5C = 100$

   $C = 10$ **mph**
   $F = 40$ **mph**

2. Rate $\cdot$ time $\cdot$ men = jobs
   Rate $\cdot d \cdot m = 1$
   Rate $= \dfrac{1}{dm}$

   $\dfrac{1}{dm} \cdot$ time $\cdot 40 = 1$

   Time $= \dfrac{dm}{40}$ **days**

3. Rate $\cdot$ time $\cdot$ men = jobs
   Rate $\cdot d \cdot k = x$
   Rate $= \dfrac{x}{dk}$

   $\dfrac{x}{dk} \cdot$ time $\cdot (k - y) = x$

   Time $= \dfrac{xdk}{x(k - y)} = \dfrac{dk}{k - y}$ **hours**

4. $\dfrac{60}{75} = \dfrac{4}{5}$

5. Rate $\cdot$ pencils = cost
   $\dfrac{d}{12} \dfrac{\text{dollar}}{\text{pencils}} \cdot mc$ pencils $= \dfrac{dmc}{12}$ **dollars**

6. Let t stand for a 2 and T stand for a 3.

T	t	2	1	$\rightarrow 2 \times 1 = 2$
t	T	2	1	$\rightarrow 2 \times 1 = 2$
2	T	t	1	$\rightarrow 2 \times 1 = 2$
2	t	T	1	$\rightarrow 2 \times 1 = 2$
2	1	T	t	$\rightarrow 2 \times 1 = 2$
2	1	t	T	$\rightarrow 2 \times 1 = 2$

                   $= 12$

7. | 9 | 9 | 4 | $= 324$

8. $y = -5 - 25 \sin x$

9. $y = -3 + 7 \cos \theta$

10. $\dfrac{(-1)^2 + 1}{2} + \dfrac{(0)^2 + 1}{2} + \dfrac{1^2 + 1}{2}$
    $+ \dfrac{2^2 + 1}{2} = 1 + \dfrac{1}{2} + 1 + \dfrac{5}{2} = 5$

11. $(x - 2)^2 + (y - 1)^2 = 9$

12. $y = \left(\dfrac{1}{2}\right)^{-x}\left(\dfrac{1}{2}\right)^{-3} = 8 \cdot 2^x$

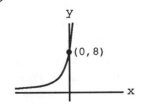

13. $[x - (3 + 2i)][x - (3 - 2i)] = 0$
    $(x - 3 - 2i)(x - 3 + 2i) = 0$
    $x^2 - 3x + 2xi - 3x + 9 - 6i - 2xi$
    $+ 6i + 4 = 0$
    $x^2 - 6x + 13 = 0$

14. $3x - \dfrac{2}{3}y = 50$
    $4x - y = 65$
    $y = 4x - 65$
    $3x - \dfrac{2}{3}(4x - 65) = 50$
    $9x - 8x + 130 = 150$
    $x = 20$
    $y = 15$

15. $\triangle ABE \sim \triangle ADC$
    $\dfrac{AB}{AD} = \dfrac{BE}{DC}$
    $\dfrac{AB}{AD} = \dfrac{AE}{AC}$
    $\dfrac{AE}{AC} = \dfrac{BE}{DC}$

16. $6^2 + 3^2 = a^2$
    $45 = a^2$
    $3\sqrt{5} = a$
    $\dfrac{6}{4} = \dfrac{3\sqrt{5}}{b}$
    $6b = 12\sqrt{5}$
    $b = 2\sqrt{5}$

17.

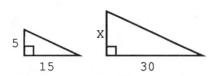

$$\frac{5}{x} = \frac{15}{30}$$
$$15x = 150$$
$$x = \textbf{10 ft}$$

18. $(x, y)\,(-3, -4) = (x, y)\,(3, 2)$
$$\sqrt{(x + 3)^2 + (y + 4)^2}$$
$$= \sqrt{(x - 3)^2 + (y - 2)^2}$$
$$x^2 + 6x + 9 + y^2 + 8y + 16$$
$$= x^2 - 6x + 9 + y^2 - 4y + 4$$
$$12x + 12y + 12 = 0$$
$$\boldsymbol{x + y + 1 = 0}$$

19. $\left(\dfrac{-4 + 6}{2}, \dfrac{-2 + 4}{2}\right) = \textbf{(1, 1)}$

20. $C_1 + F\left(C_2 - C_1\right)$
$$= -3\frac{2}{3} + \frac{4}{5}\left(4\frac{1}{4} + 3\frac{2}{3}\right)$$
$$= -\frac{11}{3} + \frac{4}{5}\left(\frac{17}{4} + \frac{11}{3}\right)$$
$$= -\frac{11}{3} + \frac{4}{5}\left(\frac{51 + 44}{12}\right)$$
$$= -\frac{11}{3} + \frac{4}{8}\left(\frac{95}{12}\right)$$
$$= -\frac{11}{3} + \frac{19}{3} = \frac{\textbf{8}}{\textbf{3}}$$

21. Arc = radius $\times$ angle in radians
$$= (20)(40)\left(\frac{\pi}{180}\right) = \textbf{14}$$

22.

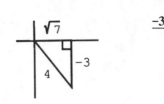

$$\frac{-3\sqrt{7}}{7}$$

23. Arctan $(-1) = \boldsymbol{-45°}$

24. $\cot(-135°) - \csc 150° = 1 - 2 = -1$

25. $\sec 390° \cos 390° = (1)(1) = \textbf{1}$

26. $\log_3 (4)(5) = \log_3 (4x + 5)$
$$20 = 4x + 5$$
$$4x = 15$$
$$x = \frac{\textbf{15}}{\textbf{4}}$$

27. $\log_7 \dfrac{6}{x - 1} = \log_7 3$
$$\frac{6}{x - 1} = 3$$
$$6 = 3x - 3$$
$$3x = 9$$
$$x = \textbf{3}$$

28. $\log_x 4^3 = 2$
$$\log_x 64 = 2$$
$$x^2 = 64$$
$$x = \textbf{8}$$

29. $\log_{15} x = \log_{15} 125^{2/3}$
$$x = 125^{2/3}$$
$$x = \textbf{25}$$

30. $(2xy^2 - 3a^2b^3)(4x^2y^4 + 6xy^2a^2b^3 + 9a^4b^6)$

PROBLEM SET 27

1. $\dfrac{R}{B} = \dfrac{2}{1}$
$$R = 2B$$
$$5(R + B) = 3W + 12$$
$$5R + 5B - 3W = 12$$
$$W = B + 4$$
$$B = W - 4$$
$$R = 2(W - 4)$$

$$R = 2W - 8$$
$$5R + 5(W - 4) - 3W = 12$$
$$5R + 2W = 32$$
$$5(2W - 8) + 2W = 32$$
$$10W - 40 + 2W = 32$$
$$W = \textbf{6}$$
$$R = \textbf{4}$$
$$B = \textbf{2}$$

2. $\boxed{\begin{array}{c} 40\% \\ x \end{array}} + \boxed{\begin{array}{c} 80\% \\ y \end{array}} = \boxed{\begin{array}{c} 50\% \\ 600 \end{array}}$

   $x + y = 600$

   $40x + 80y = 50(600)$

   $y = 600 - x$

   $40x + 80(600 - x) = 30,000$

   $40x + 48,000 - 80x = 30,000$

   $-40x = -18,000$

   $x = $ **450 ml of 40%**

   $y = $ **150 ml of 80%**

3. $C_0 + C_r = 36$

   $\dfrac{C_0}{C_r} = \dfrac{2}{1}$

   $C_0 = 2C_r$

   $2C_r + C_r = 36$

   $C_r = 12 = 12(1 \text{ oz})$

   $C_0 = 24 = 3(8 \text{ oz})$

   $3(216) + 12(106) = $ **1920 calories**

4. Painter's rate $= \dfrac{1}{m}$

   W_1 rate $= \dfrac{1}{W_1}$

   W_2 rate $= \dfrac{1}{W_2}$

   $\dfrac{1}{m} = \dfrac{1}{W_1} + \dfrac{1}{W_2}$

   $\dfrac{1}{m} = \dfrac{W_1 + W_2}{W_1 W_2}$

   $m = \dfrac{W_1 W_2}{W_1 + W_2}$

5. $\dfrac{3}{7}B = 60,000$

   $3B = 420,000$

   $B = 140,000$

   $\dfrac{1}{28}(140,000) = $ Wilbur's share $= $ **$5000**

6. $\boxed{\begin{array}{c|c|c|c} Y & 3 & 2 & 1 \end{array}} = 6$

   $\boxed{\begin{array}{c|c|c|c} P & 2 & 2 & 1 \end{array}} = 4$

   $\boxed{\begin{array}{c|c|c|c} L & 2 & 2 & 1 \end{array}} = \underline{4}$

   $= $ **14 ways**

7. $\boxed{\begin{array}{c|c|c} 2 & 8 & 5 \end{array}} = $ **80 ways**

8. $y = -5 - 20 \cos x$

9. $y = 6 - 14 \sin \theta$

10. $_4P_3 = \dfrac{(n)!}{(n-r)!} = \dfrac{4!}{1!} = 4 \cdot 3 \cdot 2 = 24$

11. $(x - 3)^2 + (y - 2)^2 = 16$

12. $y = \left(\dfrac{1}{2}\right)^x \left(\dfrac{1}{2}\right)^{-3} = 8 \cdot \left(\dfrac{1}{2}\right)^x$

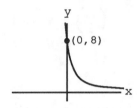

13. $x^2 - 2x + 3 = 0$

   $x = \dfrac{2 \pm \sqrt{4 - 4(1)(3)}}{2(1)}$

   $x = \dfrac{2 \pm \sqrt{-8}}{2} = \dfrac{2 \pm 2\sqrt{2}\,i}{2}$

   $x = 1 \pm \sqrt{2}\,i$

   $\left[x - \left(1 + \sqrt{2}\,i\right)\right]\left[x - \left(1 - \sqrt{2}\,i\right)\right]$

14. $\triangle ADE \sim \triangle ACB$

   $\dfrac{AD}{AC} = \dfrac{DE}{CB}$

   $\dfrac{AD}{AC} = \dfrac{AE}{AB}$

   $\dfrac{DE}{CB} = \dfrac{AE}{AB}$

15. $\dfrac{p}{1} = \dfrac{13}{2}$

   $p = \dfrac{13}{2} = 6\dfrac{1}{2}$ ft

16. $2x + y = 45$

   $y = 45 - 2x$

   $3x + 2y + 65 + 45 = 180$

   $3x + 2y = 70$

   $3x + 2(45 - 2x) = 70$

   $3x + 90 - 4x = 70$

   $x = $ **20**

   $y = $ **5**

17. Find slope: $(3, 6)$ $(8, 4)$

$$m = \frac{-4 - 6}{8 - 3} = \frac{-10}{5} = -2$$

Find $m_\perp$ and midpoint:

$$m_\perp = \frac{1}{2}$$

Midpoint: $\left(\dfrac{3 + 8}{2}, \dfrac{6 - 4}{2}\right) = \left(\dfrac{11}{2}, 1\right)$

Write equation of line:

$$y = mx + b$$

$$1 = \frac{1}{2}\left(\frac{11}{2}\right) + b$$

$$b = -\frac{7}{4}$$

$$y = \frac{1}{2}x - \frac{7}{4}$$

Put in double-intercept form:

$$4y = 2x - 7$$

$$2x - 4y = 7$$

$$\frac{2x}{7} - \frac{4y}{7} = \frac{7}{7}$$

$$\frac{x}{7/2} - \frac{y}{7/4} = 1$$

18. Find slope: $(4, -2)$ $(-2, 6)$

$$m = \frac{6 + 2}{-2 - 4} = -\frac{4}{3}$$

Find $m_\perp$ and midpoint:

$$m_\perp = \frac{3}{4}$$

Midpoint: $\left(\dfrac{4 - 2}{2}, \dfrac{-2 + 6}{2}\right) = (1, 2)$

Write equation of line:

$$y = mx + b$$

$$2 = \frac{3}{4}(1) + b$$

$$b = \frac{5}{4}$$

$$y = \frac{3}{4}x + \frac{5}{4}$$

19. $C_1 + F\left(C_2 - C_1\right)$

$$= -2\frac{1}{5} + \frac{2}{9}\left(3\frac{1}{5} + 2\frac{1}{5}\right)$$

$$= -\frac{11}{5} + \frac{2}{9}\left(\frac{16}{5} + \frac{11}{5}\right) = -\frac{11}{5} + \frac{2}{9}\left(\frac{27}{5}\right)$$

$$= -\frac{11}{5} + \frac{6}{5} = -\frac{5}{5} = -1$$

20. $\sqrt{(x + 2)^2 + (y - 1)^2}$

$$= \sqrt{(x - 3)^2 + (y - 2)^2}$$

$$x^2 + 4x + 4 + y^2 - 2y + 1$$

$$= x^2 - 6x + 9 + y^2 - 4y + 4$$

$$10x + 2y - 8 = 0$$

$$5x + y - 4 = 0$$

21. $\text{arc} = 3960\,(42.2)\left(\dfrac{\pi}{180}\right) = 2930 \text{ mi}$

22. $\sin^3(-60°) = \left(-\dfrac{\sqrt{3}}{2}\right)^3 = -\dfrac{3\sqrt{3}}{8}$

23. $\csc^2 405° - \tan^2 45°$

$$= \csc^2 45° - \tan^2 45° = \left(\sqrt{2}\right)^2 - 1 = 1$$

24. $\text{Arcsin}\left(\dfrac{1}{2}\right) = 30°$

25.

26. $\sec^2(-30°) + \sin^3(90°)$

$$= \left(\frac{2\sqrt{3}}{3}\right)^2 + 1^3 = \frac{12}{9} + 1 = \frac{7}{3}$$

27. $\log_4(5)\left(\dfrac{1}{5}\right) = \log_4(2x + 1)$

$$2x + 1 = 1$$

$$x = 0$$

28. $\log_8 \dfrac{x - 2}{3} = \log_8 16$

$$\frac{x - 2}{3} = 16$$

$$x - 2 = 48$$

$$x = 50$$

29. $\log_k x^2 = \log_k 36$

$$x^2 = 36$$

$$x = 6$$

30. $z^3 x - 4 = \sqrt{2t - 3}$

$$z^6 x^2 - 8z^3 x + 16 = 2t - 3$$

$$2t = z^6 x^2 - 8z^3 x + 19$$

$$t = \frac{z^6 x^2 - 8z^3 x + 19}{2}$$

PROBLEM SET 28

1. Rate · time · men = jobs
    Rate · b · a = c
    Rate = $\dfrac{c}{ab}$
    $\dfrac{c}{ab}$ · time · $(a - d)$ = c
    Time = $\dfrac{ab}{a - d}$ **hr**

2.
	Rate
Robill:	$\dfrac{2 \text{ jobs}}{3 \text{ days}}$
Buray:	$\dfrac{5 \text{ jobs}}{6 \text{ days}}$

    T = time together
    $R_R T_R + R_B T_B = 74$
    $\left(\dfrac{2}{3}\right)(T + 3) + \dfrac{5}{6}(T) = 74$
    $\dfrac{2}{3}T + 2 + \dfrac{5}{6}T = 74$
    $\dfrac{3}{2}T = 72$
    $T = 48$
    Jobs took $(48 + 3)$ = **51 days**

3. $\dfrac{\$240}{40}$ = \$6 per hour
    Raise = $6.00 + 0.20(6.00)$ = \$7.20
    Paycheck = $7.20(60)$ = **\$432**

4. $\text{Rate}_{\text{cats}} = \dfrac{d}{c}\dfrac{\text{dollars}}{\text{cat}}$
    $\text{Rate}_{\text{parrots}} = \dfrac{7d}{4c}\dfrac{\text{dollars}}{\text{parrot}}$
    $\text{Rate}_{\text{parrots}}$ · $\text{Number}_{\text{parrots}}$ = Cost
    $\dfrac{7d}{4c}$ · p = Cost
    Cost = $\dfrac{7dp}{4c}$ **dollars**

5. Rate · time · infants = gallons
    Rate · 11 · 5 = G
    Rate = $\dfrac{G}{11S}$
    $\left(\dfrac{G}{11S}\right)$ · time$(S + 14)$ = K
    Time = $\dfrac{11KS}{G(S + 14)}$ **days**

6. $\boxed{4\,|\,6\,|\,4\,|\,5}$ = 480

7. $\boxed{4\,|\,3\,|\,2\,|\,1\,|\,3\,|\,2\,|\,1}$ → Geometry 1st = 144
    $\boxed{3\,|\,2\,|\,1\,|\,4\,|\,3\,|\,2\,|\,1}$ → Algebra 1st = 144
    $144 + 144$ = **288**

8. $y = 1 + 5 \sin x$

9. $y = 5 - 15 \cos \theta$

10. $\dfrac{7!}{3!2!} = \dfrac{7 \cdot 6 \cdot 5 \cdot 4}{2!}$
    $= 7 \cdot 6 \cdot 5 \cdot 2 = 420$

11. $(x^2 + 2)^2 + (y + 3)^2 = 9$

12. $y = \left(\dfrac{1}{2}\right)^{-x+2} = \left(\dfrac{1}{2}\right)^{-x} \cdot \left(\dfrac{1}{2}\right)^2$
    $= 2^x \cdot \dfrac{1}{4} = \dfrac{1}{4}(2^x)$

    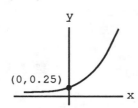

13. $[x - (2 + i)][x - (2 - i)]$
    $= (x - 2 - i)(x - 2 + 1)$
    $= x^2 - 2x + xi - 2x + 4 - 2i$
    $- xi + 2i + 1$
    $= x^2 - 4x + 5 = 0$

14. $\dfrac{5}{2}(s) = \dfrac{7}{2}$
    $s = \dfrac{7}{5}$
    $a = \left(\dfrac{7}{5}\right)$
    $b^2 = \left(\dfrac{7}{5}\right)^2 + \left(\dfrac{7}{2}\right)^2$
    $b^2 = \dfrac{49}{25} + \dfrac{49}{4}$
    $b^2 = \dfrac{196}{100} + \dfrac{1225}{100} = \dfrac{1421}{100} = \dfrac{7\sqrt{29}}{10}$

15.

$$\frac{5}{30} = \frac{12}{s}$$
$$5s = 30(12)$$
$$s = \textbf{72 m}$$

16. $4x + 2y = 70$

$\frac{3}{2}x + 2y = 30$

$\frac{5}{2}x = 40$

$x = \textbf{16}$

$4(16) + 2y = 70$

$2y = 6$

$y = \textbf{3}$

17. Midpoint $= \left(\dfrac{-2 + 6}{2}, \dfrac{-4 + 4}{2}\right) = (2, 0)$

$m = \dfrac{-4 - 4}{-2 - 6} = \dfrac{-8}{-8} = 1$

$m_\perp = -1$

$y = -1(x - 2)$

$y = -x + 2$

$\textbf{x + y - 2 = 0}$

18. Midpoint $= \left(\dfrac{-2 + 3}{2}, \dfrac{-5 + 4}{2}\right) = \left(\dfrac{1}{2}, -\dfrac{1}{2}\right)$

$m = \dfrac{-5 - 4}{-2 - 3} = \dfrac{-9}{-5} = \dfrac{9}{5}$

$m_\perp = -\dfrac{5}{9}$

$y + \dfrac{1}{2} = -\dfrac{5}{9}\left(x - \dfrac{1}{2}\right)$

$y = -\dfrac{5}{9}x + \dfrac{5}{18} - \dfrac{1}{2}$

$y = -\dfrac{5}{9}x - \dfrac{4}{18}$

$10x + 18y = -4$

$-\dfrac{5}{2}x - \dfrac{9}{2}y = 1$

$\dfrac{x}{-2/5} + \dfrac{y}{-2/9} = 1$

19. $C_1 + F\big(C_2 - C_1\big)$

$= -\dfrac{11}{3} + \dfrac{4}{9}\left(\dfrac{7}{3} + \dfrac{11}{3}\right) = -\dfrac{11}{3} + \dfrac{4}{9}\left(\dfrac{18}{3}\right)$

$= -\dfrac{11}{3} + \dfrac{8}{3} = -\dfrac{3}{3} = \textbf{-1}$

20. Midpoint $= \left(\dfrac{1 + 2}{2}, \dfrac{-1 - 6}{2}\right) = \left(\dfrac{3}{2}, -\dfrac{7}{2}\right)$

$m = \dfrac{-6 + 1}{2 - 1} = -5; \quad m_\perp = \dfrac{1}{5}$

$y + \dfrac{7}{2} = \dfrac{1}{5}\left(x - \dfrac{3}{2}\right)$

$10y + 35 = 2x - 3$

$2x - 10y - 38 = 0$

$\textbf{x - 5y - 19 = 0}$

21. $D = 0.87(200) = \textbf{174 ft}$

22. $\cos^3\left(-\dfrac{\pi}{4}\right) = \left(\dfrac{\sqrt{2}}{2}\right)^3 = \dfrac{2\sqrt{2}}{8} = \dfrac{\sqrt{2}}{4}$

23. $\sec^2\left(-\dfrac{13\pi}{6}\right) - \tan^3\dfrac{\pi}{4} = \left(\dfrac{2\sqrt{3}}{3}\right)^2 - 1^3$

$= \dfrac{4}{3} - 1 = \dfrac{1}{3}$

24. $\cos\left[\operatorname{Arcsin}\left(-\dfrac{2}{3}\right)\right] = \dfrac{\sqrt{5}}{3}$

25. $\cos\left[\operatorname{Arccos}\left(-\dfrac{2}{5}\right)\right] = -\dfrac{2}{5}$

26. $\csc^2\left(-\dfrac{\pi}{3}\right) + \sec^2\left(\dfrac{2\pi}{3}\right)$

$= \left(-\dfrac{2\sqrt{3}}{3}\right)^2 + (-2)^2 = \dfrac{4}{3} + 4 = \dfrac{16}{3}$

For problems 27–29 let $M = b^a$ and $N = b^c$.

27. $\log_b MN = \log_b b^a b^c = \log_b b^{a+c}$

$= a + c = \log_b M + \log_b N$

28. $\log_b N^x = \log_b (b^c)^x = \log_b b^{cx}$

$= cx = \big(\log_b N\big)x = x\log_b N$

29. $\log_b \dfrac{M}{N} = \log_b \dfrac{b^a}{b^c} = \log_b b^{a-c}$

$= a - c = \log_b M - \log_b N$

30. $\log_{10}(x - 2) - \log_{10} 9 = \log_{10} 4$

$\log_{10}\left(\dfrac{x - 2}{9}\right) = \log_{10} 4$

$\dfrac{x - 2}{9} = 4$

$x - 2 = 36$

$x = \textbf{38}$

1.

	Rate
Big Man:	$\dfrac{1}{12}$
Little Man:	$\dfrac{1}{4}$

$T = $ time together
$R_B T_B + R_L T_L = 30$
$\dfrac{1}{12}(T) + \dfrac{1}{4}(T + 2) = 30$
$\dfrac{1}{12}T + \dfrac{1}{4}T + \dfrac{1}{2} = 30$
$T = \textbf{88.5 hr}$

2.

	Rate
Children:	$\dfrac{1}{4}$
Adult:	$\dfrac{1}{3}$

$\dfrac{1}{4}(40) + \dfrac{1}{3}(12) = 10 + 4 = 14$

2 quarts

3.

	Now	+10 years
Sally:	S_N	$S_N + 10$
John:	J_N	$J_N + 10$

$3S_N = 5J_N + 15$
$3S_N - 5J_N = 15$

$2(S_N + 10) = 4(J_N + 10) - 20$
$2S_N - 4J_N = 0$
$S_N = 2J_N$
$3(2J_N) - 5J_N = 15$
$J_N = 15, S_N = 30$
$J_N + 15 = \textbf{30}$
$S_N + 15 = \textbf{45}$

4. Rate $\cdot$ number $=$ cost
$\left(\dfrac{D \text{ dollars}}{B \text{ big ones}}\right) b = 6 \text{ dollars}$
$b = \dfrac{6B}{D} \textbf{ big ones}$

5.

	Old	New
Rate:	$\dfrac{d}{n}$	?
Time:	h	$h - 4$
Distance:	d	d

Rate $= \dfrac{d}{h - 4} \textbf{ mph}$

6. $\boxed{5\ \ 4\ \ 2} = \textbf{40}$

7. $\boxed{5} \quad = \ 5$
$\boxed{5\ \ 5} \quad = 25$
$\boxed{1\ \ 2\ \ 5} \quad = \underline{10}$
$\phantom{\boxed{1\ \ 2\ \ 5} \quad = \ \ } \textbf{40}$

8. $y = \textbf{5} + \textbf{25} \cos x$

9. $y = \textbf{5} - \textbf{15} \cos \theta$

10. $\dfrac{1^3 - 2}{1 + 1} + \dfrac{2^3 - 2}{2 + 1} + \dfrac{3^3 - 2}{3 + 1}$
$= -\dfrac{1}{2} + 2 + \dfrac{25}{4} = \dfrac{-2 + 8 + 25}{4} = \dfrac{\textbf{31}}{\textbf{4}}$

11. $(x + 2)^2 + (y - 4)^2 = \textbf{16}$

12. $y = \left(\dfrac{1}{2}\right)^{-x}\left(\dfrac{1}{2}\right)^{-4} = 16 \cdot 2^x$

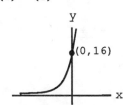

13. $x^2 - 2x + 4 = 0$
$x = \dfrac{2 \pm \sqrt{4 - 4(1)(4)}}{2(1)}$
$= \dfrac{2 \pm 2\sqrt{-12}}{2} = \dfrac{2 \pm 2\sqrt{3}\,i}{2}$
$= \left[x - \left(1 + \sqrt{3}\,i\right)\right]\left[x - \left(1 - \sqrt{3}\,i\right)\right]$

14. $c = \sqrt{5}$
$\dfrac{2}{2 + a} = \dfrac{1}{2}$
$4 = 2 + a$
$a = 2$
$\dfrac{2}{2 + 2} = \dfrac{c}{c + b}$
$\dfrac{1}{2} = \dfrac{\sqrt{5}}{\sqrt{5} + b}$
$\sqrt{5} + b = 2\sqrt{5}$
$b = \sqrt{5}$

15.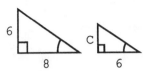

$$\frac{6}{c} = \frac{8}{6}$$
$$8c = 36$$
$$c = \frac{9}{2}\,\text{ft}$$

16. $2x + y = 40$
$y = 40 - 2x$
$4y + \dfrac{x}{2} = 55$
$8y + x = 110$
$8(40 - 2x) + x = 110$
$320 - 16x + x = 110$
$-15x = -210$
$x = 14$
$y = 12$

17. $m = \dfrac{5 - 4}{3 + 2} = \dfrac{1}{5}$
$m_\perp = -5$
Midpoint: $\left(\dfrac{-2 + 3}{2}, \dfrac{4 + 5}{2}\right) = \left(\dfrac{1}{2}, \dfrac{9}{2}\right)$
$y = -5x + b$
$\dfrac{9}{2} = -5\left(\dfrac{1}{2}\right) + b$
$b = 7$
$y = -5x + 7$
$5x + y - 7 = 0$

18. $\sqrt{(x - 6)^2 + (y - 3)^2}$
$= \sqrt{(x - 3)^2 + (y - 2)^2}$
$x^2 - 12x + 36 + y^2 - 6y + 9$
$= x^2 - 6x + 9 + y^2 - 4y + 4$
$-6x - 2y + 32 = 0$
$-3x - y + 16 = 0$
$y = -3x + 16$

19. Arc = radius × radian angle
Arc $= (300)(80)\left(\dfrac{\pi}{180}\right) = 419\,\text{m}$

20. $\theta = 45°, 315°$

21. $\sqrt{3}\sec\theta = 2$
$\sec\theta = \dfrac{2\sqrt{3}}{3}$
$\theta = 30°, 330°$

22. $\left(\dfrac{\sqrt{2}}{2}\right)^2 + \left(\dfrac{\sqrt{2}}{2}\right)^2 = \dfrac{1}{2} + \dfrac{1}{2} = 1$

23. $\left(\sqrt{2}\right)^2 - \left(\sqrt{2}\right)^2 = 0$

24.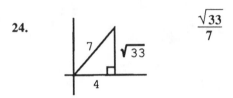

$\dfrac{\sqrt{33}}{7}$

25. $\operatorname{Arccos}\left(-\dfrac{\sqrt{3}}{2}\right) = 150°$

26. $\cot^2(-390°) - \cos 90°$
$= \cot^2(-30°) - \cos 90°$
$= \left(-\sqrt{3}\right)^2 - 0 = 3$

27. Let $M = b^a$ and $N = b^c$;
therefore,
$\log_b M = a$ and $\log_b N = c$
$\log_b MN = \log_b (b^a)(b^c)$
$= \log_b b^{a+c} = a + c$
$= \log_b M + \log_b N$

28. Let $N = b^c$; therefore $\log_b N = c$
$\log_b (N)^x = \log_b (b^c)^x = \log_b b^{cx}$
$= cx = x\log_b N$

29. $\log_3 (x - 3) = \log_3 10 = \log_3 22$
$\log_3 10(x - 3) = \log_3 22$
$10(x - 3) = 22$
$10x - 30 = 22$
$10x = 52$
$x = \dfrac{52}{10} = \dfrac{26}{5}$

30. $\log_5 3^4 = \log_5 x$
$3^4 = x = 81$

1.

	Rate
1st fellow's:	$\frac{7}{3}$
2nd fellow's:	$\frac{8}{5}$

t = time working together
$R_1T_1 + R_2T_2 = 59$
$\frac{7}{3}t + \frac{8}{5}t = 59$
$35t + 24t = 885$
$59t = 885$
$t = $ **15 hours**

2. $3 \cdot$ stamps $= 100d$ dollars
Stamps $= \dfrac{100d}{3}$ **dollars**

3.

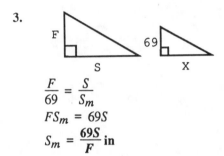

$\dfrac{F}{69} = \dfrac{S}{S_m}$
$FS_m = 69S$
$S_m = \dfrac{69S}{F}$ **in**

4. $\left(\dfrac{16 \text{ oz}}{3 \text{ cups}}\right) 15 = 80$ oz.
8 packages

5.

	Old	New
Distance:	d	d
Time:	m	$m - 60$
Rate:	$\dfrac{d}{m}$	?

Rate $= \dfrac{d}{m - 60} \dfrac{\text{mi}}{\text{min}} \cdot \dfrac{60 \text{ min}}{1 \text{ hr}} = \dfrac{60d}{m - 60}$ **mph**

6.

3	A	2	1	= 6
3	C	2	1	= 6
3	D	2	1	= 6

$\overline{\hspace{2cm} \textbf{18}}$

7.

5			=	5
5	5		=	25
4	5	5	=	100

$\overline{\hspace{2cm} \textbf{130}}$

8. $y = 5 + 25 \sin \theta$

9. $y = 10 - 20 \cos x$

10. $\dfrac{5!}{3!} = \dfrac{5 \cdot 4 \cdot 3!}{3!} = 20$

11. $(x + 3)^2 + (y - 2)^2 = 25$

12. $y = \dfrac{1}{4} \cdot \left(\dfrac{1}{2}\right)^x$

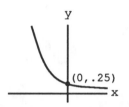
(0, .25)

13. $[x - (3 - i)][x - (3 + i)] = 0$
$(x - 3 + i)(x - 3 - i) = 0$
$x^2 - 3x - xi - 3x + 9 + 3i + xi$
$- 3i + 1 = 0$
$x^2 - 6x + 10 = 0$

14. $\triangle ABC \sim \triangle AED$
$\dfrac{AB}{AE} = \dfrac{BC}{ED}$
$\dfrac{AB}{AE} = \dfrac{AC}{AB}$
$\dfrac{BC}{ED} = \dfrac{AC}{AD}$

15.

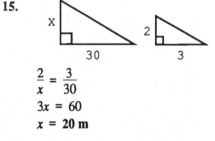

$\dfrac{2}{x} = \dfrac{3}{30}$
$3x = 60$
$x = $ **20 m**

16. Refer to Solution Set 18, problem 7.

17. $\sqrt{(x + 3)^2 + (y - 4)^2}$
$= \sqrt{(x - 6)^2 + (y + 2)^2}$
$x^2 + 6x + 9 + y^2 - 8y + 16$
$= x^2 - 12x + 36 + y^2 + 4y + 4$
$18x - 12y - 15 = 0$
$6x - 4y - 5 = 0$

18. Arc = radius angle in radians

Arc = $300 \times \dfrac{\pi}{3} = 100\pi$ meters

19. (a) **0.5441**
(b) **1.253**

20. $e^x = 3600$
$x = \ln 3600$
$3600 = e^{\ln 3600} \approx e^{8.19}$

21. $\theta = \mathbf{240°, 300°}$

22. $\cos \theta = \dfrac{-2}{\sqrt{3}}$
$\theta = \mathbf{240°, 300°}$

23. $\left(\dfrac{1}{2}\right)^2 + \left(\dfrac{\sqrt{3}}{2}\right)^2 = \dfrac{1}{4} + \dfrac{3}{4} = 1$

24. $(1)^3 - (2)^2 = 1 - 4 = \mathbf{-3}$

25.

$\dfrac{-5}{2\sqrt{6}} = \dfrac{-5\sqrt{6}}{12}$

26.

$\dfrac{\sqrt{7}}{4}$

For problems 27 and 28 let $M = b^a$; $N = b^c$

27. $\log_b \dfrac{M}{N} = \log_b \dfrac{b^a}{b^c} = \log_b b^{a \cdot c}$
$= a - c = \log_b M - \log_b N$

28. $\log_b MN = \log_b b^a b^c = \log_b b^{a + c}$
$= a + c = \log_b M + \log_b N$

29. $\log_5 (x + 2) - \log_5 6^2 = \log_5 1$
$\log_5 \dfrac{x + 2}{36} = \log_5 1$
$\dfrac{x + 2}{36} = 1$
$x + 2 = 36$
$x = \mathbf{34}$

30. $\log_7 2^3 = \log_7 3^2 + \log_7 x$
$\log_7 8 = \log_7 9(x)$
$8 = 9x$
$x = \dfrac{\mathbf{8}}{\mathbf{9}}$

PROBLEM SET 31

1.
	Rate
Rancie's:	$\dfrac{5}{4}$
Bubba's:	R_B

$R_R T_R + R_B T_B = 12$
$\dfrac{5}{4}(7) + R_B(7) = 12$
$7R_B = \dfrac{48}{4} - \dfrac{35}{4} = \dfrac{13}{4}$
$R_B = \dfrac{13}{4} \cdot \dfrac{1}{7} = \dfrac{13}{28}$
$\dfrac{13}{28} T_B = 2$
$T_B = \dfrac{\mathbf{56}}{\mathbf{13}}$ **hr**

2. Downstream: $(2W + W)(T_U + 1) = 45$
Upstream: $(2W - W)T_U = 10$

$WT_U = 10$
$3WT_U + 3W = 45$
$3(10) + 3W = 45$
$3W = 15$
$W = \mathbf{5\ mph}$
$B = \mathbf{10\ mph}$

3. $\dfrac{200}{40} = \$5.00$

40% of $5.00 = $2.00
New salary = $7.00
Weekly = $30 \times 7 = \$210$

4. $50(60) + 25(56) + 25(R) = 58(100)$
   $25R = 5800 - 300 - 1400$
   $R = \$56$

5.
	Old	New
Rate:	$\dfrac{D}{S}$	?
Time:	S	$S - 120$
Distance:	D	D

   Rate $= \dfrac{D}{S - 120} \dfrac{\text{ft}}{\text{sec}}$

6. $\boxed{6}\;\boxed{6}\;\boxed{5}\;\boxed{6}\;\boxed{1}\; = 1080$

7. $\boxed{5}$ $= 5$
   $\boxed{5}\;\boxed{5}$ $= 25$
   $\boxed{2}\;\boxed{5}\;\boxed{5}$ $= \dfrac{50}{}$
   $\overline{80}$

8. $y = 4 - 7 \sin \theta$

9. $y = 2 - 8 \cos x$

10. $(-1)^3 - 2 + 0^3 - 2 + 1^3 - 2 + 2^3$
    $- 2 + 3^3 - 2 = -3 - 2 - 1 + 6 + 25$
    $= 25$

11. $(x - h)^2 + (y - k)^2 = r^2$

12. $y = \left(\dfrac{1}{2}\right)^{-x} \cdot \left(\dfrac{1}{2}\right)^{2} = \dfrac{1}{4} \cdot 2^x$

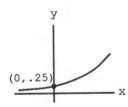

13. $x^2 + 4x + 5 = 0$
    $x = \dfrac{-4 \pm \sqrt{16 - 4(1)(5)}}{2(1)} = \dfrac{-4 \pm 2i}{2}$
    $= -2 \pm i$
    $[x - (-2 + i)][x - (-2 - i)]$
    $(x + 2 - i)(x + 2 + i)$

14. $\dfrac{2}{a + 2} = \dfrac{\frac{4}{5}}{\frac{3}{2}}$
    $3 = \dfrac{4}{5}(a + 2)$

$15 = 4a + 8$
$a = \dfrac{7}{4}$

15. $\dfrac{p}{7} = \dfrac{3}{5}$
    $5p = 21$
    $p = \dfrac{21}{5}$

16.

$\dfrac{4}{12} = \dfrac{3}{x}$
$4x = 36$
$x = 9\text{ m}$

17. $m = \dfrac{-2 - 8}{-6 + 4} = \dfrac{-10}{-2} = 5$
    $m_\perp = -\dfrac{1}{5}$
    Midpoint $= \dfrac{-4 - 6}{2}, \dfrac{8 - 2}{2} = (-5, 3)$
    $y = -\dfrac{1}{5}x + b$
    $3 = -\dfrac{1}{5}(-5) + b$
    $2 = b$
    $y = -\dfrac{1}{5}x + 2$

18. Arc = radius $\times$ angle in radians
    Arc $= 3920 \times (38.8°)\left(\dfrac{\pi}{180°}\right) = 2681$ miles

19. (a) $\log 16.3 = 1.212$
    (b) $\ln 16.3 = 2.79$

20. $\ln 3800 \approx 8.243$
    $3800 \approx e^{8.243}$

21. $\theta = 120°, 240°$

22. $\tan 3\theta = 1$
    $3\theta = 45°, 225°, 405°, 585°, 765°, 945°$
    $\theta = 15°, 75°, 135°, 195°, 255°, 315°$

23. $\sin \dfrac{\theta}{2} = \dfrac{-\sqrt{3}}{2}$

$\dfrac{\theta}{2} = 240°, 300°$

$\theta = $ **no solutions in** $0° \leq \theta \leq 360°$

24. $\left(-\dfrac{\sqrt{3}}{2}\right)^2 - \left(-\dfrac{1}{2}\right)^2 = \dfrac{3}{4} - \dfrac{1}{4} = \dfrac{1}{2}$

25. $\csc^2(-390°) - \sec^2(570°)$

$\csc^2(-30°) - \sec^2(210°)$

$(-2)^2 - \left(\dfrac{2\sqrt{3}}{-3}\right)^2 = 4 - \dfrac{4}{3} = \dfrac{8}{3}$

26. $\text{Arctan}(1) = \mathbf{45°}$

For problems 27 and 28 let $M = b^a$; $N = b^c$

27. $\log_b M = a, \log_b N = c$

$\log_b M^x = \log_b (b^a)^x = \log_b b^{ax}$

$= ax = x \log_b M$

28. $\log_b MN = \log_b (b^a)(b^c) = \log_b b^{a+c}$

$= a + c = \log_b M + \log_b N$

29. $\log_6 (x - 2) + \log_6 3^2 = \log_6 2$

$\log_6 9(x - 2) = \log_6 2$

$9(x - 2) = 2$

$x = \dfrac{20}{9}$

30. $\log_{1/2} 3^2 - \log_{1/2}(2x - 3) = 1$

$\log_{1/2} \dfrac{9}{2x - 3} = 1$

$\left(\dfrac{1}{2}\right)^1 = \dfrac{9}{2x - 3}$

$2x - 3 = 18$

$2x = 21$

$x = \dfrac{21}{2}$

PROBLEM SET 32

1.

	Rate
Mudog:	$\dfrac{8 \text{ jobs}}{3 \text{ day}}$
Jimmy:	$\dfrac{5 \text{ jobs}}{2 \text{ day}}$

$T = $ time together

$R_M T_M + R_J T_J = 39$

$\left(\dfrac{8}{3}\right)(T + 3) + \dfrac{5}{2} T = 39$

$T = \mathbf{6 \text{ days}}$

2. Rate $\cdot$ time $\cdot$ men = jobs

Rate $\cdot h \cdot m = j$

Rate $= \dfrac{j}{hm}$

$\dfrac{j}{hm} \cdot$ time $\cdot (m + p) = j$

Time $= \dfrac{hm}{m + p}$ **hr**

3. $A = $ angle

$90° - A = $ complement

$180° - A = $ supplement

$5(90° - A) - 30° = 180° - A$

$450° - 5A - 30° = 180° - A$

$420° = 180° + 4A$

$4A = 240°$

$A = \mathbf{60°}$

4.

	Old	New
Distance:	Y	$3Y$
Rate:	$\dfrac{Y}{S}$	?
Time:	S	$S + 20$

Rate $= \dfrac{3Y}{S + 20} \dfrac{\text{yd}}{\text{sec}}$

5. $2800 \text{ francs} \times \dfrac{1 \text{ dollars}}{350 \text{ francs}} \times \dfrac{400 \text{ francs}}{1 \text{ dollar}}$

$= \dfrac{2800(400)}{350}$

$= 3200$ francs for a profit of **400 francs**

6. $\boxed{3 \mid 4 \mid 5 \mid 3} = \mathbf{180}$

7. $\omega = \dfrac{v}{r} = \dfrac{50 \dfrac{\text{mi}}{\text{hr}}}{15 \text{ in}}$

$= \dfrac{10}{3} \dfrac{\text{mi}}{\text{hr} \cdot \text{in}} \times \dfrac{12 \text{ in}}{\text{ft}} \times \dfrac{5280 \text{ ft}}{\text{mi}}$

$$= \frac{10(12)(5280)}{3 \text{ hr}}$$

$$\frac{10(12)(5280)}{3} \frac{\text{rad}}{\text{hr}} \times \frac{\text{rev}}{2\pi \text{ rad}} \times \frac{1\text{hr}}{3600 \text{ sec}}$$

$$= \frac{10(12)(5280)}{6\pi(3600)} \frac{\text{rev}}{\text{sec}}$$

8. $y = 1 + 5 \cos x$

9. $y = -1 - 7 \cos x$

10. $\left[x - \left(-1 + 2\sqrt{2}i\right)\right]\left[x - \left(-1 - 2\sqrt{2}i\right)\right]$

$\left(x + 1 - 2\sqrt{2}i\right)\left(x + 1 + 2\sqrt{2}i\right) = 0$

$x^2 + x + 2\sqrt{2}xi + x + 1 + 2\sqrt{2}i$

$- 2\sqrt{2}xi - 2\sqrt{2}i + 8 = 0$

$x^2 + 2x + 9 = 0$

11. $(x - h)^2 + (y - k)^2 = 25$

12. $y = \left(\frac{1}{2}\right)^{-x} + {}^2 = \left[\left(\frac{1}{2}\right)^{-1}\right]^x \cdot \left(\frac{1}{2}\right)^2$

$$= 2^x \cdot \frac{1}{4} = \frac{1}{4}2^x$$

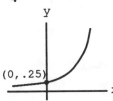

13. $\frac{50 \text{ mi}}{\text{hr}} \times \frac{1 \text{ hr}}{60 \text{ min}} \times \frac{5280 \text{ ft}}{1 \text{ mi}} \times \frac{12 \text{ in}}{1 \text{ ft}}$

$\times \frac{2.54 \text{ cm}}{1 \text{ in}} = \frac{50(5280)(12)(2.54)}{60} \frac{\text{cm}}{\text{min}}$

14. $\frac{30 \text{ liters}}{1} \times \frac{1000 \text{ cm}^3}{1 \text{ liter}} \times \frac{1^3 \text{ in}^3}{(2.54)^3 \text{ cm}^3}$

$= \frac{30(1000)}{(2.54)^3} \text{ in}^3$

15. $\frac{25}{40} = \frac{A}{26}$ $\quad\quad \frac{25}{40} = \frac{16}{B}$

$8A = 26(5)$ $\quad\quad 5B = 16(8)$

$A = \frac{26(5)}{8} = \frac{13(5)}{4}$ $\quad\quad B = \frac{16(8)}{5}$

$A = \frac{65}{4}$ $\quad\quad B = \frac{128}{5}$

16. $\frac{3}{4} = \frac{600}{s}$

$3s = 4(600)$

$s = 4(200) = \textbf{800 cm}$

17. $3x - \frac{1}{4}y = 40$

$x + 2y = 55$

$$\begin{array}{r} 24x - 2y = 320 \\ \underline{x + 2y = 55} \\ 25x = 375 \\ x = 15 \end{array}$$

$x = \textbf{15}$

$y = \textbf{20}$

18. $\sqrt{(x - 8)^2 + (y - 4)^2}$

$= \sqrt{(x + 3)^2 + (y - 4)^2}$

$x^2 - 16x + 64 + y^2 - 8y + 16$

$= x^2 + 6x + 9 + y^2 - 8y + 16$

$55 = 22x$

$x = \frac{5}{2}$

19. Arc = radius · angle in radians

$\frac{270°}{1} \times \frac{\pi \text{ rad}}{180°} = \frac{3\pi}{2} \text{ rad}$

$\frac{3\pi}{2}(2000) = \textbf{3000}\pi \text{ m}$

20. (a) $6200 = 10^{3.7924}$
    (b) $6200 = e^{8.7323}$

21. $\sin \theta = \frac{-\sqrt{3}}{2}$

$\theta = \textbf{240°, 300°}$

22. $\cos 3\theta = 1 \quad\quad 0 \le 3\theta \le 1080°$

$3\theta = 0°, 360°, 720°$

$\theta = \textbf{0°, 120°, 240°}$

23. $\sin \frac{\theta}{2} = 1 \quad\quad 0 \le \frac{\theta}{2} \le 180°$

$\frac{\theta}{2} = 90°$

$\theta = \textbf{180°}$

24. $\sec^2\left(-\frac{3\pi}{4}\right) + \cos^2\left(\frac{13\pi}{6}\right)$

$= \left(-\sqrt{2}\right)^2 + \left(\frac{\sqrt{3}}{2}\right)^2 = 2 + \frac{3}{4} = \frac{11}{4}$

25. $\cot^2\left(-\frac{\pi}{3}\right) - \sec^2 0 = \left(-\frac{\sqrt{3}}{3}\right)^2 - (1)^3$

$= \frac{3}{9} - 1 = -\frac{2}{3}$

26. $\sin\left[\operatorname{Arccos}\left(-\dfrac{5}{8}\right)\right] = \dfrac{\sqrt{39}}{8}$

27. $\log_b MN = \log_b b^a b^a = \log_b b^{a+c}$
    $= a + c = \log_b M + \log_b N$

28. $\log_{15} 4 - \log_{15} \dfrac{2}{x} = 2$

    $\log_{15} \dfrac{4}{\frac{2}{x}} = 2$

    $15^2 = 2x$

$225 = 2x$
$x = \mathbf{112.5}$

29. $\log_7 16 - \log_7 x = \log_7 4$

    $\log_7 \dfrac{16}{x} = \log_7 4$

    $\dfrac{16}{x} = 4$

    $x = \mathbf{4}$

30. $2t^2 = \sqrt{z-1} + 1$
    $2t^2 - 1 = \sqrt{z-1}$
    $4t^2 - 4t^2 + 1 = z - 1$
    $z = \mathbf{4t^4 - 4t^2 + 2}$

PROBLEM SET 33

1. $v = r\omega = \left(\dfrac{3}{2}\right) \text{ft} \cdot \dfrac{1 \text{ mile}}{5280 \text{ ft}} \cdot 30 \dfrac{\text{rev}}{\text{min}}$

   $\cdot \dfrac{2\pi \text{ rad}}{1 \text{ rev}} \cdot \dfrac{60 \text{ min}}{1 \text{ hr}} = \dfrac{3(30)(2\pi)(60)}{2(5280)} \dfrac{\text{mi}}{\text{hr}}$

2. $\omega = \dfrac{r}{v}$

   $= \dfrac{30\dfrac{\text{km}}{\text{hr}} \cdot \dfrac{1000 \text{ m}}{1 \text{ km}} \cdot \dfrac{100 \text{ cm}}{1 \text{ m}} \cdot \dfrac{1 \text{ hr}}{60 \text{ cm}}}{70 \text{ cm}}$

   $= \dfrac{(30)(1000)(100)}{(70)(60)} \dfrac{\text{rad}}{\text{min}}$

3.

	Old	New
Rate:	$\dfrac{K}{h}$	?
Time:	h	$h - 2$
Distance:	K	K

   Rate $= \dfrac{K}{h-2}$ **mph**

4. $\boxed{\begin{array}{c}5\% \\ 40\%\end{array}} + \boxed{\begin{array}{c}20\% \\ x\end{array}} = \boxed{\begin{array}{c}10\% \\ 40 + x\end{array}}$

   $5(40) \cdot 20x = 10(40 + x)$
   $200 + 20x = 400 + 10x$
   $10x = 200$
   $x = \mathbf{20 \text{ liters}}$

5.

	Rate
Hortense:	$\dfrac{1 \text{ job}}{4 \text{ hr}}$
Joe:	$\dfrac{1 \text{ job}}{8 \text{ hr}}$

   $T = $ time together

   $R_H T_H + R_J T_J = 6\dfrac{1}{4}$

   $\dfrac{1}{4}(T) + \dfrac{1}{8}(T + 2) = \dfrac{25}{4}$

   $T = \mathbf{16 \text{ hr}}$

6. $\boxed{3}\;\boxed{3}\;\boxed{4} = \mathbf{36}$

7. $x^2 + 3x - 9 = 0$

   $x = \dfrac{-3 \pm \sqrt{9 - 4(1)(-9)}}{2(1)}$

   $x = \dfrac{3 \pm 3\sqrt{5}}{2}$

   $\left[x - \left(\dfrac{-3 + 3\sqrt{5}}{2}\right)\right]\left[x - \left(\dfrac{-3 - 3\sqrt{5}}{2}\right)\right]$

   $\left(x + \dfrac{3 - 3\sqrt{5}}{2}\right)\left(x + \dfrac{3 - 3\sqrt{5}}{2}\right)$

8. $y = 9 - \sin x$

9. $y = 6 + 6 \cos \theta$

10.
$$\frac{(-3 - 1)(-3 + 1)}{-3} + \frac{(-2 - 1)(-2 + 1)}{-2}$$
$$+ \frac{(-1 - 1)(-1 + 1)}{-1}$$
$$= \frac{(-4)(-2)}{-3} + \frac{(-3)(-1)}{-2} + \frac{(-2)(0)}{-1}$$
$$= \frac{8}{-3} + \frac{3}{-2} = \frac{-16 - 9}{6} = -\frac{25}{6}$$

11. $(x - 3)^2 + (y - 2)^2 = 36$

12. $y = (x^2 - 6x + 9) + 4 - 9$
$y = (x - 3)^2 - 5$
Coefficient of x^2 term is positive;
thus it opens upward
Axis: $x = 3$
Vertex: $y = -5$

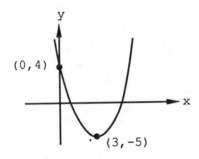

13. y-intercept $= 6$
$y = -(x^2 + 4x + 4) + 6 + 4$
$y = -(x + 2)^2 + 10$
Coefficient of x^2 term is negative;
thus it opens downward
Axis: $x = -2$
Vertex: $y = 10$

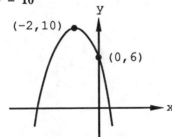

14. $y = (2)^{-x}(2)^{-3} = \left(\frac{1}{2}\right)^x\left(\frac{1}{8}\right)$

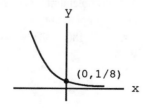

15.
$$40\,\frac{\text{mi}}{\text{hr}} \cdot \frac{5280\ \text{ft}}{1\ \text{mi}} \cdot \frac{12\ \text{in}}{1\ \text{ft}} \cdot \frac{2.54\ \text{cm}}{1\ \text{in}}$$
$$\cdot \frac{1\ \text{hr}}{60\ \text{min}} \cdot \frac{1\ \text{min}}{60\ \text{sec}}$$
$$= \frac{(40)(5280)(12)(2.54)}{(60)(60)}\,\frac{\text{cm}}{\text{sec}}$$

16.
$$12\,\frac{\text{liters}}{\text{sec}} \cdot \frac{1000\ \text{cm}}{1\ \text{liter}} \cdot \frac{60\ \text{sec}}{1\ \text{min}} \cdot \frac{60\ \text{min}}{1\ \text{hr}}$$
$$= (12)(1000)(60)(60)\,\frac{\text{cm}^3}{\text{hr}}$$

17.

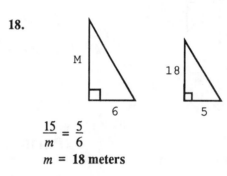

$$\frac{5}{10} = \frac{x}{12}$$
$$x = 6$$

18.

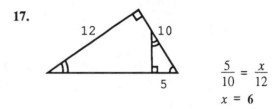

$$\frac{15}{m} = \frac{5}{6}$$
$m = 18$ **meters**

19. $5x + 2y = 40$
$5x + 6y + 80 + 40 = 180$
$x = 6$
$y = 5$

20. $\sqrt{(x - 4)^2 + (y - 6)^2}$
$= \sqrt{(x + 4)^2 + (y - 8)^2}$
$x^2 - 8x + 16 + y^2 - 12y + 36$
$= x^2 + 8x + 16 + y^2 - 16y + 64$
$-16x + 4y - 28 = 0$
$4x - y + 7 = 0$
$y = 4x + 7$

21. (a) $10^{3.491}$
(b) $e^{8.039}$

22. $\theta = 135°, 225°$

23. $\sin 3\theta = \frac{1}{2}$
$3\theta = 30°, 150°, 390°, 510°, 750°, 870°$
$\theta = 10°, 50°, 130°, 170°, 250°, 290°$

Advanced Mathematics

24. $\sec 2\theta = 1$
$2\theta = 0°, 360°$
$\theta = 0°, 180°$

25. $\csc^2(-210°) + \sec^2(210°)$

$= (2)^2 + \left(\dfrac{-2\sqrt{3}}{3}\right)^2 = 4 + \dfrac{12}{9} = \dfrac{16}{3}$

26. $\tan^2 570° - \csc^2 90°$
$= \tan^2 210° - \csc^2 90°$

$= \left(\dfrac{\sqrt{3}}{3}\right)^2 - (1)^2 = \dfrac{1}{3} - 1 = -\dfrac{2}{3}$

27.

$\dfrac{\sqrt{7}}{4}$

28. Let $M = b^a$ and $N = b^c$
so $\log_b M = a$, $\log_b N = c$
$\log_b MN = \log_b (b^a)(b^c)$
$= \log_b b^{a+c} = a + c = \log_b M - \log_b N$

29. $\log_5 6 - \log_5 \dfrac{1}{x+1} = \log_5 7$

$\log_5 \dfrac{6}{\dfrac{1}{x+1}} = \log_5 7$

$6(x + 1) = 7$
$6x + 6 = 7$
$6x = 1$
$x = \dfrac{1}{6}$

30. $\ln 5^2 - \ln x = \ln 16^{3/2}$
$\ln \dfrac{25}{x} = \ln 8$
$\dfrac{25}{x} = 8$
$x = \dfrac{25}{8}$

PROBLEM SET 34

1. $\omega = \dfrac{v}{r}$

$= \dfrac{10\,\dfrac{\text{km}}{\text{hr}} \cdot \dfrac{1000\text{ m}}{1\text{ km}} \cdot \dfrac{1\text{ hr}}{60\text{ min}} \cdot \dfrac{1\text{ min}}{60\text{ sec}}}{3\text{ m}}$

$= \dfrac{(10)(1000)}{(3)(60)(60)}\,\dfrac{\text{rad}}{\text{sec}}$

2. $v = r\omega$

$= (0.5)\text{ in} \cdot \dfrac{1\text{ yd}}{36\text{ in}} \cdot 40\,\dfrac{\text{rad}}{\text{sec}} \cdot \dfrac{60\text{ sec}}{1\text{ min}}$

$= \dfrac{(0.5)(40)(60)}{(36)}\,\dfrac{\text{yd}}{\text{min}}$

3. $R_O T_O = 400$
$R_B T_B = 400$
$R_B = 2R_O$
$T_O + T_B = 6$
$T_B = 6 - T_O$
$2R_O\left(6 - T_O\right) = 400$
$12R_O - 2R_O T_O = 400$
$12R_O - 2(400) = 400$
$12R_O = 1200$
$R_O = \textbf{100 mph}$

4. A: $2 + W = R$
B: $G + 1 = R$
C: $R + W + G = 15$

$2 + W = G + 1$
$2 + W + W + G = 15$
$2W + G = 13$

$\begin{array}{rcl} W - G &=& -1 \\ \underline{2W + G} &=& \underline{13} \\ 3W &=& 12 \\ W &=& 4 \end{array}$

$W = \textbf{4}$
$G = \textbf{5}$
$R = \textbf{6}$

5. $A = \text{angle}$
$90 - A = \text{complement}$
$180 - A = \text{supplement}$
$5(90 - A) = 2(180 - A) + 60$
$A = \textbf{10}°$

6. $(4 - 1)! = 3! = \textbf{6}$

7. $\dfrac{8!}{2!\,2!} = 10{,}080$

8. $W\ R\ W\ R\ W\ R$
$R\ W\ R\ W\ R\ W$
2 ways

9. $y = 7 + 3\sin x$

10. $y = 8 - 9\cos\theta$

11. $_7P_3 = \dfrac{7!}{4!} = 7 \cdot 6 \cdot 5 = 210$

12. $(x - h)^2 + (y - k)^2 = r^2$

13. $y = (x^2 - 8x + 16) - 2 - 16$
$y = (x - 4)^2 - 18$
Coefficient of x^2 term is positive;
thus it opens upward
Axis: $x = 4$
Vertex: $y = -18$
y-intercept $= -2$

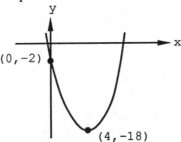

14. $y = -(x^2 + 10x + 25) + 4 + 25$
$y = -(x + 5)^2 + 29$
Coefficient of x^2 term is negative;
thus it opens downward
Axis: $x = -5$
Vertex: $y = 29$
y-intercept $= 4$

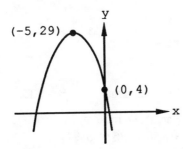

15. $20\,\dfrac{\text{m}}{\text{sec}} \cdot \dfrac{100\ \text{cm}}{1\ \text{m}} \cdot \dfrac{1\ \text{in}}{2.54\ \text{cm}} \cdot \dfrac{1\ \text{ft}}{12\ \text{in}}$
$\cdot\ \dfrac{1\ \text{mi}}{5280\ \text{ft}} \cdot \dfrac{60\ \text{sec}}{1\ \text{min}} \cdot \dfrac{60\ \text{min}}{1\ \text{hr}}$
$= \dfrac{(20)(100)(60)(60)}{(2.54)(12)(5280)}\ \dfrac{\text{mi}}{\text{hr}}$

16. $12\,\dfrac{\text{liter}}{\text{hr}} \cdot \dfrac{1000\ \text{cm}^3}{1\ \text{liter}} \cdot \dfrac{1^3\ \text{in}^3}{(2.54)^3\ \text{cm}^3}$
$\cdot\ \dfrac{1\ \text{hr}}{60\ \text{min}} = \dfrac{(12)(1000)}{(2.54)^3(60)}\ \dfrac{\text{in}^3}{\text{min}}$

17.

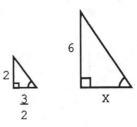

$\dfrac{k}{3} = \dfrac{4}{8}$
$8k = 12$
$k = \dfrac{12}{8} = \dfrac{3}{2}$

18.

$\dfrac{2}{6} = \dfrac{\frac{3}{2}}{x}$
$2x = 9$
$x = \dfrac{9}{2}$

19. $10x - 8y = 40$
$110^\circ + \dfrac{5}{4}x + 4y + 40 = 180$
$x = 8$
$y = 5$

20. $m = \dfrac{3 + 3}{4 + 2} = \dfrac{6}{6} = 1$
$m_\perp = -1$
Midpoint $= (1, 0)$
$y = -1x + b$
$0 = -1(1) + b$
$b = 1$
$x + y - 1 = 0$

21. (a) $10^{3.763}$

(b) $e^{8.666}$

22. $\tan \theta = \dfrac{\sqrt{3}}{3}$

$\theta = 30°, 210°$

23. $\tan 3\theta = \dfrac{\sqrt{3}}{3}$

$3\theta = 30°, 210°, 390°, 570°, 750°, 930°$

$\theta = 10°, 70°, 130°, 190°, 250°, 310°$

24. $\csc 2\theta = 1$

$2\theta = 90°, 450°$

$\theta = 45°, 225°$

25. $\sec^2 (-135°) - \cot^2 (210°)$

$= \left(-\sqrt{2}\right)^2 - \left(\sqrt{3}\right)^2 = 2 - 3 = -1$

26. $\tan^2 45° - \sin^2 (-330°)$

$= (1)^2 - \left(\dfrac{1}{2}\right)^2 = 1 - \dfrac{1}{4} = \dfrac{3}{4}$

27.

$-\dfrac{3}{4}$

28. $x^2 - 5x + 8 = 0$

$x = \dfrac{5 \pm \sqrt{25 - 4(1)(8)}}{2(1)}$

$x = \dfrac{5 \pm \sqrt{-7}}{2} = \dfrac{5 \pm \sqrt{7}i}{2}$

$\left[x - \left(\dfrac{5 + \sqrt{7}i}{2}\right)\right]\left[x - \left(\dfrac{5 - \sqrt{7}i}{2}\right)\right]$

$\left(x - \dfrac{5 + \sqrt{7}i}{2}\right)\left(x - \dfrac{5 - \sqrt{7}i}{2}\right)$

29. $\log_{18} 12x - \log_{18} 2^2 = 1$

$\log_{18} \dfrac{12x}{4} = 1$

$18^1 = 3x$

$x = 6$

30. $\ln 8^{2/3} + \ln 3^2 = \ln (x + 5)$

$\ln 4 + \ln 9 = \ln (x + 5)$

$\ln (4)(9) = \ln (x + 5)$

$36 = x + 5$

$x = 31$

PROBLEM SET 35

1. $v = r\omega = 10 \text{ in} \cdot \dfrac{2.54 \text{ cm}}{1 \text{ in}} \cdot 40 \dfrac{\text{rev}}{\text{min}}$

$\cdot \dfrac{2\pi \text{ rad}}{1 \text{ rev}} \cdot \dfrac{1 \text{ min}}{60 \text{ sec}} = \dfrac{(10)(2.54)(40)(2\pi)}{(60)} \dfrac{\text{cm}}{\text{sec}}$

2. $\omega = \dfrac{v}{r}$

$= 260 \dfrac{\text{km}}{\text{hr}} \cdot \dfrac{100 \text{ m}}{1 \text{ km}} \cdot \dfrac{100 \text{ cm}}{1 \text{ m}}$

$\cdot \dfrac{1 \text{ in}}{2.54 \text{ cm}} \cdot \dfrac{1 \text{ ft}}{12 \text{ in}} \cdot \dfrac{1 \text{ hr}}{60 \text{ min}} \cdot \dfrac{1}{1 \text{ ft}}$

$= \dfrac{(260)(1000)(100)}{(2.54)(12)(60)} \dfrac{\text{rad}}{\text{min}} \cdot \dfrac{1 \text{ rev}}{2\pi \text{ rad}}$

$= \dfrac{(260)(1000)(100)}{(2.54)(12)(60)(2\pi)} \dfrac{\text{rev}}{\text{min}}$

3.

	Now	−10 years
Ancient one:	A_N	$A_N - 10$
Youngster:	Y_N	$Y_N - 10$

$A_N = 40 + Y_N$

$A_N - 10 = 7\left(Y_N - 10\right) + 20$

$A_N = 53\dfrac{1}{3}$

$Y_N = 13\dfrac{1}{3}$

4. Hannibal's rate $= \dfrac{450}{30} = \$15.00$

Hannibal's raise $= 15 + 0.1(15) = \$16.50$

$\$16.50 \times 36 = \$594$

5. T = tens' digit
U = units' digit
$10T + U$ = original number
$10U + T$ = reversed number
$T + U = 11$
$10U + T = 10T + U - 27$
Original number = **74**

6. **11!**

7. $\dfrac{9!}{3!\,2!\,2!}$

8. $\boxed{5\ \vert\ 5\ \vert\ 5}$ = **125**

9.

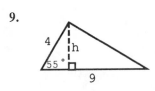

$h = 4 \sin 55° = 3.3$
Area $= \dfrac{1}{2} bh$
$= \dfrac{1}{2}(9)(3.3)$
= **14.9 m²**

10.

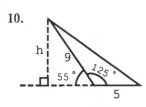

$h = 9 \sin 55° = 7.4$
Area $= \dfrac{1}{2} bh$
$= \dfrac{1}{2}(5)(7.4)$
= **18.5 cm²**

11.

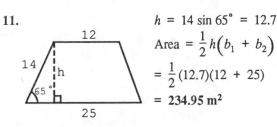

$h = 14 \sin 65° = 12.7$
Area $= \dfrac{1}{2} h\left(b_1 + b_2\right)$
$= \dfrac{1}{2}(12.7)(12 + 25)$
= **234.95 m²**

12. Area of sector $= \dfrac{A^2}{2\pi}\pi r^2 = \dfrac{0.4}{2\pi}\pi(5)^2 = $ **5 m²**

13.

$h = 10 \sin 60° \approx 8.7$
Area$_{\text{segment}}$ = area$_{\text{sector}}$ − area$_{\text{triangle}}$
$= \dfrac{60}{360}\pi(10)^2 - \dfrac{1}{2}(10)(8.7) = 52.3 - 43.5$
$= 8.8\ \text{ft}^2 \times \dfrac{12^2\ \text{in}^2}{1\ \text{ft}^2} \times \dfrac{2.54^2\ \text{cm}^2}{1\ \text{in}^2}$
= **8175 cm²**

14. $y = 3 - 9\cos x$

15. $(x - 4)^2 + (y - 5)^2 = r^2$

16. $y = (x - 2)^2 + 2$
Coefficient of x^2 term is positive;
thus it opens upward
Axis: $x = 2$
Vertex: $y = 2$
y-intercept = 6

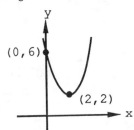

17. y-intercept = 8
$y = -(x + 3)^2 + 17$
Coefficient of x^2 term is negative;
thus it opens downward
Axis: $x = -3$
Vertex: $y = 17$

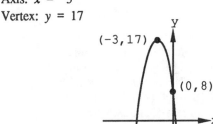

18. $70\,\dfrac{\text{km}}{\text{hr}} \cdot \dfrac{1000\ \text{m}}{1\ \text{km}} \cdot \dfrac{100\ \text{cm}}{1\ \text{m}} \cdot \dfrac{1\ \text{in}}{2.54\ \text{cm}}$
$\cdot \dfrac{1\ \text{hr}}{60\ \text{min}} = \dfrac{(70)(1000)(100)}{(2.54)(60)}\ \dfrac{\text{in}}{\text{min}}$

19. $\dfrac{3}{a} = \dfrac{a}{12}$
$a^2 = 36$
$a = $ **6**

20. Refer to Problem Set 18, problem 7.

21. $10x + 2y = 80$
$80 + 5x + 3y + 50 = 180$
$x = $ **7**
$y = $ **5**

22. $\sqrt{(x + 2)^2 + (y - 4)^2}$
    $= \sqrt{(x + 4)^2 + (y + 4)^2}$
    $x^2 + 4x + 4 + y^2 - 8y + 16$
    $= x^2 + 8x + 16 + y^2 + 8y + 16$
    $x + 4y + 3 = 0$

23. (a) $10^{4.813}$
    (b) $e^{11.082}$

24. $\tan \theta = -1$
    $\theta = 135°, 315°$

25. $\sin 3\theta = -\dfrac{\sqrt{3}}{2}$
    $3\theta = 240°, 300°, 600°, 660°, 960°, 1020°$
    $\theta = 80°, 100°, 200°, 220°, 320°, 340°$

26. $\csc 2\theta = 1$
    $2\theta = 90°, 450°$
    $\theta = 45°, 225°$

27. $\sec^2 (-120°) - \tan^2 30° = (-2)^2 - \left(\dfrac{\sqrt{3}}{3}\right)^2$
    $= 4 - \dfrac{3}{9} = \dfrac{11}{3}$

28. $-\dfrac{2\sqrt{13}}{13}$

29. Let $M = b^a$ so $\log_b M = a$
    $\log_b M^x = \log_b (b^a) = \log_b b^{ax}$
    $= ax = x\log_b M$

30. $\log_{10} 27^{2/3} + \log_{10} x = \log_{10} 12$
    $\log_{10} 9(x) = \log_{10} 12$
    $9x = 12$
    $x = \dfrac{12}{9} = \dfrac{4}{3}$

PROBLEM SET 36

1. $v = \omega r$
   $= \dfrac{400 \text{ rad}}{\text{min}} \cdot \dfrac{4 \text{ cm}}{1} \cdot \dfrac{60 \text{ min}}{\text{hr}}$
   $\cdot \dfrac{1 \text{ in}}{2.54 \text{ cm}} \cdot \dfrac{1 \text{ ft}}{12 \text{ in}} \cdot \dfrac{1 \text{ mi}}{5280 \text{ ft}}$
   $= \dfrac{(400)(4)(60)}{(2.54)(12)(5280)} \dfrac{\text{mi}}{\text{hr}}$

2. $\omega = \dfrac{v}{r} = \dfrac{40 \frac{\text{km}}{\text{hr}}}{50 \text{ cm}} = \dfrac{40}{5} \dfrac{\text{km}}{\text{hr cm}}$
   $= \dfrac{40}{5} \dfrac{\text{km}}{\text{hr cm}} \cdot \dfrac{100 \text{ cm}}{1 \text{ m}} \cdot \dfrac{1000 \text{ m}}{\text{km}}$
   $= \dfrac{40(100)(1000)}{5} \dfrac{\text{rad}}{\text{hr}}$
   $= \dfrac{40(100)(1000)}{5} \dfrac{\text{rad}}{\text{hr}} \cdot \dfrac{1 \text{ hr}}{3600 \text{ sec}}$
   $= \dfrac{40(100)(1000)}{5(3600)} \dfrac{\text{rad}}{\text{sec}}$

3. $\dfrac{P_1 V_1}{T_1} = \dfrac{P_2 V_2}{T_2}$
   $\dfrac{(40)(2)}{400} = \dfrac{P_2(4)}{1000}$
   $P_2 = \dfrac{40(2)(1000)}{400(4)} = 50 \text{ atm}$

4. $B = kF$
   $100 = 2k$
   $k = 50$
   $B = 50F$
   $B = 50(40) = 2000$

5. $B = 3W$
   $T_U = T_D - 1$
   Downstream: $(3W + W)T_D = 24$
   $\qquad\qquad 4WT_D = 24$
   $\qquad\qquad WT_D = 6$
   Upstream: $(3W - W)\left(T_D - 1\right) = 8$
   $\qquad\qquad 2WT_D - 2W = 8$
   $\qquad\qquad 2(6) - 2W = 8$
   $W = 2 \text{ mph}$
   $B = 6 \text{ mph}$

6. $\dfrac{12!}{6! \, 4! \, 2!} = \dfrac{12 \cdot 11 \cdot 10 \cdot 9 \cdot 8 \cdot 7}{4 \cdot 3 \cdot 2 \cdot 2}$
   $= 11 \cdot 90 \cdot 14 = 13860$

7. $\dfrac{15!}{3! \, 2!}$

8. $x^2 - 3x + 4 = 0$

$x = \dfrac{3 \pm \sqrt{9 - 4(4)}}{2} = \dfrac{3 \pm \sqrt{7}i}{2}$

$\left(x - \dfrac{3}{2} - \dfrac{\sqrt{7}}{2}i\right)\left(x - \dfrac{3}{2} + \dfrac{\sqrt{7}}{2}i\right) = 0$

9. $y = 6 \sin\left(x - \dfrac{\pi}{2}\right)$

10. $y = 10 \sin 2x$

11. $\sin 74° = \dfrac{h}{9}, h = 8.65$

$A = \dfrac{1}{2}(10)(8.65) = \textbf{43.3 cm}^2$

12. $\sin 55° = \dfrac{h}{9}, h = 7.37$

$A = \dfrac{1}{2}(7)(7.37)$

$= 25.8 \text{ cm}^3 \cdot \dfrac{1 \text{ in}}{2.54 \text{ cm}} \cdot \dfrac{1 \text{ in}}{2.54 \text{ cm}} = \textbf{4 in}^2$

13. $\text{Area}_{\text{trapezoid}} = \dfrac{1}{2}h\left(b_1 + b_2\right)$

$\sin 65° = \dfrac{h}{16}, h = 14.5$

$A = \dfrac{(10 + 20)14.5}{2} = \textbf{217.5 ft}^2$

14. $\text{Area}_{\text{sector}} = \dfrac{\text{radian angle}}{2\pi} \cdot \pi r^2$

$A = \pi(4)^2\left(\dfrac{0.6}{2\pi}\right) = 16\left(\dfrac{1}{2}\right)(0.6) = \textbf{4.8 m}^2$

15. $\text{Area}_{\text{segment}} = \text{area}_{\text{sector}} - \text{area}_{\text{triangle}}$

$A = \pi(10)^2\left(\dfrac{80}{360}\right) - \dfrac{10(\sin 80°(10))}{2}$

$= 100\pi\left(\dfrac{2}{9}\right) - 49.2 = \textbf{20.6 cm}^2$

16. $(x - m)^2 + (y - n)^2 = 25$

17. $y = -(x^2 + 4x + 4) + 4 + 4$

$y = -(x + 2)^2 + 8$

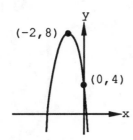

18. $\dfrac{100 \text{ mi}}{\text{hr}} \cdot \dfrac{1 \text{ hr}}{3600 \text{ sec}} \cdot \dfrac{5280 \text{ ft}}{1 \text{ mi}} \cdot \dfrac{12 \text{ in}}{1 \text{ ft}}$

$= \dfrac{100(5280)(12)}{3600} \dfrac{\text{in}}{\text{sec}}$

19. $\dfrac{5}{9} = \dfrac{M}{4}$

$9M = 20$

$M = \dfrac{20}{9}$

20. $d = \text{radius} \cdot \text{radian angle}$

$d = \left(38.3 \cdot \dfrac{\pi}{180}\right)(12000) = \textbf{8021.5 km}$

21. (a) $10000 = 10^4$
    (b) $(e^{2.3})^4 = e^{9.2}$

22. Midpoint $(0, 1)$

$m = \dfrac{14}{8} = \dfrac{7}{4}$

$m_\perp = -\dfrac{4}{7}$

$y - 1 = -\dfrac{4}{7}x$

$y = -\dfrac{4}{7}x + 1$

23. $2 \cos \theta = 1$

$\cos \theta = \dfrac{1}{2}$

$\theta = \textbf{60°, 300°}$

24. $2 \cos 3\theta = 1 \qquad 0° \le 3\theta \le 1080°$

$\cos 3\theta = \dfrac{1}{2}$

$3\theta = 60°, 300°, 420°, 660°, 780°, 1020°$

$\theta = \textbf{20°, 100°, 140°, 220°, 260°, 340°}$

25. $\cot 3\theta = 0 \qquad 0 \le 3\theta \le 1080°$

$3\theta = 90°, 270°, 450°, 630°, 810°, 990°$

$\theta = \textbf{30°, 90°, 150°, 210°, 270°, 330°}$

26. $\cot^3 \dfrac{\pi}{4} + \tan^2 480° = 1^3 + \left(-\sqrt{3}\right)^2$

$= 1 + 3 = \textbf{4}$

27. $\text{Arctan}\left(\tan \dfrac{7\pi}{6}\right) = \text{Arctan}\left(\dfrac{\sqrt{3}}{3}\right) = \textbf{60°}$ or $\dfrac{\pi}{6}$

28. $\log_b \dfrac{M}{N} = \log_b \dfrac{b^a}{b^c} = \log_b b^{a-c}$

$= a - c = \log_b M - \log_b N$

29. $\log_{1/2} 16^{3/4} - \log_{1/2}(x - 1) = 2$

$\log_{1/2} \dfrac{8}{x - 1} = 2$

$\left(\dfrac{1}{2}\right)^2 = \dfrac{8}{x - 1}$

$x - 1 = 32$

$x = \mathbf{33}$

30. $\ln 5 + \ln(x + 2) = \ln(2x + 3)$

$\ln[5(x + 2)] = \ln(2x + 3)$

$5x + 10 = 2x + 3$

$3x = -7$

$x = -\dfrac{7}{3}$

No solution

because $-\dfrac{7}{3} + 2 = -\dfrac{1}{3}$

PROBLEM SET 37

1. $v = r\omega$

$= 10 \text{ in} \cdot \dfrac{2.54 \text{ cm}}{1 \text{ in}} \cdot \dfrac{1 \text{ m}}{100 \text{ cm}}$

$\cdot \dfrac{1 \text{ km}}{1000 \text{ m}} \cdot \dfrac{525 \text{ rad}}{\text{sec}} \cdot \dfrac{60 \text{ sec}}{1 \text{ min}} \cdot \dfrac{60 \text{ min}}{1 \text{ hr}}$

$= \dfrac{(10)(2.54)(525)(60)(60)}{(100)(1000)} \dfrac{\text{km}}{\text{hr}}$

2. $\omega = \dfrac{v}{r}$

$= \dfrac{100 \dfrac{\text{mi}}{\text{hr}} \cdot \dfrac{1 \text{ hr}}{60 \text{ min}} \cdot \dfrac{1 \text{ min}}{60 \text{ sec}}}{40 \text{ cm} \cdot \dfrac{1 \text{ in}}{2.54 \text{ cm}} \cdot \dfrac{1 \text{ ft}}{12 \text{ in}}}$

$= \dfrac{(100)(2.54)(12)(5280)}{(60)(60)(40)} \dfrac{\text{rad}}{\text{sec}}$

3. Impecunious $= \ \ 14$

Destitute $\ \ \ = \ \ \dfrac{3}{17}$

$\dfrac{14}{17} = \dfrac{x}{4420}$

$x = \mathbf{3640}$

4. $\dfrac{P_1 V_1}{T_1} = \dfrac{P_2 V_2}{T_2}$

$P_2 = \dfrac{P_1 V_1 T_2}{T_1 V_2} = \dfrac{(4)(5)(500)}{(400)(7)} = \mathbf{3.57 \text{ atm}}$

5. $4(6) + 10(4) + 16A = 30(8)$

$A = \mathbf{11}$

6. $\dfrac{5!}{2! \ 2!} = \mathbf{30}$

7. $\dfrac{9!}{5! \ 4!} = \mathbf{126}$

8. $4! = \mathbf{24}$

9. $m_\perp = -2; \ (-2, 4)$

$y = mx + b$

$4 = (-2)(-2) + b$

$b = 0$

$y = -2x$

$y = \dfrac{1}{2}x - 1$

$-2x = \dfrac{1}{2}x - 1$

$x = \dfrac{2}{5} \quad y = -\dfrac{4}{5}$

$\left(\dfrac{2}{5}, -\dfrac{4}{5}\right), \ (-2, 4)$

$d = \sqrt{\left(-2 - \dfrac{2}{5}\right)^2 + \left(4 + \dfrac{4}{5}\right)^2} \approx \mathbf{5.37}$

10. $y = 2x^2 - 8x + 5$

y-intercept $= 5$

$y = 2(x^2 - 4x + 4) + 5 - 8$

$y = 2(x - 2)^2 - 3$

x^2 coefficient is positive; thus it opens upward

Axis: $x = 2$

Vertex: $y = -3$

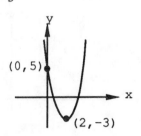

11. $y^2 = -2x^2 - 8x - 4$
$y = -2(x^2 + 4x + 4) - 4 + 8$
$y = -2(x + 2)^2 + 4$
x^2 coefficient is negative;
thus it opens downward
Axis: $x = -2$
Vertex: $y = 4$

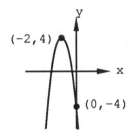

12. $y = -3 + 5\cos(x + 225°)$
or
$y = -3 + 5\cos(x - 135°)$

13. $y = 2 + 6\cos 2\theta$

14.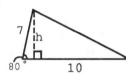

$\sin 80° = \dfrac{h}{7}$
$h = 7\sin 80° = 6.9$
$A = \dfrac{1}{2}(6.9)(10)$
$= 34.5 \text{ m}^2$

15.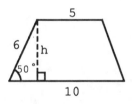

$\sin 50° = \dfrac{h}{6}$
$h = 6\sin 50° = 4.6$

$A = \dfrac{1}{2}h(b_1 + b_2) = \dfrac{1}{2}(4.6)(5 + 10) = 34.5$
$= 34.5 \text{ m}^2 \times \dfrac{100^2 \text{ cm}^2}{1^2 \text{ m}^2} = (34.5)(100)^2 \text{ cm}^2$

16.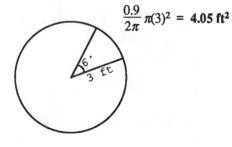

$\dfrac{0.9}{2\pi}\pi(3)^2 = 4.05 \text{ ft}^2$

17.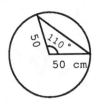

$h = 50\sin 70° = 47$
$A_{\text{segment}} = A_{\text{sector}} - A_{\text{triangle}}$
$= \dfrac{110}{360}\pi(50)^2 - \dfrac{1}{2}(50)(47)$
$= 1223.6 \text{ cm}^2 \cdot \dfrac{1^2 \text{ m}^2}{100^2 \text{ cm}^2} = 0.12 \text{ m}^2$

18. $(x - h)^2 + (y - k)^2 = r^2$

19. $\dfrac{(250)(1000)(100)(60)(60)}{(2.54)(12)(5280)} \dfrac{\text{mi}}{\text{hr}}$

20. $\dfrac{12}{b} = \dfrac{b}{9}$
$b^2 = 108$
$b = \sqrt{108} = \sqrt{36.3} = 6\sqrt{3}$

21. (a) $10^{4.3}$
(b) $e^{9.9}$

22. $\sqrt{(x + 2)^2 + (y - 3)^2}$
$= \sqrt{(x - 4)^2 + (y - 5)^2}$
$x^2 + 4x + 4 + y^2 - 6y + 9$
$= x^2 - 8x + 16 + y^2 - 10y + 25$
$12x + 4y - 28 = 0$
$3x + y - 7 = 0$

23. $\cos\theta = \dfrac{\sqrt{3}}{2}$
$\theta = 30°, 330°$

24. $\cos 5\theta = \dfrac{\sqrt{3}}{2}$
$5\theta = 30°, 330°, 390°, 690°, 750°, 1050°,$
$1110°, 1410°, 1470°, 1770°$
$\theta = 6°, 66°, 78°, 138°, 150°, 210°, 222°,$
$282°, 294°, 354°$

25. $\tan 3\theta = 1$
$3\theta = 45°, 225°, 405°, 585°, 765°, 945°$
$\theta = 15°, 75°, 135°, 195°, 225°, 315°$

26. $\sec^2 135° - 1 = \left(-\sqrt{2}\right)^2 - 1 = 2 - 1 = 1$

27. $\tan^2 (135°) = (-1)^2 = 1$

28. 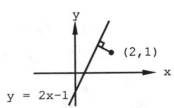 $\dfrac{\sqrt{15}}{4}$

(triangle with $\sqrt{15}$, 4, -1)

29. $\log_7 27^{2/3} - \log_7 (x + 2) = \log_7 3$

$\log_7 \dfrac{9}{(x + 2)} = \log_7 3$

$\dfrac{9}{x + 2} = 3$

$9 = 3x + 6$

$x = 1$

30. $\ln 16^{3/4} - \ln x = \ln 4$

$\ln \dfrac{8}{x} = \ln 4$

$\dfrac{8}{x} = 4$

$x = 2$

PROBLEM SET 38

1. $v = r\omega$

$= 1 \text{ ft} \cdot \dfrac{1 \text{ mi}}{5280 \text{ ft}} \cdot 400 \dfrac{\text{rad}}{\text{sec}} \cdot \dfrac{60 \text{ sec}}{1 \text{ min}} \cdot \dfrac{60 \text{ sec}}{1 \text{ hr}}$

$= \dfrac{(400)(60)(60)}{5280} \dfrac{\text{mi}}{\text{hr}}$

2. $\omega = \dfrac{v}{r} = \dfrac{40 \dfrac{\text{km}}{\text{hr}} \cdot \dfrac{1 \text{ hr}}{60 \text{ min}} \cdot \dfrac{1000 \text{ m}}{1 \text{ km}}}{8 \text{ in} \cdot \dfrac{2.54 \text{ cm}}{1 \text{ in}} \cdot \dfrac{1 \text{ m}}{100 \text{ cm}}}$

$= \dfrac{(40)(100)(1000)}{(60)(8)(2.54)} \dfrac{\text{rad}}{\text{min}} \cdot \dfrac{1 \text{ rev}}{2\pi \text{ rad}}$

$= \dfrac{(40)(100)(1000)}{(60)(8)(2.54)(2\pi)} \dfrac{\text{rev}}{\text{min}}$

3. (Rate)(number) = cost

$\left(\dfrac{2y \text{ dollars}}{4x + 4 \text{ pencils}} \right) (\text{number}) = 10 \text{ dollars}$

$\text{Number} = \dfrac{10(4x + 4)}{2y}$

$= \dfrac{20x + 20}{y} \text{ pencils}$

4. $\boxed{\dfrac{80\%}{x}} + \boxed{\dfrac{20\%}{y}} = \boxed{\dfrac{56\%}{50}}$

$x + y = 50$

$x = 50 - y$

$80x + 20y = 56(50)$

$80(50 - y) + 20y = 2800$

$4000 - 80y + 20y = 2800$

$-60y = -1200$

$y = 20$

$y = 20 \text{ gal } 20\%$

$x = 30 \text{ gal } 80\%$

5.

	Rate
Wilbur:	$\dfrac{2 \text{ jobs}}{3 \text{ days}}$
Harriet:	$\dfrac{4 \text{ jobs}}{7 \text{ days}}$

$T = \text{time together}$

$R_W T_W + R_H T_H = 8$

$\dfrac{2}{3}(T) + \dfrac{4}{7}(T + 3) = 8$

$\dfrac{2}{3}T + \dfrac{4}{7}T = \dfrac{44}{7}$

$T = \dfrac{66}{13} \text{ days}$

6. $\boxed{3|2|1|5|4|3|2|1} = 720$

7. $\dfrac{9!}{2! \, 2!} = 90,720$

8. $\boxed{9|9|8} = 648$

9.

(graph showing line $y = 2x - 1$ and point $(2, 1)$)

(1) Find equation of line $\perp$ to $y = 2x - 1$ that passes through $(2, 1)$.

$m_\perp = -\dfrac{1}{2} ; (2, 1)$

$y = -\dfrac{1}{2}x + b$

$1 = -\dfrac{1}{2}(2) + b$

$$b = 2$$
$$y = -\frac{1}{2}x + 2$$

(2) Solve $y = 2x - 1$ and $y = -\frac{1}{2}x + 2$

simultaneously.
$$-\frac{1}{2}x + 2 = 2x - 1$$
$$x = \frac{6}{5} \qquad\qquad y = \frac{7}{5}$$

(3) Distance between $(2, 1)$ and $\left(\frac{6}{5}, \frac{7}{5}\right)$

$$\sqrt{\left(2 - \frac{6}{5}\right)^2 + \left(1 - \frac{7}{5}\right)^2} =$$
$$\sqrt{\left(\frac{4}{5}\right)^2 + \left(-\frac{2}{5}\right)^2} = \sqrt{\frac{20}{25}} = \frac{2\sqrt{5}}{5}$$

10. $y = 3x^2 - 6x + 5$
y-intercept $= 5$
$y = 3(x^2 - 2x + 1) + 5 - 3$
$y = 3(x - 1)^2 + 2$
x^2 term is positive; thus it opens upward
Axis: $x = 1$
Vertex: $y = 2$

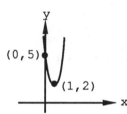

$(0,5)$
$(1,2)$

11. $y = 2x^2 + 4x + 3$
y-intercept $= 3$
$y = 2(x^2 + 2x + 1) + 3 - 2$
$y = 2(x + 1)^2 + 1$
x^2 term is positive; thus it opens upward
Axis: $x = -1$
Vertex: $y = 1$

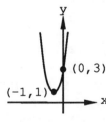

$(0,3)$
$(-1,1)$

12. $y = 3 + 8 \sin\left(x + \frac{7\pi}{4}\right)$

or

$y = 3 + 8 \sin\left(x - \frac{\pi}{4}\right)$

13. $y = 7 + 4 \sin 2\theta$

14.
$$h = 6 \sin 72° = 5.7$$
$$A = \frac{1}{2}(10)(5.7) = 28.5$$
$$28.5 \text{ m}^2 \cdot \frac{100^2 \text{ cm}^2}{1^2 \text{ m}^2}$$
$$= 28.5(100)^2 \text{ cm}^2$$

15.
$$h = 22.5 \sin 55° = 18.02$$
$$A_{\text{trapeziod}} = \frac{1}{2}h\left(b_1 + b_2\right)$$
$$A = \frac{1}{2}(18.02)(23 + 38)$$
$$= 549.65 \text{ cm}^2$$
$$A = 549.65 \text{ m}^2 \cdot \frac{100^2 \text{ cm}^2}{1 \text{ m}^2}$$
$$A = 549.65(100)^2 \text{ cm}^2$$

16. $x = \dfrac{+3 \pm \sqrt{9 - 4(1)(4)}}{2(1)} = \dfrac{3 \pm \sqrt{7}i}{2}$
$$\left(x - \frac{3 + \sqrt{7}i}{2}\right)\left(x - \frac{3 - \sqrt{7}i}{2}\right)$$

17.

$$h = 100 \sin 60°$$
$$A_{\text{segment}} = A_{\text{sector}} - A_{\text{triangle}}$$
$$= \frac{120}{360}\pi(100)^2 - \frac{1}{2}(100)(86.6)$$
$$= 10466.667 - 4330 = 6136.66 \text{ cm}^2$$
$$= 6136.66 \text{ cm}^2 \cdot \frac{1 \text{ m}^2}{100^2 \text{ cm}^2} = 0.61 \text{ m}^2$$

18. $(x - 3)^2 + (y - 2)^2 = 100$

19. $30 \dfrac{\text{cm}}{\text{sec}} \cdot \dfrac{1 \text{ m}}{100 \text{ cm}} \cdot \dfrac{1 \text{ km}}{1000 \text{ m}} \cdot \dfrac{60 \text{ sec}}{1 \text{ min}}$
$\cdot \dfrac{60 \text{ min}}{1 \text{ hr}} = \dfrac{(30)(60)(60)}{(100)(1000)} \dfrac{\text{km}}{\text{hr}}$

20. $\dfrac{2}{3} = \dfrac{5}{c}$
$2c = 15$
$c = \dfrac{15}{2}$

21.   **6**

22.   **30**

23. $\tan \theta = \dfrac{\sqrt{3}}{3}$

     $\theta = \mathbf{30°, 210°}$

24. $\tan 3\theta = \dfrac{\sqrt{3}}{3}$

     $3\theta = 30°, 210°, 390°, 570°, 750°, 930°$

     $\theta = \mathbf{10°, 70°, 130°, 190°, 250°, 310°}$

25. $\sin^2 210° + \cos^2 210°$

     $= \left(-\dfrac{1}{2}\right)^2 + \left(-\dfrac{\sqrt{3}}{2}\right)^2 = \dfrac{1}{4} + \dfrac{3}{4} = \mathbf{1}$

26. $\dfrac{1}{\sec 390°} - \cos 390° = \dfrac{1}{\sec 30°} - \cos 30°$

     $= \cos 30° - \cos 30° = \mathbf{0}$

27. $\dfrac{\sqrt{3}}{4}$

28. $\log_5 x^2 = \log_5 18 - \log_5 2$

     $\log_5 x^2 = \log_5 \dfrac{18}{2}$

     $x^2 = 9$

     $x = \pm 3$

     $x = \mathbf{+3}$

29. $\log_4 (x - 1) + \log_4 (x + 2) = 1$

     $\log_4 (x - 1)(x + 2) = 1$

     $(x - 1)(x + 2) = 4^1$

     $x^2 + x - 2 = 4$

     $x^2 + x - 6 = 0$

     $(x + 3)(x - 2) = 0$

     $x = -3, 2$

     $x = \mathbf{+2}$

30. $\log_4 x - \log_4 (2x - 1) = 1$

     $\log_4 \dfrac{x}{2x - 1} = 1$

     $4^1 = \dfrac{x}{2x - 1}$

     $4(2x - 1) = x$

     $8x - 4 = x$

     $7x = 4$

     $x = \dfrac{4}{7}$

PROBLEM SET 39

1. $v = r\omega = 16 \text{ in} \cdot \dfrac{1 \text{ ft}}{12 \text{ in}} \cdot \dfrac{1 \text{ mi}}{5280 \text{ ft}} \cdot \dfrac{367 \text{ rad}}{\text{sec}}$

     $\cdot \dfrac{60 \text{ sec}}{1 \text{ min}} \cdot \dfrac{60 \text{ min}}{1 \text{ hr}} = \dfrac{(16)(367)(60)(60)}{(12)(5280)} \dfrac{\text{mi}}{\text{hr}}$

2. $\omega = \dfrac{v}{r} = \dfrac{5 \dfrac{\text{km}}{\text{hr}} \cdot \dfrac{1 \text{ hr}}{60 \text{ min}}}{5 \text{ cm} \cdot \dfrac{1 \text{ m}}{100 \text{ cm}} \cdot \dfrac{1 \text{ km}}{1000 \text{ m}}}$

     $= \dfrac{(5)(100)(1000)}{(5)(60)} \dfrac{\text{rad}}{\text{min}}$

3. $A = 8W$

     $T_U = T_D - 1$

     Downwind: $(8W + W)T_D = 1350$

                    $9WT_D = 1350$

                    $WT_D = 150$

     Upwind: $(8W - W)(T_D - 1) = 700$

                    $7WT_D - 7W = 700$

                    $7(150) - 7W = 700$

   $W = \mathbf{50 \text{ mph}}$

   $A = \mathbf{400 \text{ mph}}$

4. $\dfrac{R}{W} = \dfrac{1}{2}$

     $\dfrac{G}{W} = \dfrac{5}{4}$

     $W = 2R$

     $4G = 5W$

     $R + W + G = 22$

     $R + 2R + G = 22$

     $4G = 5(2R) = 10R$

     $2G - 5R = 0$

     $G + 3R = 22$

     $2(22 - 3R) - 5R = 0$

     $44 - 6R - 5R = 0$

     $-11R = 4$

     $R = \mathbf{4}$

     $W = \mathbf{8}$

     $G = \mathbf{10}$

5. A = angle
    $90° - A$ = complement
    $180° - A$ = supplement
    $6(90° - A) = 2(180° - A) + 60°$
    $540° - 6A = 360° - 2A + 60°$
    $-4A = -120°$
    $A = 30°$

6. $\dfrac{11!}{3!} = 6,652,800$

7. $\boxed{3\;|\;2\;|\;1\;|\;2} = 12$

8. $\left[x - \left(-1 - \sqrt{3}i\right)\right]\left[x - \left(-1 + \sqrt{3}i\right)\right]$
    $\left(x + 1 + \sqrt{3}i\right)\left(x + 1 - \sqrt{3}i\right) =$
    $x^2 + x - \sqrt{3}xi + x + 1 - \sqrt{3}i + \sqrt{3}xi$
    $+ \sqrt{3}i + 3 = x^2 + 2x + 4 = 0$

9. (1) Find equation of line $\perp$ to $y = x + 2$
         that passes through $(-4, 6)$.
         $m_\perp = -1$
         $y = mx + b$
         $6 = -1(-4) + b$
         $b = 2$
         $y = -x + 2$
    (2) Solve $y = -x + 2$ and $y = x + 2$
         simultaneously.
         $-x + 2 = x + 2$
         $x = 0, y = 2$

    (3) Find distance between $(0, 2)$ and $(-4, 6)$.
         $\sqrt{(0 + 4)^2 + (2 - 6)^2} = \sqrt{32} = 4\sqrt{2}$

10. $y = 3x^2 + 6x$
    y-intercept $= 0$
    $y = 3(x^2 + 2x + 1) + 0 - 3$
    $y = 3(x + 1)^2 - 3$
    x^2 term coefficient is positive;
    thus the graph opens upward
    Axis: $x = -1$
    Vertex: $y = -3$

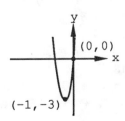

11. $y = -5 + 15 \cos (x - 45°)$

12. $y = -10 + 20 \cos 2\theta$

13.
    $\sin 60° = \dfrac{h}{22}$
    $h = 22 \sin 60° = 19.1$
    $A = \dfrac{1}{2}(19.1)(20)$
    $A = 191 \text{ m}^2 \cdot \dfrac{100^2 \text{ cm}^2}{1^2 \text{ m}^2}$
    $A = 191(100)^2 \text{ cm}^2$

14.
    $\sin 55° = \dfrac{h}{9}$
    $h = 9 \sin 55° = 7.4$
    $A = \dfrac{1}{2}(7.4)(6 + 15)$
    $A = 77.4 \text{ cm}^2 \cdot \dfrac{1 \text{ m}^2}{100^2 \text{ cm}^2}$
    $A = \dfrac{77.4}{100^2} \text{ m}^2$

15. $\dfrac{80°}{360°} \pi(20)^2 = 279.3 \text{ cm}^2$

16.
    $\sin 0.74 = \dfrac{h}{10}$
    $h = 10 \sin 0.74 = 6.7$
    $A_{\text{segment}} = A_{\text{sector}} - A_{\text{triangle}}$
    $= \dfrac{2.4}{2\pi}\pi(10)^2 - \dfrac{1}{2}(10)(6.7) = 120 - 33.5$
    $= 86.5 \text{ in}^2 \cdot \dfrac{1 \text{ ft}^2}{12^2 \text{ in}^2} = \dfrac{86.5}{12^2} \text{ ft}^2$

17. $(x - 5)^2 + (y - 6)^2 = 64$

18. $\sqrt{(x + 2)^2 + (y - 4)^2}$
    $= \sqrt{(x - 6)^2 + (y + 2)^2}$
    $x^2 + 4x + 4 + y^2 - 8y + 16$
    $= x^2 - 12x + 36 + y^2 + 4y + 4$
    $16x - 12y - 20 = 0$
    $4x - 3y - 5 = 0$

19. $2w = 2(3x + 2y) = 6x + 4y$

$10x + 6y - (6x + 4y) = \dfrac{4x + 2y}{2}$

$= 2x + y$

20. **7**

21. $3^{\log_3 3} = \mathbf{3}$

22. $\sin 3\theta = 1$
$3\theta = 90°, 450°, 810°$
$\theta = \mathbf{30°, 150°, 270°}$

23. $\cos^2 \theta - \cos \theta = 0$
$\cos \theta \, (\cos \theta - 1) = 0$

$\cos \theta = 0 \qquad\qquad \cos \theta - 1 = 0$
$\theta = 90°, 270° \qquad \cos \theta = 1$
$\qquad\qquad\qquad\qquad \theta = 0°$

$\theta = \mathbf{0°, 90°, 270°}$

24. $\sin^2 \theta - 1 = 0$
$\sin^2 \theta = 1$
$\sin \theta = \pm 1$
$\theta = \mathbf{90°, 270°}$

25. $\sin^2 135° + \cos^2 135°$

$= \left(\dfrac{\sqrt{2}}{2}\right)^2 + \left(\dfrac{\sqrt{2}}{2}\right)^2 = \dfrac{1}{2} + \dfrac{1}{2} = \mathbf{1}$

26. $\text{Arcsin}\left(\dfrac{\sqrt{2}}{2}\right) = \dfrac{\pi}{4}$

27.

$\dfrac{\sqrt{15}}{4}$

28. $\log_6 x^3 = \log_6 \dfrac{24}{3}$
$x^3 = 8$
$x = \mathbf{2}$

29. $\log_{10} x(x - 3) = 1$
$x^2 - 3x = 10^1$
$x^2 - 3x - 10 = 0$
$(x - 5)(x + 2) = 0$
$x = 5, -2$
$x = \mathbf{5}$

30. $\log_2 x^2 - \log_2 \left(x - \dfrac{1}{2}\right) = \log_{1/3} 3^{-1}$

$\log_2 \dfrac{x^2}{x - \dfrac{1}{2}} = \log_{1/3} \dfrac{1}{3}$

$\log_2 \dfrac{x^2}{x - \dfrac{1}{2}} = 1$

$\dfrac{x^2}{x - \dfrac{1}{2}} = 2$

$x^2 = 2x - 1$
$x^2 - 2x + 1 = 0$
$(x - 1)(x - 1) = 0$
$x = \mathbf{1}$

PROBLEM SET 40

1. $\omega = \dfrac{v}{r} = \dfrac{40\,\frac{\text{km}}{\text{hr}}}{14\text{ in}} \cdot \dfrac{1\text{ in}}{2.54\text{ cm}} \cdot \dfrac{100\text{ cm}}{1\text{ m}}$

$\cdot \dfrac{1000\text{ m}}{1\text{ km}} \cdot \dfrac{1\text{ hr}}{3600\text{ sec}} = \dfrac{40(100)(1000)}{14(2.54)(3600)}\,\dfrac{\textbf{rad}}{\textbf{sec}}$

2. $v = \omega r$

$= \dfrac{40\text{ rev}}{\text{sec}} \cdot \dfrac{16\text{ cm}}{1} \cdot \dfrac{2\pi}{1\text{ rev}} \cdot \dfrac{3600\text{ sec}}{1\text{ hr}}$

$\cdot \dfrac{1\text{ in}}{2.54\text{ cm}} \cdot \dfrac{1\text{ ft}}{12\text{ in}} \cdot \dfrac{1\text{ mi}}{5280\text{ ft}}$

$= \dfrac{40(16)(3600)(2\pi)}{2.54(12)(5280)}\,\dfrac{\textbf{mi}}{\textbf{hr}}$

3.

	Now	+5 yrs
Tom:	T	$T + 5$
Lucy:	L	$L + 5$

$5T = 4L + 38$
$5T - 4L = 38$
$2(T + 5) = 2(L + 5) + 8$
$2T - 2L = 8$
$T = L + 4$
$5(L + 4) - 4L = 38$
$L = 18, T = 22$
Lucy $= 18 + 13 = \mathbf{31\ years}$
Tom $= 22 + 13 = \mathbf{35\ years}$

4. Present salary $= \dfrac{\$200}{40\ \text{hr}} = \$5\,/\,\text{hr}$

New salary $= 5 + 0.30(5) = \$6.50\,/\,\text{hr}$

Paycheck $= (6.50)(38) = \mathbf{\$247}$

5. A: $\dfrac{T}{H} = \dfrac{2}{1}$

$\quad H = \dfrac{1}{2}T$

B: $2T - 1 = 5U$

$\quad U = \dfrac{2}{5}T - \dfrac{1}{5}$

C: $H + T + U = 15$

Substitute equations A and B into C.

$\dfrac{1}{2}T + T + \dfrac{2}{5}T - \dfrac{1}{5} = 15$

$\dfrac{19}{10}T = \dfrac{76}{5}$

$T = 8$

$H = \dfrac{1}{2}(8) = 4$

$U = 15 - 8 - 4 = 3$

$N = \mathbf{483}$

6. $_{12}P_3 = \dfrac{12!}{9!} = \mathbf{1320}$

7.

T	2	2	1	= 4
2	T	1	1	= 2
1	2	T	1	= 2
1	2	2	T	= 4

$\qquad\qquad\qquad\overline{\ \ \mathbf{12}\ \ }$

8. $\dfrac{11!}{(5!)(4!)(2!)} = \mathbf{6930}$

9. $3[3^2 + 1^2 + (-1)^2] - (3 + 1 - 1)^2$

$3(11) - 3^2 = 33 - 9 = \mathbf{24}$

10. $3(4)(1) + 3(9)(2) + 3(16)(3)$

$= 12 + 54 + 144 = \mathbf{210}$

11. Find the equation of the line $\perp$ to $y = x - 1$ that passes through $(2, 4)$.

$m_\perp = -1$

$y = -x + b$

$4 = -(2) + b$

$b = 6$

$y = -x + 6$

Solve $y = -x + 6$ and $y = x - 1$ simultaneously.

$-x + 6 = x - 1$

$7 = 2x$

$x = \dfrac{7}{2}$

$y = \dfrac{7}{2} - 1 = \dfrac{5}{2}$

$(x, y) = \left(\dfrac{7}{2}, \dfrac{5}{2}\right)$

$d = \sqrt{\left(2 - \dfrac{7}{2}\right)^2 + \left(4 - \dfrac{5}{2}\right)^2}$

$d = \sqrt{\left(\dfrac{3}{2}\right)^2 + \left(\dfrac{3}{2}\right)^2} = \sqrt{\dfrac{9}{4} + \dfrac{9}{4}}$

$d = \sqrt{\dfrac{18}{4}} = \dfrac{3\sqrt{2}}{2}$

12. $y = 2x^2 - 4x - 7$

$y = 2(x^2 - 2x + 1) - 7 - 2$

$y = 2(x - 1)^2 - 9$

x^2 term coefficient is positive; thus the graph opens upward

Axis: $x = 1$

Vertex: $y = -9$

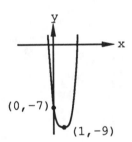

$(0, -7)$

$(1, -9)$

13. $y = -2 + 6\sin\left(x - \dfrac{\pi}{4}\right)$

14. $y = 2 + 5\sin 4\theta$

15. $\sin 60° = \dfrac{h}{0.5}$

$h = \dfrac{\sqrt{3}}{4}$

$A = \dfrac{1}{2}\left(\dfrac{1}{4}\right)\left(\dfrac{\sqrt{3}}{4}\right) = \dfrac{\sqrt{3}}{32}\,\text{m}^2$

$\dfrac{\sqrt{3}}{32}\,\text{m}^2 \left(\dfrac{100\ \text{cm}}{1\ \text{m}}\right)^2 = \dfrac{625\sqrt{3}}{2}\,\text{cm}^2$

16. $A = \pi(1)^2\left(\dfrac{1.6}{2\pi}\right) = 0.8 \text{ m}^2 \cdot \left(\dfrac{100 \text{ cm}}{1 \text{ m}}\right)^2$

$= \textbf{8000 cm}^2$

17. $A_{\text{segment}} = A_{\text{sector}} - A_{\text{triangle}}$

$A_{\text{segment}} = \pi(10)^2\left(\dfrac{150}{360}\right) - \dfrac{1}{2}(10)(5)$

$= \dfrac{125\pi}{3} - 25 = \textbf{105.9 cm}^2$

150° 10 cm

18. $(x - m)^2 + (y - n)^2 = \textbf{36}$

19. $m = \dfrac{2}{8} = \dfrac{1}{4}$

Therefore, $m_\perp = -4$.

Midpoint $(0, 3)$

$y - 3 = -4(x)$

$\boldsymbol{y = -4x + 3}$

20. Time $= \dfrac{\text{distance}}{\text{rate}}$, rate $= \dfrac{\text{distance}}{\text{time}}$

$\text{Time}_d = \dfrac{m}{d} \text{ hr}$

$\text{Time}_u = \dfrac{m}{u} \text{ hr}$

$\text{Rate} = \dfrac{2m}{\dfrac{m}{d} + \dfrac{m}{u}} = \dfrac{2m}{\dfrac{mu + md}{du}}$

$= \dfrac{2du}{u + d} \textbf{ knots}$

21. $5^{\log_5 11} = \textbf{11}$

22. $\cos 3\theta = \dfrac{\sqrt{2}}{2}$

$3\theta = 45°, 315°, 405°, 675°, 765°, 1035°$

$\theta = \textbf{15}°, \textbf{105}°, \textbf{135}°, \textbf{225}°, \textbf{255}°, \textbf{345}°$

23. $\cos\theta\left(\cos\theta - \dfrac{1}{2}\right) = 0$

$\cos\theta = 0 \qquad \text{or} \qquad \cos\theta = \dfrac{1}{2}$

$\theta = 90°, 270° \qquad\qquad \theta = 60°, 300°$

$\theta = \textbf{60}°, \textbf{90}°, \textbf{270}°, \textbf{300}°$

24. $\left(\sin\theta + \dfrac{1}{2}\right)\left(\sin\theta - \dfrac{1}{2}\right) = 0$

$\sin\theta = \pm\dfrac{1}{2}$

$\theta = \textbf{30}°, \textbf{150}°, \textbf{210}°, \textbf{330}°$

25. $2\left(\dfrac{1}{2}\right)\left(\dfrac{\sqrt{3}}{2}\right) - \dfrac{\sqrt{3}}{2} = \dfrac{\sqrt{3}}{2} - \dfrac{\sqrt{3}}{2} = \textbf{0}$

26. $0 - \dfrac{0}{-1} = 0 + 0 = \textbf{0}$

27.

$-\dfrac{5}{13}$

12

13 −5

28. $\log_5 x^2 = \log_5 4$

$x^2 = 4$

$x = \textbf{2}$

29. $\log_{10} x(x - 9) = 1$

$10 = x^2 - 9x$

$x^2 - 9x - 10 = 0$

$(x - 10)(x + 1) = 0$

$x = \textbf{10}$

30. $\log_5 (x + 4)(x - 4) = 2$

$25 = x^2 - 16$

$x^2 = 41$

$x = \boldsymbol{\sqrt{41}}$

PROBLEM SET 41

1. $C = mN + b$

$2050 = m(200) + b$

$350 = m(30) + b$

$\begin{aligned} 2050 &= 200m + b \\ (-)\,350 &= 30m + b \\ \hline 1700 &= 170m \\ 10 &= m \end{aligned}$

$b = 50;$ thus $C = 10N + 50$

2. $v = r\omega$

$v = 20\text{ cm} \cdot \dfrac{723\text{ rad}}{\text{min}} \cdot \dfrac{1\text{ in}}{2.54\text{ cm}} \cdot \dfrac{1\text{ ft}}{12\text{ in}}$

$\cdot \dfrac{1\text{ min}}{60\text{ sec}} = \dfrac{(20)(723)}{(2.54)(12)(60)} \dfrac{\text{ft}}{\text{sec}}$

3. $\dfrac{P_1 V_1}{T_1} = \dfrac{P_2 V_2}{T_2}$

$T_1 = T_2$

$(4)(500) = P_2(50)$

$P_2 = \mathbf{40\text{ atm}}$

4. $R = \dfrac{kP}{W^3}$

$k = \dfrac{RW^3}{P} = \dfrac{200(10^3)}{50} = 4000$

$R = \dfrac{4000(P)}{W^3} = \dfrac{4000(60)}{5^3} = \mathbf{1920}$

5. $B = 2W$

$T_u = T_D + 1$

Downstream: $(2W + W)T_D = 12$

$\quad\quad\quad\quad\quad 3WT_D = 12$

$\quad\quad\quad\quad\quad\ WT_D = 4$

Upstream: $(2W - W)(T_D + 1) = 6$

$\quad\quad\quad\quad\quad WT_D + W = 6$

$\quad\quad\quad\quad\quad\quad 4 + W = 6$

$W = \mathbf{2\text{ mph}}$

$B = \mathbf{4\text{ mph}}$

6. $\boxed{10\ |\ 9\ |\ 8\ |\ 7\ |\ 6} = \mathbf{30{,}240}$

7. $\boxed{4\ |\ 3\ |\ 2\ |\ 1\ |\ 1} = \mathbf{24}$

8. $\dfrac{11!}{5!\ 4!\ 2!}$

9. A: $mx + ny = c$

B: $dx + ey = f$

Multiply equation A by d, and multiply equation B by $-m$.

$\quad\quad mdx\ +\ ndy\ =\ dc$

$(+)\ -mdx\ -\ mey\ =\ -mf$

$\overline{\quad\quad\quad\quad ndy - mey\ =\ dc - mf}$

$\quad\quad\quad\quad y(nd - me)\ =\ dc - mf$

$\quad\quad\quad\quad\quad\quad y = \dfrac{dc - mf}{nd - me}$

10. $[2(4)^2 - 2] + [2(1)^2 - 1] + [2(2)^2 - 1]$

$= 30 + 1 + 7 = \mathbf{38}$

11. Find the equation of the line $\perp$ to $y = x - 4$ that passes through $(3, 1)$.

$m_\perp = -1$

$y = -x + b$

$1 = -(3) + b$

$b = 4$

$y = -x + 4$

Solve $y = -x + 4$ and $y = x - 4$ simultaneously.

$-x + 4 = x - 4$

$x = 4$

$y = 4 - 4 = 0$

$(x, y) = (4, 0)$

$d = \sqrt{(3 - 4)^2 + (1 - 0)^2}$

$= \sqrt{1 + 1} = \mathbf{\sqrt{2}}$

12. $y = 3(x^2 - 4x + 4) + 34 - 12$

$y = 3(x - 2)^2 + 22$

x^2 term coefficient is positive; thus the graph opens upward

Axis: $x = 2$

Vertex: $y = 22$

y-intercept $= 34$

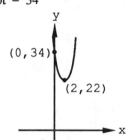

13. $y = -1 + 4 \cos (x - 135°)$

14. $y = -3 + 5 \cos \dfrac{1}{3}\theta$

15.

$h = 30 \sin 40° \approx 19.3$

$A = \dfrac{1}{2}(19.3)(40 + 25) \approx \mathbf{627.25\text{ cm}^2}$

16.

$$\frac{103}{360}\pi(10)^2 \approx \textbf{90 cm}^2$$

17.

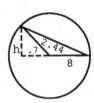

$A_{\text{segment}} = A_{\text{sector}} - A_{\text{triangle}}$

$\sin 0.7 = \dfrac{h}{8}$

$h = 8 \sin 0.7 = 5.2$

$A_{\text{segment}} = \dfrac{2.44}{2\pi}\pi(8)^2 - \dfrac{1}{2}(5.2)(8)$

$= 78.08 - 20.8 = \textbf{57.3 cm}^2$

18. $(x - a)^2 + (y - b)^2 = \textbf{16}$

19. $\sqrt{(x+4)^2 + (y+4)^2} = \sqrt{(x-6)^2 + (y-2)^2}$

$x^2 + 8x + 16 + y^2 + 8y + 16$

$= x^2 - 12x + 36 + y^2 - 4y + 4$

$20x + 12y - 8 = 0$

$\textbf{5x + 3y - 2 = 0}$

20. $\dfrac{3}{9} = \dfrac{a}{7}$ $9a = 21$ $a = \dfrac{\textbf{7}}{\textbf{3}}$

$\dfrac{3}{9} = \dfrac{2}{b}$ $3b = 18$ $b = \textbf{6}$

21. $6^{\log_6 2^2} = 6^{\log_6 4} = \textbf{4}$

22. $\cos 4\theta = 1$

$4\theta = 0°, 360°, 720°, 1080°$

$\theta = \textbf{0°, 90°, 180°, 270°}$

23. $\sin\theta\left(\sin\theta - \dfrac{\sqrt{3}}{2}\right) = 0$

$\sin\theta = 0$ or $\sin\theta = \dfrac{\sqrt{3}}{2}$

$\theta = 0°, 180°$ $\theta = 60°, 120°$

$\theta = \textbf{0°, 60°, 120°, 180°}$

24. $\tan\theta = \pm 1$

$\theta = \textbf{45°, 135°, 225°, 315°}$

25. $2\sin 570° \cos 570° - \sin 1140°$

$2\sin 210° \cos 210° - \sin 60°$

$2\left(-\dfrac{1}{2}\right)\left(-\dfrac{\sqrt{3}}{2}\right) - \left(\dfrac{\sqrt{3}}{2}\right) = \dfrac{\sqrt{3}}{2} - \dfrac{\sqrt{3}}{2} = \textbf{0}$

26. $\tan^2(-30°) + 1 = \left(-\dfrac{\sqrt{3}}{2}\right)^2 + 1$

$= \dfrac{1}{3} + 1 = \dfrac{\textbf{4}}{\textbf{3}}$

27.

$-\dfrac{\textbf{5}}{\textbf{12}}$

28. $\log_6 x^3 = \log_6 \dfrac{16}{2}$

$x^3 = 8$

$x = \textbf{2}$

29. $\log_7 \dfrac{x + 9}{x} = \log_7 7$

$\dfrac{x + 9}{x} = 7$

$7x = x + 9$

$6x = 9$

$x = \dfrac{\textbf{3}}{\textbf{2}}$

30. Let $b^a = N$

$\log_b N = a$

$\log_b N^x = \log_b (b^a)^x = \log_b b^{ax}$

$= ax = x \log_b N$

PROBLEM SET 42

1.
$R = mB + b$
$11 = m(2) + b$
$35 = m(8) + b$
$\quad\quad -11 = -2m - b$
$(+)\ 35 = \quad 8m + b$
$\quad\quad\quad 24 = \quad 6m$
$m = 4$
$b = 3$
$R = 4B + 3 = 4(6) + 3 = \mathbf{27}$

2.
$\omega = \dfrac{v}{r}$

$= \dfrac{60\,\dfrac{\text{km}}{\text{hr}} \cdot \dfrac{1\,\text{hr}}{60\,\text{min}} \cdot \dfrac{1\,\text{min}}{60\,\text{sec}}}{12\,\text{in} \cdot \dfrac{2.54\,\text{cm}}{1\,\text{in}} \cdot \dfrac{1\,\text{m}}{100\,\text{cm}} \cdot \dfrac{1\,\text{km}}{1000\,\text{m}}}$

$= \dfrac{(60)(100)(1000)}{(60)(60)(12)(2.54)}\ \dfrac{\mathbf{rad}}{\mathbf{sec}}$

3.
Onlookers: 17
Bystanders: 4
Total: 21

$\dfrac{17}{21} = \dfrac{x}{1050}$

$x = 850$
Onlookers = **850**
Bystanders = **200**

4.

	Martha	Kristel
Rate:	a	b
Time:	$\dfrac{m}{a}$	$\dfrac{m}{b}$
Distance:	m	m

$\dfrac{m}{b} - \dfrac{m}{a} = \dfrac{ma - mb}{ab}\ \mathbf{hr}$

5.

	Original	New
Rate:	a	b
Time:	b	t
Distance:	a	1000

$t = \dfrac{1000}{\dfrac{a}{b} + c} = \dfrac{1000}{\dfrac{a + bc}{b}} = \mathbf{\dfrac{1000b}{a + bc}}$

6. $\boxed{3\ |\ 2\ |\ 2\ |\ 1\ |\ 1} = \mathbf{12}$

7. $\boxed{2\ |\ 4\ |\ 3\ |\ 2\ |\ 1} = \mathbf{48}$

8. $\dfrac{7!}{4!\ 3!}$

9.
A: $ax + by = c$
B: $mx + ny = f$
Multiply equation A by n, and multiply equation B by $-b$.
$\quad\quad anx + \quad bny = \quad nc$
$(+) -bmx - \quad bmy = -bf$
$\quad\quad\quad anx - bmx = \quad nc - bf$
$\quad\quad\quad x(an - bm) = \quad nc - bf$

$\quad\quad\quad\quad x = \dfrac{nc - bf}{an - bm}$

10.
$[3(3)^2 - 2(2)] + [3(1)^2 - 2(3)]$
$+ [3(-1)^2 - 2(1)] = 23 - 3 + 1 = \mathbf{21}$

11.
$2^{1-1} + 2^{2-1} + 2^{3-1} = 2^0 + 2^1 + 2^2$
$= 1 + 2 + 4 = \mathbf{7}$

12. Find the equation of the line $\perp$ to $y = x - 6$ that passes through $(-2, 4)$.
$m_{\perp} = -1$
$y = -x + b$
$4 = -(-2) + b$
$b = 2$
$y = -x + 2$

Solve $y = -x + 2$ and $y = x - 6$ simultaneously.
$-x + 2 = x - 6$
$x = 4$
$y = 4 - 6 = -2$
$(x, y) = (4, -2)$

$d = \sqrt{(4 + 2)^2 + (-2 - 4)^2} = \sqrt{72} = 6\sqrt{2}$

13.
$y = 2x^2 - 12x + 19$
$y = 2(x^2 - 6x + 9) + 19 - 18$
$y = 2(x - 3)^2 + 1$
Coefficient of x^2 term is positive;
thus the graph opens upward
Axis: $x = 3$
Vertex: $y = 1$
y-intercept = 19

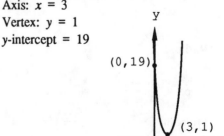
$(0, 19)$
$(3, 1)$

14. $y = 4 + 8 \sin \left(x - \frac{\pi}{4} \right)$

15. $y = -3 + 5 \sin \frac{1}{2} x$

16.

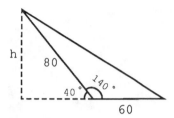

$h = 80 \sin 40° \approx 51.4$

$A = \frac{1}{2}(60)(51.4) \approx \mathbf{1542 \ cm^2}$

17. $\frac{2.4}{2\pi} \cdot \pi(40)^2 \approx \mathbf{1920 \ cm^2}$

18.

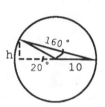

$A_{\text{segment}} = A_{\text{sector}} - A_{\text{triangle}}$

$\sin 20° = \frac{h}{10}$

$h = 10 \sin 20° \approx 3.42$

$A_{\text{segment}} = \frac{160}{360}\pi(10)^2 - \frac{1}{2}(3.42)(10)$

$= 139.6 - 17.1 \approx \mathbf{122.5 \ cm^2}$

19. $(x^2 + 8x + 16) + (y^2 - 6y + 9)$

$= 11 + 16 + 9 = 36$

$(x + 4)^2 + (y - 3)^2 = 36$

Center: (−4, 3)

Radius: 6

20. $(x^2 - 8x + 16) + (y^2 + 2y + 1)$

$= -13 + 16 + 1 = 4$

$(x - 4)^2 + (y + 1)^2 = 4$

Center: (4, −1)

Radius: 2

21. Slope $= \frac{6 - 2}{4 + 4} = \frac{4}{8} = \frac{1}{2}$

Midpoint $\left(\frac{-4 + 4}{2}, \frac{2 + 6}{2} \right) = (0, 4)$

$m_{\perp} = -2$

$y = mx + b$

$4 = (-2)(0) + b$

$b = 4$

$y = -2x + 4$

22. $\frac{9}{a} = \frac{a}{4}$ $\qquad a^2 = 36 \qquad a = 6$

23. $\cos \theta = 1$

$\theta = \mathbf{0°}$

24. $\sin \theta (\cos \theta - 1) = 0$

$\sin \theta = 0 \qquad$ or $\qquad \cos\theta = 1$

$\theta = 0°, 180° \qquad\qquad \theta = 0°$

$\theta = \mathbf{0°, 180°}$

25. $\cos^2 \theta = \frac{1}{4}$

$\cos \theta = \pm \frac{1}{2}$

$\cos \theta = \frac{1}{2} \qquad$ or $\qquad \cos\theta = -\frac{1}{2}$

$\theta = 60°, 300° \qquad\qquad \theta = 120°, 240°$

$\theta = \mathbf{60°, 120°, 240°, 300°}$

26. $\sin^2 270° + \cos^2 270° = (-1)^2 + 0^2 = 1$

27. $\cos^2 (-45°) - \sin^2 (-45°)$

$= \left(\frac{\sqrt{2}}{2} \right)^2 - \left(-\frac{\sqrt{2}}{2} \right)^2 = \frac{1}{2} - \frac{1}{2} = 0$

28.

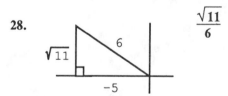

$\frac{\sqrt{11}}{6}$

29. $\log_8 x^2 = \log_8 \frac{(6)(2)}{1}$

$x^2 = 12$

$x = 2\sqrt{3}$

30. $\log_{1/2} \frac{x - 3}{x - 2} = \log_{1/2} 2$

$\frac{x - 3}{x - 2} = 2$

$x - 3 = 2x - 4$

$x = 1$

No solution

PROBLEM SET 43

1. $C = mN + b$
$15,000 = m(10) + b$
$20,000 = m(20) + b$
$\quad -15,000 = -10m - b$
$\underline{(+)\ 20,000 = \quad 20m + b}$
$\quad\quad 5000 = \quad 10m$
$m = 500$
$b = 10,000$
$C = 500N + 10,000$
$C = 500(30) + 10,000 = \$25,000$

2. $v = r\omega$
$= 10\ \text{in} \cdot \dfrac{2.54\ \text{cm}}{1\ \text{in}} \cdot \dfrac{1\ \text{m}}{100\ \text{cm}} \cdot \dfrac{1\ \text{km}}{1000\ \text{m}}$
$\cdot \dfrac{75\ \text{rad}}{1\ \text{min}} \cdot \dfrac{60\ \text{min}}{1\ \text{hr}} = \dfrac{(2.54)(10)(75)(60)}{(100)(1000)}\ \dfrac{\text{km}}{\text{hr}}$

3.

	Old	New
Rate:	$\dfrac{m}{x}$	$\dfrac{k}{y}$
Time:	x	y
Distance:	m	k

Average rate $= \dfrac{\text{total distance}}{\text{total time}} = \dfrac{m + k}{x + y}$

$r_{av}t = d$

$\dfrac{m + k}{x + y}(t) = 150$

$t = \dfrac{150(x + y)}{m + k}$

4.

	Red	Blue
Rate:	t	b
Time:	$\dfrac{m}{r}$	$\dfrac{m}{b}$
Distance:	m	m

$\dfrac{m}{b} - \dfrac{m}{r} = \dfrac{mr - mb}{br}\ \text{hr}$

5. Rate $\cdot$ number $=$ cost
$\left(\dfrac{d\ \text{dollars}}{k^2 t\ \text{pencils}}\right) \cdot \text{number} = 100\ \text{dollars}$
Number $= \dfrac{100k^2 t}{d}$ pencils

6. $\boxed{2\ |\ 5\ |\ 5} = 50$

7. $\dfrac{7!}{3!\ 4!} = 35$

8. (a)

Polar form $= r\ \text{cis}\ \theta$
$r = \sqrt{6^2 + 2^2} \approx 6.3$
$\tan \theta = \dfrac{1}{3}$
$\theta = 18.4°$
6.3 cis 18.4°

(b) $r\ \text{cis}\ \theta = r(\cos \theta + i \sin \theta)$
$= 5(\cos 30° + i \sin 30°)$
$= 5\left(\dfrac{\sqrt{3}}{2} + \dfrac{1}{2}i\right) = \dfrac{5\sqrt{3}}{2} + \dfrac{5}{2}i$

9. $(6\ \text{cis}\ 300°)(2\ \text{cis}\ 30°) = 12\ \text{cis}\ 330°$
$= 12(\cos 330° + i \sin 330°)$
$= 12\left(\dfrac{\sqrt{3}}{2} - \dfrac{1}{2}i\right) = 6\sqrt{3} - 6i$

10. $(3\ \text{cis}\ 70°)(2\ \text{cis}\ 30°) = 6\ \text{cis}\ 180°$
$= 12(\cos 180° + i \sin 180°)$
$= 6(-1 + 0i) = -6$

11. A: $cx + by = d$
B: $px + qy = f$
Multiply equation A by p, and multiply
equation B by $-c$.
$\quad\quad pcx + pby = pd$
$\underline{(+)\ -pcx - cqy = -cf}$
$\quad\quad pby - cqy = pd - cf$
$\quad\quad y(pb - cq) = pd - cf$
$\quad\quad\quad\quad\quad y = \dfrac{pd - cf}{pb - cq}$

12. $(2^2 - 3^{2-2})(2) + (2^3 - 3^{3-2})(3)$
$(4 - 1)(2) + (8 - 3)(3)$
$(3)(2) + (5)(3) = \textbf{21}$

13. Find the equation of the line $\perp$ to $y = x - 4$
that passes through $(-4, 6)$.
$m_{\perp} = -1$
$y = -x + b$
$6 = -(-4) + b$
$b = 2$
$y = -x + 2$

Solve $y = -x + 2$ and $y = x - 4$
simultaneously.
$-x + 2 = x - 4$

$x = 3$
$y = 3 - 4 = -1$
$(x, y) = (3, -1)$

$d = \sqrt{(-4 - 3)^2 + (6 + 1)^2} = \sqrt{98} = 7\sqrt{2}$

14. $y = -1 + 5\cos(x + 225°)$
or
$y = -1 + 5\cos(x - 135°)$

15. $y = 6 - 4\cos\dfrac{2}{3}x$

16.

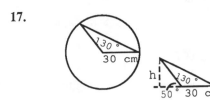

$h = 10\sin 60° \approx 8.7$
$A = \dfrac{1}{2}(8.7)(12 + 20) \approx \mathbf{138.6\ cm^2}$

17.

$A_{\text{segment}} = A_{\text{sector}} - A_{\text{triangle}}$
$h = 30\sin 50° \approx 23$
$A_{\text{segment}} = \dfrac{130}{360}\pi(30)^2 - \dfrac{1}{2}(23)(30)$
$= 1020.5 - 345 \approx \mathbf{676.5\ cm^2}$

18. $(x^2 - 4x + 4) + y^2 = 0 + 4$
$(x - 2)^2 + y^2 = 4$
Center: (2, 0)
Radius: 2

19. $(x^2 + 6x + 9) + (y^2 - 4y + 4)$
$= 9 + 9 + 4 = 22$
$(x + 3)^2 + (y - 2)^2 = 22$
Center: (-3, 2)
Radius: $\sqrt{22}$

20. $\sqrt{(x+4)^2 + (y-6)^2} = \sqrt{(x-6)^2 + (y-8)^2}$
$x^2 + 8x + 16 + y^2 - 12y + 36$
$= x^2 - 12x + 36 + y^2 - 16y + 64$
$20x + 4y - 48 = 0$
$\mathbf{5x + y - 12 = 0}$

21. $a + b = \sqrt{5^2 + 12^2} = 13$
$\dfrac{7}{12} = \dfrac{a}{a + b}$
$\dfrac{7}{12} = \dfrac{a}{13}$
$12a = 91 \qquad\qquad a = \dfrac{91}{12}$
$b = 13 - \dfrac{91}{12} \qquad b = \dfrac{65}{12}$

22. $\sin\theta = \dfrac{\sqrt{3}}{2}$
$\theta = \mathbf{60°, 120°}$

23. $\tan\theta\sin\theta - \sin\theta = 0$
$\sin\theta(\tan\theta - 1) = 0$
$\sin\theta = 0 \qquad$ or $\qquad \tan\theta = 1$
$\theta = 0°, 180° \qquad\qquad \theta = 45°, 225°$
$\theta = \mathbf{0°, 45°, 180°, 225°}$

24. $\tan^2\theta = 3$
$\tan\theta = \pm\sqrt{3}$
$\tan\theta = \sqrt{3} \quad$ or $\quad \tan\theta = -\sqrt{3}$
$\theta = 60°, 240° \qquad\quad \theta = 120°, 300°$
$\theta = \mathbf{60°, 120°, 240°, 300°}$

25. $\cos^2(225°) - \sin^2(225°)$
$= \left(-\dfrac{\sqrt{2}}{2}\right)^2 - \left(-\dfrac{\sqrt{2}}{2}\right)^2 = \dfrac{1}{2} - \dfrac{1}{2} = \mathbf{0}$

26. $\tan^3 0° - \cot^2(-45°) = 0^3 - (-1)^2 = \mathbf{-1}$

27. $-\dfrac{8}{9}$

28. $\log_8 x^2 = \log_8(2x - 1)$
$x^2 = 2x - 1$
$x^2 - 2x + 1 = 0$
$(x - 1)(x - 1) = 0$
$\mathbf{x = 1}$

29. $\log_3(x - 2)x = 1$
$3^1 = x(x - 2)$
$x^2 - 2x - 3 = 0$
$(x - 3)(x + 1) = 0$
$\mathbf{x = 3}$

30. $8^{\log_8 13^2} = 8^{\log_8 169} = \mathbf{169}$

PROBLEM SET 44

1. $C = mH + b$

$$1200 = 40m + b$$
$$(-)\ 1600 = 40m + 2b$$
$$\overline{-400 = \qquad -b}$$

$b = 400$

$800 = 20m + 400$

$20m = 400$

$m = 20$

$C = 20H + 400$

$C = 20(30) + 400 = \textbf{\$1000}$

2. $\omega = \dfrac{v}{r} = \dfrac{45 \text{ km/hr}}{30 \text{ cm}}$

$= \dfrac{45 \text{ km}}{30 \text{ hr cm}} \cdot \dfrac{1 \text{ hr}}{60 \text{ min}} \cdot \dfrac{100 \text{ cm}}{1 \text{ m}} \cdot \dfrac{1000 \text{ m}}{1 \text{ km}}$

$= \dfrac{45(100)(1000)}{30(60)} \dfrac{\textbf{rad}}{\textbf{min}}$

3.

	Old	New
Rate:	$\dfrac{m}{h}$	$\dfrac{x}{h+4}$
Time:	h	$h+4$
Distance:	m	x

$r_{av} = \dfrac{\text{total distance}}{\text{total time}} = \dfrac{m+x}{2h+4} \dfrac{\text{mi}}{\text{hr}}$

$\text{Time} = \dfrac{\text{distance}}{\text{rate}} = \dfrac{50}{\dfrac{m+x}{2h+4}}$

$= \dfrac{50(2h+4)}{m+x} \textbf{ hr}$

4.

	Peter	Roger
Rate:	P	R
Time:	$\dfrac{x}{P}$	$\dfrac{x}{R}$
Distance:	x	x

$\text{time}_{\text{Peter}} - \text{time}_{\text{Roger}} = \left(\dfrac{x}{P} - \dfrac{x}{R}\right) \textbf{ hr}$

5. $\text{Rate} \cdot \text{number} = \text{cost}$

$\left(\dfrac{d \text{ dollars}}{k^2x + m}\right) \cdot \text{number} = 500 \text{ dollars}$

$\text{Number} = \dfrac{500(k^2x + m)}{d} \textbf{ pencils}$

6.

T	5	5	= 25
F	1	1	= $\dfrac{1}{26}$

7. $\dfrac{7!}{2!} = \textbf{2520}$

8. First sketch $y = 2^x$; then reflect about $y = x$ to get $y = \log_2 x$.

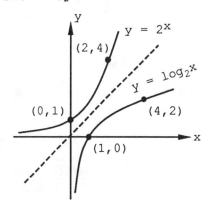

9. (*a*) Polar form $= r \text{ cis } \theta$

$r = \sqrt{3^2 + 5^2} \approx 5.8$

$\tan \theta = \dfrac{5}{3}, \ \theta \approx 59°$

$\textbf{5.8 cis 59°}$

(*b*) $r \text{ cis } \theta = r(\cos \theta + i \sin \theta)$

$= 5(\cos 60° + i \sin 60°)$

$= 5\left(\dfrac{1}{2} + \dfrac{\sqrt{3}}{2} i\right) = \textbf{3} + \textbf{3}\sqrt{\textbf{3}} \, \textbf{\textit{i}}$

10. $(5 \text{ cis } 20°)(6 \text{ cis } 70°) = 30 \text{ cis } 90°$

$= 30(\cos 90° + i \sin 90°)$

$= 30[0 + i(1)] = \textbf{30\textit{i}}$

11. $[6 \text{ cis}(-30°)](3 \text{ cis } 90°) = 18 \text{ cis } 90°$

$= 18(\cos 90° + i \sin 90°)$

$= 18\left(\dfrac{1}{2} + i\dfrac{\sqrt{3}}{2}\right) = \textbf{9} + \textbf{9}\textbf{\textit{i}}\sqrt{\textbf{3}}$

12. A: $ax + dy = g$

B: $cx + fy = h$

Multiply equation A by $-f$, and multiply equation B by d.

$$-afx - dfy = -fg$$
$$(+)\ cdx + dfy = dh$$
$$\overline{\ cdx - afx = dh - fg\ }$$

$x(cd - af) = dh - fg$

$x = \dfrac{dh - fg}{cd - af}$

13. $3(0)^2 - (-1)^2 + (-1)(-2)^2 - 0^2$
$+ (0)(3)^2 - (2)^2 = -1 - 4 - 4 = \mathbf{-9}$

14. $y = 1 + 5\sin\left(x - \dfrac{3\pi}{4}\right)$

15. $y = 6 + 10\sin\dfrac{2}{7}x$

16. $A = \dfrac{1}{2}(10)(12\sin 50°) = 5[12(0.766)]$
$= 45.96\ \text{cm}^2 \cdot \left(\dfrac{1\text{m}}{100\text{ cm}}\right)^2 \approx \mathbf{0.004596\ m^2}$

17. $\dfrac{600\text{ km}}{\text{hr}} \cdot \dfrac{1000\text{m}}{1\text{ km}} \cdot \dfrac{1\text{ in}}{2.54\text{ cm}} \cdot \dfrac{100\text{ cm}}{1\text{ m}}$
$\cdot \dfrac{1\text{ ft}}{12\text{ in}} \cdot \dfrac{1\text{ m}}{5280\text{ ft}} = \dfrac{600(1000)(100)}{2.54(12)(5280)}\dfrac{\text{mi}}{\text{hr}}$

18. Refer to Problem Set 18, problem 7.

19. $(x^2 + 10x + 25) + y^2 = 75 + 25$
$(x^2 + 5)^2 + y^2 = 100$
Center: $(-5, 0)$
Radius: 10

20. $d = \text{radius} \cdot \text{radian angle}$
$d = 3960(42.6°)\dfrac{\pi}{180} = \mathbf{2944.3\ mi}$

21.

	Down	Up
Rate:	y	z
Time:	$\dfrac{x}{y}$	$\dfrac{x}{z}$
Distance:	x	x

$\text{Rate}_{av} = \dfrac{\text{total distance}}{\text{total time}} = \dfrac{x + x}{\dfrac{x}{y} + \dfrac{x}{z}} = \dfrac{2x}{\dfrac{xz + xy}{yz}}$

$= \dfrac{2xyz}{xz + xy} = \dfrac{2yz}{z + y}$

22. $\sin x = \dfrac{\sqrt{3}}{2}$ or $\sin x = \dfrac{1}{2}$
$x = \mathbf{60°, 120°, 210°, 330°}$

23. $\cos x = \sqrt{1 - \cos^2 x}$
$\cos^2 x = 1 - \cos^2 x$
$2\cos^2 x = 1$

$\cos^2 x = \dfrac{1}{2}$

$\cos x = \pm\dfrac{\sqrt{2}}{2}$
$x = 45°, 135°, 225°, 315°$
Check all values of x.
Only $x = \mathbf{45°, 315°}$ satisfy the equation.

24. $\cos 3\theta = \dfrac{\sqrt{3}}{2}$
$3\theta = 30°, 330°, 390°, 690°, 750°, 1050°$
$\theta = \mathbf{10°, 110°, 130°, 230°, 250°, 350°}$

25. $1^3 - \left(\dfrac{\sqrt{3}}{2}\right)^2 = 1 - \dfrac{3}{4} = \dfrac{1}{4}$

26. $\left(-\dfrac{1}{2}\right)^2 + \left(-\dfrac{\sqrt{3}}{2}\right)^2 = \dfrac{1}{4} + \dfrac{3}{4} = 1$

27.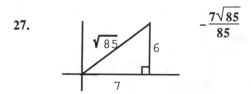
$-\dfrac{7\sqrt{85}}{85}$

28. $\ln x^2 = \ln(6 - x)$
$x^2 + x - 6 = 0$
$(x + 3)(x - 2) = 0$
$x = \mathbf{2}$

29. $\ln x^3 = \ln 64$
$x^3 = 64$
$x = \mathbf{4}$

30. $7^{\log_7 9} + 8^{\log_8 2} = 9 + 2 = \mathbf{11}$

PROBLEM SET 45

1. $\omega = \dfrac{v}{r} = \dfrac{12\,\dfrac{\text{mi}}{\text{hr}} \cdot \dfrac{1\,\text{hr}}{60\,\text{min}}}{13\,\text{in} \cdot \dfrac{1\,\text{ft}}{12\,\text{in}} \cdot \dfrac{1\,\text{mi}}{5280\,\text{ft}}}$

$= \dfrac{(12)(12)(5280)}{(60)(13)}\,\dfrac{\text{rad}}{\text{min}}$

2. $C = mD + b$

$\quad\quad -1350 = -10m - b$

$\underline{(+)\,2200 = \quad 20m + b}$

$\quad\quad\; 850 = \quad 10m$

$m = 85$

$b = 500$

$C = 85D + 500$

$C = 85(5) + 500 = \textbf{\$925}$

3.

	1st	2nd
Rate:	$\dfrac{k}{p}$	$\dfrac{z}{p+6}$
Time:	p	$p+6$
Distance:	k	z

Average rate $= \dfrac{\text{total distance}}{\text{total time}}$

$= \dfrac{k+z}{p+p+6} = \dfrac{k+z}{2p+6}$

Time $= \dfrac{740}{\dfrac{k+2}{2p+6}} = \dfrac{740(2p+6)}{k+z}\,$ hr

4.

	Mumbo	Jumbo
Rate:	a	z
Time:	$\dfrac{m}{a}$	$\dfrac{m}{z}$
Distance:	m	m

$\dfrac{m}{b} - \dfrac{m}{z} = \dfrac{mz - ma}{az}\,$ hr

5. Rate $\cdot$ number $=$ cost

$\left(\dfrac{m\,\text{dollars}}{p^2 k + m}\right) \cdot$ number $= 10{,}000$ dollars

Number $= \dfrac{10{,}000 p^2 k}{m}\,$ cars

6. $\dfrac{9!}{6!\,3!}$

7. $5!$

8. First sketch $y = 3^x$; then reflect about $y = x$ to get $y = \log_3 x$.

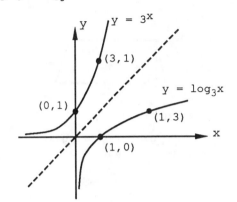

9. (a)

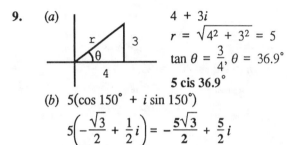

$4 + 3i$

$r = \sqrt{4^2 + 3^2} = 5$

$\tan\theta = \dfrac{3}{4},\ \theta = 36.9°$

$\textbf{5 cis 36.9}°$

(b) $5(\cos 150° + i \sin 150°)$

$5\left(-\dfrac{\sqrt{3}}{2} + \dfrac{1}{2}i\right) = -\dfrac{5\sqrt{3}}{2} + \dfrac{5}{2}i$

10. $6\,\text{cis}\,(40° - 50°) = \textbf{6 cis (-10°)}$

11. $16\,\text{cis}\,(-390°) = 16[\cos(-30°) + i\sin(-30°)]$

$= 16\left(\dfrac{\sqrt{3}}{2} - \dfrac{1}{2}i\right) = \textbf{8}\sqrt{\textbf{3}} - \textbf{8}i$

12. A: $ax + by = c$

B: $dx + fy = g$

Multiply equation A by f, and multiply equation B by $-b$.

$\quad\quad -afx + bfy = \quad cf$

$\underline{(+)-bdx - bfy = -bg}$

$\quad\quad afx - bdx = cf - bg$

$\quad\quad x(af - bd) = cf - bg$

$\quad\quad\quad\quad\quad x = \dfrac{cf - bg}{af - bd}$

13. $a = 3, b = 2, c = 6$

$d = 2, f = -4, g = 12$

$x = \dfrac{6(-4) - 2(12)}{3(-4) - 2(2)} = \dfrac{-24 - 24}{-12 - 4} = \dfrac{-48}{-16} = 3$

14. $\left[2^{1+1}(-1)\left(\dfrac{1}{4}\right)\right] + \left[2^{2+1}\left(\dfrac{1}{3}\right)(-3)\right]$

$+ \left[2^{3+1}(4)(4)\right] = -1 + (8) + 256 = \textbf{247}$

15. $y = -1 + 8 \sin 2(x - 45°)$

16. $y = 3 + 5 \cos \left(x + \dfrac{3\pi}{4} \right)$

17.

$h = 2 \sin 80° = 1.97$

$A = \dfrac{1}{2}(1.97)(4 + 5) = \textbf{8.9 m}^2$

18.

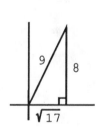

$h = 40 \sin 40° \approx 25.7$

$A_{segment} = A_{sector} - A_{triangle}$

$A_{segment} = \dfrac{140}{360}\pi(40)^2 - \dfrac{1}{2}(40)(25.7)$

$\approx \textbf{1440.5 cm}^2$

19. $(x^2 + 6x + 9) + (y^2 + 4y + 4)$
$-12 + 9 - 4$
$(x + 3)^2 + (y + 2)^2 = 1$
Center: $(-3, -2)$
Radius: 1

20. $(x^2 - 8x + 16) + (y^2 + 6y + 9)$
$= -16 + 16 + 9$
$(x - 4)^2 + (y + 3)^2 = 9$
Center: $(4, -3)$
Radius: 3

21. $\sqrt{(x+4)^2 + (y-6)^2} = \sqrt{(x-6)^2 + (y-8)^2}$
$x^2 + 8x + 16 + y^2 - 12y + 36$
$= x^2 - 12x + 36 + y^2 - 16y + 64$
$20x + 4y - 48 = 0$
$5x + y - 12 = 0$

22. $\dfrac{3}{a} = \dfrac{4}{12}$
$4a = 36$
$a = 9$
$9^2 + 12^2 = b^2 = 225$
$b = 15$

23. $\cos x = \dfrac{1}{2}$ or $\sin x = -\dfrac{1}{2}$
$x = 60°, 300°$ $\qquad x = 210°, 330°$
$x = \textbf{60°, 210°, 300°, 330°}$

24. $\tan x = \sqrt{1 - 2\tan^2 x}$
$\tan^2 x = 1 - 2\tan^2 x$
$3\tan^2 x = 1$
$\tan^2 x = \dfrac{1}{3}$
$\tan x = \pm\dfrac{\sqrt{3}}{3}$
$x = 30°, 150°, 210°, 330°$
Check: $\tan x$ must be positive.
$x = \textbf{30°, 210°}$

25. $\sin 4\theta = \dfrac{1}{2}$
$4\theta = 30°, 150°, 390°, 510°, 750°, 870°,$
$1110°, 1230°$
$\theta = \textbf{7.5°, 37.5°, 97.5°, 127.5°, 187.5°, 217.5°,}$
$\textbf{277.5°, 307.5°}$

26. $\cot^2(240°) - \tan^2(210°)$
$= \left(\dfrac{\sqrt{3}}{3}\right)^2 - \left(\dfrac{\sqrt{3}}{3}\right)^2 = \textbf{0}$

27. $\sin^2(-60°) + \sin^2 60°$
$= \left(-\dfrac{\sqrt{3}}{2}\right)^2 + \left(\dfrac{\sqrt{3}}{2}\right)^2 = \dfrac{3}{4} + \dfrac{3}{4} = \dfrac{\textbf{3}}{\textbf{2}}$

28.
$\dfrac{8\sqrt{17}}{17}$

29. $\ln x^2 = \ln(6x - 8)$
$x^2 = 6x - 8$
$x^2 - 6x + 8 = 0$
$(x - 4)(x - 2) = 0$
$x = \textbf{4, 2}$

30. $\log_{12} x^3 = \log_{12} 16^{3/4} + \log_{12} 4^{3/2}$
$\log_{12} x^3 = \log_{12} 8(8)$
$x^3 = 64$
$x = \textbf{4}$

1. E = cost of 1 dozen eggs
F = cost of 1 pound of flour
A: $3E + 5F = 550$
B: $4E + 2F = 500$
Multiply equation A by 2, and multiply equation B by −5.

$$6E + 10F = 1100$$
$$(+) -20E - 10F = -2500$$
$$\overline{\quad -14E \qquad\qquad = -1400}$$
$$E = 100 = \textbf{\$1.00}$$
$$F = 50 = \textbf{\$0.50}$$

2. T = tens' digit, U = units' digit
$10T + U$ = original number
$10U + T$ = reversed number
A: $T = 1 + U$
B: $10U + T + T = 10T + U$
$\quad 9U - 8T = 0$
Substitute equation A into B.
$9U - 8(1 + U) = 0$
$9U - 8 - 8U = 0$
$U = 8$
$T = 9$
Original number = **98**

3. T = tens' digit
U = units' digit
$10T + U$ = original number
$10U + T$ = reversed number
A: $U = 1 + 2T$
B: $10U + T + 10T + U = 77$
$\quad 11U + 11T = 77$
$\quad U + T = 7$
Substitute equation A into B.
$1 + 2T + T = 7$
$T = 2$
$U = 5$
Original number = **25**

4. $B = 16 + W$
Down: $(16 + W + W)T_D = 48$
$\qquad 16T_D + 2WT_D = 48$
Up: $\quad (16 + W - W)T_D = 32$
$\qquad 16T_D = 32$
$\qquad T_D = 2$
$16(2) + 2W(2) = 48$
$W = \textbf{4 mph}$
$B = \textbf{20 mph}$

5.

	Mickmak	Log
Rate:	$B + W$	W
Distance:	$B - W + 2$	2
Time:	$\dfrac{B - W + 2}{B + W}$	$\dfrac{2}{W} - 1$

$$\frac{B - W + 2}{B + W} = \frac{2}{W} - 1$$
$$\frac{B - W + 2}{B + W} + 1 = \frac{2}{W}$$
$$\frac{B - W + 2 + B + W}{B + W} = \frac{2}{W}$$
$$\frac{2B + 2}{B + W} = \frac{2}{W}$$
$$\frac{B + 1}{B + W} = \frac{1}{W}$$
$$WB + W = B + W$$
$$B(W - 1) = 0$$
$$W = \textbf{1 km/hr}$$

6. $\boxed{5\ |\ 4\ |\ 3} = \textbf{60}$

7. First sketch $y = e^x$; then reflect about $y = x$ to get $y = \log_e x = \ln x$.

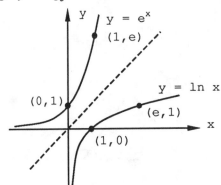

8. $5 + 12i$
$r = \sqrt{5^2 + 12^2} = 13$
$\tan \theta = \dfrac{12}{5}$
$\theta = 67.4°$
$\textbf{13 cis 67.4°}$

9. $8 \operatorname{cis} 60° = 8(\cos 60° + i \sin 60°)$
$= 8\left(\dfrac{1}{2} + \dfrac{\sqrt{3}}{2} i\right) = \textbf{4} + \textbf{4}i\sqrt{\textbf{3}}$

10. $6 \operatorname{cis}(-150°) = 6[\cos(-150°) + i \sin(-150°)]$
$= 6\left(-\dfrac{\sqrt{3}}{2} - \dfrac{1}{2} i\right) = \textbf{−3}\sqrt{\textbf{3}} - \textbf{3}i$

11. A: $cx + fy = a$
    B: $dx + gy = b$
    Multiply equation A by d, and multiply equation B by $-c$.

    $$
    \begin{aligned}
    dcx \;+\; dfy &= ad \\
    (+)\,-dcx \;-\; cgy &= -bc \\
    \hline
    dfy - cgy &= af - bc \\
    y(df - cg) &= ad - bc
    \end{aligned}
    $$

    $$y = \frac{ad - bc}{df - cg}$$

12. $c = 2, f = -3, a = 5$
    $d = 3, g = 2, b = 7$
    $$y = \frac{5(3) - 7(2)}{3(-3) - 2(2)} = \frac{15 - 14}{-9 - 4} = -\frac{1}{13}$$

13. $\left(2^0 x_2 - y_1^2\right) + \left(2^1 x_3 - y_2^2\right) + \left(2^2 x_4 - y_3^2\right)$
    $= [1(2) - 0^2] + \left[2\left(\frac{1}{4}\right) - (-2)^2\right]$
    $+ [4(-2) - 3^2]$
    $= 2 + \left(-\frac{7}{2}\right) + (-17) = -\frac{37}{2}$

14. $y = 6 + 4\sin\dfrac{2}{3}x$

15. $y = 3 + 5\cos\dfrac{1}{2}(x - 270°)$

16.

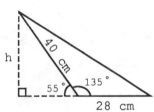

    Area $= \dfrac{1}{2}(28)(40\sin 55°) = 396$ cm^2
    $396\text{ cm}^2 \cdot \dfrac{1^2\,\text{m}^2}{100^2\,\text{cm}^2} = \dfrac{396}{100^2}\,\text{m}^2$

17. $x = \dfrac{4 \pm \sqrt{16 - 4(1)(6)}}{2(1)} = \dfrac{4 \pm \sqrt{-8}}{2}$
    $= \dfrac{4 \pm 2i\sqrt{2}}{2} = 2 \pm i\sqrt{2}$
    $= \left[x - \left(2 + i\sqrt{2}\right)\right]\left[x - \left(2 - i\sqrt{2}\right)\right]$

18. $(x^2 - 4x + 4) + (y^2 + 6y + 9)$
    $= 3 + 4 + 9 = 16$
    $(x - 2)^2 + (y + 3)^2 = 16$
    Center: (2, –3)
    Radius: 4

19. **D**

20. $\tan\theta + 1 = 0$ or $\cos\theta - \dfrac{1}{2} = 0$
    $\tan\theta = -1$ $\qquad\cos\theta = \dfrac{1}{2}$
    $\theta = 135°, 315°$ $\qquad\theta = 60°, 300°$
    $\boldsymbol{\theta = 60°, 135°, 300°, 315°}$

21. $\sqrt{\sin\theta} = \dfrac{\sqrt{2}}{2}$
    $\sin\theta = \dfrac{1}{2}$
    $\boldsymbol{\theta = 30°, 150°}$

22. $\cos 3\theta = \dfrac{1}{2}$
    $3\theta = 60°, 300°, 420°, 660°, 780°, 1020°$
    $\boldsymbol{\theta = 20°, 100°, 140°, 220°, 260°, 340°}$

23. $\tan^2(-45°) - \sec^2(-45°) = 1 - 2 = -1$

24. $\sin^2 390° + \cos^2 390°$
    $= \left(\dfrac{1}{2}\right)^2 + \left(\dfrac{\sqrt{3}}{2}\right)^2 = \dfrac{1}{4} + \dfrac{3}{4} = 1$

25. $\text{Arcsin}\left(-\dfrac{1}{2}\right) = -30°$

26. $\ln x(x) = \ln(4x - 3)$
    $x^2 = 4x - 3$
    $x^2 - 4x + 3 = 0$
    $(x - 3)(x - 1) = 0$
    $x = 3, 1$

27. $\log_7 x^3 = \log_7 \dfrac{16}{2}$
    $x^3 = 8$
    $x = 2$

28. $10^{-5.62}$
    $$
    \begin{aligned}
    6.00 &- 6 \\
    (+)\,-5.62 & \\
    \hline
    0.38 &- 6
    \end{aligned}
    $$
    2.4×10^{-6}

29. $e^2 \approx 3^2 = 9$

30. $e^{-2} \approx 3^{-2} = \dfrac{1}{9}$

Advanced Mathematics

1. A: $4R + 3B = 29$
   B: $5B + 2W = 29$
   C: $6R + 3W = 51$
   Multiply equation A by 5, equation B by -3, and equation C by 2.

   $$\begin{array}{rcl} 20R + 15B & = & 145 \\ -\,15B - 6W & = & -87 \\ \hline 20R - 6W & = & 58 \\ 12R + 6W & = & 102 \\ \hline 32R & = & 160 \end{array}$$

   $R = \textbf{5 lb}$
   $B = \textbf{3 lb}$
   $W = \textbf{7 lb}$

2. H = hundreds' digit
   T = tens' digit
   U = units' digit
   $100H + 10T + U$ = original number
   $100U + 10T + U$ = reversed number
   A: $H + T + U = 11$
   B: $U = 2 + T$
   C: $100U + 10T + H + 100H$
   $\quad + 10T + U = 1030$
   $\quad 101U + 20T + 101H = 1030$
   Substitute equation B into A.
   $H + T + 2 + T = 11$
   $H + 2T = 9$
   $H = 9 - 2T$
   Substitute equation B into C.
   $101(2 + T) + 20T + 101H = 1030$
   $121T + 101H = 828$
   $121T + 101(9 - 2T) = 828$
   $121T - 202T = 828 - 909$
   $81T = 81$
   $T = 1, H = 7, U = 3$
   Original number = **713**

3. $x = \dfrac{kyz^2}{\sqrt{w}} = \dfrac{k(2y)\left(\frac{1}{2}z\right)^2}{\sqrt{4w}} = \dfrac{k(2y)\left(\frac{1}{4}z^2\right)}{2\sqrt{w}}$

   $= \dfrac{\frac{1}{2}kyz^2}{2\sqrt{w}} = \dfrac{1}{4}\dfrac{kyz^2}{\sqrt{w}}$

   x is multiplied by $\dfrac{1}{4}$

4.

% sugar	70%		0%		40%
amount (ml)	100	+	x	=	100+x

   $70(100) + 0x = 40(100 + x)$
   $7000 = 4000 + 40x$
   $3000 = 40x$
   $x = \textbf{75 ml}$

5.

	Rate
Big guy:	$\dfrac{7 \text{ jobs}}{2 \text{ hr}}$
Little guy:	$\dfrac{5 \text{ jobs}}{3 \text{ hr}}$

   T = time together
   $R_B T_B + R_L T_L = 31$
   $\dfrac{7}{2}T + \dfrac{5}{3}T = 31$
   $21T + 10T = 186$
   $T = \textbf{6 hr}$

6. $\dfrac{10!}{3!\ 5!\ 2!}$

7. $\angle A = 180° - \angle C = 180° - 105°$
   $\angle A = \textbf{75°}$
   $\angle B = \angle C = \textbf{105°}$

8. Draw $l \parallel m$. $\angle A = \angle A'$ and $\angle C = \angle C'$ because alt. int. angles are equal. $\angle A' + \angle B' + \angle C' = 180°$ because straight angles are equal to 180°. $\angle A + \angle B + \angle C = 180°$ by substitution.

9.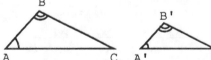

   $\angle A + \angle B + \angle C = 180°$ because the sum of the angles of a triangle is equal to 180°. $\angle A + \angle B + \angle C = \angle A + \angle B + \angle D$ by substitution. $\angle C = \angle D$ by subtraction.

10. $\angle A + \angle B + \angle C = 180°$ because the sum of the angles of a triangle is equal to 180°. $\angle A + \angle A' = 180°$ because straight angles are equal to 180°. $\angle A + \angle B + \angle C = \angle A + \angle A'$ by substitution. $\angle B + \angle C = \angle A'$ by subtraction.

11. $2x + 60 = 4x - 10 + 2x - 5$
$75 = 4x$
$x = \textbf{18.75}$

12. First sketch $y = \left(\dfrac{1}{2}\right)^y$; then reflect about
$y = x$ to get $y = \log_{1/2} x$.

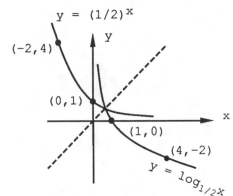

13. $r = \sqrt{6^2 + (-5)^2} \approx 7.8$
$\tan \theta = -\dfrac{5}{6}$
$\theta \approx -39.8°$
7.8 cis (−39.8°)

14. $12 \text{ cis } 45° = 12(\cos 45° + i \sin 45°)$
$12\left(\dfrac{\sqrt{2}}{2} + i\dfrac{\sqrt{2}}{2}\right) = \textbf{6}\sqrt{\textbf{2}} + \textbf{6}i\sqrt{\textbf{2}}$

15. A: $hx + gy = a$
B: $mx + ny = b$
Multiply equation A by n, and multiply
equation B by $-g$.
$\quad nhx + ngy = na$
$\underline{(+)\ -gmx - ngy = -bg}$
$\quad\quad nhx - gmx = na - bg$
$\quad\quad x(nh - gm) = na - bg$
$$x = \dfrac{na - bg}{nh - gm}$$

16. $y = 1 + 5\sin\dfrac{1}{3}(x - 135°)$

17. $y = -5 + 4\cos\dfrac{2}{3}\left(x + \dfrac{\pi}{2}\right)$

18.

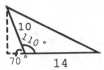

$h = 10 \sin 70° \approx 9.4$
$A = \dfrac{1}{2}(14)(9.4) = \textbf{65.8 cm}^2$

19. $(x^2 - 10x + 25) + (y^2 + 2y + 1)$
$= -22 + 25 + 1 = 4$
$(x - 5)^2 + (y + 1)^2 = 4$
Center: (5, −1)
Radius: 2

20. $\dfrac{x}{2} = \dfrac{6}{3}$
$3x = 12$
$x = \textbf{4}$

21. $\sin x = \dfrac{\sqrt{2}}{2}$ or $\cos x = \dfrac{\sqrt{2}}{2}$
$x = \textbf{45°, 135°, 315°}$

22. $\dfrac{1 - \cos x}{2} = 1$
$1 - \cos x = 2$
$\cos x = -1$
$x = \textbf{180°}$

23. $2\tan 4\theta = 0$
$\tan 4\theta = 0$
$4\theta = 0°, 180°, 360°, 540°, 720°, 900°, 1080°,$
$1260°$
$\theta = \textbf{0°, 45°, 90°, 135°, 180°, 225°, 270°, 315°}$

24. $\left(\sqrt{3}\right)^2 - 2^2 = 3 - 4 = \textbf{−1}$

25.

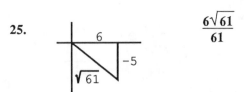

$\dfrac{6\sqrt{61}}{61}$

26. $\tan(-480°)\cot(-480°)$
$= \tan(-120°)\cot(-120°)$
$= \left(\sqrt{3}\right)\left(\dfrac{\sqrt{3}}{3}\right) = \textbf{1}$

27. $\ln \dfrac{x^3}{x} = \ln (2x + 2)(x + 1)$

$x^2 = 2x^2 + 4x + 2$

$x^2 + 4x + 2 = 0$

$x = \dfrac{-4 \pm \sqrt{16 - 4(1)(2)}}{2(1)} = \dfrac{-4 \pm 2\sqrt{2}}{2}$

$= -2 \pm \sqrt{2} \approx -0.59, -3.4$

No solution

28. $3^{\log_3 (28/4)} = 3^{\log_3 7} = \mathbf{7}$

29. $e \approx 3$

$3^3 = \mathbf{27}$

30. $10^{-5.62}$

$6.00\ -\ 6$

$\underline{(+)\ -5.62}$

$0.38\ -\ 6$

$\mathbf{2.4 \times 10^{-6}}$

PROBLEM SET 48

1. $p = \dfrac{k\sqrt{m}y^2}{x^2}$

$p = \dfrac{k\sqrt{4m}(2y)^2}{\left(\frac{1}{2}x\right)^2} = \dfrac{8k\sqrt{m}y^2}{\frac{1}{4}x^2} = 32\dfrac{k\sqrt{m}y^2}{x^2}$

p is multiplied by 32

2.

	1st	2nd
Distance:	x	x
Time:	k	$k - 20$
Rate:	$\dfrac{x}{k}$	$\dfrac{x}{k-20}\ \dfrac{\text{mi}}{\text{min}}$

3. $R_G T_G = 160$

$R_G(4) = 160$

$R_G = \mathbf{40\ mph}$

$(2)R_B = 160$

$R_B = \mathbf{80\ mph}$

4. $(3 * 2)\ \#\ 4 = [\,2(3) - 2\,]\ \#\ 4$

$= 4\ \#\ 4 = \dfrac{4}{4} + 4 = \mathbf{5}$

5. 1st year $= x$

2nd year $= x + 0.2x = 1.2x$

3rd year $= 1.2x + 0.2(1.2x) = 1.44x$

$x + 1.2x + 1.44x = 29120$

$3.64x = 29120$

$x = \mathbf{\$8000}$

6. $A = $ angle

$180° - A = $ supplement

$90° - A = $ complement

$4(90° - A) = 2(180° - A) - 40°$

$360° - 4A = 360° - 2A - 40°$

$2A = 40°$

$A = \mathbf{20°}$

7. $\begin{vmatrix} -4 & 6 \\ 5 & 2 \end{vmatrix} = -8 - 30 = \mathbf{-38}$

8. $\begin{vmatrix} x & 2 \\ 3 & x-1 \end{vmatrix} = 4$

$x(x - 1) - 6 = 4$

$x^2 - x - 10 = 0$

$x = \dfrac{-1 \pm \sqrt{1 - 4(1)(-10)}}{2(1)}$

$x = \dfrac{-1 \pm \sqrt{41}}{2}$

9. $\angle B = 180° - \angle A = 180° - 110°$

$\angle B = \mathbf{70°}$

$\angle C = \angle A = \mathbf{110°}$

10. Draw $l \parallel m$. $\angle A = \angle A'$ and $\angle C = \angle C'$ because alt. int. angles are equal. $\angle A' + \angle B' + \angle C' = 180°$ because straight angles are equal to $180°$. $\angle A + \angle B + \angle C = 180°$ by substitution.

11. $\angle A + \angle B + \angle C = 180°$ because the sum of the angles of a triangle is equal to $180°$. $\angle A + \angle A' = 180°$ because straight angles are equal to $180°$. $\angle A + \angle B + \angle C = \angle A + \angle A'$ by substitution. $\angle B + \angle C = \angle A'$ by subtraction.

12. $2a + 3a - 30° = 3a + 30°$
$2a = 60°$
$a = 30°$

13. First sketch $y = \left(\dfrac{1}{3}\right)^y$; then reflect about
$y = x$ to get $y = \log_{1/3} x$.

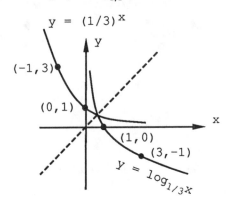

$y = (1/3)^x$

$(-1,3)$

$(0,1)$

$(1,0)$

$(3,-1)$

$y = \log_{1/3} x$

14. $12 \operatorname{cis} 60° = 12(\cos 60° + i \sin 60°)$
$12\left(\dfrac{1}{2} + \dfrac{\sqrt{3}}{2}i\right) = \mathbf{6 + 6i\sqrt{3}}$

15. (a) $r = \sqrt{6^2 + 2^2} \approx 6.3$
$\tan\theta = \dfrac{-2}{b}$
$\theta \approx -18.4°$
$\mathbf{6.3 \operatorname{cis} (-18.4°)}$

(b) $5(\cos 585° + i \sin 585°)$
$= 5(\cos 225° + i \sin 225°)$
$= 5\left[-\dfrac{\sqrt{2}}{2} + \left(-\dfrac{\sqrt{2}}{2}\right)i\right] = -\dfrac{5\sqrt{2}}{2} - \dfrac{5i\sqrt{2}}{2}$

16. A: $ax + by = c$
B: $px + qy = d$
Multiply equation A by p, and multiply
equation B by $-a$.
$\begin{array}{r} apx + pby = pc \\ (+)\,-apx - aqy = -ad \\ \hline pby - aqy = pc - ad \end{array}$
$y(pb - aq) = pc - ad$
$y = \dfrac{pc - ad}{pb - aq}$

17. Coefficient $k = \dfrac{2\pi}{\pi} = 2$
$y = 5 + 4\cos 2\left(x + \dfrac{3\pi}{8}\right)$

18. Coefficient $k = \dfrac{360°}{120°} = 3$
$y = -3 + 10 \sin 3(x - 20°)$

19.

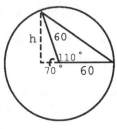

h 60
110°
70° 60

$\sin 60° = \dfrac{h}{60}$
$h = 60 \sin 60° \approx 52$
$A_{\text{segment}} = A_{\text{sector}} - A_{\text{triangle}}$
$= \dfrac{110}{360}\pi(60)^2 - \dfrac{1}{2}(60)(52) = \mathbf{1764.3 \text{ cm}^2}$

20. $\left(x^2 + x + \dfrac{1}{4}\right) + \left(y^2 + y + \dfrac{1}{4}\right)$
$= \dfrac{7}{2} + \dfrac{1}{4} + \dfrac{1}{4} = 4$
$\left(x + \dfrac{1}{2}\right)^2 + \left(y + \dfrac{1}{2}\right)^2 = 4$
Center: $\left(-\dfrac{1}{2}, -\dfrac{1}{2}\right)$
Radius: 2

21. $\dfrac{a}{2} = \dfrac{10}{a}$
$a^2 = 20$
$a = 2\sqrt{5}$
$\dfrac{b}{8} = \dfrac{10}{b}$
$b^2 = 80$
$b = 4\sqrt{5}$

22. $\begin{array}{ll} \tan\theta - \sqrt{3} = 0 & \tan\theta + \sqrt{3} = 0 \\ \tan\theta = \sqrt{3} & \tan\theta = -\sqrt{3} \\ \theta = 60°, 240° & \theta = 120°, 300° \end{array}$
$\theta = \mathbf{60°, 120°, 240°, 300°}$

23. $\sin x(1 + 2\sin x) = 0$
$\begin{array}{ll} \sin x = 0 & 1 + 2\sin x = 0 \\ x = 0°, 180° & \sin x = (1,2) \\ & x = 210°, 330° \end{array}$
$x = \mathbf{0°, 180°, 210°, 330°}$

24. $\tan^2 x = 3$
$\tan x = \pm\sqrt{3}$
$x = \mathbf{60°, 120°, 240°, 300°}$

25. $\cot^2(-150°) - \csc^2(-150°)$

$= \left(\sqrt{3}\right)^2 - (-2)^2 = 3 - 4 = -1$

26. $\sin^2(-135°) + \cos^2(-135°)$

$= \left(-\dfrac{\sqrt{2}}{2}\right)^2 + \left(-\dfrac{\sqrt{2}}{2}\right)^2 = \dfrac{1}{2} + \dfrac{1}{2} = 1$

27. Let $M = b^a$ Let $N = b^c$
$\log_b M = a$ $\log_b N = c$

$\log_b \dfrac{M}{N} = \log_b M - \log_b N$

$\log_b \dfrac{b^a}{b^c} = \log_b b^{a-c} = a - c$

$= \log_b M - \log_b N$

28. $\log_4 8^{2/3} - \log_4 x^2 = \log_4 4$

$\log_4 \dfrac{4}{x^2} = \log_4 4$

$\dfrac{4}{x^2} = 4$

$4x^2 = 4$

$x = 1$

29. $e^{-1} \approx 3^{-1} = \dfrac{1}{3}$

30. $10^{-8.12}$

$$\begin{array}{r} 9.00 - 9 \\ (+)\,-8.12 \\ \hline 0.88 - 9 \end{array}$$

$= 7.6 \times 10^{-9}$

PROBLEM SET 49

1. $(8 * 2) \# 8$
$(8 * 2) = 4(8) - 2(2) = 28$
$28 \# 8 = \dfrac{28}{8} - 8 = \dfrac{17}{2} - 8 = -\dfrac{9}{2}$

2. A: $l + w + h = 150$
B: $2(w + h) = l$
C: $2w = l + h$

$$\begin{array}{r} l + w + h = 150 \\ -l + 2w + 2h = 0 \\ \hline 3w + 3h = 150 \end{array}$$

$$\begin{array}{r} w + h = 50 \\ 2w - h = 1 \\ \hline 3w = 51 \\ w = 17 \text{ cm} \\ l = 100 \text{ cm} \\ h = 33 \text{ cm} \end{array}$$

3. $x = \dfrac{ky^2}{z\sqrt{w}}$

$x = \dfrac{k(3y)^2}{(2z)\sqrt{4w}} = \dfrac{9}{4}\dfrac{ky^2}{z\sqrt{w}}$

x is multiplied by $\dfrac{9}{4}$

4. $B = 5W$
$T_D = T_u + 2$
Upstream: $(5W - W)T_u = 64$
            $4WT_u = 64$
            $WT_u = 16$

Downstream:
            $(5W + W)(T_u + 2) = 144$
            $6WT_u + 12W = 144$
            $6(16) + 12W = 144$

$W = 4$ mph
$B = 20$ mph

5. A: $4(R + B) = 3W + 3$
       $4R + 4B - 3W = 3$
B: $5(B + W) = 8R + 13$
       $-8R + 5B + 5W = 13$
C: $B + 5 = W$
Multiply equation A by 2.

$$\begin{array}{r} 8R + 8B - 6W = 6 \\ -8R + 5B + 5W = 13 \\ \hline 13B - W = 19 \\ -B + W = 5 \\ \hline 12B = 24 \end{array}$$

$B = 2$
$R = 4$
$W = 7$

6.

| O | 3 | M | 2 | 1 | $= 6$ |

$\boxed{O\ 3\ M\ 2\ 1} = 6$
$\boxed{M\ 3\ O\ 2\ 1} = 6$
$\boxed{3\ O\ 2\ M\ 1} = 6$
$\boxed{3\ M\ 2\ O\ 1} = 6$
$\boxed{3\ 2\ O\ 1\ M} = 6$
$\boxed{3\ 2\ M\ 1\ O} = 6$
$\boxed{O\ 3\ 2\ M\ 1} = 6$
$\boxed{M\ 3\ 2\ O\ 1} = 6$
$\boxed{O\ 3\ 2\ 1\ M} = 6$
$\boxed{M\ 3\ 2\ 1\ O} = 6$
$\boxed{3\ O\ 2\ 1\ M} = 6$
$\boxed{3\ M\ 2\ 1\ O} = 6$
$$\overline{\hspace{2cm}72}$$

7. $a^2 = 16 \qquad a = 4$
$b^2 = 9 \qquad b = 3$

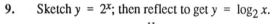

8. $\dfrac{9x^2}{36} + \dfrac{4y^2}{36} = \dfrac{36}{36}$
$\dfrac{x^2}{4} + \dfrac{y^2}{9} = 1$
$a = 3$
$b = 2$

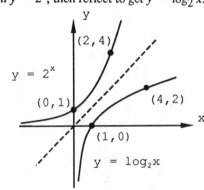

9. Sketch $y = 2^x$; then reflect to get $y = \log_2 x$.

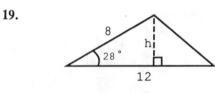

10. $r = \sqrt{7^2 + 8^2} \approx 10.6$
$\tan \theta = \dfrac{8}{7}$
$\theta \approx 48.8°$
10.6 cis 48.8°

11. $6 \operatorname{cis}(-30°) = 6[\cos(-30°) + i \sin(-30°)]$
$$= 6\left[\frac{\sqrt{3}}{2} + \left(-\frac{1}{2}i\right)\right] = 3\sqrt{3} - 3i$$

12. $(x + 1)(x - 1) - 3 = 0$
$x^2 - 1 = 3$
$x^2 = 4$
$x = \pm\,\mathbf{2}$

13. $\angle A + \angle B + \angle C = 180°$ because the sum of the angles of a triangle is equal to $180°$.
$\angle A + \angle B + \angle C = \angle A + \angle B + \angle D$ by substitution. $\angle C = \angle D$ by subtraction.

14. $\angle A + \angle B + \angle C = 180°$ because the sum of the angles of a triangle is equal to $180°$.
$\angle A + \angle A' = 180°$ because straight angles are equal to $180°$. $\angle A + \angle B + \angle C = \angle A + \angle A'$ by substitution. $\angle B + \angle C = \angle A'$ by subtraction.

15. $5c + 10 = 3c + 3c - 10$
$c = \mathbf{20}$

16. $80\,\dfrac{\text{km}}{\text{hr}} \cdot \dfrac{1000\text{ m}}{1\text{ km}} \cdot \dfrac{100\text{ cm}}{1\text{ m}} \cdot \dfrac{1\text{ in}}{2.54\text{ cm}}$
$\cdot \dfrac{1\text{ ft}}{12\text{ in}} \cdot \dfrac{1\text{ mi}}{5280\text{ ft}} = \dfrac{(80)(1000)(100)}{(2.54)(12)(5280)}\text{ mph}$

17. $y = -3 + 8\cos\dfrac{1}{4}(x - 180°)$

18. $y = 1 + 2\sin\dfrac{1}{2}\left(x + \dfrac{3\pi}{2}\right)$

19.

(triangle with side 8, angle 28°, height h, base 12)

$h = 8\sin 28° \approx 3.76$
$A = \dfrac{1}{2}(12)(3.76) = \mathbf{22.6\ cm^2}$

20. $(x^2 + 8x + 16) + (y^2 - 12y + 36)$
$= -43 + 16 + 36 = 9$
$(x + 4)^2 + (y - 6)^2 = 9$
Center: $(-4, 6)$
Radius: 3

21. $\dfrac{a}{3} = \dfrac{12}{a}$ $a^2 = 36$ $a = \mathbf{6}$

     $\dfrac{b}{9} = \dfrac{12}{b}$ $b^2 = 108$ $b = \mathbf{6\sqrt{3}}$

22. $2\cos\theta + 1 = 0$ $2\sin\theta + \sqrt{2} = 0$

     $\cos\theta = -\dfrac{1}{2}$ $\sin\theta = -\dfrac{\sqrt{2}}{2}$

     $\theta = 120°, 240°$ $\theta = 225°, 315°$

     $\theta = \mathbf{120°, 225°, 240°, 315°}$

23. $\cot^2 x = 3$

     $\cot x = \pm\sqrt{3}$

     $x = \mathbf{30°, 150°, 210°, 330°}$

24. $\cot x\,(\cot x + 1) = 0$

     $\cot x = 0$ or $\cot x = -1$

     $x = 90°, 270°$ $x = 135°, 315°$

     $x = \mathbf{90°, 135°, 270°, 315°}$

25. $\tan^2(-225°) - \sec^2(-225°) = 1 - 2 = \mathbf{-1}$

26. $\sin^2(-120°) + \cos^2(-120°)$

     $= \left(-\dfrac{\sqrt{3}}{2}\right)^2 + \left(-\dfrac{1}{2}\right)^2 = \dfrac{3}{4} + \dfrac{1}{4} = \mathbf{1}$

27. $\log_8 16^{3/4} + \log_8 x^2 = \log_8 x + \log_8 8$

     $\log_8(8x^2) = \log_8 8x$

     $8x^2 = 8x$

     $8x^2 - 8x = 0$

     $8x(x - 1) = 0$

     $x = \mathbf{1}$

28. $8^{\log_8 16/2} = 8^{\log_8 8} = \mathbf{8}$

29. $e^{-2} \approx 3^{-2} = \dfrac{1}{9}$

30.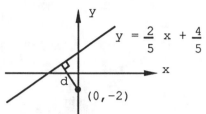

Find the equation of the line $\perp$ to $y = \dfrac{2}{5}x + \dfrac{4}{5}$

that passes through $(0, -2)$.

$m_\perp = -\dfrac{5}{2}$

$y = -\dfrac{5}{2}x + b$

$-2 = -\dfrac{5}{2}(0) + b$

$b = -2$

$y = -\dfrac{5}{2}x - 2$

Solve $y = -\dfrac{5}{2}x - 2$ and $y = \dfrac{2}{5}x + \dfrac{4}{5}$

simultaneously.

$\dfrac{2}{5}x + \dfrac{4}{5} = -\dfrac{5}{2}x - 2$

$4x + 8 = -25x - 20$

$29x = -28$

$x = -\dfrac{28}{29}$

$y = \dfrac{12}{29}$

$(x, y) = \left(-\dfrac{28}{29}, \dfrac{12}{29}\right)$

$d = \sqrt{\left(0 + \dfrac{28}{29}\right)^2 + \left(-2 - \dfrac{12}{29}\right)^2}$

$= \sqrt{\dfrac{784 + 4900}{841}} \approx \mathbf{2.6}$

PROBLEM SET 50

1. $4 * (4 \# 1)$

     $4 * \left[\dfrac{4}{2} - 2(1)\right]$

     $4 * 0$

     $2(4)^2 - 0 = \mathbf{32}$

2. $\dfrac{B}{Q} = \dfrac{14}{1}$

     $B = 14Q$

     $B + Q = 2550$

     $14Q + Q = 2550$

     $15Q = 2550$

     $Q = 170$

     $B = \mathbf{2380}$

3.

	Old	New
Distance:	y	y
Rate:	$\dfrac{y}{m}$	?
Time:	m	$m - 2$

New rate $= \dfrac{y}{m - 2} \dfrac{\text{yd}}{\text{min}}$

4. H = hundreds' digit
T = tens' digit
U = units' digit
A: $T + U = 7$
B: $H + T = 5$
C: $T = 4H$
Substitute equation C into B.
$H + 4H = 5$
$H = 1, T = 4, U = 3$
$N = \mathbf{143}$

5. $10(90° - A) = 3(180° - A) + 318°$
$900° - 10A = 540° - 3A + 318°$
$-7A = -42°$
$A = \mathbf{6°}$

6. $\dfrac{9!}{2!\,2!} = \mathbf{90{,}720}$

7. $A = 180° - 40° - 30° = 110°$

$\dfrac{8}{\sin 30°} = \dfrac{m}{\sin 40°}$

$m = \dfrac{8 \sin 40°}{\sin 30°} \approx \mathbf{10.3}$

$\dfrac{8}{\sin 30°} = \dfrac{a}{\sin 110°}$

$a = \dfrac{8 \sin 110°}{\sin 30°} \approx \mathbf{15.0}$

8. $B = 180° - 130° - 22° = \mathbf{28°}$

$\dfrac{c}{\sin 22°} = \dfrac{12}{\sin 130°}$

$c = \dfrac{12(0.3746)}{0.7660} \approx \mathbf{5.87}$

$\dfrac{b}{\sin 28°} = \dfrac{12}{\sin 130°}$

$b = \dfrac{12(0.4695)}{0.7660} \approx \mathbf{7.36}$

9. $r = \sqrt{3^2 + 4^2} = 5$

$\tan \theta = \dfrac{4}{3}$

$\theta \approx 53°$

$\mathbf{5 \text{ cis } 53°}$

10. $a = 5$
$b = 4$

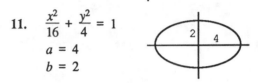

11. $\dfrac{x^2}{16} + \dfrac{y^2}{4} = 1$

$a = 4$
$b = 2$

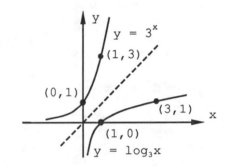

12.   Sketch $y = 3^x$; then reflect for $y = \log_3 x$.

13. $18 \text{ cis } 60° = 18(\cos 60° + i \sin 60°)$

$= 18\left(\dfrac{1}{2} + i\dfrac{\sqrt{3}}{2}\right) = \mathbf{9 + 9\sqrt{3}\,i}$

14. $a(a - 1) - 2 = 4$
$a^2 - a - 6 = 0$
$(a - 3)(a + 2) = 0$
$a = \mathbf{3, -2}$

15.   Refer to Problem Set 47, problem 8.

16.   Refer to Problem Set 47, problem 10.

17. $5x - 5 = 2x + 4x - 20$
$x = \mathbf{15}$

18. $A_{\text{segment}} = A_{\text{sector}} - A_{\text{triangle}}$

$A_{\text{segment}} = \dfrac{130}{360}\pi(80)^2 - \dfrac{1}{2}(80)(61.3)$

$= \mathbf{4809.2 \text{ cm}^2}$

19. $y = -3 + 5 \cos \dfrac{1}{2}\left(x - \dfrac{3\pi}{2}\right)$

20. $y = -10 + 20 \sin 2x$

21. $x^2 + y^2 + 4y + 4 = 5 + 4$
$x^2 + (y + 2)^2 = 9$
Center: $(0, -2)$
Radius: 3

22. $\dfrac{a}{4} = \dfrac{12}{a}$　　$a^2 = 48$　　$a = 4\sqrt{3}$
$\dfrac{b}{8} = \dfrac{12}{b}$　　$b^2 = 96$　　$b = 4\sqrt{6}$

23. $\sin^2 x \cos x - \cos x = 0$
$\cos x (\sin^2 - 1) = 0$

$\cos x = 0$　　　　　$\sin^2 x - 1 = 0$
$x = 90°, 270°$　　　$\sin^2 x = 1$
　　　　　　　　　　$\sin x = \pm 1$

$x = 90°, 270°$　　　$x = -90°, 90°$
$x = 90°, 270°$

24. $(2 \sin t - 1)(\sin t + 1) = 0$
$2 \sin t - 1 = 0$　　　　$\sin t + 1 = 0$
$\sin t = \dfrac{1}{2}$　　　　　$\sin t = -1$
$t = 30°, 150°$　　　　　$t = 270°$
$t = 30°, 150°, 270°$

25. $\sqrt{3} \tan 3\theta = 1$
$\tan 3\theta = \dfrac{1}{\sqrt{3}} = \dfrac{\sqrt{3}}{3}$
$3\theta = 30°, 210°, 390°, 570°, 750°, 930°$
$\theta = 10°, 70°, 130°, 190°, 250°, 310°$

26. $\sin^2\left(-\dfrac{2\pi}{3}\right) + \cos^2\left(-\dfrac{2\pi}{3}\right)$
$= \left(-\dfrac{\sqrt{3}}{2}\right)^2 + \left(-\dfrac{1}{2}\right)^2 = \dfrac{3}{4} + \dfrac{1}{4} = 1$

27. $0^3 - \left(-\sqrt{2}\right)^2 + 2^2 = 2$

28. $\log_7 x^2 + \log_7 49 = 2$
$\log_7 49x^2 = 2$
$49x^2 = 49$
$x^2 = 1$
$x = 1$

29. $\log_8 16^{1/2} + \log_8 x = \log_8 (x + 1)^2$
$\log_8 4x = \log_8 (x + 1)^2$
$4x = (x + 1)^2$
$4x = x^2 + 2x + 1$
$x^2 - 2x + 1 = 0$
$(x - 1)^2 = 0$
$x = 1$

30. $e^3 \approx 3^3 = 27$

PROBLEM SET 51

1. $(6 * 3) \# 3$
$(6 * 3) = 3(6) - 3 = 15$
$15 \# 3 = \dfrac{15}{2} + 2(3) = \dfrac{27}{2}$

2. $S =$ son
$W =$ woman $= 3S$
$GF =$ father $= 2W = 2(3S) = 6S$

3.

	Original	New
Total:	1000	1000
Men:	M	$M - 5$
Each:	$\dfrac{1000}{M}$	$\dfrac{1000}{M - 5}$

$\dfrac{1000}{M - 5} - \dfrac{1000}{M} = \dfrac{\$5000}{M(M - 5)}$

4. $h =$ total homework
$w =$ homework completed
$\dfrac{h - w}{h} =$ amount of homework remaining

5. $\dfrac{x + 2}{x + 1}$

6. $\dfrac{7!}{3! \, 2! \, 2!} = 210$

7. $180(n - 2) = 180(7 - 2) = 180(5) = 900°$

8. The sum of the exterior angles of any polygon is $360°$.

9.

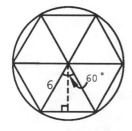

Central angle $= \dfrac{360°}{6} = 60°$

$h = 6 \sin 60° = 3\sqrt{3}$

$A_{\text{triangle}} = \dfrac{1}{2}(6)\left(3\sqrt{3}\right) = 9\sqrt{3}$

$A_{\text{hexagon}} = 6\left(9\sqrt{3}\right) = 54\sqrt{3} \approx \mathbf{93.5}$

10.

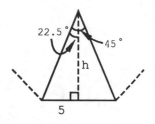

Central angle $= \dfrac{360°}{8} = 45°$

$\tan 22.5° = \dfrac{5}{h}$

$h = \dfrac{5}{\tan 22.5°} \approx 12.07$

$A_{\text{triangle}} = \dfrac{1}{2}(10)(12.07) = 60.35$

$A_{\text{octagon}} = 60.35(8) = \mathbf{482.8}$

11. $\dfrac{3^2}{1^2} = \dfrac{9}{1}$

Ratio $= \mathbf{9 : 1}$

12. $A = 180° - 130° - 30° = \mathbf{20°}$

$\dfrac{a}{\sin 20°} = \dfrac{15}{\sin 130°}$

$a = \dfrac{15 \sin 20°}{\sin 130°} \approx \mathbf{6.7}$

$\dfrac{b}{\sin 30°} = \dfrac{15}{\sin 130°}$

$b = \dfrac{15 \sin 30°}{\sin 130°} \approx \mathbf{9.8}$

13. $\dfrac{9x^2}{36} + \dfrac{4y^2}{36} = 1$

$\dfrac{x^2}{4} + \dfrac{y^2}{4} = 1$

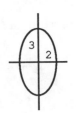

14. Sketch $y = \left(\dfrac{1}{4}\right)^y$ and reflect for

$y = \log_{1/4} x.$

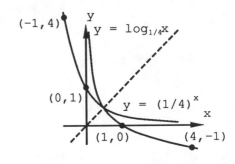

15. $12 \operatorname{cis} 30° = 12(\cos 30° + i \sin 30°)$

$= 12\left(\dfrac{\sqrt{3}}{2} + \dfrac{1}{2}i\right) = \mathbf{6\sqrt{3} + 6i}$

16. $b(b + 2) - (-12) = 12$

$b^2 + 2b + 12 = 12$

$b(b + 2) = 0$

$b = \mathbf{0, -2}$

17. Refer to Problem Set 47, problem 8.

18. Refer to Problem Set 18, problem 7.

19. $y = -3 + 2 \sin \dfrac{5}{3}(x - 27°)$

20. $y = -2 + 6 \sin\left(x - \dfrac{\pi}{4}\right)$

21. $(x^2 + 6x + 9) + y^2 = 0 + 9$

$(x + 3)^2 + y^2 = 9$

Center: $(-3, 0)$

Radius: 3

22. $\dfrac{15}{x} = \dfrac{x}{3}$

$x^2 = 45$

$x = \mathbf{3\sqrt{5}}$

$$\frac{15}{y} = \frac{y}{12}$$
$$y^2 = 180$$
$$y = 6\sqrt{5}$$

23. $\sin \theta \, (1 + 2 \sin \theta) = 0$

    $\sin \theta = 0$ or $1 + 2 \sin \theta = 0$

    $\theta = 0°, 180°$ $\sin \theta = -\dfrac{1}{2}$

                              $\theta = 210°, 330°$

    $\theta = 0°, 180°, 210°, 330°$

24. $4 \cos^2 \theta = 1$

    $\cos^2 \theta = \dfrac{1}{4}$

    $\cos \theta = \pm\dfrac{1}{2}$

    $\theta = 60°, 120°, 240°, 300°$

25. $(2 \sin x - 1)(\sin x + 1) = 0$

    $2 \sin x = 1$ or $\sin x + 1 = 0$

    $\sin x = \dfrac{1}{2}$ $\sin x = -1$

    $x = 30°, 150°$ $x = 270°$

    $x = 30°, 150°, 270°$

26. $\tan^2 (30°) - \sec^2 (30°)$

$$= \left(\frac{\sqrt{3}}{3}\right)^2 - \left(\frac{2\sqrt{3}}{3}\right)^2 = \frac{1}{3} - \frac{4}{3} = -1$$

27. $\sec^2 45° + \tan^2 45° = \left(\sqrt{2}\right)^2 + 1^2$

    $= 2 + 1 = 3$

28. $\ln 27^{1/3} + \ln x^2 = \ln (2 - x)$

    $\ln 3x^2 = \ln (2 - x)$

    $3x^2 = 2 - x$

    $3x^2 + x - 2 = 0$

    $(3x - 2)(x + 1) = 0$

    $x = \dfrac{2}{3}$

29. $\log_8 \dfrac{x - 2}{x - 3} = 2$

    $8^2 = \dfrac{x - 2}{x - 3}$

    $64(x - 3) = x - 2$

    $64x - 192 = x - 2$

    $63x = 190$

    $x = \dfrac{190}{63}$

30. $5^3 = 125$

PROBLEM SET 52

1. $L_1 = 3L_2, L_2 = 3L_3$

    $L_1 = 9L_3$

$$\frac{L_3}{L_1 + L_2 + L_3} = \frac{L_3}{9L_3 + 3L_3 + L_3} = \frac{1}{13}$$

2. $2.5(2.5w) = 16.25$

    $6.25w = 16.25$

    $w = \$2.60$

3. $\dfrac{E - P}{E}$

4. $\dfrac{D \text{ dollars} - P \text{ dollars}}{N \text{ items}} = \dfrac{D - P}{N}$

5. $y \text{ yards} - f \text{ feet} - n \text{ inches}$

    $(36y - 12f - n) \text{ inches}$

6. $3L = 2G$

    $L + G = 70$

$L = 70 - G$

$3(70 - G) = 2G$

$210 - 3G = 2G$

$5G = 210$

$G = 42, L = 28$

7.
$$x = \frac{\begin{vmatrix} -4 & -3 \\ 8 & 2 \end{vmatrix}}{\begin{vmatrix} 2 & -3 \\ 4 & 2 \end{vmatrix}} = \frac{-8 - (-24)}{4 - (-12)}$$

$$= \frac{-8 + 24}{4 + 12} = \frac{16}{16} = 1$$

$$y = \frac{\begin{vmatrix} 2 & -4 \\ 4 & 8 \end{vmatrix}}{16} = \frac{16 - (-16)}{16} = \frac{32}{16} = 2$$

$x = 1$

$y = 2$

8.

$$x = \frac{\begin{vmatrix} -2 & 1 \\ -3 & -2 \end{vmatrix}}{\begin{vmatrix} 3 & 1 \\ 1 & -2 \end{vmatrix}} = \frac{4 - (-3)}{-1}$$

$$= \frac{7}{-7} = -1$$

$$y = \frac{\begin{vmatrix} 3 & -2 \\ 1 & -3 \end{vmatrix}}{-7} = \frac{-9 - (-2)}{-7} = \frac{-7}{-7} = 1$$

$$x = -1$$
$$y = 2$$

9. $(10 - 2)180° = \mathbf{1440°}$

10. The sum of the exterior angles of any polygon is **360°**.

11. Central angle $= \dfrac{360°}{12} = 30°$

$\sin 15° = \dfrac{b}{10}$

$b = 10 \sin 15° \approx 2.6$

$2b = 5.2$

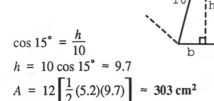

$\cos 15° = \dfrac{h}{10}$

$h = 10 \cos 15° \approx 9.7$

$A = 12\left[\dfrac{1}{2}(5.2)(9.7)\right] \approx \mathbf{303 \ cm^2}$

12. Central angle $= \dfrac{360°}{6} = 60°$

$\sin 30° = \dfrac{3}{r}$

$r = \dfrac{3}{\sin 30°} = \mathbf{4 \ cm}$

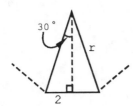

13. $\dfrac{4^2}{1^2} = \dfrac{16}{1}$

Ratio $= \mathbf{16 : 1}$

14. $A = 180° - 15° - 30° = \mathbf{135°}$

$\dfrac{b}{\sin 15°} = \dfrac{20}{\sin 30°}$

$b = \dfrac{20 \sin 15°}{\sin 30°} \approx \mathbf{10.4}$

$\dfrac{a}{\sin 135°} = \dfrac{20}{\sin 30°}$

$a = \dfrac{20 \sin 135°}{\sin 30°} \approx \mathbf{28.3}$

15. $\dfrac{25x^2}{400} + \dfrac{16y^2}{400} = 1$

$\dfrac{x^2}{16} + \dfrac{y^2}{25} = 1$

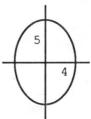

16. $24 \operatorname{cis} 60° = 24(\cos 60° + i \sin 60°)$

$= 24\left(\dfrac{1}{2} + \dfrac{\sqrt{3}}{2}i\right) = \mathbf{12 + 12i\sqrt{3}}$

17. $x(x - 1) - 15 = 5$
$x^2 - x - 15 = 5$
$x^2 - x - 20 = 0$
$(x - 5)(x + 4) = 0$
$x = \mathbf{5, -4}$

18. Refer to Problem Set 47, problem 9.

19. Refer to Problem Set 47, problem 8.

20. $y = 3 + 11 \cos \dfrac{3}{2}(x - 100°)$

21. $y = -1 + 14 \sin (x + 45°)$

22. $(x^2 + 10x + 25) + (y^2 - 4y + 4)$
$= -20 + 25 + 4 = 9$
$(x + 5)^2 + (y - 2)^2 = 9$
Center: (-5, 2)
Radius: 3

23. Overall average rate $= \dfrac{\text{total distance}}{\text{total time}}$

	1st	2nd
Distance:	m	m
Rate:	p	k
Time:	$\dfrac{m}{p}$	$\dfrac{m}{k}$

Overall rate $= \dfrac{m + m}{\dfrac{m}{p} + \dfrac{m}{k}} = \dfrac{2m}{\dfrac{km + pm}{pk}}$

$= \dfrac{2mpk}{km + pm} = \dfrac{2pk}{k + m}$ **mph**

24. $4 \cos^2 t = 3$

$\cos^2 t = \dfrac{3}{4}$

$\cos t = \pm \dfrac{\sqrt{3}}{2}$

$t = \mathbf{30°, 150°, 210°, 330°}$

25. $2 \cos 3\theta = 1$

$\cos 3\theta = \dfrac{1}{2}$

$3\theta = 60°, 300°, 420°, 660°, 780°, 1020°$

$\theta = \mathbf{20°, 100°, 140°, 220°, 260°, 340°}$

26. $\sec x = \sqrt{2 \sec x - 1}$

$\sec^2 x = 2 \sec x - 1$

$\sec^2 x - 2 \sec x + 1 = 0$

$(\sec x - 1)^2 = 0$

$\sec x = 1$

$x = \mathbf{0°}$

27. $\csc^2\left(\dfrac{3\pi}{4}\right) - \cot^2\left(-\dfrac{3\pi}{4}\right)$

$= \left(-\sqrt{2}\right)^2 - (-1)^2 = 2 - 1 = \mathbf{1}$

28. $\dfrac{1}{4} \ln 16 + 2 \ln x = \ln (6 - x)$

$\ln 2 + \ln x^2 = \ln (6 - x)$

$\ln 2x^2 = \ln (6 - x)$

$2x^2 = 6 - x$

$2x^2 + x - 6 = 0$

$(2x - 3)(x + 2) = 0$

$x = \dfrac{\mathbf{3}}{\mathbf{2}}$

29. $b^{\log_b 24/6} = b^{\log_b 4} = \mathbf{4}$

30. $e^4 \approx 3^4 = \mathbf{81}$

PROBLEM SET 53

1. Each pupil spends $\dfrac{D}{p}$ dollars. 20 drop out.

Now each spends $\dfrac{D}{p - 20}$

Difference $= \dfrac{D}{p - 20} - \dfrac{D}{p}$

$= \dfrac{Dp - Dp + 20D}{p(p - 20)} = \dfrac{20D}{p(p - 20)}$

2. $7 \dfrac{\text{mi}}{\text{gal}} + \dfrac{1}{3} = 21 \text{ mi} - 7 \text{ mi} = \mathbf{14 \ mi}$

3. $p = \dfrac{km^2}{\sqrt{N}}$

$p = \dfrac{k(4m)^2}{\sqrt{9N}} = \dfrac{16km^2}{3\sqrt{N}}$

p **is multiplied by** $\dfrac{\mathbf{16}}{\mathbf{3}}$

4. $4.40 + 1.10(m - 3)$

$= 4.40 + 1.10m - 3.30 = \mathbf{1.10 + 1.10m}$

5. $\dfrac{_8P_3}{3!} = \dfrac{8 \cdot 7 \cdot 6}{3 \cdot 2 \cdot 1} = \mathbf{56}$

6. $_8C_4 = \dfrac{_8P_4}{4!} = \dfrac{8 \cdot 7 \cdot 6 \cdot 5}{4 \cdot 3 \cdot 2 \cdot 1} = \mathbf{70}$

7. $x = \dfrac{\begin{vmatrix} -3 & -4 \\ -4 & 3 \end{vmatrix}}{\begin{vmatrix} 3 & -4 \\ 2 & 3 \end{vmatrix}} = \dfrac{-9 - 16}{9 + 8} = \dfrac{-25}{17}$

$y = \dfrac{\begin{vmatrix} 3 & -3 \\ 2 & -4 \end{vmatrix}}{17} = \dfrac{-12 + 6}{17} = -\dfrac{6}{17}$

$x = -\dfrac{25}{17}$

$y = -\dfrac{6}{17}$

8. $x = \dfrac{5 \pm \sqrt{25 - 4(2)(6)}}{2(2)}$

$= \dfrac{5 \pm \sqrt{-23}}{4} = \dfrac{5 \pm i\sqrt{23}}{4}$

$\left(x - \dfrac{5 + i\sqrt{23}}{4}\right)\left(x - \dfrac{5 - i\sqrt{23}}{4}\right)$

9. $(n - 2)180° = (13 - 2)180° = \mathbf{1980°}$

10. The sum of the exterior angles of any polygon is **360°**.

11.

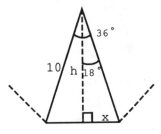

Central angle $= \dfrac{360°}{10} = 36°$

$\cos 18° = \dfrac{h}{10}$

$h = 10 \cos 18° \approx 9.5$

$\sin 18° = \dfrac{x}{10}$

$x = 10 \sin 18° \approx 3.1$

Base $= 2x = 6.2$

$A_{\text{triangle}} = \dfrac{1}{2}(6.2)(9.5) = 29.45$

$A_{\text{decagon}} = 10(29.45) \approx \mathbf{294.5\ cm^2}$

12.

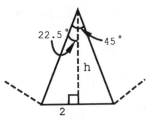

Central angle $= \dfrac{360°}{8} = 45°$

$\tan 22.5° = \dfrac{2}{h}$

$h = \dfrac{2}{\tan 22.5°} \approx 4.83$

$A_{\text{triangle}} = \dfrac{1}{2}(4)(4.83) = 9.66$

$A_{\text{octagon}} = 8(9.66) = \mathbf{77.3\ cm^3}$

13. Area $= \dfrac{\left(\frac{5}{2}\right)^2}{1^2} = \dfrac{25}{4}$

Ratio $= \mathbf{25 : 4}$

14. $A = 180° - 130° = \mathbf{50°}$

$\dfrac{b}{\sin 70°} = \dfrac{8}{\sin 60°}$

$b = \dfrac{8 \sin 70°}{\sin 60°} \approx \mathbf{8.7}$

$\dfrac{a}{\sin 50°} = \dfrac{8}{\sin 60°}$

$a = \dfrac{8 \sin 50°}{\sin 60°} \approx \mathbf{7.1}$

15. $\dfrac{5x^2}{40} + \dfrac{8y^2}{40} = \dfrac{40}{40}$

$\dfrac{x^2}{8} + \dfrac{y^2}{5} = 1$

$a = \sqrt{8} = 2\sqrt{2}$

$b = \sqrt{5}$

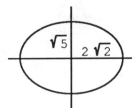

16. $[5 \operatorname{cis}(-20°)](2 \operatorname{cis} 80°) = 10 \operatorname{cis} 60°$

$= 10(\cos 60° + i \sin 60°)$

$= 10\left(\dfrac{1}{2} + i\dfrac{\sqrt{3}}{2}\right) = \mathbf{5 + 5i\sqrt{3}}$

17. $3k - k(k + 1) = 1$

$3k - k^2 - k = 1$

$k^2 - 2k + 1 = 0$

$(k - 1)^2 = 0$

$k = \mathbf{1}$

18. Refer to Problem Set 47, problem 10.

19. Refer to Problem Set 47, problem 8.

20. Period $= 540°$

Coefficient $k = \dfrac{360°}{540°} = \dfrac{2}{3}$

$y = 3 + 4 \sin \dfrac{2}{3}(\theta + 225°)$

21. Coefficient $k = \dfrac{2\pi}{4\pi} = \dfrac{1}{2}$

   $y = 10 + 6 \sin \dfrac{1}{2}\left(x - \dfrac{\pi}{2}\right)$

22. $9\left(x^2 - \dfrac{2}{3}x + \dfrac{1}{9}\right) + 9\left(y^2 + \dfrac{4}{3}y + \dfrac{4}{9}\right)$

   $= 31 + 1 + 4 = 36$

   $9\left(x - \dfrac{1}{3}\right)^2 + 9\left(y + \dfrac{2}{3}\right)^2 = 36$

   $\left(x - \dfrac{1}{3}\right)^2 + \left(y + \dfrac{2}{3}\right)^2 = 4$

   Center: $\left(\dfrac{1}{3}, -\dfrac{2}{3}\right)$

   Radius: 2

23. $\dfrac{a}{1} = \dfrac{5}{a}$ $a^2 = 5$ $a = \sqrt{5}$

   $\dfrac{b}{4} = \dfrac{5}{b}$ $b^2 = 20$ $b = 2\sqrt{5}$

24. $4 \sin^2 \theta - 3 = 0$

   $\sin^2 \theta = \dfrac{3}{4}$

   $\sin \theta = \pm\dfrac{\sqrt{3}}{2}$

   $\theta = 60°, 120°, 240°, 300°$

25. $\sin 3\theta = \dfrac{1}{2}$

   $3\theta = 30°, 150°, 390°, 510°, 750°, 870°$

   $\theta = 10°, 50°, 130°, 170°, 250°, 290°$

26. $(\sin \theta - 3)(\sin \theta - 1) = 0$

   $\sin \theta - 3 = 0$ $\sin \theta - 1 = 0$

   $\sin \theta = 3$ $\sin \theta = 1$

        $\varnothing$ $\theta = 90°$

27. $\cot^2 840° - \csc^2 840°$

   $= \cot^2 120° - \csc^2 120°$

   $= \left(\dfrac{\sqrt{3}}{3}\right)^2 - \left(\dfrac{2\sqrt{3}}{3}\right)^2 = \dfrac{1}{3} - \dfrac{4}{3} = -1$

28. $\ln 8^{1/3} + \ln x^2 = \ln(-3x + 2)$

   $\ln 2x^2 = \ln(-3x + 2)$

   $2x^2 = -3x + 2$

   $2x^2 + 3x - 2 = 0$

   $(2x - 1)(x + 2) = 0$

   $x = \dfrac{1}{2}$

29. $h^{\log_h 2^3 - \log_h 2} = h^{\log_h 8/2}$

   $h^{\log_h 4} = 4$

30. $6^{-2} = \dfrac{1}{36}$

PROBLEM SET 54

1. $x = 1 + \dfrac{3}{5}p$

   $p = \dfrac{5(x - 1)}{3}$

2. $C + 0.20C = 480$

   $1.2C = 480$

   $C = 400$

   $400 + 0.15(400) = 400 + 60 = \mathbf{\$460}$

3.
	Now	−8 years
Mary:	M_N	$M_N - 8$
Joe:	J_N	$J_N - 8$

   $M_N = J_N + 1$

   $3(M_N - 8) = 2(J_N - 8) + 6$

   $3M_N - 24 = 2J_N - 10$

   $3M_N - 2J_N = 14$

   Substitute $J_N + 1$ into equation above.

   $3(J_N + 1) - 2J_N = 14$

   $3J_N + 3 - 2J_N = 14$

   $J_N = 11$

   $J_{+17 \text{ years}} = 11 + 17 = \mathbf{28}$

   $M_{+17 \text{ years}} = 12 + 17 = \mathbf{29}$

4.
	1st	2nd
Distance:	y	y
Rate:	$\dfrac{y}{m}$	?
Time:	m	$m - 15$

   Rate $= \dfrac{y}{m - 15} \dfrac{\text{yd}}{\text{min}}$

5. $_{10}C_8 = \dfrac{_{10}P_6}{8!}$

$= \dfrac{10 \cdot 9 \cdot 8 \cdot 7 \cdot 6 \cdot 5 \cdot 4 \cdot 3}{8 \cdot 7 \cdot 6 \cdot 5 \cdot 4 \cdot 3 \cdot 2 \cdot 1} = \dfrac{10 \cdot 9}{2} = \textbf{45}$

6. $_{10}C_6 = \dfrac{_{10}P_8}{6!} = \dfrac{10 \cdot 9 \cdot 8 \cdot 7 \cdot 6 \cdot 5}{6 \cdot 5 \cdot 4 \cdot 3 \cdot 2 \cdot 1}$

$= 10 \cdot 7 \cdot 3 = \textbf{210}$

7. $\cos x \tan x = \dfrac{1}{\csc x}$

$\cos x \cdot \dfrac{\sin x}{\cos x} = \sin x = \dfrac{1}{\csc x}$

8. $-\sin(-\theta)\cos(90° - \theta)$

$= \sin^2 \theta = \sin \theta \cdot \sin \theta = \sin^2 \theta$

9. $\dfrac{\cot x}{\csc x} = \dfrac{\dfrac{\cos x}{\sin x}}{\dfrac{1}{\sin x}} = \dfrac{\cos x}{\sin x} \cdot \dfrac{\sin x}{1} = \cos x$

10. $x = \dfrac{\begin{vmatrix} 5 & -4 \\ 6 & 2 \end{vmatrix}}{\begin{vmatrix} 6 & -4 \\ 3 & 2 \end{vmatrix}} = \dfrac{10 + 24}{12 + 12} = \dfrac{34}{24} = \dfrac{17}{12}$

$y = \dfrac{\begin{vmatrix} 6 & 5 \\ 3 & 6 \end{vmatrix}}{24} = \dfrac{36 - 15}{24} = \dfrac{21}{24} = \dfrac{7}{8}$

11. $(n - 2)180° = (15 - 2)180° = 13(180°)$
    $= \textbf{2340}°$

12. The sum of the exterior angles of any polygon
    is **360°**.

13.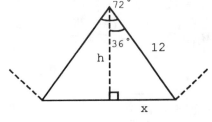

Central angle $= \dfrac{360°}{5} = 72°$

$\cos 36° = \dfrac{h}{12}$

$h = 12 \cos 36° \approx 9.7$

$\sin 36° = \dfrac{x}{12}$

$x = 12 \sin 36° \approx 7.1$

Base $= 14.2$

$A_{triangle} = \dfrac{1}{2}(14.2)(9.7) = 68.9$

$A_{pentagon} = (68.9)(5) = \textbf{1844.5 in}^2$

14.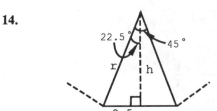

Central angle $= \dfrac{360°}{8} = 45°$

$\sin 22.5° = \dfrac{2.5}{r}$

$r = \dfrac{2.5}{\sin 22.5°} \approx \textbf{6.5 in}$

15. $\dfrac{\left(\dfrac{10}{3}\right)^2}{1^2} = \dfrac{100}{9}$

Ratio $= \textbf{100 : 9}$

16. $B = 180° - 110° - 40° = 30°$

$\dfrac{a}{\sin 110°} = \dfrac{8}{\sin 40°}$

$a = \dfrac{8 \sin 110°}{\sin 40°} \approx \textbf{11.7}$

$\dfrac{b}{\sin 30°} = \dfrac{8}{\sin 40°}$

$b = \dfrac{8 \sin 30°}{\sin 40°} \approx \textbf{6.2}$

17. $\dfrac{6x^2}{36} + \dfrac{3y^2}{36} = \dfrac{36}{36}$

$\dfrac{x^2}{6} + \dfrac{y^2}{12} = 1$

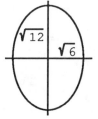

18. $18 \text{ cis } 60° = 18(\cos 60° + i \sin 60)$

$= 18\left(\dfrac{1}{2} + i\dfrac{\sqrt{3}}{2}\right) = \textbf{9} + \textbf{9}i\sqrt{3}$

19. $B = E = 90°$ and $A = D$ is given. $\angle A + \angle B + \angle C = 180°$ and $\angle D + \angle E + \angle F = 180°$ because the sum of the angles of a triangle is $180°$. $\angle A + \angle B + \angle C = \angle D + \angle E + \angle F$ by substitution. $C = F$ by subtraction.

20. $y = 3 + 6 \cos \dfrac{2}{3}(\theta - 135°)$

21. Coefficient $k = \dfrac{360°}{90°} = 4$

    $y = -3 + \dfrac{3}{2} \sin 4(\theta + 30°)$

22. $2\left(x^2 - \dfrac{1}{2}x + \dfrac{1}{16}\right) + 2\left(y^2 + \dfrac{1}{2}y + \dfrac{1}{16}\right)$

    $2\left(x - \dfrac{1}{4}\right)^2 + 2\left(y + \dfrac{1}{4}\right)^2 = \dfrac{32}{4} = 8$

    $\left(x - \dfrac{1}{4}\right)^2 + \left(y + \dfrac{1}{4}\right)^2 = 4$

    Center: $\left(\dfrac{1}{4}, -\dfrac{1}{4}\right)$

    Radius: 2

23. B

24. $\tan^2 x = 3$

    $\tan x = \pm\sqrt{3}$

    $x = 60°, 120°, 240°, 300°$

25. $\cos 4\theta = \dfrac{1}{2}$

    $4\theta = 60°, 300°, 420°, 630°, 780°, 990°, 1140°, 1350°$

    $\theta = 15°, 75°, 105°, 165°, 195°, 255°, 285°, 345°$

26. $2\cos^2 x + \cos x - 1 = 0$

    $(2\cos x - 1)(\cos x + 1) = 0$

    $2\cos x - 1 = 0 \qquad \cos x + 1 = 0$

    $\cos x = \dfrac{1}{2} \qquad\qquad \cos x = -1$

    $x = 60°, 300° \qquad\quad x = 180°$

    $x = \mathbf{60°, 180°, 300°}$

27. $\tan^2(-150°) - \sec^2(-150°)$

    $= \left(-\dfrac{\sqrt{3}}{3}\right)^2 - \left(-\dfrac{2\sqrt{3}}{3}\right)^2$

    $= \dfrac{3}{9} - \dfrac{12}{9} = \dfrac{-9}{9} = \mathbf{-1}$

28. $\log_7 (x + 1)(2x - 3) = \log_7 4x$

    $(x + 1)(2x - 3) = 4x$

    $2x^2 - x - 3 = 4x$

    $2x^2 - 5x - 3 = 0$

    $(2x + 1)(x - 3) = 0$

    $x = 3$

29. $\log_{1/2} 16^{1/4} - \log_{1/2} x^2 = 3$

    $\log_{1/2} \dfrac{2}{x^2} = 3$

    $\left(\dfrac{1}{2}\right)^3 = \dfrac{2}{x^2}$

    $\dfrac{1}{8} = \dfrac{2}{x^2}$

    $x^2 = 16$

    $x = \mathbf{4}$

30. $5^{-1} = \dfrac{1}{5}$

PROBLEM SET 55

1. $\dfrac{x + 2}{x + 1}$

2. $x(x + 2) = (x + 1) + 19$

   $x^2 + 2x = x + 20$

   $x^2 + x - 20 = 0$

   $(x + 5)(x - 4) = 0$

   $x = -5 \text{ or } x = 4$

   $\mathbf{-5, -4, -3 \text{ or } 4, 5, 6}$

3. $\dfrac{6,400,000}{100} = 64,000 \times 0.80$

   $51,200 \times 0.02 = \mathbf{\$1024}$

4. $\$200 \times 0.12 = \$24$

   $\$200 - \$24 = \$176$

   $\$200 \times 0.06 = \$12$

   $\$176 - \$12 = \$164 \times 4 = \mathbf{\$656}$

5. $\text{Rate}_{ave} = \dfrac{\text{total distance}}{\text{total time}}$

$= \dfrac{200 + 400}{4 + 10} = \dfrac{600}{14} = \dfrac{300}{7}\,\textbf{mph}$

6. $_9C_5 = \dfrac{9!}{4!\,5!} = \textbf{126}$

7.

Term:	1	2	3	4	5	6	7	8
For x:	7	6	5	4	3	2	1	0
For y:	0	1	2	3	4	5	6	7
Coeff:	1	7	21	35	35	21	7	1

$\textbf{21}\boldsymbol{x^5y^2}$

8. $\boldsymbol{x^4 + 4x^3y + 6x^2y^2 + 4xy^3 + y^4}$

9. $\sin x \sec x = \sin x \left(\dfrac{1}{\cos x}\right) = \dfrac{\sin x}{\cos x} = \tan x$

10. $\sin(-\theta)\tan(90° - \theta)$

$= -\sin\theta\cot\theta = -\sin\theta\left(\dfrac{\cos\theta}{\sin\theta}\right) = -\cos\theta$

11. $\sec x \cot x = \dfrac{1}{\cos x} \cdot \dfrac{\cos x}{\sin x} = \dfrac{1}{\sin x} = \csc x$

12. $x = \dfrac{\begin{vmatrix} 6 & -2 \\ 7 & -1 \end{vmatrix}}{\begin{vmatrix} 4 & -2 \\ 3 & -1 \end{vmatrix}} = \dfrac{-6 + 14}{-4 + 6} = \dfrac{8}{2} = 4$

$y = \dfrac{\begin{vmatrix} 4 & 6 \\ 3 & 7 \end{vmatrix}}{2} = \dfrac{28 - 18}{2} = -\dfrac{10}{2} = 5$

13. $(12 - 2)180° = (10)180° = \textbf{1800°}$

14. The sum of the exterior angles of any polygon is **360°**.

15.

Central angle $= \dfrac{360°}{6} = 60°$

$r = \textbf{6 cm}$

16. Area $= \left(\dfrac{4}{3}\right)^2 = \dfrac{16}{9}$

Ratio $= \textbf{16 : 9}$

17. $A = 180° - 120° - 30° = \textbf{30°}$

$\dfrac{a}{\sin 30°} = \dfrac{10}{\sin 30°}$

$a = \textbf{10}$

18. $\dfrac{8x^2}{16} + \dfrac{2y^2}{16} = \dfrac{16}{16}$

$\dfrac{x^2}{2} + \dfrac{y^2}{8} = 1$

19. $8 \operatorname{cis} 60° = 8(\cos 60° + i\sin 60°)$

$= 8\left(\dfrac{1}{2} + i\dfrac{\sqrt{3}}{2}\right) = \textbf{4} + \textbf{4}\boldsymbol{i}\sqrt{\textbf{3}}$

20. Find the equation of the line $\perp$ to $y = \dfrac{3}{5}x + \dfrac{2}{5}$ that passes through $(1, 4)$.

$m_\perp = -\dfrac{5}{3}$

$y = -\dfrac{5}{3}x + b$

$-2 = -\dfrac{5}{3}(1) + b$

$b = \dfrac{17}{3}$

$y = -\dfrac{5}{3}x - \dfrac{17}{3}$

Solve $y = -\dfrac{5}{3}x + \dfrac{17}{3}$ and $y = \dfrac{3}{5}x + \dfrac{2}{5}$ simultaneously.

$\dfrac{3}{5}x + \dfrac{2}{5} = -\dfrac{5}{3}x - \dfrac{17}{3}$

$9x + 6 = -25x + 85$

$34x = 79$

$x = -\dfrac{79}{34}, y = \dfrac{61}{34}$

$(x, y) = \left(-\dfrac{79}{34}, \dfrac{61}{34}\right)$

$d = \sqrt{\left(1 - \dfrac{79}{34}\right)^2 + \left(4 - \dfrac{61}{34}\right)^2}$

$= \sqrt{\left(-\dfrac{45}{34}\right)^2 + \left(\dfrac{75}{34}\right)^2} \approx \textbf{2.57}$

21. Coefficient $k = \dfrac{2\pi}{\dfrac{8\pi}{3}} = \dfrac{6}{8} = \dfrac{3}{4}$

$y = 11 + \sin\dfrac{3}{4}(x + \pi)$

22. Coefficient $k = \dfrac{360°}{540°} = \dfrac{2}{3}$

$y = \dfrac{\pi}{2} + \pi\sin\dfrac{2}{3}(x - 60°)$

23. $2(x^2 - 6x + 9) + 2(y^2 + 4y + 4) $
$= -24 + 18 + 8 = 2$
$2(x - 3)^2 + 2(y + 2)^2 = 2$
$(x - 3)^2 + (y + 2)^2 = 1$
Center: (3, –2)
Radius: 1

24. $h^2 = 4^2 + 3^2 = 16 + 9 = 25$
$h = 5$
$\dfrac{2}{4} = \dfrac{x}{5}$
$4x = 10$
$x = \dfrac{5}{2}$

25. $\tan^2 x = \dfrac{1}{3}$

$\tan x = \pm\dfrac{\sqrt{3}}{3}$

$x = 30°, 150°, 210°, 330°$

26. $\tan 3\theta = \dfrac{1}{\sqrt{3}} = \dfrac{\sqrt{3}}{3}$

$3\theta = 30°, 210°, 390°, 570°, 750°, 930°$
$\theta = 10°, 70°, 130°, 190°, 250°, 310°$

27. $\csc^2 1140° - \cot^2 1140°$
$= \csc^2 60° - \cot^2 60°$

$= \left(\dfrac{2\sqrt{3}}{3}\right)^2 - \left(\dfrac{\sqrt{3}}{3}\right)^2 = \dfrac{12}{9} - \dfrac{3}{9} = 1$

28. $\log_8 \dfrac{x - 1}{x - 2} = \log_8 3^2$

$\dfrac{x - 1}{x - 2} = 9$

$x - 1 = 9x - 18$
$8x = 17$
$x = \dfrac{17}{8}$

29. $\log_7 7^3 + 7^{\log_7 3^{2/3}} = 3 + 3 = 6$

30. $6^3 = $ **216**

ENRICHMENT LESSON 1

1. $\dfrac{x + 2}{x + 1}$

2. $x(x + 2) = x + 1 + 11$
$x^2 + 2x = x + 12$
$x^2 + x - 12 = 0$
$(x + 4)(x - 3) = 0$
$x = -4 \text{ or } x = 3$
3, 4, 5 or –4, –3, –2

3. $\dfrac{6,400,000}{100} = 64,000$
$64,000 \times 0.60 = 38,400$
$38,400 \times 0.02 = $ **\$768**

4. $\$100 - \$10 = \$90$
$\$90 - \$9 = \$81$
$\$81 \times 5 = $ **\$405**

5. rate $= \dfrac{\text{total distance}}{\text{total time}}$

$= \dfrac{100 + 200}{\dfrac{5}{3} + \dfrac{20}{3}} = \dfrac{300}{\dfrac{25}{3}} = 36\text{ mph}$

6. $_{15}C_9 = \dfrac{15!}{6!\,9!} = $ **5005**

7.
Term:	1	2	3	4	5	6	7
For x:	6	5	4	3	2	1	0
For y:	0	1	2	3	4	5	6
Coeff:	1	6	15	20	15	6	1

$20x^3y^3$

8. $x^5 + 5x^4y + 10x^3y^2 + 10x^2y^3 + 5xy^4 + y^5$

9. Jim is not a member of the set of non dogs. Therefore, statement is **invalid**.

10. Major premise is statement about the set of authors. Minor premise identifies a member of the set of gold watch wearers. Therefore, statement is **invalid**.

11. Replacing k with $k + 1$ in (b) yields:
$$\frac{(k + 1)(k + 2)}{2} = \frac{k^2 + 3k + 2}{2}$$
$$= \frac{k^2 + k + 2k + 2}{2}$$
$$= \frac{k(k + 1) + 2(k + 1)}{2}$$
$$= \frac{k(k + 1)}{2} + (k + 1)$$

12. Replacing k with $k + 1$ in (b) yields:
$(k + 1)[3(k + 1) - 1]$
$= (k + 1)(3k + 3 - 1) = (k + 1)(3k + 2)$
$= 3k^2 + 5k + 2 = 3k^2 - k + 6k + 2$
$= k(3k - 1) + (6k + 2)$

13. $\cos x \csc x = \cos x \cdot \left(\dfrac{1}{\sin x}\right)$
$= \dfrac{\cos x}{\sin x} = \cot x$

14.
$$x = \frac{\begin{vmatrix} 1 & -3 \\ 4 & -2 \end{vmatrix}}{\begin{vmatrix} 2 & -3 \\ 3 & -2 \end{vmatrix}} = \frac{-2 + 12}{-4 + 9} = \frac{10}{5} = 2$$

$$y = \frac{\begin{vmatrix} 2 & 1 \\ 3 & 4 \end{vmatrix}}{5} = \frac{8 - 3}{5} = \frac{5}{5} = 1$$

15. $(7 - 2)180° = 900°$

16. Area $= \left(\dfrac{5}{3}\right)^2 = \dfrac{25}{9}$
Ratio $= \mathbf{25 : 9}$

17. $B = 180° - 50° - 60° = \mathbf{70°}$

$\dfrac{30}{\sin 60°} = \dfrac{b}{\sin 70°}$

$b = \dfrac{30 \sin 70°}{\sin 60°} \approx \mathbf{32.6}$

18. $\dfrac{4x^2}{36} + \dfrac{9y^2}{36} = \dfrac{36}{36}$

$\dfrac{x^2}{9} + \dfrac{y^2}{4} = 1$

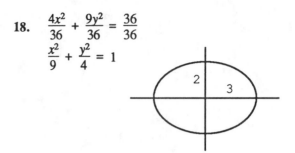

19. $16 \text{ cis } 0° = 16(\cos 0° + i \sin 0°)$
$= 16(1 + 0i) = \mathbf{16}$

20. Refer to Problem Set 47, problem 10.

21. Coefficient $k = \dfrac{360°}{720°} = \dfrac{1}{2}$

$y = -1 + \sin\dfrac{1}{2}(x - 90°)$

22. Coefficient $k = \dfrac{2\pi}{\frac{\pi}{2}} = 4$

$y = 10 + 2 \sin 4\left(x + \dfrac{\pi}{6}\right)$

23. $(x^2 - 4x + 4) + (y^2 + 2y + 1)$
$= 4 + 4 + 1 = 9$
$(x - 2)^2 + (y + 1)^2 = 9$
Center: (2, −1)
Radius: 3

24. $\dfrac{a}{3} = \dfrac{12}{a}$
$a^2 = 36$
$a = \mathbf{6}$

$\dfrac{b}{9} = \dfrac{12}{b}$
$b^2 = 108$
$b = \mathbf{6\sqrt{3}}$

25. $\tan 2\theta = \dfrac{1}{\sqrt{3}} = \dfrac{\sqrt{3}}{3}$

$2\theta = 30°, 210°, 390°, 570°$
$\theta = \mathbf{15°, 105°, 195°, 285°}$

26. $\sin^2 \theta = \dfrac{1}{2}$

$\sin \theta = \pm\dfrac{\sqrt{2}}{2}$

$\theta = \mathbf{45°, 135°, 225°, 315°}$

27. $\tan^2 960° - \sec^2 960°$
     $= \tan^2 240° - \sec^2 240°$
     $= \left(\sqrt{3}\right)^2 - (2)^2 = -1$

$-2x = 5$

$x = -\dfrac{5}{2}$

No solution

28. $\log_3 \dfrac{2x - 1}{x + 1} = \log_3 2^2$

$\dfrac{2x - 1}{x + 1} = 4$

$2x - 1 = 4(x + 1)$

$2x - 1 = 4x + 4$

29. $3^{\log_3 6/2} = 3^{\log_3 3} = \mathbf{3}$

30. $2^4 = \mathbf{16}$

PROBLEM SET 56

1. (a) $\dfrac{W}{H} = \dfrac{7}{9}$

$9W = 7H$

(b) $\dfrac{H}{I} = \dfrac{9}{5}$

$5H = 9I$

(c) $W + H - 2I = 12$

Multiply equation a by 5 and equation b by 7.

$\begin{array}{rrrr} 45W & - & 35H & & = 0 \\ & + & 35H & - & 63I = 0 \\ \hline 45W & & & - & 63I = 0 \end{array}$

Divide by 9.

(d) $5W - 7I = 0$

Multiply equation c by 35 and add to equation a.

$\begin{array}{rrrrr} 45W & - & 35H & & = & 0 \\ 35W & + & 35H & - & 70I = & 420 \\ \hline 80W & & & - & 70I = & 420 \end{array}$

Divide by 10.

(e) $8W - 7I = 42$

Subtract equation e from equation d.

$\begin{array}{rrrrr} & 5W & - & 7I & = & 0 \\ (-) & 8W & - & 7I & = & 42 \\ \hline & -3W & & & = & -42 \\ & W & & & = & \mathbf{14} \end{array}$

$5(14) - 7I = 0$

$I = \mathbf{70}$

$14 + H = 2(10) + 12$

$H = \mathbf{18}$

2. A = angle
    $180° - A$ = supplement
    $90° - A$ = complement
    $2(180° - A) = 3(90° - A) + 120°$
    $360° - 2A = 270° - 3A + 120°$
    $A = \mathbf{30°}$

3. h = hundreds' digit
    t = tens' digit
    u = units' digit
    A: $h + t + u = 8$
    B: $100t + 10h + u$
        $= 180 + 100h + 10t + u$
        $90h - 90t = -180$
        $h - t = -2$
    C: $t + 1 = u$

    $h = t - 2$
    Substitute into equation A.
    $(t - 2) + t + (t + 1) = 8$
    $3t - 1 = 8$
    $t = 3$
    $u = 3 + 1 = 4$
    $h = 3 - 2 = 1$
    Original number = **134**

4. $R = \dfrac{kGw^2}{B}$

$80 = \dfrac{k(2)(2)^2}{4}$

$k = 40$

$R = \dfrac{40(5)(3)^2}{3} = \mathbf{600}$

5. Average price = $\dfrac{\text{total cost}}{\text{number}}$

$\dfrac{1000 + 1000 + 100x}{100 + 200 + 100} = 10$

$\dfrac{2000 + 100x}{400} = 10$

$100x = 2000$

$x = \mathbf{\$20}$

6. $_8C_5 = \dfrac{8!}{3!\,5!} = 56$

7. Construction

8. Triangle cannot be constructed

9. Construction

10. Construction

11. Construction

12.

Term:	1	2	3	4	5	6	7	8	9
For a:	8	7	6	5	4	3	2	1	0
For b:	0	1	2	3	4	5	6	7	8
Coeff:	1	8	28	56	70	56	28	8	1

$56a^5b^3$

13. $x^5 + 5x^4y + 10x^3y^2 + 10x^2y^3 + 5xy^4 + y^5$

14. $\tan\theta\sec(90^\circ - \theta) = \tan\theta\csc\theta$

$= \dfrac{\sin\theta}{\cos\theta} \cdot \dfrac{1}{\sin\theta} = \dfrac{1}{\cos\theta} = \sec\theta$

15. $\dfrac{\csc x}{\sec x} = \dfrac{\dfrac{1}{\sin x}}{\dfrac{1}{\cos x}} = \dfrac{1}{\sin x} \cdot \dfrac{\cos x}{1}$

$= \dfrac{\cos x}{\sin x} = \cot x$

16.

$x = \dfrac{\begin{vmatrix} 5 & -2 \\ 6 & 5 \end{vmatrix}}{\begin{vmatrix} 3 & -2 \\ 2 & 5 \end{vmatrix}} = \dfrac{25 + 12}{15 + 4} = \dfrac{37}{19}$

$y = \dfrac{\begin{vmatrix} 3 & 5 \\ 2 & 6 \end{vmatrix}}{19} = \dfrac{18 - 10}{19} = \dfrac{8}{19}$

17. $(4 - 2)180^\circ = 360^\circ$

18. (a) $\dfrac{36}{9} = 4$ in

(b)

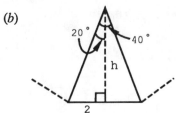

$\tan 20^\circ = \dfrac{2}{h}$

$h = \dfrac{2}{\tan 20^\circ} \approx 5.5$

$A = \dfrac{1}{2}(4)(5.5) = 11$

$A_{\text{nonagon}} = 9(11) = 99$ in^2

19. Area $= \left(\dfrac{3}{2}\right)^2 = \dfrac{9}{4}$

Ratio $= 9:4$

20. $Y = 180^\circ - 40^\circ - 30^\circ = 110^\circ$

$\dfrac{y}{\sin 110^\circ} = \dfrac{6.000}{\sin 30^\circ}$

$y = \dfrac{6.000 \sin 110^\circ}{\sin 30^\circ} \approx 11.28$

21. $\dfrac{3x^2}{36} + \dfrac{9y^2}{36} = \dfrac{36}{36}$

$\dfrac{x^2}{12} + \dfrac{y^2}{4} = 1$

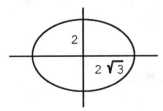

22. $12\,\text{cis}\,60^\circ = 12(\cos 60^\circ + i\sin 60^\circ)$

$= 12\left(\dfrac{1}{2} + i\dfrac{\sqrt{3}}{2}\right) = 6 + 6i\sqrt{3}$

23. Refer to Problem Set 47, problem 10.

24. Coefficient $k = \dfrac{2\pi}{\dfrac{2\pi}{3}} = 3$

$y = -1 + 2\cos 3\left(x - \dfrac{5\pi}{18}\right)$

25. $3(x^2 - 2x + 1) + 3\left(y^2 + \dfrac{2}{3}y + \dfrac{1}{9}\right)$

$= 2 + 3 + \dfrac{1}{3} = \dfrac{16}{3}$

$3(x - 1)^2 + 3\left(y + \dfrac{1}{3}\right)^2 = \dfrac{16}{3}$

$(x - 1)^2 + \left(y + \dfrac{1}{3}\right)^2 = \dfrac{16}{9}$

Center: $\left(1, -\dfrac{1}{3}\right)$

Radius: $\dfrac{4}{3}$

26. $\dfrac{y}{4} = \dfrac{1}{2}$

$y = 2$

27. $2\sin^2 x - 3\sin x + 1 = 0$

$(2\sin x - 1)(\sin x - 1) = 0$

$2\sin x - 1 = 0$ or $\sin x - 1 = 0$

$\sin x = \dfrac{1}{2}$ $\sin x = 1$

$x = 30°, 90°, 150°$

28.

(figure) $-\dfrac{2\sqrt{13}}{13}$

29. $\log_5 (x - 2)(x - 1) = \log_5 x^2$

$(x - 2)(x - 1) = x^2$

$x^2 - 3x + 2 = x^2$

$-3x + 2 = 0$

$x = \dfrac{2}{3}$

No solution

30. Let $N = b^c$

$\log_b N = c$

$\log_b N^x = \log_b (b^c)^x = \log_b b^{cx}$

$= cx = x\log_b N$

EP

1. **Invalid**

2. $\dfrac{k(k + 1)}{2} + (k + 1) = \dfrac{k(k + 1) + 2(k + 1)}{2}$

$= \dfrac{k^2 + 3k + 2}{2} = \dfrac{(k + 1)(k + 2)}{2}$

$= \dfrac{(k + 1)[(k + 1) + 1]}{2}$

PROBLEM SET 57

1. Average $= \dfrac{\text{total points}}{\text{number of tests}} = \dfrac{288 + x}{5}$

$= 70$

$x = \mathbf{62}$

2. $A + B = 3000$

$B = 3000 - A$

$0.06A + 0.08B = 220$

$6A + 8(3000 - A) = 22{,}000$

$6A + 24000 - 8A = 22{,}000$

$2A = 2000$

$A = \mathbf{\$1000\ at\ 6\%}$

$B = \mathbf{\$2000\ at\ 8\%}$

3. $R_P T_P + R_L T_L = 6$

$\dfrac{5}{3}T_P + \dfrac{2}{3}\left(T_P + 2\right) = 6$

$5T_P + 2T_P + 4 = 18$

$7T_P = 14$

$T_P = \mathbf{2\ hr}$

4. Average $= \dfrac{\text{total temp.}}{\text{number of days}}$

$= \dfrac{400° + T}{6} = 80°$

$T = 83°(6) - 400° = \mathbf{98°}$

5. $(K)(a) = $ cost of articles

$\mathbf{25Q - Ka = change}$

6. $_9C_5 = \dfrac{9!}{4!\ 5!} = \mathbf{126}$

7. $a = \sqrt{16} = 4$

$b = \sqrt{4} = 2$

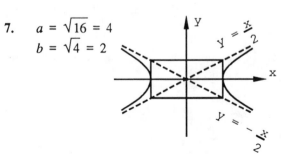

8. $\dfrac{4y^2}{36} - \dfrac{9x^2}{36} = \dfrac{36}{36}$

$\dfrac{y^2}{9} - \dfrac{x^2}{4} = 1$

$a = \sqrt{9} = 3$

$b = \sqrt{4} = 2$

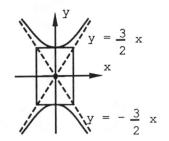

$y = \dfrac{3}{2}x$

$y = -\dfrac{3}{2}x$

9. Construction

10. Construction

11. Construction

12.

Term:	1	2	3	4	5	6	7
For a:	6	5	4	3	2	1	0
For b:	0	1	2	3	4	5	6
Coeff:	1	6	15	20	15	6	1

$15a^2b^4$

13. $a^4 + 4a^3b + 6a^2b^2 + 4ab^3 + b^4$

14. $\sin\theta \csc\theta\,(90° - \theta) = \sin\theta \sec\theta$

$= \sin\theta \left(\dfrac{1}{\cos\theta}\right) = \tan\theta$

15. $\sec(90° - \theta)\tan\theta = \csc\theta\tan\theta$

$= \dfrac{1}{\sin\theta}\left(\dfrac{\sin\theta}{\cos\theta}\right) = \dfrac{1}{\cos\theta} = \sec\theta$

16.

$x = \dfrac{\begin{vmatrix} 5 & -3 \\ -3 & -4 \end{vmatrix}}{\begin{vmatrix} 4 & -3 \\ 2 & -4 \end{vmatrix}} = \dfrac{-20 - 9}{-416 + 6} = \dfrac{29}{10}$

$y = \dfrac{\begin{vmatrix} 4 & 5 \\ 2 & -3 \end{vmatrix}}{-10} = \dfrac{-12 - 10}{-10} = \dfrac{-22}{-10} = \dfrac{11}{5}$

17. The sum of the exterior angles of any polygon is **360°**.

18. (a) side $= \dfrac{50}{10} = $ **5 cm**

(b)

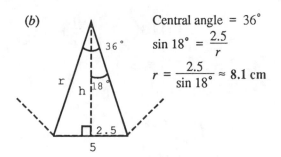

Central angle $= 36°$

$\sin 18° = \dfrac{2.5}{r}$

$r = \dfrac{2.5}{\sin 18°} \approx $ **8.1 cm**

19. Side ratio $= 5 : 3$

Area ratio $= \left(\dfrac{5}{3}\right)^2 = \dfrac{25}{9} = 25 : 9$

20. $A = 180° - 130° - 20° = 30°$

$\dfrac{a}{\sin 30°} = \dfrac{6}{\sin 20°}$

$a = \dfrac{6\sin 30°}{\sin 20°} \approx$ **8.8**

$\dfrac{b}{\sin 130°} = \dfrac{6}{\sin 20°}$

$b = \dfrac{6\sin 130°}{\sin 20°} \approx$ **13.4**

21. $\dfrac{49x^2}{196} + \dfrac{4y^2}{196} = \dfrac{196}{196}$

$\dfrac{x^2}{4} + \dfrac{y^2}{49} = 1$

$a = \sqrt{49} = 7$

$b = \sqrt{4} = 2$

22. $6\operatorname{cis} 150° = 6(\cos 150° + i\sin 150°)$

$= 6\left(-\dfrac{\sqrt{3}}{2} + i\dfrac{1}{2}\right) = -3\sqrt{3} + 3i$

23. Refer to Solution Set 47, problem 8.

24. Coefficient $k = \dfrac{2\pi}{3\pi} = \dfrac{2}{3}$

$y = 5 + 4\sin\dfrac{2}{3}\left(x - \dfrac{3\pi}{2}\right)$

25. $3(x^2 + 2x + 1) + 3(y^2 + 2y + 1)$

$= -4 + 3 + 3 = 2$

$3(x + 1)^2 + 3(y + 1)^2 = 2$

$(x + 1)^2 + (y + 1)^2 = \dfrac{2}{3}$

Center: (−1, −1)

Radius: $\dfrac{\sqrt{2}}{\sqrt{3}} = \dfrac{\sqrt{6}}{3}$

Advanced Mathematics

26. $a^2 = 7^2 + 20^2 = 449$

$a = \sqrt{\mathbf{449}}$

$\dfrac{14}{20} = \dfrac{b}{7}$

$20b = 98$

$b = \dfrac{98}{20} = \dfrac{\mathbf{49}}{\mathbf{10}}$

27. $\tan 3\theta = \dfrac{1}{\sqrt{3}} = \dfrac{\sqrt{3}}{3}$

$3\theta = 30°, 210°, 390°, 570°, 750°, 930°$

$\theta = \mathbf{10°, 70°, 130°, 190°, 250°, 310°}$

28. $\text{Arccos}\left(-\dfrac{\sqrt{3}}{2}\right) = \mathbf{150°}$

29. $\ln x^2 - \ln\left(x - \dfrac{1}{2}\right) = \ln 2$

$\ln \dfrac{x^2}{x - \dfrac{1}{2}} = \ln 2$

$\dfrac{x^2}{x - \dfrac{1}{2}} = 2$

$x^2 = 2x - 1$

$x^2 - 2x + 1 = 0$

$(x - 1)^2 = 0$

$x = \mathbf{1}$

30. $e^{-3} \approx 3^{-3} = \dfrac{\mathbf{1}}{\mathbf{27}}$

EP

3. **Valid**

PROBLEM SET 58

1. $B = 3C$

$T_D = T_U - 2$

Upstream: $(3C - C)T_U = 32$

               $2CT_U = 32$

               $CT_U = 16$

Downstream: $(3C + C)(T_U - 2) = 16$

               $4CT_U - 8C = 16$

               $4(16) - 8C = 16$

$C = \mathbf{6\ mph}$

$B = \mathbf{18\ mph}$

2. $\dfrac{b}{2}N + \dfrac{b}{2}(2N) = \dfrac{bN + 2bN}{2}$

$= \dfrac{\mathbf{3bN}}{\mathbf{2}} \textbf{ inches}$

3. $C = mN + b$

$5100 = m(10) + b$

$2600 = m(5) + b$

$5100 = 10m + b$

$\underline{(-)\ 2600 = 5m + b}$

$2500 = 5m$

$m = 500$

$b = 100$

$C = 500N + 100$

$C = 500(2) + 100 = \mathbf{\$1100}$

4. $A = $ angle

$90° - A = $ complement

$180° - A = $ supplement

$4(90° - A) = 2(180° - A) - 80°$

$360° - 4A = 360° - 2A - 80°$

$2A = 80°$

$A = \mathbf{40°}$

5. Rate $\cdot$ time $\cdot$ men $=$ jobs

Rate $\cdot\ 24\ \cdot\ 81 = 1$

Rate $= \dfrac{1}{1944}$

$\dfrac{1}{1944} \cdot t \cdot 108 = 1$

$t = 18$

6 days saved

6. $\dfrac{8!}{2!} = \mathbf{20{,}160}$

7. $25^{1/4} \text{ cis } \dfrac{80°}{4}$

First root $= \sqrt{5} \text{ cis } 20°$

Angles differ by $\dfrac{360°}{4} = 90°$

$\mathbf{\sqrt{5} \text{ cis } 110°, \sqrt{5} \text{ cis } 200°, \sqrt{5} \text{ cis } 290°}$

8. $16 \operatorname{cis} 90°$

First root $= \sqrt[3]{16} \operatorname{cis} \dfrac{90°}{3} = \sqrt[3]{16} \operatorname{cis} 30°$

Angles differ by $\dfrac{360°}{3} = 120°$

$\sqrt[3]{16} \operatorname{cis} 150°, \sqrt[3]{16} \operatorname{cis} 270°$

9. $1 \operatorname{cis} 180°$

First root $= \sqrt{1} \operatorname{cis} \dfrac{180°}{2} = 1 \operatorname{cis} 90°$

Angles differ by $\dfrac{360°}{2} = 180°$

$1 \operatorname{cis} 270°$

$1(\cos 90° + i \sin 90°) = i$

$1(\cos 270° + i \sin 270°) = -i$

10. Construction

11. Triangle cannot be constructed.

12. Construction

13.

Term:	1	2	3	4	5	6	7	8	9	10
For a:	9	8	7	6	5	4	3	2	1	0
For b:	0	1	2	3	4	5	6	7	8	9
Coeff:	1	9	36	84	126	126	84	36	9	1

$126a^4b^5$

14. $x^6 + 6x^5y + 15x^4y^2 + 20x^3y^3$
$+ 15x^2y^4 + 6xy^5 + y^6$

15. $\sin(90° - \theta)\sec(90° - \theta) = \cos\theta \csc\theta$

$= \cos\theta\left(\dfrac{1}{\sin\theta}\right) = \dfrac{\cos\theta}{\sin\theta} = \cot\theta$

16. $\dfrac{\tan\theta}{\sec\theta} = \dfrac{\dfrac{\sin\theta}{\cos\theta}}{\dfrac{1}{\cos\theta}} = \dfrac{\sin\theta}{\cos\theta} \cdot \dfrac{\cos\theta}{1} = \sin\theta$

17.

$x = \dfrac{\begin{vmatrix} 8 & -3 \\ 5 & 2 \end{vmatrix}}{\begin{vmatrix} 5 & -3 \\ 4 & 2 \end{vmatrix}} = \dfrac{16 + 15}{10 + 12} = \dfrac{31}{22}$

$y = \dfrac{\begin{vmatrix} 5 & 8 \\ 4 & 5 \end{vmatrix}}{22} = \dfrac{25 - 32}{22} = -\dfrac{7}{22}$

18. $(16 - 2)180° = 14(180°) = 2520°$

19. (a) $l = \dfrac{96}{12} = 8 \text{ ft}$

(b) Central angle $= \dfrac{360°}{12} = 30°$

$\tan 15° = \dfrac{4}{h}$

$h = \dfrac{4}{\tan 15°} \approx 14.93$

$A_{\text{triangle}} = \dfrac{1}{2}(8)(14.93) = 59.71 \text{ ft}^2$

$A_{\text{dodecahedron}} = (59.71)(12) = 716.6 \text{ ft}^2$

20. $B = 180° - 120° - 20° = 40°$

$\dfrac{a}{\sin 120°} = \dfrac{5}{\sin 20°}$

$a = \dfrac{5 \sin 120°}{\sin 20°} \approx 12.7$

$\dfrac{b}{\sin 40°} = \dfrac{5}{\sin 20°}$

$b = \dfrac{5 \sin 40°}{\sin 20°} \approx 9.4$

21. $\dfrac{16x^2}{64} + \dfrac{4y^2}{64} = \dfrac{64}{64}$

$\dfrac{x^2}{4} + \dfrac{y^2}{16} = 1$

22.

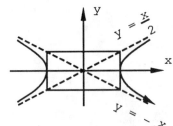

23. $\dfrac{9x^2}{36} - \dfrac{4y^2}{36} = \dfrac{36}{36}$

$\dfrac{x^2}{4} - \dfrac{y^2}{9} = 1$

Vertices: $(2, 0), (-2, 0)$

Asymptotes: $y = \pm\dfrac{3}{2}x$

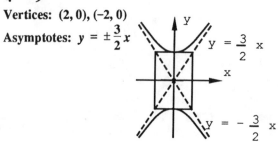

24. $8 \text{ cis } 90° = 8(\cos 90° + i \sin 90°)$
$= 8(0 + 1i) = \mathbf{8i}$

25. Refer to Problem Set 18, problem 7.

26. Coefficient $k = \dfrac{360°}{120°} = 3$

$\mathbf{y = -1 + 5 \cos 3(x - 50°)}$

27. $2\left(x^2 + x + \dfrac{1}{4}\right) + 2(y^2 - 2y + 1)$

$= 0 + \dfrac{1}{2} + 2 = \dfrac{5}{2}$

$2\left(x + \dfrac{1}{2}\right)^2 + 2(y - 1)^2 = \dfrac{5}{2}$

$\left(x + \dfrac{1}{2}\right)^2 + (y - 1)^2 = \dfrac{5}{4}$

Center: $\left(-\dfrac{1}{2}, 1\right)$

Radius: $\dfrac{\sqrt{5}}{2}$

28. $\dfrac{5}{7} = \dfrac{x}{4}$

$7x = 20$

$x = \dfrac{20}{7}$

29. $\cos 4\theta = \dfrac{1}{2}$

$4\theta = 60°, 300°, 420°, 660°, 780°, 1020°,$
$1140°, 1380°$

$\boldsymbol{\theta = 15°, 75°, 105°, 165°, 195°, 255°, 285°,}$
$\mathbf{345°}$

30. $\ln \dfrac{x - 2}{3x - 4} = \ln 3$

$\dfrac{x - 2}{3x - 4} = 3$

$x - 2 = 9x - 12$

$-8x = -10$

$x = \dfrac{5}{4}$

No solution

EP

4. $\dfrac{k(k + 2) + 1}{(k + 1)(k + 2)} = \dfrac{k^2 + 2k + 1}{(k + 1)(k + 2)}$

$= \dfrac{(k + 1)^2}{(k + 1)(k + 2)} = \dfrac{k + 1}{k + 2} = \dfrac{k + 1}{(k + 1) + 1}$

PROBLEM SET 59

1. $2 \text{ hr} = \dfrac{4}{7}$

$1 \text{ hr} = \dfrac{2}{7}$

$\dfrac{2}{7} T = \dfrac{3}{7}$

$T = \dfrac{3}{2} \mathbf{hr}$

2. Rate $\cdot$ time $\cdot$ men = jobs
Rate $\cdot$ 1 $\cdot$ M = 50
Rate $= \dfrac{50}{M}$

$\dfrac{50}{M} \cdot T \cdot 10 = 20$

$T = \dfrac{m}{25} \mathbf{days}$

3. $H = $ hundreds' digit
$T = $ tens' digit

$U = $ units' digit
A: $H + T + U = 17$
B: $T = H - 5$
$\quad H = T + 5$
C: $2U = 4T + 8$
$\quad U = 2T + 4$
Substitute equations B and C into A.
$(T + 5) + T + (2T + 4) = 17$
$4T = 8$
$T = 2$
$H = 2 + 5 = 7$
$U = 2(2) + 4 = 8$
$N = \mathbf{728}$

4. Distance $= hm$
Time $= h$
Rate $= m$
Distance $= \mathbf{300 - hm}$

5. 1 cup brown = $\frac{3}{4}$ cup white

$\frac{1}{4}$ (1 cup white) = $\frac{1}{4}\left(\frac{4}{3}$ cup brown$\right)$

$\frac{1}{4}$ cup white = $\frac{1}{3}$ **cup brown**

6. | 4 | 3 | T | 2 | 1 | = **24 ways**

7. $(27 \text{ cis } 36°)^{1/3}$

First root = $\sqrt[3]{27}$ cis $\frac{36°}{3}$ = **3 cis 12°**

Angles differ by $\frac{360°}{3}$ = 120°

3 cis 132°, 3 cis 252°

8. $(16 \text{ cis } 180°)^{1/4}$

First root = $\sqrt[4]{16}$ cis $\frac{180°}{4}$ = **2 cis 45°**

Angles differ by $\frac{360°}{4}$ = 90°

2 cis 135°, 2 cis 225°, 2 cis 315°

$2 \text{ cis } 45° = 2\left(\frac{\sqrt{2}}{2}+\frac{\sqrt{2}}{2}i\right) = \sqrt{2}+i\sqrt{2}$

$2 \text{ cis } 135° = 2\left(-\frac{\sqrt{2}}{2}+\frac{\sqrt{2}}{2}i\right) = -\sqrt{2}+i\sqrt{2}$

$2 \text{ cis } 225° = 2\left(-\frac{\sqrt{2}}{2}-\frac{\sqrt{2}}{2}i\right) = -\sqrt{2}-i\sqrt{2}$

$2 \text{ cis } 315° = 2\left(\frac{\sqrt{2}}{2}-\frac{\sqrt{2}}{2}i\right) = \sqrt{2}-i\sqrt{2}$

9. Construction

10. Construction

11.

Term:	1	2	3	4	5	6	7
For x:	6	5	4	3	2	1	0
For y:	0	1	2	3	4	5	6
Coeff:	1	6	15	20	15	6	1

$15x^4y^2$

12. $a^3 + 3a^2b + 3ab^2 + b^3$

13. $\dfrac{\sec^2 x - \tan^2 x}{1 + \cot^2 x} = \dfrac{1}{\csc^2 x} = \sin^2 x$

14. $\dfrac{\cos A}{1 + \sin A} + \dfrac{1 + \sin A}{\cos A}$

$= \dfrac{\cos^2 A + (1 + \sin A)^2}{\cos A \, (1 + \sin A)}$

$= \dfrac{\cos^2 A + 1 + 2 \sin A + \sin^2 A}{\cos A \, (1 + \sin A)}$

$= \dfrac{2 + 2 \sin A}{\cos A \, (1 + \sin A)} = \dfrac{2(1 + \sin A)}{\cos A \, (1 + \sin A)}$

$= \dfrac{2}{\cos A} = 2 \sec A$

15. $\dfrac{1}{\tan A} + \tan A = \dfrac{1 + \tan^2 A}{\tan A}$

$= \dfrac{\sec^2 A}{\tan A} = \dfrac{\dfrac{1}{\cos^2 A}}{\dfrac{\sin A}{\cos A}} = \dfrac{1}{\cos^2 A} \cdot \dfrac{\cos A}{\sin A}$

$= \dfrac{1}{\cos A} \cdot \dfrac{1}{\sin A} = \sec A \csc A$

16. $x = \dfrac{\begin{vmatrix} 7 & -2 \\ 9 & 4 \end{vmatrix}}{\begin{vmatrix} 4 & -2 \\ 3 & 4 \end{vmatrix}} = \dfrac{28 + 18}{16 + 6} = \dfrac{46}{22} = \dfrac{23}{11}$

$y = \dfrac{\begin{vmatrix} 4 & 7 \\ 3 & 9 \end{vmatrix}}{23} = \dfrac{36 - 21}{22} = \dfrac{15}{22}$

17. $(15 - 2)180° = 13(180°) = 2340°$

18. (a) $l = \dfrac{39}{13} = 3 \text{ in}$

(b)

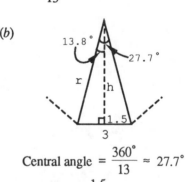

Central angle = $\dfrac{360°}{13} \approx 27.7°$

$\tan 13.8° = \dfrac{1.5}{h}$

$h = \dfrac{1.5}{\tan 13.8°} \approx 6.1$

$A_{\text{triangle}} = \dfrac{1}{2}(3)(6.1) = 9.15$

$A_{\text{polygon}} = (9.15)(13) = \textbf{118.9 in}^2$

(c) $\sin 13.8 = \dfrac{1.5}{r}$

$r = \dfrac{1.5}{\sin 13.8°} \approx \mathbf{6.3\ in}$

19. $C = 180° - 145° - 20° = \mathbf{15°}$

$\dfrac{b}{\sin 145°} = \dfrac{12}{\sin 20°}$

$b = \dfrac{12 \sin 145°}{\sin 20°} \approx \mathbf{20.1}$

$\dfrac{c}{\sin 15°} = \dfrac{12}{\sin 20°}$

$c = \dfrac{12 \sin 15°}{\sin 20°} \approx \mathbf{9.1}$

20. $\dfrac{9x^2}{225} + \dfrac{25y^2}{225} = \dfrac{225}{225}$

$\dfrac{x^2}{25} + \dfrac{y^2}{9} = 1$

Major axis: 10
Minor axis: 6
Center: (0, 0)

21. $\dfrac{16x^2}{400} - \dfrac{25y^2}{400} = \dfrac{400}{400}$

$\dfrac{x^2}{25} - \dfrac{y^2}{16} = 1$

Vertices: (±5, 0)

Asymptotes: $y = \pm\dfrac{4}{5}x$

22. $(3 \text{ cis } 20°)(4 \text{ cis } 40°) = 12 \text{ cis } 60°$
$= 12(\cos 60° + i \sin 60°)$

$= 12\left(\dfrac{1}{2} + i\dfrac{\sqrt{3}}{2}\right) = \mathbf{6 + 6i\sqrt{3}}$

23. Refer to Problem Set 47, problem 8.

24. Coefficient $k = \dfrac{360°}{240°} = \dfrac{3}{2}$

$y = -4 + 6 \cos \dfrac{3}{2}(x + 110°)$

25. $3(x^2 + 2x + 1) + 3(y^2 - 4y + 4)$
$= 1 + 3 + 12 = 16$
$3(x + 1)^2 + 3(y - 2)^2 = 16$
$(x + 1)^2 + (y - 2)^2 = \dfrac{16}{3}$

Center: (–1, 2)

Radius: $\sqrt{\dfrac{16}{3}} = \dfrac{4\sqrt{3}}{3}$

26. $\dfrac{a}{35} = \dfrac{15}{25}$

$a = \mathbf{21}$

$\dfrac{b}{24} = \dfrac{15}{25}$

$b = \dfrac{72}{5}$

27. $\tan 4\theta = \dfrac{1}{\sqrt{3}} = \dfrac{\sqrt{3}}{3}$

$4\theta = 30°, 210°, 390°, 570°, 750°, 930°,$
$1110°, 1290°$
$\theta = \mathbf{7.5°, 52.5°, 97.5°, 142.5°, 187.5°, 232.5°,}$
$\mathbf{277.5°, 322.5°}$

28.
$-\dfrac{4}{3}$

29. $\log_7 \dfrac{2x - 1}{3x + 3} = \log_7 5$
$2x - 1 = 15x + 15$
$-13x = 16$
$x = -\dfrac{16}{13}$
No solution

30. $\log_6 6^2 + 6^{\log_6 3} = 2 + 3 = \mathbf{5}$

EP

5. **Invalid**

PROBLEM SET 60

1.   A: $x + y = 150$

     B: $\dfrac{x}{27} + \dfrac{y}{23} = 6$

        $23x + 27y = 3726$

     Multiply equation A by 23.

$$\begin{array}{r} 23x + 23y = 3450 \\ (-)\ 23x + 27y = 3726 \\ \hline -4y = -276 \\ y = \quad 69 \end{array}$$

     $x + 69 = 150$

     $x = \mathbf{81}$

     $y = \mathbf{69}$

2. 1st angle $= A$

     2nd angle $= A + 10$

     3rd angle $= A + 35$

     $A + A + 10 + A + 35 = 180$

     $A = 45°$

     $\mathbf{45°, 55°, 80°}$

3.   Rate · time · workers = jobs

     Rate · 2 · 5 = 3

     Rate $= \dfrac{3}{10}$

     $\dfrac{3}{10}(10)$ · workers $= 18$

     Workers $= \mathbf{6}$

4.   (Cost of each)(number) = total cost

     $\left(\dfrac{c \text{ cents}}{p \text{ pencil}}\right)(N) = 500$ cents

     $N = 500 \text{ cents} \cdot \dfrac{p \text{ pencils}}{c \text{ cents}} = \dfrac{500\,p}{c}$ pencils

5.   Average $= \dfrac{\text{total}}{\text{number}}$

     $\dfrac{280 + G}{5} = 60$

     $G = \mathbf{20}$

6. $_{10}C_6 = \dfrac{10!}{4!\,6!} = \mathbf{210}$

7. $(16 \text{ cis } 180°)^{1/4}$

     First root $= \sqrt[4]{16} \text{ cis } \dfrac{180°}{4} = 2 \text{ cis } 45°$

     Angles differ by $\dfrac{360°}{4} = 90°$

     $2 \text{ cis } 135°, 2 \text{ cis } 225°, 2 \text{ cis } 315°$

$$2 \text{ cis } 45° = 2\left(\frac{\sqrt{2}}{2} + \frac{\sqrt{2}}{2}i\right) = \sqrt{2} + i\sqrt{2}$$

$$2 \text{ cis } 135° = 2\left(-\frac{\sqrt{2}}{2} + \frac{\sqrt{2}}{2}i\right) = -\sqrt{2} + i\sqrt{2}$$

$$2 \text{ cis } 225° = 2\left(-\frac{\sqrt{2}}{2} - \frac{\sqrt{2}}{2}i\right) = -\sqrt{2} - i\sqrt{2}$$

$$2 \text{ cis } 315° = 2\left(\frac{\sqrt{2}}{2} - \frac{\sqrt{2}}{2}i\right) = \sqrt{2} - i\sqrt{2}$$

8. $(8 \text{ cis } 45°)^{1/3}$

     First root $= \sqrt[3]{8} \text{ cis } \dfrac{45°}{3} = \mathbf{2 \text{ cis } 15°}$

     Angles differ by $\dfrac{360°}{3} = 120°$

     $\mathbf{2 \text{ cis } 135°, 2 \text{ cis } 255°}$

9.   Construction

10.   Construction

11.

Term:	1	2	3	4	5	6	7	8
For x:	7	6	5	4	3	2	1	0
For y:	0	1	2	3	4	5	6	7
Coeff:	1	7	21	35	35	21	7	1

     $\mathbf{35x^4y^3}$

12. $m^4 + 4m^3n + 6m^2n^2 + 4mn^3 + n^4$

13. $\dfrac{1 - \cos^2 x}{\sec^2 x - 1} = \dfrac{1 - \cos^2 x}{\dfrac{1}{\cos^2 x} - 1}$

     $= \dfrac{1 - \cos^2 x}{\dfrac{1 - \cos^2 x}{\cos^2 x}} = \cos^2 x$

14. $\dfrac{1}{1 + \sin A} + \dfrac{1}{1 - \sin A}$

     $= \dfrac{1 - \sin A + 1 + \sin A}{1 - \sin^2 A}$

     $= \dfrac{2}{1 - \sin^2 A} = \dfrac{2}{\cos^2 A} = 2 \sec^2 A$

15. $\dfrac{1}{\cot A} + \cot A = \dfrac{1 + \cot^2 A}{\cot A}$

$= \dfrac{\csc^2 A}{\cot A} = \dfrac{\dfrac{1}{\sin^2 A}}{\dfrac{\cos A}{\sin A}} = \dfrac{1}{\sin^2 A} \cdot \dfrac{\sin A}{\cos A}$

$= \dfrac{1}{\sin A \cos A} = \csc A \sec A$

16.

$x = \dfrac{\begin{vmatrix} 4 & 6 \\ 1 & -5 \end{vmatrix}}{\begin{vmatrix} 3 & 6 \\ 2 & -5 \end{vmatrix}} = \dfrac{-20 - 6}{-15 - 12} = \dfrac{-26}{-27} = \dfrac{26}{27}$

$y = \dfrac{\begin{vmatrix} 3 & 4 \\ 2 & 1 \end{vmatrix}}{-27} = \dfrac{3 - 8}{-27} = \dfrac{-5}{-27} = \dfrac{5}{27}$

17. $(13 - 2)180° = \mathbf{1980°}$

18. Central angle $= \dfrac{360°}{12} = 30°$

Side $= \dfrac{36}{12} = 3$ in

$\tan 15° = \dfrac{1.5}{h}$

$h = \dfrac{1.5}{\tan 15°} \approx 5.6$

$A_{\text{triangle}} = \dfrac{1}{2}(3)(5.6) = 8.4$

$A_{\text{dodecahedron}} = (8.4)(12) = \mathbf{100.8 \ in^2}$

19. $a^2 = 6^2 + 8^2 - 2(6)(8)\cos 40°$

$a = \sqrt{6^2 + 8^2 - 2(6)(8)\cos 40°}$

$a \approx \mathbf{5.14}$

$\sin B = \dfrac{(8)(\sin 40°)}{\sqrt{6^2 + 8^2 - 2(6)(8)\cos 40°}}$

$B = \sin^{-1}(0.9996886)$

$B = \mathbf{91.43°}$

$C = 180° - 40° - 91.43° = \mathbf{48.57°}$

20. $\cos A = \dfrac{5^2 + 10^2 - 7^2}{2(5)(10)} = 0.76$

$A \approx \mathbf{40.5°}$

$\cos B = \dfrac{5^2 + 7^2 - 10^2}{2(5)(7)} \approx -0.37$

$B \approx \mathbf{111.7°}$

$C = 180° - 40.5° - 111.7° = \mathbf{27.8°}$

21. $\dfrac{x^2}{25} + \dfrac{y^2}{4} = 1$

Major axis: **10**

Minor axis: **4**

22. $\dfrac{x^2}{25} - \dfrac{y^2}{4} = 1$

Vertices: **(±5, 0)**

Asymptotes: $y = \pm\dfrac{2}{5}x$

23. $8 \operatorname{cis}(0°) = 8[\cos(-60°) + i \sin(-60°)]$

$= 8\left(\dfrac{1}{2} - i\dfrac{\sqrt{3}}{2}\right) = \mathbf{4 - 4i\sqrt{3}}$

24. Refer to Problem Set 47, problem 10.

25. Period $= 90° - (-230°) = 320°$

Coefficient $k = \dfrac{360°}{320°} = \dfrac{9}{8}$

$y = 10 + 2\sin\dfrac{9}{8}(x - 90°)$

26. $2(x^2 - 2x + 1) + 2(y^2 + 4y + 4)$

$= -1 + 2 + 8 = 9$

$2(x - 1)^2 + 2(y + 2)^2 = 9$

$(x - 1)^2 + (y + 2)^2 = \dfrac{9}{2}$

Center: **(1, −2)**

Radius: $\sqrt{\dfrac{9}{2}} = \dfrac{3\sqrt{2}}{2}$

27. $\dfrac{x}{3} = \dfrac{12}{x}$ $\dfrac{y}{9} = \dfrac{12}{y}$

$x^2 = 36$ $y^2 = 108$

$x = 6$ $y = \sqrt{108} = 6\sqrt{3}$

28. $\tan 3\theta = -\dfrac{1}{\sqrt{3}} = -\dfrac{\sqrt{3}}{3}$

$3\theta = 150°, 330°, 510°, 690°, 870°, 1050°$

$\theta = \mathbf{50°, 110°, 170°, 230°, 290°, 350°}$

29.

$\dfrac{3}{5}$

30. $\log_{1/2}(3x + 2) - \log_{1/2}(x - 2) = \log_{1/2} 4^{-1}$

$\log_{1/2} \dfrac{3x + 2}{x - 2} = \log_{1/2} \dfrac{1}{4}$

$\dfrac{3x + 2}{x - 2} = \dfrac{1}{4}$

$x - 2 = 12x + 8$

$-10 = 11x$

$x = -\dfrac{10}{11}$

No solution

EP

6. $(k + 1)^2 = k^2 + 2k + 1$

PROBLEM SET 61

1. A: $L + W + H = 18$

B: $H = \dfrac{4}{5}(L + W)$

$5H = 4L + 4W$

C: $H = 4(L - W)$

$H = 4L - 4W$

Add equations B and C.

$\quad 5H = 4L + 4W$

$\underline{(+)\ H = 4L - 4W}$

$\quad 6H = 8L$

D: $L = \dfrac{3}{4}H$

Substitute equation D into B.

$5H = 4\left(\dfrac{3}{4}H\right) + 4W$

$2H = 4W$

E: $W = \dfrac{1}{2}H$

Substitute equations D and E into A.

$\dfrac{3}{4}H + \dfrac{1}{2}H + H = 18$

$\dfrac{9}{4}H = 18$

$H = \textbf{8 ft}$

$L = \textbf{6 ft}$

$W = \textbf{4 ft}$

2. Distance $= rh$

Rate $= r$

Time $= h$

Distance left $= \textbf{\textit{t} - \textit{rh}}$

3. $RTM = J$

$R(5)(7) = 3$

$R = \dfrac{3}{35}$

$\dfrac{3}{35}T(9) = 27$

$T = \dfrac{27(35)}{(9)(3)} = \textbf{35 days}$

4. $R_1T_1 + R_2T_2 = 13$

$\left(\dfrac{a}{3}\right)T + \left(\dfrac{3}{b}\right)T = 13$

$\dfrac{aT}{3} + \dfrac{3T}{b} = 13$

$abT + 9T = 39b$

$T(ab + 9) = 39b$

$T = \dfrac{39b}{ab + 9}\ \textbf{days}$

5. $RTM = J$

$R(5)(10) = p$

$R = \dfrac{p}{50}$

$T = \dfrac{50k}{15p} = \dfrac{10k}{3p}\ \textbf{days}$

6. $\dfrac{20!}{10!\ 6!\ 4!}$

7. $(1 \text{ cis } 180°)^{1/3}$

First root $= \sqrt[3]{1} \text{ cis } \dfrac{180°}{3} = 1 \text{ cis } 60°$

Angles differ by $\dfrac{360°}{3} = 120°$

$1 \text{ cis } 180°,\ 1 \text{ cis } 300°$

$1 \text{ cis } 60° = \left(\dfrac{1}{2} + i\dfrac{\sqrt{3}}{2}\right) = \dfrac{1}{2} + i\dfrac{\sqrt{3}}{2}$

$1 \text{ cis } 180° = (-1 + 0i) = -1$

$1 \text{ cis } 300° = \left(\dfrac{1}{2} - i\dfrac{\sqrt{3}}{2}\right) = \dfrac{1}{2} - i\dfrac{\sqrt{3}}{2}$

8. $(16 \text{ cis } 60°)^{1/4}$

First root $= \sqrt[4]{16} \text{ cis } \dfrac{60°}{4} = \textbf{2 cis 15}°$

Angles differ by $\dfrac{360°}{4} = 90°$

2 cis 105°, 2 cis 195°, 2 cis 285°

9. Construction

10. Triangle cannot be constructed.

11. $p^5 + 5p^4q + 10p^3q^2 + 10p^2q^3 + 5pq^4 + q^5$

12. $\dfrac{\sin A}{1 + \cos A} + \dfrac{1 + \cos A}{\sin A}$

$= \dfrac{\sin^2 A + (1 + \cos A)^2}{(1 + \cos A)\sin A}$

$= \dfrac{\sin^2 A + 1 + 2\cos A + \cos^2 A}{(1 + \cos A)\sin A}$

$= \dfrac{2 + 2\cos A}{(1 + \cos A)\sin A} = \dfrac{2(1 + \cos A)}{(1 + \cos A)\sin A}$

$= \dfrac{2}{\sin A} = 2\csc A$

13. $\dfrac{\csc^2 \theta - \cot^2 \theta}{1 + \cot^2 \theta} = \dfrac{1}{\csc^2 \theta} = \sin^2 \theta$

14. $\dfrac{\sin x}{\csc x} + \dfrac{\cos x}{\sec x}$

$= \dfrac{\sin x}{\dfrac{1}{\sin x}} + \dfrac{\cos x}{\dfrac{1}{\cos x}} = \sin^2 x + \cos^2 x = 1$

15. Central angle $= \dfrac{360°}{14} \approx 25.7°$

Side $= \dfrac{42}{14} = 3$

$\sin 12.9° = \dfrac{1.5}{r}$

$r = \dfrac{1.5}{\sin 12.9°} \approx \textbf{6.7}$

16. $(10 - 2)180° = \textbf{1440}°$

17. $a^2 = 9^2 + 10^2 - 2(9)(10)\cos 45°$

$= 181 - 180\left(\dfrac{\sqrt{2}}{2}\right) \approx 53.7$

$a \approx \textbf{7.33}$

$\cos B = \dfrac{7.33^2 + 9^2 - 10^2}{2(7.33)(9)} \approx 0.263$

$B \approx \textbf{74.7}°$

$C = 180° - 45° - 74.7° = \textbf{60.3}°$

18. $\cos A = \dfrac{4^2 + 12^2 - 10^2}{2(4)(12)} = 0.625$

$A \approx \textbf{51.3}°$

$\cos B = \dfrac{10^2 + 4^2 - 12^2}{2(10)(4)} = -0.35$

$B \approx \textbf{110.5}°$

$C = 180° - 51.3° - 110.5° = 18.2°$

19. $\dfrac{x^2}{36} + \dfrac{y^2}{9} = 1$

Major axis: 12

Minor axis: 6

20. $\dfrac{x^2}{36} - \dfrac{y^2}{9} = 1$

Vertices: (±6, 0)

Asymptotes: $y = \pm\dfrac{1}{2}x$

21. $6 \text{ cis } (-60°) = 6[\cos (-60°) + i \sin (-60°)]$

$= 6\left[\dfrac{1}{2} + i \sin\left(-\dfrac{\sqrt{3}}{2}\right)\right] = 3 - 3i\sqrt{3}$

22. Find the equation of the line $\perp$ to
$y = -2x + 3$ that passes through $(2, 1)$.

$m_\perp = \dfrac{1}{2}$

$1 = \dfrac{1}{2}(2) + b$

$b = 0$

$y = \dfrac{1}{2}x$

Set $y = -2x + 3$ equal to $y = \dfrac{1}{2}x$ to get:

$-2x + 3 = \dfrac{1}{2}x$

$x = \dfrac{6}{5}$

$y = \dfrac{1}{2}\left(\dfrac{6}{5}\right) = \dfrac{3}{5}$

$(x, y) = \left(\dfrac{6}{5}, \dfrac{3}{5}\right)$

$d = \sqrt{\left(2 - \dfrac{6}{5}\right)^2 + \left(1 - \dfrac{3}{5}\right)^2}$

$= \sqrt{\left(\dfrac{4}{5}\right)^2 + \left(\dfrac{2}{5}\right)^2} = \sqrt{\dfrac{16 + 4}{25}}$

$= \dfrac{\sqrt{20}}{5} = \dfrac{2\sqrt{5}}{5}$

23. $y = 2 + 9 \sin 4\left(x - \dfrac{\pi}{8}\right)$

24. $2(x^2 + 2x + 1) + 2(y^2 - 6y + 9)$
$= -1 + 2 + 18 = 19$
$2(x + 1)^2 + 2(y - 3)^2 = 19$
$(x + 1)^2 + (y - 3)^2 = \dfrac{19}{2}$

Center: $(-1, 3)$

Radius: $\sqrt{\dfrac{19}{2}} = \dfrac{\sqrt{38}}{2}$

25. $x^2 = 5^2 + \left(\dfrac{5}{2}\right)^2 = 25 + \dfrac{25}{4} = \dfrac{125}{4}$

$x = \dfrac{5\sqrt{5}}{2}$

$\dfrac{\frac{5\sqrt{5}}{2}}{a} = \dfrac{5}{9}$

$5a = \dfrac{45\sqrt{5}}{2}$

$a = \dfrac{9\sqrt{5}}{2}$

$\dfrac{\frac{5}{2}}{b} = \dfrac{5}{3}$

$5b = \dfrac{15}{2}$

$b = \dfrac{3}{2}$

26. $\sin^2 x = \dfrac{1}{4}$

$\sin x = \pm\dfrac{1}{2}$

$x = 30°, 150°, 210°, 330°$

27. $(3x + 2)(\log 6) = (2x - 1)(\log 4)$
$(3x + 2)(0.7782) = (2x - 1)(0.6021)$
$2.3346x + 1.5564 = 1.2042x - 0.6021$
$1.1304x = -2.1585$
$x \approx -1.91$

28. $(-3x - 4)(\log 10) = (2x - 1)(\log 5)$
$(-3x - 4)(1) = (2x - 1)(0.699)$
$-3x - 4 = 1.398x - 0.699$
$0.398x = 3.301$
$x \approx -0.75$

29. $(1.02)^8 \approx 1.17$

30. $\log_7 \dfrac{8^{2/3}(x)}{x + 2} = \log_7 9$

$\dfrac{4x}{x + 2} = 9$

$4x = 9x + 18$

$x = -\dfrac{18}{5}$

No solution

EP

7.   Invalid

PROBLEM SET 62

1. $\dfrac{6 \text{ numbers} > 9}{36 \text{ possible numbers}} = \dfrac{1}{6}$

2. $\dfrac{5}{17} \times \dfrac{2}{17} = \dfrac{60}{289}$

3. $\dfrac{5}{17} \times \dfrac{12}{16} = \dfrac{5}{17} \times \dfrac{3}{4} = \dfrac{15}{68}$

4. $v = r\omega$
$v = (r \text{ in}) \times \left(\dfrac{40 \text{ rev}}{\text{min}} \cdot \dfrac{2\pi \text{ rad}}{\text{rev}}\right)$

$\times \left(\dfrac{1 \text{ ft}}{12 \text{ in}}\right) \times \left(\dfrac{1 \text{ min}}{60 \text{ sec}}\right)$

$= \dfrac{(r)(40)(2\pi)}{(12)(60)} \dfrac{\text{ft}}{\text{sec}} = \dfrac{\pi r}{9} \dfrac{\text{ft}}{\text{sec}}$

5. $C = mN + b$
$\qquad 450 = m(10) + b$
$(-) \; 850 = m(20) + b$
$\qquad\overline{-400 = -10m}$
$\qquad\quad 40 = \quad\; m$
$b = 450 - (10)(40) = 50$
$C = 40N + 50 = 40(2) + 50 = \$130$

6. $RTM = J$

$R(1)(M) = J$

$R = \dfrac{J}{M}$

$\dfrac{J}{M}(T)(M - 5) = k$

$T = \dfrac{Mk}{J(M - 5)}$ **days**

7. $(32 \text{ cis } 60°)^{1/5}$

First root $= \sqrt[5]{32} \text{ cis } \dfrac{60°}{5} = \textbf{2 cis 12}°$

Angles differ by $\dfrac{360°}{5} = 72°$

**2 cis 84°, 2 cis 156°, 2 cis 228°,
2 cis 300°**

8. Construction

9. Construction

10. $x^6 + 6x^5z + 15x^4z^2 + 20x^3z^3$
$+ \ 15x^2z^4 + 6xz^5 + z^6$

11. $\dfrac{\sin A}{1 - \cos A} + \dfrac{1 - \cos A}{\sin A}$

$= \dfrac{\sin^2 A + (1 - \cos A)^2}{(1 - \cos A)(\sin A)}$

$= \dfrac{\sin^2 A + 1 - 2\cos A + \cos^2 A}{(1 - \cos A)(\sin A)}$

$= \dfrac{2 - 2\cos A}{(1 - \cos A)(\sin A)} = \dfrac{2(1 - \cos A)}{(1 - \cos A)(\sin A)}$

$= \dfrac{2}{\sin A} = 2 \csc A$

12. $\dfrac{\sec^2 \theta - \tan^2 \theta}{\tan^2 \theta + 1} = \dfrac{1}{\sec^2 \theta} = \cos^2 \theta$

13. $\dfrac{1}{\tan (-x)} + \tan (-x) = \dfrac{1}{-\tan x} - \tan x$

$= \dfrac{1 + \tan^2 x}{-\tan x} = \dfrac{\sec^2 x}{-\tan x} = \dfrac{\dfrac{1}{\cos^2 x}}{\dfrac{-\sin x}{\cos x}}$

$= \dfrac{1}{\cos^2 x}\left(-\dfrac{\cos x}{\sin x}\right) = -\dfrac{1}{\cos x \sin x}$

$= -\sec x \csc x$

14. Central angle $= \dfrac{360°}{12} = 30°$

Side $= \dfrac{96 \text{ cm}}{12} = 8 \text{ cm}$

$\tan 15° = \dfrac{4}{h}$

$h = \dfrac{4}{\tan 15°} \approx 14.9$

$A_{\text{triangle}} = \dfrac{1}{2}(8)(14.9) = 59.7$

$A_{\text{dodecahedron}} = (59.7)(12) = \textbf{716.6 cm}^2$

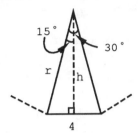

15. The sum of the exterior angles of any polygon is **360°**.

16. $a^2 = 8^2 + 12^2 - 2(8)(12)\cos 60°$

$= 208 - 192\left(\dfrac{1}{2}\right) = 112$

$a = \sqrt{112} = 4\sqrt{7} \approx 10.58$

$\cos B = \dfrac{8^2 + \left(4\sqrt{7}\right)^2 - 12^2}{2(8)\left(4\sqrt{7}\right)}$

$= \dfrac{32}{64\sqrt{7}} = \dfrac{1}{2\sqrt{7}} \approx 0.189$

$B = \cos^{-1} 0.189 \approx \textbf{79}°$

$C = 180° - 60° - 79° = \textbf{41}°$

17. $\cos A = \dfrac{14^2 + 8^2 - 10^2}{2(14)(8)} \approx 0.7143$

$A = \cos^{-1} 0.7143 \approx \textbf{44.4}°$

$\cos B = \dfrac{8^2 + 10^2 - 14^2}{2(8)(10)} = -0.2$

$B = \cos^{-1}(-0.2) \approx \textbf{101.5}°$

$C = 180° - 44.4° - 101.5° = \textbf{34.1}°$

18. $\dfrac{x^2}{9} + \dfrac{y^2}{16} = 1$

Major axis: 8
Minor axis: 6

19. $\dfrac{y^2}{16} - \dfrac{x^2}{9} = 1$

Vertices: $(0, \pm 4)$

Asymptotes: $y = \pm \dfrac{4}{3}x$

Center: $(0, 0)$

20. $1 \text{ cis } 0° = 1(\cos 0° + i \sin 0°)$
$= 1 + 0i = \mathbf{1}$

21. Refer to Problem Set 18, problem 7.

22. Period $= 30 - (-50°) = 80°$
Coefficient $k = \dfrac{360°}{80°} = \dfrac{9}{2}$
$y = \mathbf{-8 + 6\cos\dfrac{9}{2}(x - 30°)}$

23. $(x^2 + 2x + 1) + (y^2 - 6y + 9)$
$= 6 + 1 + 9 = 16$
$(x + 1)^2 + (y - 3)^2 = \mathbf{16}$
Center: $\mathbf{(-1, 3)}$
Radius: $\mathbf{4}$

24. $(a + b)^2 = 5^2 + 12^2 = 169$
$a + b = 13$
$\dfrac{9}{12} = \dfrac{b}{13}$
$12b = 117$
$b = \dfrac{117}{12} = \dfrac{\mathbf{39}}{\mathbf{4}}$
$a = 13 - \dfrac{39}{4} = \dfrac{\mathbf{13}}{\mathbf{4}}$

25. $(\sec\theta + 2)(\sec\theta - 1) = 0$
$\sec\theta = -2$ or $\sec\theta = 1$
$\cos\theta = (1,2)$ $\cos\theta = 1$
$\theta = 120°, 240°$ $\theta = 0°$
$\theta = \mathbf{0°, 120°, 240°}$

26. Tangent is the reciprocal of cotangent.
Therefore, $\tan\left[\text{Arccot}\left(-\dfrac{4}{3}\right)\right] = \mathbf{-\dfrac{5}{4}}$

27. $(2x - 4)\log 7 = (3x + 2)\log 5$
$(2x - 4)(0.8451) = (3x + 2)(0.6990)$
$1.6902x - 3.3804 = 2.097x + 1.398$
$-0.4068x = 4.7784$
$x \approx \mathbf{-11.75}$

28. $(3x - 1)(\log 10) = (4x - 2)(\log 5)$
$(3x - 1)(1) = (4x - 2)(0.6990)$
$3x - 1 = 2.796x - 1.398$
$0.204x = -0.398$
$x \approx \mathbf{-2}$

29. $(1.41)^8 \approx \mathbf{15.6}$

30. $\log_8 \dfrac{16}{4} = x$
$\log_8 4 = x$
$8^x = 4$
$2^{3x} = 2^2$
$3x = 2$
$x = \dfrac{\mathbf{2}}{\mathbf{3}}$

EP

8. $(k + 1)\left[(k + 1) + 1\right]$
$= (k + 1)(k + 2) = k^2 + 3k + 2$
$= k^2 + k + 2k + 2 = k(k + 1) + 2(k + 1)$

PROBLEM SET 63

1. $\dfrac{500 + T}{6} = 90$
$500 + T = 540$
$T = \mathbf{40°}$

2. Distance: k k
Rate: $\dfrac{k}{p}$?
Time: p $p + m$
New rate $= \dfrac{k}{p + m}\dfrac{\text{yd}}{\text{min}}$

3. $R_J T_J + R_B T_B = 11$
$\dfrac{4}{3}(6) + R_B(6) = 11$

$8 + 6R_B = 11$
$R_B = \dfrac{1}{2}$
$\dfrac{1}{2}(4) = \mathbf{2 \text{ jobs}}$

4. $N_1 = 11N$
$N_2 = 11(N + 1)$
$N_3 = 11(N + 2)$
$4(N_1 + N_3) + 66 = 10N_2$
$4[11N + 11(N + 2)] + 66 = 10[11(N + 1)]$
$4(11N + 11N + 22) + 66 = 10(11N + 11)$
$44N + 44N + 88 + 66 = 110N + 110$
$44N + 44N - 110N = 110 - 66 - 88$

$-22N = -44$
$N = 2$
$N_1 = \mathbf{22}$
$N_2 = \mathbf{33}$
$N_3 = \mathbf{44}$

5. $\dfrac{1}{2} \cdot \dfrac{1}{2} \cdot \dfrac{1}{2} = \dfrac{\mathbf{1}}{\mathbf{8}}$

6. (a) $\dfrac{4}{7} \cdot \dfrac{4}{7} = \dfrac{\mathbf{16}}{\mathbf{49}}$

    (b) $\dfrac{4}{7} \cdot \dfrac{3}{6} = \dfrac{\mathbf{2}}{\mathbf{7}}$

7. $(16 \operatorname{cis} 120°)^{1/4}$

    First root $= \sqrt[4]{16} \operatorname{cis} \dfrac{120°}{4} = 2 \operatorname{cis} 30°$

    Angles differ by $\dfrac{360°}{4} = 90°$

    $2 \operatorname{cis} 120°, 2 \operatorname{cis} 210°, 2 \operatorname{cis} 300°$

    $2 \operatorname{cis} 30° = 2\left(\dfrac{\sqrt{3}}{2} + \dfrac{1}{2}i\right) = \mathbf{\sqrt{3} + i}$

    $2 \operatorname{cis} 120° = 2\left(-\dfrac{1}{2} + \dfrac{\sqrt{3}}{2}i\right) = \mathbf{-1 + i\sqrt{3}}$

    $2 \operatorname{cis} 210° = 2\left(-\dfrac{\sqrt{3}}{2} - \dfrac{1}{2}i\right) = \mathbf{-\sqrt{3} - i}$

    $2 \operatorname{cis} 300° = 2\left(\dfrac{1}{2} - \dfrac{\sqrt{3}}{2}i\right) = \mathbf{1 - i\sqrt{3}}$

8. Construction

9. Construction

10. $a^7 + 7a^6c + 21a^5c^2 + 35a^4c^3 + 35a^3c^4 + 21a^2c^5 + 7ac^6 + c^7$

11. $\dfrac{(\csc^2 x - \cot^2 x)(\csc^2 x + \cot^2 x)}{\csc^2 x + \cot^2 x}$
    $+ \cot^2 x = \csc^2 x - \cot^2 x + \cot^2 x$
    $= \csc^2 x$

12. $\cos x - \cos x \sin^2 x = \cos x(1 - \sin^2 x)$
    $= \cos x \cos^2 x = \cos^3 x$

13. $\dfrac{\sec^2 \theta - 1}{\cot \theta} = \dfrac{\tan^2 \theta}{\cot \theta} = \dfrac{\tan^2 \theta}{\dfrac{1}{\tan \theta}} = \tan^3 \theta$

14. $\cos(-\theta)\csc(-\theta) = \cos \theta(-\csc \theta)$
    $= -\cos \theta \csc \theta = -\cos \theta \cdot \dfrac{1}{\sin \theta}$
    $= -\dfrac{\cos \theta}{\sin \theta} = -\cot \theta = \cot(-\theta)$

15.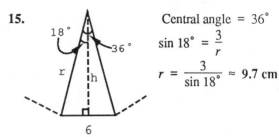

    Central angle $= 36°$

    $\sin 18° = \dfrac{3}{r}$

    $r = \dfrac{3}{\sin 18°} \approx \mathbf{9.7 \text{ cm}}$

16. $\cos A = \dfrac{8^2 + 10^2 - 7^2}{2(8)(10)} \approx 0.7188$
    $A = \cos^{-1} .7188 \approx \mathbf{44.1°}$
    $\cos B = \dfrac{8^2 + 7^2 - 10^2}{2(8)(7)} \approx 0.1161$
    $B = \cos^{-1} 0.1161 \approx \mathbf{83.3°}$
    $C = 180° - 44.1° - 83.3° = \mathbf{52.6°}$

17. $\sin 50° = \dfrac{h}{8}$
    $h = 8 \sin 50° \approx 6.13 \text{ cm}$
    $A = \dfrac{1}{2}(10)(6.13) = \mathbf{30.6 \text{ cm}^2}$

    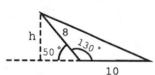

18. $\dfrac{x^2}{25} + \dfrac{y^2}{4} = 1$
    Center: (0, 0)
    Major axis: 10
    Minor axis: 4

19. $\dfrac{x^2}{25} - \dfrac{y^2}{4} = 1$
    Center: (0, 0)
    Vertices: (±5, 0)
    Asymptotes: $y = \pm\dfrac{2}{5}x$

20. Refer to Problem Set 47, problem 8.

21. Period $= \dfrac{2\pi}{2} = \pi$

22. Period $= \dfrac{360°}{2} = 180°$

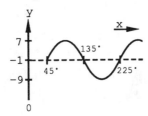

23. $(x^2 + 6x + 9) + (y^2 - 4y + 4)$
$= 15 + 9 + 4 = 28$
$(x + 3)^2 + (y - 2)^2 = 28$
Center: (–3, 2)
Radius: $2\sqrt{7}$

24. $\dfrac{6}{9} = \dfrac{10}{y}$
$6y = 90$
$y = \mathbf{15}$

25. $2\cos 3\theta = \sqrt{3}$
$\cos 3\theta = \dfrac{\sqrt{3}}{2}$
$3\theta = 30°, 330°, 390°, 690°, 750°, 1050°$
$\theta = \mathbf{10°, 110°, 130°, 230°, 250°, 350°}$

26. $4\sin^2 x = 3$
$\sin^2 x = \dfrac{3}{4}$
$\sin x = \pm\dfrac{\sqrt{3}}{2}$
$x = \mathbf{60°, 120°, 240°, 300°}$

27. $(3x - 1)(\log 8) = (2x + 1)(\log 5)$
$(3x - 1)(0.903) = (2x + 1)(0.6990)$
$2.71x - 0.903 = 1.398x + 0.6990$
$1.312x = 1.602$
$x \approx \mathbf{1.2}$

28. $(2x - 3)(\log 10) = (2x + 1)(\log 4)$
$(2x - 3)(1) = (2x + 1)(0.602)$
$2x - 3 = 1.204x + 0.602$
$0.796x = 3.602$
$x \approx \mathbf{4.5}$

29. $x = \dfrac{-4 \pm \sqrt{16 - 4(1)(6)}}{2(1)}$
$= \dfrac{-4 \pm \sqrt{-8}}{2} = \dfrac{-4 \pm 2i\sqrt{2}}{2} = -2 \pm i\sqrt{2}$
$\left[x - \left(-2 + i\sqrt{2}\right)\right]\left[x - \left(-2 - i\sqrt{2}\right)\right]$

30. $\log_8 4^{3/2} + \log_8 x^2 = \log_8 16$
$\log_8 8x^2 = \log_8 16$
$8x^2 = 16$
$x^2 = 2$
$x = \mathbf{\sqrt{2}}$

EP

9. **Invalid**

PROBLEM SET 64

1.

	Old	New
Distance:	m	$m + 60$
Time:	h	?
Rate:	$\dfrac{m}{h}$	$\dfrac{2m}{h}$

Time $= \dfrac{m + 60}{\frac{2m}{h}} = \dfrac{h(m + 60)}{2m}$ hr

2. $n = 1^{\text{st}}$ number
$n + 1 = 2^{\text{nd}}$ number
$n + 2 = 3^{\text{rd}}$ number
$n(n + 1) - 14 = n + 2$

$n^2 + n - 14 = n + 2$
$n^2 = 16$
$n = \pm 4$
4, 5, 6 or **–4, –3, –2**

3. $\dfrac{1}{2} \cdot \dfrac{1}{2} = \dfrac{1}{4}$

4.

	Uphill	Downhill
Distance:	200	160
Rate:	50	r
Time:	4	$\dfrac{160}{r}$

Average rate $= \dfrac{\text{total distance}}{\text{total time}}$

$60 = \dfrac{200 + 160}{\dfrac{200}{50} + \dfrac{160}{r}} = \dfrac{360}{4 + \dfrac{160}{r}}$

$60 = \dfrac{360}{\dfrac{4r + 160}{r}} = \dfrac{360r}{4r + 160}$

$60(4r + 160) = 360r$

$240r + 9600 = 360r$

$120r = 9600$

$r = \mathbf{80\ mph}$

5.   (a) $\dfrac{5}{9} \cdot \dfrac{4}{9} = \dfrac{\mathbf{20}}{\mathbf{81}}$

     (b) $\dfrac{5}{9} \cdot \dfrac{4}{8} = \dfrac{20}{72} = \dfrac{\mathbf{5}}{\mathbf{18}}$

6. $\boxed{10\ |\ 4\ |\ 5} = \mathbf{200}$

7. $\begin{bmatrix} 3 & -2 & -1 \\ 2 & 3 & 8 \end{bmatrix} = \begin{bmatrix} 1 & -\dfrac{2}{3} & -\dfrac{1}{3} \\ 0 & \dfrac{13}{3} & \dfrac{26}{3} \end{bmatrix}$

     $= \begin{bmatrix} 1 & 0 & 1 \\ 0 & 1 & 2 \end{bmatrix}$

     $x = \mathbf{1}$

     $y = \mathbf{2}$

8. $\begin{bmatrix} 1 & 2 & 0 \\ 2 & -3 & 5 \end{bmatrix} = \begin{bmatrix} 1 & 2 & 0 \\ 0 & -7 & 5 \end{bmatrix}$

     $= \begin{bmatrix} 1 & 0 & \dfrac{10}{7} \\ 0 & 1 & -\dfrac{5}{7} \end{bmatrix}$

     $x = \dfrac{\mathbf{10}}{\mathbf{7}}$

     $y = -\dfrac{\mathbf{5}}{\mathbf{7}}$

9.   Construction

10. $(8\text{ cis }90°)^{1/3}$

     First root $= \sqrt[3]{8}\text{ cis }\dfrac{90°}{3} = 2\text{ cis }30°$

     Angles differ by $\dfrac{360°}{3} = 120°$

     $2\text{ cis }150°,\ 2\text{ cis }270°$

     $2\text{ cis }30° = 2\left(\dfrac{\sqrt{3}}{2} + \dfrac{1}{2}i\right) = \sqrt{3} + i$

$2\text{ cis }150° = 2\left(-\dfrac{\sqrt{3}}{2} + \dfrac{1}{2}i\right) = -\sqrt{3} + 1$

$2\text{ cis }270° = 2(0 - 1i) = -2i$

11. $p^8 + 8p^7q + 28p^6q^2 + 56p^5q^3$
     $+ 70p^4q^4 + 56p^3q^5 + 28p^2q^6$
     $+ 8pq^7 + q^8$

12. $\sec^2 x - \sec^2 x \cos^2 x$

     $= \sec^2 x(1 - \cos^2 x) = \dfrac{1}{\cos^2 x} \cdot \sin^2 x$

     $= \dfrac{\sin^2 x}{\cos^2 x} = \tan^2 x$

13. $\dfrac{(\sec^2 x - \tan^2 x)(\sec^2 x + \tan^2 x)}{\sec^2 x + \tan^2 x}$

     $= \sec^2 x - \tan^2 x = 1$

14. $\cos(-x)\tan(-x)\csc(-x)$

     $= \cos x\,(-\tan x)(-\csc x)$

     $= \cos x \cdot \dfrac{\sin x}{\cos x} \cdot \dfrac{1}{\sin x} = 1$

15. $\dfrac{\sin^2 x + \cos^2 x}{\sec^2 x - 1} = \dfrac{1}{\tan^2 x} = \cot^2 x$

16. $\dfrac{6^2}{5^2} = \dfrac{36}{25}$

     Ratio $= \mathbf{36 : 25}$

17. $c = \sqrt{64 + 100 - 2(8)(10)\cos 20°}$

     $\approx \sqrt{13.65} \approx \mathbf{3.7}$

     $\cos B = \dfrac{8^2 + (3.7)^2 - 10^2}{2(8)(3.7)} \approx -0.3769$

     $B = \cos^{-1}(-.3769) \approx \mathbf{112.2°}$

     $A = 180° - 20° - 112.2° = \mathbf{47.8°}$

18.

     $\sin 30° = \dfrac{h}{8}$

     $h = 8\sin 30° = 4$

     $A = \dfrac{1}{2}(6 + 14) = 2(20) = 40\text{ m}^2$

     $A = 40\text{ m}^2 \times \left(\dfrac{100^2\text{ cm}^2}{\text{m}^2}\right) = \mathbf{400{,}000\text{ cm}^2}$

19. $\dfrac{80 \text{ mi}}{\text{hr}} \cdot \dfrac{5280 \text{ ft}}{\text{mi}} \cdot \dfrac{12 \text{ in}}{\text{ft}} \cdot \dfrac{2.54 \text{ cm}}{\text{in}}$

$\cdot \dfrac{1 \text{ m}}{100 \text{ cm}} \cdot \dfrac{1 \text{ km}}{1000 \text{ m}} \cdot \dfrac{1 \text{ hr}}{60 \text{ min}} \cdot \dfrac{1 \text{ min}}{60 \text{ sec}}$

$= \dfrac{(80)(5280)(12)(2.54)}{(100)(1000)(60)(60)} \dfrac{\text{km}}{\text{sec}}$

20. $\dfrac{9x^2}{144} - \dfrac{16y^2}{144} = \dfrac{144}{144}$

$\dfrac{x^2}{16} - \dfrac{y^2}{9} = 1$

Vertices: $(\pm 4, 0)$

Asymptotes: $y = \pm \dfrac{3}{4}x$

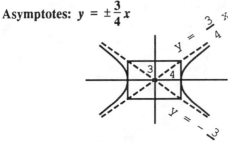

21. Refer to Problem Set 18, problem 7.

22. $(x^2 - 4x + 4) + y^2 = 0 + 4$
$(x - 2)^2 + y^2 = 4$
Center: $(2, 0)$
Radius: 2

23. Period $= \dfrac{360°}{3} = 120°$

24. Period $= \dfrac{2\pi}{2} = \pi$

25. $(2x^2y^4 - 3p^3)(4x^4y^8 + 6x^2y^4p^3 + 9p^6)$

26. $2 \sin 4\theta = 1$

$\sin 4\theta = \dfrac{1}{2}$

$4\theta = 30°, 150°, 390°, 510°, 750°, 870°,$
$1110°, 1230°$
$\theta = \textbf{7.5°}, \textbf{37.5°}, \textbf{97.5°}, \textbf{127.5°}, \textbf{187.5°}, \textbf{217.5°},$
$\textbf{277.5°}, \textbf{307.5°}$

27. $4 \sin^2 x - 1 = 0 \qquad\qquad \sec x - 2 = 0$

$\sin^2 x = \dfrac{1}{4} \qquad\qquad\qquad \sec x = 2$

$\sin x = \pm \dfrac{1}{2} \qquad\qquad\quad \cos x = \dfrac{1}{2}$

$x = \textbf{30°}, \textbf{60°}, \textbf{150°}, \textbf{210°}, \textbf{300°}, \textbf{330°}$

28. $6^{3x-2} = 5^{2x-1}$
$\log 6^{3x-2} = \log 5^{2x-1}$
$(3x - 2)(\log 6) = (2x - 1)(\log 5)$
$(3x - 2)(0.7782) = (2x - 1)(0.6990)$
$2.3346x - 1.5564 = 1.398x - 0.6990$
$0.9366x = 0.8574$
$x \approx \textbf{0.92}$

29. $(2.02)^5$
$\log 2.02^5 = 5 \log 2.02 \approx 1.5268$
$\text{antilog } (1.5268) \approx \textbf{33.6}$

30. $\left(\dfrac{1}{2}\right)^{-3} = x = 2^3 = \textbf{8}$

EP

10. $(n + 1)^2 = n^2 + 2n + 1$

PROBLEM SET 65

1.

<u>Little Hand</u>	<u>Big Hand</u>	$T_L = T_B$
$R_L T_L = S$	$R_B T_B = S + 30$	$\dfrac{1}{12}T = 1(T) - 30$
$R_L = \dfrac{1}{12}$	$R_B = 1$	

$$\frac{11}{12}T = 30$$

$$T = 32\frac{8}{11}\text{ min}$$

2.
Little Hand	Big Hand

$R_L T_L = S$ $R_B T_B = S + 45$

$R_L = \dfrac{1}{12}$ $R_B = 1$

$T_L = T_B$

$\dfrac{1}{12}T = 1(T) - 45$

$\dfrac{11}{12}T = 45$

$T = 49\dfrac{1}{11}\text{ min}$

3. $N_1 = N$
$N_2 = N + 2$
$N_3 = N + 4$
$N_1 N_2 = 3N_3$
$N(N + 2) = 3(N + 4)$
$N^2 + 2N = 3N + 12$
$N^2 - N - 12 = 0$
$(N - 4)(N + 3) = 0$
$N = 4$
4, 6, 8

4.
	1st	2nd
Distance:	d	d
Rate:	10	25
Time:	$t + 5$	$t - 1$

$(10)(t + 5) = (25)(t - 1)$
$10t + 50 = 25t - 25$
$15t = 75$
$t = 5$
$d = 25(5 - 1) = \textbf{100 mi}$

5. $\dfrac{4}{7}$

6. $(6 - 1)! = 5! = \textbf{120}$

7. $\begin{bmatrix} 1 & 2 & 8 \\ 2 & -3 & -5 \end{bmatrix} = \begin{bmatrix} 1 & 2 & 8 \\ 0 & -7 & -21 \end{bmatrix}$

$= \begin{bmatrix} 1 & 0 & 2 \\ 0 & 1 & 3 \end{bmatrix}$

$x = \textbf{2}$
$y = \textbf{3}$

8. Construction

9. $x^9 + 9x^8 y + 36x^7 y^2 + 84x^6 y^3 + 126x^5 y^4 +$
$126x^4 y^5 + 84x^3 y^6 + 36x^2 y^7 + 9xy^8 + y^9$

10. $(16 \text{ cis } 120°)^{1/4}$

First root $= \sqrt[4]{16}\text{ cis }\dfrac{120°}{4} = 2\text{ cis }30°$

Angles differ by $\dfrac{360°}{4} = 90°$

$2\text{ cis }120°, 2\text{ cis }210°, 2\text{ cis }300°$

$2\text{ cis }30° = 2\left(\dfrac{\sqrt{3}}{2} + \dfrac{1}{2}i\right) = \sqrt{3} + i$

$2\text{ cis }120° = 2\left(-\dfrac{1}{2} + \dfrac{\sqrt{3}}{2}i\right) = -1 + i\sqrt{3}$

$2\text{ cis }210° = 2\left(-\dfrac{\sqrt{3}}{2} - \dfrac{1}{2}i\right) = -\sqrt{3} - i$

$2\text{ cis }300° = 2\left(\dfrac{1}{2} - \dfrac{\sqrt{3}}{2}i\right) = 1 - i\sqrt{3}$

11. $3\tan^2\theta - 7\sec\theta + 5 = 0$
$3(\sec^2\theta - 1) - 7\sec\theta + 5 = 0$
$3\sec^2\theta - 3 - 7\sec\theta + 5 = 0$
$3\sec^2\theta - 7\sec\theta + 2 = 0$
$(3\sec\theta - 1)(\sec\theta - 2) = 0$
$\sec\theta = \dfrac{1}{3}$ $\sec\theta = 2$
$\varnothing$ $\theta = 60°, 300°$

12. $2\sin^2\theta = 3 + 3\cos\theta$
$2(1 - \cos^2\theta) - 3 - 3\cos\theta = 0$
$2 - 2\cos^2\theta - 3 - 3\cos\theta = 0$
$2\cos^2\theta + 3\cos\theta + 1 = 0$
$(2\cos\theta + 1)(\cos\theta + 1) = 0$
$\cos\theta = -\dfrac{1}{2}$ $\cos\theta = -1$
$\theta = \textbf{120°, 180°, 240°}$

13. $2\tan^2\theta - \sec\theta + 1 = 0$
$2(\sec^2\theta - 1) - \sec\theta + 1 = 0$
$2\sec^2\theta - 2 - \sec\theta + 1 = 0$
$2\sec^2\theta - \sec\theta - 1 = 0$
$(2\sec\theta + 1)(\sec\theta - 1) = 0$
$\sec\theta = -\dfrac{1}{2}$ $\sec\theta = 1$
$\varnothing$ $\theta = 0°$

14. $\dfrac{\cos^4 x - \sin^4 x}{\cos^2 x - \sin^2 x}$

$= \dfrac{(\cos^2 x + \sin^2 x)(\cos^2 x - \sin^2 x)}{\cos^2 x - \sin^2 x}$

$= \cos^2 x + \sin^2 x = 1$

15. $\tan x + \cot x = \dfrac{\sin x}{\cos x} + \dfrac{\cos x}{\sin x}$

$= \dfrac{\sin^2 x + \cos^2 x}{\cos x \sin x} = \dfrac{1}{\cos x \sin x}$

$= \sec x \csc x$

16. $\dfrac{1}{1 + \cos x} + \dfrac{1}{1 - \cos x}$

$= \dfrac{1 - \cos x + 1 + \cos x}{1 - \cos^2 x}$

$= \dfrac{2}{1 - \cos^2 x} = \dfrac{2}{\sin^2 x} = 2 \csc^2 x$

17. Central angle $= \dfrac{360°}{8} = 45°$

$h = \dfrac{2}{\tan 22.5°} \approx 4.828$

$A_{\text{triangle}} = \dfrac{1}{2}(4)(4.828) = 9.656$

$A_{\text{octagon}} = (9.656)(8) \approx \mathbf{77.25\ cm^2}$

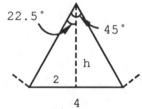

18. $\cos B = \dfrac{4^2 + 7^2 - 5^2}{2(4)(7)} \approx 0.7143$

$B = \cos^{-1} 0.7143 \approx \mathbf{44.4°}$

$\cos A = \dfrac{4^2 + 5^2 - 7^2}{2(4)(5)} = -0.2$

$A = \cos^{-1}(-0.2) \approx \mathbf{101.5°}$

$C = 180° - 101.5° - 44.4° = \mathbf{34.1°}$

19. $h = 8 \sin 40° \approx 5.14$

$A = \dfrac{1}{2}(10)(5.14) \approx \mathbf{25.7}$

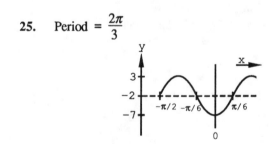

20. $(n - 2) = 180°$

$(12 - 2)(180°) = \mathbf{1800°}$

21.

$A_{\text{segment}} = A_{\text{sector}} - A_{\text{triangle}}$

$= \left(\dfrac{50°}{360°}\right)(\pi)(10^2) - \dfrac{1}{2}(10)(10 \sin 50°)$

$\approx 43.6 - 38.3 \approx \mathbf{5.3\ cm^2}$

22. Refer to Problem Set 47, problem 8.

23. $\dfrac{9x^2}{36} + \dfrac{4y^2}{36} = \dfrac{36}{36}$

$\dfrac{x^2}{4} + \dfrac{y^2}{9} = 1$

Center: (0, 0)

Major axis: 6

Minor axis: 4

24. $\dfrac{4y^2}{36} - \dfrac{9x^2}{36} = \dfrac{36}{36}$

$\dfrac{y^2}{9} - \dfrac{x^2}{4} = 1$

Vertices: $(0, \pm 3)$

Asymptotes: $y = \pm \dfrac{3}{2} x$

25. Period $= \dfrac{2\pi}{3}$

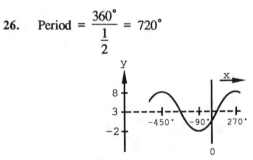

26. Period $= \dfrac{360°}{\dfrac{1}{2}} = 720°$

27. ***D***

28. $\log 10^{3x-2} = \log 7^{2x+3}$
$(3x - 2)(\log 10) = (2x + 3)(\log 7)$
$(3x - 2)(1) = (2x + 3)(0.845)$
$3x - 2 = 1.69x + 2.535$
$1.31x = 4.535$
$x \approx \textbf{3.46}$

$-8x = 0$
$x = 0$
No solution

29. $\log_3 8^{2/3} - \log_3 (3x - 2) + \log_3 (x - 2) = \log_3 4$
$\log_3 \dfrac{4(x - 2)}{3x - 2} = \log_3 4$
$4x - 8 = 12x - 8$

30. $y = 1.04^6$
$\log y = \log 1.04^6 = 6 \log 1.04 \approx 0.1022$
$y \approx \textbf{1.27}$

EP

11. Valid

ENRICHMENT LESSON 2

1. A: $\dfrac{1}{12}T = S$

B: $1T = S + 45$

Substitute equation A into B.

$T = \dfrac{1}{12}T + 45$

$\dfrac{11}{12}T = 45$

$T = \dfrac{540}{11} = \textbf{49}\dfrac{\textbf{1}}{\textbf{11}}\textbf{ min}$

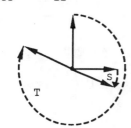

2. A: $\dfrac{1}{12}T = S$

B: $T = S + 50$

Substitute equation A into B.

$T = \dfrac{1}{12}T + 50$

$\dfrac{11}{12}T = 50$

$T = \dfrac{600}{11} = \textbf{54}\dfrac{\textbf{6}}{\textbf{11}}\textbf{ min}$

3. $n = 1^{st}$ number
$n + 2 = 2^{nd}$ number
$n + 4 = 3^{rd}$ number
$n(n + 4) - 8 = n + 2$
$n^2 + 4n - 8 = n + 2$
$n^2 + 3n - 10 = 0$
$(n + 5)(n - 2) = 0$
$n = 2$
2, 4, 6

4.

	First trip	Second trip
Distance:	d	d
Rate:	10	20
Time:	$t + 5$	$t + 2$

$10(t + 5) = 20(t + 2)$
$10t + 50 = 20t + 40$
$10t = 10$
$t = 1$
$d = 10(1 + 5) = \textbf{60 mi}$

5. $\dfrac{4}{7}$

6. $(6 - 1)! = 5! = 120$

7. $\dfrac{1}{6}k(k + 1)(2k + 1) + (k + 1)^2$

$= (k + 1)\left[\dfrac{1}{6}k(2k + 1) + (k + 1)\right]$

$= (k + 1)\left(\dfrac{1}{3}k^2 + \dfrac{1}{6}k + k + 1\right)$

$= (k + 1)\left(\dfrac{1}{3}k^2 + \dfrac{7}{6}k + 1\right)$

$$= (k + 1)\left(\frac{1}{6}\right)(2k^2 + 7k + 6)$$

$$= \frac{1}{6}(k + 1)(k + 2)(2k + 3)$$

$$= \frac{1}{6}(k+1)[(k+1) + 1][2(k+1) + 1]$$

8. $2^{k+1} - 2 + 2^{k+1} = 2(2^{k+1}) - 2$
$= 2^{k+2} - 2 = 2^{(k+1)+1} - 2$

9. Yes

10. $\begin{bmatrix} 1 & 2 & -3 \\ 2 & -1 & 4 \end{bmatrix} = \begin{bmatrix} 1 & 2 & -3 \\ 0 & -5 & 10 \end{bmatrix}$

$= \begin{bmatrix} 1 & 0 & 1 \\ 0 & 1 & -2 \end{bmatrix}$

$x = 1$
$y = -2$

11. Construction

12. $x^5 + 5x^4y + 10x^3y^2 + 10x^2y^3 + 5xy^4 + y^5$

13. $(16 \text{ cis } 240°)^{1/4}$

First root $= \sqrt[4]{16} \text{ cis } \dfrac{240°}{4} = 2 \text{ cis } 60°$

Angles differ by $\dfrac{360°}{4} = 90°$

$2 \text{ cis } 150°, 2 \text{ cis } 240°, 2 \text{ cis } 330°$

$2 \text{ cis } 60° = 2\left(\dfrac{1}{2} + \dfrac{\sqrt{3}}{2}i\right) = 1 + i\sqrt{3}$

$2 \text{ cis } 150° = 2\left(-\dfrac{\sqrt{3}}{2} + \dfrac{1}{2}i\right) = -\sqrt{3} + i$

$2 \text{ cis } 240° = 2\left(-\dfrac{1}{2} - \dfrac{\sqrt{3}}{2}i\right) = -1 - i\sqrt{3}$

$2 \text{ cis } 330° = 2\left(\dfrac{\sqrt{3}}{2} - \dfrac{1}{2}i\right) = \sqrt{3} - i$

14. $\tan^2 x + \tan x = 0$
$(\tan x)(\tan x + 1) = 0$
$\tan x = 0 \qquad\qquad \tan x = -1$
$x = 0°, 180° \qquad x = 135°, 315°$
$x = 0°, 135°, 180°, 315°$

15. $3(\sec^2 x - 1) + 5 \sec x + 1 = 0$
$3 \sec^2 x - 3 + 5 \sec x + 1 = 0$
$3 \sec^2 x + 5 \sec x - 2 = 0$
$(3 \sec x - 1)(\sec x + 2) = 0$

$\sec x = \dfrac{1}{3} \qquad\qquad \sec x = -2$
$\emptyset \qquad\qquad\qquad x = 120°, 240°$

16. $\dfrac{\tan^2 x - 1}{\tan x} = \tan x - \dfrac{1}{\tan x} = \tan x - \cot x$

17. $\sec x - \cos x = \dfrac{1}{\cos x} - \cos x$

$= \dfrac{1 - \cos^2 x}{\cos x} = \dfrac{\sin^2 x}{\cos x}$

$= \sin x \left(\dfrac{\sin x}{\cos x}\right) = \sin x \tan x$

18. Central angle $= \dfrac{360°}{8} = 45°$

$\tan 22.5° = \dfrac{3}{h}$

$h = \dfrac{3}{\tan 22.5°} \approx 7.24$

$A_{\text{triangle}} = \dfrac{1}{2}(6)(7.24) = 21.72$

$A_{\text{octagon}} = (21.72)(8) \approx \textbf{173.8 cm}^2$

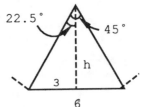

19. $c^2 = 10^2 + 8^2 - 2(10)(8) \cos 30°$

$= 100 + 64 - 160\left(\dfrac{\sqrt{3}}{2}\right) \approx 25.44$

$c \approx \textbf{5.04}$

$\cos A = \dfrac{(5.04)^2 + 10^2 - 8^2}{2(5.04)(10)} \approx 0.6091$

$A = \cos^{-1} .6091 \approx \textbf{52.5}°$

$B = 180° - 52.5° - 30° = \textbf{97.5}°$

20. $(10 - 2)180° = \textbf{1440}°$

21. $A_{\text{segment}} = A_{\text{sector}} - A_{\text{triangle}}$

$= \dfrac{60°}{360°}\pi(10^2) - \dfrac{1}{2}(10)(10 \sin 60°)$

$\approx 52.36 - 43.3 \approx \textbf{9.1 cm}^2$

22. $(x^2 - 4x + 4) + y^2 = 5 + 4 = 9$

$(x - 2)^2 + y^2 = 9$

Center: (2, 0)

Radius: 3

23. Period $= \dfrac{2\pi}{2} = \pi$

24. $\dfrac{60 \text{ mi}}{\text{hr}} \cdot \dfrac{5280 \text{ ft}}{\text{mi}} \cdot \dfrac{12 \text{ in}}{\text{ft}} \cdot \dfrac{2.54 \text{ cm}}{\text{in}}$

$\cdot \dfrac{1 \text{ m}}{100 \text{ cm}} \cdot \dfrac{1 \text{ hr}}{60 \text{ min}} \cdot \dfrac{1 \text{ min}}{60 \text{ sec}}$

$= \dfrac{(60)(5280)(12)(2.54)}{(100)(60)(60)} \dfrac{\text{m}}{\text{sec}}$

25. $\dfrac{a}{24} = \dfrac{6}{a}$

$a^2 = 144$

$a = 12$

26. $2 \sin 2\theta - 1 = 0$

$\sin 2\theta = \dfrac{1}{2}$

$2\theta = 30°, 150°, 390°, 510°$

$\theta = \mathbf{15°, 75°, 195°, 255°}$

27. $4 \cos^2 x = 1$

$\cos^2 x = \dfrac{1}{4}$

$\cos x = \pm\dfrac{1}{2}$

$x = \mathbf{60°, 120°, 240°, 300°}$

28. $\log 3^{2x-1} = \log 4^{3x+2}$

$(2x - 1)(\log 3) = (3x + 2)(\log 4)$

$(2x - 1)(0.477) = (3x + 2)(0.602)$

$0.954x - 0.477 = 1.81x + 1.204$

$0.856x = -1.681$

$x = \mathbf{-1.97}$

29. $y = 1.04^6$

$\log y = \log 1.04^6 = 6 \log 1.04$

≈ 0.1022

$y \approx \mathbf{1.3}$

30. $\log_6 x^2 - \log_6 27^{2/3} = \log_6 x$

$\log_6 \dfrac{x^2}{9} = \log_6 x$

$\dfrac{x^2}{9} = x$

$x^2 - 9x = 0$

$x(x - 9) = 0$

$x = \mathbf{9}$

PROBLEM SET 66

1.

<u>Little Hand</u>	<u>Big Hand</u>
$R_L T_L = S$	$R_B T_B = S + 60$

$R_L = \dfrac{1}{12}$ $\qquad R_B = 1$

$T_L = T_B$

$\dfrac{1}{12} T = S \qquad 1T = S + 60$

$T = \dfrac{1}{12} T + 60$

$T = \dfrac{720}{11} = 65\dfrac{5}{11} \text{ min}$

2.

	<u>Original</u>	<u>New</u>
Distance:	m	$A + 10$
Time:	k	?
Rate:	$\dfrac{m}{k}$	$\dfrac{3m}{k}$

New time $= \dfrac{A + 10}{\dfrac{3m}{k}} = \dfrac{k(A + 10)}{3m}$

3. $n = 1^{\text{st}}$ number

$n + 2 = 2^{\text{nd}}$ number

$n + 4 = 3^{\text{rd}}$ number

$n(n + 2) = (n + 4) + 8$

$n^2 + 2n = n + 12$

$n^2 + n - 12 = 0$

$(n + 4)(n - 3) = 0$

$n = 3$

$\mathbf{3, 5, 7}$

4.

	1st trip	2nd trip
Distance:	d	d
Rate:	400	200
Time:	$t - 2$	$t + 2$

$400(t - 2) = 200(t + 2)$
$400t - 800 = 200t + 400$
$200t = 1200$
$t = 6$
$d = 400(6 - 2) = \mathbf{1600\ mi}$

5. $\dfrac{13}{52} \cdot \dfrac{13}{52} = \dfrac{1}{4} \cdot \dfrac{1}{4} = \dfrac{1}{16}$

6. $\dfrac{5}{36} \cdot \dfrac{6}{36} = \dfrac{5}{216}$

7. $\begin{bmatrix} 2 & -3 & 5 \\ 3 & 4 & -1 \end{bmatrix} = \begin{bmatrix} 1 & -\dfrac{3}{2} & \dfrac{5}{2} \\ 0 & \dfrac{17}{2} & -\dfrac{17}{2} \end{bmatrix}$

$= \begin{bmatrix} 1 & 0 & 1 \\ 0 & 1 & -1 \end{bmatrix}$

$x = 1$
$y = -1$

8. Construction

9. Coefficient = 56, term = p^3q^5
$\mathbf{56p^3q^5}$

10. $(27 \text{ cis } 180°)^{1/3}$

First root $= \sqrt[3]{27} \text{ cis } \dfrac{180°}{3} = 3 \text{ cis } 60°$

Angles differ by $\dfrac{360°}{3} = 120°$

$3 \text{ cis } 180°, 3 \text{ cis } 300°$

$3 \text{ cis } 60° = 3\left(\dfrac{1}{2} + \dfrac{\sqrt{3}}{2}i\right) = \dfrac{3}{2} + \dfrac{3i\sqrt{3}}{2}$

$3 \text{ cis } 180° = 3(-1 + 0i) = -3$

$3 \text{ cis } 300° = 3\left(\dfrac{1}{2} - \dfrac{\sqrt{3}}{2}i\right) = \dfrac{3}{2} - \dfrac{3i\sqrt{3}}{2}$

11. $3\cot^2\theta = 7\csc\theta - 5$
$3(\csc^2\theta - 1) - 7\csc\theta + 5 = 0$
$3\csc^2\theta - 3 - 7\csc\theta + 5 = 0$
$3\csc^2\theta - 7\csc\theta + 2 = 0$
$(3\csc\theta - 1)(\csc\theta - 2) = 0$
$\csc\theta = \dfrac{1}{3} \qquad\qquad \csc\theta = 2$
$\quad\varnothing \qquad\qquad\qquad \theta = 30°, 150°$

12. $2\cos^2\theta = 3 + 3\sin\theta$
$2(1 - \sin^2\theta) = 3 + 3\sin\theta$
$2 - 2\sin^2\theta = 3 + 3\sin\theta$
$2\sin^2\theta + 3\sin\theta + 1 = 0$
$(2\sin\theta + 1)(\sin\theta + 1) = 0$
$\sin\theta = -\dfrac{1}{2} \qquad\qquad \sin\theta = -1$
$\theta = 210°, 330° \qquad\qquad \theta = 270°$
$\theta = \mathbf{210°, 270°, 330°}$

13. $2\tan^2\theta = \sec\theta - 1$
$2(\sec^2\theta - 1) = \sec\theta - 1$
$2\sec^2\theta - 2 = \sec\theta - 1$
$2\sec^2\theta - \sec\theta - 1 = 0$
$(2\sec\theta + 1)(\sec\theta - 1) = 0$
$\sec\theta = -\dfrac{1}{2} \qquad\qquad \sec\theta = 1$
$\quad\varnothing \qquad\qquad\qquad \theta = 0°$

14. $\dfrac{1}{\sec^2\theta} + \dfrac{1}{\csc^2\theta} = \cos^2\theta + \sin^2\theta = 1$

15. $\sec\theta - \tan\theta\sin\theta = \dfrac{1}{\cos\theta} - \dfrac{\sin\theta}{\cos\theta} \cdot \sin\theta$

$= \dfrac{1 - \sin^2\theta}{\cos\theta} = \dfrac{\cos^2\theta}{\cos\theta} = \cos\theta$

16. $\dfrac{\sec^2\theta}{\sec^2\theta - 1} = \dfrac{\sec^2\theta}{\tan^2\theta}$

$= \dfrac{1}{\cos^2\theta} \cdot \dfrac{\cos^2\theta}{\sin^2\theta} = \dfrac{1}{\sin^2\theta} = \csc^2\theta$

17. Central angle $= \dfrac{360°}{8} = 45°$

$\sin 22.5° = \dfrac{25}{r}$

$r = \dfrac{25}{\sin 22.5°} \approx \mathbf{6.53\ cm}$

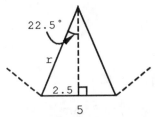

18. $c^2 = 7^2 + 8^2 - 2(7)(8)\cos 35° \approx 21.255$
$c \approx \mathbf{4.6}$
$\cos B = \dfrac{4.6^2 + 8^2 - 7^2}{2(4.6)(8)} \approx 0.4913$
$B = \cos^{-1} 0.4913 = \mathbf{60.6°}$
$A = 180° - 60.6° - 35° = \mathbf{84.4°}$

19. $\angle A = \angle A'$ and $\angle B = \angle B'$ are given. $\angle A + \angle B + \angle C = 180°$ and $\angle A' + \angle B' + \angle C' = 180°$ because the sum of the angles in a triangle equals $180°$. $\angle A + \angle B + \angle C = \angle A' + \angle B' + \angle C'$ by substitution. $\angle C = \angle C'$ by subtraction.

20. Since $\angle Y = \angle A$, $\angle X = \angle B$ because alternate interior angles are equal. $\angle M = \angle M$ because vertical angles are equal. Therefore $\triangle ABM \sim \triangle YXM$ because of the angle–angle–angle theorem. $\dfrac{XY}{BA} = \dfrac{XM}{BM}$ because they are corresponding parts.

21. Refer to Example 66.A.3.

22. $\dfrac{y}{16} = \dfrac{4}{y}$

$y^2 = 64, y = \mathbf{8}$

$4^2 + x^2 = 8^2$

$x^2 = 64 - 16 = 48, x = \mathbf{4\sqrt{3}}$

$12^2 + \left(4\sqrt{3}\right)^2 = z^2$

$z^2 = 144 + 48 = 192$

$z = \sqrt{192} = \mathbf{8\sqrt{3}}$

23. $\dfrac{16x^2}{400} + \dfrac{25y^2}{400} = \dfrac{400}{400}$

$\dfrac{x^2}{25} + \dfrac{y^2}{16} = 1$

Center: $(0, 0)$

Major axis: 10

Minor axis: 8

24. $\dfrac{16x^2}{400} - \dfrac{25y^2}{400} = \dfrac{400}{400}$

$\dfrac{x^2}{25} - \dfrac{y^2}{16} = 1$

Vertices: $(\pm 5, 0)$

Asymptotes: $y = \pm\dfrac{4}{5}x$

25. $A = 10$, coefficient $k = \dfrac{1}{3}$

Period $= \dfrac{360°}{1/3} = 1080°$

Phase shift $= 180°$ right

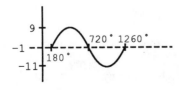

26. $A = 1$, coefficient $k = \dfrac{1}{4}$

Period $= \dfrac{2\pi}{1/4} = 8\pi$

Phase shift $= \dfrac{9\pi}{4}$ right

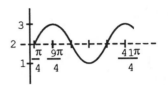

27. $\log 12^{2x-3} = \log 2^{3x+2}$

$(2x - 3)(\log 12) = (3x + 2)(\log 2)$

$(2x - 3)(1.08) = (3x + 2)(0.3)$

$2.16x - 3.24 = 0.9x + 0.6$

$1.26x = 3.84$

$x \approx \mathbf{3.05}$

28. $\log_2 16^{3/4} + \log_2 x^2 = \log_2 4^2$

$\log_2 8x^2 = \log_2 16$

$8x^2 = 16$

$x^2 = 2$

$x = \mathbf{\sqrt{2}}$

29. $b^a = M, \qquad\qquad b^c = N$

$\log_b M = a \qquad\qquad \log_b N = c$

$\log_b MN = \log_b \left(b^a\right)\left(b^c\right) = \log_b b^{a+c}$

$= a + c = \log_b M + \log_b N$

30. $y = 1.02^3$

$\log y = \log 1.02^3 = 3 \log 1.02$

≈ 0.0258

$y \approx \mathbf{1.06}$

EP

12. $\dfrac{1}{6}k(k + 1)(2k + 1) + (k + 1)^2$

$= (k + 1)\left[\dfrac{1}{6}k(2k + 1) + (k + 1)\right]$

$= (k + 1)\left(\dfrac{1}{3}k^2 + \dfrac{1}{6}k + k + 1\right)$

$= (k + 1)\left(\dfrac{1}{3}k^2 + \dfrac{7}{6}k + 1\right)$

$= (k + 1)\left(\dfrac{1}{6}\right)(2k^2 + 7k + 6)$

$= \dfrac{1}{6}(k + 1)(k + 2)(2k + 3)$

$= \dfrac{1}{6}(k + 1)[(k + 1) + 1][2(k + 1) + 1]$

PROBLEM SET 67

1.

Little Hand	Big Hand
$R_L T_L = S$	$R_B T_B = S + 15$
$R_L = \dfrac{1}{12}$	$R_B = 1$
$T_L = T_B$	
$\dfrac{1}{12} T = S$	$1T = S + 15$

$$T = \frac{1}{12} T + 15$$

$$T = \frac{180}{11} = 16 \frac{4}{11} \text{ min}$$

2.

$$O = Im + b$$
$$45 = 10m + b$$
$$\underline{(-)\ 37 = 8m + b}$$
$$8 = 2m$$
$$m = 4$$
$$45 = 10(4) + b$$
$$b = 5$$
$$\mathbf{O = 4I + 5}$$

3.

$n = 1^{\text{st}}$ number
$n + 2 = 2^{\text{nd}}$ number
$n + 4 = 3^{\text{rd}}$ number
$n(n + 4) = -(n + 4) + 18$
$n^2 + 4n = -n - 4 + 18$
$n^2 + 5n - 14 = 0$
$(n - 2)(n + 7) = 0$
$n = 2$
2, 4, 6

4.

	1st trip	2nd trip
Distance:	d	d
Rate:	30	64
Time:	$t + 2$	t

$$30(t + 2) = 64t$$
$$30t + 60 = 64t$$
$$34t = 60$$
$$t = \frac{30}{17}$$
$$d = 30\left(\frac{30}{17} + 2\right) \approx \frac{\mathbf{1920}}{\mathbf{17}} \text{ km}$$

5. $\dfrac{13}{52} \cdot \dfrac{39}{51} = \dfrac{1}{4} \cdot \dfrac{13}{17} = \dfrac{\mathbf{13}}{\mathbf{68}}$

6. $\dfrac{6}{36} = \dfrac{\mathbf{1}}{\mathbf{6}}$

7. $\begin{bmatrix} 2 & -3 & 1 \\ 3 & 4 & 10 \end{bmatrix} = \begin{bmatrix} 1 & -\dfrac{3}{2} & \dfrac{1}{2} \\ 0 & \dfrac{17}{2} & \dfrac{17}{2} \end{bmatrix}$

$= \begin{bmatrix} 1 & 0 & 2 \\ 0 & 1 & 1 \end{bmatrix}$

$\mathbf{x = 2, y = 1}$

8. Construction

9. $a_1 = -10, d = 6$
−10, −4, 2, 8, 14

10. $a_1 = 5, d = -4$
$a_{30} = a_1 + 29d = 5 + 29(-4) = \mathbf{-111}$

11. $a_1 = 3, a_5 = -13$
$a_5 = a_1 + 4d$
$-13 = 3 + 4d$
$d = -4$
−1, −5, −9

12. $a_{10} = -30, a_{20} = 40$

$$a_1 + 9d = -30$$
$$\underline{(-)\ a_1 + 19d = 40}$$
$$-10d = -70$$
$$d = 7$$
$$a_1 + 9(7) = -30$$
$$a_1 = -93$$
−93, −86, −79, −72, − 65

13. $a_1 = 2x + 3y, a_6 = 7x + 8y$
$a_6 = a_1 + 5d$
$7x + 8y = 2x + 3y + 5d$
$5d = 5x + 5y$
$d = x + y$
$a_8 = 2x + 3y + 7(x + y) = \mathbf{9x + 10y}$

14. $(8 \text{ cis } 270°)^{1/3}$

First root $= \sqrt[3]{8} \text{ cis } \dfrac{270°}{3} = 2 \text{ cis } 90°$

Angles differ by $\dfrac{360°}{3} = 120°$

$2 \text{ cis } 210°, 2 \text{ cis } 300°$

$2 \text{ cis } 90° = 2(0 + i) = 2i$

$2 \text{ cis } 210° = 2\left(-\dfrac{\sqrt{3}}{2} - \dfrac{1}{2}i\right) = -\sqrt{3} - i$

$2 \text{ cis } 300° = 2\left(\dfrac{\sqrt{3}}{2} - \dfrac{1}{2}i\right) = \sqrt{3} - i$

15. $2\sin^2 x + 3\sin x + 1 = 0$

$(2\sin x + 1)(\sin x + 1) = 0$

$\sin x = -\dfrac{1}{2}$ $\qquad\qquad \sin x = -1$

$x = 210°, 330°$ $\qquad\qquad x = 270°$

$x = \mathbf{210°, 270°, 330°}$

16. $2(\sec^2 \theta - 1) = 3\sec \theta - 3$

$2\sec^2 \theta - 2 - 3\sec \theta + 3 = 0$

$2\sec^2 \theta - 3\sec \theta + 1 = 0$

$(2\sec \theta - 1)(\sec \theta - 1) = 0$

$\sec \theta = \dfrac{1}{2}$ $\qquad\qquad \sec \theta = 1$

$\varnothing$ $\qquad\qquad\qquad \theta = \mathbf{0°}$

17. $\tan 3\theta = -\dfrac{\sqrt{3}}{3}$

$3\theta = 150°, 330°, 510°, 690°, 870°, 1050°$

$\theta = \mathbf{50°, 110°, 170°, 230°, 290°, 350°}$

18. $\dfrac{\sec^2 x}{\tan^2 x} = \dfrac{1}{\cos^2 x} \cdot \dfrac{\cos^2 x}{\sin^2 x} = \dfrac{1}{\sin^2 x} = \csc^2 x$

19. $\dfrac{\cos^2 \theta + \sin^2 \theta}{\sin \theta} = \dfrac{1}{\sin \theta} = \csc \theta$

20. $\dfrac{\cos x}{(-\sin x)(-\cot x)} = \dfrac{\cos x}{\dfrac{\sin x}{1} \cdot \dfrac{\cos x}{\sin x}} = 1$

21. $\cos A = \dfrac{7^2 + 8^2 - 10^2}{2(7)(8)} \approx 0.1161$

$A = \cos^{-1} 0.1161 \approx \mathbf{83.3°}$

$\cos B = \dfrac{7^2 + 10^2 - 8^2}{2(7)(8)} \approx 0.6071$

$B = \cos^{-1} 0.6071 \approx \mathbf{52.6°}$

$C = 180° - 52.6° - 83.3° = \mathbf{44.1°}$

22. Find the equation of the line $\perp$ to

$y = -x + 4$ that passes through $(0, 0)$.

$m_\perp = 1$

$y = -x + b$

$0 = 0 + b$

$b = 0$

$y = x$

Solve $y = -x + 4$ and $y = x$ simultaneously.

$-x + 4 = x$

$x = 2$

$y = 2$

$(x, y) = (2, 2)$

$d = \sqrt{(0 - 2)^2 + (0 - 2)^2} = \sqrt{8} = 2\sqrt{2}$

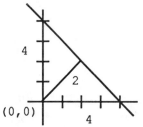

23. $\angle A = \angle E$ is given. $\angle C = \angle C'$ because vertical angles are equal. $\angle B = \angle D$ because the third angle must be equal if the other two are equal. $\triangle ABC \sim \triangle ECD$ by AAA. Therefore $\dfrac{BC}{CD} = \dfrac{AB}{DE}$ by corresponding parts.

24. Refer to Example 66.A.4.

25. Period $= \dfrac{2\pi}{2} = \pi$

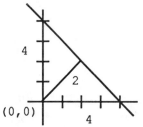

26. Refer to Problem Set 47, problem 16.

27. $\log 10^{3x-2} = \log 5^{2x-1}$

$(3x - 2)(\log 10) = (2x - 1)(\log 5)$

$(3x - 2)(1) = (2x - 1)(0.699)$

$3x - 2 = 1.4x - 0.699$

$1.6x = 1.3$

$x \approx \mathbf{0.81}$

28. $\log_5 8^{2/3} - \log_5 (x - 4) = 1$

$\log_5 \dfrac{4}{x - 4} = 1$

$5^1 = \dfrac{4}{x - 4}$

$5x - 20 = 4$

$x = \dfrac{\mathbf{24}}{\mathbf{5}}$

29. $y = 1.04^4$

$\log y = \log 1.04^4 = 4 \log 1.04 \approx 0.068$

$y \approx \mathbf{1.17}$

30. $\dfrac{x^2}{9} - \dfrac{y^2}{16} = 1$

Vertices: $(\pm 3, 0)$

Asymptotes: $y = \pm \dfrac{4}{3}x$

EP

13. *b*

PROBLEM SET 68

1.

Little Hand	Big Hand
$R_L T_L = S$	$R_B T_B = S + 25$

$R_L = \dfrac{1}{12}$ $R_B = 1$

$T_L = T_B$

$\dfrac{1}{12}T = S$ $1T = S + 25$

$T = \dfrac{1}{12}T + 25$

$T = \dfrac{300}{11} = 27\dfrac{3}{11}$ **min**

2. $3n = 1^{st}$ number

$3(n + 1) = 2^{nd}$ number

$3(n + 2) = 3^{rd}$ number

$3[3n + 3(n + 2)] - 42 = 4[3(n + 1)]$

$3(6n + 6) - 42 = 4(3n + 3)$

$18n + 18 - 42 = 12n + 12$

$n = 6$

18, 21, 24

3.

	1st trip	2nd trip
Distance:	d	d
Rate:	60	90
Time:	$t + 1$	$t - 1$

$60(t + 1) = 90(t - 1)$

$60t + 60 = 90t - 90$

$30t = 150$

$t = 5$

$d = 60(5 + 1) = \mathbf{360 \ km}$

4.

	1st trip	2nd trip
Distance:	x	x
Rate:	$\dfrac{x}{y}$	?
Time:	y	$y - k$

$\dfrac{x}{y} \cdot y = r(y - k)$

$x = r(y - k)$

$r = \dfrac{x}{y - k} \dfrac{\mathbf{yd}}{\mathbf{min}}$

5. $\dfrac{2}{9} \cdot \dfrac{1}{8} = \dfrac{1}{36}$

6. $\dfrac{3}{36} + \dfrac{10}{36} = \dfrac{13}{36}$

7.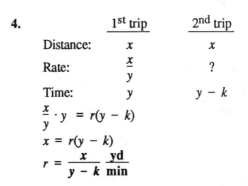

$= \begin{bmatrix} 1 & 0 & -2 \\ 0 & 1 & -2 \end{bmatrix}$

$x = \mathbf{-2}, y = \mathbf{-2}$

8. Triangle cannot be constructed.

9. $a_1 = 6, d = -3$

$a_{10} = 6 + 9(-3) = \mathbf{-21}$

10. $a_1 = 6, a_6 = 106$

$106 = 6 + 5d$

$100 = 5d$

$d = 20$

26, 46, 66, 86

Advanced Mathematics

11. $a_{10} = 39, a_4 = 15$

$$a_1 + 9d = 39$$
$$\underline{(-)\ a_1 + 3d = 15}$$
$$6d = 24$$
$$d = 4$$
$$15 = a_1 + 3(4)$$
$$a_1 = 3$$

3, 7, 11, 15

12. $(16 \text{ cis } 40°)^{1/4}$

First root $= \sqrt[4]{16} \text{ cis } \dfrac{40°}{4} = 2 \text{ cis } 10°$

Angles differ by $\dfrac{360°}{4} = 90°$

2 cis 100°, 2 cis 190°, 2 cis 280°

13. $\sin 15° = \sin(60° - 45°)$
$= \sin 60° \cos 45° - \cos 60° \sin 45°$

$$= \left(\frac{\sqrt{3}}{2}\right)\left(\frac{\sqrt{2}}{2}\right) - \left(\frac{1}{2}\right)\left(\frac{\sqrt{2}}{2}\right)$$

$$= \frac{\sqrt{6} - \sqrt{2}}{4} \approx \textbf{0.259}$$

14. $\cos\left(\theta - \dfrac{\pi}{4}\right) = \cos\theta \cos\dfrac{\pi}{4} + \sin\theta \sin\dfrac{\pi}{4}$

$$= \cos\theta\left(\frac{\sqrt{2}}{2}\right) + \sin\theta\left(\frac{\sqrt{2}}{2}\right)$$

$$= \frac{\sqrt{2}}{2}(\cos\theta + \sin\theta)$$

15. Refer to Example 68.B.1.

16. $\tan 75° = \tan(30° + 45°)$

$$= \frac{\tan 30° + \tan 45°}{1 - \tan 30° \tan 45°}$$

$$= \frac{\dfrac{1}{\sqrt{3}} + 1}{1 - \dfrac{1}{\sqrt{3}}} = \frac{1 + \sqrt{3}}{\sqrt{3} - 1}$$

17. $2\cos^2 x + \sin x + 1 = 0$
$2(1 - \sin^2 x) + \sin x + 1 = 0$
$2 - 2\sin^2 x + \sin x + 1 = 0$
$2\sin^2 x - \sin x - 3 = 0$
$(2\sin x - 3)(\sin x + 1) = 0$

$\sin x = \dfrac{3}{2}$ $\sin x = -1$

$\varnothing$ $x = \textbf{270}°$

18. $2\tan^2 x - 3\sec x = -3$
$2(\sec^2 x - 1) - 3\sec x = -3$
$2\sec^2 x - 2 - 3\sec x + 3 = 0$
$2\sec^2 x - 3\sec x + 1 = 0$
$(2\sec x - 1)(\sec x - 1) = 0$

$\sec x = \dfrac{1}{2}$ $\sec x = 1$

$\varnothing$ $x = \textbf{0}°$

19. $2\cos 4\theta = -1$

$\cos 4\theta = -\dfrac{1}{2}$

$4\theta = 120°, 240°, 480°, 600°, 840°, 960°,$
$1200°, 1320°$

$\theta = \textbf{30}°, \textbf{60}°, \textbf{120}°, \textbf{150}°, \textbf{210}°, \textbf{240}°, \textbf{300}°,$
$\textbf{330}°$

20. $\sec x + \sec x \tan^2 x = (\sec x)(1 + \tan^2 x)$
$= \sec x \cdot \sec^2 x = \sec^3 x$

21. $\dfrac{\sin^2 x}{\cos x} + \cos x = \dfrac{\sin^2 x + \cos^2 x}{\cos x}$

$= \dfrac{1}{\cos x} = \sec x$

22. $\dfrac{\tan(-\theta)\cos(-\theta)}{\sin(-\theta)} = \dfrac{-\tan\theta \cos\theta}{-\sin\theta}$

$= \tan\theta \cot\theta = 1$

23. $a = \sqrt{11^2 + 10^2 - 2(10)(11)\cos 20°} \approx \textbf{3.8}$

$\cos B = \dfrac{3.8^2 + 11^2 - 10^2}{2(3.8)(11)} \approx 0.4239$

$B = \cos^{-1} 0.4239 \approx \textbf{65}°$

$C = 180° - 65° - 20° = \textbf{95}°$

24. Refer to Solution Set 18, problem 7.

25. $\angle A = \angle A$ by reflexive property; $\angle ADE$ $= \angle ABC$ by corresponding angles. So $\triangle ADE \sim \triangle ABC$ by angle–angle. Therefore,
$\dfrac{AD}{AB} = \dfrac{AE}{AC}$

26. $\dfrac{a}{21} = \dfrac{3}{a}$

$a^2 = 63$

$a \approx \textbf{7.9}$

$\dfrac{b}{21} = \dfrac{18}{b}$

$b^2 = 378$

$b \approx \textbf{19.4}$

$$3^2 + h^2 = 7.9^2$$
$$h^2 = 7.9^2 - 3^2 = 53.41$$
$$h \approx \mathbf{7.3}$$

$$x^2 - x - 6 = 0$$
$$(x - 3)(x + 2) = 0$$
$$x = \mathbf{3}$$

27. Period $= \dfrac{360°}{\frac{2}{3}} = 540°$

28. $(2x - 4)(\log 6) = (3x + 1)(\log 10)$
$(2x - 4)(0.7782) = (3x + 1)(1)$
$1.5564x - 3.1128 = 3x + 1$
$1.4436x = -4.1128$
$x \approx \mathbf{-2.85}$

29. $\log_2 (x + 1)(x - 2) = 2$
$2^2 = (x + 1)(x - 2)$
$x^2 - x - 2 = 4$

30. $\log_3 7x + \log_3 27^{2/3} = 7^{\log_7 2^3 - \log_7 2}$
$\log_3 (7x)(9) = 7^{\log_7 4}$
$\log_3 63x = 4$
$3^4 = 63x$
$81 = 63x$
$x = \dfrac{81}{63} = \dfrac{9}{7}$

EP

14. $\dfrac{5k(k + 1)}{2} + 5(k + 1)$

$= \dfrac{5k^2 + 5k + 10k + 10}{2}$

$= \dfrac{5k^2 + 15k + 10}{2} = \dfrac{5(k^2 + 3k + 2)}{2}$

$= \dfrac{5(k + 1)[(k + 1) + 1]}{2}$

PROBLEM SET 69

1.
Little Hand	Big Hand
$R_L T_L = S$	$R_B T_B = S + 15$
$R_L = \dfrac{1}{12}$	$R_B = 1$
$T_L = T_B$	
$\dfrac{1}{12} T = S$	$1T = S + 15$

$T = \dfrac{1}{12} T + 15$

$T = \dfrac{180}{11} = \mathbf{16\dfrac{4}{11}}$ min

2. A: $C + B = 100$
$B = 100 - C$

B: $\dfrac{3}{4} C + \dfrac{2}{3} B = 70$

Substitute equation A into B.
$\dfrac{3}{4} C + \dfrac{2}{3} (100 - C) = 70$

$\dfrac{3}{4} C + \dfrac{200}{3} - \dfrac{2}{3} C = 70$

$\dfrac{1}{12} C = \dfrac{10}{3}$

$C = \mathbf{\$40}$
$B = \mathbf{\$60}$

3. $\dfrac{4}{10} \cdot \dfrac{3}{9} \cdot \dfrac{2}{8} = \dfrac{24}{720} = \dfrac{1}{30}$

4. $\dfrac{30}{36} \cdot \dfrac{6}{36} = \dfrac{180}{1296} = \dfrac{5}{36}$

5. T = tens' digit
U = units' digit
A: $T + U = 11$

B: $10U + T = 10T + U + 45$
$9U - 9T = 45$
$U - T = 5$
Substitute equation A into B.
$U - (11 - U) = 5$

$2U = 16$
$U = 8$
$T = 11 - 8 = 3$
$N = \mathbf{38}$

6. H = hundreds' digit
   T = tens' digit
   U = units' digit
   A: $T = H + U$
   B: $4U - 4 = H$
   C: $T = 3U$
   Substitute equations C and B into A.
   $3U = (4U - 4) + U$
   $-2U = -4$
   $U = 2$
   $T = 3(2) = 6$
   $H = 6 - 2 = 4$
   $N = \mathbf{462}$

7. $\begin{bmatrix} 2 & -1 & -1 \\ 3 & 2 & 9 \end{bmatrix} = \begin{bmatrix} 1 & -\frac{1}{2} & -\frac{1}{2} \\ 3 & 2 & 9 \end{bmatrix}$

   $= \begin{bmatrix} 1 & -\frac{1}{2} & -\frac{1}{2} \\ 0 & \frac{5}{2} & \frac{29}{2} \end{bmatrix} = \begin{bmatrix} 1 & -\frac{1}{2} & -\frac{1}{2} \\ 0 & 1 & 3 \end{bmatrix}$

   $= \begin{bmatrix} 1 & 0 & 1 \\ 0 & 1 & 3 \end{bmatrix}$

   $x = \mathbf{1}$
   $y = \mathbf{3}$

8. Construction

9. $a_1 = 10, a_6 = 25$
   $25 = 10 + 5d$
   $d = 3$
   $\mathbf{13, 16, 19, 22}$

10. $a_4 = -3, a_{10} = -15$
    $-3 = a_1 + 3d$
    $\underline{(-)\,-15 = a_1 + 9d}$
    $-6d = 12$
    $d = -2$
    $-3 = a_1 + 3(-2)$
    $a_1 = 3$
    $\mathbf{3, 1, -1, -3}$

11. $(32 \text{ cis } 60°)^{1/5}$
    First root $= \sqrt[5]{32} \text{ cis } \dfrac{60°}{5} = \mathbf{2 \text{ cis } 12°}$

Angles differ by $\dfrac{360°}{5} = 72°$

$\mathbf{2 \text{ cis } 84°, \ 2 \text{ cis } 156°, \ 2 \text{ cis } 228°, \ 2 \text{ cis } 300°}$

12. $\cos(30° + 45°)$
    $= \cos 30° \cos 45° - \sin 30° \sin 45°$
    $= \left(\dfrac{\sqrt{3}}{2}\right)\left(\dfrac{\sqrt{2}}{2}\right) - \left(\dfrac{1}{2}\right)\left(\dfrac{\sqrt{2}}{2}\right)$
    $= \dfrac{\sqrt{6} - \sqrt{2}}{4} \approx \mathbf{0.259}$

13. $\sin\left(\theta + \dfrac{\pi}{6}\right) = \sin\theta \cos\dfrac{\pi}{6} + \cos\theta \sin\dfrac{\pi}{6}$
    $= \sin\theta\left(\dfrac{\sqrt{3}}{2}\right) + \cos\theta\left(\dfrac{1}{2}\right)$
    $= \mathbf{\dfrac{1}{2}\left(\sqrt{3}\sin\theta + \cos\theta\right)}$

14. Refer to Example 68.B.2.

15. $2\sin^2 x + 3\cos x = 0$
    $2(1 - \cos^2 x) + 3\cos x = 0$
    $2 - 2\cos^2 x + 3\cos x = 0$
    $2\cos^2 x - 3\cos x - 2 = 0$
    $(2\cos x + 1)(\cos x - 2) = 0$
    $\cos x = -\dfrac{1}{2} \qquad\qquad \cos x = 2$
    $x = \mathbf{120°, 240°} \qquad\qquad \varnothing$

16. $2\sin^2\theta + 15\cos\theta - 9 = 0$
    $2(1 - \cos^2\theta) + 15\cos\theta - 9 = 0$
    $2 - 2\cos^2\theta + 15\cos\theta - 9 = 0$
    $2\cos^2\theta - 15\cos\theta + 7 = 0$
    $(2\cos\theta - 1)(\cos\theta - 7) = 0$
    $\cos\theta = \dfrac{1}{2} \qquad\qquad \cos\theta = 7$
    $\theta = \mathbf{60°, 300°} \qquad\qquad \varnothing$

17. $6\sin 4\theta = 3$
    $\sin 4\theta = \dfrac{1}{2}$
    $4\theta = 30°, 150°, 390°, 510°, 750°, 870°,$
    $1110°, 1230°$
    $\theta = \mathbf{7.5°, 37.5°, 97.5°, 127.5°, 187.5°, 217.5°,}$
    $\mathbf{277.5°, 307.5°}$

18. $\csc x + \csc x \cot^2 x = (\csc x)(1 + \cot^2 x)$
    $= (\csc x)(\csc^2 x) = \csc^3 x$

19. $\dfrac{1 - \cos^2\theta}{1 + \tan^2\theta} = \dfrac{\sin^2\theta}{\sec^2\theta} = \sin^2\theta \cos^2\theta$

20. $\sin^2 \theta = 1 - \cos^2 \theta$
$= (1 - \cos \theta)(1 + \cos \theta)$

21. $a^2 = 6^2 + 8^2 - 2(6)(8) \cos 20° \approx 9.7895$
$a \approx \mathbf{3.1}$
$\dfrac{\sin B}{6} = \dfrac{\sin 20°}{3.129}$
$\sin B = \dfrac{6 \sin 20°}{3.129} \approx 0.6558$
$B = \sin^{-1} 0.6558 \approx \mathbf{41.0°}$
$C = 180° - 41° - 20° = \mathbf{119.0°}$

22. $\angle ADE = \angle ABC, \angle AED = \angle ACB$
Therefore, $\triangle ADE \sim \triangle ABC$, and $\dfrac{AB}{AD} = \dfrac{AC}{AE}$.
$\dfrac{AD + DB}{AD} = \dfrac{AE + EC}{AE}$
$1 + \dfrac{DB}{AD} = 1 + \dfrac{EC}{AE}$
$\dfrac{DB}{AD} = \dfrac{EC}{AE}$
$\dfrac{AD}{DB} = \dfrac{AE}{EC}$

23. $\dfrac{3}{6} = \dfrac{6}{a}$
$3a = 36$
$a = \mathbf{12}$

24. $c = 2(5) = \mathbf{10}$

25. $a = \dfrac{3}{2}(5) = \dfrac{\mathbf{15}}{\mathbf{2}}$

26. $\dfrac{a}{12} = \dfrac{4}{a}$
$a^2 = 48$
$a = \sqrt{48} = 4\sqrt{3} \approx \mathbf{6.9}$

$\dfrac{b}{8} = \dfrac{12}{b}$
$b^2 = 96$
$b = \sqrt{96} = 4\sqrt{6} \approx \mathbf{9.8}$

$\dfrac{h}{4} = \dfrac{8}{h}$
$h^2 = 32$
$h = \sqrt{32} = 4\sqrt{2} \approx \mathbf{5.7}$

27. $y = 1 + \cos\left(x - \dfrac{5\pi}{3}\right)$

28. $\log 8^{4x+2} = \log 5^{2x-3}$
$(4x + 2)(\log 8) = (2x - 3)(\log 5)$
$(4x + 2)(0.903) = (2x - 3)(0.699)$
$3.612x + 1.806 = 1.398x - 2.097$
$2.214x = -3.903$
$x \approx \mathbf{-1.76}$

29. $\log_4 16^{3/4} - \log_4 (3x + 2) = 2$
$\log_4 \dfrac{8}{3x + 2} = 2$
$4^2 = \dfrac{8}{3x + 2}$
$16(3x + 2) = 8$
$48x + 32 = 8$
$x = -\dfrac{1}{2}$

30. $(x^2 + 4x + 4) + (y^2 + 2y + 1)$
$= -1 + 1 + 4 = 4$
$(x + 2)^2 + (y + 1)^2 = 4$
Center: (2, −1)
Radius: 2

EP

15. **Valid**

PROBLEM SET 70

1. $A_t = A_0 e^{kt}$
$4000 = 400 e^{10k}$
$10 = e^{10k}$
$\ln 10 = \ln e^{10k}$

$2.3 = 10k$
$k = 0.23$
$A_{12} = 400 e^{0.23(12)} = 400 e^{2.76} \approx 6320$

2. $A_t = A_0 e^{kt}$
   $20 = 40e^{50k}$
   $0.5 = e^{50k}$
   $\ln 0.5 = \ln e^{50k}$
   $0.693 = 50k$
   $k \approx -0.014$
   $A_{100} = 40e^{-0.014(100)} = 40e^{-1.4} \approx$ **9.86 g**

3. $A_t = A_0 e^{kt}$
   $20 = 100e^{4k}$
   $0.2 = e^{4k}$
   $\ln 0.2 = \ln e^{4k}$
   $-1.609 = 4k$
   $k \approx -0.4024$
   $A_t = 100e^{-0.4024t}$
   $50 = 100e^{-0.4024t}$
   $0.5 = e^{-0.4024t}$
   $\ln 0.5 = -0.4024t$
   $t \approx$ **1.7 years**

4. | Little Hand | Big Hand |
   |---|---|
   | $R_L T_L = S$ | $R_B T_B = S + 15$ |
   | $R_L = \dfrac{1}{12}$ | $R_B = 1$ |
   | $T_L = T_B$ | |
   | $\dfrac{1}{12}T = S$ | $1T = S + 15$ |

   $T = \dfrac{1}{12}T + 15$

   $\dfrac{11}{12}T = 15$

   $T = \dfrac{180}{11} = 16\dfrac{4}{11}$ min

   $3 : 16\dfrac{4}{11}$

5. $\dfrac{26}{52} \cdot \dfrac{25}{51} = \dfrac{1}{2} \cdot \dfrac{25}{51} = \dfrac{25}{102}$

6. $\dfrac{6}{36} \cdot \dfrac{6}{36} = \dfrac{1}{6} \cdot \dfrac{1}{6} = \dfrac{1}{36}$

7. $x = \dfrac{\begin{vmatrix} 2 & -4 \\ 4 & 3 \end{vmatrix}}{\begin{vmatrix} 3 & -4 \\ 2 & 3 \end{vmatrix}} = \dfrac{6 + 16}{9 + 8} = \dfrac{22}{17}$

   $y = \dfrac{\begin{vmatrix} 3 & 2 \\ 2 & 4 \end{vmatrix}}{17} = \dfrac{12 - 4}{17} = \dfrac{8}{17}$

8. Construction

9. $a_{20} = a_1 + 19d = 2 + 19(-4) = -74$

10. $a_8 = -8, a_{10} = -12$
    $-8 = a_1 + 7d$
    $(-)\ -12 = a_1 + 9d$
    _____
    $\quad -2d = \quad 4$
    $\quad\quad d = -2$
    $-8 = a_1 + 7(-2)$
    $a_1 = 6$
    6, 4, 2

11. $(27 \text{ cis } 30°)^{1/3}$

    First root $= \sqrt[3]{27} \text{ cis } \dfrac{30°}{3} = 3 \text{ cis } 10°$

    Angles differ by $\dfrac{360°}{3} = 120°$

    3 cis 130°, 3 cis 250°

12. $\sin 75° = \sin(45° + 30°)$
    $= \sin 45° \cos 30° + \cos 45° \sin 30°$
    $\approx (0.707)(0.866) + (0.707)(0.5) \approx$ **0.9659**

13. $\sin\left(\theta - \dfrac{\pi}{6}\right) = \sin\theta \cos\dfrac{\pi}{6} - \cos\theta \sin\dfrac{\pi}{6}$

    $= \sin\theta\left(\dfrac{\sqrt{3}}{2}\right) - \cos\theta\left(\dfrac{1}{2}\right)$

    $= \dfrac{1}{2}\left(\sqrt{3}\sin\theta - \cos\theta\right)$

14. Refer to Example 56.B.5.

15. $\sqrt{3}\tan^2 x + 2\tan x - \sqrt{3} = 0$
    $\left(\sqrt{3}\tan x - 1\right)\left(\tan x + \sqrt{3}\right) = 0$
    $\tan x = \dfrac{1}{\sqrt{3}} = \dfrac{\sqrt{3}}{3}$ $\quad\quad \tan x = -\sqrt{3}$
    $x =$ **30°, 120°, 210°, 300°**

16. $\tan^2\theta - 5\tan\theta + 6 = 0$
    $(\tan\theta - 3)(\tan\theta - 2) = 0$
    $\tan\theta = 3$ $\quad\quad\quad \tan\theta = 2$
    $\theta \approx 72°, 252°$ $\quad\quad \theta \approx 63°, 243°$
    $\theta \approx$ **63°, 72°, 243°, 252°**

17. $\sec 4\theta = 1$
    $4\theta = 0°, 360°, 720°, 1080°$
    $\theta =$ **0°, 90°, 180°, 270°**

18.

$$\frac{\cos \theta}{1 - \sin \theta} - \frac{\cos \theta}{1 + \sin \theta}$$

$$= \frac{(\cos \theta)(1 + \sin \theta) - (\cos \theta)(1 - \sin \theta)}{1 - \sin^2 \theta}$$

$$= \frac{\cos \theta + \cos \theta \sin \theta - \cos \theta + \cos \theta \sin \theta}{1 - \sin^2 \theta}$$

$$= \frac{2 \cos \theta \sin \theta}{\cos^2 \theta} = \frac{2 \sin \theta}{\cos \theta} = 2 \tan \theta$$

19.

$$\frac{\cos^3 x + \sin^3 x}{\cos x + \sin x}$$

$$= \frac{(\cos x + \sin x)(\cos^2 x - \sin x \cos x + \sin^2 x)}{\cos x + \sin x}$$

$$= \cos^2 x + \sin^2 x - \sin x \cos x$$

$$= 1 - \sin x \cos x$$

20. $(1 - \sin \theta)(1 + \sin \theta) = 1 - \sin^2 \theta$
$$= \cos^2 \theta$$

21. $a^2 = 8^2 + 9^2 - 2(8)(9) \cos 120° = 217$
$$a = \sqrt{217} \approx \mathbf{14.7}$$

22. $\dfrac{4}{3} = \dfrac{6}{EC}$

$4EC = 18, EC = \dfrac{9}{2}$

23. $d = \dfrac{7}{4}(8) = \dfrac{56}{4} = \mathbf{14}$

24. $\dfrac{a}{15} = \dfrac{5}{a}$

$a^2 = 75$

$a = \sqrt{75} = 5\sqrt{3} \approx \mathbf{8.7}$

$b^2 = 15^2 - 75 = 225 - 75 = 150$

$b = \sqrt{150} = 5\sqrt{6} \approx \mathbf{12.2}$

$h^2 = 75 - 25 = 50$

$h = \sqrt{50} = 5\sqrt{2} \approx \mathbf{7.1}$

25. Central angle $= \dfrac{360°}{5} = 72°$

$h = \dfrac{3}{\tan 36°} \approx 4.1$

$A_{\text{triangle}} = \dfrac{1}{2}(6)(4.1) = 12.39$

$A_{\text{pentagon}} = 12.39(5) \approx \mathbf{61.9 \ cm^2}$

26. Period $= \dfrac{360°}{\frac{9}{5}} = 200°$

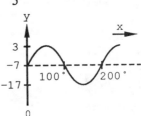

27. $\log 9^{8x-3} = \log 5^{2x-3}$
$(8x - 3)(\log 9) = (2x - 3)(\log 5)$
$(8x - 3)(0.95) = (2x - 3)(0.70)$
$7.6x - 2.85 = 1.4x - 2.1$
$6.2x = 0.75$
$x \approx \mathbf{0.12}$

28. $\log_2 27^{2/3} + \log_2 (3x + 2) = 2$
$\log_2 9(3x + 2) = 2$
$27x + 18 = 4$
$x = -\dfrac{14}{27}$

29. $2^{\log_2 3^2 - \log_2 3} = 2^{\log_2 9/3} = 2^{\log_2 3} = \mathbf{3}$

30. Refer to Problem Set 47, problem 10.

EP

16. $\dfrac{a(1 - r^k)}{1 - r} + ar^k = \dfrac{a - ar^k}{1 - r} + \dfrac{ar^k(1 - r)}{1 - r}$

$= \dfrac{a - ar^k + ar^k - ar^{k+1}}{1 - r}$

$= \dfrac{a - ar^{k+1}}{1 - r} = \dfrac{a(1 - r^{k+1})}{1 - r}$

PROBLEM SET 71

1. $A_t = A_0 e^{kt}$
$2000 = 40e^{6k}$
$50 = e^{6k}$
$\ln 50 = \ln e^{6k}$

$3.91 = 6k$
$k \approx 0.652$
$A_8 = 40e^{0.652(8)} \approx \mathbf{7251}$

2. $A_t = A_0 e^{kt}$
   $3000 = 40,000 e^{10k}$
   $0.75 = e^{10k}$
   $\ln 0.75 = \ln e^{10k}$
   $-0.2877 = 10k$
   $k = -0.0288$
   $20,000 = 40,000 e^{-0.0288t}$
   $0.5 = e^{-0.0288t}$
   $\ln 0.5 = \ln e^{-0.0288t}$
   $-0.693 = -0.0288t$
   $t \approx \textbf{23.9 years}$

3. <u>Little Hand</u>   <u>Big Hand</u>
   $R_L T_L = S$ $R_B T_B = S + 10$
   $R_L = \dfrac{1}{12}$ $R_B = 1$
   $T_L = T_B$
   $\dfrac{1}{12} T = S$ $1T = S + 10$

   $T = \dfrac{1}{12} T + 10$

   $T = \dfrac{120}{11} = \textbf{10} \dfrac{\textbf{10}}{\textbf{11}} \textbf{ min}$

4. $\dfrac{3}{7} \cdot \dfrac{3}{7} \cdot \dfrac{2}{6} = \dfrac{18}{294} = \dfrac{3}{49}$

5. $\dfrac{26}{52} \cdot \dfrac{25}{51} \cdot \dfrac{24}{50} = \dfrac{2}{17}$

6. $n = 1^{\text{st}}$ number
   $n + 2 = 2^{\text{nd}}$ number
   $n + 4 = 3^{\text{rd}}$ number

   $n + (n + 4) - 6 = n + 2$
   $n = 4$
   4, 6, 8

7. $b^2 = 4^2 - 3^2 = 7$
   $\dfrac{x^2}{16} + \dfrac{y^2}{7} = 1$

8. $b^2 = 7^2 - 5^2 = 24$
   $\dfrac{x^2}{24} + \dfrac{y^2}{49} = 1$

9. $2a = 10$ $2b = 4$
   $a = 5$ $b = 2$

   $\dfrac{x^2}{4} + \dfrac{y^2}{25} = 1$

10. $\begin{bmatrix} 2 & -3 & -7 \\ 3 & 2 & 9 \end{bmatrix} = \begin{bmatrix} 1 & -\frac{3}{2} & -\frac{7}{2} \\ 3 & 2 & 9 \end{bmatrix}$

   $= \begin{bmatrix} 1 & -\frac{3}{2} & -\frac{7}{2} \\ 0 & \frac{13}{2} & \frac{39}{2} \end{bmatrix} = \begin{bmatrix} 1 & -\frac{3}{2} & -\frac{7}{2} \\ 0 & 1 & 3 \end{bmatrix}$

   $= \begin{bmatrix} 1 & 0 & 1 \\ 0 & 1 & 3 \end{bmatrix}$

   $x = 1$
   $y = 3$

11. $a_1 = 3, d = -3$
   $a_{16} = 3 + 15(-3) = \textbf{-42}$

12. $a_9 = -46, a_4 = -16$
   $\qquad -46 = a_1 + 8d$
   $\underline{(-) -16 = a_1 + 3d}$
   $\qquad\quad 5d = -30$
   $\qquad\quad\; d = -6$
   $-16 = a_1 + 3(-6)$
   $a_1 = 2$
   2, -4, -10, -16

13. $\sin x \cos \dfrac{\pi}{2} - \cos x \sin \dfrac{\pi}{2}$
   $= (\sin x)(0) - (\cos x)(1) = \textbf{-cos } x$

14. $\tan(45° + 30°) = \dfrac{\tan 45° + \tan 30°}{1 - \tan 45° \tan 30°}$
   $\approx \dfrac{1 + 0.577}{1 - 1(0.577)} \approx \textbf{3.73}$

15. $\tan(60° - 45°) = \dfrac{\tan 60° - \tan 45°}{1 + \tan 60° \tan 45°}$
   $= \dfrac{\sqrt{3} - 1}{1 + \sqrt{3}}$

16. $\sqrt{3} \cot^2 x + 2 \cot x - \sqrt{3} = 0$
   $\left(\sqrt{3} \cot x - 1\right)\left(\cot x + \sqrt{3}\right) = 0$
   $\cot x = \dfrac{\sqrt{3}}{3}$ $\cot x = -\sqrt{3}$
   $x = 60°, 240°$ $x = 150°, 330°$
   $x = \textbf{60°, 150°, 240°, 330°}$

17. $3\cos^2 x + 5\cos x - 2 = 0$
$(3\cos x - 1)(\cos x + 2) = 0$
$\cos x = \dfrac{1}{3}$ $\cos x = -2$
$x \approx \mathbf{70.5°, 289.5°}$ $\varnothing$

18. $\csc 4x = 2$
$\sin 4x = \dfrac{1}{2}$
$4x = 30°, 150°, 390°, 510°, 750°, 870°,$
$1110°, 1230°$
$x = \mathbf{7.5°, 37.5°, 97.5°, 127.5°, 187.5°, 217.5°,}$
$\mathbf{277.5°, 307.5°}$

19. $\dfrac{(\sin\theta)(1 + \cos\theta) - (\sin\theta)(1 - \cos\theta)}{1 - \cos^2\theta}$
$= \dfrac{\sin\theta + \sin\theta\cos\theta - \sin\theta + \sin\theta\cos\theta}{\sin^2\theta}$
$= \dfrac{2\sin\theta\cos\theta}{\sin^2\theta} = \dfrac{2\cos\theta}{\sin\theta} = 2\cot\theta$

20. $\dfrac{(\tan x + 1)(\tan^2 x - \tan x + 1)}{\tan x + 1}$
$= \tan^2 x - \tan x + 1 = \sec^2 x - \tan x$

21. $\cos A = \dfrac{8^2 + 14.7^2 - 10^2}{2(14.7)(8)} \approx 0.7657$
$A = \cos^{-1} 0.7657 \approx \mathbf{40°}$
$B = 180° - 40° - 109° = \mathbf{31°}$

22. $\angle ABD = \angle ACE, \angle ADB = \angle AEC$
Therefore, $\triangle ABD \sim \triangle ACE$, and $\dfrac{AC}{AB} = \dfrac{AE}{AD}$.
$\dfrac{AB + BC}{AB} = \dfrac{AD + DE}{AD}$
$1 + \dfrac{BC}{AB} = 1 + \dfrac{DE}{AD}$
$\dfrac{BC}{AB} = \dfrac{DE}{AD}$

23. $c = \dfrac{3}{2}(8) = \dfrac{24}{2} = \mathbf{12}$

24. $\dfrac{a}{4} = \dfrac{13}{a}$
$a^2 = 52$
$a \approx \mathbf{7.2}$

$\dfrac{b}{9} = \dfrac{13}{b}$
$b^2 = 117$
$b \approx \mathbf{10.8}$

$\dfrac{h}{4} = \dfrac{9}{h}$
$h^2 = 36$
$h = \mathbf{6}$

25. $(14 - 2)180° = \mathbf{2160°}$

26. Refer to Problem Set 48, problem 18.

27. $(3x - 1)(\log 8) = (2x - 1)(\log 4)$
$(3x - 1)(0.903) = (2x - 1)(0.602)$
$2.709x - 0.903 = 1.204x - 0.602$
$1.505x = 0.301$
$x \approx \mathbf{0.2}$

28. $\ln 16^{3/4} + \ln x^2 = \ln(2x + 1)$
$\ln 8x^2 = \ln(2x + 1)$
$8x^2 - 2x - 1 = 0$
$(2x - 1)(4x + 1) = 0$
$x = \dfrac{1}{2}$

29. $3^4 = \mathbf{81}$

30. Refer to Problem Set 47, problem 8.

EP

17. **Invalid**

PROBLEM SET 72

1. $A_t = A_0 e^{kt}$
$400 = 80 e^{k(2)}$
$5 = e^{2k}$
$\ln 5 = \ln e^{2k}$
$1.6094 = 2k$

$k \approx 0.8047$
$2000 = 80 e^{0.8047t}$
$25 = e^{0.8047t}$
$3.2189 = 0.8047t$
$t \approx \mathbf{4\ years}$

2. $A_t = A_0 e^{kt}$
    $500 = 2000 e^{4k}$
    $0.25 = e^{4k}$
    $-1.3863 = 4k$
    $k \approx -0.35$
    $A_t = 2000 e^{-0.35t}$

3. $\dfrac{1}{2}$

4. $10M + 20W + 30C = 3825$
    $M = W$
    $M = 2C$

    $10M + 20M + 30\left(\dfrac{1}{2}M\right) = 3285$

    $M = \$85$
    $\dfrac{M}{7}$ = one day's work $= \dfrac{\$85}{7} \approx \mathbf{\$12.14}$

5. $\dfrac{13}{52} \cdot \dfrac{13}{52} = \dfrac{169}{2704} = \dfrac{1}{16}$

6. $\dfrac{1}{6} \cdot \dfrac{1}{6} \cdot \dfrac{3}{6} = \dfrac{1}{72}$

7. $\cos 2A = \cos(A + A)$
    $= \cos A \cos A - \sin A \sin A$
    $= \cos^2 A - \sin^2 A$

8. Refer to Example 72.B.1.

9. Refer to Example 72.A.2.

10. $b^2 = 5^2 - 3^2 = 16$
    $\dfrac{x^2}{25} + \dfrac{y^2}{16} = 1$

11. $b^2 = 8^2 - 4^2 = 48$
    $\dfrac{x^2}{48} + \dfrac{y^2}{64} = 1$

12. $2a = 12$ $2b = 4$
    $a = 6$ $b = 2$
    $a^2 = 36$ $b^2 = 4$
    $\dfrac{x^2}{36} + \dfrac{y^2}{4} = 1$

13. $a_{18} = 4 + 17(2) = \mathbf{38}$

14. $a_{10} = -22,\ a_3 = -8$
    $-22 = a_1 + 9d$
    $\underline{(-)\ -8 = a_1 + 2d}$
    $7d = -14$
    $d = -2$
    $-8 = a_1 + 2(-2)$
    $a_1 = -4$
    $\mathbf{-4, -6, -8}$

15. $\sin(60° + 45°)$
    $= \sin 60° \sin 45° + \cos 60° \cos 45°$
    $= \left(\dfrac{\sqrt{3}}{2}\right)\left(\dfrac{\sqrt{2}}{2}\right) + \left(\dfrac{\sqrt{2}}{2}\right)\left(\dfrac{1}{2}\right) = \dfrac{\sqrt{6} + \sqrt{2}}{4}$

16. $\sin 15° = \sqrt{\dfrac{1 - \cos 30°}{2}}$
    $\approx \sqrt{\dfrac{1 - 0.866}{2}} \approx \mathbf{0.259}$

17. $2\cos^2 y - 9\sin y + 3 = 0$
    $2(1 - \sin^2 y) - 9\sin y + 3 = 0$
    $2\sin^2 y + 9\sin y - 5 = 0$
    $(2\sin y - 1)(\sin y + 5) = 0$
    $\sin y = \dfrac{1}{2}$ $\sin y = -5$
    $y = \mathbf{30°, 150°}$ $\varnothing$

18. $\sec 2x = 2$
    $\cos 2x = \dfrac{1}{2}$
    $2x = 120°, 240°, 480°, 600°$
    $x = \mathbf{60°, 120°, 240°, 300°}$

19. $\sec^2 x \sin^2 x + \sin^2 x \csc^2 x$
    $= \dfrac{1}{\cos^2 x} \cdot \sin^2 x + \sin^2 x \cdot \dfrac{1}{\sin^2 x}$
    $= \dfrac{\sin^2 x}{\cos^2 x} + 1 = \tan^2 x + 1 = \sec^2 x$

20. $\sin^2 \theta + \tan^2 \theta + \cos^2 \theta = 1 + \tan^2 \theta$
    $= \sec^2 \theta$

21. $\cos A = \dfrac{8^2 + 12^2 - 10^2}{2(10)(12)} = 0.5625$
    $A = \cos^{-1} 0.5625 \approx \mathbf{55.8°}$

22. $\dfrac{x}{3} = \dfrac{5}{4}$
    $4x = 15$
    $x = \dfrac{15}{4}$

23. $C = \dfrac{4}{3}(4) = \dfrac{16}{3}$

24. $\angle ABC = \angle CDE$ is given. $\angle ACB = \angle DCE$ because vertical angles are eqaul. Therefore, $\triangle ACB \sim \triangle ECD$ and $\dfrac{BC}{CD} = \dfrac{AB}{DE}$.

25. Period $= \dfrac{360°}{\dfrac{10}{7}} = 252°$

26. The sum of the exterior angles of any polygon is **360°**.

27. $(2x - 1)(\log 7) = (3x + 2)(\log 8)$
$(2x - 1)(0.8451) = (3x + 2)(0.9031)$

$1.69x - 0.8451 = 2.709x + 1.806$
$1.019x = -2.6511$
$x \approx \mathbf{-2.60}$

28. $\ln x + \ln x = \ln 2^2$
$\ln x^2 = \ln 4$
$x^2 = 4$
$x = \mathbf{2}$

29. $M = b^a, N = b^c$
$\log_b M = a, \log_b N = c$
$\log_b MN = \log_b (b^a)(b^c)$
$= \log_b b^{a+c} = a + c = \log_b M + \log_b N$

30. $4^{-1} = \dfrac{1}{4}$

EP

18. $1 - \dfrac{1}{2^k} + \dfrac{1}{2^{k+1}} = 1 - \dfrac{2}{2}\dfrac{1}{2^k} + \dfrac{1}{2^{k+1}}$
$= 1 - \dfrac{2}{2^{k+1}} + \dfrac{1}{2^{k+1}} = 1 - \dfrac{1}{2^{k+1}}$

PROBLEM SET 73

1. $A_t = A_0 e^{kt}$
$900 = 30e^{3k}$
$30 = e^{3k}$
$3.401 = 3k$
$k \approx 1.13$
$A_t = \mathbf{30e^{1.13t}}$

2. $A_t = A_0 e^{kt}$
$7 = 42e^{10k}$
$-1.792 = 10k$
$k \approx -0.1792$
$30 = 42e^{-0.1792t}$
$-0.3365 = -0.1792t$
$t \approx \mathbf{1.88\ years}$

3.

Little Hand	Big Hand
$R_L T_L = S$	$R_B T_B = S + 40$
$R_L = \dfrac{1}{12}$	$R_B = 1$
$T_L = T_B$	
$\dfrac{1}{12}T = S$	$T = S + 40$

$T = \dfrac{1}{12}T + 40$
$T = \dfrac{480}{11} = 43\dfrac{7}{11}$ min

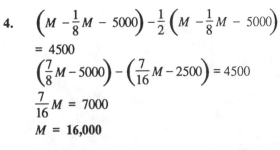

4. $\left(M - \dfrac{1}{8}M - 5000\right) - \dfrac{1}{2}\left(M - \dfrac{1}{8}M - 5000\right)$
$= 4500$
$\left(\dfrac{7}{8}M - 5000\right) - \left(\dfrac{7}{16}M - 2500\right) = 4500$
$\dfrac{7}{16}M = 7000$
$M = \mathbf{16,000}$

5. $\dfrac{T}{20} + \dfrac{T}{30} = 1$
$30T + 20T = 600$

$$50T = 600$$
$$T = \textbf{12 hr}$$

6. $\dfrac{1}{6} \cdot \dfrac{1}{6} \cdot \dfrac{4}{6} = \dfrac{1}{\textbf{54}}$

7. Refer to Example 72.A.1.

8. Refer to Example 72.B.1.

9. $a_6 = a_1 r^5 = (-4)(-2)^5 = (-4)(-32) = \textbf{128}$

10. $a_4 = a_1 r^3$
    $a_4 = 4r^3$
    $4r^3 = 108$
    $r^3 = 27$
    $r = 3$
    12, 36

11. $a_5 = a_1 r^4$
    $32 = 2r^4$
    $r^4 = 16$
    $r = \pm 2$
    4, 8, 16 or **−4, 8, −16**

12. $b^2 = 6^2 - 2^2 = 32$
    $\dfrac{x^2}{36} + \dfrac{y^2}{32} = 1$

13. $a = 7 \qquad\quad a^2 = 49$
    $b = 5 \qquad\quad b^2 = 25$
    $\dfrac{x^2}{25} + \dfrac{y^2}{49} = 1$

14. $-30 = 6 + 9d$
    $d = -4$
    6, 2, −2, −6

15. $\cos(45° + 60°)$
    $= \cos 45° \cos 60° - \sin 45° \sin 60°$
    $= \left(\dfrac{\sqrt{2}}{2}\right)\left(\dfrac{1}{2}\right) - \left(\dfrac{\sqrt{2}}{2}\right)\left(\dfrac{\sqrt{3}}{2}\right) = \dfrac{\sqrt{2} - \sqrt{6}}{4}$

16. $\cos 15° = \sqrt{\dfrac{1 + 0.866}{2}}$
    $= \sqrt{\dfrac{1 + \dfrac{\sqrt{3}}{2}}{2}} \approx \textbf{0.966}$

17. $2\sin^2 y - 9\cos y + 3 = 0$
    $2(1 - \cos^2 y) - 9\cos y + 3 = 0$
    $2 - 2\cos^2 y - 9\cos y + 3 = 0$
    $2\cos^2 y + 9\cos y - 5 = 0$
    $(2\cos y - 1)(\cos y + 5) = 0$
    $\cos y = \dfrac{1}{2} \qquad\qquad \cos y = -5$
    $y = \textbf{60}°, \textbf{300}° \qquad\qquad \varnothing$

18. $2\cos 3\theta = -\sqrt{3}$
    $\cos 3\theta = -\dfrac{\sqrt{3}}{2}$
    $3\theta = 150°, 210°, 510°, 570°, 870°, 930°$
    $\theta = \textbf{50}°, \textbf{70}°, \textbf{170}°, \textbf{190}°, \textbf{290}°, \textbf{310}°$

19. $\dfrac{1 - \cos^2 \theta}{1 + \tan^2 \theta} = \dfrac{\sin^2 \theta}{\sec^2 \theta} = \sin^2 \theta \cos^2 \theta$

20. $\csc^2 y \sec^2 y - \sec^2 y$
    $= (\sec^2 y)(\csc^2 y - 1) = \sec^2 y \cdot \cot^2 y$
    $= \dfrac{1}{\cos^2 y} \cdot \dfrac{\cos^2 y}{\sin^2 y} = \dfrac{1}{\sin^2 y} = \csc^2 y$

21. $\cos a = \dfrac{10^2 + 19.04^2 - 11^2}{2(10)(19.04)} \approx 0.8969$
    $a = \cos^{-1} 0.8969 \approx \textbf{26.3}°$

    $b = 180° - 26.3° - 130° = \textbf{23.7}°$

22. Refer to Example 69.B.1.

23. $\dfrac{7}{6}m = 10$
    $m = 10\left(\dfrac{6}{7}\right) = \dfrac{60}{7}$

24. $\dfrac{a}{2} = \dfrac{16}{a}$
    $a^2 = 32$
    $a = \sqrt{32} \approx \textbf{5.7}$

    $\dfrac{b}{16} = \dfrac{14}{b}$
    $b^2 = 224$
    $b = \sqrt{224} \approx \textbf{15.0}$

    $\dfrac{h}{14} = \dfrac{2}{h}$
    $h^2 = 28$
    $h = \sqrt{28} \approx \textbf{5.3}$

25. $y = \dfrac{3}{2} + \dfrac{3}{2}\sin 2\left(x + \dfrac{\pi}{6}\right)$

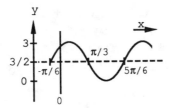

26. Side $= \dfrac{48}{6} = 8$ in

Central angle $= \dfrac{360°}{6} = 60°$

$\sin 30° = \dfrac{4}{r}$

$r = \dfrac{4}{\sin 30°} = \mathbf{8\ in}$

27. $(3x - 4)(\log 16) = (2x + 1)(\log 4)$
$(3x - 4)(1.204) = (2x + 1)(0.602)$
$3.612x - 4.816 = 1.204x + 0.602$

$2.408x = 5.418$
$x \approx \mathbf{2.25}$

28. $\ln \dfrac{2x - 3}{3x} = \ln 27^{2/3}$

$\dfrac{2x - 3}{3x} = 9$

$2x - 3 = 27x$

$25x = -3$

$x = -\dfrac{3}{25}$

No solution

29. $4^{-2} = \dfrac{1}{4^2} = \dfrac{1}{\mathbf{16}}$

30. Refer to Problem Set 28, problem 29.

EP

19. Invalid

PROBLEM SET 74

1. $A_t = A_0 e^{kt}$
$100 = 500 e^{100k}$
$0.2 = e^{10k}$
$-1.60 = 10k$
$k \approx -0.016$
$50 = 500 e^{-0.016t}$
$0.1 = e^{-0.016t}$
$-2.303 = -0.016t$
$t \approx \mathbf{143.9\ days}$

2. $A_t = A_0 e^{kt}$
$2000 = 10 e^{k(3)}$
$200 = e^{3k}$
$5.298 = 3k$
$k \approx 1.77$
$A_6 = 10 e^{1.77(6)} \approx \mathbf{400{,}000}$

3. $(m - 2) - \dfrac{1}{6}(m - 2)$

$- \dfrac{1}{2}\left[(m - 2) - \dfrac{1}{6}(m - 2)\right] = 9$

$m - 2 - \dfrac{1}{6}m + \dfrac{1}{3}$

$- \dfrac{1}{2}\left(m - 2 - \dfrac{1}{6}m + \dfrac{1}{3}\right) = 9$

$m - 2 - \dfrac{1}{6}m + \dfrac{1}{3} - \dfrac{1}{2}m + 1 + \dfrac{1}{12}m - \dfrac{1}{6} = 9$
$12m - 24 - 2m + 4 - 6m + 12 + m - 2 = 108$
$5m = 118$
$m = \mathbf{\$23.60}$

4. $u = $ units' digit
$t = $ tens' digit
A $u = t + 2$
B: $\dfrac{10t + u + 6}{t + u} = 5$
Substitute equation B into A.
$\dfrac{10t + t + 2 + 6}{t + t + 2} = 5$
$\dfrac{11t + 8}{2t + 2} = 5$
$11t + 8 = 10t + 10$
$t = 2$
$u = 2 + 2 = 4$
$N = \mathbf{24}$

5. Rate $\cdot$ time $\cdot$ men $=$ jobs
Rate $\cdot K \cdot 14 = M$
$\dfrac{M}{14K} \cdot$ time $\cdot 21 = $ F
Time $= \dfrac{14KF}{21M} = \dfrac{2KF}{3M}$ **days**

6. *AD* bisects $\angle BAC$ and $\angle BDC$
   $\angle BAD = \angle CAD$, $\angle BDA = \angle CDA$ by
   definition of angle bisector. $AD = AD$ by
   reflexive property. $\triangle ABD \cong \triangle ACD$ by ASA.
   $AB = AC$ by CPCTE.

7. $AO = CO, DO = BO$
   $\angle DOA = \angle BOC$ because vertical angles are
   equal. $\triangle AOD \cong \triangle OCB$ by SAS. $\angle DAO =$
   $\angle OCB$ by CPCTE.

8. $\overline{WX} \perp \overline{UV}$, $UW = WV$.
   $\angle UWX = \angle VWX, WX = WX$
   $\triangle VWX \cong \triangle UWX$ by SAS. $UX = VX$ by
   CPCTE.

9. Refer to Example 72.A.2.

10. Refer to Example 72.B.1.

11. $a_5 = (-3)(-2)^4 = -3(16) = \mathbf{-48}$

12. Find the equation of the line $\perp$ to $y = x - 1$
    that passes through $(-1, 0)$.
    $m_\perp = -1$
    $y = -x + b$
    $0 = -(-1) + b$
    $b = -1$
    $y = -x - 1$

    Solve $y = -x - 1$ and $y = x - 1$
    simultaneously.
    $-x - 1 = x - 1$
    $0 = 2x$
    $x = 0$
    $y = 0 - 1 = -1$
    $(x, y) = (0, -1)$

    $d = \sqrt{(-1 - 0)^2 + (0 + 1)^2}$
    $\sqrt{1 + 1} = \sqrt{2}$

13. $b^2 = 5^2 - 2^2 = 21$
    $\dfrac{x^2}{21} + \dfrac{y^2}{25} = 1$

14. $2a = 16$
    $a = 8$
    $a^2 = 64$
    $2b = 8$

$b = 4$
$b^2 = 16$
$\dfrac{x^2}{64} + \dfrac{y^2}{16} = 1$
$\mathbf{x^2 + 4y^2 - 64 = 0}$

15. $a_{10} = 52, a_{15} = 82$
    $\quad\quad 52 = a_1 + 9d$
    $\underline{(-)\ 82 = a_1 + 14d}$
    $\quad -5d = -30$
    $\quad\quad d = 6$
    $52 = a_1 + 9(6)$
    $a_1 = -2$
    $\mathbf{-2, 4, 10}$

16. $\tan(60° + 45°)$
    $= \dfrac{\tan 60° + \tan 45°}{1 - \tan 60° \tan 45°} = \dfrac{\sqrt{3} + 1}{1 - \sqrt{3}}$

17. $\cos 15° = \sqrt{\dfrac{1 + \cos 30°}{2}}$
    $= \sqrt{\dfrac{1 + 0.866}{2}} \approx \mathbf{0.966}$

18. $\tan^2 x - \sec x - 5 = 0$
    $\sec^2 x - 1 - \sec x - 5 = 0$
    $\sec^2 x - \sec x - 6 = 0$
    $(\sec x - 3)(\sec x + 2) = 0$
    $\sec x = 3 \quad\quad\quad\quad \sec x = -2$
    $\cos x = \dfrac{1}{3} \quad\quad\quad\quad \cos x = -\dfrac{1}{2}$
    $x \approx 71°, 289° \quad\quad x = 120°, 240°$
    $x = \mathbf{71°, 120°, 240°, 289°}$

19. $\tan 4\theta = \sqrt{3}$
    $4\theta = 60°, 240°, 420°, 600°, 780°, 960°,$
    $1140°, 1320°$
    $\theta = \mathbf{15°, 60°, 105°, 150°, 195°, 240°, 285°,}$
    $\mathbf{330°}$

20. $\dfrac{1 - \sin^2 \theta}{1 + \cot^2 \theta} = \dfrac{\cos^2 \theta}{\csc^2 \theta} = \cos^2 \theta \sin^2 \theta$

21. $\sin^2 x \sec^2 x + \sin^2 x \csc^2 x$
    $= \sin^2 x \cdot \dfrac{1}{\cos^2 x} + \sin^2 x \cdot \dfrac{1}{\sin^2 x}$
    $= \dfrac{\sin^2 x}{\cos^2 x} + 1 = \tan^2 x + 1 = \sec^2 x$

22. $a^2 = 64 + 100 - 2(8)(10 \cos 140°)$
$\approx 164 - 122.57 \approx 286.57$
$a \approx \textbf{16.9}$

23. $a = \dfrac{3}{4}(8) = \dfrac{24}{4} = \textbf{6}$

24. $\dfrac{m}{h} = \dfrac{a}{b}$
$\dfrac{a}{b} = \dfrac{h}{n}$
$\dfrac{h}{n} = \dfrac{m}{h}$

25.

26. $A_{\text{segment}} = A_{\text{sector}} - A_{\text{triangle}}$
$= \dfrac{40°}{360°}\pi(10)^2 - \dfrac{1}{2}(10)(6.43) \approx \textbf{2.8 in}^2$

27. $(2x + 2)(\log 16) = (x + 1)(\log 4)$
$(2x + 2)(1.204) = (x + 1)(0.602)$
$2.408x + 2.408 = 0.602x + 0.602$
$1.806x = -1.806$
$x = \textbf{-1}$

28. $\ln \dfrac{x^2}{\frac{1}{2}x + 1} = \ln 2$

$\dfrac{x^2}{\frac{1}{2}x + 1} = 2$

$x^2 = 2\left(\dfrac{1}{2}x + 1\right)$

$x^2 = x + 2$
$x^2 - x - 2 = 0$
$(x - 2)(x + 1) = 0$
$x = \textbf{2}$

29. $3^{-2} = \dfrac{1}{9}$

30. Refer to Lesson 28.B.

EP

20. $\dfrac{k(k+1)(k+2)}{3} + (k + 1)(k + 2)$

$= \dfrac{k(k+1)(k+2) + 3(k+1)(k+2)}{3}$

$= \dfrac{(k+1)(k+2)(k+3)}{3}$

$= \dfrac{(k+1)[(k+1)+1][(k+1)+2]}{3}$

21. **Valid**

PROBLEM SET 75

1. $N = mT + b$
$8 = 10m + b$
$\underline{(-)\ 13 = 20m + b}$
$5 = 10m$

$m = \dfrac{1}{2}$

$b = 3$

$N = \dfrac{1}{2}T + 3 = \dfrac{1}{2}(8) + 3 = \textbf{7}$

2. $A_t = A_0 e^{kt}$
$9000 = 10{,}000 e^{40k}$
$0.9 = e^{40k}$
$-0.01536 = 40k$
$k \approx -0.00263$
$A_t = 10{,}000 e^{-0.00263t}$
$5000 = 10{,}000 e^{-0.00263t}$

$0.5 = e^{-0.00263t}$
$-0.6921 = -0.00263t$
$t \approx \textbf{263 min}$

3. $A_t = A_0 e^{kt}$
$1000 = 100 e^{6k}$
$10 = e^{6k}$
$2.3 = 6k$
$k \approx 0.3838$
$A_t = 100 e^{0.3838t}$
$2000 = 100 e^{0.3838t}$
$20 = e^{0.3838t}$
$2.9957 = 0.3838t$
$t \approx \textbf{7.8 months}$

4. $\dfrac{4}{52} + \dfrac{26}{52} - \dfrac{2}{52} = \dfrac{28}{52} = \dfrac{7}{13}$

5. $_8P_5 = \dfrac{8!}{3!} = 6720$

    $_8C_5 = \dfrac{8!}{3!\,5!} = 56$

6. $AB = AC, BD = DC$
    $AD = AD$ by reflexive property, $\triangle ABD$
    $\cong \triangle ADC$ by SSS. $\angle BAD = \angle DAC$ and
    $\angle BCA = \angle CDA$ by CPCTE. AD bisects
    $\angle BAC$ and $\angle BDC$ by definition of angle
    bisector.

7. $AO = CO, DO = BO$
    $\angle AOD = \angle BOC$ because vertical angles are
    equal. $\triangle AOD \cong \triangle BOC$ by SAS. $AD = BC$
    by CPCTE.

8. $UX = VX, \angle UXW = \angle VXW$
    $WX = WX$ by reflexive property. $\angle UWX$
    $\cong \angle VWX$ by CPCTE.

9. $\cos(A + A) = \cos A \cos A - \sin A \sin A$
    $= \cos^2 A - \sin^2 A$
    $= (1 - \sin^2 A) - \sin^2 A$
    $= 1 - 2\sin^2 A$
    $\sin^2 A = \dfrac{1 - \cos 2A}{2}$

    $\sin A = \pm\sqrt{\dfrac{1 - \cos 2A}{2}}$

    $\sin \dfrac{1}{2}x = \pm\sqrt{\dfrac{1 - \cos x}{2}}$

10. $(16 \text{ cis } 120°)^{1/4}$

    First root $= \sqrt[4]{16} \text{ cis } \dfrac{120°}{4} = 2 \text{ cis } 30°$

    Angles differ by $\dfrac{360°}{4} = 90°$

    $2 \text{ cis } 120°, 2 \text{ cis } 210°, 2 \text{ cis } 300°$

    $2 \text{ cis } 30° = 2\left(\dfrac{\sqrt{3}}{2} + \dfrac{1}{2}i\right) = \sqrt{3} + i$

    $2 \text{ cis } 120° = 2\left(-\dfrac{1}{2} + \dfrac{\sqrt{3}}{2}i\right) = -1 + \sqrt{3}\,i$

    $2 \text{ cis } 210° = 2\left(-\dfrac{\sqrt{3}}{2} - \dfrac{1}{2}i\right) = -\sqrt{3} - i$

    $2 \text{ cis } 300° = 2\left(\dfrac{1}{2} - \dfrac{\sqrt{3}}{2}i\right) = 1 - \sqrt{3}\,i$

11. $a_4 = a_1 r^4 = 2\left(-\dfrac{1}{2}\right)^3 = 2\left(-\dfrac{1}{8}\right) = -\dfrac{1}{4}$

12. $a_4 = a_1 r^3$
    $-16 = 2r^3$
    $-8 = r^3$
    $r = -2$
    $-4, 8$

13. $2a = 10$ $2b = 8$
    $a = 5$ $b = 4$
    $a^2 = 25$ $b^2 = 16$
    $\dfrac{x^2}{16} + \dfrac{y^2}{25} = 1$

14. $\dfrac{x^2}{25} - \dfrac{y^2}{16} = 1$
    Vertices: $(\pm 5, 0)$
    Asymptotes: $y = \pm\dfrac{4}{3}x$

15. $a_4 = -2, a_{10} = 10$
    $-2 = a_1 + 3d$
    $\underline{(-)\,10 = a_1 + 9d}$
    $-12 = -6d$
    $d = 2$
    $-2 = a_1 + 3(2)$
    $a_1 = -8$
    $-8, -6, -4, -2$

16. $\sin 15° = \sqrt{\dfrac{1 - \cos 30°}{2}}$

    $= \sqrt{\dfrac{1 - 0.866}{2}} \approx 0.259$

17. $\cos\left(x + \dfrac{\pi}{2}\right) = \cos x \cos \dfrac{\pi}{2} - \sin x \sin \dfrac{\pi}{2}$

    $= (\cos x)(0) - (\sin x)(1) = -\sin x$

18. $\tan^2 \theta - \sec \theta - 1 = 0$
    $\sec^2 \theta - 1 - \sec \theta - 1 = 0$
    $\sec^2 \theta - \sec \theta - 2 = 0$
    $(\sec \theta - 2)(\sec \theta + 1) = 0$
    $\sec \theta = 2$ $\sec \theta = -1$
    $\theta = 60°, 300°$ $\theta = 180°$
    $\theta = 60°, 180°, 300°$

19. $\sin 5\theta = 0$
    $5\theta = 0°, 180°, 360°, 540°, 720°, 900°, 1080°,$
    $1260°, 1440°, 1620°$
    $\theta = 0°, 36°, 72°, 108°, 144°, 180°, 216°,$
    $252°, 288°, 324°$

20.
$$\frac{(\sin^2\theta + \cos^2\theta)(\sin^2\theta - \sin^2\theta)}{\sin^2\theta - \cos^2\theta}$$
$$= \sin^2\theta + \cos^2\theta = 1$$

21.
$$\frac{\dfrac{1}{\cos^2 x}}{\dfrac{1}{\cos^2 x} - 1} = \frac{\dfrac{1}{\cos^2 x}}{\dfrac{1 - \cos^2 x}{\cos^2 x}}$$
$$= \frac{1}{\cos^2 x} \cdot \frac{\cos^2 x}{1 - \cos^2 x}$$
$$= \frac{1}{1 - \cos^2 x} = \frac{1}{\sin^2 x} = \csc^2 x$$

22.
$$\cos A = \frac{5^2 + 8^2 - 6^2}{2(5)(8)} = 0.6625$$
$$A = \cos^{-1} 0.6625 \approx \mathbf{48.5°}$$

$$\cos B = \frac{5^2 + 6^2 - 8^2}{2(5)(6)} = -0.05$$
$$B = \cos^{-1}(0.05) \approx \mathbf{92.9°}$$

23.
$$c = 8\left(\frac{4}{3}\right) = \frac{32}{3}$$

24.
$$\frac{a}{3} = \frac{12}{a}$$
$$a^2 = 36, a = \mathbf{6}$$
$$6^2 + b^2 = 12^2$$
$$b^2 = 144 - 36 = 108$$
$$b = \sqrt{108} \approx \mathbf{10.4}$$

25. Period $= \dfrac{2\pi}{1/2} = 4\pi$

26.

Central angle $= \dfrac{360°}{10} = 36°$

$h = \dfrac{2}{\tan 18°} \approx 6.16$

$A_{\text{triangle}} = \dfrac{1}{2}(4)(6.16) = 12.31$

$A_{\text{decagon}} = (12.31)(10) = \mathbf{123.1\ cm^2}$

27.
$$(\log 16)(3x - 2) = (\log 2)(4x - 1)$$
$$1.2(3x - 2) = 0.3(4x - 1)$$
$$3.6x - 1.2x = 2.4 - 0.3$$
$$2.4x = 2.1$$
$$x \approx 0.875 = \frac{7}{8}$$

28.
$$\log_7 \frac{8^{2/3}}{x - 1} = 1$$
$$7^1 = \frac{4}{x - 1}$$
$$7x - 7 = 4$$
$$x = \frac{11}{7}$$

29.
$$8^{\log_8 4^2 - \log_8 3} = 8^{\log_8 16/3} = \frac{16}{3}$$

30.
$$4^{-2} = \frac{1}{16}$$

EP

22.
$$\frac{1}{2}n[2a + (n - 1)d] + a + nd$$
$$= na + \frac{1}{2}n(n - 1)d + a + nd$$
$$= na + \frac{1}{2}n^2 d - \frac{1}{2}nd + a + nd$$
$$= na + a + \frac{1}{2}n^2 d + \frac{1}{2}nd$$
$$= a(n + 1) + \frac{1}{2}nd(n + 1)$$
$$= \frac{1}{2}(n + 1)(2a + nd)$$
$$= \frac{1}{2}(n + 1)\{2a + [(n + 1) - 1]d\}$$

23. **Invalid**

PROBLEM SET 76

1. $A_t = A_0 e^{kt}$
$80 = 10e^{40k}$
$8 = e^{40k}$
$2.079 = 40k$
$k \approx 0.052$
$A_{100} = 10e^{0.052(100)} \approx \mathbf{5120}$

2. $A_t = A_0 e^{kt}$
$300 = 400e^{30k}$
$0.75 = e^{30k}$
$-0.2877 = 30k$
$k \approx -0.0096$
$A_t = 400e^{-0.0096t}$
$200 = 400e^{-0.0096t}$
$0.5 = e^{-0.0096t}$
$-0.69314 = -0.0096t$
$t \approx \mathbf{72.3\ hr}$

3.

Little Hand	Big Hand
$R_L T_L = S$	$R_B T_B = S + 25$
$R_L = \dfrac{1}{12}$	$R_B = 1$
$T_L = T_B$	
$\dfrac{1}{12}T = S$	$1T = S + 25$

$T = \dfrac{1}{12}T + 25$

$T = \dfrac{300}{11} = 27\dfrac{3}{11}\ \text{min}$

$\mathbf{4 : 27\dfrac{3}{11}\ min}$

4. $P(G) + P(S) - P(G, S)$
$\dfrac{4}{9} + \dfrac{5}{9} - \dfrac{2}{9} = \dfrac{7}{9}$

5. $_9P_6 = \dfrac{9!}{(9-6)!} = \dfrac{9!}{3!} = \mathbf{60{,}480}$
$_9C_6 = \dfrac{9!}{(9-6)!\,6!} = \dfrac{9!}{3!\,6!} = \mathbf{84}$

6. $\dfrac{a}{c} = \dfrac{m}{a}$ $\qquad\qquad$ $\dfrac{b}{c} = \dfrac{n}{b}$
$a^2 = cm$ $\qquad\qquad$ $b^2 = cn$

$c = m + n$
$a^2 + b^2 = cm + cn$
$a^2 + b^2 = c(m + n)$
$a^2 + b^2 = c^2$

7. $AD \perp BC$ and AD bisects $\overline{BC}$ are given.
$BD = DC$ by def. of bisector. $AD = AD$ by reflexive property. $\angle ABD = \angle ADC = 90°$. $\triangle ADB \cong \triangle ADC$ by SAS. Therefore, $AB = AC$ by CPCTE.

8. AD bisects $\angle BAC$ and $AB = AC$ are given. $\angle BAC = \angle CAD$ by def. of bisector. $AD = AD$ by reflexive property. $\triangle ADB \cong \triangle ADC$ by SAS. Therefore, $BD = DC$ by CPCTE.

9. $AO = CO$ and $BO = DO$ are given. $\angle AOB = \angle COD$ by vertical angles. $\triangle AOB \cong \triangle COD$ by SAS. Therefore, $\angle AOB = \angle OCD$ by CPCTE.

10. $\cos(A + A) = \cos A \cos A - \sin A \sin A$
$= \cos^2 A - \sin^2 A$

11. $(32\ \text{cis}\ 20°)^{1/5}$
First root $= \sqrt[5]{32}\ \text{cis}\ \dfrac{20°}{5} = \mathbf{2\ cis\ 4°}$
Angles differ by $\dfrac{360°}{5} = 72°$
**2 cis 76, 2 cis 148°, 2 cis 220°,
2 cis 292°**

12. $a_5 = a_1 r^4$
$162 = 2r^4$
$r^4 = 81$
$r = \pm 3$
6, 18, 54 or -6, 18, -54

13. $2a = 8$
$a = 4$
$a^2 = 16$
$2b = 6$
$b = 3$
$b^2 = 9$
$\dfrac{x^2}{9} + \dfrac{y^2}{16} = 1$
$\mathbf{16x^2 + 9y^2 - 144 = 0}$

14. $\dfrac{x^2}{4} - \dfrac{y^2}{9} = 1$
Vertices: $(\pm 2, 0)$
Asymptotes: $y = \pm \dfrac{3}{2}x$

15. $a_5 = 12, a_{13} = -4$

$a_5 = a_1 + 4d$

$a_{13} = a_1 + 12d$

$\quad a_1 + 4d = 12$

$\underline{(-)\, a_1 + 12d = -4}$

$\qquad\qquad 8d = -16$

$\qquad\qquad\ d = -2$

$a_1 = 12 - 4(-2) = 20$

20, 18, 16, 14

16. $\sin(285°) = \sin(240° + 45°)$

$= \sin 240° \cos 45° + \cos 240° \sin 45°$

$= (-0.866)(0.707) + (-0.5)(0.707) \approx \textbf{-0.966}$

17. $\sin\left(x - \dfrac{\pi}{4}\right) = \sin x \cos\dfrac{\pi}{4} - \cos x \sin\dfrac{\pi}{4}$

$= (\sin x)\left(\dfrac{\sqrt{2}}{2}\right) - (\cos x)\left(\dfrac{\sqrt{2}}{2}\right)$

$= \dfrac{\sqrt{2}}{2}\sin x - \dfrac{\sqrt{2}}{2}\cos x = \dfrac{\sqrt{2}}{2}(\sin x - \cos x)$

18. $2\sin^2 x + 7\cos x + 2 = 0$

$2(1 - \cos^2 x) + 7\cos x + 2 = 0$

$2 - 2\cos^2 x + 7\cos x + 2 = 0$

$2\cos^2 x - 7\cos x - 4 = 0$

$(2\cos x + 1)(\cos x - 4) = 0$

$\cos x = -\dfrac{1}{2} \qquad\qquad \cos x = 4$

$x = \textbf{120°, 240°} \qquad\qquad \varnothing$

19. $\cot 3x = -\dfrac{\sqrt{3}}{3}$

$3x = 120°, 300°, 480°, 660°, 840°, 1020°$

$x = \textbf{40°, 100°, 160°, 220°, 280°, 340°}$

20. $\dfrac{1 + \sin B}{\cos B} \cdot \dfrac{\cos B}{\cos B} = \dfrac{(1 + \sin B)\cos B}{\cos^2 B}$

$= \dfrac{(1 + \sin B)\cos B}{1 - \sin^2 B}$

$= \dfrac{(1 + \sin B)\cos B}{(1 + \sin B)(1 - \sin B)} = \dfrac{\cos B}{1 - \sin B}$

21. $\dfrac{\tan B + 1}{\tan B - 1} = \dfrac{\dfrac{\sin B}{\cos B} + 1}{\dfrac{\sin B}{\cos B} - 1}$

$= \dfrac{\dfrac{\sin B + \cos B}{\cos B}}{\dfrac{\sin B - \cos B}{\cos B}} = \dfrac{\sin B + \cos B}{\sin B - \cos B}$

$= \dfrac{\dfrac{1}{\csc B} + \dfrac{1}{\sec B}}{\dfrac{1}{\csc B} - \dfrac{1}{\sec B}} = \dfrac{\dfrac{\sec B + \csc B}{\csc B \sec B}}{\dfrac{\sec B - \csc B}{\csc B \sec B}}$

$= \dfrac{\sec B + \csc B}{\sec B - \csc B}$

22. $(y^2 \sin^2\theta + 2xy \sin\theta \cos\theta + x^2 \cos^2\theta)$

$+ (y^2 \cos^2\theta - 2xy \sin\theta \cos\theta + x^2 \sin^2\theta)$

$= y^2 \sin^2\theta + y^2 \cos^2\theta + x^2 \cos^2\theta + x^2 \sin^2\theta$

$= y^2(\sin^2\theta + \cos^2\theta) + x^2(\cos^2\theta + \sin^2\theta)$

$= y^2 + x^2$

23. $a^2 = 8^2 + 9^2 - 2(8)(9)\cos 30°$

$= 64 + 81 - 144\left(\dfrac{\sqrt{3}}{2}\right) \approx 20.3$

$a \approx \sqrt{20.3} \approx \textbf{4.5}$

24. $8\left(\dfrac{2}{3}\right) = \dfrac{\textbf{16}}{\textbf{3}}$

25. Period $= \dfrac{2\pi}{\dfrac{1}{2}} = 4\pi$

26. $(10 - 2)180° = \textbf{1440°}$

27. $\log 27^{2x+3} = \log 3^{x-4}$

$(2x + 3)(\log 27) = (x - 4)(\log 3)$

$(2x + 3)(1.43) = (x - 4)(0.477)$

$2.86x - 0.477x = -4.29 - 1.79$

$2.38x = -6.08$

$x \approx \textbf{-2.6}$

28. $\log_8 16^{3/4} + \log_8 (3x - 2) = 2$

$\log_8 8(3x - 2) = 2$

$8^2 = 8(3x - 2)$

$8 = 3x - 2$

$x = \dfrac{\textbf{10}}{\textbf{3}}$

29. $6^{-2} = \dfrac{1}{36}$

30. $M = b^a, N = b^c$
$\log_b M = a, \log_b N = c$
$\log_b MN = \log_b (b^a)(b^c) = \log_b b^{a+c}$
$= a + c = \log_b M + \log_b N$

25. **Invalid**

ENRICHMENT LESSON 3

1. $A_t = A_0 e^{kt}$
$50 = 10e^{10k}$
$5 = e^{10k}$
$1.61 = 10k$
$k \approx 0.161$
$A_{30} = 10e^{0.161(30)} \approx \mathbf{1250}$

2. $A_t = A_0 e^{kt}$
$150 = 200e^{10k}$
$0.75 = e^{10k}$
$-0.2877 = 10k$
$k \approx -0.02877$
$100 = 200e^{-0.02877t}$
$0.5 = e^{-0.02877t}$
$-0.6931 = -0.02877t$
$t \approx \mathbf{24\ hr}$

3.
Little Hand	Big Hand
$R_L T_L = S$	$R_B T_B = S + 25$
$R_L = \dfrac{1}{12}$	$R_B = 1$
$T_L = T_B$	
$\dfrac{1}{12}T = S$	$1T = S + 25$

$T = \dfrac{1}{12}T + 25$

$T = \dfrac{300}{11} = 27\dfrac{3}{11}$ min

$3{:}27\dfrac{3}{11}$ min

4. $P(G) + P(RS) - P(G \cap RS) = P(G \cup RS)$
$\dfrac{6}{11} + \dfrac{4}{11} - \dfrac{2}{11} = \dfrac{8}{11}$

5. $\dfrac{k(k + 1)}{2} + (k + 1)$
$= \dfrac{k^2 + k}{2} + k + 1 = \dfrac{1}{2}k^2 + \dfrac{3}{2}k + 1$
$= \dfrac{1}{2}(k^2 + 3k + 2) = \dfrac{1}{2}(k + 1)(k + 2)$
$= \dfrac{(k + 1)[(k + 1) + 1]}{2}$

6. Refer to Problem Set 76, problem 6.

7. $(a)\ -3$　　　　$(b)\ 6$　　　　$(c)\ 4$

8. $(a)\ \begin{bmatrix} 4 & 3 \\ 2 & 1 \end{bmatrix} + \begin{bmatrix} 1 & 4 \\ -3 & 2 \end{bmatrix} = \begin{bmatrix} 5 & 7 \\ -1 & 3 \end{bmatrix}$

$(b)\ \begin{bmatrix} 0 & 0 \\ 0 & 0 \end{bmatrix} - \begin{bmatrix} 4 & 3 \\ 2 & 1 \end{bmatrix} = \begin{bmatrix} -4 & -3 \\ -2 & -1 \end{bmatrix}$

9. $\begin{bmatrix} 0 & 0 & 0 \\ 0 & 0 & 0 \\ 0 & 0 & 0 \end{bmatrix}$

10. $\angle B = \angle C$ and $\overline{AD}$ bisects $\angle A$ are given.
$\angle BAD = \angle CAD$ by def. of angle bisector.
$\overline{AD} = \overline{AD}$ by reflexive property.
$\triangle ABD \cong \triangle ACD$ by AAS.

11. Refer to Problem Set 72, problem 7.

12. $(32 \text{ cis } 30°)^{1/5}$

First root $= \sqrt[5]{32} \text{ cis } \dfrac{30°}{5} = 2 \text{ cis } 6°$

Angles differ by $\dfrac{360°}{5} = 72°$

2 cis 78°, 2 cis 150°, 2 cis 222°, 2 cis 294°

13. $-16 = 2r^3$
$-8 = r^3$
$r = -2$
$\mathbf{-4, 8}$

14. $2a = 8$
$a = 4, a^2 = 16$
$2b = 6$
$b = 3, b^2 = 9$
$\dfrac{x^2}{16} + \dfrac{y^2}{9} = 1$
$\mathbf{9x^2 + 16y^2 - 144 = 0}$

15. $\dfrac{16x^2}{144} - \dfrac{9y^2}{144} = \dfrac{144}{144}$

$\dfrac{x^2}{9} - \dfrac{y^2}{16} = 1$

Vertices: $(\pm 3, 0)$

Asymptotes: $y = \pm\dfrac{4}{3}x$

16. $a_6 = a_1 + 5d = 17$
$a_8 = a_1 + 7d = 25$

$\quad a_1 + 5d = 17$

$\underline{(-)\ a_1 + 7d = 25}$

$\qquad\qquad 2d = 8$

$\qquad\qquad d = 4$

$17 = a_1 + 5(4)$

$a_1 = -3$

$-3, 1, 5$

17. $\cos 285° = \cos(240° + 45°)$
$= \cos 240° \cos 45° - \sin 240° \sin 45°$

$= \left(-\dfrac{1}{2}\right)\left(\dfrac{\sqrt{2}}{2}\right) - \left(-\dfrac{\sqrt{3}}{2}\right)\left(\dfrac{\sqrt{2}}{2}\right) = \dfrac{\sqrt{6} - \sqrt{2}}{4}$

18. $\cos\left(x - \dfrac{\pi}{4}\right) = \cos x \cos\dfrac{\pi}{4} + \sin x \sin\dfrac{\pi}{4}$

$= (\cos x)\left(\dfrac{\sqrt{2}}{2}\right) + (\sin x)\left(\dfrac{\sqrt{2}}{2}\right)$

$= \dfrac{\sqrt{2}}{2}(\cos x + \sin x)$

19. $2(1 - \sin^2 x) + 7\sin x + 2 = 0$
$2 - 2\sin^2 x + 7\sin x + 2 = 0$
$2\sin^2 x - 7\sin x - 4 = 0$
$(2\sin x + 1)(\sin x - 4) = 0$

$\sin x = -\dfrac{1}{2} \qquad\qquad \sin x = 4$

$x = 210°, 330° \qquad\qquad \varnothing$

20. $\sqrt{2}\cos 2\theta = -1$

$\cos 2\theta = -\dfrac{1}{\sqrt{2}} = -\dfrac{\sqrt{2}}{2}$

$2\theta = 135°, 225°, 495°, 585°$

$\theta = 67.5°, 112.5°, 247.5°, 292.5°$

21. $(x\sin\theta + y\cos\theta)^2 + (y\cos\theta - y\sin\theta)^2$
$= x^2\sin^2\theta + 2xy\sin\theta\cos\theta + y^2\cos^2\theta$
$+ x^2\cos^2\theta - 2xy\sin\theta\cos\theta + y^2\sin^2\theta$
$= x^2(\sin^2\theta + \cos^2\theta) + y^2(\cos^2\theta - \sin^2\theta)$
$= x^2(1) + y^2(1) = x^2 + y^2$

22. $\dfrac{\cos B}{1 + \sin B} = \dfrac{\cos B}{1 + \sin B} \cdot \dfrac{1 - \sin B}{1 - \sin B}$

$= \dfrac{\cos B(1 - \sin B)}{1 - \sin^2 B}$

$= \dfrac{\cos B(1 - \sin B)}{\cos^2 B} = \dfrac{1 - \sin B}{\cos B}$

23. $a^2 = 6^2 + 7^2 - 2(6)(7)\cos 130°$
$= 36 + 49 - 84(-0.6428) \approx 139$
$a = \sqrt{139} \approx 11.8$

24. $a = \dfrac{3}{4}(8) = 6$

25. Refer to Problem Set 46, problem 15.

26. The sum of the exterior angles of any polygon is $360°$.

27. $6^{3x-2} = 2^{2x+4}$
$(3x - 2)(\log 6) = (2x + 4)(\log 2)$
$(3x - 2)(0.778) = (2x + 4)(0.301)$
$2.334x - 1.556 = 0.602x + 1.204$
$1.732x = 2.76$
$x \approx 1.6$

28. $\dfrac{1}{4}\log_3 16 - \log_3(2x + 3) = 1$

$\log_3 16^{1/4} - \log_3(2x + 3) = 1$

$\log_3 \dfrac{2}{2x + 3} = 1$

$3^1 = \dfrac{2}{2x + 3}$

$3(2x + 3) = 2$

$6x + 9 = 2$

$x = -\dfrac{7}{6}$

29. $3^{-2} = \dfrac{1}{9}$

30. $M = b^a, N = b^c$
$\log_b M = a, \log_b N = c$

$\log_b \dfrac{M}{N} = \log_b \dfrac{b^a}{b^c} = \log_b b^{a-c}$

$= a - c = \log_b M - \log_b N$

PROBLEM SET 77

1. Rate · time · men = jobs
   Rate · 9 · X = P
   Rate = $\dfrac{P}{9X}$
   $\dfrac{P}{9X}$ · time · Y = 20
   Time = $\dfrac{20(9X)}{YP} = \dfrac{180X}{YP}$ **days**

2. $0.95817 = e^{100k}$
   $-0.04273 = 100k$
   $k = -0.000427$
   $0.5 = e^{0.000427t}$
   $t \approx$ **1622.2 years**

3. $A_t = A_0 e^{kt}$
   $200 = 4e^{20k}$
   $50 = e^{20k}$
   $3.912 = 20k$
   $k \approx 0.196$
   $A_t = 4e^{0.196t}$

4. $\dfrac{4}{10} + \dfrac{7}{10} - \dfrac{3}{10} = \dfrac{8}{10} = \dfrac{4}{5}$

5. $\dfrac{7!}{3!} =$ **840**

6. (a)
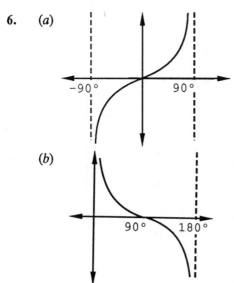
   (b)

7. (a) $y = 4 + 4\sec x$
   (b) $y = -2 + 4\csc x$

8. Refer to Problem Set 76, problem 6.

9. $\overline{AD}$ is ⊥ bisector of $\overline{BC}$ is given.
   $BD = DC$ by def. of bisector. $\angle ADB$
   $= \angle ADC = 90°$. $AD = AD$ by reflexive
   property. $\triangle ADB \cong \triangle ADC$ by SAS. AB
   $= AC$ by CPCTE.

10. $\overline{AD}$ is ∠ bisector of $\angle A$ and $AB = AC$ are
    given. $\angle BAD = \angle CAD$ by def. of ∠ bisector.
    $\triangle BAD \cong \triangle CAD$ by SAS.
    $\angle B = \angle C$ by CPCTE.

11. $AO = CO, BO = DO$ are given.
    $\angle AOB = \angle COD$ because vertical angles are
    equal. $\triangle AOB \cong \triangle COD$ by SAS. $\angle OBA$
    $= \angle ODC$ by CPCTE.

12. Refer to Example 72.A.2.

13. $(81 \text{ cis } 24°)^{1/4}$
    First root = $\sqrt[4]{81}$ cis $\dfrac{24°}{4} = 3$ cis $6°$
    Angles differ by $\dfrac{360°}{4} = 90°$
    3 cis 96°, 3 cis 186°, 3 cis 276°

14. $a_4 = a_1 r^3$
    $16 = -2r^3$
    $r^3 = -8, r = -2$
    4, −8

15. $2a = 10$
    $a = 5$
    $a^2 = 25$
    $2b = 8$
    $b = 4$
    $b = 16$
    $\dfrac{x^2}{25} + \dfrac{y^2}{16} = 1$
    $16x^2 + 25y^2 - 400 = 0$

16. $a_8 = a_1 + 7d = 19$
    $a_{10} = a_1 + 9d = 25$
    $\quad a_1 + 7d = 19$
    $(-)\,a_1 + 9d = 25$
    $\overline{\qquad 2d = 6}$
    $\qquad d = 3$
    $a_1 = 19 - 7(3) = -2$
    −2, 1, 4

17. $\cos(-285°) = \cos(285°)$
$= \cos(240° + 45°)$
$= \cos 240° \cos 45° - \sin 240° \sin 45°$
$$= \left(-\frac{1}{2}\right)\left(\frac{\sqrt{2}}{2}\right) - \left(-\frac{\sqrt{3}}{2}\right)\left(\frac{\sqrt{2}}{2}\right)$$
$$= \frac{-\sqrt{2} + \sqrt{6}}{4}$$

18. $\cos\left(x + \frac{\pi}{2}\right) = \cos x \cos \frac{\pi}{2} - \sin x \sin \frac{\pi}{2}$
$= (\cos x)(0) - (\sin x)(1) = -\sin x$

19. $2(1 - \sin^2 x) + 7 \sin x + 2 = 0$
$2 - 2\sin^2 x + 7 \sin x + 2 = 0$
$2\sin^2 x - 7 \sin x - 4 = 0$
$(2 \sin x + 1)(\sin x - 4) = 0$
$\sin x = -\frac{1}{2}$ $\sin x = 4$
$x = 210°, 330°$ $\varnothing$

20. $\cot 3x = \frac{\sqrt{3}}{3}$
$3x = 60°, 240°, 420°, 600°, 780°, 960°$
$x = 20°, 80°, 140°, 200°, 260°, 320°$

21. $\dfrac{1 + \cos x}{\sin x} \cdot \dfrac{\sin x}{\sin x} = \dfrac{(1 + \cos x)\sin x}{\sin^2 x}$
$= \dfrac{(1 + \cos x)\sin x}{1 - \cos^2 x} = \dfrac{(1 + \cos x)\sin x}{(1 + \cos x)(1 - \cos x)}$
$= \dfrac{\sin x}{1 - \cos x}$

22. $\dfrac{\tan B + 1}{\tan B - 1} = \dfrac{\tan B + 1}{\tan B - 1} \cdot \dfrac{\frac{1}{\sin B}}{\frac{1}{\sin B}}$
$= \dfrac{\sec B + \csc B}{\sec B - \csc B}$

23. $(1 + \sin x)^2 + (1 - \sin x)^2$
$= 1 + 2\sin x + \sin^2 x + 1 - 2\sin x + \sin^2 x$
$= 2 + 2\sin^2 x = 2 + 2(1 - \cos^2 x)$
$= 4 - 2\cos^2 x$

24. $c^2 = 6^2 + 8^2 - 2(6)(8)\cos 60°$
$= 36 + 64 - 48 = 52$
$c = \sqrt{52} \approx 7.2$

25. $a = \frac{4}{3}(5) = \frac{20}{3}$

26. Period $= \dfrac{360°}{\frac{5}{3}} = 216°$

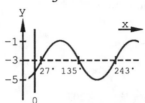

27. $(\log 12)(2x - 2) = (\log 4)(3x + 1)$
$(1.08)(2x - 2) = (0.6)(3x + 1)$
$2.16x - 1.8x = 2.16 + 0.6$
$0.36x = 2.76$
$x = 7.7$

28. $\log_3 27^{2/3} - \log_3(2x - 1) = 1$
$\log_3 \dfrac{9}{2x - 1} = 1$
$3 = \dfrac{9}{2x - 1}$
$6x - 3 = 9$
$x = 2$

29. $2^{-3} = \dfrac{1}{8}$

30. $e^{\ln 3^2 - \ln 2} = e^{\ln 9/2} = \dfrac{9}{2}$

EP

26. $\begin{bmatrix} 1 & -1 \\ 2 & -2 \\ 3 & -3 \end{bmatrix} + \dfrac{1}{6}\begin{bmatrix} -1 & 1 \\ -2 & 2 \\ 3 & 3 \end{bmatrix}$

$= \begin{bmatrix} 1 & -1 \\ 2 & -2 \\ 3 & -3 \end{bmatrix} + \begin{bmatrix} -\frac{1}{6} & \frac{1}{6} \\ -\frac{1}{3} & \frac{1}{3} \\ \frac{1}{2} & \frac{1}{2} \end{bmatrix}$

$= \begin{bmatrix} \frac{5}{6} & -\frac{5}{6} \\ \frac{5}{3} & -\frac{5}{3} \\ \frac{7}{2} & -\frac{5}{2} \end{bmatrix}$

27. $[k(2k - 1) + 1] + (4k + 1)$
$= 2k^2 + 3k + 2 = (k + 1)(2k + 1) + 1$
$= (k + 1)[2(k + 1) - 1] + 1$

PROBLEM SET 78

1.

% alcohol	20%		100%		44%
amount (lit)	140	+	x	=	$140+x$

$0.20(140) + 1.00x = 0.44(140 + x)$
$28 + x = 61.6 + 0.44x$
$0.56x = 33.6$
$x = \textbf{60 liters}$

2. $A_t = A_0 e^{kt}$
$1000 = 600e^{60k}$
$1.667 = e^{60k}$
$0.5108 = 60k$
$k \approx 0.0085$
$A_t = 600e^{0.0085t}$
$5000 = 600e^{0.0085t}$
$8.333 = e^{0.0085t}$
$t \approx \textbf{249 min}$

3. $580 = 600e^{60k}$
$0.9667 = e^{60k}$
$-0.0339 = 60k$
$k \approx -0.000565$
$300 = 600e^{-0.000565t}$
$0.5 = e^{-0.000565t}$
$-0.69315 = -0.000565t$
$t \approx \textbf{1226.8 min}$

4. $\dfrac{2}{3} = \dfrac{1}{3} + \dfrac{1}{2} - P(RG) \rightarrow P(RG) = \dfrac{\mathbf{1}}{\mathbf{6}}$

5. $\dfrac{3}{10} \cdot \dfrac{3}{10} \cdot \dfrac{2}{9} = \dfrac{18}{900} = \dfrac{\mathbf{1}}{\mathbf{50}}$

6. $r = \sqrt{3^2 + 4^2} = 5$
$\tan \theta = \dfrac{4}{3}, \theta \approx 53°$
$(5 \text{ cis } 53°)^{1/4}$
First root $= \sqrt[4]{5} \text{ cis } \dfrac{53°}{4} \approx \textbf{1.5 cis 13.25}°$
Angles differ by $\dfrac{360°}{4} = 90°$
1.5 cis 103.25°, 1.5 cis 193.25°,
1.5 cis 283.25°

7. $r = \sqrt{2^2 + 3^2} \approx 3.6$
$\tan \theta = \dfrac{3}{2}, \theta \approx 56.3°$
$(3.6 \text{ cis } 56.3°)^{1/3}$
First root $= \sqrt[3]{3.6} \text{ cis } \dfrac{56.3°}{3} = \textbf{1.5 cis 18.77}°$
Angles differ by $\dfrac{360°}{3} = 120°$
1.5 cis 138.77°, 1.5 cis 258.77°

8. C is midpoint of $\overline{AD}$ and $\overline{BE}$ is given. BC = CE, $AC = CD$ by def. of midpoint. $\angle ACB$ = $\angle ECD$ by vertical angles. $\triangle ACB \cong \triangle ECD$ by SAS. $AB = ED$ by CPCTE.

9. $\angle B = \angle D$ and $\overline{AD} \parallel \overline{BC}$ is given. $\angle DAC = \angle BCA$ because alt. int. angles are equal. $\triangle ADC \cong \triangle CBA$ by AAS.

10. $\dfrac{z}{x} = \dfrac{x}{m}$ $\qquad$ $\dfrac{y}{z} = \dfrac{n}{y}$
$x^2 = zm$ $\qquad\qquad$ $y^2 = zn$

$x^2 + y^2 = zm + zn = z(m + n)$
$x^2 + y^2 = z^2$

11. Refer to Solution Set 47, problem 8.

12. $a_4 = a_1 r^3$
$-24 = 3r^3$
$-8 = r^3$
$r = -2$
-6, 12

13. $2a = 10$
$a = 5, a^2 = 25$
$2b = 4$
$b = 2, b^2 = 4$
$\dfrac{x^2}{25} + \dfrac{y^2}{4} = 1$

14. $\dfrac{x^2}{9} - \dfrac{y^2}{16} = 1$
Vertices: $(\pm 3, 0)$
Asymptotes: $y = \pm \dfrac{4}{3} x$

15. $a_4 = a_1 + 3d = 4$
$a_{13} = a_1 + 12d = 28$

$a_1 + 3d = 4$
$\underline{(-)\, a_1 + 12d = 28}$
$9d = 24$
$d = \dfrac{8}{3}$

$a_1 = 4 - 3\left(\dfrac{8}{3}\right) = -4$

$\mathbf{-4, -\dfrac{4}{3}, \dfrac{4}{3}, 4, \dfrac{20}{3}}$

16. $\cos 285° = \cos (240° + 45°)$
$= \cos 240° \cos 45° - \sin 240° \sin 45°$
$\approx (-0.5)(0.707) + (-0.866)(0.707) \approx \mathbf{0.259}$

17. $\sin \left(x - \dfrac{\pi}{4} \right) = \sin x \cos \dfrac{\pi}{4} - \cos x \sin \dfrac{\pi}{4}$
$= \dfrac{\sqrt{2}}{2} \sin x - \dfrac{\sqrt{2}}{2} \cos x = \dfrac{\sqrt{2}}{2} (\sin x - \cos x)$

18. $3(\sec^2 x - 1) + 5 \sec x + 1 = 0$
$3 \sec^2 x - 3 + 5 \sec x + 1 = 0$
$3 \sec^2 x + 5 \sec x - 2 = 0$
$(3 \sec x - 1)(\sec x + 2) = 0$
$\sec x = \dfrac{1}{3}$ $\qquad\qquad$ $\sec x = -2$
$\varnothing$ $\qquad\qquad\qquad$ $x = \mathbf{120°, 240°}$

19. $\tan 3x = 1$
$3x = 45°, 225°, 405°, 585°, 765°, 945°$
$x = \mathbf{15°, 75°, 135°, 195°, 255°, 315°}$

20. $\dfrac{\sin x}{1 + \cos x} + \dfrac{1 + \cos x}{\sin x}$
$= \dfrac{\sin^2 x + 1 + 2 \cos x + \cos^2 x}{(1 + \cos x) \sin x}$
$= \dfrac{2 + 2 \cos x}{(1 + \cos x) \sin x} = \dfrac{2(1 + \cos x)}{(1 + \cos x) \sin x}$
$= \dfrac{2}{\sin x} = 2 \csc x$

21. $\dfrac{\csc x + \cot x}{\tan x + \sin x} = \dfrac{\dfrac{1}{\sin x} + \dfrac{\cos x}{\sin x}}{\dfrac{\sin x}{\cos x} + \sin x}$

$= \dfrac{\dfrac{1 + \cos x}{\sin x}}{\dfrac{\sin x + \sin x \cos x}{\cos x}}$

$= \dfrac{1 + \cos x}{\sin x} \cdot \dfrac{\cos x}{(\sin x)(1 + \cos x)}$

$= \dfrac{\cos x}{\sin^2 x} = \dfrac{\cos x}{\sin x} \cdot \dfrac{1}{\sin x} = \cot x \csc x$

22. $\dfrac{(\sin^2 x + \cos^2 x)(\sin^2 x - \cos^2 x)}{2 \sin^2 x - 1}$
$= \dfrac{(1) \sin^2 x - (1 - \sin^2 x)}{2 \sin^2 x - 1}$
$= \dfrac{2 \sin^2 x - 1}{2 \sin^2 x - 1} = 1$

23. $\cos A = \dfrac{4^2 + 6^2 - 8^2}{2(4)(6)} = -0.25$
$A = \cos^{-1} (-0.25) \approx \mathbf{104.5°}$

24. $\dfrac{8}{3} x = 9$
$x = 9 \left(\dfrac{3}{8} \right) = \dfrac{27}{8}$

25. $\text{Period} = \dfrac{360°}{\dfrac{3}{2}} = 240°$

26. (a) $y = 3 + 4 \csc x$

(b) $y = \cot \theta$

27. $(\log 9)(3x - 2) = (\log 3)(2x - 1)$
$(0.95)(3x - 2) = (0.48)(2x - 1)$
$2.85x - 0.96x = 1.9 - 0.48$
$1.89x = 1.42$
$x = \mathbf{0.75}$

28. $\log_2 27^{1/3} - \log_2 (2x - 1) = 2$
$\log_2 \dfrac{3}{2x - 1} = 2$
$4 = \dfrac{3}{2x - 1}$
$8x - 4 = 3$
$x = \dfrac{7}{8}$

29. $x = \log_{1/3} \dfrac{18}{6}$
$\left(\dfrac{1}{3} \right)^x = 3$
$x = \mathbf{-1}$

30. $3^3 = \mathbf{27}$

EP

28. $\begin{bmatrix} 1 \\ -2 \\ 3 \end{bmatrix} + \begin{bmatrix} 3 \\ 2 \\ 1 \end{bmatrix} = \begin{bmatrix} 4 \\ 0 \\ 4 \end{bmatrix}$

29. **Invalid**

1. Downstream: A: $(B + 4)T = 27$
$$BT + 4T = 27$$

Upstream: B: $(B - 4)T = 3$
$$BT - 4T = 3$$

Add equation A and B.
$$\begin{array}{r} BT + 4T = 27 \\ (+)\, BT - 4T = 3 \\ \hline 2BT = 30 \\ BT = 15 \end{array}$$

Substitute in equation A.
$$15 + 4T = 27$$
$$T = 3$$
$$B(3) + 4(3) = 27$$
$$B = 5 \text{ mph}$$

2. $A_t = A_0 e^{kt}$
$$4000 = 500e^{0.005t}$$
$$8 = e^{0.005t}$$
$$2.0794 = 0.005t$$
$$t \approx 415.9 \text{ time units}$$

3. $50{,}000 = 60{,}000e^{5k}$
$$0.8333 = e^{5k}$$
$$-0.1823 = 5k$$
$$k \approx -0.0365$$
$$10{,}000 = 60{,}000e^{-0.0365t}$$
$$-1.792 = -0.0365t$$
$$t \approx 49.1 \text{ min}$$

4.
Little Hand
$$R_L T_L = S$$
$$R_L = \frac{1}{12}$$
$$T_L = T_B$$
$$\frac{1}{12}T = S$$
$$T = \frac{1}{12}T + 5$$
$$\frac{11}{12}T = 25$$
$$T = \frac{60}{11} = 5\frac{5}{11} \text{ min}$$

Big Hand
$$R_B T_B = S + 5$$
$$R_B = 1$$

$$T = S + 5$$

5. $_8P_3 = \dfrac{8!}{(8 - 3)!} = \dfrac{8!}{5!} = 336$

6. $\dfrac{\frac{\pi}{3}}{2\pi}\pi(6)^2 = \dfrac{1}{6}(36\pi) = 6\pi \approx 18.8 \text{ in}^2$

7. $r = \sqrt{3^2 + 4^2} = 5$
$$\tan\theta = \frac{4}{3}, \theta \approx 53.1°$$
First root $= \sqrt{5}\,\text{cis}\,\dfrac{53.1°}{2} \approx$
2.2 cis 26.6°
Angles differ by $\dfrac{360°}{2} = 180°$
2.2 cis 206.6°

8. $\overline{AD}$ is bisector of $\overline{BC}$ and $BD = DC$ are given. $\angle ADB = \angle ADC$ by def. of bisector. $AD = AD$ by reflexive property. $\triangle ADB \cong \triangle ADC$ by SAS. $AB = AC$ by CPCTE.

9. $\overline{AB} \parallel \overline{DE}$ and $AC = CE$ are given. $\angle BAC = \angle CED$ because alt. int. angles are equal. $\angle ACB = \angle DCE$ by vert. angles. $\triangle ACE \cong \triangle DCE$ by ASA. $BC = CD$ by CPCTE.

10. Refer to Problem Set 76, problem 6.

11.

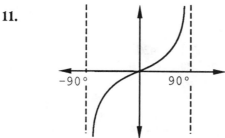

12. $a_4 = a_1 r^3$
$$16 = -2r^3$$
$$-8 = r^3, r = -2$$
4, −8

13. $c^2 = a^2 - b^2$
$$36 = 100 - b^2$$
$$b^2 = 64, b = 8$$
$$\frac{x^2}{64} + \frac{y^2}{100} = 1$$
$25x^2 + 16y^2 - 1600 = 0$

14. $\dfrac{x^2}{16} - \dfrac{y^2}{9} = 1$

 Vertices: $(\pm 4, 0)$

 Asymptotes: $y = \pm \dfrac{3}{4} x$

15. $a_3 = a_1 + 2d = -8$
$a_5 = a_1 + 4d = 0$

$\quad a_1 + 2d = -8$

$(-) a_1 + 4d = \quad 0$
$\overline{\qquad\qquad\qquad\quad}$
$\qquad\quad 2d = \quad 8$

$\qquad\qquad d = \quad 4$

$a_1 = -8 - 2(4) = -16$

$-16, -12, -8$

16. $\sin(-15°) = \sin(30° - 45°)$

$= \sin 30° \cos 45° - \cos 30° \sin 45°$

$= \left(\dfrac{1}{2}\right)\left(\dfrac{\sqrt{2}}{2}\right) - \left(\dfrac{\sqrt{3}}{2}\right)\left(\dfrac{\sqrt{2}}{2}\right) = \dfrac{\sqrt{2} - \sqrt{6}}{4}$

17. $\cos\left(x + \dfrac{\pi}{2}\right) = \cos x \cos\dfrac{\pi}{2} - \sin x \sin\dfrac{\pi}{2}$

$= (\cos x)(0) - (\sin x)(1) = -\sin x$

18. $2\tan^2 x + 3\sec x = 0$
$2(\sec^2 x - 1) + 3\sec x = 0$
$2\sec^2 x + 3\sec x - 2 = 0$
$(2\sec x - 1)(\sec x + 2) = 0$

$\sec x = \dfrac{1}{2} \qquad\qquad \sec x = -2$

$\qquad \emptyset \qquad\qquad\qquad x = 120°, 240°$

19. $\sin 3\theta = \dfrac{\sqrt{3}}{2}$

$3\theta = 60°, 120°, 420°, 480°, 780°, 840°$

$\theta = 20°, 40°, 140°, 160°, 260°, 280°$

20. $\dfrac{\cos^4 x - \sin^4 x}{\cos 2x}$

$= \dfrac{(\cos^2 x + \sin^2 x)(\cos^2 x - \sin^2 x)}{\cos^2 x - \sin^2 x}$

$= \cos^2 x + \sin^2 x = 1$

21. $(\sin x + \cos x)^2$

$= \sin^2 x + 2\sin x \cos x + \cos^2 x$

$= 1 + 2\sin x \cos x = 1 + \sin 2x$

22. $\dfrac{1 - \cos x}{\sin x} = \dfrac{1 - \cos x}{\sin x} \cdot \dfrac{\sin x}{\sin x}$

$= \dfrac{(1 - \cos x)\sin x}{\sin^2 x} = \dfrac{(1 - \cos x)\sin x}{1 - \cos^2 x}$

$= \dfrac{(1 - \cos x)\sin x}{(1 + \cos x)(1 - \cos x)} = \dfrac{\sin x}{1 + \cos x}$

23. $\dfrac{\sin A}{10} = \dfrac{\sin 70°}{12}$

$\sin A = \dfrac{10 \sin 70°}{12} \approx 0.7831$

$A = \sin^{-1} 0.7831 \approx \mathbf{51.5°}$

24. $c = \dfrac{8}{5}(10) = \mathbf{16}$

25. Period $= \dfrac{2\pi}{3/4} = \dfrac{8\pi}{3}$

26. The sum of the exterior angles of any polygon is **360°**.

27. $(\log 12)(4x + 2) = (\log 8)(2x - 3)$
$(1.1)(4x + 2) = (0.9)(2x - 3)$
$4.4x - 1.8x = -2.2 - 2.7$
$2.6x = -4.9$
$x \approx \mathbf{-1.94}$

28. $\log_{12} 8^{2/3} - \log_{12}(3x + 2) = \log_{12} 10{,}000^{1/2}$

$\log_{12}\left(\dfrac{4}{3}x + 2\right) = \log_{12} 100$

$\dfrac{4}{3x + 2} = 100$

$4 = 300x + 200$

$x = -\dfrac{196}{300} = -\dfrac{49}{75}$

29. $e^{\ln 2^2} + e^{\ln 8^2 - \ln 2} = e^{\ln 4} + e^{\ln 64/2}$

$= e^{\ln 4} + e^{\ln 32} = 4 + 32 = \mathbf{36}$

30. $e^2 \approx 3^2 = \mathbf{9}$

EP

30. $\begin{bmatrix} -1 & -3 & 4 \\ 2 & 0 & 3 \end{bmatrix} + \begin{bmatrix} 1 & 0 & -1 \\ 0 & 1 & -1 \end{bmatrix}$

$= \begin{bmatrix} \mathbf{0} & \mathbf{-3} & \mathbf{3} \\ \mathbf{2} & \mathbf{1} & \mathbf{2} \end{bmatrix}$

31. $2k(k + 1) + 4(k + 1) = (k + 1)(2k + 4)$
$= (k + 1)(2)(k + 2)$
$= 2(k + 1)[(k + 1) + 1]$

1. $H + C + S = 128$

   $\frac{1}{2}S + 12 = C$

   $\frac{1}{2}C + 12 = H$

   $\frac{1}{2}\left(\frac{1}{2}S + 12\right) + 12 + \frac{1}{2}S + 12 + S = 128$

   $\frac{1}{4}S + 6 + 12 + \frac{1}{2}S + 12 + S = 128$

   $\frac{7}{4}S + 30 = 128$

   $\frac{7}{4}S = 98$

   $S = 56$

   $C = \frac{1}{2}(56) + 12 = 28 + 12 = 40$

   $H = \frac{1}{2}(40) + 12 = 20 + 12 = 32$

2. $A_t = A_0 e^{kt}$

   $300 = 50 e^{30k}$

   $6 = e^{30k}$

   $\ln 6 = \ln e^{30k}$

   $1.7918 \approx 30k$

   $0.05973 \approx k$

   $1500 \approx 50 e^{0.05973t}$

   $30 \approx e^{0.05973t}$

   $3.401197 \approx 0.05973t$

   $t \approx 56.95$ min

3. $\frac{4}{52} + \frac{13}{52} - \frac{1}{52} = \frac{16}{52} = \frac{4}{13}$

4. $\frac{4}{7} \cdot \frac{7}{10} = \frac{2}{5}$

5. $WY = 500$

   $(W + 5)Y = 750$

   $WY + 5Y = 750$

   $500 + 5Y = 750$

   $5Y = 250$

   $Y = 50$ yd

6. $\frac{\sin B}{7} = \frac{\sin 27°}{5}$

   $\sin B = \frac{7 \sin 27°}{5} \approx 0.6356$

   $B \approx 39.5°$

   $B' \approx 140.5°$

   $C \approx 180° - 27° - 39.5° \approx 113.5°$

   $C' \approx 180° - 27° - 140.5° \approx 12.5°$

   $\frac{c}{\sin 113.5°} = \frac{5}{\sin 27°}$

   $c = \frac{5 \sin 113.5°}{\sin 27°} \approx 10.1$

   $\frac{c'}{\sin 12.5°} = \frac{5}{\sin 27°}$

   $c' = \frac{5 \sin 12.5°}{\sin 27°} \approx 2.38$

   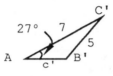 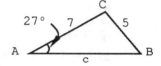

7. $\frac{\sin x}{10} = \frac{\sin 40°}{5}$

   $\sin x = \frac{10 \sin 40°}{5} \approx 1.28$

   No such triangle exists

8. $r = \sqrt{5^2 + 8^2} \approx 9.4$

   $\tan \theta = \frac{8}{5}, \theta \approx 58°$

   $(9.4 \text{ cis } 58°)^{1/3}$

   First root is $9.4^{1/3} \text{ cis } \frac{58°}{3} \approx 2.1 \text{ cis } 19.3°$

   Angles of the cube root differ by $\frac{360°}{3} = 120°$

   2.1 cis 139.3°, 2.1 cis 259.3°

9. Area $= \frac{30°}{360°} \pi(r)^2 = \frac{1}{12}(25\pi) \approx 6.54$ cm²

10. Given $\overline{AB} \parallel \overline{CD}$ and $\overline{AC} \parallel \overline{BD}$.
    Thus $\angle ADC = \angle BAD$ and $\angle BDA = \angle CAD$
    (by alt. int. angles), $AD = AD$ (reflexive
    property). Therefore $\triangle BAD \cong \triangle CDA$ by ASA.
    So $AC = BD$ by CPCTE.

11. Given $\overline{AB} \parallel \overline{DE}, AB = DE$
    $\angle A = \angle E, \angle B = \angle D$ (alt. int. angles)
    Therefore $\triangle ABC \cong \triangle EDC$ by ASA,
    $AC = CE$ by CPCTE

12. Given $\angle A = \angle B, DC = CE,$
$\angle ACE \cong \angle BCE$ (vert. angles)
$\triangle ACD \cong \triangle BCE$ by AAS,
$AD = BE$ by CPCTE

13. Refer to Problem Set 76, problem 6.

14. $a_5 = a_1 r^4$
$32 = 2r^4$
$16 = r^4$
$r = \pm 2$
4, 8, 16 and $-4, 8, -16$

15. $c^2 = a^2 - b^2$
$16 = 25 - b^2$
$b^2 = 25 - 16 = 9$
$\dfrac{x^2}{9} + \dfrac{y^2}{25} = 1$
$25x^2 + 9y^2 - 225 = 0$

16. $\dfrac{x^2}{4} - \dfrac{y^2}{4} = 1$
Vertices: $(\pm 2, 0)$
Asymptotes: $y = \pm x$

17.
$a_5 = a_1 + 4d = 0$
$(-)\ a_8 = a_1 + 7d = 9$
$\overline{ -3d = -9}$
$d = 3$
$a_1 = 0 - 4(3) = -12$
$-12, -9, -6$

18. $\sin 30° = 2 \sin 15° \cos 15° = \dfrac{1}{2}$

19. $2(1 - \sin^2 x) - 1 + \sin x = 0$
$2 - 2 \sin^2 x - 1 + \sin x = 0$
$2 \sin^2 x - \sin x - 1 = 0$
$(2 \sin x + 1)(\sin x - 1) = 0$

$2 \sin x + 1 = 0$	$\sin x - 1 = 0$
$2 \sin x = -1$	$\sin x = 1$
$\sin x = -\dfrac{1}{2}$	$x = 90°$

$x = 210°, 330°$

20. $\sec 3\theta = 2$
$3\theta = 60°, 300°, 420°, 660°, 780°, 1020°$
$\theta = \mathbf{20°, 100°, 140°, 220°, 260°, 340°}$

21. $(\cos 2x) + 2 \sin^2 x = 1$
$(1 - 2 \sin^2 x) + 2 \sin^2 x = 1$

22. $\dfrac{\cos x}{1 - \sin x} - \dfrac{\cos x}{1 + \sin x}$
$= \dfrac{\cos x + \cos x \sin x - \cos x + \cos x \sin x}{1 - \sin^2 x}$
$= \dfrac{2 \cos x \sin x}{\cos^2 x} = \dfrac{2 \sin x}{\cos x} = 2 \tan x$

23. $\dfrac{2 \sin x}{2 \sin x \cos x} = \dfrac{1}{\cos x} = \sec x$

24. $c^2 = 7^2 + 10^2 - 2(7)(10) \cos 20° = 17.44$
$c = \sqrt{17.44} \approx \mathbf{4.2}$

25. $\dfrac{c}{6} = \dfrac{4}{3}$
$c = 6 \left(\dfrac{4}{3}\right) = \mathbf{8}$

26. Period $= \dfrac{360°}{2/3} = 540°$

27. $y = \cot x$

28. $\log_e 16^{3/4} - \log_e (2x - 4) = \log_e 3$
$\log_e \left(\dfrac{8}{2x - 4}\right) = \log_e 3$
$\dfrac{8}{2x - 4} = 3$
$8 = 6x - 12$
$6x = 20$
$x = \dfrac{10}{3}$

29. $(\log 10)(2x - 4) = (\log 100)(3x)$
$2x - 4 = 6x$
$4x = -4$
$x = -1$

30. $6^{-3} = \dfrac{1}{216}$

EP

32. $\begin{bmatrix} 1 & -2 & 3 \\ -4 & 6 & -5 \\ 0 & 1 & 0 \end{bmatrix} + \begin{bmatrix} 0 & 0 & 0 \\ 0 & 0 & 0 \\ 0 & 0 & 0 \end{bmatrix} = \begin{bmatrix} 1 & -2 & 3 \\ -4 & 6 & -5 \\ 0 & 1 & 0 \end{bmatrix}$

33. **Invalid**

PROBLEM SET 81

1. $20x - 2(30 - x) = 424$
$20x - 60 + 2x = 424$
$22x = 484$
$x = \textbf{22}$

2. $\dfrac{30}{36} \cdot \dfrac{6}{36} = \dfrac{5}{6} \cdot \dfrac{1}{6} = \dfrac{5}{36}$

3. $150 = 10e^{0.003t}$
$15 = e^{0.003t}$
$2.708 \approx 0.003t$
$t \approx \textbf{902.7 time units}$

4. $(L + 0.20L)(W - 0.20W) = (1.2L)(0.8W)$
$= 0.96LW$
4% decrease

5. $pj = 360, \quad (p + 7)j = 640$
$pj + 7j = 640$
$360 + 7j = 640$
$j = \textbf{40}$

6. Refer to Lesson 81, Example 81.A.1.

7. Refer to Lesson 81, Example 81.B.1.

8. Refer to Lesson 81, Example 81.C.1.

9. $\dfrac{\sin B}{6} = \dfrac{\sin 30°}{4}$

$\sin B = \dfrac{6 \sin 30°}{4} \approx .75$

$B \approx 48.6°, B' \approx 131.4°$
$C \approx 180° - 30° - 48.6° \approx 101.4°$
$C' \approx 180° - 30° - 131.4° \approx 18.6°$

$\dfrac{c}{\sin 101.4°} = \dfrac{4}{\sin 30°}$

$c = \dfrac{4 \sin 101.4°}{\sin 30°} \approx \textbf{7.84}$

$\dfrac{c'}{\sin 18.6°} = \dfrac{4}{\sin 30°}$

$c' = \dfrac{4 \sin 18.6°}{\sin 30°} \approx \textbf{2.55}$

10. $\dfrac{\sin B}{10} = \dfrac{\sin 50°}{6}$

$\sin B = \dfrac{10 \sin 50°}{6} \approx 1.2$

No such triangle exists

11. Linear $=$ angular $\cdot$ radius
$= 10{,}000 \dfrac{\text{rev}}{\text{min}} \cdot 2\pi \dfrac{\text{rad}}{\text{rev}} \cdot 2 \text{ ft} \approx 40{,}000\pi \dfrac{\text{ft}}{\text{min}}$

12. $r = \sqrt{8^2 + 15^2} = 17$
$\tan \theta = \dfrac{15}{8}, \ \theta \approx 61.9°$
$(17 \text{ cis } 61.9°)^{1/2}$
First root is $\sqrt{17} \text{ cis } \dfrac{61.9}{2} \approx \textbf{4.1 cis 30.97°}$
Angles of the square root differ by $\dfrac{360°}{2} =$
$180°$
4.1 cis 210.97°

13. $a_5 = a_1 \cdot r^4$
$81 = 1 \cdot r^4$
$r^4 = 81$
$r = \pm 3$
-3, 9, -27 or 3, 9, 27

14. Refer to Problem Set 76, problem 6.

15. $\dfrac{x^2}{25} + \dfrac{y^2}{16} = 1$

16. $\dfrac{x^2}{4} - \dfrac{y^2}{16} = 1$

Vertices: $(\pm 2, 0)$

Asymptotes: $y = \pm 2x$

17. $a_{25} = a_1 + 24d = -6 + 24(2) = 42$

18. $2 \sin 30° \cos 30° = 2\left(\dfrac{1}{2}\right)\left(\dfrac{\sqrt{3}}{2}\right) = \dfrac{\sqrt{3}}{2}$

19. $\tan x = \sqrt{1 - 2\tan^2 x}$

$\tan^2 x = 1 - 2\tan^2 x$

$3\tan^2 x = 1$

$\tan^2 x = \dfrac{1}{3}$

$\tan x = \pm\dfrac{\sqrt{3}}{3}$

$x = 30°, 150°, 210°, 330°$

20. $\csc 3\theta = 2$

$\sin 3\theta = \dfrac{1}{2}$

$3\theta = 30°, 150°, 390°, 510°, 750°, 870°$

$\theta = 10°, 50°, 130°, 170°, 250°, 290°$

21. $4\cos^2 x - 2\cos 2x$

$= 4\cos^2 x - 2(2\cos^2 x - 1)$

$= 4\cos^2 x - 4\cos^2 x + 2 = 2$

22. $\dfrac{2\cos x}{\sin 2x} = \dfrac{2\cos x}{2\sin x \cos x} = \dfrac{1}{\sin x} = \csc x$

23. $\dfrac{\cos x}{\sec x - 1} - \dfrac{\cos x}{\sec x + 1}$

$= \dfrac{\cos x\,(\sec x + 1) - \cos x\,(\sec x - 1)}{\sec^2 x - 1}$

$= \dfrac{2\cos x}{\tan^2 x} = 2\cos x \cdot \dfrac{\cos^2 x}{\sin^2 x}$

$= 2\cos^3 x \csc^2 x$

24. $a = \sqrt{100 + 64 - 2(10)8 \cos 110°} \approx 14.8$

25. $\dfrac{a}{8} = \dfrac{b}{\frac{4}{3}b}$

$a = 8\left(\dfrac{3}{4}\right) = \dfrac{24}{4} = 6$

26. $y = -1 + 2\sin 3\left(x - \dfrac{\pi}{9}\right)$

27. (a) $y = -2 + 3\sec x$

(b) $y = \tan\theta$

28. $\log_{10} x(x - 3) = 1$

$x(x - 3) = 10$

$x^2 - 3x - 10 = 0$

$(x + 2)(x - 5) = 0$

$x = 5$

29. $(3x + 2)\log 10 = (2x - 1)\log 5$

$(3x + 2)(1) \approx (2x - 1)(0.7)$

$3x + 2 \approx 1.4x - 0.7$

$1.6x \approx -2.7$

$x \approx -\dfrac{2.7}{1.6} = -1.69$

30. $3^{-2} = \dfrac{1}{3^2} = \dfrac{1}{9}$

EP

34. $\begin{bmatrix} 2 & 3 \\ 4 & -5 \end{bmatrix} - \begin{bmatrix} 3 & -4 \\ 1 & 0 \end{bmatrix} = \begin{bmatrix} -1 & 7 \\ 3 & -5 \end{bmatrix}$

35. $\dfrac{3(3^k - 1)}{2} + 3^{k+1} = \dfrac{3^{k+1} - 3}{2} + 3^{k+1}$

$= \dfrac{3^{k+1} - 3 + 2(3^{k+1})}{2} = \dfrac{3(3^{k+1}) - 3}{2}$

$= \dfrac{3(3^{k+1} - 1)}{2}$

PROBLEM SET 82

1. $\frac{1}{m}(t) + \frac{1}{f}(t) = 1$

    $\frac{t}{m} + \frac{t}{f} = 1$

    $ft + mt = mf$

    $t(f + m) = mf$

    $t = \frac{mf}{m + f}$ **hr**

2. $300 = 400\, e^{60k}$

    $0.75 = e^{60k}$

    $k \approx -0.0047947$

    $A_{180} \approx 400\, e^{180(-0.005)}$

    $A_{180} \approx \mathbf{168.75}$

3.

	2 hr. ea.	1 hr. la.
Distance:	m	m
Time:	h	$h + 3$
Rate:	$\frac{m}{h}$	$\frac{m}{h+3}$ mph

4. $p \cdot l = 1350$

    $(p + 2)l = 2250$

    $pl + 2l = 2250$

    $1350 + 2l = 2250$

    $2l = 900$

    $l = \mathbf{450\ laps}$

5. $C_5^{10} = \frac{10!}{5!(10-5)!} = \frac{10 \cdot 9 \cdot 8 \cdot 7 \cdot 6}{5 \cdot 4 \cdot 3 \cdot 2 \cdot 1}$

    $= \mathbf{252}$

6. $\log_6 81 = y$

    $6^y = 81$

    $y \log 6 = \log 81$

    $y = \frac{\log 81}{\log 6} \approx \mathbf{2.45}$

7. $4y = 2x + 2$

    $y = \frac{1}{2}x + \frac{1}{2}$

    $(1, 3)\ m = -2$

    $3 = -2(1) + b$

    $b = 5;\ y = -2x + 5$

    $\frac{1}{2}x + \frac{1}{2} = -2x + 5$

$x + 1 = -4x + 10$

$5x = 9$

$x = \frac{9}{5}$

$y = -2\left(\frac{9}{5}\right) + 5$

$y = \frac{7}{5}$

$\left(\frac{9}{5}, \frac{7}{5}\right), (1, 3)$

$\sqrt{\left(1 - \frac{9}{5}\right)^2 + \left(3 - \frac{7}{5}\right)^2}$

$= \sqrt{\left(\frac{4}{5}\right)^2 + \left(\frac{8}{5}\right)^2}$

$= \sqrt{\frac{16 + 64}{25}} = \sqrt{\frac{80}{25}} = \frac{4\sqrt{5}}{5}$

8. $\triangle ACD$ and $\triangle CDB$ are right triangles. $AC = CB, CD = CD$; therefore $\triangle ACD \cong \triangle BCD$ by HL, which gives $\angle A = \angle B$ by CPCTE.

9. $AB = DC, AD = BC, AC = AC$, so $\triangle DCA \cong \triangle BAC$ by SSS; then $\angle 1 = \angle 2$ by CPCTE. Therefore $\overline{AB} \parallel \overline{DC}$ (alt. int. angles).

10. $\overline{AB} \parallel \overline{DC}$ so $\angle CDB = \angle DBA$; $AB = DC$ and $DB = DB$. Thus $\triangle CDB \cong \triangle ABD$ by SAS; finally $DA = CB$.

11. $\frac{\sin 45°}{4} = \frac{\sin B}{8}$

    $\sin B \approx 1.4142$

    No such triangle exists

12. $\frac{\sin B}{10} = \frac{\sin 20°}{6}$

    $\sin B = \frac{10 \sin 20°}{6} \approx 0.57$

    $B \approx 34.75°, B' \approx 145.25°$

    $C \approx 180° - 20° - 34.75° \approx 125.3°$

    $C' \approx 180° - 20° - 145.25° \approx 14.75°$

    $\frac{c}{\sin 125.3°} = \frac{6}{\sin 20°}$

$$c = \frac{6 \sin 125.3°}{\sin 20°} \approx \mathbf{14.3}$$

$$\frac{c'}{\sin 14.75°} = \frac{6}{\sin 20°}$$

$$c' = \frac{6 \sin 14.75°}{\sin 20°} \approx \mathbf{4.47}$$

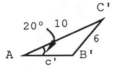 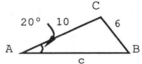

13. $r = \sqrt{6^2 + 2^2} \approx 6.32$

$\tan \theta = -\frac{2}{6}$ (in Q IV), $\theta \approx 341.6$

$(6.32 \text{ cis } 341.6°)^{1/3}$

First root is $6.32^{1/3} \text{ cis } \dfrac{341.6°}{3}$

$= \mathbf{1.8 \text{ cis } 113.86°}$; angles differ by $120°$
1.8 cis 233.86°, 1.8 cis 353.86°

14. $a_4 = a_1 r^3 = 2(4)^3 = \mathbf{128}$

15. Refer to Problem Set 76, problem 6.

16. $\dfrac{x^2}{4} + \dfrac{y^2}{16} = 1$

$16x^2 + 4y^2 = 64$

$16x^2 + 4y^2 - 64 = 0$

$\mathbf{4x^2 + y^2 - 16 = 0}$

17. $\left(\dfrac{5}{4}\right)^2 = \dfrac{25}{16}$; ratio $= \mathbf{25 : 16}$

18. $\cos^2 15° - \sin^2 15° = \cos 30° = \dfrac{\sqrt{3}}{2}$

19. $2\cos^2 x - \sqrt{3}\cos x = 0$

$\cos x (2\cos x - \sqrt{3}) = 0$

$\cos x = 0 \qquad\qquad 2\cos x - \sqrt{3} = 0$

$x = \mathbf{90°, 270°} \qquad \cos x = \dfrac{\sqrt{3}}{2}$

$\qquad\qquad\qquad\qquad x = \mathbf{30°, 330°}$

20. $\sec 3\theta = \dfrac{2}{\sqrt{3}}$

$\cos 3\theta = \dfrac{\sqrt{3}}{2}$

$3\theta = 30°, 330°, 390°, 690°, 750°, 1050°$
$\theta = \mathbf{10°, 110°, 130°, 230°, 250°, 350°}$

21. $\dfrac{2\cos 2x}{\sin 2x} = \dfrac{2(\cos^2 x - \sin^2 x)}{2\sin x \cos x}$

$= \dfrac{2\cos^2 x}{2\sin x \cos x} - \dfrac{2\sin^2 x}{2\sin x \cos x}$

$= \dfrac{\cos x}{\sin x} - \dfrac{\sin x}{\cos x} = \cot x - \tan x$

22. $2 \csc 2x \cos x = \dfrac{2}{\sin 2x}\cos x$

$= \dfrac{2\cos x}{2\sin x \cos x} = \dfrac{1}{\sin x} = \csc x$

23. $\dfrac{2\tan x}{1 + \tan^2 x} = \dfrac{2\tan x}{\sec^2 x} = \dfrac{2\sin x}{\cos x} \cdot \dfrac{\cos^2 x}{1}$

$= 2\sin x \cos x = \sin 2x$

24. $\cos A = \dfrac{8^2 + 8^2 - 5^2}{2(8)(8)} = \dfrac{103}{128} \approx 0.8047$

$A \approx \mathbf{36.4°}$

25. $\dfrac{c}{15} = \dfrac{a}{\frac{8}{3}a}$

$c = 15\left(\dfrac{3}{8}\right) = \dfrac{\mathbf{45}}{\mathbf{8}}$

26. Refer to Lesson 58, problem 26.

27. $2^3 = \log_2 x = 8$

$2^8 = x = \mathbf{256}$

28. $\sqrt{\log x}\, \log x = 8 \log 10$

$(\log x)^{3/2} = 8$

$((\log x)^{3/2})^{2/3} = 8^{2/3}$

$\log x = 4$

$10^4 = x = \mathbf{10,000}$

29. $\dfrac{1}{2}\log_3 x = \sqrt{\log_3 x}$

$\dfrac{1}{4}\left(\log_3 x\right)^2 - \log_3 x = 0$

$\log_3 x \left(\dfrac{1}{4}\log_3 x - 1\right) = 0$

$\log_3 x = 0 \qquad\qquad \dfrac{1}{4}\log_3 x - 1 = 0$

$3^0 = x = \mathbf{1} \qquad\qquad \log_3 x = 4$

$\qquad\qquad\qquad\qquad\quad 3^4 = x = \mathbf{81}$

30. Refer to Lesson 77.B.

EP

36. $\begin{bmatrix} 2 & 3 \\ 4 & 5 \end{bmatrix} + \begin{bmatrix} 2 & 1 \\ 2 & -1 \end{bmatrix} = \begin{bmatrix} \mathbf{4} & \mathbf{4} \\ \mathbf{6} & \mathbf{4} \end{bmatrix}$

Advanced Mathematics

PROBLEM SET 83

1. $\dfrac{m}{4}(t) + R_s(t) = 2$

   $mt + 4R_s t = 8$

   $4R_s t = 8 - mt$

   $R_s = \dfrac{8 - mt}{4t}$ $\dfrac{\text{jobs}}{\text{hr}}$

2. $500 = 600\, e^{10k}$

   $0.83 \approx e^{10k}$

   $k \approx -0.0182$

   $300 = 600\, e^{-0.0182t}$

   $0.5 = e^{-0.0182t}$

   $t \approx$ **31 years**

3. $\dfrac{20}{60} + \dfrac{50}{60} - \dfrac{10}{60} = \dfrac{60}{60} = 1$

4. $V = kS^2\sqrt{E}$

   $k(3S)^2\sqrt{4E} = k9S^2(2\sqrt{E}) = 18kS^2\sqrt{E}$

   Multiplied by factor of 18

5.

	Original speed	Speed + 4
Distance:	F	$F + 4$
Rate:	r	$r + 4$
Time:	$\dfrac{F}{r}$	$\dfrac{F + 6}{r + 4}$

6. $\log_5 60 = \dfrac{\log 60}{\log 5} \approx$ **2.54**

7. $\log_6 50 = \dfrac{\log 50}{\log 6} \approx$ **2.18**

8. $\overline{CD} \perp \overline{AB}$ so $\angle CDA = \angle CDB = 90°$, $\angle A = \angle B$; thus $\triangle ADC \sim \triangle BDC$ by AA; $CD = CD$ so $SF = 1$. This implies $\triangle ADC \cong \triangle BDC$; therefore $AC = CB$.

9. $AB = DC, AD = BC, DB = DB$; thus $\triangle ADB \cong \triangle CBD$ by SSS. Therefore $\angle A = \angle C$.

10. $\overline{AB} \parallel \overline{DC}$ so $\angle 1 = \angle 2, AB = DC, DB = DB$. Thus $\triangle DBA \cong \triangle BDC$ by SAS; therefore $\angle 3 = \angle 4$ and $\overline{DA} \parallel \overline{CB}$.

11. $\dfrac{\sin B}{10} = \dfrac{\sin 50°}{9}$

    $\sin B = \dfrac{10 \sin 50°}{9} \approx 0.8512$

    $B \approx 58.3°, B' \approx 126.7°$

    $C \approx 180° - 50° - 58.3° \approx 76.7°$

    $C' \approx 180° - 50° - 126.7° \approx 3.3°$

    $\dfrac{c}{\sin 76.7°} = \dfrac{9}{\sin 50°}$

    $c = \dfrac{9 \sin 76.7°}{\sin 50°} \approx 11.4$

    $\dfrac{c'}{\sin 3.3°} = \dfrac{9}{\sin 50°}$

    $c' = \dfrac{9 \sin 3.3°}{\sin 50°} \approx 1.7$

 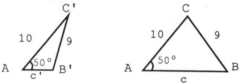

12. $r = \sqrt{3^2 + 2^2} = \sqrt{13} \approx 3.6$

    $\tan \theta = \dfrac{2}{3}$ (in Q I); $\theta \approx 33.7$

    $(3.6 \text{ cis } 33.7°)^{1/4}$

    First root is $3.6^{1/4} \text{ cis } \dfrac{33.7°}{4}$

    $\approx$ **1.38 cis 8.42°**; angles differ by $90°$

    1.38 cis 98.42°, 1.38 cis 188.42°,

    1.38 cis 278.42°

13. $a_4 = a_1 r^3 = 128\left(\dfrac{1}{2}\right)^3 = \dfrac{128}{8} = 16$ ft

14. $\sqrt{xy} = 9$ (a) $x - y = 24$

    $xy = 81$ $x = 24 + y$

    $(24 + y)y = 81$

    $y^2 + 24y - 81 = 0$

    $(y + 27)(y - 3) = 0$

    $y = -27, 3$

    Substitute these numbers into equation (a) to find x

    -27, -3 and 3, 27

15. $r = \dfrac{3 + 2\sqrt{2}}{1 + \sqrt{2}} \cdot \left(\dfrac{1 - \sqrt{2}}{1 - \sqrt{2}}\right)$

$= \dfrac{3 + 2\sqrt{2} - 3\sqrt{2} - 4}{1 - 2}$

$= \dfrac{-1 + \sqrt{2}}{-1} = 1 + \sqrt{2}$

$a_4 = \left(1 + \sqrt{2}\right)\left(1 + \sqrt{2}\right)^3$

$= 17 + 12\sqrt{2}$

16. $\dfrac{8 + 22}{2} = \dfrac{30}{2} = 15$

17. Refer to Problem Set 76, problem 6.

18. $2\cos^2 15° - 1 = \cos 30° = \dfrac{\sqrt{3}}{2}$

19. $2\cos^2 x + \sin x - 1 = 0$
$2(1 - \sin^2 x) + \sin x - 1 = 0$
$2 - 2\sin^2 x + \sin x - 1 = 0$
$2\sin^2 x - \sin x - 1 = 0$
$(2\sin x + 1)(\sin x - 1) = 0$
$\sin x = -\dfrac{1}{2}$ $\qquad \sin x = 1$
$x = 210°, 330°$ $\qquad x = 90°$

20. $\sec 3\theta = -\dfrac{2}{\sqrt{3}}$

$\cos 3\theta = -\dfrac{\sqrt{3}}{2}$

$3\theta = 150°, 210°, 510°, 570°, 870°, 930°$
$\theta = 50°, 70°, 170°, 190°, 290°, 310°$

21. $\dfrac{\cos^3 x - \sin^3 x}{\cos x - \sin x}$

$= \dfrac{(\cos x - \sin x)(\cos^2 x + \cos x \sin x + \sin^2 x)}{\cos x - \sin x}$

$= \cos^2 x + \cos x \sin x + \sin^2 x$

$= 1 + \cos x \sin x = 1 + \dfrac{1}{2}(2\cos x \sin x)$

$= 1 + \dfrac{1}{2}\sin 2x$

22. $\dfrac{\cos 2x}{\cos^2 x} = \dfrac{\cos^2 x - \sin^2 x}{\cos^2 x}$

$= \dfrac{\cos^2 x}{\cos^2 x} - \dfrac{\sin^2 x}{\cos^2 x} = 1 - \tan^2 x$

23. $\tan 2x = \dfrac{2\tan x}{1 - \tan^2 x}$

$= \dfrac{\dfrac{2\tan x}{\tan x}}{\dfrac{1}{\tan x} - \dfrac{\tan^2 x}{\tan x}} = \dfrac{2}{\cot x - \tan x}$

24. $a = \sqrt{49 + 25 - 2(5)(7\cos 60°)} \approx 6.24$

25. $\dfrac{2}{3}y = 12$

$y = \dfrac{36}{2} = 18$

26.

27. $\log_2 x = 2^2 = 4$
$2^4 = x = 16$

28. $\log_2 x^2 = 2(\log_2 x)^2$
$2\log_2 x = 2(\log_2 x)^2$
$(\log_2 x)^2 - \log_2 x = 0$
$(\log_2 x)(\log_2 x - 1) = 0$
$\log_2 x = 0$ $\qquad \log_2 x - 1 = 0$
$2^0 = x = 1$ $\qquad 2^1 = x = 2$

29. $\log_3 \sqrt[3]{x} = \sqrt{\log_3 x}$

$\dfrac{1}{3}\log_3 x = \sqrt{\log_3 x}$

$\dfrac{1}{9}(\log_3 x)^2 = \log_3 x$

$\dfrac{1}{9}(\log_3 x)^2 - \log_3 x$

$= (\log_3 x)\left(\dfrac{1}{9}\log_3 x - 1\right) = 0$

$\log_3 x = 0$ $\qquad \dfrac{1}{9}\log_3 x - 1 = 0$
$3^0 = x = 1$ $\qquad \log_3 x = 9$
$\qquad\qquad x = 3^9$

30. (a) $y = \cot\theta$
(b) $y = -3 + \sec x$

EP

37. **Invalid**

38. $\begin{bmatrix} 1 & -2 \\ -1 & 2 \end{bmatrix} + \begin{bmatrix} 6 & 4 \\ 2 & 0 \end{bmatrix} = \begin{bmatrix} 7 & 2 \\ 1 & 2 \end{bmatrix}$

PROBLEM SET 84

1.

	Original	Increased
Distance:	m	$m + 5$
Time:	$\dfrac{m}{R}$	$\dfrac{m}{R}$
Rate:	R	$\dfrac{R(m+5)}{m} \dfrac{\text{mi}}{\text{hr}}$

2. $G = \dfrac{k\sqrt{R}}{W^2}$

$\dfrac{k\sqrt{16R}}{(2W)^2} = \dfrac{4k\sqrt{R}}{4W^2} = \dfrac{k\sqrt{R}}{W^2}$

G **remains the same**

3. $_{11}P_4 = \dfrac{11!}{(11-4)!} = \dfrac{11!}{7!} = \mathbf{7920}$

$_{11}C_4 = \dfrac{11!}{4!(11-4)!} = \dfrac{11!}{4!\,7!} = \mathbf{330}$

4. $T = S + 15, \qquad \dfrac{1}{12}T = S$

$T = \dfrac{1}{12}T + 15$

$T = \dfrac{180}{11} = \mathbf{16\dfrac{4}{11}\ min}$

5. $x\left(\dfrac{d}{m} + k\right) = 14$

$x\left(\dfrac{d + km}{m}\right) = 14$

$x = \dfrac{14m}{d + km}$

6. Refer to Example 84.A.3.

7. Refer to Example 84.A.4.

8. Refer to Example 84.B.2.

9. Refer to Example 84.B.4.

10. $\log_8 50 = \dfrac{\log 50}{\log 8} \approx \mathbf{1.88}$

11. $\log_5 60 = \dfrac{\log 60}{\log 5} \approx \mathbf{2.54}$

12. $CD \perp$ bisector of $\overline{AB}$ implies $\angle CDA$ $= \angle CDB = 90°$. $\angle 1 = \angle 2$; thus $\triangle ACD$ $\sim \triangle BCD$ by AA. $CD = CD$ so $SF = 1$; this implies $\triangle ACD \cong \triangle BCD$ and $AC = CB$.

13. $\overline{AB} \parallel \overline{CD}$ so $\angle ABO = \angle ODC$ and $\angle BAO = \angle OCD$; which implies $\triangle AOB$ $\cong \triangle COD$. Since $CD = AB$, $SF = 1$; therefore $\triangle AOB \cong \triangle COD$; which gives $AO = OC$ and $DO = OB$.

14. $\dfrac{\sin B}{8} = \dfrac{\sin 35°}{4}$

$\sin B = \dfrac{8 \sin 35°}{4} \approx 1.15$

No such triangle exists

15. $r = \sqrt{4^2 + 3^2} = 5$

$\tan \theta = -\dfrac{3}{4}$

$\theta \approx 323.1°$

$(5 \text{ cis } 323.1°)^{1/4}$

First root is $5^{1/4} \text{ cis } \dfrac{323.1°}{4}$

$\approx \mathbf{1.5 \ cis \ 80.8°}$; angles differ by $90°$

1.5 cis 170.8°, 1.5 cis 260.8°

1.5 cis 350.8°

16. $\dfrac{9 + 21}{2} = \dfrac{30}{2} = \mathbf{15}$

17. $a_4 = a_1 r^3 = 81\left(\dfrac{2}{3}\right)^3 = 81\left(\dfrac{8}{27}\right) = \mathbf{24\ ft}$

18. $\sqrt{LS} = 8 \qquad\qquad L - S = 12$

$LS = 64 \qquad (a)\ L = S + 12$

$(S + 12)S = 64$

$S^2 + 12S - 64 = 0$

$(S + 16)(S - 4) = 0$

$S = -16, 4$

Substitute these numbers into equation (a) to find L.

−16, −4 or 16, 4

19. $2(1 - \cos^2 x) + 15 \cos x - 9 = 0$

$2 \cos^2 x + 15 \cos x + 7 = 0$

$(2 \cos x - 1)(\cos x + 7) = 0$

$\cos x = \dfrac{1}{2} \qquad\qquad \cos x = -7$

$x = \mathbf{60°, 300°} \qquad\qquad \emptyset$

20. $\cot 2\theta = \sqrt{3}$

$\tan 2\theta = \dfrac{\sqrt{3}}{3}$

$2\theta = 30°, 210°, 390°, 570°$

$\theta = \mathbf{15°, 105°, 195°, 285°}$

21. $2 \csc 2x = \dfrac{2}{\sin 2x} = \dfrac{2}{2\sin x \cos x}$

$= \dfrac{1}{\sin x \cos x} = \dfrac{\sin^2 x + \cos^2 x}{\sin x \cos x}$

$= \dfrac{\sin x}{\cos x} + \dfrac{\cos x}{\sin x} = \tan x + \cot x$

22. $\dfrac{\sin 2x}{\tan x} = \dfrac{2 \sin x \cos x}{\dfrac{\sin x}{\cos x}} = 2 \cos^2 x$

23. $(\tan^2 x)(1 + \cot^2 x) = \tan^2 x + \tan^2 x \cot^2 x$

$= \tan^2 x + 1 = \sec^2 x = \dfrac{1}{\cos^2 x} = \dfrac{1}{1 - \sin^2 x}$

24. $\dfrac{\sin A}{10} = \dfrac{\sin 100°}{18}$

$\sin A = \dfrac{10 \sin 100°}{18} \approx 0.5471$

$A \approx \mathbf{33.2°}$

25. $\dfrac{5}{3} x = 5$

$x = \dfrac{15}{5} = \mathbf{3}$

26. Refer to Lesson 77.B.

27. $\log_2 x = 2^3 = 8$

$2^8 = x = \mathbf{256}$

28. $2 \log_3 x = \log_3 x$

$2 \log_3 x - \log_3 x = 0$

$\log_3 x = 0$

$3^0 = x = \mathbf{1}$

29. $\log_e \dfrac{8^{2/3}(x)}{3x - 2} = \log_e 3$

$\dfrac{4x}{3x - 2} = 3$

$4x = 3(3x - 2)$

$4x = 9x - 6$

$-5x = -6$

$x = \dfrac{6}{5}$

30. $\log x = 4$

$10^4 = x = \mathbf{10{,}000}$

EP

39. **Valid**

40. $\begin{bmatrix} 3 & 2 \\ 1 & 0 \end{bmatrix} + \begin{bmatrix} 1 & -2 \\ -1 & 2 \end{bmatrix} = \begin{bmatrix} 4 & 0 \\ 0 & 2 \end{bmatrix}$

PROBLEM SET 85

1. $\dfrac{R}{G} = \dfrac{4}{3}$

$R + G = 63$

$3R = 4G$

$R = 63 - G$

$3(63 - G) = 4G$

$189 - 3G = 4G$

$7G = 189$

$G = \dfrac{189}{7} = 27$

$R = 63 - 27 = \mathbf{36}$

2. $760 = 800 e^{-20k}$

$0.95 = e^{-20k}$

$\ln 0.95 = \ln e^{-20k}$

$-0.05129 \approx -20k$

$k \approx 0.0026$

$400 \approx 800 e^{-0.0026t}$

$0.5 \approx e^{-0.0026t}$

$\ln 0.5 \approx \ln e^{-0.0026t}$

$-0.693 \approx -0.0026t$

$t \approx \mathbf{270.3 \ min}$

3. $\dfrac{1}{3}\left(\dfrac{4}{11}\right) = \dfrac{4}{33}$

4. $(a \ \# \ b) \ * \ b = [2(10) - 3(2)] - 2$

$= (20 - 6) - 2 = (14) - 2 = \mathbf{12}$

5. $R_o T_o = 360$
    $R_b = 2R_o$
    $T_o + T_b = 9$
    $T_b = 9 - T_o$
    $R_b T_b = 360$
    $(2R_o)(9 - T_o) = 360$
    $18R_o - 2R_o T_o = 360$
    $18R_o - 2(360) = 360$
    $18R_o = 1080$
    $R_o = \dfrac{1080}{18} = \mathbf{60\ mph}$

6. $\begin{vmatrix} 2 & 0 & -1 \\ 0 & 3 & -2 \\ 3 & 4 & -1 \end{vmatrix}$
    $= -6 + 0 + 0 + 9 + 16 + 0 = \mathbf{19}$

7. $z = \dfrac{\begin{vmatrix} 2 & 3 & 2 \\ 0 & 1 & 5 \\ 1 & 2 & -1 \end{vmatrix}}{\begin{vmatrix} 2 & 3 & 2 \\ 0 & 1 & 5 \\ 1 & 2 & -1 \end{vmatrix}}$
    $= \dfrac{-2 + 15 + 0 - 2 - 20 - 0}{0 + 6 + 0 - 1 - 8 - 0} = \dfrac{-9}{-3} = \mathbf{3}$

8. Refer to Example 84.A.2.

9. Refer to Example 84.B.1.

10. $\log_5 35 = \dfrac{\log 35}{\log 5} \approx \mathbf{2.21}$

11. $\log_6 40 = \dfrac{\log 40}{\log 6} \approx \mathbf{2.06}$

12. $AB = CD, AD = BC, DB = DB$ implies
    $\triangle DAB \cong \triangle BCD$ so $\angle ADB = \angle DBC$. Also
    $CA = CA$, which implies $\triangle DAC \cong \triangle BCA$, so
    $\angle BAC = \angle ACD$.

13. $\overline{AB} \parallel \overline{FC}$ so $\angle 1 = \angle 2, \angle 3 = \angle 4$. This
    implies $\triangle ADE \sim \triangle CFE$. E is the midpoint of
    $\overline{AC}$ so $AE = EC$ and $SF = 1$; therefore
    $\triangle ADE \cong \triangle CFE$ and $DE = EF$.

14. $\dfrac{\sin B}{8} = \dfrac{\sin 20^\circ}{4}$
    $\sin B = \dfrac{8 \sin 20^\circ}{4} \approx 0.684$
    $B \approx 43.2^\circ, B' \approx 136.8^\circ$

$C \approx 180^\circ - 20^\circ - 43.2^\circ \approx 116.8^\circ$
$C' \approx 180^\circ - 20^\circ - 136.8^\circ \approx 23.2^\circ$

$\dfrac{c}{\sin 116.8^\circ} = \dfrac{4}{\sin 20^\circ}$
$c = \dfrac{4 \sin 116.8^\circ}{\sin 20^\circ} \approx \mathbf{10.4}$

$\dfrac{c'}{\sin 23.2^\circ} = \dfrac{4}{\sin 20^\circ}$
$c' = \dfrac{4 \sin 23.2^\circ}{\sin 20^\circ} \approx \mathbf{4.6}$

15. $r = \sqrt{4^2 + 2^2} = \sqrt{20} \approx 4.5$
    $\tan \theta = \dfrac{2}{4}$, (in Q I) $\theta \approx 26.6^\circ$
    $(4.5 \text{ cis } 26.6^\circ)^{1/3}$
    First root is $4.5^{1/3} \text{ cis } \dfrac{26.6^\circ}{3}$
    $\approx \mathbf{1.65 \text{ cis } 8.86^\circ}$; angles differ by 120°
    $\mathbf{1.65 \text{ cis } 128.6^\circ, 1.65 \text{ cis } 248.6^\circ}$

16. $a_5 = a_1 r^4 = 256 \left(\dfrac{3}{4}\right)^4 = 256 \left(\dfrac{81}{256}\right) = \mathbf{81\ ft}$

17. $\sqrt{xy} = 4$ (a) $\dfrac{x + y}{2} = 5$
    $xy = 16$ $x + y = 10$
    $y = 10 - x$
    $x(10 - x) = 16$
    $x^2 - 10x + 16 = 0$
    $(x - 8)(x - 2) = 0$
    $x = \mathbf{8, 2}$
    Substitute the numbers into equation (a) for y.
    $y = \mathbf{2, 8}$

18. $-\sqrt{xy} = -10$ $x - y = 15$
    $xy = 100$ $x = 15 + y$
    $(15 + y)y = 100$
    $y^2 + 15y - 100 = 0$
    $(y + 20)(y - 5) = 0$
    $y = \mathbf{-20, 5}$
    Substitute these numbers into equation (a) to
    find x.
    $x = \mathbf{-5, 20}$

19. $\csc 3x = -2$

$\sin 3x = -\dfrac{1}{2}$

$3x = 210°, 330°, 570°, 690°, 930°, 1050°$

$x = \mathbf{70°, 110°, 190°, 230°, 310°, 350°}$

20. $2(1 - \sin^2 x) + 15 \sin x - 9 = 0$

$2 - 2 \sin^2 x + 15 \sin x - 9 = 0$

$2 \sin^2 x - 15 \sin x + 7 = 0$

$(2 \sin x + 1)(\sin x - 7) = 0$

$\sin x = -\dfrac{1}{2}$ $\qquad\qquad$ $\sin x = 7$

$x = \mathbf{30°, 150°}$ $\qquad\qquad$ $\varnothing$

21. $\dfrac{\sec 2x - 1}{2 \sec 2x} = \dfrac{\dfrac{1}{\cos 2x} - 1}{\dfrac{2}{\cos 2x}}$

$= \dfrac{1 - \cos 2x}{2} = \dfrac{1 - (1 - 2\sin^2 x)}{2}$

$= \dfrac{2 \sin^2 x}{2} = \sin^2 x$

22. $(\cot^2 x)(1 + \tan^2 x) = \cot^2 x + 1 = \csc^2 x$

$= \dfrac{1}{\sin^2 x} = \dfrac{1}{1 - \cos^2 x}$

23. $\dfrac{1}{2} \cot x \sec^2 x = \dfrac{\cos x}{2 \sin x} \cdot \dfrac{1}{\cos^2 x}$

$= \dfrac{1}{2 \sin x \cos x} = \dfrac{1}{\sin 2x} = \csc 2x$

24. Area $= \dfrac{1}{2}(8)(10)\sin 110° \approx \mathbf{37.6 \ units^2}$

25. $(13 - 2)180° = \mathbf{1980°}$

26.

27. $x^{\ln x} = e^4$

$(\ln x)(\ln x) = 4 \ln e$

$(\ln x)^2 = 4(1)$

$\ln x = 4^{1/2} = \pm 2$

$x = e^{\pm 2}$

28. $\log_4 [(x + 3)(x - 3)] = 2$

$\log_4[x^2 - 9] = 2$

$4^2 = x^2 - 9$

$16 + 9 = x^2 = 25$

$x = \mathbf{5}$

29. $\dfrac{1}{4} \log_4 x = \sqrt{\log_4 x}$

$\dfrac{1}{16}(\log_4 x)^2 = \log_4 x$

$\dfrac{1}{16}(\log_4 x)^2 - \log_4 x = 0$

$(\log_4 x)\left(\dfrac{1}{16}\log_4 x - 1\right) = 0$

$\log_4 x = 0$ $\qquad\qquad$ $\dfrac{1}{16}\log_4 x - 1 = 0$

$4^0 = x = \mathbf{1}$ $\qquad\qquad$ $\log_4 x = 16$

$\qquad\qquad\qquad\qquad\qquad$ $x = \mathbf{4^{16}}$

30. $4^3 = \mathbf{64}$

EP

41. $\begin{bmatrix} 6 & 2 \\ 3 & 1 \end{bmatrix} + \begin{bmatrix} -1 & 2 \\ 3 & 4 \end{bmatrix} = \begin{bmatrix} 5 & 4 \\ 6 & 5 \end{bmatrix}$

42. $2(2^{k+1} - 1) = 2 \cdot 2^{k+1} - 2$

$= 2^{k+1} + 2^{k+1} - 2 = 2^{k+1} - 2 + 2^{k+1}$

$= 2(2^k - 1) + 2^{k+1}$

PROBLEM SET 86

1. $4(90 - A_1) = (180 - A_2) - 40$

$360 - 4A_1 = 140 - A_2$

$A_2 = 4A_1 - 220$

$A_1 + A_2 = 80$

$A_2 = 80 - A_1$

$4A_1 - 220 = 80 - A_1$

$5A_1 = 300$

$A_1 = \dfrac{300}{5} = \mathbf{60°}$

$A_2 = 80 - 60 = \mathbf{20°}$

2. $W = 5P$

$W - 5 = 6(P - 5) + 19$

$5P - 5 = 6P - 30 + 19$

$P = -5 + 30 - 19 = 6$

$W = 5(6) = 30$

Seventeen years later

$P = 6 + 17 = \textbf{23}$

$W = 30 + 17 = \textbf{47}$

3. $\dfrac{4}{52} + \dfrac{26}{52} - \dfrac{2}{52} = \dfrac{28}{52} = \dfrac{7}{13}$

4. $2.6 = 0.04\, e^{20k}$

$65 = e^{20k}$

$\ln 65 = \ln e^{20k}$

$4.174 \approx 20k$

$k \approx \dfrac{4.174}{20} \approx 0.2087$

$16 = 0.04\, e^{0.2087t}$

$400 = e^{0.2087t}$

$t \approx \textbf{28.7 sec}$

5. $(B + W)T_D = 33,\ (B - W)T_U = 20$

$T_D = T_U - 1,\ B = 2W$

$(2W + W)(T_U - 1) = 33$

$3WT_U - 3W = 33$

$(2W - W)T_U = 20$

$T_U W = 20$

$3(20) - 3W = 33$

$3W = 27$

$W = \textbf{9 mph}$

$B = 2W = \textbf{18 mph}$

6.

Term	1	2	3	4	5	6	7	8
For x:	7	6	5	4	3	2	1	0
For y:	0	1	2	3	4	5	6	7
Coeff:	1	7	21	35	35	21	7	1

$35x^4(-y)^3 = \mathbf{-35x^4y^3}$

7. $(2a^2)^3 - 3(2a^2)^2(b^3) + 3(2a^2)(b^3)^2 + (b^3)^3$

$= \mathbf{8a^6 - 12a^4b^3 + 6a^2b^6 - b^9}$

8.

$x = \dfrac{\begin{vmatrix} 0 & -1 & 1 \\ 4 & 3 & 2 \\ 5 & 2 & 0 \end{vmatrix}}{\begin{vmatrix} 3 & -1 & 1 \\ 0 & 3 & 2 \\ 1 & 2 & 0 \end{vmatrix}}$

$= \dfrac{0 - 10 + 8 - 15 - 0 - 0}{0 - 2 + 0 - 3 - 12 - 0} = \dfrac{-17}{-17} = \textbf{1}$

9. Refer to Example 84.B.3.

10. Refer to Example 84.A.2.

11. $\log_6 40 = \dfrac{\log 40}{\log 6} \approx \textbf{2.06}$

12. $AB = CD, AD = BC, DB = DB$ implies $\triangle ADB \cong \triangle CBD$; thus $\angle ABD = \angle BDC$. Also $AC = AC$ implies $\triangle ADC \cong \triangle CBA$; thus $\angle BAC = \angle ACD$. Now $\triangle AOB \sim \triangle COD$, $AB = CD$; thus $SF = 1$ and $\triangle AOB \cong \triangle COD$.

13. D is the midpoint of $\overline{AB}$ and E is the midpoint of $\overline{AC}$ implies $AD = \dfrac{1}{2}AB$ and $AE = \dfrac{1}{2}AC$. $\dfrac{AD}{AB} = \dfrac{AE}{AC} = \dfrac{1}{2}$, $\angle A = \angle A$ implies $\triangle ADE \sim \triangle ABC$ by SAS; therefore $\angle ADE = \angle ABC$ and $\overline{DE} \parallel \overline{BC}$.

14. $\dfrac{\sin 50^\circ}{9} = \dfrac{\sin B}{10}$

$\sin B = \dfrac{10 \sin 50^\circ}{9} \approx 0.85116$

$B \approx 58.34^\circ,\ B' \approx 121.66^\circ$

$C \approx 180^\circ - 50^\circ - 58.34^\circ \approx 71.66^\circ$

$C' \approx 180^\circ - 50^\circ - 121.66^\circ \approx 8.34^\circ$

$\dfrac{c}{\sin 71.66^\circ} = \dfrac{9}{\sin 50^\circ}$

$c = \dfrac{9 \sin 71.66^\circ}{\sin 50^\circ} \approx \textbf{11.2}$

$\dfrac{c'}{\sin 8.34^\circ} = \dfrac{9}{\sin 50^\circ}$

$c' = \dfrac{9 \sin 8.34^\circ}{\sin 50^\circ} \approx \textbf{1.7}$

15. $r = \sqrt{8^2 + 2^2} = \sqrt{68} \approx 8.246$

$\tan \theta = -\dfrac{8}{2} = -4$ (in Q II), $\theta \approx 104.04^\circ$

$(8.25 \text{ cis } 104.04^\circ)^{1/5}$. First root is

$8.25^{1/5} \text{ cis } \dfrac{104.04^\circ}{5} \approx \textbf{1.5 cis 20.8}^\circ$

The fifth roots differ by $\dfrac{360^\circ}{5} = 72^\circ$

1.5 cis 92.8°, 1.5 cis 164.8°,
1.5 cis 236.8°, 1.5 cis 308.8°

16. $243\left(\dfrac{1}{3}\right)^3 = 243\left(\dfrac{1}{27}\right) = \mathbf{9\ ft}$

17. $-\sqrt{LS} = -12$ (a) $\dfrac{L + S}{2} = 20$

$LS = 144$ $L = 40 - S$

$(40 - S)S = 144$

$S^2 - 40S + 144 = 0$

$(S - 36)(S - 4) = 0$

$S = 36$ $S = 4$

$L = 36$

18. $\text{Area}_\Delta = \dfrac{1}{2}(5)\left(\dfrac{5}{2}\sqrt{3}\right) = \dfrac{25\sqrt{3}}{4}$

$\text{Area}_{\text{Hex}} = 6\left(\dfrac{25\sqrt{3}}{4}\right) = \dfrac{75\sqrt{3}}{2}$

19. $\cot 3\theta = 0$

$\tan 3\theta = \infty$ or undefined

$3\theta = 90°, 270°, 450°, 630°, 810°, 990°$

$\theta = \mathbf{30°, 90°, 150°, 210°, 270°, 330°}$

20. $3(\sec^2 x - 1) + 5\sec x + 1 = 0$

$3\sec^2 x + 5\sec x - 2 = 0$

$(3\sec x - 1)(\sec x + 2) = 0$

$\sec x = \dfrac{1}{3}$ $\sec x = -2$

$\cos x = 3$ $\cos x = -\dfrac{1}{2}$

    $\varnothing$ $x = \mathbf{120°, 240°}$

21. $\dfrac{\sin x \tan x}{1 - \cos x} - 1 = \dfrac{\sin x \cdot \dfrac{\sin x}{\cos x}}{1 - \cos x} - 1$

$= \dfrac{\dfrac{\sin^2 x}{\cos x}}{(\cos x)(1 - \cos x)} - 1$

$= \dfrac{\sin^2 x - \cos x + \cos^2 x}{(\cos x)(1 - \cos x)}$

$= \dfrac{1 - \cos x}{(\cos x)(1 - \cos x)} = \dfrac{1}{\cos x} = \sec x$

22. $\dfrac{\cos 2x}{\sin^2 x} = \dfrac{\cos^2 x - \sin^2 x}{\sin^2 x} = \dfrac{\cos^2 x}{\sin^2 x} - 1$

$= \cot^2 x - 1$

23. $\dfrac{1 + \sin x}{\cos x} + \dfrac{\cos x}{1 + \sin x}$

$= \dfrac{1 + 2\sin x + \sin^2 x + \cos^2 x}{(\cos x)(1 + \sin x)}$

$= \dfrac{2 + 2\sin x}{(\cos x)(1 + \sin x)} = \dfrac{2(1 + \sin x)}{(\cos x)(1 + \sin x)}$

$= \dfrac{2}{\cos x} = \dfrac{2}{\cos x} \cdot \dfrac{2\sin x}{2\sin x}$

$= \dfrac{4\sin x}{2\sin x \cos x} = \dfrac{4\sin x}{\sin 2x}$

24. (a) $y = 6 + 8\csc x$

    (b) $y = \cot\theta$

25. The sum of the exterior angles of any polygon is $\mathbf{360°}$.

26. Refer to Lesson 77, #7b.

27. $\log_{81} x = 4(\log_{81} x)^2$

$4(\log_{81} x)^2 - \log_{81} x = 0$

$(\log_{81} x)(4\log_{81} x - 1) = 0$

$\log_{81} x = 0$ $\log_{81} x = \dfrac{1}{4}$

$81^0 = x = 1$ $81^{1/4} = x = 3$

28. $\log_2 \dfrac{x + 1}{x - 1} = 1$

$2^1 = 2 = \dfrac{x + 1}{x - 1}$

$2x - 2 = x + 1$

$x = 3$

29. $(\ln x)(x - 1) = \ln 20$

$x^2 - x - 20 = 0$

$(x - 5)(x + 4) = 0$

$x = 5$

30. $4^2 = 16$

EP

43. $\begin{bmatrix} 2 & 0 \\ -1 & 1 \end{bmatrix} + \begin{bmatrix} -1 & 0 \\ 1 & -2 \end{bmatrix} = \begin{bmatrix} -2 & 0 \\ 2 & -2 \end{bmatrix}$

44. $\begin{bmatrix} 2 & 3 \\ 1 & 7 \end{bmatrix} + \begin{bmatrix} 9 & -4 \\ 2 & 0 \end{bmatrix} = \begin{bmatrix} 11 & -1 \\ 3 & 7 \end{bmatrix}$

1. $3(90° - A_1) = 100° + 180° - A_2$
$A_1 + A_2 = 130°$
$A_1 = 130° - A_2$
$3(90° - 130° + A_2) = 100° + 180° - A_2$
$180° - 390° + 3A_2 = 280° - A_2$
$4A_2 = 400°$
$A_2 = \mathbf{100°}$
$A_1 = 130° - 100° = \mathbf{30°}$

2. $K = 2M$
$K - 5 = 3(M - 5)$
$2M - 5 = 3M - 15$
$M = \mathbf{10}$
$K = 2(10) = \mathbf{20}$

3. $\dfrac{4}{52} + \dfrac{13}{52} - \dfrac{1}{52} = \dfrac{16}{52} = \mathbf{\dfrac{4}{13}}$

4. $15 = 5\,e^{4k}$
$3 = e^{4k}$
$\ln 3 = 4k$
$k \approx 0.2747$

$A_9 \approx 5\,e^{0.2747t}$
$A_9 \approx 5\,e^{0.2747(9)} \approx 5(11.84) \approx \mathbf{59.2\ m}$

5. $B = 2C$
$(2C + C)(T - 4) = 30$
$3CT - 12C = 30$
$(2C - C)T = 30$
$CT = 30$
$3(30) - 12C = 30$
$60 = 12C$
$C = \mathbf{5\ mph}$
$B = 2(5) = \mathbf{10\ mph}$

6.
term:	1	2	3	4	5	6	7
for x:	6	5	4	3	2	1	0
for y:	0	1	2	3	4	5	6
coeff:	1	6	15	20	15	6	1

$15x^4(-y)^2 = \mathbf{15x^4y^2}$

7. $(2a^2)^3 + 3(2a^2)^2(-b^4) + 3(2a^2)(-b^4) + (-b^4)^3$
$= \mathbf{8a^6 - 12a^4b^4 + 6a^2b^8 - b^{12}}$

8. $x = \dfrac{\begin{vmatrix} 7 & -1 & 1 \\ 5 & 2 & 3 \\ -5 & 3 & 0 \end{vmatrix}}{\begin{vmatrix} 2 & -1 & 1 \\ 0 & 2 & 3 \\ 1 & 3 & 0 \end{vmatrix}}$

$= \dfrac{0 + 15 + 15 + 10 - 63 - 0}{0 - 3 + 0 - 2 - 18 - 0}$

$= \dfrac{-23}{-23} = \mathbf{1}$

9. $\begin{bmatrix} 5 & 0 \\ 6 & -2 \end{bmatrix} - \begin{bmatrix} 3 & -1 \\ -2 & 2 \end{bmatrix} = \begin{bmatrix} 2 & 1 \\ 8 & -4 \end{bmatrix}$

10. $3\begin{bmatrix} 2 & -1 \\ 6 & 3 \end{bmatrix} = \begin{bmatrix} 6 & -3 \\ 18 & 9 \end{bmatrix}$

11. $\begin{bmatrix} 2 & -1 \\ 3 & 4 \end{bmatrix}\begin{bmatrix} -3 & -2 \\ 2 & 1 \end{bmatrix}$
$a_{11} = (2)(-3) + (-1)(2) = -8$
$a_{21} = (3)(-3) + (4)(2) = -1$
$a_{12} = (2)(-2) + (-1)(1) = -5$
$a_{22} = (3)(-2) + (4)(1) = -2$
$= \begin{bmatrix} \mathbf{-8} & \mathbf{-5} \\ \mathbf{-1} & \mathbf{-2} \end{bmatrix}$

12. Refer to Lesson 84.B.1.

13. Refer to Lesson 84.A.1.

14. $\log_5 30 = \dfrac{\log 30}{\log 5} \approx \mathbf{2.1}$

15. $AB = CD, AD = BC, DB = DB$ implies $\triangle ADB \cong \triangle CBD$; so $\angle ABO = \angle ODC$, $\angle AOB = \angle DOC$, and $AB = DC$. Thus the $SF = 1$ and $\triangle AOB \cong \triangle COD$.

16. D is the midpoint of $\overline{AB}$ and E is the midpoint of $\overline{AC}$ so $AD = \dfrac{1}{2}AB$ and $AE = \dfrac{1}{2}AC$. $\angle A = \angle A$ implies $\triangle DAE$ $\sim \triangle BAC$ with $SF = 2$; therefore $DE = \dfrac{1}{2}BC$.

17. $\dfrac{\sin B}{8} = \dfrac{\sin 70°}{5}$

$\sin B = \dfrac{8 \sin 70°}{5} \approx 1.504$

No such triangle exists

18. $r = \sqrt{3^2 + 4^2} = 5$

$\tan \theta = -\dfrac{4}{3}$ (in Q II), $\theta \approx 126.9°$

$(5 \text{ cis } 126.9°)^{1/3}$ First root is $5^{1/3} \text{ cis } \dfrac{126.9°}{3}$

$\approx$ **1.7 cis 42.3°**, angles differ by 120°

1.7 cis 162.3°, 1.7 cis 282.3°

19. $\sqrt{xy} = 20$

$xy = 400$

$(104 - y)y = 400$

$y^2 - 104y + 400 = 0$

$(y - 100)(y - 4) = 0$

$y = 100, 4$

(a) $\dfrac{x + y}{2} = 52$

$x = 104 - y$

Substitute into (a) to get x values.

$x = 4, 100$

Either way the two numbers are **4, 100**

20. $\tan 2\theta = 0$

$2\theta = 0°, 180°, 360°, 540°$

$\theta = \mathbf{0°, 90°, 180°, 270°}$

21. $2(1 - \sin^2 x) - 9 \sin x + 3 = 0$

$2 - 2 \sin^2 x - 9 \sin x + 3 = 0$

$2 \sin^2 x + 9 \sin x - 5 = 0$

$(2 \sin x - 1)(\sin x + 5) = 0$

$\sin x = \dfrac{1}{2}$ $\qquad$ $\sin x = -5$

$x = \mathbf{30°, 150°}$ $\qquad$ $\varnothing$

22. $\dfrac{2 \sec 2x}{\sec 2x - 1} = \dfrac{\dfrac{2}{\cos 2x}}{\dfrac{1}{\cos 2x} - 1}$

$= \dfrac{2}{1 - \cos 2x} = \dfrac{2}{1 - (1 - 2 \sin^2 x)}$

$= \dfrac{2}{2 \sin^2 x} = \dfrac{1}{\sin^2 x} = \csc^2 x$

23. $\dfrac{1 + \cos 2x}{1 - \cos 2x} = \dfrac{1 + (2 \cos^2 x - 1)}{1 - (1 - 2 \sin^2 x)}$

$= \dfrac{2 \cos^2 x}{2 \sin^2 x} = \cot^2 x$

24. (a) $y = 1 + \sin (x + 40°)$

(b) $y = 3 + 2 \sin 2\left(x - \dfrac{\pi}{6}\right)$

25. **No**

26. Refer to Lesson 45, problem 16.

27. $2^2 = \sqrt{x} = 4$

$x = \mathbf{16}$

28. $\log_2 \dfrac{2x - 1}{x - 1} = 2$

$2^2 = \dfrac{2x - 1}{x - 1} = 4$

$4(x - 1) = 2x - 1$

$2x = 3$

$x = \dfrac{3}{2}$

29. $(\ln x)(x + 1) = \ln 6$

$x(x + 1) = 6$

$x^2 + x - 6 = 0$

$(x + 3)(x - 2) = 0$

$x = \mathbf{2}$

30. $2^{-2} = \dfrac{1}{4}$

PROBLEM SET 87

1. $\dfrac{P_1 V_1}{T_1} = \dfrac{P_2 V_2}{T_2}$

$P_1 V_1 = P_2 V_2$

$(4)(10) = P_2(2)$

$P_2 = \dfrac{40}{2} = \mathbf{20 \text{ atm}}$

2. $39 = 42\,e^{30k}$
   $0.929 \approx e^{30k}$
   $30k \approx \ln 0.929$
   $k \approx -0.00247$

   $12.5 \approx 42\,e^{-0.00247t}$
   $0.2976 \approx e^{-0.00247t}$
   $-0.00247t \approx \ln 0.2976$
   $t \approx \mathbf{490.6\ min}$

3. $\dfrac{1}{2} \cdot \dfrac{1}{2} \cdot \dfrac{1}{2} \cdot \dfrac{1}{2} = \dfrac{1}{16}$

4. $35(180) + 100x = 50(180 + x)$
   $6300 + 100x = 9000 + 50x$
   $50x = 2700$
   $x = \mathbf{54\ g}$

5.
	Original	Increased
Distance:	k	12
Rate:	$\dfrac{k}{p}$	$\dfrac{k}{p} + s$
Time:	p	$\dfrac{12}{\dfrac{k}{p} + s}$

   $= \dfrac{12}{\dfrac{k + ps}{p}} = \dfrac{\mathbf{12p}}{\mathbf{k + ps}}$

6. $\log y = \log (6.3 \times 10^{-9}) + \log (5.0 \times 10^{5})$
   $\log y = (0.7993 - 9) + (0.6990 + 5)$
   $= -8.2007 + 5.6990 = -2.5017$
   $y = \text{antilog}\,(-2.5017) = \mathbf{3.15 \times 10^{-3}}$

7. $\log y = \log (5.25 \times 10^{5})^{1/6}$
   $\quad - \log (6.3 \times 10^{3})^{1.5}$
   $\log y = \dfrac{1}{6}(0.7202 + 5) - 1.5(0.7993 + 3)$
   $\log y = 0.9534 - 5.6989 = -4.7456$
   $y = \text{antilog}\,(-4.7456) = \mathbf{1.8 \times 10^{-5}}$

8. $\text{pH} = -\log \text{H}^{+} = -(\log 5.3 \times 10^{-5})$
   $= (0.72 - 5) = -(-4.28) \approx \mathbf{4.3}$

9. $\text{H} = 10^{-\text{pH}} = 10^{-6.5} = 10^{-6.5 + 7 - 7}$
   $= 10^{0.5 - 7} \approx \mathbf{3.16 \times 10^{-7}\ mole/liter}$

10.
Term:	1	2	3	4	5	6	7	8	9
For x:	8	7	6	5	4	3	2	1	0
For y:	0	1	2	3	4	5	6	7	8
Coeff:	1	8	28	56	70	56	28	8	1

   $70(x)^{4}(-y)^{4} = \mathbf{70x^4y^4}$

11. $(3a^2)^4 + 4(3a^2)^3(b^3) + 6(3a^2)^2(b^3)^2$
    $\quad + 4(3a^2)(b^3)^3 + (b^3)$
    $= \mathbf{81a^8 - 108a^6b^3 + 54a^4b^6}$
    $\quad \mathbf{- 12a^2b^9 + b^{12}}$

12. $x = \dfrac{\begin{vmatrix} -3 & 1 & 3 \\ 5 & 3 & 4 \\ 3 & 2 & 0 \end{vmatrix}}{\begin{vmatrix} 2 & 1 & 3 \\ 0 & 3 & 4 \\ 1 & 2 & 0 \end{vmatrix}}$

    $= \dfrac{0 + 12 + 30 - 27 + 24 - 0}{0 + 4 + 0 - 9 - 16 - 0}$
    $= \dfrac{39}{-21} = \mathbf{-\dfrac{13}{7}}$

13. Refer to Example 84.B.2.

14. Refer to Example 84.A.4.

15. $\log_5 22 = \dfrac{\log 22}{\log 5} \approx \mathbf{1.92}$

16. $\overline{AD}$ bisects $\angle A$ implies $\angle BAD = \angle CAD$;
    $AB = AC$, $AD = AD$ so $\triangle DAB \cong \triangle DAC$
    (SAS with $SF = 1$). Thus $\angle ADB = \angle ADC$,
    $\angle ADB + \angle ADC = 180°$; therefore $\angle ADB$
    $= \angle ADC = 90°$.

17. D is the midpoint of $\overline{AB}$ and E is the
    midpoint of $\overline{AC}$ so $AD = \dfrac{1}{2} AB$ and
    $AE = \dfrac{1}{2} AC$. $\angle A = \angle A$ so $\triangle ADE$
    $\sim \triangle ABC$ by SAS; therefore $\dfrac{DE}{BC} = \dfrac{AD}{AB}$
    $= \dfrac{1}{2}$ and $DE = \dfrac{1}{2} BC$.

18. $\dfrac{\sin B}{8} = \dfrac{\sin 25^\circ}{5}$

$\sin B = \dfrac{8 \sin 25^\circ}{5} \approx 0.6761$

$B = 42.6^\circ, B' = 137.4^\circ$

$C = 180^\circ - 25^\circ - 42.6^\circ = 112.4^\circ$

$C' = 180^\circ - 25^\circ - 137.4^\circ = 17.6^\circ$

$\dfrac{c}{\sin 112.4^\circ} = \dfrac{5}{\sin 25^\circ}$

$c = \dfrac{5 \sin 112.4^\circ}{\sin 25^\circ} \approx \textbf{10.9}$

$\dfrac{c'}{\sin 17.6^\circ} = \dfrac{5}{\sin 25^\circ}$

$c' = \dfrac{5 \sin 17.6^\circ}{\sin 25^\circ} \approx \textbf{3.6}$

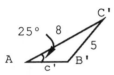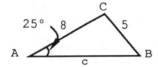

19. $r = \sqrt{3^2 + 4^2} = 5$

$\tan \theta = \dfrac{4}{-3}$ (in Q II), $\theta \approx 126.87^\circ$

$(5 \text{ cis } 126.87^\circ)^{1/3}$

First root is $5^{1/3}$ cis $\dfrac{126.87^\circ}{3}$

$\approx \textbf{1.7 cis 42.3}^\circ$; angles differ by 120°

1.7 cis 162.3°, 1.7 cis 282.3°

20. $128\left(\dfrac{1}{4}\right)^4 = 128\left(\dfrac{1}{256}\right) = \dfrac{1}{2}\,\text{ft}$

21. Area $= \dfrac{1}{2}(5)(8) \sin 120^\circ \approx \textbf{17.3}$

22. $\tan 3\theta = -2$

$3\theta = 117^\circ, 297^\circ, 477^\circ, 657^\circ, 837^\circ, 1017^\circ$

$\theta = \textbf{39}^\circ, \textbf{99}^\circ, \textbf{159}^\circ, \textbf{219}^\circ, \textbf{279}^\circ, \textbf{339}^\circ$

23. $3(\sec^2 x - 1) + 5 \sec x + 1 = 0$

$3 \sec^2 x - 3 + 5 \sec x + 1 = 0$

$3 \sec^2 x + 5 \sec x - 2 = 0$

$(3 \sec x - 1)(\sec x + 2) = 0$

$\sec x = \dfrac{1}{3}$ $\sec x = -2$

$\cos x = 3$ $\cos x = -\dfrac{1}{2}$

   $\varnothing$ $x = \textbf{120}^\circ, \textbf{240}^\circ$

24. $\dfrac{\cos 2x + 1}{2} = \dfrac{2 \cos^2 x - 1 + 1}{2}$

$= \dfrac{2 \cos^2 x}{2} = \cos^2 x$

25. $\dfrac{2 \cot x}{\tan 2x} = \dfrac{2 \cot x}{\dfrac{\sin 2x}{\cos 2x}} = \dfrac{2 \cot x \cos 2x}{\sin 2x}$

$= \dfrac{2 \cos x (\cos^2 x - \sin^2 x)}{\sin x \, 2 \sin x \cos x}$

$= \dfrac{\cos^2 x - \sin^2 x}{\sin^2 x} = \dfrac{\cos^2 x}{\sin^2 x} - 1$

$= \cot^2 x - 1 = \csc^2 x - 1 - 1$

$= \csc^2 x - 2$

26. Refer to Lesson 77, problem 7a.

27. $5^1 = \sqrt{x^2 + 16}$

$25 = x^2 + 16$

$x^2 = 9$

$x = \pm\textbf{3}$

28. $\log \dfrac{8^{2/3}}{3x - 2} = 2$

$4^2 = \dfrac{4}{3x - 2}$

$16(3x - 2) = 4$

$3x = \dfrac{9}{4}$

$x = \dfrac{3}{4}$

29. $4 \log_3 x^{1/4} = \log_3 (3x + 1)$

$\left(\dfrac{1}{4}\right) 4 \log_3 x = \log_3 (3x + 1)$

$\log_3 x = \log_3 (3x + 1)$

$x = 3x + 1$

$2x = -1$

$x = -\dfrac{1}{2}$ **No solution**

30. $2^1 = \log_2 x$

$2^2 = x = \textbf{4}$

EP

45. $-2\begin{bmatrix} -4 & 1 \\ 3 & 6 \end{bmatrix}\begin{bmatrix} 1 & 0 \\ 1 & 1 \end{bmatrix}$

$a_{11} = (-4)(1) + (1)(1) = -3$

$a_{21} = (3)(1) + (6)(1) = 9$

$a_{12} = (-4)(0) + (1)(1) = 1$

$a_{22} = (3)(0) + (6)(1) = 6$

$= -2\begin{bmatrix} -3 & 1 \\ 9 & 6 \end{bmatrix} = \begin{bmatrix} 6 & -2 \\ -18 & -12 \end{bmatrix}$

46. $2(k + 1)^2 + 3(k + 1) = 2k^2 + 4k + 2 +$
$3k + 3 = 2k^2 + 3k + 4k + 5$
$= (2k^2 + 3k) + (4k + 5)$

PROBLEM SET 88

1. $T + U = 9$
$U = 9 - T$
$10U + T = 10T + U + 9$
$-9 = 9T - 9U$
$-1 = T - U$
$-1 = T - 9 + T$
$8 = 2T$
$T = 4$
$U = 9 - 4 = 5$
Original number = **45**

2. $\dfrac{4}{52} + \dfrac{26}{52} - \dfrac{2}{52} = \dfrac{28}{52} = \dfrac{7}{13}$

3. $0.6B = W \qquad\qquad 5R = 10 + 2W$
$W = \dfrac{3}{5}B \qquad\qquad 5R = 10 + 2\left(\dfrac{3B}{5}\right)$
$R = \dfrac{1}{5}\left[10 + 2\left(\dfrac{3B}{5}\right)\right]$
$R + W + B = 140$
$\dfrac{1}{5}\left[10 + 2\left(\dfrac{3B}{5}\right)\right] + \dfrac{3}{5}B + B = 140$
$2 + \dfrac{6}{25}B + \dfrac{3}{5}B + B = 140$
$B = \dfrac{25}{46}(138) = \mathbf{75}$
$W = \dfrac{3}{5}(75) = \mathbf{45}$
$R = \dfrac{1}{5}\left[10 + 2\left(\dfrac{3(75)}{5}\right)\right] = \mathbf{20}$

4. $140g + fg + sg = 4200$
$g(140 + f + s) = 4200$
$g = \dfrac{4200}{140 + f + s}$

5. $\dfrac{4}{\dfrac{14}{a + b} + 3} = \dfrac{4}{\dfrac{14 + 3a + 3b}{a + b}}$

$= \dfrac{4a + 4b}{14 + 3a + 3b}$

6. (a) $\dfrac{n}{2}(a_1 + a_2)$
(b) $a_n = a_1 + (n - 1)d$
$100 = 2 + (n - 1)2$
$n = 50$
$S = \dfrac{50}{2}(2 + 100) = 25(102) = \mathbf{2550}$

7. (a) $s = \dfrac{a_1(1 - r^n)}{1 - r}$
(b) $s = \dfrac{2(1 - (-2)^5)}{1 - (-2)} = \dfrac{2(1 + 32)}{3}$
$= \dfrac{66}{3} = \mathbf{22}$

8. $x^2 + x + 3 = 0$
$x = \dfrac{-1 \pm \sqrt{1 - 4(1)(3)}}{2(1)} = \dfrac{-1 \pm \sqrt{11}\,i}{2}$
$\left(x + \dfrac{1}{2} - i\dfrac{\sqrt{11}}{2}\right)\left(x + \dfrac{1}{2} + i\dfrac{\sqrt{11}}{2}\right)$

9. $\log y = \dfrac{1}{3}\log(5.3 \times 10^4) - 2.5\log(3.2 \times 10^3)$
$\log y = \dfrac{1}{3}(0.7243 + 4) - 2.5(0.5052 + 3)$
$= 1.5748 - 8.7630 = -7.1882$
$y = \text{antilog}\,(-7.1882) = \mathbf{6.5 \times 10^{-8}}$

10. $\text{pH} = -\log H^+ = -(\log 6.2 \times 10^{-4})$
$= -(0.7924 - 4) = \mathbf{3.21}$

11. $H^+ = 10^{-\text{pH}} = 10^{-8.5} = 10^{-8.5 + 9 - 9}$
$= 10^{0.5 - 9} \approx \mathbf{3.2 \times 10^{-9}}$

12.

Term:	1	2	3	4	5	6	7
For x:	6	5	4	3	2	1	0
For y:	0	1	2	3	4	5	6
Coeff:	1	6	15	20	15	6	1

$20x^3(2y)^3 = \mathbf{160x^3y^3}$

13. $x^4 - 4x^3y + 6x^2y^2 - 4xy^3 + y^4$

14.

$$x = \frac{\begin{vmatrix} 0 & 3 & 1 \\ 4 & 0 & 2 \\ -4 & 1 & -3 \end{vmatrix}}{\begin{vmatrix} 2 & 3 & 1 \\ 1 & 0 & 2 \\ 0 & 1 & -3 \end{vmatrix}}$$

$$= \frac{0 - 24 + 4 - 0 - 0 + 36}{0 + 0 + 1 - 0 - 4 + 9} = \frac{16}{6} = \frac{8}{3}$$

15. Refer to Example 84.B.3.

16. Refer to Example 84.A.1.

17. $\log_6 45 = \dfrac{\log 45}{\log 6} \approx 2.12$

18. $AB = DC, AC = DB, BC = BC$ implies $\triangle ABC \cong \triangle DCB$ (SSS).

19.

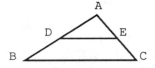

$AD = \frac{1}{2}AB, AE = \frac{1}{2}AC, \angle A = \angle A$
implies $\triangle ADE \sim \triangle ABC$; so $\angle ADE$
$= \angle ABC$. Thus $\overline{DE} \parallel \overline{BC}$; $\dfrac{AD}{AB} = \dfrac{DE}{BC}$
so $\dfrac{DE}{BC} = \dfrac{1}{2}$ and $DE = \dfrac{1}{2}BC$.

20. $(1 \operatorname{cis} 90°)^{1/3}$

$1(\cos 30° + i \sin 30°) = \dfrac{\sqrt{3}}{2} + \dfrac{1}{2}i$

$1(\cos 150° + i \sin 150°) = \dfrac{-\sqrt{3}}{2} + \dfrac{1}{2}i$

$1(\cos 270° + i \sin 270°) = 0 - i$

21.
$$\sqrt{xy} = 6 \qquad\qquad \frac{x + y}{2} = 10$$
$$xy = 36 \qquad\qquad y = 20 - x$$
$$x(20 - x) = 36$$
$$x^2 - 20x + 36 = 0$$
$$(x - 18)(x - 2) = 0$$
$$x = 18, 2$$
$$y = 2, 18$$
2, 18

22. $\sin 3\theta = \dfrac{1}{\sqrt{2}} = \dfrac{\sqrt{2}}{2}$

$3\theta = 45°, 135°, 405°, 495°, 765°, 855°$
$\theta = \mathbf{15°, 45°, 135°, 165°, 255°, 285°}$

23.
$$2(\sec^2 x - 1) + 3 \sec x = 0$$
$$2\sec^2 x + 3 \sec x - 2 = 0$$
$$(2 \sec x - 1)(\sec x + 2) = 0$$

$\sec x = \dfrac{1}{2}$ $\qquad\qquad$ $\sec x = -2$

$\cos x = 2$ $\qquad\qquad$ $\cos x = \dfrac{1}{2}$

$\varnothing$ $\qquad\qquad\qquad$ $x = \mathbf{120°, 240°}$

24.
$$\frac{1 - \cos 2x}{2} = \frac{1 - (1 - 2\sin^2 x)}{2}$$
$$= \frac{2 \sin^2 x}{2} = \sin^2 x$$

25.
$$\frac{2 + \cos 2y - 5 \sin y}{3 + \sin y}$$
$$= \frac{2 + (1 - 2 \sin^2 y) - 5 \sin y}{3 + \sin y}$$
$$= \frac{-2 \sin^2 y - 5 \sin y + 3}{3 + \sin y}$$
$$= \frac{-(2 \sin^2 y + 5 \sin y - 3)}{3 + \sin y}$$
$$= \frac{-(2 \sin y - 1)(\sin y + 3)}{\sin y + 3}$$
$$= 1 - 2 \sin y$$

26.

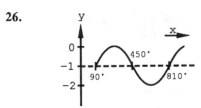

27. $\log_2 x = \dfrac{1}{4}(\log_2 x)^2$

$\dfrac{1}{4}(\log_2 x)^2 - \log_2 x = 0$

$(\log_2 x)\left(\dfrac{1}{4}\log_2 x - 1\right) = 0$

$\log_2 x = 0$ $\qquad\qquad$ $\dfrac{1}{4}\log_2 x - 1 = 0$

$x = 2^0 = \mathbf{1}$ $\qquad\qquad$ $\log_2 x = 4$

$\qquad\qquad\qquad\qquad$ $x = 2^4 = \mathbf{16}$

28. $\ln \dfrac{x^2}{2x - 2} = \ln 2$

$x^2 = 2(2x - 2)$
$x^2 - 4x + 4 = 0$

$$(x - 2)^2 = 0$$
$$x = 2$$

29. $2^1 = \log_3 x$
    $x = 3^2 = 9$

30. $2^3 = 8$

47. $\begin{bmatrix} -1 & 2 \\ 1 & 0 \end{bmatrix} + \begin{bmatrix} 2 & 1 \\ -3 & 0 \end{bmatrix} = \begin{bmatrix} 1 & 3 \\ -2 & 0 \end{bmatrix}$

48. **Valid**

PROBLEM SET 89

1. $S = mT + b$

   $\begin{aligned} 2 &= 40m + b \\ (-) \; 12 &= 80m + b \\ \hline -10 &= -40m \end{aligned}$

   $\dfrac{1}{4} = m$

   $2 = \dfrac{1}{4}(40) + b$

   $b = -8$

   $S = \dfrac{1}{4}(60) - 8 = 7$

2. $\dfrac{1}{12}T = S$

   $T = S + 5$

   $T = \dfrac{1}{12}T + 5$

   $\dfrac{11}{12}T = 5$

   $T = \dfrac{60}{11} = 5\dfrac{5}{11}$ **min**

3. $4100 = 4200\, e^{20k}$
   $0.976 = e^{20k}$
   $\ln 0.976 = \ln e^{20k}$
   $20k \approx -0.02429$
   $k \approx -0.0012$

   $2100 = 4200\, e^{-0.0012t}$
   $0.5 = e^{-0.0012t}$
   $\ln 0.5 = \ln e^{-0.0012t}$
   $-0.0012t \approx -0.693$
   $t \approx$ **575.3 min**

4. Rate $\cdot$ time $\cdot$ men $=$ jobs
   Rate $\cdot h \cdot K = 40$
   Rate $= \dfrac{40}{hK}$

   $\dfrac{40}{hK} \cdot 14 \cdot$ men $= m$

   Men $= \dfrac{mhK}{560}$

5. $\dfrac{10!}{6!4!} = 210$

6. $-2 \begin{vmatrix} 1 & 2 \\ 1 & 0 \end{vmatrix} - 0 \begin{vmatrix} 3 & 2 \\ 1 & 0 \end{vmatrix} + 1 \begin{vmatrix} 3 & 1 \\ 1 & 1 \end{vmatrix}$
   $= (-2)(0 - 2) - 0 + 1(3 - 1) = 4 + 2 = 6$

7. $-2 \begin{vmatrix} 1 & 2 \\ 1 & -1 \end{vmatrix} - 0 \begin{vmatrix} 0 & 2 \\ 3 & -1 \end{vmatrix} + 1 \begin{vmatrix} 0 & 1 \\ 3 & 1 \end{vmatrix}$
   $= -2(-1 - 2) + 3(0 - 3) = 6 - 9 = -3$

8. (a) $S_n = \dfrac{n}{2}(a_1 + a_n)$

   (b) $46 = -2 + (n - 1)6$
   $46 = -2 + 6n - 6$
   $54 = 6n$
   $n = 9$

   $S_n = \dfrac{9}{2}(-2 + 46) = \dfrac{9}{2}(44) = 198$

9. (a) $S_n = \dfrac{a_1(1 - r^n)}{1 - r}$

   (b) $S_6 = \dfrac{1\left[1 - \left(-\dfrac{1}{2}\right)^6\right]}{1 - \left(-\dfrac{1}{2}\right)}$

   $= \dfrac{1 - \dfrac{1}{64}}{\dfrac{3}{2}} = \dfrac{\dfrac{63}{64}}{\dfrac{3}{2}} = \dfrac{21}{32}$

10. $\log y = \log (3.3 \times 10^{10}) - \log (2.2 \times 10^6)$
$= 10.5185 - 6.3424 = 4.1761$
$y = $ antilog $4.1761 = \mathbf{1.5 \times 10^4}$

11. $x - 3y + 5 = 0$
The point $(1, 2)$ gives $1 - 3(2) + 5 = 0$;
$0 = 0$; the distance is **0**.

12. $\text{pH} = -\log \text{H}^+ = -\log (4.4 \times 10^{-4})$
$= -(0.6435 - 4) = -(-3.3565) = \mathbf{3.4}$

13.

Term:	1	2	3	4	5	6	7
For x:	6	5	4	3	2	1	0
For y:	0	1	2	3	4	5	6
Coeff:	1	6	15	20	15	6	1

$15x^2(-2y)^4 = \mathbf{240x^2y^4}$

14. $(3x)^2 + 3(3x)^2(-2y) + 3(3x)(-2y)^2 + (-2y)^3$
$= \mathbf{27x^3 - 54x^2y + 36xy^2 - 8y^3}$

15.
$$x = \frac{\begin{vmatrix} 0 & 1 & 1 \\ 5 & 2 & 3 \\ 1 & 3 & 0 \end{vmatrix}}{\begin{vmatrix} 2 & 1 & 1 \\ 0 & 2 & 3 \\ 1 & 3 & 0 \end{vmatrix}}$$
$$= \frac{0 + 3 + 15 - 2 - 0 - 0}{0 + 3 + 0 - 2 - 18 - 0} = -\frac{16}{17}$$

16. Refer to Example 84.B.4.

17. $\log_5 30 = \dfrac{\log 30}{\log 5} \approx \mathbf{2.1}$

18. $AB = DC, AC = DB, BC = BC$ implies
$\triangle ABC \cong \triangle DCB$; therefore $\angle A = \angle D$.

19. $\triangle CDA$ and $\triangle ABC$ are right triangles. CD
$= AB$ and $CA = CA$ so $\triangle CDA \cong \triangle ABC$
(HL); therefore $CB = AD$.

20. $(1 \text{ cis } 180°)^{1/3}$

$1(\cos 60° + i \sin 60°) = \dfrac{1}{2} + \dfrac{\sqrt{3}}{2}i$

$1(\cos 180° + i \sin 180°) = -1$

$1(\cos 300° + i \sin 300°) = \dfrac{1}{2} - \dfrac{\sqrt{3}}{2}i$

21. $a_4 = a_1 r^3 = 256\left(\dfrac{1}{4}\right)^3 = 256\left(\dfrac{1}{64}\right) = \mathbf{4 \text{ ft}}$

22. $\cos 3x = \dfrac{2}{\sqrt{2}} = \dfrac{\sqrt{2}}{2}$
$3x = 45°, 315°, 405°, 675°, 765°, 1035°$
$x = \mathbf{15°, 105°, 135°, 225°, 255°, 345°}$

23. $(\tan^2 \theta + 1) - 2 \tan \theta - 4 = 0$
$\tan^2 \theta - 2 \tan \theta - 3 = 0$
$(\tan \theta + 1)(\tan \theta - 3) = 0$
$\tan \theta = -1 \qquad\qquad \tan \theta = 3$
$\theta = \mathbf{135°, 315°} \qquad \theta \approx \mathbf{71.6°, 251.6°}$

24. $\dfrac{1}{2} \sin 2x \sec x = \dfrac{1}{2}(2 \sin x \cos x)\dfrac{1}{\cos x} = \sin x$

25. $\dfrac{1 + \cos 2x}{\sin 2x} = \dfrac{1 + (2\cos^2 x - 1)}{2 \cos x \sin x}$
$= \dfrac{2\cos^2 x}{2 \sin x \cos x} = \dfrac{\cos x}{\sin x} = \cot x$

26. (a) $y = \mathbf{\tan x}$

(b) $y = \mathbf{-7 + 4 \sec x}$

27. $\log_3 x = \dfrac{1}{4}(\log_3 x)^2$

$\dfrac{1}{4}(\log_3 x)^2 - \log_3 x = 0$

$(\log_3 x)\left(\dfrac{1}{4}\log_3 x - 1\right) = 0$

$\log_3 x = 0 \qquad\qquad \dfrac{1}{4}\log_3 x = 1$
$x = 3^0 = \mathbf{1} \qquad\qquad \log_3 x = 4$
$\qquad\qquad\qquad\qquad x = 3^4 = \mathbf{81}$

28. $3^1 = \log_2 x$
$x = 2^3 = \mathbf{8}$

29. $\ln \dfrac{2x + 6}{x - 3} = \ln x$
$\dfrac{2x + 6}{x - 3} = x$
$2x + 6 = x(x - 3)$
$x^2 - 5x - 6 = 0$
$(x - 6)(x + 1) = 0$
$x = \mathbf{6}$

30. $3^{-2} = \dfrac{1}{3^2} = \dfrac{1}{9}$

49. $\begin{bmatrix} 0 & 1 \\ -5 & 6 \end{bmatrix} \cdot \begin{bmatrix} 3 & -4 \\ 4 & 7 \end{bmatrix}$

$= \begin{bmatrix} 0(3) + (1)(4) & (0)(-4) + (1)(7) \\ (-5)(3) + (6)(4) & (-5)(-4) + (6)(7) \end{bmatrix}$

$= \begin{bmatrix} 4 & 7 \\ 9 & 62 \end{bmatrix}$

50. $\dfrac{(k + 1)[3(k + 1) - 1]}{2}$

$= \dfrac{(k + 1)[3k + 3 - 1]}{2}$

$= \dfrac{(k + 1)(3k + 2)}{2} = \dfrac{3k^2 + 5k + 2}{2}$

$= \dfrac{3k^2 - k + 6k + 2}{2} = \dfrac{3k^2 - k}{2} + \dfrac{6k + 2}{2}$

$= \dfrac{k(3k - 1)}{2} + (3k + 1)$

PROBLEM SET 90

1. $60 = 42\,e^{8k}$

$1.4285 = e^{8k}$

$\ln 1.4285 = \ln e^{8k}$

$8k \approx 0.35667$

$k \approx 0.04458$

$A_t = 42\,e^{0.04458} = 42\,e^{0.04458(30)} = \mathbf{160}$

2. $R_M T_M + R_D T_D = \text{jobs}$

$\dfrac{4}{5}t + \dfrac{7}{3}t = 47$

$\dfrac{47}{15}t = 47$

$t = \mathbf{15\ hr}$

3. Rate $\cdot$ time $\cdot$ men = jobs

Rate $\cdot c \cdot 8 = b$

Rate $= \dfrac{b}{8c}$

$\dfrac{b}{8c} \cdot \text{time} \cdot (8 + d) = 9$

Time $= \dfrac{72c}{8b + bd}$

4. $\dfrac{10!}{4!6!} = \mathbf{210}$

5. Linear = radius × angular

$20\ \text{in}\left(\dfrac{1\ \text{ft}}{12\ \text{in}}\right)\left(\dfrac{1\ \text{mi}}{5280\ \text{ft}}\right)$

$\times \left(200\dfrac{\text{rad}}{\text{sec}}\right)\left(\dfrac{60\ \text{sec}}{1\ \text{min}}\right)\left(\dfrac{60\ \text{min}}{1\ \text{hr}}\right)$

$= \dfrac{(20)(200)(60)(60)}{(12)(5280)}\ \dfrac{\text{mi}}{\text{hr}}$

6. $\dfrac{x + 3}{10} = \dfrac{x + 4.2}{12}$

$12(x + 3) = 10(x + 4.2)$

$2x = 6$

$x = 3$

7. $\overline{AB} \parallel \overline{DE}$ implies $\dfrac{DC}{AD} = \dfrac{CE}{EB}$, $\angle EDC$

$= \angle BAD$. $\overline{DE}$ is an angle bisector so $\angle BDE$

$= \angle EDC$; $\angle BDE = \angle DBA$ implies $\angle DBA$

$= \angle BDE = \angle EDC = \angle BAD$. Therefore

$\angle DBA = \angle BAD$ and $AD = DB$; thus

$\dfrac{DC}{DB} = \dfrac{EC}{BE}$

8. $AD = BC$, $DB = AC$, $AB = AB$ so

$\triangle ADB \cong \triangle BCA$ and $\angle DBA = \angle CAB$.

9. $\dfrac{8}{x} = \dfrac{12}{8}$

$12x = 64$

$x = \dfrac{64}{12} = \dfrac{16}{3}$

10.

Term:	1	2	3	4	5
For x:	4	3	2	1	0
For y:	0	1	2	3	4
Coeff:	1	4	65	4	1

$4(2x)^1(-3y)^3 = -216xy^3$

11. $-1\begin{vmatrix} 2 & 0 \\ 0 & -2 \end{vmatrix} - 0\begin{vmatrix} 3 & 0 \\ 1 & -2 \end{vmatrix} + 2\begin{vmatrix} 3 & 2 \\ 1 & 0 \end{vmatrix}$

$= -1(-4 - 0) + 2(0 - 2) = 4 - 4 = 0$

12.

$$x = \dfrac{\begin{vmatrix} -3 & 1 & 2 \\ 5 & 0 & -1 \\ 1 & 2 & 1 \end{vmatrix}}{\begin{vmatrix} 1 & 1 & 2 \\ 2 & 0 & -1 \\ 0 & 2 & 1 \end{vmatrix}}$$

$$= \dfrac{-3\begin{vmatrix} 0 & -1 \\ 2 & 1 \end{vmatrix} - 1\begin{vmatrix} 5 & -1 \\ 1 & 1 \end{vmatrix} + 2\begin{vmatrix} 5 & 0 \\ 1 & 2 \end{vmatrix}}{1\begin{vmatrix} 0 & -1 \\ 2 & 1 \end{vmatrix} - 1\begin{vmatrix} 2 & -1 \\ 0 & 1 \end{vmatrix} + 2\begin{vmatrix} 2 & 0 \\ 0 & 2 \end{vmatrix}}$$

$$= \dfrac{-3(0+2) - 1(5+1) + 2(10-0)}{1(0+2) - 1(2-0) + 2(4-0)}$$

$$= \dfrac{-6 - 6 + 20}{2 - 2 + 8} = \dfrac{8}{8} = 1$$

13. (a) Refer to Lesson 88.

(b) $S_n = \dfrac{n}{2}(a_1 + a_n)$

$a_n = a_1 + (n-1)d$

$36 = -4 + (n-1)4$

$36 = -4 + 4n - 4$

$44 = 4n$

$n = 11$

$S_n = \dfrac{11}{2}(-4 + 36) = 176$

14. (a) $S_n = \dfrac{a_1(1 - r^n)}{1 - r}$

(b) $S_7 = \dfrac{5(1 - 3^7)}{1 - 3} = \dfrac{5(1 - 2187)}{-2}$

$S_7 = \dfrac{-10930}{-2} = 5465$

15. $\log y = \dfrac{1}{3}(\log 2.2 \times 10^4) - 1.5(\log 10^3)$

$= \dfrac{1}{3}(0.34 + 4) - 1.5(3)$

$= 1.45 - 4.5 = -3.05 + 4 - 4$

$= 0.95 - 4$

$y = \text{antilog } (0.95) - 4 \approx 8.9 \times 10^{-4}$

16. $\log y = \log (3.6 \times 10^{11}) + \log (2.5 \times 10^{20})$

$= 11.56 + 20.4 = 31.96$

$y = \text{antilog } 31.96 \approx 9 \times 10^{31}$

17. $H^+ = 10^{-pH} = 10^{-8.5} = 10^{-8.5 + 9 - 9}$

$= 10^{0.5 - 9} \approx 3.16 \times 10^{-9}$

18. Refer to Example 84.B.2.

19. $\log_6 22 = \dfrac{\log 22}{\log 6} \approx 1.73$

20. $r = \sqrt{3^2 + 5^2} = \sqrt{34} \approx 5.8$

$\tan \theta = \dfrac{3}{-5}$ (in Q II), $\theta \approx 149°$

$(5.8 \text{ cis } 149°)^{1/3}$ First root is

$5.8^{1/3} \text{ cis } \dfrac{149°}{3} \approx 1.8 \text{ cis } 49.7°$

Angles of cube root differ by $\dfrac{360°}{3} = 120°$

$1.8 \text{ cis } 169.7°, 1.8 \text{ cis } 289.7°$

21. $-\sqrt{xy} = -8 \qquad\qquad \dfrac{x+y}{2} = -10$

$xy = 64 \qquad\qquad\qquad y = -20 - x$

$x(-20 - x) = 64$

$-20x - x^2 = 64$

$x^2 + 20x + 64 = 0$

$(x + 16)(x + 4) = 0$

$x = -16, -4$

$y = -4, -16$

$-4, -16$

22. $\cos 2x = \dfrac{\sqrt{2}}{2}$

$2x = 45°, 315°, 405°, 675°$

$x = 22.5°, 157.5°, 202.5°, 337.5°$

23. $\tan^2 x = 1 - 2\tan^2 x$

$3\tan^2 x = 1$

$\tan^2 x = \dfrac{1}{3}$

$\tan x = \pm\dfrac{\sqrt{3}}{3}$

$x = 30°, 150°, 210°, 330°$

The values that work are $150°, 330°$.

24. $(\cos x - \sin x)(\cos x + \sin x)$

$= \cos^2 x - \sin^2 x = \cos 2x$

25. $\dfrac{\tan x + 1}{\tan x - 1} = \dfrac{\dfrac{\sin x}{\cos x} \cdot \dfrac{1}{\sin x} + 1 \cdot \dfrac{1}{\sin x}}{\dfrac{\sin x}{\cos x} \cdot \dfrac{1}{\sin x} - 1 \cdot \dfrac{1}{\sin x}}$

$= \dfrac{\sec x + \csc x}{\sec x - \csc x}$

26. Refer to Lesson 77.B.

27. $\log_4 x = \frac{1}{4}(\log_4 x)^2$

$\frac{1}{4}(\log_4 x)^2 - \log_4 x = 0$

$(\log_4 x)\left(\frac{1}{4}\log_4 x - 1\right) = 0$

$\log_4 x = 0 \qquad\qquad \log_4 x = 4$

$x = 4^0 = \mathbf{1} \qquad\quad x = 4^4 = \mathbf{256}$

28. $4^1 = \log_2 x$

$x = 2^4 = \mathbf{16}$

29. $4 \log x = (\log x)^2$

$(\log x)^2 - 4\log x = 0$

$(\log x)(\log x - 4) = 0$

$\log x = 0 \qquad\qquad \log x = 4$

$x = 10^0 = \mathbf{1} \qquad\quad x = \mathbf{10^4}$

30. $(e^{\ln 3})^2 \cdot (e^{\ln 2})^{-1} = 3^2 \cdot 2^{-1} = 9 \cdot \frac{1}{2} = \dfrac{\mathbf{9}}{\mathbf{2}}$

EP

51. $-\frac{1}{2}X = \begin{bmatrix} 3 & 4 \\ 2 & \end{bmatrix} - \begin{bmatrix} -1 & 2 \\ 4 & -5 \end{bmatrix} = \begin{bmatrix} 4 & 2 \\ -2 & -1 \end{bmatrix}$

$X = -2\begin{bmatrix} 4 & 2 \\ -2 & -1 \end{bmatrix} = \begin{bmatrix} \mathbf{-8} & \mathbf{-4} \\ \mathbf{4} & \mathbf{2} \end{bmatrix}$

52. $\dfrac{k(2k - 1)(2k + 1) + 3(2k + 1)^2}{3}$

$= \dfrac{(2k + 1)[k(2k - 1) + 3(2k + 1)]}{3}$

$= \dfrac{(2k + 1)(2k^2 - k + 6k + 3)}{3}$

$= \dfrac{(2k + 1)(2k^2 + 5k + 3)}{3}$

$= \dfrac{(k + 1)(2k + 1)(2k + 3)}{3}$

$= \dfrac{(k + 1)[2(k + 1) - 1][2(k + 1) + 1]}{3}$

PROBLEM SET 91

1. $\frac{3}{7}x = 12{,}600$

$x = 29{,}400$

$\frac{4}{21}(29{,}400) = \mathbf{\$5600}$

2.

	Trip back	Trip out
Distance:	72 mi	72 mi
Time:	18 hr	6 hr
Rate:	4 mph	**12 mph**

The times come from $t + \frac{1}{3}t = 24$

3. $380 = 400\,e^{20k}$

$0.95 = e^{20k}$

$\ln 0.95 = \ln e^{20k}$

$20k \approx -0.05129$

$k \approx -0.00256$

$200 = 400e^{-0.00256t}$

$0.5 = e^{-0.00256t}$

$\ln 0.5 = \ln e^{-0.00256t}$

$-0.00256t \approx -0.693$

$t \approx \mathbf{270.3\ min}$

4. $v = \omega r$

$300\,\dfrac{\text{rad}}{\text{min}} \times 1\,\text{m} \times \dfrac{100\,\text{cm}}{1\,\text{m}}$

$\times \dfrac{1\,\text{in}}{2.54\,\text{cm}} \times \dfrac{1\,\text{ft}}{12\,\text{in}} \times \dfrac{1\,\text{mi}}{5280\,\text{ft}}$

$= \dfrac{(30)(1)(100)}{(2.54)(12)(5280)}\,\dfrac{\text{mi}}{\text{min}} \approx 1.12\,\dfrac{\text{mi}}{\text{min}}$

5. $(9 - 1)! = 8! = \mathbf{40{,}320}$

6. $(x + 2)^2 + (y - 3)^2 = 3^2$

$(x + 2)^2 + (y - 3)^2 = 9$

$x^2 + 4x + 4 + y^2 - 6y + 9 = 9$

$\mathbf{x^2 + y^2 + 4x - 6y + 4 = 0}$

7. $(x^2 - 10x + 25) + 2(y^2 + 4y + 4)$

$= -29 + 25 + 8$

$(x - 5)^2 + 2(y + 2)^2 = 4$

$\dfrac{(x - 5)^2}{4} + \dfrac{(y + 2)^2}{2} = 1$

Center: (5, –2)

Major axis: 4

Minor axis: $2\sqrt{2}$

8. $9(x^2 + 6x + 9) + 4(y^2 - 2y + 1)$
$= -49 + 81 + 4$
$\dfrac{9(x + 3)^2}{36} + \dfrac{4(y - 1)^2}{36} = \dfrac{36}{36}$
$\dfrac{(x + 3)^2}{4} + \dfrac{(y - 1)^2}{9} = 1$
Center: **(−3, 1)**
Major axis: **6**
Minor axis: **4**

9. $(x^2 - 2x + 1) - (y^2 + 4y + 4)$
$= 4 + 1 - 4$
$(x - 1)^2 - (y + 2)^2 = 1$
Center: **(1, −2)**
Vertices: **(2, −2), (0, −2)**
Asymptotes: $y = -x - 1$
$\qquad\qquad\quad y = x - 3$

10. $4(x^2 + 2x + 1) - (y^2 + 4y + 4)$
$= 4 + 4 - 4$
$\dfrac{4(x + 1)^2}{4} - \dfrac{(y + 2)^2}{4} = \dfrac{4}{4}$
$\dfrac{(x + 1)^2}{1} - \dfrac{(y + 2)^2}{4} = 1$
Center: **(−1, −2)**
Vertices: **(0, −2), (−2, −2)**
Asymptotes: $y = 2x$
$\qquad\qquad\quad y = -2x - 4$

11. $\overline{DE}$ is the angle bisector of $\angle BDC$ implies
$\angle BDE = \angle EDC,\ \overline{AB}\ \|\ \overline{DE}$ implies
$\angle BDE = \angle ABD$ and $\angle EDC = \angle BAD$; so
$\angle ABD = \angle BAD$ and $AD = DB$.
$\overline{AB}\ \|\ \overline{DE}$ implies $\dfrac{DC}{AD} = \dfrac{EC}{BE}$. Substitute
to get $\dfrac{DC}{DB} = \dfrac{EC}{BE}$.

12. $\dfrac{9}{12} = \dfrac{6}{x}$
$9x = 72$
$x = 8$

13. $\overline{BD} \perp \overline{AC},\ \overline{EC} \perp \overline{AB}$ implies
$\triangle BDA$ and $\triangle CEA$ are right triangles. $\angle A$
$= \angle A$ implies $\triangle BDA \sim \triangle CEA$. $AB = AC$
so $SF = 1$, and $\triangle BDA \cong \triangle CEA$ so $BD = CE$.

14. $\dfrac{x}{8} = \dfrac{15}{10}$
$10x = 120$
$x = 12$

15.

Term:	1	2	3	4	5	6	7
For x:	6	5	4	3	2	1	0
For y:	0	1	2	3	4	5	6
Coeff:	1	6	15	20	15	6	1

$15(3x)^4(-2y)^2 = 15(81x^4)(4y^2)$
$= \mathbf{4860x^4y^2}$

16. $y = \dfrac{\begin{vmatrix} 2 & 2 & 2 \\ 0 & 5 & 1 \\ 1 & 2 & 0 \end{vmatrix}}{\begin{vmatrix} 2 & 1 & 2 \\ 0 & 2 & 1 \\ 1 & 3 & 0 \end{vmatrix}}$

$= \dfrac{2\begin{vmatrix} 5 & 1 \\ 2 & 0 \end{vmatrix} - 2\begin{vmatrix} 0 & 1 \\ 1 & 0 \end{vmatrix} + 2\begin{vmatrix} 0 & 5 \\ 1 & 2 \end{vmatrix}}{2\begin{vmatrix} 2 & 1 \\ 3 & 0 \end{vmatrix} - 1\begin{vmatrix} 0 & 1 \\ 1 & 0 \end{vmatrix} + 2\begin{vmatrix} 0 & 2 \\ 1 & 3 \end{vmatrix}}$

$= \dfrac{2(0 - 2) - 2(0 - 1) + 2(0 - 5)}{2(0 - 3) - 1(0 - 1) + 2(0 - 2)}$
$= \dfrac{-12}{-9} = \dfrac{4}{3}$

17. (a) Refer to Lesson 88.A.
(b) $a_n = a_1 + (n - 1)d$
$24 = -8 + (n - 1)(4)$
$32 = 4n - 4$
$36 = 4n$
$n = 9$
$S_n = \dfrac{n}{2}(a_1 + a_n) = \dfrac{9}{2}(-8 + 24)$

$S_n = \dfrac{9}{2}(16) = \mathbf{72}$

18. (a) Refer to Example 88.B.1
(b) $S_n = \dfrac{4[1 - (-2)^7]}{1 - (-2)}$
$= \dfrac{4[1 - (-128)]}{1 + 2}$
$= \dfrac{4(129)}{3} = \mathbf{172}$

19. $\log y = \frac{1}{4} \log (6.4 \times 10^4)$

$\quad\quad - 1.4 \log (2.1 \times 10^3)$

$\log y = \frac{1}{4} (0.8062 + 4) - 1.4(0.3222 + 3)$

$\log y = \frac{1}{4} (4.8062) - 1.4(3.3222)$

$\log y = 1.2016 - 4.6511 = -3.4495$

$y = \text{antilog} (-3.4495 + 4) - 4$

$\quad = \text{antilog} (0.5505) - 4 = \mathbf{3.6 \times 10^{-4}}$

20. $H^+ = 10^{-pH} = 10^{-3.5}$

$H^+ = \mathbf{3.16 \times 10^{-4} \frac{mole}{liter}}$

21. Refer to Example 84.A.1.

22. $\log_5 45 = \frac{\log 45}{\log 5} \approx \mathbf{2.37}$

23. $r = \sqrt{(-6)^2 + 4^2} = \sqrt{52} \approx 7.2$

$\tan \theta = \frac{4}{6}$ (in Q II) $\theta \approx 146.3°$

$(7.2 \text{ cis } 142.3°)^{1/4} = 7.2^{1/4} \text{ cis } \frac{142.3°}{4}$

$\approx \mathbf{1.6 \text{ cis } 36.6°}$; angles differ by $90°$

$\mathbf{1.6 \text{ cis } 126.6°, \ 1.6 \text{ cis } 216.6°, \ 1.6 \text{ cis } 306.6°}$

24. $\tan 36° = \frac{2.5}{h}$

$h = \frac{2.5}{\tan 36°} \approx 3.44$

$\text{Area}_\Delta = \frac{1}{2} (5)(3.44) \approx 8.6$

$\text{Area}_{pent} = 5(8.6) \approx \mathbf{43 \ cm^2}$

25. $2 \sin^2 x + \sqrt{3} \cos^2 x = 0$

$\sin x (2 \sin x + \sqrt{3}) = 0$

$\sin x = 0 \quad\quad\quad\quad 2 \sin x + \sqrt{3} = 0$

$x = \mathbf{0°, 180°} \quad\quad\quad x = \mathbf{240°, 300°}$

26. $\frac{\sin^3 x + \cos^3 x}{\sin x + \cos x} = \sin x + \cos x$

$\times \ \frac{\sin^2 x - \sin x \cos x + \cos^2 x}{\sin x + \cos x}$

$= 1 - \sin x \cos x = 1 - \frac{1}{2} \sin 2x$

27. $\frac{\cot x + 1}{\cot x - 1} = \frac{\frac{\cos x}{\sin x} + 1}{\frac{\cos x}{\sin x} - 1} \cdot \frac{\frac{1}{\cos x}}{\frac{1}{\cos x}}$

$= \frac{\frac{1}{\sin x} + \frac{1}{\cos x}}{\frac{1}{\sin x} - \frac{1}{\cos x}} = \frac{\csc x + \sec x}{\csc x - \sec x}$

28.

29. $\log_3 25^{1/2} - \log_3 (2x - 5) = 2$

$\log_3 \frac{5}{2x - 5} = 2$

$3^2 = \frac{5}{2x - 5}$

$9(2x - 5) = 5$

$18x = 50$

$x = \frac{25}{9}$

30. $\log_2 3 = \log_2 x^2$

$x^2 = 3$

$x = \sqrt{3}$

EP

53. $\frac{k(2k + 3) + 1}{(2k + 1)(2k + 3)} = \frac{2k^2 + 3k + 1}{(2k + 1)(2k + 3)}$

$= \frac{(2k + 1)(k + 1)}{(2k + 1)(2k + 3)} = \frac{k + 1}{[2(k + 1) + 1]}$

54. $\begin{bmatrix} 1 & -2 \\ -1 & 1 \end{bmatrix} \cdot \begin{bmatrix} 1 & -2 \\ -1 & 2 \end{bmatrix}$

$= \begin{bmatrix} (1)(1) + (-2)(-1) & (1)(-2) + (-2)(2) \\ (-1)(1) + (1)(-1) & (-1)(-2) + (1)(2) \end{bmatrix}$

$= \begin{bmatrix} 3 & -6 \\ -2 & 4 \end{bmatrix}$

PROBLEM SET 92

1. $\omega = \dfrac{v}{r}$

$$\dfrac{2\pi \times \dfrac{200\ \text{mi}}{\text{hr}} \times \dfrac{1\ \text{hr}}{60\ \text{min}}}{4\ \text{m}} \times \dfrac{100\ \text{cm}}{1\ \text{m}}$$

$$\times \dfrac{1\ \text{in}}{2.54\ \text{cm}} \times \dfrac{1\ \text{ft}}{12\ \text{in}} \times \dfrac{1\ \text{mi}}{5280\ \text{ft}}$$

$$= \dfrac{(2\pi)(200)(2.54)(12)(5280)}{(0.4)(100)(60)}\ \dfrac{\text{rad}}{\text{min}}$$

$$\approx 84{,}265\ \dfrac{\text{rad}}{\text{min}}$$

2.

	Driver 1	Driver 2
Time:	h hr	$(h - 2)$ hr
Rate:	35 mph	40 mph
Distance:	$(35\ \text{mph})(h\ \text{hr})$	$(40\ \text{mph})[(h - 2)\text{hr}]$

dist 1 − dist 2 $= 35h - (40h - 80)$

$\qquad\qquad\qquad = 80 - 5h$

Driver 1 drove **$(80 - 5h)$ mi** farther.

3.

	Nellie	Captain
Distance:	k	$\dfrac{k}{2}$
Time:	m	$3m$
Rate:	$\dfrac{k}{m}$	$\dfrac{\frac{k}{2}}{3m} = \dfrac{k}{6m}$

4. Overall average speed $= \dfrac{\text{total distance}}{\text{total time}}$

$$= \dfrac{a + c}{b + d}$$

$$\left(\dfrac{a + c}{b + d}\right)\text{Time} = 1000$$

$$\text{Time} = \dfrac{1000\ (b + d)}{a + c}\ \text{hr}$$

5. $(0.62) + (0.35) + P = (0.80)$

$P = (0.62) + (0.35) - (0.80) = \mathbf{0.17}$

6. $(x - 2)^2 + (y - 3)^2 = 4$

$x^2 - 4x + 4 + y^2 - 6y + 9 = 4$

$\mathbf{x^2 + y^2 - 4x - 6y + 9 = 0}$

7. $(x^2 + 10x + 25) + 4(y^2 + 6y + 9)$

$= -45 + 25 + 36$

$\dfrac{(x + 5)^2}{16} + \dfrac{4(y + 3)^2}{16} = \dfrac{16}{16}$

$\dfrac{(x + 5)^2}{16} + \dfrac{(x + 3)^2}{4} = 1$

Center: $(-5, -3)$

Major axis: 8

Minor axis: 4

8. $4(x^2 - 4x + 4) + 9(y^2 + 2y + 1)$

$= 11 + 16 + 9$

$\dfrac{4(x - 2)^2}{36} + \dfrac{9(y + 1)^2}{36} = \dfrac{36}{36}$

$\dfrac{(x - 2)^2}{9} + \dfrac{(y + 1)^2}{4} = 1$

Center: $(2, -1)$

Major axis: 6

Minor axis: 4

9. $4(x^2 + 4x + 4) - (y^2 + 4y + 4)$

$= 4 + 16 - 4$

$\dfrac{4(x + 2)^2}{16} - \dfrac{(y + 2)^2}{16} = \dfrac{16}{16}$

$\dfrac{(x + 2)^2}{4} - \dfrac{(y + 2)^2}{16} = 1$

Center: $(-2, -2)$

Vertices: $(0, -2), (-4, -2)$

Asymptotes: $y = 2x + 2$

$\qquad\qquad\quad y = -2x - 6$

10. $(x^2 - 2x + 1) - (y^2 + 4y + 4) = 4 + 1 - 4$

$(x - 1)^2 - (y + 2)^2 = 1$

Center: $(1, -2)$

Vertices: $(0, -2), (2, -2)$

Asymptotes: $y = x - 3$

$\qquad\qquad\quad y = -x - 1$

11. Refer to Lesson 90.B.

12. $\dfrac{4}{x} = \dfrac{6}{4}$

$6x = 16$

$x = \dfrac{16}{6} = \dfrac{8}{3}$

13. $\triangle ABD$ and $\triangle ACE$ are right triangles. $\angle A = \angle A$ implies $\triangle ABD \sim \triangle ACE$. $AE = AD$; thus $\triangle ABD \cong \triangle ACE$ and $AB = AC$. Therefore $\triangle ABC$ is an isosceles triangle.

14. $\dfrac{x}{3} = \dfrac{8}{4}$

$4x = 24$

$x = \dfrac{24}{4} = 6$

15.

Term:	1	2	3	4	5	6	7	8
For x:	7	6	5	4	3	2	1	0
For y:	0	1	2	3	4	5	6	7
Coeff:	1	7	21	35	45	21	7	1

$35(x)^4(-3y)^3 = -945x^4y^3$

16.

$$\begin{bmatrix} 2 & 1 & 1 & 0 \\ 0 & 2 & -1 & -1 \\ 3 & -1 & 0 & -7 \end{bmatrix} = \begin{bmatrix} 1 & \frac{1}{2} & \frac{1}{2} & 0 \\ 0 & 2 & -1 & -1 \\ 0 & -\frac{5}{2} & -\frac{3}{2} & -7 \end{bmatrix}$$

$$= \begin{bmatrix} 1 & 0 & \frac{1}{2} & -\frac{1}{2} \\ 0 & 1 & -\frac{1}{2} & -\frac{1}{2} \\ 0 & 0 & -\frac{11}{4} & -\frac{33}{4} \end{bmatrix} = \begin{bmatrix} 1 & 0 & 0 & -2 \\ 0 & 1 & 0 & 1 \\ 0 & 0 & 1 & 3 \end{bmatrix}$$

$x = -2, y = 1, z = 3$

17. (a) $\dfrac{a_1(1 - r^n)}{1 - r}$

(b) $S_n = \dfrac{-4(1 - r^n)}{1 - r} = \dfrac{-4[1 - (-2)^8]}{1 - (-2)}$

$= \dfrac{-4(1 + 256)}{3} = \dfrac{1020}{3} = 340$

18. (a) $a_n = a_1 + (n - 1)d$

(b) $30 = -2 + (n - 1)(4)$

$32 = 4n - 4$

$36 = 4n$

$n = 9$

$S_n = \dfrac{n}{2}(a_1 + a_n)$

$S_9 = \dfrac{9}{2}(-2 + 30) = \dfrac{9}{2}(28) = 126$

19. $\text{pH} = -\log H^+ = -\log 6.5 \times 10^{-6} = 5.19$

20. $\log y = \dfrac{1}{3}\log(2.8 \times 10^4) - 0.8\log(3.6 \times 10^3)$

$\log y = \dfrac{1}{3}(0.4472 + 4) - 0.8(0.5563 + 3)$

$= 1.4824 - 2.8450 = -1.3626$

$y = \text{antilog}(-1.3626) = 4.3 \times 10^{-2}$

21. Refer to Example 84.A.4.

22. $r = \sqrt{2^2 + (-3)^2} = \sqrt{13} \approx 3.6$

$\tan\theta = \dfrac{2}{3}$ (in QII), $\theta \approx 146.3°$

$(3.6 \text{ cis } 146.3°)^{1/2} = 3.6^{1/2}\text{ cis }\dfrac{146.3°}{2}$

$\approx$ **1.9 cis 73.15°**; angles differ by $180°$

1.9 cis 253.15°

23. $\log_5 60 = \dfrac{\log 60}{\log 5}$

24. **360°**

25. $2\sin^2 x + 15\cos x - 9 = 0$

$2(1 - \cos^2 x) + 15\cos x - 9 = 0$

$2 - 2\cos^2 x + 15\cos x - 9 = 0$

$2\cos^2 x - 15\cos x + 7 = 0$

$(2\cos x - 1)(\cos x - 7) = 0$

$\cos x = \dfrac{1}{2}$ $\qquad\qquad \cos x = 7$

$x = 60°, 300°$ $\qquad\qquad \varnothing$

26. $\dfrac{\sin x + \cos x}{\tan^2 x - 1} = \dfrac{\sin x + \cos x}{\dfrac{\sin^2 x}{\cos^2 x} - 1}$

$= \dfrac{\sin x + \cos x}{\dfrac{\sin^2 x - \cos^2 x}{\cos^2 x}} = \dfrac{(\cos^2 x)(\sin x + \cos x)}{\sin^2 x - \cos^2 x}$

$= \dfrac{(\cos^2 x)(\sin x + \cos x)}{(\sin x - \cos x)(\sin x + \cos x)}$

$= \dfrac{\cos^2 x}{\sin x - \cos x}$

27. $\dfrac{2\cos 2x}{\sin 2x} = \dfrac{2(\cos^2 x - \sin^2 x)}{2\sin x\cos x}$

$= \dfrac{\cos^2 x}{\sin x\cos x} - \dfrac{\sin^2 x}{\sin x\cos x}$

$= \cot x - \tan x$

28. Refer to Problem Set 77, problem 7a.

29. $\log_4 8^{2/3} + \log_4(2x - 3) = -1$

$(\log_4 4)(2x - 3) = -1$

$4^{-1} = 4(2x - 3)$

$\dfrac{1}{4} = 8x - 12$

$1 = 32x - 48$

$32x = 49$

$x = \dfrac{49}{32}$

30. $\log_3 (\log_2 x) = 2$
$3^2 = \log_2 x = 9$
$2^9 = x$
$x = 512$

55. $\begin{bmatrix} 1 & 2 \\ 3 & 4 \end{bmatrix} \cdot \begin{bmatrix} 1 & 0 \\ 0 & 1 \end{bmatrix}$

$= \begin{bmatrix} (1)(1) + (2)(0) & (1)(0) + (2)(1) \\ (3)(1) + (4)(0) & (3)(0) + (4)(1) \end{bmatrix} = \begin{bmatrix} 1 & 2 \\ 3 & 4 \end{bmatrix}$

56. **Valid** (use the contrapositive).

PROBLEM SET 93

1. $1360 = 1440\, e^{50k}$
$0.944 \approx e^{50k}$
$\ln 0.944 \approx \ln e^{50k}$
$50k \approx -0.0572$
$k \approx -0.001143$
$400 = 1440\, e^{-0.001143t}$
$0.278 \approx e^{-0.001143t}$
$\ln 0.278 \approx \ln e^{-0.001143t}$
$-0.001143t \approx -1.280$
$t \approx \textbf{1120.5 hr}$

2. Rate · time · men = jobs
Rate · d · 4 = 15
Rate $= \dfrac{15}{4d}$

$\dfrac{15}{4d} \cdot$ time $\cdot (4 + w) = 135$

Time $= \dfrac{135(4d)}{15(4 + w)} = \dfrac{9(4d)}{4 + w}$

$= \dfrac{36d}{4 + w}$ **days**

3. $200 = 40\, e^{300k}$
$5 = e^{300k}$
$\ln 5 = \ln e^{500k}$
$500k \approx 1.609$
$k \approx 0.00536$
$1800 = 40\, e^{0.00536t}$
$45 = e^{0.00536t}$
$\ln 45 = \ln e^{0.00536t}$
$0.00536t \approx 3.807$
$t \approx \textbf{709.6 min}$

4. $\dfrac{4}{52} + \dfrac{13}{52} - \dfrac{1}{52} = \dfrac{16}{52} = \dfrac{4}{13}$

5. $_7C_4 = \dfrac{7!}{3!4!} = \textbf{35}$

6. $\overline{SR}$ is $\perp$ bisector of $\overline{QT}$ so ΔQVS and ΔTVS are right triangles. $QV = VT$ and $SV = SV$ implies $\Delta QVS \cong \Delta TVS$ and $QS = ST$. $\overline{QR}$ is $\perp$ bisector of $\overline{PS}$ so ΔPVQ and ΔSUQ are right triangles. $PU = US$ and $QU = QU$ implies $\Delta PUQ \cong \Delta SUQ$ and $PQ = QS$. Thus, $PQ = SQ = ST$ so $PQ = ST$.

7. P and Q are midpoints of $\overline{AD}$ and $\overline{AB}$ implies $PQ = \dfrac{1}{2}DB$. S and R are midpoints of $\overline{DC}$ and $\overline{BC}$ implies $SR = \dfrac{1}{2}DB$.

Thus, $SR = \dfrac{1}{2}DB = PQ$ so $SR = PQ$.

8. Refer to Problem Set 90, problem 7.

9. Let P be any point on the $\perp$ bisector of $\overline{AB}$. $\overline{PC}$ is the $\perp$ bisector so ΔACP and ΔBCP are right triangles. $AC = CB$ and $PC = PC$ implies $\Delta ACP \cong \Delta BCP$; thus $PA = PB$ so P is equidistant from A and B.

10. $(x^2 - 10x + 25) + 2(y^2 + 4y + 4)$
$= -29 + 25 + 8$
$\dfrac{(x - 5)^2}{4} + \dfrac{2(y + 2)^2}{4} = \dfrac{4}{4}$
$\dfrac{(x - 5)^2}{4} + \dfrac{(y + 2)^2}{2} = 1$
Center: (5, -2)
Major axis: 4
Minor axis: $2\sqrt{2}$

11. $36\left(x^2 - \frac{2}{3}x + \frac{1}{9}\right) - 9(y^2 - 6y + 9) = 113$

$\qquad + 4 - 81$

$\dfrac{36\left(x - \frac{1}{3}\right)^2}{36} - \dfrac{9(y - 3)^2}{36} = \dfrac{36}{36}$

$\dfrac{\left(x - \frac{1}{3}\right)^2}{1} - \dfrac{(y - 3)^2}{4} = 1$

Center: $\left(\frac{1}{3}, 3\right)$

Vertices: $\left(\frac{4}{3}, 5\right)\left(-\frac{2}{3}, 3\right)$

Asymptotes: $y = -2x + \dfrac{11}{3}$

$\qquad\qquad\quad y = 2x + \dfrac{7}{3}$

12. $(x - 3)^2 + (y - 0)^2 = 4$

$x^2 - 6x + 9 + y^2 - 4 = 0$

$x^2 + y^2 - 6x + 5 = 0$

13. $i^{1/3} = (1 \operatorname{cis} 90°)^{1/3}$; angles differ by $120°$

$1 \operatorname{cis} 30° = \dfrac{\sqrt{3}}{2} + \dfrac{1}{2}i$

$1 \operatorname{cis} 150° = -\dfrac{\sqrt{3}}{2} + \dfrac{1}{2}i$

$1 \operatorname{cis} 270° = 0 - i$

14.

$x = \dfrac{\begin{vmatrix} 0 & 2 & 1 \\ 11 & -1 & 3 \\ -2 & 3 & 4 \end{vmatrix}}{\begin{vmatrix} 1 & 2 & 1 \\ 2 & -1 & 3 \\ 0 & 3 & 4 \end{vmatrix}}$

$= \dfrac{0\begin{vmatrix} -1 & 3 \\ 3 & 4 \end{vmatrix} - 2\begin{vmatrix} 11 & 3 \\ -2 & 4 \end{vmatrix} + 1\begin{vmatrix} 11 & -1 \\ -2 & 3 \end{vmatrix}}{1\begin{vmatrix} -1 & 3 \\ 3 & 4 \end{vmatrix} - 2\begin{vmatrix} 2 & 3 \\ 0 & 4 \end{vmatrix} + 1\begin{vmatrix} 2 & -1 \\ 0 & 3 \end{vmatrix}}$

$= \dfrac{0 - 2(44 + 6) + 1(33 - 2)}{1(-4 - 9) - 2(8 - 0) + 1(6 - 0)}$

$= \dfrac{-69}{-23} = 3$

$y = \dfrac{\begin{vmatrix} 1 & 0 & 1 \\ 2 & 11 & 3 \\ 0 & -2 & 4 \end{vmatrix}}{-23}$

$= \dfrac{1\begin{vmatrix} 11 & 3 \\ -2 & 4 \end{vmatrix} - 0\begin{vmatrix} 2 & 3 \\ 0 & 4 \end{vmatrix} + 1\begin{vmatrix} 2 & 11 \\ 0 & -2 \end{vmatrix}}{-23}$

$= \dfrac{1(44 + 6) - 0 + 1(-4 - 0)}{-23} = \dfrac{46}{-23} = -2$

$z = \dfrac{\begin{vmatrix} 1 & 2 & 0 \\ 2 & -1 & 11 \\ 0 & 3 & -2 \end{vmatrix}}{-23}$

$= \dfrac{1\begin{vmatrix} -1 & 11 \\ 3 & -2 \end{vmatrix} - 2\begin{vmatrix} 2 & 11 \\ 0 & -2 \end{vmatrix} + 0}{-23}$

$= \dfrac{1(2 - 33) - 2(-4 + 0)}{-23} = \dfrac{-23}{-23} = 1$

15.

$\begin{bmatrix} 2 & 1 & 1 & 3 \\ 0 & 3 & 2 & 0 \\ 3 & 2 & 0 & -1 \end{bmatrix} = \begin{bmatrix} 1 & \frac{1}{2} & \frac{1}{2} & \frac{3}{2} \\ 0 & 3 & 2 & 0 \\ 0 & \frac{1}{2} & -\frac{3}{2} & -\frac{11}{2} \end{bmatrix}$

$= \begin{bmatrix} 1 & 0 & \frac{1}{6} & \frac{3}{2} \\ 0 & 1 & \frac{2}{3} & 0 \\ 0 & 0 & -\frac{11}{6} & -\frac{11}{2} \end{bmatrix} = \begin{bmatrix} 1 & 0 & 0 & 1 \\ 0 & 1 & 0 & -2 \\ 0 & 0 & 1 & 3 \end{bmatrix}$

$x = 1$

$y = -2$

$z = 3$

16. (a) Refer to Example 84.B.3.

(b) $\cos 75° + \cos 15°$

$= 2\cos \dfrac{75° + 15°}{2} \cos \dfrac{75° - 15°}{2}$

$= 2 \cos 45° \cos 30°$

$= 2(0.707)(0.866) \approx 1.22$

17. (a) Refer to Example 84.B.4.

(b) $\cos 75° - \cos 15°$

$= -2 \sin \dfrac{75° + 15°}{2} \sin \dfrac{75° - 15°}{2}$

$= -2 \sin 45° \sin 30°$

$= -2 \left(\dfrac{\sqrt{2}}{2}\right)\left(\dfrac{1}{2}\right) = -\dfrac{\sqrt{2}}{2}$

18. (a) $a_{10} = 4 + 9(-5) = -41$

(b) $S_{10} = \dfrac{10}{2}(4 - 41) = 5(-37) = -185$

19. $H^+ = 10^{-pH} = 10^{-7.6} \approx 2.51 \times 10^{-8} \dfrac{\text{mole}}{\text{liter}}$

20. $\log y = \dfrac{1}{5} (\log 6.39 \times 10^4)$

$\quad - 0.4(\log 2.1 \times 10^3)$

$= \dfrac{1}{5}(0.8055 + 4) - 0.4(0.3222 + 3)$

$= \dfrac{1}{5}(4.8055) - 0.4(3.3222)$

$= 0.9611 - 1.3289 = -0.3678$

$y = \text{antilog} (-0.3678 + 1) - 1$

$= \text{antilog} (0.6322) - 1 = \mathbf{0.43}$

21.

$\dfrac{\sin B}{10} = \dfrac{\sin 30°}{8}$

$\sin B = \dfrac{10 \sin 30°}{8} \approx 0.625$

$B \approx 38.7°, B' \approx 180° - 38.7° \approx 141.3°$

$C \approx 180° - (38.7° + 30°) \approx 111.3°$

$C' \approx 180° - (141.3° + 30°) \approx 8.7°$

$\dfrac{c}{\sin 111.3°} = \dfrac{8}{\sin 30°}$

$c = \dfrac{8 \sin 111.3°}{\sin 30°} \approx \mathbf{14.9}$

$\dfrac{c'}{\sin 8.7°} = \dfrac{8}{\sin 30°}$

$c' = \dfrac{8 \sin 8.7°}{\sin 30°} \approx \mathbf{2.4}$

22. $\log_6 40 = \dfrac{\log 40}{\log 6}$

23. $243 \left(\dfrac{2}{3}\right)^3 = 243 \left(\dfrac{8}{27}\right) = \mathbf{72 \ ft}$

24. Refer to Lesson 77.B.

25. $4 \sin^2 x \tan x = \tan x$

$4 \sin^2 x \tan x - \tan x = 0$

$\tan x(4 \sin^2 x - 1) = 0$

$\tan x = 0 \qquad 4 \sin^2 x - 1 = 0$

$x = 0°, 180° \qquad x = 30°, 150°, 210°, 330°$

$x = \mathbf{0°, 30°, 150°, 180°, 210°, 330°}$

26. $2 \csc 2x \sin x = \dfrac{2 \sin x}{\sin 2x} = \dfrac{2 \sin x}{2 \sin x \cos x}$

$= \dfrac{1}{\cos x} = \sec x$

27. $(\tan \theta - \sec \theta)^2$

$= \tan^2 \theta - 2 \tan \theta \sec \theta + \sec^2 \theta$

$= \dfrac{\sin^2 \theta}{\cos^2 \theta} - \dfrac{2 \sin \theta}{\cos^2 \theta} + \dfrac{1}{\cos^2 \theta}$

$= \dfrac{\sin^2 \theta - 2 \sin \theta + 1}{\cos^2 \theta}$

$= \dfrac{(\sin \theta - 1)(\sin \theta - 1)}{1 - \sin^2 \theta}$

$= \dfrac{(\sin \theta - 1)(\sin \theta - 1)}{(1 + \sin \theta)(1 - \sin \theta)}$

$= \dfrac{(1 - \sin \theta)(1 - \sin \theta)}{(1 + \sin \theta)(1 - \sin \theta)}$

$= \dfrac{1 - \sin \theta}{1 + \sin \theta}$

28. $(\log 5)(2x - 1) = (\log 6)(2x + 1)$

$0.699(2x - 1) \approx 0.778(2x + 1)$

$1.398x - 0.699 \approx 1.56x + 0.778$

$-1.487 \approx 0.162x$

$x \approx \mathbf{-9.3}$

29. $\log_2 (x^2 + 3x + 4) = 2$

$2^2 = x^2 + 3x + 4 = 4$

$x^2 + 3x = 0$

$x(x + 3) = 0$

$x = \mathbf{0} \qquad\qquad x = \mathbf{-3}$

30. $\log_2 \dfrac{8}{4} = x$

$\log_2 2 = x$

$2^x = 2$

$x = \mathbf{1}$

EP

57.
$$\begin{bmatrix} -9 & 6 \\ 20 & -5 \end{bmatrix} \cdot \begin{bmatrix} -2 & 1 \\ 2 & -1 \end{bmatrix}$$

$$= \begin{bmatrix} (-9)(-2) + (6)(2) & (-9)(1) + (6)(-1) \\ (20)(-2) + (-5)(2) & (20)(1) + (-5)(-1) \end{bmatrix}$$

$$= \begin{bmatrix} 30 & -15 \\ -50 & 25 \end{bmatrix}$$

58.
$$\frac{k^2(k+1)^2}{4} + (k+1)^3$$

$$= \frac{k^2(k+1)^2 + 4(k+1)^3}{4}$$

$$= \frac{(k+1)^2\,[k^2 + 4(k+1)]}{4}$$

$$= \frac{(k+1)^2(k^2 + 4k + 4)}{4}$$

$$= \frac{(k+1)^2(k+2)^2}{4}$$

$$= \frac{(k+1)^2[(k+1)+1]^2}{4}$$

PROBLEM SET 94

1.
$$\frac{1.0 + 0.8 + 0.2 + x}{4} = 0.6$$
$$1.0 + 0.8 + 0.2 + x = 0.6(4)$$
$$2 + x = 2.4$$
$$x = 0.4$$

2.
$$\frac{m + n}{2} = A$$
$$m + n = 2A$$
$$n = 2A - m$$

3.
$$0.10\,G + 0.20B = 16$$
$$G + 2B = 160$$

$$\frac{G}{B} = \frac{2}{3}$$
$$2B = 3G$$

$$G + 3G = 160$$
$$G = \frac{160}{4} = 40$$
$$B = \frac{3}{2}(40) = 60$$

4.
$$\frac{1}{12}T = S, \qquad T = S + 30$$
$$\frac{1}{12}T = T - 30$$
$$-\frac{11}{12}T = -30$$
$$T = -30\left(-\frac{12}{11}\right) = 32\frac{8}{11}$$
Time = **6:32 $\frac{8}{11}$ p.m.**

5.
$$R_E T_E + R_T T_T = \text{jobs}$$
$$\frac{1}{x}(2) + R_T(2) = 1$$
$$\frac{2}{x} + R_T(2) = 1$$
$$2R_T = 1 - \frac{2}{x} = \frac{x-2}{x}$$
$$R_T = \frac{x-2}{2x}$$
$$T_T = \frac{2x}{x-2}\,\text{days}$$

6.
$$S_\infty = \frac{a_1}{1-r} = \frac{4}{1-\frac{1}{3}} = \frac{4}{\frac{2}{3}} = 6$$

7.
$$S_\infty = \frac{a_1}{1-r} = \frac{4}{1-\frac{1}{2}} = \frac{4}{\frac{1}{2}}$$
$$S_\infty = \textbf{8 miles}$$

8.
$$(x-1)^2 + (y+3)^2 = 1$$
$$x^2 - 2x + 1 + y^2 + 6y + 9 = 1$$
$$x^2 + y^2 - 2x + 6y + 9 = 0$$

9. $\triangle PQR$ and $\triangle PSR$ are right triangles. $PQ = PS$, $PR = PR$ implies $\triangle PQR \cong \triangle PSR$ and $QR = RS$. $\angle QRP = \angle SRP$ and $OR = OR$ implies $\triangle RQO \cong \triangle RSO$ and $QO = OS$.

10. Refer to Problem Set 76, problem 6.

11. P and S are midpoints of $\overline{AD}$ and $\overline{DC}$

implies $PS = \frac{1}{2}AC$. Q and R are midpoints

of $\overline{AB}$ and $\overline{CB}$ implies $QR = \frac{1}{2}AC$.

So $QR = \frac{1}{2}AC = PS$; thus $QR = PS$.

12. $9(x^2 + 6x + 9) + 4(y^2 - 2y + 1)$

$= -49 + 81 + 4$

$\dfrac{9(x + 3)^2}{36} + \dfrac{4(y - 1)^2}{36} = \dfrac{36}{36}$

$\dfrac{(x + 3)^2}{4} + \dfrac{(y - 1)^2}{9} = 1$

Center: $(-3, 1)$

Major axis: **6**

Minor axis: **4**

13. $(x^2 - 14x + 49) - (y^2 + 8y + 16)$

$= -29 + 49 - 16$

$\dfrac{(x - 7)^2}{4} - \dfrac{(y + 4)^2}{4} = \dfrac{4}{4}$

$\dfrac{(x - 7)^2}{4} - \dfrac{(y + 4)^2}{4} = 1$

Center: $(7, -4)$

Vertices: $(5, -4), (9, -4)$

Asymptotes: $y = x - 11$

$\qquad\qquad\quad y = -x + 3$

14. $x = \dfrac{\begin{vmatrix} 7 & 1 & -1 \\ 1 & 2 & 3 \\ -8 & -3 & 0 \end{vmatrix}}{\begin{vmatrix} -2 & 1 & -1 \\ 0 & 2 & 3 \\ 1 & -3 & 0 \end{vmatrix}}$

$= \dfrac{7\begin{vmatrix} 2 & 3 \\ -3 & 0 \end{vmatrix} - 1\begin{vmatrix} 1 & 3 \\ -8 & 0 \end{vmatrix} - 1\begin{vmatrix} 1 & 2 \\ -8 & -3 \end{vmatrix}}{-2\begin{vmatrix} 2 & 3 \\ -3 & 0 \end{vmatrix} - 1\begin{vmatrix} 0 & 3 \\ 1 & 0 \end{vmatrix} - 1\begin{vmatrix} 0 & 2 \\ 1 & -3 \end{vmatrix}}$

$= \dfrac{7(0 + 9) - 1(0 + 24) - 1(-3 + 16)}{-2(0 + 9) - 1(0 - 3) - 1(0 - 2)}$

$= \dfrac{26}{-13} = -2$

$y = \dfrac{\begin{vmatrix} -2 & 7 & -1 \\ 0 & 1 & 3 \\ 1 & -8 & 0 \end{vmatrix}}{-13}$

$= \dfrac{-2\begin{vmatrix} 1 & 3 \\ -8 & 0 \end{vmatrix} - 7\begin{vmatrix} 0 & 3 \\ 1 & 0 \end{vmatrix} - 1\begin{vmatrix} 0 & 1 \\ 1 & -8 \end{vmatrix}}{-13}$

$= \dfrac{-2(0 + 24) - 7(0 - 3) - 1(0 - 1)}{-13}$

$= \dfrac{-26}{-13} = 2$

$z = \dfrac{\begin{vmatrix} -2 & 1 & 7 \\ 0 & 2 & 1 \\ 1 & -3 & -8 \end{vmatrix}}{-13}$

$= \dfrac{-2\begin{vmatrix} 2 & 1 \\ -3 & -8 \end{vmatrix} - 1\begin{vmatrix} 0 & 1 \\ 1 & -8 \end{vmatrix} + 7\begin{vmatrix} 0 & 2 \\ 1 & -3 \end{vmatrix}}{-13}$

$= \dfrac{-2(-16 + 3) - 1(0 - 1) + 7(0 - 2)}{-13}$

$= \dfrac{13}{-13} = -1$

15. $\begin{bmatrix} 3 & 1 & 1 & 4 \\ 0 & 2 & -1 & 2 \\ 2 & 1 & 0 & 1 \end{bmatrix} = \begin{bmatrix} 1 & \frac{1}{3} & \frac{1}{3} & \frac{4}{3} \\ 0 & 2 & -1 & 2 \\ 0 & \frac{1}{3} & -\frac{2}{3} & -\frac{5}{3} \end{bmatrix}$

$= \begin{bmatrix} 1 & 0 & \frac{1}{2} & 1 \\ 0 & 1 & -\frac{1}{2} & 1 \\ 0 & 0 & -\frac{1}{2} & -2 \end{bmatrix} = \begin{bmatrix} 1 & 0 & 0 & -1 \\ 0 & 1 & 0 & 3 \\ 0 & 0 & 1 & 4 \end{bmatrix}$

$x = -1, y = 3, z = 4$

16. (a) Refer to Example 84.A.1

(b) $\sin 75° \cos 15°$

$= \dfrac{1}{2}[\sin (75° + 15°) + \sin (75° - 15°)]$

$= \dfrac{1}{2}[\sin 90° + \sin 60°]$

$= \dfrac{1}{2}\left(1 + \dfrac{\sqrt{3}}{2}\right) = \dfrac{2 + \sqrt{3}}{4}$

17. (a) Refer to Example 84.B.1

(b) $\sin 15° + \sin 75°$

$$= 2 \sin \frac{15° + 75°}{2} \cos \frac{15° - 75°}{2}$$
$$= 2 \sin 45° \cos -30°$$
$$\approx 2(0.707)(0.866) \approx \mathbf{1.22}$$

18. $H^+ = 10^{-pH} = 10^{-8.5}$
   $H^+ = \mathbf{3.16 \times 10^{-9}} \dfrac{\mathbf{mole}}{\mathbf{liter}}$

19. (a) $a_n = a_1 + (n - 1)d$

   (b) $S_n = \dfrac{n}{2}(a_1 + a_n)$

   $= \dfrac{n}{2}[a_1 + a_1 + (n - 1)d]$

   $= \dfrac{n}{2}[2a_1 + (n - 1)d]$

20. $(-i)^{1/3} = (1 \text{ cis } 270°)^{1/3}$; angles differ by $120°$
   $1 \text{ cis } 90° = i$

   $1 \text{ cis } 210° = -\dfrac{\sqrt{3}}{2} - \dfrac{1}{2}i$

   $1 \text{ cis } 330° = \dfrac{\sqrt{3}}{2} - \dfrac{1}{2}i$

21. $\log y = \dfrac{1}{4} \log (4.2 \times 10^4) + \dfrac{1}{3} \log (2.3 \times 10^3)$

   $\log y = \dfrac{1}{4}(0.6232 + 4) + \dfrac{1}{3}(0.3617 + 3)$

   $\log y = \dfrac{1}{4}(4.6232) + \dfrac{1}{3}(3.3617)$

   $\log y = 1.1558 + 1.1206 = 2.2764$
   $y = \text{antilog } 2.2764 \approx \mathbf{188.97}$

22. $\ln 22 = \log_e 22 = \dfrac{\log 22}{\log e}$

23.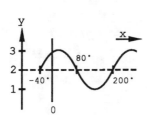

24. **360°**

25. **Construction**

26. $\sqrt{3} \tan 3\theta - 1 = 0$
   $\sqrt{3} \tan 3\theta = 1$

   $\tan 3\theta = \dfrac{1}{\sqrt{3}} = \dfrac{\sqrt{3}}{3}$

   $3\theta = 30°, 210°, 390°, 570°, 750°, 930°$
   $\theta = \mathbf{10°, 70°, 130°, 190°, 250°, 310°}$

27. $\sec x - \sin x \tan x = \dfrac{1}{\cos x} - \sin x \dfrac{\sin x}{\cos x}$

   $= \dfrac{1 - \sin^2 x}{\cos x} = \dfrac{\cos^2 x}{\cos x} = \cos x$

28. $\dfrac{\sec^2 x}{2 - \sec^2 x} = \dfrac{\dfrac{1}{\cos^2 x}}{2 - \dfrac{1}{\cos^2 x}}$

   $= \dfrac{\dfrac{1}{\cos^2 x}}{\dfrac{2 \cos^2 x - 1}{\cos^2 x}} = \dfrac{1}{\cos^2 x} \cdot \dfrac{\cos^2 x}{2 \cos^2 x - 1}$

   $= \dfrac{1}{2 \cos^2 x - 1} = \dfrac{1}{\cos 2x} = \sec 2x$

29. $2^{3x-2} = 2^2$
   $3x - 2 = 2$
   $3x = 4$
   $x = \dfrac{4}{3}$

30. $\log_6 (x - 1)(x - 2) = \log_6 6$
   $(x - 1)(x - 2) = 6$
   $x^2 - 3x + 2 = 6$
   $x^2 - 3x - 4 = 0$
   $(x - 4)(x + 1) = 0$
   $x = 4$

EP

59. $k^2(2k^2 - 1) + (2k + 1)^3$
   $= 2k^4 - k^2 + 8k^3 + 12k^2 + k + 1$
   $= 2k^4 + 8k^3 + 11k^2 + 6k + 1$
   $= (k^2 + 2k + 1)(2k^2 + 4k + 1)$
   $= (k + 1)^2[2(k + 1)^2 - 1]$

60. $X = \begin{bmatrix} -2 & 3 \\ -1 & -2 \end{bmatrix} - \begin{bmatrix} 1 & 0 \\ 2 & 1 \end{bmatrix} = \begin{bmatrix} -3 & 3 \\ -3 & -3 \end{bmatrix}$

PROBLEM SET 95

1. $B = mF + b$

$$\begin{array}{r} 30 = 40m + b \\ (-)\,40 = 80m + b \\ \hline -10 = -40m \end{array}$$

$m = \dfrac{1}{4}$

$b = 20$

$B = \dfrac{1}{4}F + 20$

$B = \dfrac{1}{4}(4) + 20 = \mathbf{21}$

2. $S = \dfrac{k}{d^2}$

$16 = \dfrac{k}{25}$

$k = 16(25) = 400$

$S = \dfrac{400}{10^2} = \mathbf{4}$

3. $\dfrac{\text{part}}{\text{whole}} = \dfrac{R}{M + R} = \dfrac{I}{K}$

$I = \dfrac{RK}{M + R}$

4. $\dfrac{7}{10} - \dfrac{1}{5} = \dfrac{5}{10} = \dfrac{1}{2}$

$\dfrac{1}{2}x = 160$

$x = \mathbf{320\ gal}$

5. $2(1) + 2(5) + 1(10) = 22$

$\dfrac{22}{25}$

6. $A_1 = l \cdot w \cdot h$

$A_2 = 2l \cdot 2w \cdot 2h = 8 \cdot l \cdot w \cdot h$

Ratio $= \mathbf{8 : 1}$

7. $\dfrac{1}{3}Bh = \dfrac{1}{3}\left(24\sqrt{3}\right)(10) = \mathbf{80\sqrt{3}\ cm^3}$

8. (a) $V = \dfrac{1}{3}\pi r^2 h = \dfrac{1}{3}(\pi)(10)^2(10)$

$\quad = \dfrac{1000}{3}\pi\ \mathbf{cm^3}$

(b) $SA = \pi r^2 + \pi rs$

$\quad = \pi(10)^2 + \pi(10)\left(10\sqrt{2}\right)$

$\quad = (100\pi + 100\sqrt{2}\,\pi)\ \mathbf{cm^2}$

9. $AC = \sqrt{l^2 + w^2 + h^2}$

$\quad = \sqrt{9 + 4 + n^2} = \sqrt{13 + n^2}$

10. (a) $V = \dfrac{4}{3}\pi r^3 = \dfrac{4}{3}\pi(10)^3 = \left(\dfrac{4000}{3}\pi\right)\ \mathbf{cm^3}$

(b) $SA = 4\pi r^2 = 4\pi(10)^2 = \mathbf{400\pi\ cm^2}$

11. $r = \dfrac{-\dfrac{3}{2}}{3} = -\dfrac{1}{2}$

$S_n = \dfrac{a_1}{1 - r} = \dfrac{3}{1 - \left(-\dfrac{1}{2}\right)} = \dfrac{3}{\dfrac{3}{2}} = \mathbf{2}$

12. Down: $\dfrac{10}{1 - \dfrac{1}{2}} = 20$

Up: down − firstfall $= 20 - 10 = 10$

Distance = down + up $= 20 + 10 = \mathbf{30\ ft}$

13. $\overline{PR}$ is the perpendicular bisector of $\overline{SQ}$ implies $SO = OQ$; also $\triangle SOP$ and $\triangle QOP$ are right triangles. $OP = OP$ implies $\triangle SOP \cong \triangle QOP$ and $PS = PQ$. $PR = PR$ implies $\triangle PSR \cong \triangle PQR$ and $RS = QR$.

14. $16(y^2 - 4y + 4) - 9(x^2 + 2x + 1)$

$= 89 + 64 - 9$

$\dfrac{16(y - 2)^2}{144} - \dfrac{9(x + 1)^2}{144} = \dfrac{144}{144}$

$\dfrac{(y - 2)^2}{9} - \dfrac{(x + 1)^2}{16} = 1$

Center: $\mathbf{(-1, 2)}$

Vertices: $\mathbf{(-1, 5), (-1, -1)}$

Asymptotes: $y = \dfrac{3}{4}x + \dfrac{11}{4}$

$\qquad\qquad\quad y = -\dfrac{3}{4} + \dfrac{5}{4}$

15. $3(x^2 + 4x + 4) + 4(y^2 - 2y + 1)$

$= 176 + 12 + 4$

$\dfrac{3(x + 2)^2}{192} + \dfrac{4(y - 1)^2}{192} = \dfrac{192}{192}$

$\dfrac{(x + 2)^2}{64} + \dfrac{(y - 1)^2}{48} = 1$

Center: $\mathbf{(-2, 1)}$

Major axis: **16**

Minor axis: $\mathbf{8\sqrt{3}}$

16.

$$\begin{bmatrix} 2 & -3 & 1 & 7 \\ 0 & 2 & -1 & -8 \\ 1 & 1 & 0 & -5 \end{bmatrix} = \begin{bmatrix} 1 & -\dfrac{3}{2} & \dfrac{1}{2} & \dfrac{7}{2} \\ 0 & 2 & -1 & -8 \\ 0 & \dfrac{5}{2} & -\dfrac{1}{2} & -\dfrac{17}{2} \end{bmatrix}$$

$$= \begin{bmatrix} 1 & 0 & -\dfrac{1}{4} & -\dfrac{5}{2} \\ 0 & 1 & -\dfrac{1}{2} & -4 \\ 0 & 0 & \dfrac{3}{4} & \dfrac{3}{2} \end{bmatrix} = \begin{bmatrix} 1 & 0 & 0 & -2 \\ 0 & 1 & 0 & -3 \\ 0 & 0 & 1 & 2 \end{bmatrix}$$

$x = -2$
$y = -3$
$z = 2$

17. (a) Refer to Example 84.B.3
   (b) $\cos 255° + \cos 15°$

$$= 2 \cos \frac{255° + 15°}{2} \cos \frac{255° - 15°}{2}$$

$$= 2 \cos 135° \cos 120°$$

$$= 2(-0.707)(-0.5) = \mathbf{0.707}$$

18. (a) Refer to Example 84.A.3
   (b) $\cos 255° \cos 15°$

$$= \frac{1}{2}[\cos(255° + 15°) + \cos(255° - 15°)]$$

$$= \frac{1}{2}[\cos 270° + \cos 240°]$$

$$= \frac{1}{2}\left(0 - \frac{1}{2}\right) = -\frac{1}{4}$$

19. (a) $a_n = a_1 + (n - 1)d$

   (b) $S_n = \dfrac{n}{2}(a_1 + a_n)$

$$= \frac{n}{2}[a_1 + a_1 + (n - 1)d]$$

$$= \frac{n}{2}[2a_1 + (n - 1)d]$$

20. $r = \sqrt{4^2 + 5^2} = \sqrt{41} \approx 6.4$

$\tan \theta = \dfrac{5}{4}$ (in Q I) $\theta \approx 51.3°$

$(6.4 \text{ cis } 51.3°)^{1/3} = 6.4^{1/3} \text{ cis } \dfrac{51.3°}{3}$

$\approx \mathbf{1.86 \text{ cis } 17.1°}$; angles differ by $120°$
$\mathbf{1.86 \text{ cis } 137.1°, 1.86 \text{ cis } 257.1°}$

21. $\log y = \dfrac{1}{5}(\log 6.3 \times 10^4) + 1.5(\log 4.5 \times 10^3)$

$$= \frac{1}{5}(0.7993 + 4) + 1.5(0.6532 + 3)$$

$$= \frac{1}{5}(4.7993) + 1.5(3.6532)$$

$$= 0.9599 + 5.4798 = 6.4397$$

$y = $ antilog $6.4397 = \mathbf{2.75 \times 10^6}$

22. $a^2 = 6^2 + 7^2 - 2(6)(7)\cos 30° = 12.25$
   $a = \sqrt{12.25} = \mathbf{3.5}$

23. $\ln 35 = \log_e 35 = \dfrac{\log 35}{\log e}$

24. Construction.

25. Refer to Lesson 77.A.

26. $(\cos 2x)(\sec^2 x) = (2\cos^2 x - 1)\left(\dfrac{1}{\cos^2 x}\right)$

$$= \frac{2\cos^2 x - 1}{\cos^2 x} = 2 - \frac{1}{\cos^2 x}$$

$$= 2 - \sec^2 x = 2 - (1 + \tan^2 x)$$

$$= 2 - 1 - \tan^2 x = 1 - \tan^2 x$$

27. $6\cos^2 x + 5\cos x + 1 = 0$
   $(3\cos x + 1)(2\cos x + 1) = 0$

$\cos x = -\dfrac{1}{3}$ $\qquad\qquad$ $\cos x = -\dfrac{1}{2}$

$x = \mathbf{109.5°, 250.5°}$ $\qquad$ $x = \mathbf{120°, 240°}$

28. $\dfrac{1 + \cos 2x}{\sin 2x} = \dfrac{1 + (2\cos^2 x - 1)}{2\sin x \cos x}$

$$= \frac{2\cos^2 x}{2\sin x \cos x} = \frac{\cos x}{\sin x} = \cot x$$

29. $(\log 3)(2x - 4) = (\log 4)(3x - 2)$
   $0.477(2x - 4) = 0.602(3x - 2)$
   $0.954x - 1.908 = 1.806x - 1.204$
   $-0.703 = 0.852x$
   $x = \mathbf{-0.83}$

30. $\log_4 8^{2/3} + \log_4 (x - 2) = \log_4 (2x - 3)$
   $(\log_4 4)(x - 2) = \log_4 (2x - 3)$
   $4(x - 2) = 2x - 3$
   $4x - 8 = 2x - 3$
   $2x = 5$
   $x = \dfrac{5}{2}$

61. $\begin{bmatrix} 1 & 1 \\ -1 & 1 \end{bmatrix} \cdot \begin{bmatrix} 3 & 3 \\ 4 & -4 \end{bmatrix}$

$= \begin{bmatrix} (1)(3) + (1)(4) & (1)(3) + (1)(-4) \\ (-1)(3) + (1)(4) & (-1)(3) + (1)(-4) \end{bmatrix}$

$= \begin{bmatrix} 7 & -1 \\ 1 & -7 \end{bmatrix}$

62. $\dfrac{k(k + 1)(k + 2)}{6} + \dfrac{(k + 1)(k + 2)}{2}$

$= \dfrac{k(k + 1)(k + 2) + 3(k + 1)(k + 2)}{6}$

$= \dfrac{(k + 1)(k + 2)(k + 3)}{6}$

$= \dfrac{(k + 1)[(k + 1) + 1][(k + 1) + 2]}{6}$

ENRICHMENT LESSON 5

1. $S = mP + b$

$\begin{array}{r} 60 = 80m + b \\ (-)\ 45 = 50m + b \\ \hline 15 = 30m \end{array}$

$\dfrac{1}{2} = m$

$60 = 80\left(\dfrac{1}{2}\right) + b$

$b = 60 - 40 = 20$

$S = \dfrac{1}{2}P + 20$

$S = \dfrac{1}{2}(10) + 20 = \textbf{25}$

2. $F = \dfrac{k}{I^2}$

$9 = \dfrac{k}{2^2}$

$k = 36$

$F = \dfrac{36}{I^2}$

$F = \dfrac{36}{3^2} = \dfrac{36}{9} = \textbf{4}$

3. $C = 3, I = 7, C + I = 10$

$\dfrac{I}{C + I} = \dfrac{7}{10} = \dfrac{I}{700}$

$I = \dfrac{7(700)}{10} = \textbf{490}$

4. $\left(\dfrac{1}{5}F + 100\right) = \dfrac{3}{5}F$

$100 = \dfrac{2}{5}F$

$F = \dfrac{5(100)}{2} = \textbf{250 lb}$

5. (A) Downstream $(2W + W)(T - 4) = 60$
$3WT - 12W = 60$
(B) Upstream: $(2W - W)T = 60$
$WT = 60$
$3(60) - 12W = 60$
$-12W = -120$
$W = \dfrac{-120}{-12} = 10$
Boat $= 2W = \textbf{20 mph}$
Water $= W = \textbf{10 mph}$

6. $\dfrac{1}{2}n(n + 1) + (n + 1) = \dfrac{1}{2}n^2 + \dfrac{3}{2}n + 1$

$= \dfrac{1}{2}(n + 1)(n + 2)$

$= \dfrac{1}{2}(n + 1)[(n + 1) + 1]$

7. $\dfrac{1}{2}n[2a + (n - 1)d] + a + nd$

$= na + \dfrac{1}{2}n^2d - \dfrac{1}{2}nd + a + nd$

$= a(n + 1) + \dfrac{1}{2}n^2d + \dfrac{1}{2}nd$

$= a(n + 1) + \dfrac{1}{2}n(n + 1)d$

$= \dfrac{1}{2}(n + 1)(2a + nd)$

$= \dfrac{1}{2}(n + 1)[2a + (n + 1 - 1)d]$

8. $\dfrac{1 - r^{n+1}}{1 - r} + r^{n+1} = \dfrac{1 - r^{n+1} + r^{n+1} - r^{n+2}}{1 - r}$

$= \dfrac{1 - r^{n+2}}{1 - r} = \dfrac{1 - r^{(n+1)+1}}{1 - r}$

9. $\left(\dfrac{3}{1}\right)^3 = \dfrac{27}{1}$

Ratio $= \textbf{27 : 1}$

10.　$B = 6\left(\frac{1}{2}(5)\frac{5}{2}\sqrt{3}\right) = \frac{150}{4}\sqrt{3} = \frac{75\sqrt{3}}{2}$

　　　$V = \frac{1}{3}Bh = \frac{1}{3}\left(\frac{75\sqrt{3}}{2}\right)(6) = 75\sqrt{3}\text{ cm}^3$

11.　(a)　$V = \frac{1}{3}\pi r^2 h = \frac{1}{3}\pi(6)^2(6) = 72\pi\text{ cm}^3$

　　　(b)　$SA = \pi r^2 + \pi r s = \pi(6)^2 + \pi(6)(6\sqrt{2})$
　　　　　$= (36\pi + 36\sqrt{2}\,\pi)\text{ cm}^2$

12.　$AC = \sqrt{l^2 + w^2 + h^2} = \sqrt{x^2 + y^2 + 9}$

13.　(a)　$V = \frac{4}{3}\pi r^3 = \frac{4}{3}(\pi)(6)^3 = 288\pi\text{ cm}^3$

　　　(b)　$SA = 4\pi r^2 = 4(\pi)(6)^2 = 144\pi\text{ cm}^2$

14.　$2r = -\frac{4}{3}$

　　　$r = \frac{-\frac{4}{3}}{2} = -\frac{2}{3}$

　　　$S_\infty = \frac{a_1}{1-r} = \frac{2}{1-\left(-\frac{2}{3}\right)} = \frac{2}{\frac{5}{3}} = \frac{6}{5}$

15.　$\overline{PR}$ is the angle bisector of $\angle P$ and $\angle QRS$
　　　implies $\angle QPR = \angle SPR$ and $\angle QRP$
　　　$= \angle SRP$. $PR = PR$ implies $\triangle PQR$
　　　$\cong \triangle PSR$, and thus $QR = RS$.

16.　$4(x^2 + 6x + 9) - (y^2 - 4y + 4)$
　　　$= -28 + 36 - 4$
　　　$\frac{4(x+3)^2}{4} - \frac{(y-2)^2}{4} = \frac{4}{4}$
　　　$\frac{(x+3)^2}{1} - \frac{(y-2)^2}{4} = 1$
　　　Center: $(-3, 2)$
　　　Vertices: $(-2, 2), (-4, 2)$
　　　Asymptotes: $y = 2x + 8$
　　　　　　　　　　$y = -2x - 4$

17.　$9(x^2 + 6x + 9) + 4(y^2 - 2y + 1)$
　　　$= -49 + 81 + 4$
　　　$\frac{9(x+3)^2}{36} + \frac{4(y-1)^2}{36} = \frac{36}{36}$
　　　$\frac{(x+3)^2}{4} + \frac{(y-1)^2}{9} = 1$
　　　Center: $(-3, 1)$
　　　Major axis: 6
　　　Minor axis: 4

18.
$$\begin{bmatrix} 3 & 2 & 1 & 5 \\ 0 & 3 & -2 & 5 \\ 2 & 3 & 0 & 7 \end{bmatrix} = \begin{bmatrix} 1 & \frac{2}{3} & \frac{1}{3} & \frac{5}{3} \\ 0 & 3 & -2 & 5 \\ 0 & \frac{5}{3} & -\frac{2}{3} & \frac{11}{3} \end{bmatrix}$$

$$= \begin{bmatrix} 1 & 0 & \frac{7}{9} & \frac{5}{9} \\ 0 & 1 & -\frac{2}{3} & \frac{5}{3} \\ 0 & 0 & \frac{4}{9} & \frac{8}{9} \end{bmatrix} = \begin{bmatrix} 1 & 0 & 0 & -1 \\ 0 & 1 & 0 & 3 \\ 0 & 0 & 1 & 2 \end{bmatrix}$$

　　　$x = -1$
　　　$y = 3$
　　　$z = 2$

19.　$\sin 285^\circ + \sin 15^\circ$
　　　$= 2\sin\frac{285^\circ + 15^\circ}{2}\cos\frac{285^\circ - 15^\circ}{2}$
　　　$= 2\sin 150^\circ \cos 135^\circ$
　　　$= 2\left(\frac{1}{2}\right)\left(-\frac{\sqrt{2}}{2}\right) = -\frac{\sqrt{2}}{2}$

20.　(a)　$a_n = a_1 + (n-1)d$

　　　(b)　$S_n = \frac{n}{2}(a_1 + a_n)$

　　　　　$S_n = \frac{n}{2}[a_1 + a_1 + (n-1)d]$

　　　　　$S_n = \frac{n}{2}[2a_1 + (n-1)d]$

21.　$(3 + 4i)^{1/3} = (5\text{ cis }53.1^\circ)^{1/3}$
　　　$= 5^{1/3}\text{ cis }\frac{53.1^\circ}{3} \approx 1.7\text{ cis }17.7^\circ$
　　　Angles differ by 120°
　　　$1.7\text{ cis }137.7^\circ, 1.7\text{ cis }257.7^\circ$

22.　$a = \sqrt{4^4 + 6^2 - 2(4)(6)\cos 120^\circ} = 8.7$

23.　$\ln 10 = \log_e 10 = \frac{\log 10}{\log e} = \frac{1}{\log e}$

24.　Construction.

25.　Refer to Problem Set 48, problem 18.

26.　$(\sin 2x)(\sec^2 x) = (2\sin x \cos x)\left(\frac{1}{\cos^2 x}\right)$
　　　$= \frac{2\sin x}{\cos x} = 2\tan x$

27. $6\sin^2 x + 5\sin x + 1 = 0$
$(3\sin x + 1)(2\sin x + 1) = 0$
$\sin x = -\dfrac{1}{3}$ $\sin x = -\dfrac{1}{2}$
$x = \mathbf{199.5°, 340.5°}$ $x = \mathbf{210°, 330°}$

28. $(\log 2)(3x - 1) = (\log 8)(2x)$
$0.301(3x - 1) = 0.903(2x)$
$0.903x - 0.301 = 1.806x$
$-0.301 = 0.903x$
$x = -\dfrac{0.301}{0.903} = -\dfrac{1}{3}$

29. $\log_3 4^{3/2} - \log_3 (2x + 1) = \log_3 (x + 1)^{-1}$
$\log_3 \dfrac{8}{2x + 1} = \log_3 \dfrac{1}{x + 1}$
$\dfrac{8}{2x + 1} = \dfrac{1}{x + 1}$
$8(x + 1) = 2x + 1$
$8x + 8 = 2x + 1$
$6x = -7$
$x = -\dfrac{7}{6}$
No solution

30. **No**

PROBLEM SET 96

1. $(M - 10) = 2(J - 10) + 6$
$M = 2J - 20 + 6 + 10$
$3(M + 10) = 4(J + 10) + 30$
$3M = 4J + 40$

$M = 2J - 4$
$3M = 4J + 4$
$3(2J - 4) = 4J + 40$
$6J - 12 = 4J + 40$
$2J = 52$
$J = 26$
Jim $= 26 + 15 = \mathbf{41\ years}$
$M = 2(26) - 4 + 15$
Mary $= 52 + 11 = \mathbf{63\ years}$

2.

	Jimjoe	Whortle & Jimjoe
Jobs:	5	10
Time:	H	3
Rate:	$\dfrac{5}{H}$	$\dfrac{10}{3}$

Whortle's = Whortle & Jimjoe's − Jimjoe's
Whortle's $= \dfrac{10}{3} - \dfrac{5}{H} = \dfrac{10H - 15}{3H} \dfrac{\text{jobs}}{\text{hr}}$

3. $1300 = 1400e^{20k}$
$0.9286 \approx e^{20k}$
$\ln 0.9286 \approx \ln e^{20k}$
$-0.0741 \approx 20k$
$k \approx -0.0037$
$A_{180} = 1400e^{(-0.0037)(180)}$
$A_{180} \approx \mathbf{718.6}$

4. (Cost each)(number) = total price
$\left(\dfrac{d}{n} + 3\right)(x) = 400$
$\left(\dfrac{d + 3n}{n}\right)x = 400$
$x = \dfrac{400n}{d + 3n}$

5. $\dfrac{3}{7} \cdot \dfrac{2}{6} = \dfrac{3}{7} \cdot \dfrac{1}{3} = \dfrac{1}{7}$

6. $S_\infty = \dfrac{0.00031}{1 - 0.01} = \dfrac{0.00031}{0.99} = \dfrac{31}{99{,}000}$

7. $S_\infty = \dfrac{0.017}{1 - 0.01} = \dfrac{0.017}{0.99} = \dfrac{17}{990} + 6$
$= \dfrac{6(990) + 17}{990} = \dfrac{5957}{990}$

8. $\dfrac{8}{1} = \dfrac{s^3}{6^3}$
$s^3 = 8(6^3) = 8(216) = 1728$
$s = \sqrt[3]{1728} = \mathbf{12}$

9. $B = \left(\dfrac{20}{4}\right)^2 = (5)^2$
$V = \dfrac{1}{3}Bh = \dfrac{1}{3}(5)^2(5) = \dfrac{125}{3}$ cm^3

10. $V = \sqrt{l^2 + w^2 + h^2}$
$= \sqrt{3^2 + 4^2 + 5^2} = \sqrt{50} = \mathbf{5\sqrt{2}}$

11. (a) $V = \frac{1}{3}\pi r^2 h = \frac{1}{3}\pi(6)^2(8)$

$= \frac{288\pi}{3} = 96\pi \text{ cm}^3$

(b) $SA = \pi r^2 + \pi rs = \pi(6)^2 + \pi(6)(10)$
$= 36\pi + 60\pi = 96\pi \text{ cm}^2$

12. $V = \frac{4}{3}\pi r^3 = \frac{4}{3}\pi(6)^3 = 288\pi \text{ m}^3$

$SA = 4\pi r^2 = 4\pi(6)^2 = 144\pi \text{ m}^2$

13. Down: $\dfrac{132}{1 - \frac{1}{4}} = \dfrac{132}{\frac{3}{4}} = 176$

Up: down − firstfall = 176 − 132 = 44
Distance = down + up = 176 + 44 = **220 ft**

14. Construction

15. Draw diagonals $\overline{DB}$ and $\overline{AC}$. P, Q, S, R are midpoints of $\overline{AD}$, $\overline{AB}$, $\overline{BC}$, and $\overline{DC}$, respectively. So $PQ = \frac{1}{2}DB = SR$ and $PS = \frac{1}{2}AC = QR$.

16. Refer to Problem Set 76, problem 6.

17. $AC = BC, DC = EC, \angle C = \angle C$ implies $\triangle AEC \cong \triangle BDC$ and $\angle AEC = \angle BDC$.

18. $4(x^2 + 6x + 9) - (y^2 - 4y + 4)$
$= -28 + 36 - 4$
$\dfrac{4(x + 3)^2}{4} - \dfrac{(y - 2)^2}{4} = \dfrac{4}{4}$
$\dfrac{(x + 3)^2}{1} - \dfrac{(y - 2)^2}{4} = 1$
Center: (−3, 2)
Vertices: (−2, 2), (−4, 2)
Asymptotes: $y = 2x + 8$
$\qquad\qquad\quad y = -2x - 4$

19. $9(x^2 - 4x + 4) + 25(y^2 + 6y + 9)$
$= -260 + 36 + 225$
$9(x - 2)^2 + 25(y + 3)^2 = 1$
$\dfrac{(x - 2)^2}{\frac{1}{9}} + \dfrac{(y + 3)^2}{\frac{1}{25}} = 1$
Center: (2, −3)

Major axis: $\frac{2}{3}$
Minor axis: $\frac{2}{5}$

20. (a) Refer to Example 84.B.2
(b) $\sin 255° - \sin 15°$
$= 2\cos\dfrac{255° + 15°}{2}\sin\dfrac{255° - 15°}{2}$
$= 2\cos 135° \sin 120°$
$= 2\left(-\dfrac{\sqrt{2}}{2}\right)\left(\dfrac{\sqrt{3}}{2}\right) = -\dfrac{\sqrt{6}}{2}$

21. (a) $a_{12} = a_1 r^{11} = (2)(-2)^{11} = -4096$
(b) $S_{12} = \dfrac{a_1(1 - r^n)}{1 - r} = \dfrac{2[1 - (-2)^{12}]}{1 - (-2)}$
$S_{12} = \dfrac{2[1 - 4096]}{3} = -2730$

22. $\ln 42 = \log_e 42 = \dfrac{\log 42}{\log e}$

23. $\cos A = \dfrac{3^2 + 8^2 - 7^2}{2(2)(3)} = \dfrac{1}{2}$
$A = \text{Arccos}\dfrac{1}{2} = 60°$

24. $\dfrac{40 \text{ mi}}{\text{hr}} \cdot \dfrac{1 \text{ hr}}{60 \text{ min}} \cdot \dfrac{1 \text{ min}}{60 \text{ sec}} \cdot \dfrac{5280}{1 \text{ mi}} \cdot \dfrac{12 \text{ in}}{1 \text{ ft}}$
$\cdot \dfrac{2.54 \text{ cm}}{1 \text{ in}} \cdot \dfrac{1 \text{ m}}{100 \text{ cm}} \cdot \dfrac{1 \text{ km}}{1000 \text{ m}}$
$= \dfrac{(40)(5280)(12)(2.54) \text{ km}}{(60)(60)(100)(1000) \text{ sec}}$

25. (a) $y = 10 + 6\csc x$

(b) $y = -7 + 4\sec x$

26. $(\sin x - \cos x)^2$
$= \sin^2 x - 2\sin x \cos x + \cos^2 x$
$= 1 - 2\sin x \cos x = 1 - \sin 2x$

27. $\dfrac{\tan^2 x}{\sec x + 1} = \dfrac{\sec^2 x - 1}{\sec x +}$
$= \dfrac{(\sec x + 1)(\sec x - 1)}{\sec x + 1} = \sec x - 1$

28. $-2\cos 3x = -\sqrt{2}$
$\cos 3x = \dfrac{\sqrt{2}}{2}$
$3x = 45°, 315°, 405°, 675°, 765°, 1035°$
$x = 15°, 105°, 135°, 225°, 255°, 345°$

29. $\log_5 16^{3/4} - \log_5 (3x - 2) = \log_5 (2x + 1)^{-1}$

$\log_5 \dfrac{8}{3x - 2} = \log_5 \dfrac{1}{2x + 1}$

$\dfrac{8}{3x - 2} = \dfrac{1}{2x + 1}$

$8(2x + 1) = 3x - 2$

$x = -\dfrac{10}{13}$

No solution

30. (1) Find the line perpendicular to the first.

$y = -5x - 13$

$m_\perp = \dfrac{1}{5}$ at $(0, 2)$

$2 = \dfrac{1}{5}(0) + b$

$y = \dfrac{1}{5}x + 2$

(2) Set the equations equal to find their point of intersection.

$-5x - 13 = \dfrac{1}{5}x + 2$

$-15 = \dfrac{26}{5}x$

$x = -\dfrac{75}{26}$

$y = \dfrac{1}{5}\left(-\dfrac{75}{26}\right) + 2 = -\dfrac{15}{26} + \dfrac{52}{26} = \dfrac{37}{26}$

(3) Find the distance between the two points, $(0, 2)$ and $\left(-\dfrac{75}{26}, \dfrac{37}{26}\right)$.

$\sqrt{\left(-\dfrac{75}{26} - 0\right)^2 + \left(\dfrac{37}{26} - 2\right)^2}$

$= \sqrt{\left(-\dfrac{75}{26}\right)^2 + \left(-\dfrac{15}{26}\right)^2}$

$= \sqrt{\dfrac{5625}{26^2} + \dfrac{225}{26^2}} = \sqrt{\dfrac{5850}{26^2}}$

$= \dfrac{\sqrt{5850}}{26} = \dfrac{15\sqrt{26}}{26}$

EP

63. $\begin{bmatrix} 1 & 0 \\ 0 & 1 \end{bmatrix} \cdot \begin{bmatrix} 3 & -4 \\ 4 & 7 \end{bmatrix}$

$= \begin{bmatrix} (1)(3) + (0)(4) & (1)(-4) + (0)(7) \\ (0)(3) + (1)(4) & (0)(-4) + (1)(7) \end{bmatrix}$

$= \begin{bmatrix} 3 & -4 \\ 4 & 7 \end{bmatrix}$

64. For $k = 1$ we get $1 = \dfrac{1(1 + 1)}{2}$ and also

$\dfrac{k(k + 1)}{2} + (k + 1) = \dfrac{k(k + 1)}{2} + \dfrac{2(k + 1)}{2}$

$= \dfrac{(k + 2)(k + 1)}{2} = \dfrac{(k + 1)[(k + 1) + 1]}{2}$

PROBLEM SET 97

1. $\boxed{\begin{matrix} 10\% \\ x \end{matrix}} + \boxed{\begin{matrix} 2\% \\ y \end{matrix}} = \boxed{\begin{matrix} 6\% \\ 1400 \end{matrix}}$

$x + y = 1400$

$y = 1400 - x$

$10x + 2y = 6(1400)$

$10x + 2(1400 - x) = 8400$

$10x + 2800 - 2x = 8400$

$8x = 5600$

$x = \textbf{700 ml of 10\%}$

$y = \textbf{700 ml of 2\%}$

2. $B = 3R - 4$

$2B = W$

$R + B + W = 28$

$R + B + 2B = 28$

$R + 3B = 28$

$R + 3(3R - 4) = 28$

$10R = 40$

$R = 4$

$B = 3(4) - 4 = \textbf{8}$

$W = 2(8) = \textbf{16}$

3. $2(180 - A) = 4(90 - B) + 200$

$360 - 2A = 360 - 4B + 200$

$4B - 2A = 200$

$2B - A = 100$

$A = 2B - 100$

$A + B = 110$

$(2B - 100) + B = 110$

$3B = 210$

$B = \textbf{70}°$

$A = 110° - 70° = \textbf{40}°$

4. H = hundreds' digit
T = tens' digit
U = units' digit
$100H + 10T + U$ = number
$100U + 10T + H$ = reversed number
A: $\dfrac{H}{U} = 4$ thus $H = 4U$
B: $100U + 10T + H = 100H + 10T + U - 297$
$99U - 99H = -297$
C: $H + T + U = 13$
Substitute equation A into B.
$99U - 99(4U) = -297$
$-297U = -297$
$U = 1$
$H = 4(1) = 4$
$T = 13 - (4) - (1) = 8$
Number = $100(4) + 10(8) + (1) =$ **481**

5. Down: $(2C + C)(B - 1) = 60$
$3CB - 3C = 60$
Up: $(2C - C)B = 45$
$CB = 45$
$3(45) - 3C = 60$
$3C = 75$
$C = 25$
Water = $C =$ **25 mph**
Jewel Ann = $2C =$ **50 mph**

6. $S_\infty = \dfrac{0.00029}{1 - 0.01} = \dfrac{0.00029}{0.99} = \dfrac{29}{99,000}$

7. $S_\infty = \dfrac{0.019}{1 - 0.01} = \dfrac{0.019}{0.99}$
$S_\infty = \dfrac{19}{990} + 2 = \dfrac{1999}{990}$

8. $B = \left(\dfrac{40}{4}\right)^2 = (10)^2$
$V = \dfrac{1}{3}Bh = \dfrac{1}{3}(10)^2(6) =$ **200 cm³**

9. $\left(\dfrac{3}{1}\right)^3 = \dfrac{27}{1}$
Ratio = **27 : 1**

10. (a) $V = \dfrac{4}{3}\pi r^3 = \dfrac{4}{3}\pi(4)^3 = \dfrac{256\pi}{3}$ cm³
(b) $SA = 4\pi r^2 = 4\pi(4)^2 =$ **64π cm²**

11. $d = \sqrt{l^2 + w^2 + h^2}$
$= \sqrt{2^2 + m^2 + 4^2} = \sqrt{20 + m^2}$

12. (a) $V = \dfrac{1}{3}\pi r^2 h = \dfrac{1}{3}\pi(5)^2(10) = \dfrac{250\pi}{3}$ cm³
(b) $SA = \pi r^2 + \pi r s = \pi(5)\left(5\sqrt{5}\right)$
$= \left(25 + 25\sqrt{5}\,\pi\right)$ cm²

13. $S = \dfrac{a_1}{1 - r} = \dfrac{\frac{1}{4}}{1 - \left(-\frac{1}{2}\right)} = \dfrac{\frac{1}{4}}{\frac{3}{2}} = \dfrac{1}{6}$

14. $x^2 + 3x + 9 = 0$
$x = \dfrac{-3 \pm \sqrt{9 - 4(1)(9)}}{2(1)} = \dfrac{-3 \pm 3\sqrt{3}\,i}{2}$
$= \left[x - \left(\dfrac{-3 + 3\sqrt{3}\,i}{2}\right)\right]\left[x - \left(\dfrac{-3 - 3\sqrt{3}\,i}{2}\right)\right]$
$= \left(x + \dfrac{3}{2} - \dfrac{3\sqrt{3}\,i}{2}\right)\left(x + \dfrac{3}{2} + \dfrac{3\sqrt{3}\,i}{2}\right)$

15. $AB = AD, BC = CD, AC = AC$ implies
$\triangle ABC \cong \triangle ADC$ and $\angle BAO = \angle DAO$.
$AO = AO$ implies $\triangle ABO \cong \triangle ADO$ and
$\angle AOB = \angle AOD$. $\angle AOB + \angle AOD = 180°$
implies $\angle AOB = \angle AOD = 90°$. Therefore
$\overline{AC} \perp \overline{BD}$.

16. $\overline{BD}$ and $\overline{KJ}$ bisect each other. $KE = EJ$,
$DE = EB, \angle DEK = \angle JEB$ implies $\triangle DEK$
$\cong \triangle BEJ$; and $\angle DKE = \angle BJE$ implies $\angle CKE$
$= \angle AJE$. $\angle CEK = \angle EJA$ implies $\triangle CKE$
$\sim \triangle AJE$. $KE = EJ$ so $SF = 1$,;therefore
$\triangle CKE \cong \triangle AJE$ and $KC = AJ$.

17. Draw $\overline{IK}$ and $\overline{MK}$. $IJ = ML, JK = LK$,
$\angle IJK = \angle MLK$ implies $\triangle IJK \cong \triangle MLK$ and
$IK = MK$. $IH = HM, HK = HK$ implies
$\triangle HIK \cong \triangle HMK$ and $\angle IHK = \angle MHK$.

18. $4(x^2 - 2x + 1) - 25(y^2 + 4y + 4)$
$= 196 + 4 - 100$
$\dfrac{4(x - 1)^2}{100} - \dfrac{25(y + 2)^2}{100} = \dfrac{100}{100}$
$\dfrac{(x - 1)^2}{25} - \dfrac{(y + 2)^2}{4} = 1$
Center: (1, −2)
Vertices: (6, −2), (−4, −2)
Asymptotes: $y = \dfrac{2}{5}x - \dfrac{12}{5}$
$y = -\dfrac{2}{5}x - \dfrac{8}{5}$

19. $25(x^2 + 6x + 9) + 9(y^2 - 4y + 4)$
$= -36 + 225 + 36$
$$\frac{25(x + 3)^2}{225} + \frac{9(y - 2)^2}{225} = \frac{225}{225}$$
$$\frac{(x + 3)^2}{9} + \frac{(y - 2)^2}{25} = 1$$
Center: $(-3, 2)$
Major axis: 10
Minor axis: 6

20. (a) Refer to Example 84.B.3.
(b) $\cos 285° + \cos 15°$
$$= 2 \cos \frac{285° + 15°}{2} \cos \frac{285° - 15°}{2}$$
$= 2 \cos 150° \cos 135°$
$$= 2\left(-\frac{\sqrt{3}}{2}\right)\left(-\frac{\sqrt{2}}{2}\right) = \frac{\sqrt{6}}{2}$$

21. (a) $a_{16} = a_1 + 15d = -5 + 15\left(\frac{2}{5}\right)$
$= -5 + 6 = 1$
(b) $S_n = \frac{n}{2}(a_1 + a_n) = \frac{16}{2}(-5 + 1)$
$= 8(-4) = -32$

22. $\cos B = \frac{8^2 + 9^2 - 15^2}{2(8)(9)} = -\frac{80}{144}$
$B \approx 123.7°$

23. $\ln 200 = \log_e 200 = \frac{\log 200}{\log e}$

24. $360°$

25. $(-i)^{1/3} = (1 \text{ cis } 270°)^{1/3}$
$1 \text{ cis } 90° = i$
$1 \text{ cis } 210° = -\frac{\sqrt{3}}{2} - \frac{1}{2}i$
$1 \text{ cis } 330° = \frac{\sqrt{3}}{2} - \frac{1}{2}i$

26. $\sin (-x) \sec (-x) = -\sin x \sec x$
$= -\sin x \frac{1}{\cos x} = \frac{-\sin x}{\cos x} = -\tan x$

27. $\dfrac{\cot x - 1}{1 - \tan x} = \dfrac{\dfrac{\cos x}{\sin x} - 1}{1 - \dfrac{\sin x}{\cos x}} = \dfrac{\dfrac{\cos x - \sin x}{\sin x}}{\dfrac{\cos x - \sin x}{\cos x}}$
$= \dfrac{\cos x - \sin x}{\sin x} \cdot \dfrac{\cos x}{\cos x - \sin x}$
$= \dfrac{\cos x}{\sin x} = \dfrac{\dfrac{1}{\sec x}}{\dfrac{1}{\csc x}} = \dfrac{\csc x}{\sec x}$

28. $\sin^2 x - \sin x = 0$
$(\sin x)(\sin x - 1) = 0$
$\sin x = 0 \qquad\qquad \sin x - 1 = 0$
$x = 0°, 180° \qquad \sin x = 1$
$\qquad\qquad\qquad\qquad x = 90°$

29. $\log_8 8^{2/3} + \log_8 (4x - 2) = 1$
$(\log_8 4)(4x - 2) = 1$
$8^1 = 4(4x - 2)$
$8 = 16x - 8$
$16x = 16$
$x = 1$

30. $H^+ = 10^{-pH} = 10^{-3} = 1 \times 10^{-3}$

EP

65. For $k = 1$, we get $\dfrac{1}{1 \cdot 2}$ and
$$\frac{k}{k + 1} + \frac{1}{(k + 1)(k + 2)} = \frac{k(k + 2) + 1}{(k + 1)(k + 2)}$$
$$= \frac{k^2 + 2k + 1}{(k + 1)(k + 2)} = \frac{(k + 1)^2}{(k + 1)(k + 2)}$$
$$= \frac{k + 1}{k + 2} = \frac{k + 1}{(k + 1) + 1}$$

66. Invalid

PROBLEM SET 98

1. $\dfrac{V_1}{T_1} = \dfrac{V_2}{T_2}$

$\dfrac{4}{4000} = \dfrac{V}{2000}$

$V = \dfrac{4(2000)}{4000} = $ **2 liters**

2. Sweets = 7
Sour = 2
Total = 9

$\dfrac{2}{9} = \dfrac{\text{Sour}}{18{,}000}$

$\text{Sour} = \dfrac{2(18{,}000)}{9} = $ **4000**

3. $m = \dfrac{kkw^2}{\sqrt{x}}$

$\dfrac{k(2k)(3w)^2}{\sqrt{8x}} = \dfrac{18kkw^2}{2\sqrt{2}\,\sqrt{x}}$

Multiply by $\dfrac{9}{\sqrt{2}}$

4. (Cost each)(number) = total price

$\left(\dfrac{c}{m} + p\right)N = 4000$

$\dfrac{c + pm}{m}N = 4000$

$N = \dfrac{4000m}{c + pm}$

5. $\dfrac{1}{4}F + 14 = F$

$\dfrac{3}{4}F = 14$

$F = \dfrac{56}{3}\,\textbf{gal}$

6. Refer to Example 98.A.1.

7. Refer to Example 98.A.3.

8. $BD = EC, AD = AE, BD + AD = AE + EC$
implies $AB = AC, \angle A = \angle A$. Therefore
$\triangle AEB \cong \triangle ADC$ and $BE = CD$.

9. Trapezoid $ABCD$ is an isosceles trapezoid
implies $\angle ACD = \angle BDC$. $AC = BD$
and $CD = CD$ implies $\triangle ACD \cong \triangle BCD$
and $AD = BC$.

10. $\dfrac{0.0037}{1 - 0.01} = \dfrac{0.0037}{0.99} = \dfrac{37}{9900}$

11. $S_\infty = \dfrac{a_1}{1 - r} = \dfrac{\frac{2}{3}}{1 - \left(-\frac{1}{3}\right)} = \dfrac{\frac{2}{3}}{\frac{4}{3}} = \dfrac{2}{4} = \dfrac{1}{2}$

12. $d = \sqrt{l^2 + w^2 + h^2}$
$= \sqrt{3^2 + 5^2 + x^2} = \sqrt{34 + x^2}$

13. $\tan 36° = \dfrac{3}{h}$; thus $h = \dfrac{3}{\tan 36°} \approx 4.13$

$\text{Area}_\Delta \approx \dfrac{1}{2}(6)(4.13) \approx 12.39$

$B \approx 12.39(5) \approx 62$

$V = \dfrac{1}{3}Bh = \dfrac{1}{3}(62)(10) = $ **206.5 cm³**

14. Ratio of sides $= \dfrac{3}{1}$

Ratio of area $= \dfrac{9}{1}$

Ratio of volume $= \dfrac{27}{1}$

$\dfrac{9}{1} = \dfrac{x}{4}$

$x = 4(9) = $ **36 square units**

15. (a) $V = \dfrac{4}{3}\pi r^3 = \dfrac{4}{3}\pi(6)^3 = 288\pi\,\text{cm}^3$

(b) $SA = 4\pi r^2 = 4\pi(6)^2 = 144\pi\,\text{cm}^2$

16. (a) $V = \dfrac{1}{3}\pi r^2 h = \dfrac{1}{3}\pi(6)^2(4) = 48\pi\,\text{cm}^3$

(b) $SA = \pi r^2 + \pi rs = \pi(6)^2 + \pi(6)\left(2\sqrt{13}\right)$

$SA = (36\pi + 12\sqrt{13}\,\pi)\,\text{cm}^2$

17. $9(x^2 - 6x + 9) - 4(y^2 + 4y + 4)$
$= 79 + 81 - 16$

$\dfrac{9(x - 3)^2}{36} - \dfrac{4(y + 2)^2}{36} = \dfrac{36}{36}$

$\dfrac{(x - 3)^2}{4} - \dfrac{(y + 2)^2}{9} = 1$

Center: $(3, -2)$

Vertices: $(7, -2), (-1, -2)$

Asymptotes: $y = \dfrac{3}{2}x - \dfrac{13}{2}$

$y = -\dfrac{3}{2}x + \dfrac{5}{2}$

18. $25(x^2 - 6x + 9) + 4(y^2 + 8y + 16)$
     $= -189 + 225 + 64$
     $\dfrac{25(x - 3)^2}{100} + \dfrac{4(y + 4)^2}{100} = \dfrac{100}{100}$
     $\dfrac{(x - 3)^2}{4} + \dfrac{(y + 4)^2}{25} = 1$
     Center: $(3, -4)$
     Major axis: **10**
     Minor axis: **4**

19. (a) Refer to Example 84.A.4
     (b) $\sin 225° \sin 15°$
         $= \dfrac{1}{2}[(\cos(225° - 15°) - \cos(225° + 15°)]$
         $= \dfrac{1}{2}[\cos 210° - \cos 240°]$
         $= \dfrac{1}{2}\left[-\dfrac{\sqrt{3}}{2} - \left(-\dfrac{1}{2}\right)\right] = \dfrac{-\sqrt{3} + 1}{4}$

20. $a_{17} = a_1 + 16d = 3 + 16(3) = \mathbf{51}$
     $S_{17} = \dfrac{n}{2}(a_1 + a_n) = \dfrac{17}{2}(3 + 51) = \mathbf{459}$

21. $\dfrac{\sin A}{4} = \dfrac{\sin 40°}{12}$
     $\sin A = \dfrac{4 \sin 40°}{12} \approx 0.2142$
     $A = \text{Arcsin}(0.2142) \approx \mathbf{12.4°}$

22. $\ln 305 = \log_e 305 = \dfrac{\log 305}{\log e}$

23. $(-1)^{1/3} = (1 \text{ cis } 180°)^{1/3}$
     $1 \text{ cis } 60° = \dfrac{1}{2} + \dfrac{\sqrt{3}}{2}i$
     $1 \text{ cis } 180° = -1$
     $1 \text{ cis } 300° = \dfrac{1}{2} - \dfrac{\sqrt{3}}{2}i$

24. Refer to Lesson 77.B.

25. $\sqrt{(x + 3)^2 + (y + 4)^2} = \sqrt{(x - 3)^2 + (y - 4)^2}$
     $x^2 + 6x + 9 + y^2 + 8y + 16$
     $= x^2 - 6x + 9 + y^2 - 8y + 16$
     $12x + 16y = 0$
     $16y = -12x$
     $y = -\dfrac{12}{16}x$
     $y = -\dfrac{3}{4}x$

26. $(1 + \tan x)(1 - \tan x) + 2\tan^2 x$
     $= 1 - \tan^2 x + 2\tan^2 x = 1 + \tan^2 x$
     $= \sec^2 x$

27. $\dfrac{\sin x}{1 + \cos x} + \dfrac{1 + \cos x}{\sin x}$
     $= \dfrac{\sin^2 x + (1 + \cos x)^2}{(1 + \cos x)\sin x}$
     $= \dfrac{\sin^2 x + 1 + 2\cos x + \cos^2 x}{(1 + \cos x)\sin x}$
     $= \dfrac{2 + 2\cos x}{(1 + \cos x)\sin x}$
     $= \dfrac{2(1 + \cos x)}{(1 + \cos x)\sin x} = \dfrac{2}{\sin x} = 2\csc x$

28. $2 \sin 3x = -1$
     $\sin 3x = -\dfrac{1}{2}$
     $3x = 210°, 330°, 570°, 690°, 930°, 1050°$
     $x = \mathbf{70°, 110°, 190°, 230°, 310°, 350°}$

29. $\log \dfrac{x^2 - 1}{x - 1} = 1$
     $10^1 = \dfrac{x^2 - 1}{x - 1}$
     $10(x - 1) = x^2 - 1$
     $x^2 - 10x + 9 = 0$
     $(x - 9)(x - 1) = 0$
     $x = \mathbf{9}$

30. $2^{-2} = \dfrac{1}{2^2} = \dfrac{1}{4}$

EP

67. For $k = 1$, we get $1 = (1)^3$ and also
     $k^2 + (2k + 1) = (k + 1)^2$

68. $2X = \begin{bmatrix} 9 & 4 \\ 8 & 4 \end{bmatrix} - \begin{bmatrix} 1 & 0 \\ 0 & 2 \end{bmatrix} = \begin{bmatrix} 8 & 4 \\ 8 & 2 \end{bmatrix}$
     $X = \dfrac{1}{2}\begin{bmatrix} 8 & 4 \\ 8 & 2 \end{bmatrix} = \begin{bmatrix} 4 & 2 \\ 4 & 1 \end{bmatrix}$

PROBLEM SET 99

1. $R_1T_1 + R_2T_2 = 1$

$\frac{1}{10}(T + 2) + \frac{1}{8}T = 1$

$\frac{1}{10}T + \frac{1}{5} + \frac{1}{8}T = 1$

$4T + 8 + 5T = 40$

$9T = 32$

$T = \frac{32}{9}$ hr

2. $400 = 120e^{5k}$

$3.33 \approx e^{5k}$

$\ln 3.33 \approx \ln e^{5k}$

$1.204 \approx 5k$

$k \approx 0.2408$

$A_{25} = 120e^{25(0.2408)} = 120e^{6.02}$

$= 120(411.58) = \mathbf{49,382.7}$

3. $\frac{1}{12}T = S$ $\qquad T = 30 + S$

$\frac{11}{12}T = 30$

$T = \frac{30(12)}{11} = 32\frac{8}{11}$ min

4. Down: $(3W + W)(B - 1) = 48$

$4WB - 4W = 48$

Up: $(3W - W)B = 32$

$2WB = 32$

$WB = 16$

$4(16) - 4W = 48$

$-4W = -16$

$W = 4$

Water $= W = \mathbf{4\,mph}$

Mary Ann $= 3W = \mathbf{12\,mph}$

5. $\frac{4}{52} + \frac{26}{52} - \frac{2}{52} = \frac{28}{52} = \frac{7}{13}$

6. Refer to Lesson 99.A.

7. $AD = BE, DC = EC$ implies $AD + DC$ $= BE + EC$; so $AC = BC$. $\angle C = \angle C$ implies $\triangle ACE \cong \triangle BCD$ and $\angle A = \angle B$.

8. $\overline{RC} \parallel \overline{AB}$ implies $\angle DRX = \angle XSA$,

$\angle RXD = \angle AXS$ implies $\triangle XRD \sim \triangle XSA$; $RX = XS$ so $SF = 1$. $\triangle XRD \cong \triangle XSA$

implies $\overline{RD} = \overline{SA}$. $RSBC$ is a parallelogram since $\overline{RC} \parallel \overline{SB}$, $\overline{RS} \parallel \overline{CB}$, which implies $RS = CB$. X, Y are midpoints implies $XS = \frac{1}{2}RS = \frac{1}{2}CB = YB$.

$\overline{XS} \parallel \overline{YB}$ implies $XSBY$ is a parallelogram so $\overline{XY} \parallel \overline{SB}$. XY

$= RD + DC, AS = RD$ implies XY $= AS + DC$. $XY = SB$ implies $2XY$ $= AS + DC + SB$; so $2XY = DC + AB$.

Therefore $XY = \frac{1}{2}(DC + AB)$ and

$\overline{RC} \parallel \overline{XY} \parallel \overline{AB}$.

9. Refer to Lesson 98.A.

10. Refer to Lesson 76.B.

11. $S_\infty = \frac{a_1}{1 - r} = \frac{0.0041}{1 - 0.01} = \frac{0.0041}{0.99} = \frac{41}{9900}$

12. $S_\infty = \frac{a_1}{1 - r} = \frac{\frac{1}{4}}{1 + \frac{3}{4}} = \frac{\frac{1}{4}}{\frac{7}{4}} = \frac{1}{7}$

13. $d = \sqrt{l^2 + w^2 + h^2}$

$= \sqrt{7^2 + 3^2 + x^2} = \sqrt{58 + x^2}$

14. $V = \frac{1}{3}Bh = \frac{1}{3}\left[\frac{1}{2}(6)(3\sqrt{3})\right](10)$

$= \mathbf{30\sqrt{3}\ cm^3}$

15. $\left(\frac{8}{27}\right)^{1/3} = \frac{2}{3}$

Ratio $= \mathbf{2:3}$

16. (a) $V = \frac{4}{3}\pi r^3 = \frac{4}{3}\pi(10)^3 = \frac{4000}{3}\pi\ cm^3$

(b) $SA = 4\pi r^2 = 4\pi(10)^2 = 400\pi\ cm^2$

17. (a) $V = \frac{1}{3}\pi r^2 h = \frac{1}{3}\pi(10)^2(6) = 200\pi\ cm^3$

(b) $SA = \pi r^2 + \pi r s$

$= \pi(10)^2 + \pi(10)2\sqrt{34}$

$= (100\pi + 20\sqrt{34}\,\pi)\ cm^2$

18. $25(x^2 - 8x + 16) + 9(y^2 + 2y + 1)$
$= -184 + 400 + 9$
$\dfrac{25(x - 4)^2}{225} + \dfrac{9(y + 1)^2}{225} = \dfrac{225}{225}$
$\dfrac{(x - 4)^2}{9} + \dfrac{(y + 1)^2}{25} = 1$
Center: (4, -1)
Major axis: 10
Minor axis: 6

19. $(x^2 + 4x + 4) - 4(y^2 - 8y + 16)$
$= 96 + 4 - 64$
$\dfrac{(x + 2)^2}{36} - \dfrac{4(y - 4)^2}{36} = \dfrac{36}{36}$
$\dfrac{(x + 2)^2}{36} - \dfrac{(y - 4)^2}{9} = 1$
Center: (-2, 4)
Vertices: (4, 4), (-8, 4)
Asymptotes: $y = \dfrac{1}{2}x + 5$
$\qquad\qquad\quad y = -\dfrac{1}{2}x + 3$

20. (a) Refer to Example 84.A.1.

(b) $\sin 225° \cos 15°$
$= \dfrac{1}{2}\left[\sin(225° + 15°) + \sin(x - y)\right]$
$= \dfrac{1}{2}(\sin 240° + \sin 210°)$
$= \dfrac{1}{2}[-0.866 - 0.5] = \mathbf{-0.683}$

21. $a_{15} = a_1 r^{14} = 4(2)^{14} = \mathbf{65{,}536}$

22. $\cos A = \dfrac{8^2 + 4^2 - 7^2}{2(8)(4)} = 0.4844$
$A = \text{Arccos } 0.4844 \approx \mathbf{61.0°}$

23. $\log_4 8 = \dfrac{\log 8}{\log 4}$

24. $(1)^{1/3} = (1 \text{ cis } 0°)^{1/3}$; angles differ by $120°$
$1 \text{ cis } 0° = \mathbf{1}$
$1 \text{ cis } 120° = \mathbf{-\dfrac{1}{2} + \dfrac{\sqrt{3}}{2}i}$
$1 \text{ cis } 240° = \mathbf{-\dfrac{1}{2} - \dfrac{\sqrt{3}}{2}i}$

25.

26. $\dfrac{1}{2} \sec x \csc(-x) = \dfrac{1}{2 \cos x} \cdot \dfrac{1}{-\sin x}$
$= -\dfrac{1}{2 \cos x \sin x} = -\dfrac{1}{\sin 2x}$

27. $-2 \sin 3x = 1$
$\sin 3x = -\dfrac{1}{2}$
$3x = 210°, 330°, 570°, 690°, 930°, 1050°$
$x = \mathbf{70°, 110°, 190°, 230°, 310°, 350°}$

28. $\dfrac{\cos x}{\sec x - 1} - \dfrac{\cos x}{\sec x + 1}$
$= \dfrac{(\cos x)(\sec x + 1) - (\cos x)(\sec x - 1)}{\sec^2 x - 1}$
$= \dfrac{1 + \cos x - 1 + \cos x}{\sec^2 x - 1} = \dfrac{2 \cos x}{\tan^2 x}$
$= \dfrac{2 \cos x}{\dfrac{\sin^2 x}{\cos^2 x}} = \dfrac{2 \cos^3 x}{\sin^2 x} = 2 \cos^3 x \csc^2 x$

29. $\log x^{2/3} + \log x^{4/3} = \log \dfrac{1}{23}$
$\log (x^{2/3})(x^{4/3}) = \log \dfrac{1}{8}$
$x^2 = \dfrac{1}{8}$
$x = \pm\dfrac{1}{\sqrt{8}} = \pm\dfrac{1}{2\sqrt{2}} = \pm\dfrac{\sqrt{2}}{4}$

30. $5^{\log_5 4 - \log_5 2} = 5^{\log_5 4/2} = \dfrac{4}{2} = \mathbf{2}$

EP

69. For $k = 1$, we get $2 = 1(1 + 1)$. Also
$k(k + 1) + 2(k + 1) = (k + 1)(k + 2)$
$= (k + 1[(k + 1) + 1]$

70. $\dfrac{1}{2}\begin{bmatrix} 4 & 6 \\ 2 & -2 \end{bmatrix} \cdot \begin{bmatrix} -2 & 0 \\ 2 & 4 \end{bmatrix}$
$= \dfrac{1}{2}\begin{bmatrix} (4)(-2) + (6)(2) & (4)(0) + (6)(4) \\ (2)(-2) + (-2)(2) & (2)(0) + (-2)(4) \end{bmatrix}$
$= \dfrac{1}{2}\begin{bmatrix} 4 & 24 \\ -8 & -8 \end{bmatrix} = \begin{bmatrix} 2 & 12 \\ -4 & -4 \end{bmatrix}$

1. $2(180° - A) = 5(90° - A) + 30°$
   $360° - 2A = 450° - 5A + 30°$
   $3A = 120°$
   $A = \mathbf{40°}$

2.
	Late	On time
Distance:	$f \cdot t$	$f \cdot t$
Time:	t	$t - 2$
Rate:	f	$\dfrac{f \cdot t}{t - 2}\dfrac{\text{ft}}{\text{hr}}$

3. $2 \, \# \, (4 * 3)$
   $2 \, \# \, [5(4) + 4(3)]$
   $2 \, \# \, 32$
   $2(2) + 3(32) = \mathbf{100}$

4. $\dfrac{1}{2} \cdot \dfrac{1}{2} = \dfrac{1}{4}$

5. $_8P_6 = \dfrac{8!}{2!} = \mathbf{20,160}$
   $_8C_6 = \dfrac{8!}{2!6!} = \mathbf{28}$

6. $\log y = \dfrac{1}{2} \log (3.01 \times 10^2) + \dfrac{1}{4} \log (2.6 \times 10^3)$
   $= \dfrac{1}{2}(0.4786 + 2) + \dfrac{1}{4}(0.4150 + 3)$
   $= \dfrac{1}{2}(2.4786) + \dfrac{1}{4}(3.4150)$
   $= 1.2393 + 0.8538 = 2.0931$
   $y = \text{antilog } 2.0931 = \text{antilog } (0.0931) + 2$
   $= 1.239 \times 10^2 = \mathbf{123.9}$

7. $\log y = \dfrac{2}{3} \log (2.03 \times 10^6) - \dfrac{1}{2} \log (8.04 \times 10^{18})$
   $= \dfrac{2}{3}(0.3075 + 6) - \dfrac{1}{2}(0.9053 + 18)$
   $= \dfrac{2}{3}(6.3075) - \dfrac{1}{2}(18.9053)$
   $= 4.2050 - 9.4527 = -5.2476$
   $y = \text{antilog } (-5.2476) = \text{antilog } (0.7524) - 6$
   $= \mathbf{5.7 \times 10^{-6}}$

8. $\log_3 (x - 2) < 3$
   $(x - 2) < 3^3$ and $x - 2 > 0$
   $x - 2 < 27 \qquad x > 2$
   $x < 29$
   $\mathbf{2 < x < 29}$

9. $\log_{1/2} (x - 3) > 3$
   $x - 3 < \left(\dfrac{1}{2}\right)^3$ and $x - 3 > 0$
   $x - 3 < \dfrac{1}{8} \qquad x > 3$
   $x < \dfrac{25}{8}$
   $3 < x < \dfrac{25}{8}$

10. $\log_5 6 = \dfrac{\log 6}{\log 5}$

11. (a) Refer to Lesson 99.B.

    (b) Refer to Lesson 99.B.

12. $AD = BE, DC = EC$ implies $AD + DC$
    $= BE + EC$; so $AC = BC$. $\angle DCE$
    $= \angle DCE$ implies $\triangle AEC \cong \triangle BDC$ and
    $AE = BD$.

13. $AD = BE, DC = EC$ implies $AD + DC$
    $= BE + EC$; so $AC = BC$. $\angle DCE$
    $= \angle DCE$ so $\triangle AEC \cong \triangle BDC$ and $\angle A$
    $= \angle B$. $\angle AFD = \angle BFE$ implies $\triangle AFD$
    $\sim \triangle BFE$, $AD = BE$; so $SF = 1$ and
    $\triangle AFD \cong \triangle BFE$.

14. Refer to Problem Set 47, problem 8.

15. $\overline{RS} \parallel \overline{CB}$, $\angle XRD = \angle XSA$, $\angle RXD$
    $= \angle AXS$ implies $\triangle RXD \sim \triangle SXA$.
    $AX = XD$ so $SF = 1$; thus $\triangle RXD$
    $\cong \triangle SXA$ and $RX = \overline{XS}$. $RCBS$ is a
    parallelogram since $\overline{RC} \parallel \overline{AB}$,
    $\overline{RS} \parallel \overline{CB}$ implies $RS = CB$.
    $XS = \dfrac{1}{2}RS = \dfrac{1}{2}CB = YB$; $\overline{XS} \parallel \overline{YB}$
    implies $XSBY$ is a parallelogram so $\overline{XY}$
    $\parallel \overline{AB}$. $XY = RD + DC, XY = SB$
    implies $2XY = RD + DC + SB$. AS
    $= RD$ implies $2XY = AS + SB + DC$
    $= DC + AB$ implies $XY = \dfrac{1}{2}(DC + AB)$.

16. $S_\infty = \dfrac{0.0043}{1 - 0.01} = \dfrac{0.0043}{0.99} = \dfrac{43}{9900}$

17. $a_4 = a_1 r^4 = 256\left(\dfrac{3}{4}\right)^4 = 256\left(\dfrac{81}{256}\right)$

$= \mathbf{81\ ft}$

18. $d = \sqrt{l^2 + w^2 + h^2}$

$= \sqrt{3^2 + 5^2 + x^2} = \sqrt{34 + x^2}$

19. $\tan 22.5° = \dfrac{2.5}{h}$

$h = \dfrac{2.5}{\tan 22.5°} \approx 6.04$

$\text{Area}_\Delta = \dfrac{1}{2}(5)(6.04) \approx 15.1$

$B = \text{Area}_{\text{octagon}} = 8(15.1) \approx 120.8$

$V = \dfrac{1}{3}Bh = \dfrac{1}{3}(120.8)(9) \approx \mathbf{362.4\ cm^3}$

20. $\left(\dfrac{3}{5}\right)^2 = \dfrac{9}{25}$

21. (a) $V = \dfrac{4}{3}\pi r^3 = \dfrac{4}{3}\pi(9)^3 = \mathbf{972\pi\ cm^3}$

(b) $SA = 4\pi r^2 = 4\pi(9)^2 = \mathbf{324\pi\ cm^2}$

22. (a) $V = \dfrac{1}{3}\pi r^2 h = \dfrac{1}{3}\pi(8)^2(8) = \dfrac{512}{3}\pi\ \mathbf{cm^3}$

(b) $SA = \pi r^2 + \pi rs$

$= \pi(8)^2 + \pi(8)\left(8\sqrt{2}\right)$

$= \left(64\pi + 64\sqrt{2}\,\pi\right)\mathbf{cm^2}$

23. $25(x^2 + 2x + 1) + 9(y^2 - 4y + 4)$

$= 164 + 25 + 36$

$\dfrac{25(x + 1)^2}{225} + \dfrac{9(y - 2)^2}{225} = \dfrac{225}{225}$

$\dfrac{(x + 1)^2}{9} + \dfrac{(y - 2)^2}{25} = 1$

Center: (-1, 2)

Major axis: 10

Minor axis: 6

24. $4(x^2 - 10x + 25) - 36(y^2 - 6y + 9)$

$= 368 + 100 - 324$

$\dfrac{4(x - 5)^2}{144} - \dfrac{36(y - 3)^2}{144} = \dfrac{144}{144}$

$\dfrac{(x - 5)^2}{36} - \dfrac{(y - 3)^2}{4} = 1$

Center: (5, 3)

Vertices: (11, 3), (-1, 3)

Asymptotes: $y = \dfrac{1}{3}x + \dfrac{4}{3}$

$y = -\dfrac{1}{3}x + \dfrac{14}{3}$

25. $\cos x - \cos y = -2\sin\dfrac{x+y}{2}\sin\dfrac{x-y}{2}$

$\cos 255° - \cos 15°$

$= -2\sin\dfrac{255° + 15°}{2}\sin\dfrac{255° - 15°}{2}$

$= -2\sin 135°\ \sin 120°$

$= -2\left(\dfrac{\sqrt{2}}{2}\right)\left(\dfrac{\sqrt{3}}{2}\right) = -\dfrac{\sqrt{6}}{2}$

26. $a = \sqrt{8^2 + 10^2 - 2(8)(10)\cos 140°} \approx 16.9$

27. $\sec x \csc x = \left(\dfrac{1}{\cos x}\right)\left(\dfrac{1}{\sin x}\right)$

$= \dfrac{1}{\cos x \sin x}\dfrac{2}{2} = \dfrac{2}{2\cos x \sin x}$

$= \dfrac{2}{\sin 2x} = 2\csc 2x$

28. $\sqrt{3}\tan 3x = 1$

$\tan 3x = \dfrac{1}{\sqrt{3}} = \dfrac{\sqrt{3}}{3}$

$3x = 30°, 210°, 390°, 570°, 750°, 930°$

$x = \mathbf{10°, 70°, 130°, 190°, 250°, 310°}$

29. $\dfrac{2\tan\theta}{1 + \tan^2\theta} = \dfrac{2\tan\theta}{\sec^2\theta} = \dfrac{2\dfrac{\sin\theta}{\cos\theta}}{\dfrac{1}{\cos^2\theta}}$

$= \dfrac{2\sin\theta}{\cos\theta}\cdot\cos^2\theta = 2\sin\theta\cos\theta = \sin 2\theta$

30. $4^{-3} = \dfrac{1}{4^3} = \dfrac{1}{64}$

EP

71. For $k = 1$, we get 1^2

$= \dfrac{1(1 + 1)(2 + 1)}{6} = \dfrac{(2)(3)}{6} = 1$

Also $\dfrac{k(k + 1)(2k + 1)}{6} + (k + 1)^2$

$= \dfrac{k(k + 1)(2k + 1) + 6(k + 1)^2}{6}$

$= \dfrac{(k + 1)[k(2k + 1) + 6(k + 1)]}{6}$

$$= \frac{(k + 1)(2k^2 + 7k + 6)}{6}$$

$$= \frac{(k + 1)[(k + 2)(2k + 3)]}{6}$$

$$= \frac{(k+1)[(k+1) + 1][2(k+1) + 1]}{6}$$

72. $\begin{bmatrix} -1 & 2 \\ 3 & 0 \end{bmatrix} \cdot \begin{bmatrix} -1 & 7 \\ 3 & -5 \end{bmatrix}$

$= \begin{bmatrix} (-1)(-1) + (2)(3) & (-1)(7) + (2)(-5) \\ (3)(-1) + (0)(3) & (3)(7) + (0)(-5) \end{bmatrix}$

$= \begin{bmatrix} 7 & -17 \\ -3 & 21 \end{bmatrix}$

PROBLEM SET 101

1. $2.20 + 0.90(p - 3)$
$= 2.20 + 0.90p - 2.70$
$= \mathbf{(0.9p - 0.5)}$ **dollars**

2. $c + 0.80c = 900$
$1.8c = 900$
$c = 500$
Markup $= 0.50(500) = 250$
$500 + 250 = \$750$

3. $0.60(80,000) = 48,000$
$0.04(48,000) = \$1920$

4. $_7C_3 = \frac{7!}{(7 - 3)!3!} = 35$

5. $0.4 + 0.6 - 0.2 = \mathbf{0.8}$

6. $\frac{6!}{3! \, 3!} (2x^2)^3(-y)^3 = \mathbf{-160x^6y^3}$

7. $\frac{8!}{4! \, 4!} (a^2)^4(-2b)^4 = \mathbf{1120a^8b^4}$

8. $\log y = \frac{2}{3} \log (3.01 \times 10^6)$
$- \frac{1}{2} \log (9.01 \times 10^{17})$
$= \frac{2}{3}(0.4786 + 6) - \frac{1}{2}(0.9547 + 17)$
$= \frac{2}{3}(6.4786) - \frac{1}{2}(17.9547)$
$= 4.3191 - 8.9774 = -4.6583$
antilog $y = $ antilog $(-4.6583 + 5) - 5$
$= $ antilog $(0.3417) - 5 = \mathbf{2.2 \times 10^{-5}}$

9. $(x - 2) < 5^3$ also $x - 2 > 0$
$x - 2 < 125$ $x > 2$
$x < 127$
$\mathbf{2 < x < 127}$

10. $x + 1 > \left(\frac{1}{3}\right)^2$ also $x + 1 > 0$
$x + 1 > \frac{1}{9}$ $x > -1$
$x > -\frac{8}{9}$
$\mathbf{x > -\frac{8}{9}}$

11. $AD = BE, DC = EC$ implies $AD + DC$
$= BE + EC$ so $AC = BC$. $\angle C = \angle C$
so $\triangle AEC \cong \triangle BDC$; this implies $\angle A = \angle B$
and $\angle AFD = \angle BFE$. Now $\triangle AFD \sim \triangle BFE$
and $AD = BE$ so $SF = 1$ and thus $\triangle AFD$
$\cong \triangle BFE$. This implies $AF = BF, AC = BC,$
$FC = FC$ so $\triangle AFC \cong \triangle BFC.$

12. $\angle DBC = \angle ACB$ implies $BE = EC$; AE
$= ED, \angle AEB = DEC$ implies $\triangle AEB$
$\cong \triangle DEC$ implies $AB = DC.$

13. Draw $\overline{BE} \parallel \overline{AD}$ where E is on the
extension of AC. $\overline{AD} \parallel \overline{EB}$ implies
$\angle 2 = \angle 4, \angle 1 = \angle 3, \frac{AE}{AC} = \frac{BD}{DC}.$
$\overline{AD}$ is an angle bisector so $\angle 1 = \angle 2$, which
implies $\angle 3 = \angle 4$, and thus $AE = AB$; so
$\frac{AB}{AC} = \frac{BD}{DC}.$

14. Refer to Problem Set 47, problem 8.

15. (a) Refer to Lesson 99.A.

    (b) Refer to Lesson 99.B.

16. $S_\infty = \frac{a_1}{1 - r} = \frac{0.017}{1 - 0.01} = \frac{0.017}{0.99} = \frac{17}{990}$

17. $S_\infty = \dfrac{a_1}{1 - r} = \dfrac{128}{1 - \dfrac{1}{3}} = \dfrac{128}{\dfrac{2}{3}} = 192$ downs

$192 - 128 = 64$ ups

Total = **256 ft**

18. $d = \sqrt{l^2 + w^2 + h^2}$
$= \sqrt{3^2 + 6^2 + 5^2} = \sqrt{70}$

19. $h = 3\sqrt{3}$

$\text{Area}_\Delta = \dfrac{1}{2}(6)(3\sqrt{3}) = 9\sqrt{3}$

$B = \text{Area}_{\text{hexagon}} = 6(9\sqrt{3}) = 54\sqrt{3}$

$V = \dfrac{1}{3}Bh = \dfrac{1}{3}(54\sqrt{3})(12) = \textbf{216}\sqrt{\textbf{3}}\ \textbf{cm}^3$

20. (a) $V = \dfrac{4}{3}\pi(1)^2 = \dfrac{\textbf{4}}{\textbf{3}}\boldsymbol{\pi}\ \textbf{cm}^3$

(b) $SA = 4\pi r^2 = 4\pi(1)^2 = \textbf{4}\boldsymbol{\pi}\ \textbf{cm}^2$

21. $\left(\dfrac{4}{5}\right)^3 = \dfrac{\textbf{64}}{\textbf{125}}$

22. (a) $V = \dfrac{1}{3}\pi r^2 h = \dfrac{1}{3}\pi(6)^2(8) = \textbf{96}\boldsymbol{\pi}\ \textbf{cm}^3$

(b) $SA = \pi r^2 + \pi rs = \pi(6)^2 + \pi(6)(10)$
$= 36\pi + 60\pi = \textbf{96}\boldsymbol{\pi}\ \textbf{cm}^2$

23. $(x^2 - 14x + 49) - (y^2 + 8y + 16)$
$= -37 + 49 - 16$

$\dfrac{(y + 4)^2}{4} - \dfrac{(x - 7)^2}{4} = \dfrac{4}{4}$

$\dfrac{(y + 4)^2}{4} - \dfrac{(x - 7)^2}{4} = 1$

Center: **(7, −4)**
Vertices: **(7, −2), (7, −6)**
Asymptotes: $y = x - 11$
$\qquad\qquad\quad y = -x + 3$

24. $16(x^2 - 8x + 16) + (y^2 + 20y + 100)$
$= -292 + 256 + 100$

$\dfrac{16(x - 4)^2}{64} + \dfrac{(y + 10)^2}{64} = \dfrac{64}{64}$

$\dfrac{(x - 4)^2}{4} + \dfrac{(y + 10)^2}{64} = 1$

Center: **(4, −10)**
Major axis: **16**
Minor axis: **4**

25. $a = \sqrt{8^2 + 12^2 - 2(8)(12)\cos 150^\circ} \approx \textbf{19.3}$

26. $\cos 75^\circ - \cos 15^\circ$
$= -2 \sin \dfrac{75^\circ + 15^\circ}{2}\ \sin \dfrac{75^\circ - 15^\circ}{2}$
$= -2 \sin 45^\circ \sin 30^\circ = -2\left(\dfrac{\sqrt{2}}{2}\right)\left(\dfrac{1}{2}\right) = -\dfrac{\sqrt{2}}{2}$

27. $2 \sin^2 x + 3 \sin x + 1 = 0$
$(2 \sin x + 1)(\sin x + 1) = 0$
$\sin x = -\dfrac{1}{2} \qquad \sin x = -1$
$x = \textbf{210}^\circ, \textbf{330}^\circ, \textbf{270}^\circ$

28. $\tan 2x = \dfrac{\sin 2x}{\cos 2x}$

$= \dfrac{2 \sin x \cos x}{\cos^2 x - \sin^2 x} \cdot \dfrac{\dfrac{1}{\cos^2 x}}{\dfrac{1}{\cos^2 x}}$

$= \dfrac{\dfrac{2 \sin x \cos x}{\cos^2 x}}{\dfrac{\cos^2 x}{\cos^2 x} - \dfrac{\sin^2 x}{\cos^2 x}} = \dfrac{2 \tan x}{1 - \tan^2 x}$

29. $\dfrac{1 + \cos \theta}{\sin \theta} + \dfrac{\sin \theta}{\cos \theta}$

$= \dfrac{(\cos \theta)(1 + \cos \theta) + \sin^2 \theta}{\sin \theta \cos \theta}$

$= \dfrac{\cos \theta + \cos^2 \theta + \sin^2 \theta}{\sin \theta \cos \theta}$

$= \dfrac{\cos \theta + 1}{\sin \theta \cos \theta}$

30. $\text{pH} = -\log \text{H}^+ = -\log 2.3 \times 10^{-4}$
$= -(-3.6) = \textbf{3.6}$

EP

73. For $k = 1$, we get $5 = \dfrac{5(1)(1 + 1)}{2}$

Also $\dfrac{5k(k + 1)}{2} + 5(k + 1)$

$= \dfrac{5k(k + 1) + 10(k + 1)}{2}$

$= \dfrac{5(k + 1)(k + 2)}{2} = \dfrac{5(k + 1)[(k + 1) + 1]}{2}$

74. **Valid**

PROBLEM SET 102

1. Down: $(3C + C)(T - 1) = 64$
   Up: $\quad (3C - C)T = 40$
   $2CT = 40$
   $CT = 20$
   $4CT - 4C = 64$
   $4(20) - 4C = 64$
   $-4C = -16$
   $C = 4 \text{ mph}$
   $B = 12 \text{ mph}$

2. Rate $\cdot$ time $\cdot$ men = jobs
   Rate $\cdot d \cdot 7 = c$
   Rate $= \dfrac{c}{7d}$
   $\left(\dfrac{c}{7d}\right) \cdot 11 \cdot \text{men} = 25$
   Men $= \dfrac{25(7d)}{11c} = \dfrac{175d}{11c}$ workers

3. $R_B T_B + R_L T_L = \text{jobs}$
   $\dfrac{4}{x}(14) + \dfrac{m}{k}(14) = \text{jobs}$
   $\dfrac{56}{x} + \dfrac{14m}{k} = \text{jobs}$
   $= \dfrac{56k + 14mx}{xk} \text{jobs}$

4. $\dfrac{(w + 4 + g)!}{w!\, 4!\, g!}$

5. $\dfrac{4}{9} \cdot \dfrac{3}{8} = \dfrac{1}{6}$

6. Refer to Example 102.A.2.

7. $AD = BE, DC = EC$ implies AC
   $= AD + DC = BE + EC = BC.$
   $\angle C = \angle C$ implies $\triangle AEC \cong \triangle BDC$ implies
   $\angle A = \angle B. \angle AFD = \angle BFE$ implies $\triangle AFD$
   $\sim \triangle BFE; AD = BE$ so $SF = 1. \triangle AFD$
   $\cong \triangle BFE$ implies $AF = FB, FC = FC$ and AC
   $= BC$ implies $\triangle AFC \cong \triangle BFC$ so $\angle ACF$
   $= \angle BCF.$

8. Refer to Example 102.B.1.

9. Refer to Example 102.B.3.

10. Refer to Example 102.B.4.

11. $\dfrac{14!}{9!\, 5!} (2x)^9 (-y^2)^5 = -1{,}025{,}024\, x^9 y^{10}$

12. $\dfrac{8!}{4!\, 4!} (2x)^4 (y^3)^4 = 1120 x^4 y^{12}$

13. $\log y = \dfrac{3}{4}(\log 6.2 \times 10^9)$
    $\quad - \dfrac{1}{2}(\log 2.1 \times 10^7)$
    $= \dfrac{3}{4}(0.7924 + 9) - \dfrac{1}{2}(0.3222 + 7)$
    $= \dfrac{3}{4}(9.7924) - \dfrac{1}{2}(7.3222)$
    $= 7.3443 - 3.6611 = 3.6832$
    antilog $y =$ antilog 3.6832
    $=$ antilog $(0.6832) + 3 \approx 4.8 \times 10^3$

14. $x + 2 < 3^3$ $\quad$ and $\quad x + 2 > 0$
    $x + 2 < 27$ $\qquad\qquad x > -2$
    $x < 25$
    $-2 < x < 25$

15. $x - 1 > \left(\dfrac{1}{4}\right)^2$ and $x - 1 > 0$
    $x - 1 > \dfrac{1}{16}$ $\qquad\qquad x > 1$
    $x > \dfrac{17}{16}$
    $x > \dfrac{17}{16}$

16. (a) Refer to Lesson 99.A.

    (b) Refer to Lesson 99.B.

17. $S_\infty = \dfrac{a_1}{1 - r} = \dfrac{0.016}{1 - 0.01}$
    $= \dfrac{0.016}{0.99} = \dfrac{16}{990} = \dfrac{8}{495}$

18. Downs: $\dfrac{81}{1 - \dfrac{2}{3}} = \dfrac{81}{\dfrac{1}{3}} = 243$

    Ups: $\quad 243 - 81 = 162$
    Total $= 243 + 162 = 405 \text{ ft}$

19. $d = \sqrt{3^2 + 5^2 + n^2} = \sqrt{34 + n^2}$

20. $V = \frac{1}{3}Bh = \frac{1}{3}(25)(10) = \frac{250}{3}$ cm³

21. (a) $V = \frac{4}{3}\pi r^3$ cm³

    (b) $SA = 4\pi r^2$ cm²

22. $\left(\frac{8}{125}\right)^{1/3} = \frac{2}{5}$

    Ratio = 2 : 5

23. (a) $V = \frac{1}{3}\pi r^2 h = \frac{1}{3}\pi(10)^2(9) = 300\pi$ cm³

    (b) $SA = \pi r^2 + \pi rs$
    $= \pi(10)^2 + \pi(10)\left(\sqrt{181}\right)$
    $= (100\pi + 10\sqrt{181}\,\pi)$ cm²

24. $4(x^2 + 4x + 4) - 9(y^2 - 12y + 36)$
    $= 344 + 16 - 324$
    $\frac{4(x+2)^2}{36} - \frac{9(y-6)^2}{36} = \frac{36}{36}$
    $\frac{(x+2)^2}{9} - \frac{(y-6)^2}{9} = 1$
    Center: (−2, 6)
    Vertices: (1, 6), (−5, 6)
    Asymptotes: $y = \frac{2}{3}x + \frac{22}{3}$
    $y = -\frac{2}{3}x + \frac{14}{3}$

25. $16(x^2) + 25(y^2 - 12y + 36) = -500 + 900$
    $\frac{16(x-0)^2}{400} + \frac{25(y-6)^2}{400} = \frac{400}{400}$
    $\frac{(x-0)^2}{25} + \frac{(y-6)^2}{16} = 1$
    center: (0, 6)
    major axis: 10
    minor axis: 8

26. $\cos A = \frac{8^2 + 10^2 - 17^2}{2(8)(10)} = -\frac{125}{160}$
    $A \approx 141.4°$

27. $\sin 15° \cos 285°$
    $= \frac{1}{2}(\sin(15° + 285°) + \sin(15° - 285°))$
    $= \frac{1}{2}(\sin 300° - \sin 270°)$
    $= \frac{1}{2}\left(-\frac{\sqrt{3}}{2} - (-1)\right) = \frac{-\sqrt{3} + 2}{4}$

28. $2\cos^2 x + \sqrt{3}\cos x = 0$
    $\cos x(2\cos x + \sqrt{3}) = 0$
    $\cos x = 0 \qquad 2\cos x + \sqrt{3} = 0$
    $\qquad\qquad\qquad \cos x = -\frac{\sqrt{3}}{2}$
    $x = 90°, 270° \qquad x = 150°, 210°$

29. $\frac{\cot x}{\cot x - 1} - \frac{\tan x}{\tan x + 1}$
    $= \frac{(\cot x)(\tan x + 1) - (\tan x)(\cot x - 1)}{(\cot x - 1)(\tan x + 1)}$
    $= \frac{1 + \cot x - 1 + \tan x}{\cot x \tan x + \cot x - \tan x - 1}$
    $= \frac{\cot x + \tan x}{\cot x - \tan x}$

30. $\log_2 27^{1/3} - \log_2(x - 2) = \log_2 x^{-1}$
    $\log_2 \frac{3}{x-2} = \log_2 \frac{1}{x}$
    $\frac{3}{x-2} = \frac{1}{x}$
    $3x = x - 2$
    $2x = -2$
    $x = -1$
    No solution

EP

75. For $k = 1$, we get $1 \cdot 2 = \frac{1(1+1)(1+2)}{3}$
    $2 = \frac{(2)(3)}{3} = 2.$ Also
    $\frac{k(k+1)(k+2)}{3} + (k+1)(k+2)$
    $= \frac{k(k+1)(k+2) + 3(k+1)(k+2)}{3}$
    $= \frac{(k+1)(k+2)(k+3)}{3}$
    $= \frac{(k+1)[(k+1)+1][(k+1)+2]}{3}$

76. $\begin{bmatrix} 3 & 1 \\ 0 & 2 \end{bmatrix} \cdot \begin{bmatrix} 1 & 0 \\ 1 & 1 \end{bmatrix}$
    $= \begin{bmatrix} (3)(1)+(1)(1) & (3)(0)+(1)(1) \\ (0)(1)+(2)(1) & (0)(0)+(2)(1) \end{bmatrix}$
    $= \begin{bmatrix} 4 & 1 \\ 2 & 2 \end{bmatrix}$

1. $R_O T_O = 600$ $\qquad$ $R_O = 3R_B$
   $R_B T_B = 600$ $\qquad$ $T_O = 40 - T_B$
   $3R_B(40 - T_B) = 600$
   $120R_B - 3R_B T_B = 600$
   $120R_B - 3(600) = 600$
   $120R_B = 2400$
   $R_B = \mathbf{20\ mph}$
   $R_O = \mathbf{60\ mph}$

2. Distance traveled $= hk$
   Distance after resting $= \mathbf{400 - hk}$

3. $5000 = 10{,}000e^{14k}$
   $0.5 = e^{14k}$
   $\ln 0.5 = \ln e^{14k}$
   $-0.693 \approx 14k$
   $k \approx -0.0495$
   $4000 = 10{,}000e^{-0.0495t}$
   $0.4 = e^{-0.0495t}$
   $\ln 0.4 = \ln e^{-0.0495t}$
   $-0.91629 \approx -0.0495t$
   $t \approx \mathbf{18.5\ years}$

4. $\dfrac{7}{11} \cdot \dfrac{4}{10} = \dfrac{7}{11} \cdot \dfrac{2}{5} = \dfrac{\mathbf{14}}{\mathbf{55}}$

5. Linear $= k \text{ in} \cdot \left(r\,\dfrac{\text{rad}}{\text{sec}} \right) \cdot \left(\dfrac{2.54 \text{ cm}}{1 \text{ in}} \right)$
   $\cdot \left(\dfrac{1 \text{ m}}{100 \text{ cm}} \right) \cdot \left(\dfrac{60 \text{ sec}}{1 \text{ min}} \right) \cdot \left(\dfrac{60 \text{ min}}{1 \text{ hr}} \right)$
   $= \dfrac{k(r)(2.54)(60)(60)}{100}\ \dfrac{\text{m}}{\text{hr}}$

6. $\begin{array}{r|rrrr} 2 & 1 & -5 & 0 & 12 \\ & & 2 & -6 & -12 \\ \hline & 1 & -3 & -6 & 0 \end{array}$
   $x^2 - 3x - 6$

7. $\begin{array}{r|rrrrr} -2 & 4 & -4 & 1 & -3 & 2 \\ & & -8 & 24 & -50 & 106 \\ \hline & 4 & -12 & 25 & -53 & 108 \end{array}$
   $4x^3 - 12x^2 + 25x - 53 + \dfrac{108}{x + 2}$

8. $\begin{array}{r|rrrr} -1 & 1 & 2 & -3 & -4 \\ & & -1 & -1 & 4 \\ \hline & 1 & 1 & -4 & 0 \end{array}$
   Yes, it is a zero.

9. $\begin{array}{r|rrrr} -2 & 2 & -1 & 2 & -4 \\ & & -4 & 10 & -24 \\ \hline & 2 & -5 & 12 & -28 \end{array}$
   No, it is not a zero.

10. Refer to Lesson 102.

11. $\angle 1 = \angle 2$, $CD = CE$, $FC = FC$ implies $\triangle DFC \cong \triangle EFC$ so $DF = FE$. $\angle FDC = \angle FEC$ implies $\angle ADF = \angle BEF$; $\angle AFD = \angle BFE$ implies $\triangle AFD \cong \triangle BFE$ implies $AF = BF$.

12. Refer to Lesson 102.

13. Draw $\overline{OC}$ and $\overline{OD}$. $\overset{\frown}{CD} = \overset{\frown}{BD}$ implies $\angle COB = \angle DOB$. $OC = OD$, $OE = OE$ implies $\triangle COE \cong \triangle DOE$ so $CE = ED$ and $\angle OEC = \angle OED = 90°$.

14. $\dfrac{15!}{11!\ 4!}\,(2x^2)^4(-y^3)^4 = 2{,}795{,}520x^{22}y^{12}$

15. $\dfrac{8!}{5!\ 3!}\,(3x^3)^5(-y^2)^3 = -13{,}608x^{15}y^6$

16. (1) $m_\perp = 1$ $(4, -1)$
    $-1 = 1(4) + b$
    $-5 = b$
    $y = x - 5$

    (2) $-x + 5 = x - 5$
    $2x = 10$
    $x = 5$
    $y = 0$
    $(5, 0), (4, -1)$
    $\sqrt{(4 - 5)^2 + (-1 - 0)^2} = \sqrt{1^2 + 1^2} = \sqrt{2}$

17. $\text{pH} = -\log(6.3 \times 10^{-4}) = -(0.7993 - 4)$
    $= -(-3.2) = \mathbf{3.2}$

18. $\log_4(2x - 1) < 2$

    $(2x - 1) > 0$ and $2x - 1 < 4^2$
    $2x > 1$ $2x - 1 < 16$
    $x > \dfrac{1}{2}$ $2x < 17$

    $\qquad\qquad\qquad x < \dfrac{17}{2}$

    $\dfrac{1}{2} < x < \dfrac{17}{2}$

19. $\log_{1/3}(2x + 1) < 2$

    $2x + 1 > 0$ and $2x + 1 > \left(\dfrac{1}{3}\right)^2$

    $x > -\dfrac{1}{2}$ $2x + 1 > \dfrac{1}{9}$

    $\qquad\qquad\qquad 2x > -\dfrac{8}{9}$

    $\qquad\qquad\qquad x > -\dfrac{8}{18} = -\dfrac{4}{9}$

    $\qquad\qquad\qquad x > -\dfrac{4}{9}$

20. Refer to Lesson 99.

21. $S_\infty = \dfrac{a_1}{1 - r} = \dfrac{0.013}{1 - 0.01} = \dfrac{0.013}{0.99} = \dfrac{13}{990}$

22. (a) $V = \dfrac{1}{3}\pi r^2 h = \dfrac{1}{3}\pi(6)^2(10) = \mathbf{120\pi\ cm^2}$

    (b) $SA = \pi r^2 + \pi r s$
    $= \pi(6)^2 + \pi(6)(2\sqrt{34})$
    $= \mathbf{(36\pi + 12\sqrt{34}\,\pi)\ cm^2}$

23. $\tan 20° = \dfrac{1.5}{h_1}$

    $h_1 \approx 4.121$

    $\text{Area}_\Delta = \dfrac{1}{2}(3)(4.121) = 6.1815$

    $\text{Area } B = (6.1815)(9) = 55.63$

    $V = \dfrac{1}{3}Bh = \dfrac{1}{3}(55.63)(3) = \mathbf{55.63\ cm^3}$

24. $\mathbf{360°}$

25. $36(x^2 - 6x + 9) + 9(y^2) = 324$
    $\dfrac{(x - 3)^2}{9} + \dfrac{y^2}{6} = 1$
    Center: (3, 0)

Major axis: 12
Minor axis: 6

26. $\cos 285° - \cos 15° = -2\sin 150° \sin 135°$

    $= -2\left(\dfrac{1}{2}\right)\left(\dfrac{\sqrt{2}}{2}\right) = -\dfrac{\sqrt{2}}{2}$

27. $2\sin^2 x + \sin x - 1 = 0$
    $(2\sin x - 1)(\sin x + 1) = 0$
    $\sin x = \dfrac{1}{2}\qquad\qquad \sin x = -1$
    $x = \mathbf{30°, 150°}\qquad x = \mathbf{270°}$

28. $\dfrac{\tan x}{\tan x - 1} - \dfrac{\cot x}{\cot x + 1}$

    $= \dfrac{(\tan x)(\cot x + 1) - (\cot x)(\tan x - 1)}{(\tan x - 1)(\cot x + 1)}$

    $= \dfrac{1 + \tan x - 1 + \cot x}{1 + \tan x - \cot x - 1} = \dfrac{\tan x + \cot x}{\tan x - \cot x}$

29. $\dfrac{\log 3}{\log 5} \approx \mathbf{0.683}$

30. $6^{2\log_6 3} = 6^{\log_6 3^2} = 6^{\log_6 9} = \mathbf{9}$

EP

77. **Invalid**

78. $\begin{bmatrix} \dfrac{1}{2} & -\dfrac{1}{3} \\[2mm] 2 & \dfrac{1}{2} \end{bmatrix} \cdot \begin{bmatrix} 6 & 0 \\ 0 & 6 \end{bmatrix}$

    $= \begin{bmatrix} \dfrac{1}{2}(6) + \left(-\dfrac{1}{3}\right)(0) & \dfrac{1}{2}(0) + \left(-\dfrac{1}{3}\right)(6) \\[3mm] 2(6) + \dfrac{1}{2}(0) & 2(0) + \dfrac{1}{2}(6) \end{bmatrix}$

    $= \begin{bmatrix} 3 & -2 \\ 12 & 3 \end{bmatrix}$

1.

$$V = Nm + b$$
$$60 = 4m + b$$
$$\underline{30 = 2m + b}$$
$$30 = 2m$$
$$15 = m$$
$$b = 0$$
$$V = 15N$$
$$V = 15(10) = \mathbf{150}$$

2. $L + B = 300$
$$L = 300 - B$$
$$40L + 10B = 30(300)$$
$$40(300 - B) + 10B = 9000$$
$$B = \mathbf{100\ ml\ 10\%}$$
$$L = \mathbf{200\ ml\ 40\%}$$

3. $R_S = 2R_T \qquad T_S = T_T - 3$
$$R_S = 2(50)$$
$$R_S = 100$$
$$R_S T_S = R_T T_T$$
$$100(T_T - 3) = 50T_T$$
$$100T_T - 300 = 50T_T$$
$$50T_T = 300$$
$$T_T = 6$$
$$\text{Distance} = R_T T_T = (50)(6) = \mathbf{300\ mi}$$

4. $N, N + 2, N + 4$
$$N(N + 4) = 9(N + 2) - 24$$
$$N^2 - 5N + 6 = 0$$
$$(N - 3)(N - 2) = 0$$
$$N - 2 = 0$$
$$N = \mathbf{2}$$
$$N + 2 = \mathbf{4}$$
$$N + 4 = \mathbf{6}$$

5. $B - 10 = J$
$$3(B + 10) = 4(J + 10) - 16$$
$$3B - 4J = -6$$

$$3B - 4(B - 10) = -6$$
$$3B - 4B + 40 = -6$$
$$-B = -46$$
$$B = \mathbf{46}$$
$$J = \mathbf{36}$$

6. $xy = 4$

x	y
1	4
4	1
2	2
−1	−4
−4	−1
−2	−2

7. (a) **Circle**
(b) **Ellipse**
(c) **Hyperbola**
(d) **Parabola**
(e) **Circle**

8. $(x^2 + 8x + 16) + (y^2 - 6y + 9)$
$$= 15 + 16 + 9$$
$$\mathbf{(x + 4)^2 + (y - 3)^2 = 40}$$
Center: $\mathbf{(-4, 3)}$
Radius: $\sqrt{40} = 2\sqrt{10}$

9.

$$
\begin{array}{r|rrrrr}
1 & 1 & 0 & -3 & -2 & 1 \\
  &   & 1 & 1 & -2 & -4 \\
\hline
  & 1 & 1 & -2 & -4 & -3
\end{array}
$$

$$x^3 + x^2 - 2x - 4 - \frac{3}{x - 1}$$

10.

$$
\begin{array}{r|rrrr}
2 & 1 & -2 & 1 & -3 \\
  &   & 2 & 0 & 2 \\
\hline
  & 1 & 0 & 1 & -1
\end{array}
$$

$$x^2 + 1 - \frac{1}{x - 2}$$

11.

$$
\begin{array}{r|rrrr}
-2 & 1 & 2 & -3 & -6 \\
   &   & -2 & 0 & 6 \\
\hline
   & 1 & 0 & -3 & 0
\end{array}
$$
Yes

12.

$$
\begin{array}{r|rrrr}
-2 & 1 & -2 & -4 & 3 \\
   &   & -2 & 8 & -8 \\
\hline
   & 1 & -4 & 4 & -5
\end{array}
$$
No

13. $CD = CE, \angle 1 = \angle 2, FC = FC$ implies $\triangle FDC \cong \triangle FEC$ and $DF = FE$; $\angle CDF = \angle CEF$ implies $\angle ADF = \angle BEF$. $\angle AFD = \angle BFE$ implies $\triangle AFD \sim \triangle BFE$ since $DF = FE$. Then $SF = 1$ and $\triangle AFD \cong \triangle BFE$; $AD = BE, CD = CE$ implies $AC = AD + DC = BE + EC = BC$.

14. Draw radii OC, OD. $\overset{\frown}{CB} = \overset{\frown}{BD}$ implies $\angle COB = \angle BOD$; $OE = OE$ implies $\triangle COE \cong \triangle DOE$ implies $CE = ED$. $\angle OEC = \angle OED = 90°$.

15. P and Q are midpoints of $\overline{AD}$ and $\overline{AB}$ implies $AP = \frac{1}{2}AD, AQ = \frac{1}{2}AB$. $\angle A = \angle A$ implies $\triangle APQ \sim \triangle ADB$ with $SF = 2$; $\angle APQ = \angle ADB$; $\overline{PQ} \parallel \overline{DB}, PQ = \frac{1}{2}DB$ and $SR = \frac{1}{2}DB$, $\overline{SR} \parallel \overline{DB}$. Thus, $\overline{PQ} \parallel \overline{SR}, PQ = SR$ implies $PQRS$ is a parallelogram.

16. Refer to Lesson 102.

17. $\dfrac{8!}{5!\,3!}(2x^2)^5(-y^4)^3 = -1792x^{10}y^{12}$

18. $\log y = \frac{4}{3}\log(5.1 \times 10^8)$
    $\quad - \frac{1}{2}\log(3.61 \times 10^7)$
    $= \frac{4}{3}(8.7075) - \frac{1}{2}(7.5575)$
    $= 11.6100 - 3.7788 = 7.8312$
    antilog y = antilog $7.8312 \approx \mathbf{6.8 \times 10^7}$

19. pH $= -(\log H^+) = -(\log 4.3 \times 10^{-4})$
    $= -(0.6335 - 4) = -(-3.37) \approx \mathbf{3.4}$

20. $\log_{1/2}(x - 3) < 3$

    $x - 3 > 0 \qquad\qquad x - 3 > \left(\frac{1}{2}\right)^3$

    $x > 3 \qquad\qquad\quad x - 3 > \frac{1}{8}$

    $\qquad\qquad\qquad\qquad x > 3\frac{1}{8} = \frac{25}{8}$

    $x > \dfrac{25}{8}$

21. $a_{10} = 42$ and $a_5 = 17$

    $\begin{aligned} a_1 + 4d &= 17 \\ a_1 + 9d &= 42 \\ \hline 5d &= 25 \\ d &= 5 \end{aligned}$

    $a_1 = 17 - 4(5) = -3$
    $a_{13} = a_1 + 12d = -3 + 12(5) = 57$

22. (a) $V = \frac{4}{3}\pi r^3 = \frac{4}{3}\pi(8)^3 = \dfrac{2048}{3}\pi$ cm^3

    (b) $SA = 4\pi R^2 = 4\pi(8)^2 = 256\pi$ cm^2

23. Sides $= \dfrac{\frac{5}{2}}{1}$; $V = \dfrac{\frac{5^3}{2^3}}{1^3}$ thus, ratio $= \dfrac{125}{8} : 1$

24. $\begin{bmatrix} 2 & -3 & -1 & 4 \\ 1 & -2 & 2 & 5 \\ 3 & -1 & 1 & 5 \end{bmatrix} = \begin{bmatrix} 1 & -2 & 2 & 5 \\ 2 & -3 & -1 & 4 \\ 3 & -1 & 1 & 5 \end{bmatrix}$

    $= \begin{bmatrix} 1 & -2 & 2 & 5 \\ 0 & 1 & -5 & -6 \\ 0 & 5 & -5 & -10 \end{bmatrix} = \begin{bmatrix} 1 & 0 & -8 & -7 \\ 0 & 1 & -5 & -6 \\ 0 & 0 & 20 & 20 \end{bmatrix}$

    $= \begin{bmatrix} 1 & 0 & 0 & 1 \\ 0 & 1 & 0 & -1 \\ 0 & 0 & 1 & 1 \end{bmatrix}$

    $x = 1, y = -1, z = 1$

25. $a = \sqrt{36 + 64 - 2(6)(8)\cos 20°} \approx 3.1$

26. $\cos 315° \cos 15° = \frac{1}{2}(\cos 330° + \cos 300°)$

    $= \frac{1}{2}\left(\dfrac{\sqrt{3}}{2} + \dfrac{1}{2}\right) = \dfrac{\sqrt{3} + 1}{4}$

27. $\dfrac{\cot^2 x + \sec^2 x + 1}{\cot^2 x}$

    $= \dfrac{\csc^2 x + \sec^2 x}{\cot^2 x} = \dfrac{\dfrac{1}{\sin^2 x} + \dfrac{1}{\cos^2 x}}{\dfrac{\cos^2 x}{\sin^2 x}}$

    $= \dfrac{\cos^2 x + \sin^2 x}{\sin^2 x \cos^2 x} \cdot \dfrac{\sin^2 x}{\cos^2 x}$

    $= \dfrac{1}{\cos^4 x} = \sec^4 x$

28. $-\tan 3\theta = \sqrt{3}$
    $\tan 3\theta = -\sqrt{3}$
    $3\theta = 120°, 300°, 480°, 660°, 840°, 1020°$
    $\theta = \mathbf{40°, 100°, 160°, 220°, 280°, 340°}$

29. $3^{4\log_3 2} = 3^{\log_3 2^4} = 3^{\log_3 16} = \mathbf{16}$

30. $\dfrac{\log 5}{\log 6}$

EP

79. For $k = 1$, we get $a = \dfrac{(1 - r^1)a}{1 - r}$. Also

$$\dfrac{(1 - r^k)a}{1 - r} + ar^k = \dfrac{(1 - r^k)a + ar^k(1 - r)}{1 - r}$$
$$= \dfrac{a - ar^k + ar^k - ar^{k+1}}{1 - r} = \dfrac{a(1 - r^{k+1})}{1 - r}$$

80. $\begin{bmatrix} -2 & 3 \\ 4 & -1 \end{bmatrix} \cdot \begin{bmatrix} 1 & x \\ 2 & 4 \end{bmatrix}$

$$= \begin{bmatrix} (-2)(1) + (3)(2) & (-2)(x) + (3)(4) \\ (4)(1) + (-1)(2) & (4)(x) + (-1)(4) \end{bmatrix}$$

$$= \begin{bmatrix} 4 & -2x + 12 \\ 2 & 4x - 4 \end{bmatrix}$$

PROBLEM SET 105

1.
$380 = 260e^{5k}$
$1.46154 = e^{5k}$
$e^{0.3795} = e^{5k}$
$k \approx 0.0759$
$2000 = 260e^{0.0759k}$
$7.6923 = e^{0.0759t}$
$2.0402 = 0.0759t$
$t \approx 26.9 \text{ hr}$
$26.9 + 5 = \mathbf{31.9 \text{ hr}}$

2.

Little Hand	Big Hand
$R_L T_L = S$	$R_B T_B = S + 60$
$R_L = \dfrac{1}{12}$	$R_B = 1$
$T_L = T_B$	
$\dfrac{1}{12}T = S$	$1T = S + 60$

$T = \dfrac{1}{12}T + 60$

$\dfrac{11}{12}T = 15$

$T = \dfrac{360}{11} = 65\dfrac{5}{11}\text{ min}$

$\mathbf{1{:}05\dfrac{5}{11}\text{ p.m.}}$

3.

% salt	5%		20%		10%
amount (lit)	40	+	x	=	40+x

$5(40) + 20x = 10(40 + x)$
$200 + 20x = 400 + 10x$
$10x = 200$
$x = \mathbf{20 \text{ liters}}$

4.

	Trot	Walk
Total distance:	152	152
Rate:	10	4
Time:	T	$20 - T$

$R_1 T_1 + R_2 T_2 = 152$
$10T + 4(20 - T) = 152$
$10T + 80 - 4T = 152$
$6T = 72$
$T = 12$
$D_T = 10(12) = \mathbf{120 \text{ mi}}$
$D_W = 4(20 - 12) = \mathbf{32 \text{ mi}}$

5. A: $\dfrac{W}{S} = \dfrac{7}{10}$

$\quad\quad 10W = 7S$

$\quad\quad W = \dfrac{7}{10}S$

B: $10S = 4W + 216$

$\quad\quad 5S = 2W + 108$

Substitute equation A into B.

$5S = 2\left(\dfrac{7}{10}S\right) + 108$

$5S = \dfrac{7}{5}S + 108$

$S = \mathbf{30}$

$W = \dfrac{7}{10}(30) = \mathbf{21}$

6. Refer to Example 105.A.2.

7. $\angle ABC = \dfrac{1}{2}\overset{\frown}{AC}$, $\angle ADC = \dfrac{1}{2}\overset{\frown}{AC}$ is given.

$\angle ABC = \angle ADC$ by substitution. $\angle BEA = \angle DEC$ because vertical angles are equal. $\triangle BAE \sim \triangle DCE$ by AA.

8. $\angle 1 = \angle 2, CD = CE$ is given. $FC = FC$ by reflexive property. $\triangle FDC \cong \triangle FEC$ by SAS. $DF = FE$ and $\angle CDF = \angle CEF$ by CPCTE. $\angle ADF = \angle BEF$ because if two angles are equal then the supplements of those angles are equal. $\angle AFD = \angle BFE$ because vertical angles are equal. $\triangle AFD \cong \triangle BFE$ by SAS. $AF = BF$ by CPCTE.

9. $x = 2(80°) = 160°$
$y = 2(30°) = 60°$
$z = 2(70°) = 140°$

10. Refer to Example 102.A.2.

11. (a) **Circle**
(b) **Parabola**
(c) **Hyperbola**
(d) **Hyperbola**
(e) **Ellipse**

12. $xy = 8$

x	y
-4	-2
-1	-8
1	8
2	4
4	2

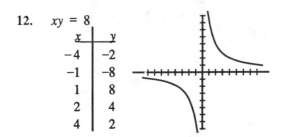

13. $9(x^2 + 6x + 9) - 4(y^2 - 2y + 1)$
$= -41 + 81 - 4 = 36$
$9(x + 3)^2 - 4(y - 1)^2 = 36$
$\dfrac{(x + 3)^2}{4} - \dfrac{(y - 1)^2}{9} = 1$
Center: **(-3, 1)**
Vertices: **(-5, 1), (-1, 1)**
Asymptotes: $y = \dfrac{3}{2}x + \dfrac{11}{2}$
$\qquad\qquad y = \dfrac{3}{2}x - \dfrac{7}{2}$

14.
$$\begin{array}{r|rrrrrr} 2 & 1 & -6 & 0 & -3 & -2 & 1 \\ & & 2 & -8 & -16 & -38 & -80 \\ \hline & 1 & -4 & -8 & -19 & -40 & -79 \end{array}$$

$x^4 - 4x^3 - 8x^2 - 19x - 40 - \dfrac{79}{x - 2}$

15.
$$\begin{array}{r|rrrr} -1 & 1 & -2 & 3 & 6 \\ & & -1 & 3 & -6 \\ \hline & 1 & -3 & 6 & 0 \end{array}$$

Yes, it is a zero.

16.
$$\begin{array}{r|rrrr} -1 & 1 & 2 & -3 & -6 \\ & & -1 & -1 & 4 \\ \hline & 1 & 1 & -4 & 2 \end{array}$$

No, it is not a zero.

17. $\dfrac{9!}{5!\,4!}(x^2)^5(-2y^3)^4 = \mathbf{2016x^{10}y^{12}}$

18. $\dfrac{3}{2}\log(6.2 \times 10^{11}) = \dfrac{3}{2}(11.7924) = 17.6886$
$\dfrac{1}{3}\log(3.1 \times 10^3) = \dfrac{1}{3}(3.4914) = 1.1638$
$17.6886 + 1.1638 = 18.8524$
antilog $18.8524 \approx \mathbf{7.1 \times 10^{18}}$

19. $H^+ = 10^{-pH} = 10^{-9.2} = \mathbf{6.3 \times 10^{-10}}$

20. $a_{13} = 34$
$a_8 = 19$
$a_1 + 12d = 34$
$\underline{a_1 + 7d = 19}$
$5d = 15$
$d = 3$
$a_1 = 19 - 7(3) = -2$
$a_{10} = a_1 + 9d = -2 + 9(3) = \mathbf{25}$

21. $2x - 1 > 0 \qquad\qquad 2x - 1 < 2$
$x > \dfrac{1}{2} \qquad\qquad\qquad x < \dfrac{3}{2}$
$\dfrac{1}{2} < x < \dfrac{3}{2}$

22. Base $= 4^2 = 16$
$V = \dfrac{1}{3}(16)(4) = \dfrac{64}{3}\ \text{cm}^3$

23. (a) $V = \dfrac{1}{3}\pi r^2 h = \dfrac{1}{3}\pi(10)^2(8) = \dfrac{800}{3}\pi\ \text{cm}^3$
(b) $S = \pi r^2 + \pi rs = \pi(10)^2 + \pi(10)(2\sqrt{41})$
$\qquad = \left(100\pi + 20\pi\sqrt{41}\right)\ \text{cm}^2$

24.

$$x = \frac{\begin{vmatrix} 9 & 1 & 2 \\ -1 & 2 & -1 \\ -1 & 3 & 0 \end{vmatrix}}{\begin{vmatrix} -1 & 1 & 2 \\ 0 & 2 & -1 \\ 2 & 3 & 0 \end{vmatrix}}$$

$$= \frac{9\begin{vmatrix} 2 & -1 \\ 3 & 0 \end{vmatrix} - 1\begin{vmatrix} -1 & -1 \\ -1 & 0 \end{vmatrix} + 2\begin{vmatrix} -1 & 2 \\ -1 & 3 \end{vmatrix}}{\begin{vmatrix} 2 & -1 \\ 3 & 0 \end{vmatrix} - \begin{vmatrix} 0 & -1 \\ 2 & 0 \end{vmatrix} + 2\begin{vmatrix} 0 & 2 \\ 2 & 3 \end{vmatrix}}$$

$$= \frac{9(0+3) - 1(0-1) + 2(-3+2)}{-1(0+3) - 1(0+2) + 2(0-4)}$$

$$= \frac{27 + 1 - 2}{-3 - 2 - 8} = -\frac{26}{13} = -2$$

25. $y = 2 + 4\sec x$

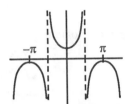

26. (a) Refer to Example 84.A.4.

(b) $\sin 315° \sin 15°$

$$= \frac{1}{2}(\cos 300° - \cos 330°)$$

$$= \frac{1}{2}\left(\frac{1}{2} - \frac{\sqrt{3}}{2}\right) = \frac{1 - \sqrt{3}}{4}$$

27. $\dfrac{\cos^2 x}{1 - \sin x} = \dfrac{1 - \sin^2 x}{1 - \sin x}$

$$= \frac{(1 + \sin x)(1 - \sin x)}{1 - \sin x} = 1 + \sin x$$

$$= 1 + \frac{1}{\csc x} = \frac{\csc x + 1}{\csc x}$$

28. $2\sin^2 x - \sin x = 0$

$(\sin x)(2\sin x - 1) = 0$

$\sin x = 0$ $2\sin x - 1 = 0$

$x = 0°, 180°$ $\sin x = \dfrac{1}{2}$

                       $x = 30°, 150°$

$x = \mathbf{0°, 30°, 150°, 180°}$

29. $2\sin^2 x = 1$

$\sin^2 x = \dfrac{1}{2}$

$\sin x = \pm\dfrac{\sqrt{2}}{2}$

$x = \mathbf{45°, 135°, 225°, 315°}$

30. $\log_2 x = 3$

$x = 2^3 = \mathbf{8}$

EP

81. $\begin{bmatrix} 1 & -1 \\ 1 & -2 \end{bmatrix}\begin{bmatrix} 5 & -5 \\ -5 & 5 \end{bmatrix}$

$$= \begin{bmatrix} 1(5) - 1(-5) & 1(-5) - 1(5) \\ 1(5) - 2(-5) & 1(-5) - 2(5) \end{bmatrix}$$

$$= \begin{bmatrix} \mathbf{10} & \mathbf{-10} \\ \mathbf{15} & \mathbf{-15} \end{bmatrix}$$

82. For $k = 1$, we get $1^2 = \dfrac{1(2-1)(2+1)}{3}$

$1 = \dfrac{1(3)}{3}$ and $\dfrac{k(2k-1)(2k+1)}{3} + (2k+1)^2$

$$= \frac{k(2k-1)(2k+1) + 3(2k+1)^2}{3}$$

$$= \frac{(2k+1)[k(2k-1) + 3(2k+1)]}{3}$$

$$= \frac{(2k+1)(2k^2 + 5k + 3)}{3}$$

$$= \frac{(2k+1)[(2k+3)(k+1)]}{3}$$

$$= \frac{(k+1)[2(k+1)-1][2(k+1)+1]}{3}$$

1. $\omega = \dfrac{v}{r} = \dfrac{\dfrac{60 \text{ ft}}{\text{sec}} \cdot \dfrac{60 \text{ sec}}{\text{min}}}{35 \text{ cm} \cdot \dfrac{1 \text{ in}}{2.54 \text{ cm}} \cdot \dfrac{1 \text{ ft}}{12 \text{ in}}}$

$= \dfrac{(60)(2.54)(12)(60)}{35} \dfrac{\text{rad}}{\text{min}}$

2. A: $R = 4W + 2$
B: $7W = 4P - 14$
$\quad W = \dfrac{4}{7}P - 2$
C: $4(W + P) = 3R + 6$

Substitute equation A into C.
D: $4(W + P) = 3(4W + 2) + 6$
$\quad 4W + 4P = 12W + 12$
$\quad 8W = 4P - 12$
$\quad 2W = P - 3$
Substitute equation B into D.

$2\left(\dfrac{4}{7}P - 2\right) = P - 3$

$\dfrac{8}{7}P - 4 = P - 3$

$\dfrac{1}{7}P = 1$

$P = 7$

$W = \dfrac{1}{2}P - \dfrac{3}{2} = 2$

$R = 4(4) + 2 = 10$

3. $\dfrac{4}{52} + \dfrac{13}{52} - \dfrac{1}{52} = \dfrac{16}{52} = \dfrac{4}{13}$

4.

	1st	2nd
Distance:	m	m
Rate:	k	?
Time:	$\dfrac{m}{k}$	$\dfrac{m}{k} - p$

$\text{Rate} = \dfrac{m}{\dfrac{m}{k} - p} = \dfrac{m}{\dfrac{m - pk}{k}} = \dfrac{mk}{m - pk}$

5. A: $D + S = 200$
$\quad D = 200 - S$
B: $\dfrac{1}{2}D + \dfrac{1}{10}S = 76$

Substitute equation A into B.

$\dfrac{1}{2}(200 - S) + \dfrac{1}{10}S = 76$

$100 - \dfrac{1}{2}S + \dfrac{1}{10}S = 76$

$\dfrac{2}{5}S = 24$

$S = \$60$
$D = \$140$

6.

$\begin{array}{r|rrrr} -2 & 3 & -9 & -3 & 4 \\ & & -6 & 30 & -54 \\ \hline & 3 & -15 & 27 & -50 \end{array}$

$f(-2) = 3(-2)^3 - 9(-2)^2 - 3(-2) + 4 = -50$
$= (x + 2)(3x^2 - 15x + 27) - 50$
$= (-2 + 2)[3(-2)^2 - 15(-2) + 27] - 50$
$= -50$

7.

$\begin{array}{r|rrrrrr} 2 & 1 & -3 & 0 & 0 & 3 & -4 \\ & & 2 & -2 & -4 & -8 & -10 \\ \hline & 1 & -1 & -2 & -4 & -5 & -14 \end{array}$

$f(2) = -14$

8. Refer to Example 105.A.3.

9. $ABCD$ is a parallelogram is given. $\overline{AB} \parallel \overline{CD}$, $AB = DC$ by def. of a parallelogram. $\angle ABE = \angle EDC$, $\angle BAE = \angle ECD$ because alt. int. angles are equal. $\triangle AEB \cong \triangle CED$ by ASA. $AE = EC$, $BE = ED$ by CPCTE. AC and BD bisect each other by def. of bisector.

10. $\angle ABC = \dfrac{1}{2}\overset{\frown}{AC}$, $\angle ADC = \dfrac{1}{2}\overset{\frown}{AC}$,

$\angle BAD = \dfrac{1}{2}\overset{\frown}{BD}$ and $\angle BCD = \dfrac{1}{2}\overset{\frown}{BD}$ because the measure of an inscribed angle is one-half the intercepted arc. $\angle ABC = \angle ADC$ and $\angle BAD = \angle BCD$ by substitution. $\triangle BAE \sim \triangle DCE$ by AA.

11. Refer to Example 98.A.3.

12. $x = 2(70°) = 140°$
$y = 2(40°) = 80°$
$z = 2(70°) = 140°$

13. (a) Ellipse
(b) Hyperbola
(c) Hyperbola
(d) Parabola
(e) Circle

14. Refer to Problem Set 77, problem 6b.

15. $(x^2 + 2x + 1) + (y^2 - 8y + 16)$
$= 1 + 16 - 13 = 4$
$(x + 1)^2 + (y - 4)^2 = 4$
Center: **(-1, 4)**
Radius: **2**

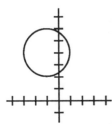

16.
$$\underline{2|\quad 1 \quad -4 \quad 6}$$
$$\underline{\quad\quad 2 \quad -4 \quad -4}$$
$$1 \quad -2 \quad 2$$

No, it is not a zero.

17.
$$\underline{1|\quad 1 \quad -5 \quad 0 \quad 4 \quad -2 \quad 1}$$
$$\underline{\quad\quad 1 \quad -4 \quad -4 \quad 0 \quad -2}$$
$$1 \quad -4 \quad -4 \quad 0 \quad -2 \quad -1$$
$$x^5 - 4x^4 - 4x^2 - 2 - \frac{1}{x - 1}$$

18. $\frac{10!}{4!\,6!} (x^4)^4 (-y^3)^6 = \mathbf{210x^{16}y^{18}}$

19. $\text{pH} = -\log(6.5 \times 10^{-4}) = -(0.8 - 4) = \mathbf{3.2}$

20. $\dfrac{\frac{1}{4}}{1 - \frac{2}{3}} = \frac{1}{4} \cdot \frac{3}{1} = \frac{3}{4}$

21. $\frac{1}{2}n(a_1 + a_n) = \frac{n}{2}\left[a_1 + a_1 + (n-1)d\right]$
$= \frac{n}{2}\left[2a_1 + (n-1)d\right]$

22.
$3x - 2 > 0$ $3x - 2 > \frac{1}{3}$
$x > \frac{2}{3}$ $x > \frac{7}{9}$
$x > \frac{7}{9}$

23. Base $= 6\left[\frac{1}{2}(6)(3\sqrt{3})\right] = 54\sqrt{3}$
$V = \frac{1}{3}bh = \frac{1}{3}\left(54\sqrt{3}\right)(1) = \mathbf{18\sqrt{3}\ m^3}$

24. (a) $V = \frac{4}{3}\pi r^3 = \frac{4}{3}\pi(6)^3 = \mathbf{288\pi\ in^3}$
(b) $S = 4\pi r^2 = 4(\pi)(6)^2 = \mathbf{144\pi\ in^2}$

25.
$$\begin{bmatrix} 2 & 1 & -1 & 0 \\ 0 & 2 & 3 & 7 \\ 2 & -3 & 0 & 7 \end{bmatrix} = \begin{bmatrix} 1 & \frac{1}{2} & -\frac{1}{2} & 0 \\ 0 & 2 & 3 & 7 \\ 0 & -4 & 1 & 7 \end{bmatrix}$$
$$\begin{bmatrix} 1 & 0 & -\frac{5}{4} & -\frac{7}{4} \\ 0 & 1 & \frac{3}{2} & \frac{7}{2} \\ 0 & 0 & 7 & 21 \end{bmatrix} = \begin{bmatrix} 1 & 0 & 0 & 2 \\ 0 & 1 & 0 & -1 \\ 0 & 0 & 1 & 3 \end{bmatrix}$$
$x = 2, y = -1, z = 3$

26. $\cos(x + y) = \cos x \cos y - \sin x \sin y$
$\cos 75° = \cos(30° + 45°)$
$= \cos 30° \cos 45° - \sin 30° \sin 45°$
$= \left(\frac{\sqrt{3}}{2}\right)\left(\frac{\sqrt{2}}{2}\right) - \left(\frac{1}{2}\right)\left(\frac{\sqrt{2}}{2}\right) = \dfrac{\sqrt{6} - \sqrt{2}}{4}$

27. $\dfrac{\cot(\tan x + 1) - \tan x(\cot x - 1)}{(\cot x - 1)(\tan x + 1)}$
$= \dfrac{1 + \cot x - 1 + \tan x}{1 + \cot x - \tan x - 1} = \dfrac{\cot x + \tan x}{\cot x - \tan x}$

28. $-2\sin 3\theta = -\sqrt{2}$
$\sin 3\theta = \dfrac{\sqrt{2}}{2}$
$3\theta = 45°, 135°, 405°, 495°, 765°, 855°$
$\theta = \mathbf{15°, 45°, 135°, 165°, 255°, 285°}$

29. $\log_3 x = 4$
$x = 3^4 = \mathbf{81}$

30. $\frac{1}{2}\log_2 x = \sqrt{\log_2 x}$
$\frac{1}{4}(\log_2 x)^2 = \log_2 x$
$\frac{1}{4}(\log_2 x)^2 - \log_2 x = 0$
$(\log_2 x)\left(\frac{1}{4}\log_2 x - 1\right) = 0$

$\log_2 x = 0$ $\frac{1}{4}\log_2 x - 1 = 0$
$x = 2^0 = \mathbf{1}$ $\log_2 x = 4$
           $2^4 = x = \mathbf{16}$

EP

83. **Invalid**

84.
$$\begin{bmatrix} -1 & 7 \\ 3 & -5 \end{bmatrix}\begin{bmatrix} -1 & 2 \\ 3 & 0 \end{bmatrix} = \begin{bmatrix} 22 & -2 \\ -18 & 6 \end{bmatrix}$$

$$= \begin{bmatrix} (-1)(-1)+(7)(3) & (-1)(2)+(7)(0) \\ (3)(-1)+(-5)(3) & (3)(2)+(-5)(0) \end{bmatrix}$$

PROBLEM SET 107

1. Refer to Example 75.B.1.

2. A $h = 4u$
   B: $t = 5 + u$
   C: $100u + 10t + h = 100h + 10t + u - 297$
   $\quad\;\; 99u - 99h = -297$
   $\qquad\; u - h = -3$
   Substitute equation A into C.
   $u - 4u = -3$
   $u = 1$
   $t = 5 + 1 = 6$
   $h = 4(1) = 4$
   Number = **461**

3. $470 = 480e^{30k}$
   $0.9792 = e^{30k}$
   $e^{-0.0210} = e^{30k}$
   $k \approx -0.0007$
   $240 = 480e^{-0.0007t}$
   $0.5 = e^{-0.0007t}$
   $e^{-0.693} = e^{-0.0007t}$
   $t \approx$ **987.7 min**

4. Rate · time · men = jobs
   Rate · 5 · 4 = k
   Rate = $\dfrac{k}{20}$
   $\dfrac{k}{20} \cdot t \cdot (4 + m) = 49$
   $\left(\dfrac{4k + mk}{20}\right)t = 49$
   $t = \dfrac{49(20)}{4k + mk} = \dfrac{980}{4k + mk}$ hr

5. $R_B T_B + R_G T_G = $ jobs
   $\dfrac{3}{2}(10) + \dfrac{p}{h}(10) = $ jobs
   $15 + \dfrac{10p}{h} = $ jobs $= \dfrac{15h + 10p}{h}$ jobs

6. **Yes**

7. **No**

8. $y = 3x - 4$
   $x = 3y - 4$
   $3y = x + 4$
   $y = \dfrac{1}{3}x + \dfrac{4}{3}$

9. $y = \dfrac{1}{3}x - 4$
   $x = \dfrac{1}{3}y - 4$
   $3x = y - 12$
   $y = 3x + 12$

10.
$$\begin{array}{r|rrrr} -2 & 2 & -9 & 3 & -4 \\ & & -4 & 26 & -58 \\ \hline & 2 & -13 & 29 & 2 \end{array}$$
   $p(-2) = 2(-2)^3 - 9(-2)^2 + 3(-2) - 4 = $ **-62**

11.
$$\begin{array}{r|rrrrr} -1 & 1 & 4 & -6 & 0 & -1 \\ & & -1 & -3 & 9 & -9 \\ \hline & 1 & 3 & -9 & 9 & -10 \end{array}$$
   $p(-1) = (-1)^4 + 4(-1)^3 - 6(-1)^2 - 1 = $ **-10**

12. Refer to Example 105.A.1.

13. Refer to Lesson 90.B.

14. Refer to Example 102.B.1.

15. $AN = NB, AD = BC$, and $\angle NDC = \angle NCD$ are given. $\triangle NDC$ is an isosceles $\triangle$ and $ND = NC$ by the def. of an isosceles triangle. $\triangle ADN \cong \triangle DCN$ by SSS. $\angle DAN = \angle CBN$ by CPCTE. $AB = AB$ by reflexive property. $\triangle ADB \cong \triangle BCA$ by SAS. $DB = AC$ by CPCTE.

16. $x = 2(50°) = 100°$
$y = 2(60°) = 120°$
$z = 2(70°) = 140°$

17. (a) **Ellipse**   (d) **Circle**
(b) **Hyperbola**   (e) **Ellipse**
(c) **Parabola**

18. $4(x^2 - 4x + 4) - 9(y^2 - 4y + 4)$
$= 344 + 16 - 36 = 324$
$$\frac{(x - 2)^2}{81} - \frac{(y - 2)^2}{36} = 1$$
Center: **(2, 2)**
Vertices: **(11, 2), (–7, 2)**
Asymptotes: $y = \dfrac{2}{3}x + \dfrac{2}{3}$
$\ y = -\dfrac{2}{3}x + \dfrac{10}{3}$

19. Find the equation of the line $\perp$ to $y = x - 4$
that passes through $(0, 0)$.
$m_\perp = -1$
$y = -x + b$
$0 = -(0) + b, \ b = 0$
$y = -x$
Solve $y = -x$ and $y = x - 4$ simultaneously:
$-x = x - 4$
$4 = 2x \quad$ thus $\quad x = 2$
$y = -2$
$(x, y) = (2, -2)$
$d = \sqrt{(2 - 0)^2 + (-2 - 0)^2}$
$= \sqrt{2^2 + 2^2} = \sqrt{8} = 2\sqrt{2}$

20.
$$\underline{3}\ \begin{array}{rrrr} 1 & -2 & 2 & -1 \\ & 3 & 3 & 15 \\ \hline 1 & 1 & 5 & 14 \end{array}$$
No, it is not a zero.

21.
$$\underline{2}\ \begin{array}{rrrrrr} 1 & 0 & -4 & 2 & -3 & 1 \\ & 2 & 4 & 0 & 4 & 2 \\ \hline 1 & 2 & 0 & 2 & 1 & 3 \end{array}$$
$x^4 + 2x^3 + 2x + 1 + \dfrac{3}{x - 2}$

22. $S_n = \dfrac{n}{2}\Big[2a_1 + (n - 1)d\Big]$

23. $\dfrac{9!}{6!\,3!}(2x^2)^6(-y^3)^3 = $ **–5376** $x^{12}y^9$

24. $\text{pH} = -\log(8.4 \times 10^{-6})$
$= -(0.9243 - 6) \approx$ **5.1**

25. $\sqrt{4}$ to $\sqrt{9x}$ to $\sqrt{60y} = 2 : 3\sqrt{x} : 2\sqrt{15y}$

26.
$$x = \frac{\begin{vmatrix} -1 & 3 & 1 \\ 8 & 2 & 3 \\ -10 & -1 & 0 \end{vmatrix}}{\begin{vmatrix} 2 & 3 & 1 \\ 0 & 2 & 3 \\ 3 & -1 & 0 \end{vmatrix}}$$

$$= \frac{-1\begin{vmatrix} 2 & 3 \\ -1 & 0 \end{vmatrix} - 3\begin{vmatrix} 2 & 3 \\ -1 & 0 \end{vmatrix} + 1\begin{vmatrix} 2 & 3 \\ -1 & 0 \end{vmatrix}}{2\begin{vmatrix} 2 & 3 \\ -1 & 0 \end{vmatrix} - 3\begin{vmatrix} 2 & 3 \\ -1 & 0 \end{vmatrix} + 1\begin{vmatrix} 2 & 3 \\ -1 & 0 \end{vmatrix}}$$

$$= \frac{-1(0 + 3) - 3(0 + 30) + 1(-8 + 20)}{2(0 + 3) - 3(0 - 9) + 1(0 - 6)}$$
$$= \frac{-3 - 90 + 12}{6 + 27 - 6} = -\frac{81}{27} = -3$$

27. $\sin(x + y) = \sin x \cos y + \cos x \sin y$
$\sin 75° = \sin(30° + 45°)$
$= \sin 30° \cos 45° + \cos 30° \sin 45°$
$= \left(\dfrac{1}{2}\right)\left(\dfrac{\sqrt{2}}{2}\right) + \left(\dfrac{\sqrt{3}}{2}\right)\left(\dfrac{\sqrt{2}}{2}\right) = \dfrac{\sqrt{2} + \sqrt{6}}{4}$

28. $(\sin x - \cos x)^2$
$= \sin^2 x - 2\sin x \cos x + \cos^2 x$
$= 1 - 2\sin x \cos x = 1 - \sin 2x$

29. $-2\cos 2\theta = -\sqrt{2}$
$\cos 2\theta = \dfrac{\sqrt{2}}{2}$
$2\theta = 45°, 315°, 405°, 675°$
$\theta =$ **22.5°, 157.5°, 202.5°, 337.5°**

30. $\log_2 x^{1/3} = \left(\log_2 x\right)^2$
$\dfrac{1}{3}\log_2 x = \left(\log_2 x\right)^2$
$\left(\log_2 x\right)^2 - \dfrac{1}{3}\log_2 x = 0$
$(\log_2 x)\left(\log_2 x - \dfrac{1}{3}\right) = 0$

$\log_2 x = 0 \qquad\qquad \log_2 x = \dfrac{1}{3}$

$x = 2^0 = 1 \qquad\qquad x = 2^{1/3} = \sqrt[3]{2}$

85. For $k = 1$, we get $\dfrac{1}{2^1} = 1 - \dfrac{1}{2^1}$ and

$1 - \dfrac{1}{2^k} + \dfrac{1}{2^{k+1}} = 1 - \dfrac{2}{2} \cdot \dfrac{1}{2^k} + \dfrac{1}{2^{k+1}}$

$= 1 - \dfrac{2}{2^{k+1}} + \dfrac{1}{2^{k+1}} = 1 - \dfrac{1}{2^{k+1}}$

86. $\begin{bmatrix} 2 & 1 \\ 0 & 0 \end{bmatrix} \begin{bmatrix} 0 & 0 \\ 0 & 0 \end{bmatrix} = \begin{bmatrix} 0 & 0 \\ 0 & 0 \end{bmatrix}$

PROBLEM SET 108

1. $1300 = 1400e^{17k}$
$0.92857 = e^{17k}$
$e^{-0.07411} = e^{17k}$
$k \approx -0.00436$
$A_t = 1400e^{-0.0044(53)} \approx \mathbf{1111.2}$

2.

Little Hand	Big Hand
$R_L T_L = S$	$R_B T_B = S + 20$

$R_L = \dfrac{1}{12}$ $\qquad R_B = 1$

$T_L = T_B$

$\dfrac{1}{12} T = S \qquad\qquad 1T = S + 20$

$T = \dfrac{1}{12} T + 20$

$\dfrac{11}{12} T = 20$

$T = \dfrac{240}{11} = \mathbf{21\dfrac{9}{11} \, min}$

3. Rate $\cdot$ time $\cdot$ men = jobs
Rate $\cdot$ $7(5 + w) = 2$
Rate $= \dfrac{2}{7(5 + w)}$

$\dfrac{2}{2(5 + w)} \cdot t(m + 4) = c$

$t = \dfrac{c(7)(5 + w)}{2(m + 4)}\,\mathbf{hr}$

4. $\dfrac{6}{9} \cdot \dfrac{3}{8} = \dfrac{1}{4}$

5. $S = Tm + b$
$\quad 20m + b = 15$
$\quad \underline{40m + b = 25}$
$\quad 20m \quad\quad = 10$
$\qquad m \quad\quad = \dfrac{1}{2}$
$b = 15 - 20\left(\dfrac{1}{2}\right) = 5$

$S = \dfrac{1}{2} T + 5$

$= \dfrac{1}{2}(100) + 5 = \mathbf{55}$

6. **No**

7. $y = x^3 - 2x^2 - 5x + 6$

x	y
−2	0
−1	8
0	6
1	0
2	−4
3	0

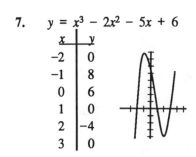

8. $y = x^3 + 2x^2 - 5x + 6$

x	y
−3	0
−2	4
−1	0
0	−6
1	−8
2	0

9. $d = 5 - 3 = \mathbf{2}$

10. $y = 4x - 2$
$x = 4y - 2$
$4y = x + 2$
$y = \dfrac{1}{4} x + \dfrac{1}{2}$

11.
$\begin{array}{r|rrrrr} 3 & 1 & -3 & 2 & -3 & 4 \\ & & 3 & 0 & 6 & 9 \\ \hline & 1 & 0 & 2 & 3 & 13 \end{array}$

$x^3 + 2x + 3 + \dfrac{13}{x - 3}$

12. Refer to Example 105.A.2.

13. $AP = AQ, PB = QC$ are given.
$AB = AP + PB, AC = AQ + QC$ by def. of betweenness. $AB = AC$ by substitution. $\angle A = \angle A$ by reflexive property. $\triangle ABQ \cong \triangle ACP$ by SAS. $BQ = PC$ by CPCTE.

14. Refer to Lesson 90.B.

15. $AN = NB, AD = BC$, and $\angle NDC = \angle NCD$ are given. $\triangle DNC$ is an isosceles triangle by the def. of an isosceles triangle. $DN = CN$ by CPCTE. $\triangle ADN \cong \triangle BCN$ by SSS. $\angle DAB = \angle CBA, \angle ADN = \angle NCB$ by CPCTE. $\angle ADN + \angle NDC = \angle BCN + \angle NCD$ by addition. $\angle ADC = \angle BCD$ by substitution. $\triangle DCB \cong \triangle CDA$ by SAS. $AC = BD$ by CPCTE.

16. $x = 2(40°) = 80°$
$y = 2(60°) = 120°$
$z = 2(80°) = 160°$

17. (a) **Ellipse**
(b) **Hyperbola**
(c) **Circle**
(d) **Parabola**
(e) **Circle**

18. $xy = 8$

x	y
-8	-1
-4	-2
-1	-8
1	8
4	2
8	1

19. $(x^2 - 10x + 25) + (y^2 + 8y + 16)$
$= -5 + 25 + 16 = 36$
$(x - 5)^2 + (y + 4)^2 = 36$
Center: $(5, -4)$
Radius: 6

20. $\dfrac{12!}{7!\,5!}(x^3)^7(-2y^3)^5 = -25{,}344x^{21}y^{15}$

21. $S_n = \dfrac{n}{2}\left[2a_1 + (n - 1)d\right]$

22. $H^+ = 10^{-pH} = 10^{-9.2}$
$\approx 6.3 \times 10^{-10}$ mole/liter

23. $S = \dfrac{a_1}{1 - r}$ $\qquad r = \dfrac{\dfrac{2}{9}}{-\dfrac{1}{3}} = -\dfrac{2}{3}$

$S = \dfrac{-\dfrac{1}{3}}{1 - \left(-\dfrac{2}{3}\right)} = -\dfrac{1}{3} \cdot \dfrac{3}{5} = -\dfrac{1}{5}$

24. (a) $\dfrac{1}{3}\pi r^2 h = \dfrac{1}{3}\pi(6^2)(10) = 120\pi$ cm³

(b) $A = \pi r^2 + \pi r s = \pi(6^2) + \pi(6)\left(2\sqrt{34}\right)$
$= \pi\left(36 + 12\sqrt{34}\right)$ cm²

25. (a) $V = \dfrac{4}{3}\pi r^3$ in³

(b) $A = 4\pi r^2$ in²

26. $\begin{bmatrix} -1 & 2 & 1 & 9 \\ 0 & 1 & -2 & 0 \\ 2 & 3 & 0 & -2 \end{bmatrix} = \begin{bmatrix} 1 & -2 & -1 & -9 \\ 0 & 1 & -2 & 0 \\ 0 & 7 & 2 & 16 \end{bmatrix}$

$= \begin{bmatrix} 1 & 0 & -5 & -9 \\ 0 & 1 & -2 & 0 \\ 0 & 0 & 16 & 16 \end{bmatrix} = \begin{bmatrix} 1 & 0 & 0 & -4 \\ 0 & 1 & 0 & 2 \\ 0 & 0 & 1 & 1 \end{bmatrix}$

$x = -4$
$y = 2$
$z = 1$

27. $\tan(a + b) = \dfrac{\tan a + \tan b}{1 - \tan a \tan b}$
$\tan 75° = \tan(30° + 45°)$
$= \dfrac{\tan 30° + \tan 45°}{1 - \tan 30° \tan 45°}$
$= \dfrac{\dfrac{\sqrt{3}}{3} + 1}{1 - \dfrac{\sqrt{3}}{3}} = \dfrac{\dfrac{\sqrt{3} + 3}{3}}{\dfrac{3 - \sqrt{3}}{3}}$
$= \dfrac{\sqrt{3} + 3}{3 - \sqrt{3}} \cdot \dfrac{3 + \sqrt{3}}{3 + \sqrt{3}}$
$= \dfrac{3\sqrt{3} + 9 + 3 + 3\sqrt{3}}{9 - 3}$
$= \dfrac{12 + 6\sqrt{3}}{6} = 2 + \sqrt{3}$

28.

$$-2 \sin 3\theta = \sqrt{2}$$

$$\sin 3\theta = -\frac{\sqrt{2}}{2}$$

$$3\theta = 225°, 315°, 585°, 675°, 945°, 1035°$$

$$\theta = \mathbf{75°, 105°, 195°, 225°, 315°, 345°}$$

29.

$$\frac{\cos^2 x}{1 - \sin x} = \frac{1 - \sin^2 x}{1 - \sin x}$$

$$= \frac{(1 + \sin x)(1 - \sin x)}{1 - \sin x} = 1 + \sin x$$

$$= 1 + \frac{1}{\csc x} = \frac{\csc x + 1}{\csc x}$$

30.

$$\log_3\left(\frac{x^2}{\frac{2}{3}x - \frac{1}{3}}\right) = 1$$

$$3^1 = \frac{x^2}{\frac{2}{3}x - \frac{1}{3}}$$

$$x^2 = 2x - 1$$

$$x^2 - 2x + 1 = 0$$

$$(x - 1)^2 = 0$$

$$x = 1$$

EP

87. **Valid**

88.

$$x + \begin{bmatrix} (3)(0) + (5)(-1) & (3)(1) + (5)(1) \\ (2)(0) + (1)(-1) & (2)(1) + (1)(1) \end{bmatrix}$$

$$= \begin{bmatrix} 6 & 5 \\ 3 & 2 \end{bmatrix}$$

$$x + \begin{bmatrix} -5 & 8 \\ -1 & 3 \end{bmatrix} = \begin{bmatrix} 6 & 5 \\ 3 & 2 \end{bmatrix}$$

$$x = \begin{bmatrix} 11 & -3 \\ 4 & -1 \end{bmatrix}$$

PROBLEM SET 109

1.
Total $= s + L$

$$\frac{\text{Small}}{\text{Total}} = \frac{s}{s + L}$$

2.

$$\frac{L}{s + L}(100) = \frac{100L}{s + L}$$

3.
$$P = kv^3$$
$$400 = k(10^3)$$
$$k = \frac{400}{1000} = 0.4$$
$$P = 0.4(20^3) = \mathbf{3200}$$

4.
$$V = \frac{kp^2}{\sqrt{w}}$$
$$V = \frac{k(9p)^2}{\sqrt{4w}} = \frac{81kp^2}{2\sqrt{w}}$$
V is multiplied by $\frac{81}{2}$

5.
(Cost of each)(number) = total price
$$(c + p)n = 3000$$
$$n = \frac{3000}{c + n}$$

6. Refer to Example 102.A.2.

7. $AP = AQ, PB = QC$ are given. $AB = AP + PB$ and $AC = AQ + QC$ by the def. of betweenness. $AB = AC$ by addition. $\angle A = \angle A$ by reflexive property. $\triangle ABQ \cong \triangle ACP$ by SAS. $\angle ABQ = \angle ACP$ by CPCTE. Since $AB = AC$, $\triangle ABC$ is an isosceles triangle, and $\angle ABC = \angle ACB$. $\angle ABC - \angle ABQ = \angle ACB - \angle ACP$ by substitution and subtraction. $\angle QBC = \angle PCB$ by substitution.

8. Refer to Example 105.A.3.

9. $\angle BAD = \angle BCD$ because if two angles intercept the same arc, then the two angles are equal (Lesson 105). $\angle AEB = \angle CED$ because vert. angles are equal. $\triangle AEB \sim \triangle CED$ by AA. Therefore, $\frac{BE}{AE} = \frac{ED}{EC}$

10. Refer to Problem Set 76, problem 6.

11.
$$x = 2(30°) = \mathbf{60°}$$
$$y = 2(80°) = \mathbf{160°}$$
$$z = 2(70°) = \mathbf{140°}$$

12.

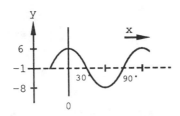

13. (a) Ellipse   (d) Circle
    (b) Hyperbola   (e) Ellipse
    (c) Parabola

14. Yes

15. $9(x^2 - 6x + 9) - 4(y^2 + 4y + 4)$
$= 79 + 81 - 16 = 144$
$9(x - 3)^2 - 4(y + 2)^2 = 144$
$\dfrac{(x - 3)^2}{16} - \dfrac{(y + 2)^2}{36} = 1$
Center $(3, -2)$
Vertices: $(7, -2), (-1, -2)$
Asymptotes: $y = \dfrac{3}{2}x - \dfrac{13}{2}$
$\qquad\qquad\quad y = -\dfrac{3}{2}x + \dfrac{5}{2}$

16. $y = x^3 - 4x^2 + x + 6$

x	y
-1	0
0	6
1	8
2	0
3	0

17. $y = x^3 + x^2 - 10x + 8$

x	y
-4	8
0	0
1	0
2	0

18. $y = 3x - 2$
$x = 3y - 2$
$3y = x + 2$
$y = \dfrac{1}{3}x + \dfrac{2}{3}$

19. $y = \dfrac{1}{5}x - 6$
$x = \dfrac{1}{5}y - 6$
$5x = y - 30$
$y = 5x + 30$

20. $S_n = \dfrac{n}{2}\left[2a_1 + (n - 1)d\right]$

21. $\dfrac{6!}{3!\,3!}(x^2)^3(-3y^2)^3 = -540x^6y^6$

22. $S_n = \dfrac{a_1(1 - r^n)}{1 - r}$

$r = \dfrac{-\dfrac{3}{4}}{\dfrac{1}{2}} = -\dfrac{3}{2}$

$S_7 = \dfrac{\dfrac{1}{2}\left[1 - \left(-\dfrac{3}{2}\right)^7\right]}{1 + \dfrac{3}{2}}$

$= \dfrac{\dfrac{1}{2}\left(1 + \dfrac{2187}{128}\right)}{\dfrac{5}{2}} = \dfrac{1}{5}\left(1 + \dfrac{2187}{128}\right)$

$= \dfrac{1}{5}\left(\dfrac{2315}{128}\right) = \dfrac{463}{128}$

23. $H^+ = 10^{-pH} = 10^{-7.4}$
$\approx 4.0 \times 10^{-8}$ mole/liter

24. $d = \sqrt{2^2 + 5^2 + x^2} = \sqrt{29 + x^2}$

25. Base $= 6\left[\dfrac{1}{2}(4)(2\sqrt{3})\right] = 24\sqrt{3}$
$V = \dfrac{1}{3}\left(24\sqrt{3}\right)(9) = 72\sqrt{3}$ in³

26.
$$x = \dfrac{\begin{vmatrix} 2 & -1 & -1 \\ 10 & 2 & 3 \\ -5 & 2 & 0 \end{vmatrix}}{\begin{vmatrix} -2 & -1 & -1 \\ 0 & 2 & 3 \\ 3 & 2 & 0 \end{vmatrix}}$$

$$= \dfrac{2\begin{vmatrix} 2 & 3 \\ 2 & 0 \end{vmatrix} + 1\begin{vmatrix} 10 & 3 \\ -5 & 0 \end{vmatrix} - 1\begin{vmatrix} 10 & 2 \\ -5 & 2 \end{vmatrix}}{-2\begin{vmatrix} 2 & 3 \\ 2 & 0 \end{vmatrix} + 1\begin{vmatrix} 0 & 3 \\ 3 & 0 \end{vmatrix} - 1\begin{vmatrix} 0 & 2 \\ 3 & 2 \end{vmatrix}}$$

$$= \dfrac{2(0 - 6) + 1(0 + 15) - 1(20 + 10)}{-2(0 - 6) + 1(0 - 9) - 1(0 - 6)}$$

$$\dfrac{-12 + 15 - 30}{12 - 9 + 6} = -\dfrac{27}{9} = -3$$

27. $\sin 15° = \sqrt{\dfrac{1 - \cos 30°}{2}}$

$= \sqrt{\dfrac{1 - \dfrac{\sqrt{3}}{2}}{2}} \approx \sqrt{\dfrac{1 - 0.866}{2}} \approx \mathbf{0.259}$

28. $\dfrac{\sin^2 x}{1 - \cos x} = \dfrac{1 - \cos^2 x}{1 - \cos x}$

$= \dfrac{(1 + \cos x)(1 - \cos x)}{1 - \cos x}$

$= 1 + \cos x = 1 + \dfrac{1}{\sec x} = \dfrac{\sec x + 1}{\sec x}$

29. $3 \tan^2 x + 5 \sec x + 1 = 0$
$3(\sec^2 x - 1) + 5 \sec x + 1 = 0$
$3 \sec^2 x - 3 + 5 \sec x + 1 = 0$
$3 \sec^2 x + 5 \sec x - 2 = 0$
$(3\sec x - 1)(\sec x + 2) = 0$

$\sec x = \dfrac{1}{3}$ $\sec x = -2$

$\varnothing$ $\cos x = -\dfrac{1}{2}$

$x = \mathbf{120°, 240°}$

30. $\log_3 x = 4$
$x = 3^4 = \mathbf{81}$

EP

89. For $k = 1$, we get $(4 \cdot 1 - 3) = 1(2 - 1)$
$4 - 3 = 1$. And $k(2k - 1) + (4k + 1)$
$= 2k^2 + 3k + 1 = (k + 1)(2k + 1)$
$= (k + 1)[2(k + 1) - 1]$

90. $\begin{bmatrix} 1 & -2 \\ -1 & 2 \end{bmatrix} \begin{bmatrix} 1 & -2 \\ -1 & 1 \end{bmatrix}$

$= \begin{bmatrix} (1)(1) + (-2)(-1) & (1)(-2) + (-2)(1) \\ (-1)(1) + (2)(-1) & (-1)(-2) + (2)(1) \end{bmatrix}$

$= \begin{bmatrix} \mathbf{3} & \mathbf{-4} \\ \mathbf{-3} & \mathbf{4} \end{bmatrix}$

PROBLEM SET 110

1. $R = \dfrac{kG}{P^2}$

$40 = \dfrac{k(10)}{5^2}$

$k = 100$

$R = \dfrac{100(20)}{16} = \mathbf{125}$

2. $0.7 + 0.5 + x = 0.9$
$x = \mathbf{0.3}$

3. $482 = 470e^{4k}$
$1.025 = e^{4k}$
$e^{0.0252} = e^{4k}$
$k = 0.0063$
$1460 = 470e^{0.0063t}$
$3.1064 = e^{0.0063t}$
$e^{1.1335} = e^{0.0063t}$
$t \approx 179.9 + 6 = \mathbf{185.8\ hr}$

4. $w(w + 10) = 200$
$w^2 + 10w - 200 = 0$
$(w + 20)(w - 10) = 0$
$w = 10\ ft$

$l = w + 10 = 10 + 10 = 20\ ft$
$P = 2(10) + 2(20) = \mathbf{60\ ft}$

5. $\pi r^2 h = \pi(r + 2)^2\left(\dfrac{1}{4}h\right)$

$\pi r^2 h = \pi(r^2 + 4r + 4)\left(\dfrac{1}{4}h\right)$

$4r^2 = r^2 + 4r + 4$
$3r^2 - 4r - 4 = 0$
$(3r + 2)(r - 2) = 0$
$r = \mathbf{2\ cm}$

6.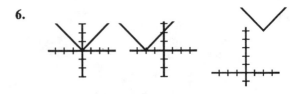

7. $f(x) = \begin{cases} -1 & x \leq -2 \\ \dfrac{1}{2}x & -2 \leq x < 0 \\ 1 & x \geq 0 \end{cases}$

8.

9. $AP = AQ, PB = QC$ are given. $AB = AP$ $+ PB, AC = AQ + QC$ by the def. of betweenness. $AB = AC$ by substitution. $\angle A = \angle A$ by reflexive property. $\triangle ABQ$ $\cong \triangle ACP$ by SAS. $BQ = CP$ and $\angle ABQ$ $= \angle ACP$ by CPCTE. $\triangle ABC$ is an isosceles $\triangle$ and $\angle ABC = \angle ACB$ by the def. of an isosceles $\triangle$. $\angle ABC - \angle ABQ = \angle ACB$ $- \angle ACP$ by subtraction. $\angle QBC = \angle PCB$ by substitution. $\triangle BQR \cong \triangle CPR$ by SAS. $\angle BQR = \angle CPR$ by CPCTE.

10. Refer to Example 109.A.3.

11. $\angle BAD = \frac{1}{2}\overset{\frown}{BD}$, $\angle BCD = \frac{1}{2}\overset{\frown}{BD}$ because the measure of an inscribed angle is one-half the measure of the intercepted arc. $\angle BAD$ $= \angle BCD$ by substitution. $\angle BEA = \angle CED$ because vertical angles are equal. $\triangle AEB$ $\sim \triangle CED$ by AA. $\frac{BE}{ED} = \frac{AE}{EC}$. Therefore, $(BE)(EC) = (AE)(ED)$

12. Refer to Example 105.A.3.

13. $x = 2(80°) = 160°$
$y = 2(30°) = 60°$
$z = 2(70°) = 140°$

14. No

15. (a) **Ellipse**
(b) **Circle**
(c) **Hyperbola**
(d) **Parabola**
(e) **Ellipse**

16. $\frac{7!}{3!\,4!}\,(a^2)^3(-2b^5)^4 = \mathbf{560a^6b^{20}}$

17. $x = -5(y^2 + 6y + 9) - 11 + 45$
$x = -5(y + 3)^2 + 34$
Vertex : (34, –3)
Axis of symmetry: $y = -3$
Opens to the left

18. $y = x^3 - 2x^2 - 9x + 18$

x	y
–3	0
–1	24
0	18
2	0
3	0

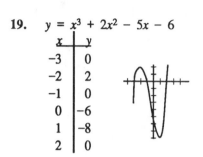

19. $y = x^3 + 2x^2 - 5x - 6$

x	y
–3	0
–2	2
–1	0
0	–6
1	–8
2	0

20. $y = 4x - 2$
$x = 4y - 2$
$4y = x + 2$
$y = \frac{1}{4}x + \frac{1}{2}$

21. $y = \frac{1}{3}x + 3$
$x = \frac{1}{3}y + 3$
$y = 3x - 9$

22. $S_n = \frac{n}{2}\left[2a_1 + (n - 1)d\right]$

23. Downs $= \frac{a_1(1 - r^n)}{1 - r}$

$= \frac{64\left[1 - \left(\frac{1}{2}\right)^8\right]}{1 - \frac{1}{2}} = 127.5$

Ups $= 127.5 - 64 = 63.5$
Total $= 127.5 + 63.5 =$ **191 ft**

24. $H^+ = 10^{-pH} = 10^{-3} = 1 \times 10^{-3} \dfrac{\text{mole}}{\text{liter}}$

25. (a) $V = \frac{1}{3}\pi r^2 h = \frac{1}{3}\pi(8)^2(10) = \frac{640}{3}\pi \text{ cm}^3$

(b) $A = \pi r^2 + \pi r s$
$= \pi(8)^2 + \pi(2)\left(2\sqrt{41}\right)$
$= \pi\left(64 + 16\sqrt{41}\right) \text{ cm}^2$

26.

$$\begin{bmatrix} -2 & -1 & 1 & -2 \\ 1 & 2 & 0 & 3 \\ 0 & 3 & 2 & 2 \end{bmatrix} = \begin{bmatrix} 1 & 2 & 0 & 3 \\ 0 & 3 & 2 & 2 \\ -2 & -1 & 1 & -2 \end{bmatrix}$$

$$= \begin{bmatrix} 1 & 2 & 0 & 3 \\ 0 & 3 & 2 & 2 \\ 0 & 2 & 1 & 4 \end{bmatrix} = \begin{bmatrix} 1 & 0 & -\frac{4}{3} & \frac{5}{3} \\ 0 & 1 & \frac{2}{3} & \frac{2}{3} \\ 0 & 0 & -1 & 2 \end{bmatrix}$$

$$= \begin{bmatrix} 1 & 0 & 0 & -1 \\ 0 & 1 & 0 & 2 \\ 0 & 0 & 1 & -2 \end{bmatrix}$$

$x = -1$
$y = 2$
$z = -2$

27. $\cos 15° = \sqrt{\dfrac{1 + \cos 30°}{2}} = \sqrt{\dfrac{1 + \dfrac{\sqrt{3}}{2}}{2}}$

$$= \sqrt{\dfrac{\dfrac{2 + \sqrt{3}}{2}}{2}} = \dfrac{\sqrt{2 + \sqrt{3}}}{2}$$

28. $2\cos^2 x - 9\sin x + 3 = 0$
$2(1 - \sin^2 x) - 9\sin x + 3 = 0$
$2 - 2\sin^2 x - 9\sin x + 3 = 0$

$2\sin^2 x + 9\sin x - 5 = 0$
$(2\sin x - 1)(\sin x + 5) = 0$

$\sin x = \dfrac{1}{2}$ $\qquad\qquad \sin x = -5$

$x = 30°, 150°$ $\qquad\qquad \emptyset$

29. $\dfrac{\sec^3 x - 8}{\sec^2 x + \sec x - 6}$

$= \dfrac{(\sec x - 2)(\sec^2 x + 2\sec x + 4)}{(\sec x - 2)(\sec x + 3)}$

$= \dfrac{\sec^2 x + 2\sec x + 4}{\sec x + 3}$

30. $\log_b MN = \log_b b^a b^c = \log_b b^{a+c}$
$= a + c = \log_b M + \log_b N$

EP

91. **Invalid**

92. $\begin{bmatrix} (3)(1) + (0)(-1) & (3)(-2) + (0)(2) \\ (0)(1) + (1)(-1) & (0)(-2) + (1)(2) \end{bmatrix}$

$= \begin{bmatrix} 3 & -6 \\ -1 & 2 \end{bmatrix}$

PROBLEM SET 111

1. $V = lwh$

$(6l)\left(\dfrac{w}{2}\right)\left(\dfrac{h}{\sqrt{2}}\right) = \dfrac{6}{2\sqrt{2}} lwh$

$= \dfrac{6\sqrt{2}}{4} lwh = \dfrac{3\sqrt{2}}{2} lwh$

Multiplied by $\dfrac{3\sqrt{2}}{2}$

2.

	1st	2nd
Distance:	m	$m + 30$
Rate:	$\dfrac{m}{h}$	?
Time:	h	$\dfrac{h}{2}$

Rate $= \dfrac{m + 30}{\dfrac{h}{2}} = \dfrac{2(m + 30)}{h}$ mph

3. $450 = 1460e^{50k}$
$0.30822 = e^{50k}$
$e^{-1.1769} = e^{50k}$
$k \approx -0.02354$

$730 = 1460e^{-0.02354t}$
$0.5 = e^{-0.02354t}$
$e^{-0.6931} = e^{-0.02354t}$
$t \approx$ **29.4 hr**

4. Overall average $= \dfrac{\text{total}}{\text{number of tosses}}$

$37 = \dfrac{19A + x}{20}$

$20(37) = 19A + x$
$x = [20(37) - 19A]$ ft

5. Rate · time · men = jobs
    Rate · 3 · 5 = k
    Rate = $\dfrac{k}{15}$

    $\dfrac{k}{15} \cdot T \cdot 12 = 13m$

    $\dfrac{12k}{15} T = 13m$

    $T = \dfrac{13m(15)}{12k} = \dfrac{65m}{4k}$ hr

6. Refer to Example 111.B.1.

7. Draw $\overline{CB}$. $\angle DCB = \dfrac{1}{2}\overset{\frown}{DB}$,

    $\angle ABC = \dfrac{1}{2}\overset{\frown}{AC}$ because the measure of an
    inscribed angle is equal to one-half the
    measure of the intercepted arc. $\angle AEC$
    $= \angle DCB + \angle ABC = \dfrac{1}{2}\left(\overset{\frown}{DB} + \overset{\frown}{AC}\right)$

8. Refer to Example 111.B.2.

9. Refer to Example 111.B.3.

10. $AP = AQ, PB = QC$ are given. $AB = AP$
    $+ PB, AC = AQ + QC$ by the def. of
    betweenness. $AB = AC$ by substitution.
    $\angle A = \angle A$ by reflexive property. $\triangle ABQ$
    $\cong \triangle ACP$ by SAS. $BQ = PC$ by CPCTE.

11. $x = 2(80°) = \mathbf{160°}$
    $y = 2(30°) = \mathbf{60°}$
    $z = 2(70°) = \mathbf{140°}$

12.

13. $f(x) = \begin{cases} -1 & x \le 0 \\ x & 0 < x \le 1 \\ 1 & x > 1 \end{cases}$

14.

15. (*a*) **Hyperbola**
    (*b*) **Ellipse**
    (*c*) **Circle**
    (*d*) **Parabola**
    (*e*) **Ellipse**

16. **No**

17. $25(x^2 - 4x + 4) - 16(y^2 + 6y + 9)$
    $= 444 + 100 - 144 = 400$
    $25(x - 2)^2 - 16(y + 3)^2 = 400$
    $\dfrac{(x - 2)^2}{16} - \dfrac{(y + 3)^2}{25} = 1$
    Center: (2, −3)
    Vertices: (6, −3), (−2, −3)
    Asymptotes: $y = \dfrac{5}{4}x - \dfrac{11}{2}$
    $y = \dfrac{5}{4}x - \dfrac{1}{2}$

18. $y = x^3 - x^2 - 10x - 8$

x	y
−2	0
−1	0
0	−8
2	−24
4	0

    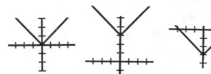

19. $y = x^3 + 2x^2 - 5x - 6$

x	y
−3	0
−2	4
−1	0
0	−6
1	−8
2	0

20. $x = 2y - 3$
    $2y = x + 3$
    $y = \dfrac{1}{2}x + \dfrac{3}{2}$

21. $x = \dfrac{1}{4}y - 4$
    $\dfrac{1}{4}y = x + 4$
    $y = 4x + 16$

22. $a_9 = 37, a_4 = 12$

$$a_1 + 8d = 37$$
$$(-)\; a_1 + 3d = 12$$
$$\overline{\qquad 5d = 25}$$
$$d = 5$$
$$a_1 = 37 - 8(5) = -3$$
$$a_{13} = -3 + 12(5) = \mathbf{57}$$

23. $-\sqrt{xy} = -12$

(1) $xy = 144$

$$\frac{x + y}{2} = 20$$
$$x + y = 40$$

(2) $y = 40 - x$

Substitute equation (2) into (1).

$$x(40 - x) = 144$$
$$40x - x^2 = 144$$
$$x^2 - 40x + 144 = 0$$
$$(x - 36)(x - 4) = 0$$
$$x = 36, x = 4$$

Numbers = **36, 4**

24. Sides = $\dfrac{3\sqrt{2}}{1}$

Volumes = $\dfrac{\left(3\sqrt{2}\right)^3}{1^3} = \dfrac{54\sqrt{2}}{1}$

Ratio = $\mathbf{54\sqrt{2}:1}$

25. pH $= -\log H^+ = -\log(4.3 \times 10^{-9})$
$$\approx -(0.6335 - 9) \approx \mathbf{8.4}$$

26.

$$z = \frac{\begin{vmatrix} 2 & -3 & 2 \\ 3 & -1 & 2 \\ 6 & 2 & 11 \end{vmatrix}}{\begin{vmatrix} 2 & -3 & 1 \\ 3 & -1 & 0 \\ 0 & 2 & 3 \end{vmatrix}}$$

$$= \frac{2\begin{vmatrix} -1 & 2 \\ 2 & 11 \end{vmatrix} + 3\begin{vmatrix} 3 & 2 \\ 0 & 11 \end{vmatrix} + 2\begin{vmatrix} 3 & -1 \\ 0 & 2 \end{vmatrix}}{2\begin{vmatrix} -1 & 0 \\ 2 & 3 \end{vmatrix} + 3\begin{vmatrix} 3 & 0 \\ 0 & 3 \end{vmatrix} + 1\begin{vmatrix} 3 & -1 \\ 0 & 2 \end{vmatrix}}$$

$$= \frac{2(-11-4) + 3(33-0) + 2(6-0)}{-2(-3+0) + 3(9-0) + 1(6-0)}$$
$$= \frac{-30 + 99 + 12}{-6 + 27 + 6} = -\frac{81}{27} = \mathbf{3}$$

27. $a = \sqrt{10^2 + 11^2 - 2(10)(11)\cos 130°}$
$$\approx \sqrt{221 - 220(-.6428)} \approx \sqrt{362} \approx \mathbf{19.0}$$

28. $2(1 - \cos^2 x) - 9\cos x + 3 = 0$
$$2 - 2\cos^2 x - 9\cos x + 3 = 0$$
$$2\cos^2 x + 9\cos x - 5 = 0$$
$$(2\cos x - 1)(\cos x + 5) = 0$$

$\cos x = \dfrac{1}{2}$ \qquad\qquad $\cos x = -5$

$x = \mathbf{60°, 300°}$ \qquad\qquad $\varnothing$

29. $(\sec x - \tan x)^2$
$$= \sec^2 x - 2\sec x \tan x + \tan^2 x$$
$$= \frac{1}{\cos^2 x} + \frac{2}{\cos x} \cdot \frac{\sin x}{\cos x} + \frac{\sin^2 x}{\cos^2 x}$$
$$= \frac{1 - 2\sin x + \sin^2 x}{\cos^2 x}$$
$$= \frac{(1 - \sin x)(1 - \sin x)}{1 - \sin^2 x}$$
$$= \frac{(1 - \sin x)(1 - \sin x)}{(1 + \sin x)(1 - \sin x)} = \frac{1 - \sin x}{1 + \sin x}$$

30. $\log_{10} 6 = \dfrac{\log_e 6}{\log_e 10} = \dfrac{\ln 6}{\ln 10}$

EP

93. For $k = 1$, we get $1^3 = 1^2(2 \cdot 1^2 - 1)$
$$1 = 2 - 1.$$
And $k^2(2k^2 - 1) + (2k + 1)^3$
$$= 2k^4 - k^2 + 8k^3 + 12k^2 + 6k + 1$$
$$= 2k^4 + 8k^3 + 11k^2 + 6k + 1$$
$$= (k + 1)^2(2k^2 + 4k + 1)$$
$$= (k + 1)^2[2(k + 1)^2 - 1]$$

94.
$$\begin{bmatrix} 3 & 3 \\ 4 & -4 \end{bmatrix} \cdot \begin{bmatrix} 1 & -1 \\ 2 & -2 \end{bmatrix}$$
$$= \begin{bmatrix} (3)(1) + (3)(2) & (3)(-1) + (3)(-2) \\ (4)(1) + (-4)(2) & (4)(-1) + (-4)(-2) \end{bmatrix}$$
$$= \begin{bmatrix} \mathbf{9} & \mathbf{-9} \\ \mathbf{-4} & \mathbf{4} \end{bmatrix}$$

PROBLEM SET 112

1. $0.4 + 0.7 - 0.25 =$ **0.85**

2. $\dfrac{6}{36} + \dfrac{2}{36} = \dfrac{8}{36} = \dfrac{2}{9}$

3. Rate $\cdot$ time $\cdot$ men = jobs
   Rate $\cdot$ $m \cdot 4 = k$
   Rate $= \dfrac{k}{4m}$

   $\dfrac{k}{4m} \cdot T \cdot 7 = 35$
   $T = \dfrac{35(4m)}{7k} = \dfrac{20m}{k}$ **hr**

4.
	1st	2nd
Distance:	m	k
Rate:	$\dfrac{m}{60h}$	$\dfrac{k}{m}$
Time:	$60h$	m

   Overall rate $= \dfrac{\text{total distance}}{\text{total time}} = \dfrac{m + k}{60h + m}$

   $\dfrac{m + k}{60h + m} T = 30$

   $T = \dfrac{30(60h + m)}{m + k}$ **min**

5. $\omega = \dfrac{v}{r} = \dfrac{m\dfrac{\text{mi}}{\text{hr}} \cdot \dfrac{1\ \text{hr}}{60\ \text{min}} \cdot \dfrac{1\ \text{min}}{60\ \text{sec}}}{c\ \text{cm} \cdot \dfrac{1\ \text{in}}{2.54\ \text{cm}} \cdot \dfrac{1\ \text{ft}}{12\ \text{in}} \cdot \dfrac{1\ \text{mi}}{5280\ \text{ft}}}$

   $= \dfrac{m(2.54)(12)(5280)}{(60)(60)(c)} \dfrac{\text{rad}}{\text{sec}}$

6. Yes. They have no common factor.

7. Yes. They have no common factor.

8. Refer to Example 112.B.1.

9. $\dfrac{\text{Integer factors of } 3}{\text{Integer factors of } 4} = \dfrac{\pm 1, \pm 3}{\pm 1, \pm 2, \pm 4}$

   Possible roots: $\pm\dfrac{1}{4}, \pm\dfrac{1}{2}, \pm\dfrac{3}{4}, \pm 1, \pm\dfrac{3}{2}, \pm 3$

10. Refer to Example 111.B.1.

11. Refer to Example 111.B.2.

12. Refer to Problem Set 111, problem 7.

13. Refer to Example 111.B.3.

14. Refer to Problem Set 76, problem 6.

15. $x = 2(50°) =$ **100°**
    $y = 2(60°) =$ **120°**
    $z = 2(70°) =$ **140°**

16.

17. $f(x) = \begin{cases} -1 & x \le 1 \\ 2x - 2 & 1 < x \le 2 \\ 2 & x > 2 \end{cases}$

18.

19. (a) **Circle**
    (b) **Ellipse**
    (c) **Ellipse**
    (d) **Hyperbola**
    (e) **Parabola**

20. **Yes**

21. $(x^2 - 10x + 25) + (y^2 + 8y + 16)$
    $= -5 + 16 + 25 = 36$
    $(x - 5)^2 + (y + 4)^2 = 36$
    Center: (5, −4)
    Radius: 6

22. $x = \dfrac{-1 \pm \sqrt{1 - 4(1)(2)}}{2(1)} = \dfrac{-1 \pm i\sqrt{7}}{2}$

    $\left[x - \left(-\dfrac{1}{2} + \dfrac{i\sqrt{7}}{2} \right) \right]\left[x - \left(-\dfrac{1}{2} - \dfrac{i\sqrt{7}}{2} \right) \right]$

    $= \left(x + \dfrac{1}{2} - \dfrac{i\sqrt{7}}{2} \right)\left(x + \dfrac{1}{2} + \dfrac{i\sqrt{7}}{2} \right)$

23. $y = x^3 - 3x^2 - x + 3$

x	y
0	3
−1	0
1	0
2	3
3	0

24. $\sqrt{xy} = 15$

(1) $xy = 225$

$\dfrac{x + y}{2} = 39$

$x + y = 78$

(2) $y = 78 - x$

Substitute equation (2) into (1).

$x(78 - x) = 225$

$78x - x^2 = 225$

$x^2 - 78x + 225 = 0$

$(x - 3)(x - 75) = 0$

$x = 3, x = 75$

Numbers = **3, 75**

25. Central angle $= \dfrac{360°}{5} = 72°$

$h = \dfrac{2}{\tan 36°} \approx 2.75$

Base $= 5\left(\dfrac{1}{2}(4)(2.75)\right) = 27.5$

$V = \dfrac{1}{3}(27.5)(10) = $ **91.8 cm³**

26. $\text{pH} = -\log(5.2 \times 10^{-8})$

$\approx -(0.716 - 8) \approx$ **7.3**

27.

$$\begin{bmatrix} 2 & -1 & 1 & 4 \\ 0 & 2 & -1 & -3 \\ 3 & -2 & 0 & 5 \end{bmatrix} = \begin{bmatrix} 1 & -\frac{1}{2} & \frac{1}{2} & 2 \\ 0 & 2 & -1 & -3 \\ 0 & -\frac{1}{2} & -\frac{3}{2} & -1 \end{bmatrix}$$

$$\begin{bmatrix} 1 & 0 & \frac{1}{4} & \frac{5}{4} \\ 0 & 1 & -\frac{1}{2} & -\frac{3}{2} \\ 0 & 0 & -\frac{7}{4} & -\frac{7}{4} \end{bmatrix} = \begin{bmatrix} 1 & 0 & 0 & 1 \\ 0 & 1 & 0 & -1 \\ 0 & 0 & 1 & 1 \end{bmatrix}$$

$x = 1$

$y = -1$

$z = 1$

28. $(1 + \tan^2 x)^2 = 1 + 2\tan x + \tan^2 x$

$= \sec^2 x + 2\tan x$

29. $3(1 + \tan^2 x) - 2\sqrt{3}\tan x - 6 = 0$

$3 + 3\tan^2 x - 2\sqrt{3}\tan x - 6 = 0$

$\left(3\tan x + \sqrt{3}\right)\left(\tan x - \sqrt{3}\right) = 0$

$3\tan x = -\sqrt{3} \qquad\qquad \tan x = \sqrt{3}$

$\tan x = -\dfrac{\sqrt{3}}{3} \qquad\qquad x = 60°, 240°$

$x = 150°, 330°$

$x =$ **60°, 150°, 240°, 330°**

30. $2^{-3} = \dfrac{1}{8}$

EP

95. For $k = 1$, we get $4 = 2 \cdot 1(1 + 1)$.

$4 = (2)(2)$

And $2k(k + 1) + 4(k + 1)$

$= (k + 1)(2k + 4) = 2(k + 1)(k + 2)$

$= 2(k + 1)[(k + 1) + 1]$

96.

$$\begin{bmatrix} (3)(2) + (2)(0) & (3)(1) + (2)(-1) \\ (-1)(2) + (1)(0) & (-1)(1) + (1)(-1) \end{bmatrix}$$

$$+ 3x = \begin{bmatrix} 1 & 12 \\ 1 & 6 \end{bmatrix}$$

$$\begin{bmatrix} 6 & 1 \\ -2 & -2 \end{bmatrix} + 3x = \begin{bmatrix} 1 & 12 \\ 1 & 6 \end{bmatrix}$$

$$3x = \begin{bmatrix} 1 & 12 \\ 1 & 6 \end{bmatrix} - \begin{bmatrix} 6 & 1 \\ -2 & -2 \end{bmatrix}$$

$$3x = \begin{bmatrix} -5 & 11 \\ 3 & 8 \end{bmatrix}$$

$$x = \begin{bmatrix} -\dfrac{5}{3} & \dfrac{11}{3} \\ 1 & \dfrac{8}{3} \end{bmatrix}$$

1. $R_R T_R + R_S T_S = 12$

$$\left(\frac{p}{6}\right) T + \frac{1}{m}(T + 2) = 12$$

$$\frac{pT}{6} + \frac{T + 2}{m} = 12$$

$$mpT + 6T + 12 = 12$$

$$T(mp + 6) = 72m - 12$$

$$T = \frac{72m - 12}{mp + 6} \text{ min}$$

2. $_7C_3 = \frac{7!}{3! \, 4!} = 35$

3.

	1st	2nd
Distance	m	$m + 5$
Rate:	$\frac{m}{h}$	$\frac{m}{h}$
Time:	h	$\frac{m + 5}{\frac{m}{h}}$

$$T = h + \frac{m + 5}{\frac{m}{h}} = \frac{hm + h(m + 5)}{m}$$

4. $C = mN + b$

$\quad 55 = m(10) + b$

$\quad \underline{85 = m(20) + b}$

$\quad 30 = \quad 10m$

$\quad \ 3 = \quad m$

$b = 55 - 10(3) = 25$

$C = 3N + 25 = 3(1) + 25 = \$28$

5. $\dfrac{4}{\dfrac{7}{x + y} - 3} = \dfrac{4}{\dfrac{7 - 3(x + y)}{x + y}} = \dfrac{4(x + y)}{7 - 3(x + y)}$

6.

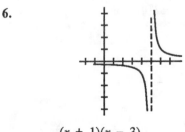

7. $y = \dfrac{(x + 1)(x - 3)}{x + 1}$

$y = x - 3$

Hole at $\begin{cases} x = -1 \\ y = -4 \end{cases}$

8.

9. $y = \dfrac{(x + 2)(x + 1)}{x + 2}$

$y = x + 1$

Hole at $\begin{cases} x = -2 \\ y = -1 \end{cases}$

10.

11. **Yes.** They have no common factor.

12. **No.** They both contain factor of 3.

13. $\dfrac{\text{Integer factors of 3}}{\text{Integer factors of 5}} = \dfrac{\pm 1, \pm 3}{\pm 1, \pm 5}$

possible roots: $\pm\dfrac{1}{5}, \pm\dfrac{3}{5}, \pm 1, \pm 3$

14. Refer to Example 111.B.2.

15. $\angle BAD = \dfrac{1}{2}\overset{\frown}{BD}$, $\angle BCD = \dfrac{1}{2}\overset{\frown}{BD}$ because the measure of an inscribed angle is one-half the measure of the intercepted arc. $\angle BAD = \angle BCD$ by substitution. $\angle P = \angle P$ by reflexive property. $\triangle PAD \sim \triangle PCD$ by AA.

16. Refer to Example 111.B.3.

17. $\angle ACD = \dfrac{1}{2}\overset{\frown}{AD}$, $\angle ABD = \dfrac{1}{2}\overset{\frown}{AD}$ because the measure of an inscribed angle is one-half the measure of the intercepted arc. $\angle ACD = \angle ABD$ by substitution. $\angle AEC = \angle DEB$ because vertical $\angle$'s are equal. $\triangle AEC \sim \triangle DEB$ by AA. $\dfrac{AE}{CE} = \dfrac{ED}{EB}$ by proportion. $(AE)(EB) = (CE)(ED)$ by multiplication.

18. Refer to Solution Set 47, problem 8.

19. $f(x) = \begin{cases} -2 & x \le 1 \\ x - 1 & 1 < x \le 3 \\ 2 & x > 3 \end{cases}$

20. (a) **Hyperbola**
(b) **Ellipse**
(c) **Circle**
(d) **Parabola**
(e) **Hyperbola**

21. $x = -3(y^2 + 4y + 4) - 5 + 12$
$x = -3(y + 2)^2 + 7$
Parabola with vertex: $(7, -2)$
Axis of symmetry: $y = -2$
Opens to the left

22. Find the equation of the line $\perp$ to
$y = -x + 5$ that passes through $(2, 5)$.
$m_\perp = -1$
$y = x + b$
$5 = 2 + b$
$b = 3$
$y = x + 3$

Solve $y = -x + 5$ and $y = x + 3$
simultaneously.
$-x + 5 = x + 3$
$2x = 2$
$x = 1$
$y = 1 + 3 = 4$
$(x, y) = (1, 4)$

$d = \sqrt{(1 - 2)^2 + (4 - 5)^2} = \sqrt{2}$

23. $x = 5y - 3$
$5y = x + 3$
$y = \dfrac{1}{5}x + \dfrac{3}{5}$

24. $\dfrac{\frac{1}{4}}{1 - \left(-\frac{3}{4}\right)} = \dfrac{1}{4} \cdot \dfrac{4}{7} = \dfrac{1}{7}$

25. Base $= 6^2 = 36$
$V = \dfrac{1}{3}(36)(8) = \mathbf{96\ cm^3}$

26.
$x = \dfrac{\begin{vmatrix} -1 & 3 & 1 \\ -4 & 2 & -3 \\ -5 & 4 & 0 \end{vmatrix}}{\begin{vmatrix} 2 & 3 & 1 \\ 0 & 2 & -3 \\ 3 & 4 & 0 \end{vmatrix}}$

$= \dfrac{-1\begin{vmatrix} 2 & -3 \\ 4 & 0 \end{vmatrix} - 3\begin{vmatrix} -4 & -3 \\ -5 & 0 \end{vmatrix} + 1\begin{vmatrix} -4 & 2 \\ -5 & 4 \end{vmatrix}}{2\begin{vmatrix} 2 & -3 \\ 4 & 0 \end{vmatrix} - 3\begin{vmatrix} 0 & -3 \\ 3 & 0 \end{vmatrix} + 1\begin{vmatrix} 0 & 2 \\ 3 & 4 \end{vmatrix}}$

$= \dfrac{-1(0 + 12) - 3(0 - 15) + 1(-16 + 10)}{2(0 + 12) - 3(0 + 9) + 1(0 - 6)}$

$= \dfrac{-12 + 45 - 6}{24 - 27 - 6} = -\dfrac{27}{9} = -3$

27. $(8\ \text{cis}\ 270°)^{1/3}$

First root $= \sqrt[3]{8}\ \text{cis}\ \dfrac{270°}{3} = 2\ \text{cis}\ 90°$

Angles differ by $\dfrac{360°}{3} = 120°$

$2\ \text{cis}\ 210°,\ 2\ \text{cis}\ 330°$
$2\ \text{cis}\ 90° = 2(0 + i) = 2i$

$2\ \text{cis}\ 210° = 2\left(-\dfrac{\sqrt{3}}{2} - \dfrac{1}{2}i\right) = -\sqrt{3} - i$

$2\ \text{cis}\ 330° = 2\left(\dfrac{\sqrt{3}}{2} - \dfrac{1}{2}i\right) = \sqrt{3} - i$

28. $3\tan^2 x = 1$
$\tan^2 x = \dfrac{1}{3}$

$\tan x = \pm\dfrac{\sqrt{3}}{3}$
$x = \mathbf{30°, 150°, 210°, 330°}$

29. $\dfrac{2\sec 2x}{\sec 2x + 1} = \dfrac{\dfrac{2}{\cos 2x}}{\dfrac{1}{\cos 2x} + 1}$

$= \dfrac{\dfrac{2}{\cos 2x}}{\dfrac{1 + \cos 2x}{\cos 2x}} = \dfrac{2}{\cos 2x} \cdot \dfrac{\cos 2x}{1 + \cos 2x}$

$= \dfrac{2}{1 + \cos 2x} = \dfrac{2}{1 + (2\cos^2 x - 1)}$

$= \dfrac{2}{2\cos^2 x} = \dfrac{1}{\cos^2 x} = \sec^2 x$

30. $x - 1 > 0$ $x - 1 < 2^2$
   $x > 1$ $x < 5$
   $1 < x < 5$

EP

97. $x = \begin{bmatrix} -1 & -3 \\ 2 & -7 \end{bmatrix} + \begin{bmatrix} 1 & 3 \\ 2 & 4 \end{bmatrix} = \begin{bmatrix} 0 & 0 \\ 4 & -3 \end{bmatrix}$

98. For $k = 1$, we get $3^1 = \dfrac{3(3^1 - 1)}{2}$

$3 = \dfrac{3(2)}{2}$

And $\dfrac{3(3^k - 1)}{2} + 3^{k+1} = \dfrac{3^{k+1} - 3 + 2\,(3^{k+1})}{2}$

$= \dfrac{3(3^{k+1}) - 3}{2} = \dfrac{3(3^{k+1} - 1)}{2}$

PROBLEM SET 114

1. $5 \, \# \, (4 * 3)$
   $5 \, \# \, (4 - 3(3))$
   $5 \, \# \, (-5)$
   $2(5) + 3(-5) = \mathbf{-5}$

2. $4(90 - A) = 180 - B + 70$
   $360 - 4A = 180 - B + 70$
   $-4A + B = -110$
   (1) $B = 4A - 110$

   $5(90 - B) = 3(180 - A) - 220$
   $450 - 5B = 540 - 3A - 220$
   (2) $3A - 5B = -130$
   Substitute equation (1) into (2).
   $3A - 5(4A - 110) = -130$
   $3A - 20A + 550 = -130$
   $A = \mathbf{40^\circ}$
   $B = 4(40) - 110 = \mathbf{50^\circ}$

3. $m = \dfrac{kpv^3}{\sqrt{k}} = \dfrac{k(3p)(3v)^3}{\sqrt{4k}} = \dfrac{81kpv^3}{2\sqrt{k}}$

   Multiplied by $\dfrac{81}{2}$

4. $0.2 + 0.5 - 0.3 = \mathbf{0.4}$

5. | 26 | 25 | 24 | 10 | 9 | 8 | 7 | $= \mathbf{78{,}624{,}000}$

6. $x(4 + x) = 8(5)$
   $4x + x^2 = 40$
   $x^2 + 4x - 40 = 0$
   $x = \dfrac{-4 \pm \sqrt{16 - 4(1)(-4)}}{2(1)}$
   $= \dfrac{-4 \pm \sqrt{176}}{2} = \dfrac{-4 \pm 4\sqrt{11}}{2} = \mathbf{-2 + 2\sqrt{11}}$

7. $\angle SRU = \dfrac{1}{2}\overset{\frown}{SU}$, $\angle STU = \dfrac{1}{2}\overset{\frown}{SU}$ because the measure of an inscribed angle is one-half the measure of the intercepted arc. $\angle SRU = \angle STU$ by substitution. $\angle P = \angle P$ because vertical $\angle$'s are equal. $\triangle RPU \sim \triangle TPS$ by AA. $\dfrac{PR}{TP} = \dfrac{UP}{SP}$ by proportion. $(PR)(SP) = (TP)(UP)$ by multiplication.

8. $(9 + x)x = 8^2$
   $x^2 + 9x - 64 = 0$
   $x = \dfrac{-9 \pm \sqrt{81 - 4(1)(4)}}{2(1)} = \dfrac{-9 \pm \sqrt{337}}{2}$

9. $\angle TRS = \dfrac{1}{2}\overset{\frown}{TS}$, $\angle STK = \dfrac{1}{2}\overset{\frown}{TS}$ because the measure of an inscribed angle is one-half the measure of the intercepted arc. $\angle TRS = \angle STK$ by substitution. $\angle K = \angle K$ by reflexive property. $\triangle RKT \sim \triangle TKS$ by AA. $\dfrac{KT}{RK} = \dfrac{KS}{KT}$ by proportion. $(KT)^2 = (KS)(RK)$ by multiplication.

10. $\angle C = \dfrac{1}{2}\overset{\frown}{AD}$, $\angle B = \dfrac{1}{2}\overset{\frown}{AD}$ because the measure of an inscribed angle is one-half the measure of the intercepted arc. $\angle C = \angle B$ by substitution. $\angle AEC = \angle DEB$ because vertical $\angle$'s are equal. $\triangle AEC \sim \triangle DEB$ by AA. $\dfrac{AE}{ED} = \dfrac{CE}{EB}$ by proportion. $(AE)(EB) = (CE)(ED)$ by multiplication.

11. Refer to Example 111.B.3.

12.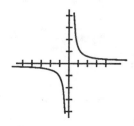

13. $y = \dfrac{(x + 2)(x - 3)}{x + 2}$

$y = x - 3$

Hole at $\begin{cases} x = -2 \\ y = -5 \end{cases}$

14. $y = \dfrac{(x - 2)(x + 3)}{x - 2}$

$y = x + 3$

Hole at $\begin{cases} x = 2 \\ y = 5 \end{cases}$

15.

16. $\dfrac{\text{Integer factors of 2}}{\text{Integer factors of 6}} = \dfrac{\pm 1, \pm 2}{\pm 1, \pm 2, \pm 3, \pm 6}$

Possible roots $\pm\dfrac{1}{6}, \pm\dfrac{1}{3}, \pm\dfrac{1}{2}, \pm\dfrac{2}{3}, \pm 1, \pm 2$

17. No. They could have a common factor.

18. Refer to Solution Set 77, problem 6.

19. $f(x) = \begin{cases} -1 & x < -2 \\ -x - 2 & -2 \le x \le 0 \\ 2x & 0 < x \le 1 \\ 2 & x > 1 \end{cases}$

20. $y = x^3 - x^2 - 10x - 8$

x	y
0	-8
-2	0
-1	0
2	24
4	0

21. Downs $= \dfrac{a_1(1 - r^n)}{1 - r}$

$a_1 = 256, r = \dfrac{3}{4} = \dfrac{256\left[1 - \left(\dfrac{3}{4}\right)^5\right]}{1 - \dfrac{3}{4}} = 781$

Ups $= 781 - 256 = 525$

Total $= 781 + 525 = \mathbf{1306\ ft}$

22. $x = 2y + 4$

$2y = x - 4$

$y = \dfrac{1}{2}x - 2$

23.
(a) **Hyperbola**
(b) **Parabola**
(c) **Circle**
(d) **Parabola**
(e) **Ellipse**

24. Base $= 9^2 = 81$

$V = \dfrac{1}{3}(81)(4) = \mathbf{108\ m^3}$

25. $(x^2 + 4x + 4) - 4(y^2 - 8y + 16)$

$= 96 + 4 - 64 = 36$

$(x + 2)^2 - 4(y - 4)^2 = 36$

$\dfrac{(x + 2)^2}{36} - \dfrac{(y - 4)^2}{9} = 1$

Center: (-2, 4)

Vertices: (4, 4), (-8, 4)

Asymptotes: $y = \dfrac{1}{2}x + 5$

$y = -\dfrac{1}{2}x + 3$

26. $\begin{bmatrix} 1 & 2 & 1 & 7 \\ 0 & 3 & -2 & 0 \\ 2 & -1 & 0 & -2 \end{bmatrix} = \begin{bmatrix} 1 & 2 & 1 & 7 \\ 0 & 3 & -2 & 0 \\ 0 & -5 & -2 & -16 \end{bmatrix}$

$= \begin{bmatrix} 1 & 0 & \dfrac{7}{3} & 7 \\ 0 & 1 & -\dfrac{2}{3} & 0 \\ 0 & 0 & -\dfrac{16}{3} & -16 \end{bmatrix} = \begin{bmatrix} 1 & 0 & 0 & 0 \\ 0 & 1 & 0 & 2 \\ 0 & 0 & 1 & 3 \end{bmatrix}$

$x = 0$

$y = 2$

$z = 3$

27. $(4 + 6i)^{1/3}$

$r = \sqrt{4^2 + 6^2} = \sqrt{52} = 2\sqrt{13}$

$\theta = \tan^{-1}\left(\dfrac{6}{4}\right) \approx 56.3°$

$\left(2\sqrt{13} \text{ cis } 56.3°\right)^{1/3}$

First root $= \dfrac{2\sqrt{13}}{3} \text{ cis } \dfrac{56.3°}{3} \approx$ **2.4 cis 18.8°**

Angles differ by $\dfrac{360°}{3} = 120°$

2.4 cis 138.8°, 2.4 cis 258.8°

28. $\dfrac{1}{2}\cot x \sec^2 x = \dfrac{1}{2}\dfrac{\cos x}{\sin x} \cdot \dfrac{1}{\cos^2 x}$

$= \dfrac{1}{2\sin x \cos x} = \dfrac{1}{\sin 2x} = \csc 2x$

29. $3(\sec^2 x - 1) + 5\sec x + 1 = 0$

$3\sec^2 x - 3 + 5\sec x + 1 = 0$

$3\sec^2 x + 5\sec x - 2 = 0$

$(3\sec x - 1)(\sec x + 2) = 0$

$\sec x = \dfrac{1}{3}$ $\qquad$ $\sec x = -2$

$\varnothing$ $\qquad\qquad$ $\cos x = -\dfrac{1}{2}$

$x = \mathbf{120°, 240°}$

30. $\sqrt{\log_2 x} = \dfrac{1}{3}\log_2 x$

$\log_2 x = \dfrac{1}{9}\left(\log_2 x\right)^2$

$\dfrac{1}{9}(\log_2 x)^2 - \log_2 x = 0$

$(\log_2 x)\left(\dfrac{1}{9}\log_2 x - 1\right) = 0$

$\log_2 x = 0$ $\qquad$ $\dfrac{1}{9}\log_2 x - 1 = 0$

$x = 2^0$ $\qquad\qquad$ $x = 2^9$

$x = \mathbf{1, 2^9}$

EP

99. For $k = 1$, we get $2^1 = 2(2^1 - 1)$
And $2(2^k - 1) + 2^{k+1}$
$= 2(2^{k+1}) - 2 = 2(2^{k+1} - 1)$

100. $\begin{bmatrix} x(2) + (2)(3) & x(-1) + (2)(4) \\ (2)(2) + (1)(3) & (2)(-1) + (1)(4) \end{bmatrix}$

$= \begin{bmatrix} 2x + 6 & -x + 8 \\ 7 & 2 \end{bmatrix}$

PROBLEM SET 115

1. Downstream: $\quad (3C + C)(T - 1) = 90$
$\qquad\qquad\qquad 4CT - 4C = 90$

   Upstream: $\qquad (3C - C)T = 48$
   $\qquad\qquad\qquad 2CT = 48$
   $\qquad\qquad\qquad CT = 24$

   $4(24) - 4C = 90$
   $-4C = -6$
   $C = \dfrac{3}{2}$ **mph**

   $B = 3C = 3\left(\dfrac{3}{2}\right) = \dfrac{9}{2}$ **mph**

2. $\dfrac{R}{B} = \dfrac{1}{2}$

   A: $2R = B$
   $\quad G - R = 7$
   B: $G = R + 7$
   $\quad R + B = 1 + G$
   C: $R + B - G = 1$
   Substitute equations A and B into C.
   $R + 2R - (R + 7) = 1$
   $2R = 8$

   $R = \mathbf{4}$
   $B = 2(4) = \mathbf{8}$
   $G = 4 + 7 = \mathbf{11}$

3. $\dfrac{P_1 V_1}{T_1} = \dfrac{P_2 V_2}{T_2}$
   $P_1 V_1 = P_2 V_2$
   $(5)(40) = (1)P_2$
   $P_2 = \mathbf{200 \text{ atm}}$

4. $\qquad 4(90 - A) = 2(180 - B) + 40$
   $\qquad 360 - 4A = 360 - 2B + 40$
   A: $-4A + 2B = 40$
   $\qquad 180 - A = 2(90 - B) + 70$
   $\qquad 180 - A = 180 - 2B + 70$
   B: $-A + 2B = 70$
   Subtract equation B from A.
   $-3A = -30$
   $A = \mathbf{10°}$
   $B = \dfrac{1}{2}(70 + 10) = \mathbf{40°}$

5. $440 = 1460e^{360k}$
$0.30137 = e^{360k}$
$e^{-1.1994} = e^{360k}$
$k \approx -0.00333$

$730 = 1460e^{-0.00333t}$
$0.5 = e^{-0.00333t}$
$e^{-0.693} = e^{-0.00333t}$
$t \approx \mathbf{208\ min}$

6. Refer to Example 115.A.1.

7. $x_f = x_1 + \dfrac{4}{11}\left(x_2 - x_1\right)$

$= x_1 + \dfrac{4}{11}x_2 - \dfrac{4}{11}x_1 = \dfrac{7x_1 + 4x_2}{11}$

$y_f = y_1 + \dfrac{4}{11}\left(y_2 - y_1\right)$

$= y_1 + \dfrac{4}{11}y_2 - \dfrac{4}{11}y_1 = \dfrac{7y_1 + 4y_2}{11}$

8. $x_f = 2 + \dfrac{1}{4}(6 - 2) = 2 + 1 = 3$

$y_f = 4 + \dfrac{1}{4}(6 - 4) = 4 + \dfrac{1}{2} = \dfrac{9}{2}$

$\left(3, \dfrac{9}{2}\right)$

9. $6(4) = (5 + a)(a)$
$24 = 5a + a^2$
$a^2 + 5a - 24 = 0$
$(a + 8)(a - 3) = 0$
$a = \mathbf{3}$

10. Refer to Solution Set 114, problem 7.

11. $(12 + x)(x) = 8^2$
$12x + x^2 = 64$
$x^2 + 12x - 64 = 0$
$(x + 16)(x - 4) = 0$
$x = \mathbf{4}$

12. Refer to Solution Set 114, problem 9.

13. $36z = 9(12)$
$36z = 108$
$z = \mathbf{3}$

14. Refer to Solution Set 114, problem 10.

15.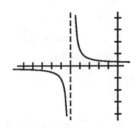

16.

17. $y = \dfrac{(x + 2)(x - 1)}{x + 2}$
$y = x - 1$
Hole at $\begin{cases} x = -2 \\ y = -3 \end{cases}$

18. **No.** All nonzero even integers have a factor of 2.

19. $\dfrac{\text{Integer factors of 5}}{\text{Integer factors of 8}} = \dfrac{\pm 1, \pm 5}{\pm 1, \pm 2, \pm 4, \pm 8}$

Possible roots: $\pm\dfrac{1}{8}, \pm\dfrac{1}{4}, \pm\dfrac{1}{2}, \pm\dfrac{5}{8}, \pm 1, \pm\dfrac{5}{4}, \pm\dfrac{5}{2}, \pm 5$

20. $y = x^3 + 2x^2 - 9x - 18$

x	y
-3	0
-2	0
0	-18
3	0

21. $f(x) = \begin{cases} x + 1 & x \le -1 \\ -2 & -1 < x < 1 \\ x - 1 & x \ge 1 \end{cases}$

22. $S_n = \dfrac{n}{2}\left[2a_1 + (n - 1)d\right]$

23. (*a*) **Circle**
(*b*) **Hyperbola**
(*c*) **Hyperbola**
(*d*) **Parabola**
(*e*) **Ellipse**

24. Construction

25. $16x^2 + 25(y^2 - 12y + 36)$
$= -500 + 900 = 400$
$\dfrac{x^2}{25} + \dfrac{(y - 6)^2}{16} = 1$
Center: $(0, 6)$
Major axis: 10
Minor axis: 8

26. Base $= 3^2 = 9$
$V = \dfrac{1}{3}(9)(6) = 18 \text{ cm}^3$

27. $(8 \operatorname{cis} 90°)^{1/3}$
First root $= \sqrt[3]{8} \operatorname{cis} \dfrac{90°}{3} = 2 \operatorname{cis} 30°$
Angles differ by $\dfrac{360°}{3} = 120°$
$2 \operatorname{cis} 150°, 2 \operatorname{cis} 270°$
$2 \operatorname{cis} 30° = 2\left(\dfrac{\sqrt{3}}{2} + \dfrac{1}{2}i\right) = \sqrt{3} + i$
$2 \operatorname{cis} 150° = 2\left(-\dfrac{\sqrt{3}}{2} + \dfrac{1}{2}i\right) = -\sqrt{3} + i$
$2 \operatorname{cis} 270° = 2(0 - i) = -2i$

28. $\cos\theta = \dfrac{1}{\sqrt{2}} = \dfrac{\sqrt{2}}{2}$
$\theta = 45°, 315°$

29. $\dfrac{\sin x}{\tan x + 3 \sin x}$
$= \dfrac{\sin x}{\dfrac{\sin x}{\cos x} + \dfrac{3\sin x\cos x}{\cos x}} = \dfrac{\sin x}{\dfrac{\sin x(1 + 3\cos x)}{\cos x}}$
$= \dfrac{\sin x}{1} \cdot \dfrac{\cos x}{\sin x(1 + 3\cos x)}$
$= \dfrac{\cos x}{1 + 3\cos x} = \dfrac{\dfrac{1}{\sec x}}{1 + 3\left(\dfrac{1}{\sec x}\right)}$
$= \dfrac{\dfrac{1}{\sec x}}{\dfrac{\sec x + 3}{\sec x}} = \dfrac{1}{\sec x + 3}$

30. $\sqrt{\log_3 x} = \dfrac{1}{4}\log_3 x$
$\log_3 x = \dfrac{1}{16}\left(\log_3 x\right)^2$
$\dfrac{1}{16}\left(\log_3 x\right)^2 - \log_3 x = 0$
$(\log_3 x)\left(\dfrac{1}{16}\log_3 x - 1\right) = 0$
$\log_3 x = 0 \qquad\qquad \log_3 x = 16$
$x = 3^0 \qquad\qquad\quad x = 3^{16}$
$x = 1, 3^{16}$

EP

101. **Invalid**

102. $\begin{bmatrix} 1 & -1 \\ 1 & 0 \end{bmatrix} - x = \begin{bmatrix} 2 & -1 \\ -2 & 1 \end{bmatrix}$
$x = \begin{bmatrix} 1 & -1 \\ 1 & 0 \end{bmatrix} - \begin{bmatrix} 2 & -1 \\ -2 & 1 \end{bmatrix}$
$= \begin{bmatrix} -1 & 0 \\ 3 & -1 \end{bmatrix}$

PROBLEM SET 116

1. $1100 = 960e^{14k}$
$1.1458 = e^{14k}$
$e^{0.13613} = e^{14k}$
$k \approx 0.009724$
$2400 = 960e^{0.009724t}$
$2.5 = e^{0.009724t}$
$e^{0.91629} = e^{0.009724t}$
$t \approx 94.2 \text{ min}$
$94.2 + 6 \approx \textbf{100.2 min}$

2. $R = \dfrac{kG}{p^2}$
$25 = \dfrac{k(10)}{20^2}$
$k = 1000$

$R = \dfrac{1000(30)}{2^2} = \textbf{7500}$

3. $0.4 + 0.7 - x = 0.85$
$x = \textbf{0.25}$

4. Refer to Solution Set 75, problem 5.

5. Cost + markup = selling price
$C + 0.40C = 2800$
$1.4C = 2800$
$C = 2000$
$2000 + 0.20(2000) = \$2400$

6.

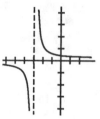

7. $y = \dfrac{-2(x + 3)}{(x + 3)(x + 1)}$

$y = \dfrac{-2}{x + 1}$

Hole at $\begin{cases} x = -3 \\ y = 1 \end{cases}$

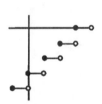

8.

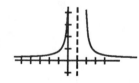

9. Asymptote: $x = 1$

10. $y = -x^3 + x^2 + 10x + 8$

x	y
-2	0
-1	0
0	8
1	18
4	0

11. $\dfrac{\text{Integer factors of } 56}{\text{Integer factors of } 6} = \dfrac{\pm 1, \pm 5}{\pm 1, \pm 2, \pm 3, \pm 6}$

Possible roots: $\pm\dfrac{1}{6}, \pm\dfrac{1}{3}, \pm\dfrac{1}{2}, \pm\dfrac{5}{6}, \pm 1, \pm\dfrac{5}{3}, \pm\dfrac{5}{2}, \pm 5$

12. $f(x) = \begin{cases} -x - 1 & x \le -1 \\ -2 & -1 < x < 1 \\ x - 1 & x \ge 1 \end{cases}$

13. Downs $= \dfrac{a_1}{1 - r} = \dfrac{100}{1 - \dfrac{1}{4}} = \dfrac{400}{3}$

Ups $= \dfrac{400}{3} - 100 = \dfrac{100}{3}$

Total $= \dfrac{400}{3} + \dfrac{100}{3} = \dfrac{500}{3}$ ft

15. (a) **Ellipse**
(b) **Ellipse**
(c) **Hyperbola**
(d) **Parabola**
(e) **Circle**

16. (a) $V = \dfrac{1}{3}\pi r^2 h = \dfrac{1}{3}\pi(6^2)(4) = \mathbf{48\pi}$ **in³**

(b) $SA = \pi r^2 + \pi r s$
$= \pi(6^2) + \pi(6)\left(2\sqrt{13}\right)$
$= \left(\mathbf{36\pi + 12\pi\sqrt{13}}\right)$ **in²**

17. $25(x^2 - 8x + 16) - 4(y^2 + 2y + 1)$
$= -796 - 4 + 400 = -400$
$\dfrac{25(x - 4)^2}{-400} - \dfrac{4(y + 1)^2}{-400} = \dfrac{-400}{-400}$
$\dfrac{(y + 1)^2}{100} - \dfrac{(x + 4)^2}{16} = 1$
Center: (4, −1)
Vertices: (4, 9), (4, −11)
Asymptotes: $y = \dfrac{5}{2}x - 11$
$y = -\dfrac{5}{2}x + 9$

18. $(3 + a)3 = (a + 3)a$
$9 + 3a = a^2 + 3a$
$a^2 = 9$
$a = 3$

19. $\angle SRU = \dfrac{1}{2}\overset{\frown}{SU} = \angle STU$ because the

measure of an inscribed angle is equal to one-half the measure of the intercepted arc. $\angle P = \angle P$ by reflexive property. $\triangle PRU \sim \triangle PTS$ by AA. $\dfrac{RP}{UP} = \dfrac{PT}{SP}$ by proportion. $(RP)(SP) = (UP)(PT)$ by multiplication.

20. $(3x + x)x = 10^2$
$4x^2 = 100$
$x^2 = 25$
$x = 5$

21. Refer to Solution Set 114, problem 9.

22. Refer to Solution Set 114, problem 10.

23. $\overline{QS}$ is $\perp$ bisector of $\overline{PR}$ is given. $PU = UR$, $\angle QUP$ and $\angle QUR$ are right $\angle$'s by def. of bisector. $QU = QU$ by reflexive property. $\Delta PQU \cong \Delta RQU$ by SAS. $PQ = QR$ by CPCTE. $\overline{RS}$ is $\perp$ bisector of $\overline{QT}$ is given. $QV = VT$, ΔQVR and ΔRVT are right triangles by def. of bisector. $RV = RV$ by reflexive property. $\Delta QVR \cong \Delta TVR$ by SAS. $QR = RT$ by CPCTE. $PQ = RT$ by substitution.

24. $\sqrt{xy} = 10$
$xy = 100$
$\dfrac{x + y}{2} = 26$
$x + y = 52$
$y = 52 - x$
$x(52 - x) = 100$
$52x - x^2 = 100$
$x^2 - 52x + 100 = 0$
$(x - 50)(x - 2) = 0$
$x = 50, 2$
Numbers = **50, 2**

25. Sides = $\dfrac{4}{1}$
Volume = $\left(\dfrac{4}{1}\right)^3 = \dfrac{64}{1}$
Ratio = **64 : 1**

26. $pH = -\log(4.5 \times 10^{-6})$
$= -(0.6532 - 6) \approx$ **5.3**

27.
$$\begin{bmatrix} 2 & 1 & 1 & 2 \\ 0 & 2 & -3 & -9 \\ 3 & 0 & -2 & 4 \end{bmatrix} = \begin{bmatrix} 1 & \frac{1}{2} & \frac{1}{2} & 1 \\ 0 & 2 & -3 & -9 \\ 0 & -\frac{3}{2} & -\frac{7}{2} & 1 \end{bmatrix}$$

$$\begin{bmatrix} 1 & 0 & 0 & \frac{13}{4} \\ 0 & 1 & -\frac{3}{2} & -\frac{9}{2} \\ 0 & 0 & -\frac{23}{2} & -\frac{23}{2} \end{bmatrix} = \begin{bmatrix} 1 & 0 & 0 & 2 \\ 0 & 1 & 0 & -3 \\ 0 & 0 & 1 & 1 \end{bmatrix}$$

$x = 2$
$y = -3$
$z = 1$

28. $(\sin^2 x + 1)(\cot^2 x + 1)$
$= (\sin^2 x + 1)(\csc^2 x)$
$= \sin^2 x \csc^2 x + \csc^2 x = 1 + \csc^2 x$

29. $2(1 - \sin^2 x) - 9\sin x + 3 = 0$
$2 - 2\sin^2 x - 9\sin x + 3 = 0$
$2\sin^2 x + 9\sin x - 5 = 0$
$(2\sin x - 1)(\sin x + 5) = 0$
$\sin x = \dfrac{1}{2}$ $\sin x = 5$
$x = 30°, 150°$ $\emptyset$

30. $3^{-4} = \dfrac{1}{81}$

EP

103. For $k = 1$, we get $4 \cdot 1 + 1 = 2 \cdot 1 + 3 \cdot 1$
$5 = 2 + 3$
And $2k^2 + 3k + (4k + 5)$
$= (2k^2 + 4k + 2) + (3k + 3)$
$= 2(k + 1)^2 + 3(k + 1)$

104. **Valid**

PROBLEM SET 117

1. $1180 = 1200e^{10k}$
$0.983 = e^{10k}$
$e^{-0.01681} = e^{10k}$
$k \approx -0.00168$

$600 = 1200e^{-0.00168t}$
$0.5 = e^{-0.00168t}$
$e^{-0.693} = e^{-0.00168t}$
$t \approx$ **412.4 min**

2. T = tens' digit
U = units' digit
$10T + U$ = original number
$10U + T$ = reversed number
A $4T = 2U + 2$
   $U = 2T - 1$
B: $10U + T = 10T + U + 27$
   $9U = 9T + 27$
   $U = T + 3$
$2T - 1 = T + 3$
$T = 4$
$U = 4 + 3 = 7$
Original number = **47**

3. Rate · time · men = jobs
Rate · 7 · 5 = 3
Rate = $\dfrac{3}{35}$

$\dfrac{3}{35} \cdot (p - 2) \cdot (k + 5)$ = jobs

$\dfrac{3(p - 2)(k + 5)}{35}$ jobs

4. $R_R T_R + R_G T_G$ = jobs
$\left(\dfrac{1}{2}\right)h + R_G h = k$

$R_G h = k - \dfrac{h}{2}$

$R_G = \dfrac{k - \dfrac{h}{2}}{h} = \dfrac{\dfrac{2k - h}{2}}{h} = \dfrac{2k - h}{2h}$

$T_G = \dfrac{2h}{2k - h}$ hr

5. $\dfrac{280}{40}$ = \$7.00
$7.00 \times 0.20 = 1.40$
$8.40(50)$ = **\$420**

6. Construction

7. Construction

8. Construction

9. $(5x)(3x) = (16 + 2x)(2x + 2)$
$15x^2 = 32x + 32 + 4x^2 + 4x$
$11x^2 - 36x - 32 = 0$
$(11x + 8)(x - 4) = 0$
$x = \mathbf{4}$

10. $(7 + x)x = 12^2$
$x^2 + 7x = 144$
$x^2 + 7x - 144 = 0$
$(x - 9)(x + 16) = 0$
$x = \mathbf{9}$

11. Refer to Solution Set 114, problem 7.

12. Refer to Example 111.B.3.

13. $\angle TRS = \dfrac{1}{2}\overset{\frown}{SK} = \angle STK$ because the measure of an inscribed angle is one-half the measure of the intercepted arc. $\angle K = \angle K$ by reflexive property. $\triangle TSK \sim \triangle RTK$ by AA. $\dfrac{KR}{KT} = \dfrac{RT}{TS}$ by proportion. $(KR)(TS) = (KT)(RT)$ by multiplication.

14. Asymptote: $x = 2$

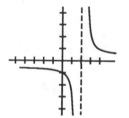

15. $y = \dfrac{-2(x - 1)}{(x + 3)(x - 1)}$
$y = \dfrac{-2}{x + 3}$
Asymptote: $x = -3$
Hole at $\begin{cases} x = 1 \\ y = -\dfrac{1}{2} \end{cases}$

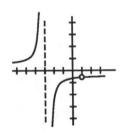

16.

17.

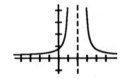

18. $y = x^3 + x^2 - 36x - 36$

x	y
-6	0
-1	0
0	-36
6	0

19. $\dfrac{\text{Integer factors of 3}}{\text{Integer factors of 8}} = \dfrac{\pm 1, \pm 3}{\pm 1, \pm 2, \pm 4, \pm 8}$

Possible roots: $\pm\dfrac{1}{8}, \pm\dfrac{1}{4}, \pm\dfrac{3}{8}, \pm\dfrac{1}{2}, \pm\dfrac{3}{4}, \pm 1, \pm\dfrac{3}{2}, \pm 3$

20. $S_n = \dfrac{n}{2}\left[2a_1 + (n-1)d\right]$

21. $f(x) = \begin{cases} -4 & x \le -3 \\ -2 & -3 < x \le 0 \\ x & 0 < x \le 2 \\ 3 & x > 2 \end{cases}$

22. $x = x_1 + \dfrac{2}{3}\left(x_2 - x_1\right)$

$= 4 + \dfrac{2}{3}(-2 - 4) = 4 + (-4) = 0$

$y = y_1 + \dfrac{2}{3}\left(y_2 - y_1\right)$

$= -2 + \dfrac{2}{3}(-5 + 2) = -2 - 2 = -4$

$(0, -4)$

23. (a) Circle
(b) Ellipse
(c) Hyperbola
(d) Parabola
(e) Parabola

24. $V = \dfrac{4}{3}\pi r^3$

$A = 4\pi r^2$

25. $y = -4\left(x^2 - 5x + \dfrac{25}{4}\right) - 41 + 25$

$y = -4\left(x - \dfrac{5}{2}\right)^2 - 16$

Vertex: $\left(\dfrac{5}{2}, -16\right)$

Axis of symmetry: $x = \dfrac{5}{2}$

Opens down

26. Yes

27. $16^{1/4} = (16 \text{ cis } 0°)^{1/4}$

First root $= \sqrt[4]{16}\text{ cis }\dfrac{0°}{4} = 2\text{ cis }0°$

Angles differ by $\dfrac{360°}{4} = 90°$

$2\text{ cis }0° = 2(1 + 0i) = 2$

$2\text{ cis }90° = 2(0 + i) = 2i$

$2\text{ cis }180° = 2(-1 + 0i) = -2$

$2\text{ cis }270° = 2(0 - i) = -2i$

28. $\dfrac{\cos x}{1 + 3\sin x} = \dfrac{\cos x}{\dfrac{\cos x}{\sin x} + \dfrac{3\cos x \sin x}{\sin x}}$

$= \dfrac{\cos x}{\dfrac{\cos x(1 + 3\sin x)}{\sin x}} = \dfrac{\sin x}{1 + 3\sin x}$

$= \dfrac{\dfrac{1}{\csc x}}{1 + \dfrac{3}{\csc x}} = \dfrac{\dfrac{1}{\csc x}}{\dfrac{\csc x + 3}{\csc x}} = \dfrac{1}{\csc x + 3}$

29. $2\sin x + \dfrac{2}{\sin x} - 5 = 0$

$2\sin^2 x + 2 - 5\sin x = 0$

$(2\sin x - 1)(\sin x - 2) = 0$

$\sin x = \dfrac{1}{2} \qquad\qquad \sin x = 2$

$x = 30°, 150° \qquad\qquad \varnothing$

30. $\log_b \dfrac{M}{N} = \log_b \dfrac{b^a}{b^c} = \log_b b^{a-c}$

$= a - c = \log_b M - \log_b N$

EP

105. For $k = 1$, we get $\dfrac{1 \cdot 2}{2}$

$= \dfrac{1(1+1)(1+1)}{6} \cdot \dfrac{2}{2} = \dfrac{2(3)}{6}$

$\dfrac{k(k+1)(k+2)}{6} + \dfrac{(k+1)(k+2)}{2}$

$= \dfrac{k(k+1)(k+2) + 3(k+1)(k+2)}{6}$

$= \dfrac{(k+1)(k+2)(k+3)}{6}$

$= \dfrac{(k+1)[(k+1)+1][(k+1)+2]}{6}$

PROBLEM SET 118

1. $2800 = 400e^{26k}$
$7 = e^{26k}$
$e^{1.9459} = e^{26k}$
$k = 0.07484$

$5000 = 400e^{0.074843t}$
$12.5 = e^{0.074843t}$
$e^{2.52572} = e^{0.074843t}$
$t \approx 33.74$
$33.47 + 14 \approx \textbf{47.7 years}$

2. $R_B T_B = 1120$
$R_W T_W = 400$
$R_B = R_W + 20$
$T_B = 2T_W$

$\left(R_W + 20\right)\left(2T_W\right) = 1120$
$2R_W T_W + 40T_W = 1120$
$2(400) + 40T_W = 1120$
$40T_W = 320$
$T_W = \textbf{8 hr}$
$T_B = 2(8) = \textbf{16 hr}$
$R_W = \dfrac{400}{8} = \textbf{50 mph}$
$R_B = \dfrac{1120}{16} = \textbf{70 mph}$

3. A: $10F = 2S - 180$
$5F = S - 90$
$S = 5F + 90$

B: $\dfrac{1}{2}S = 3F + 40$
$S = 6F + 80$
$5F + 90 = 6F + 80$
$F = \textbf{10}$
$S = 5(10) + 90 = \textbf{140}$

4. $R_1 T_1 + R_2 T_2 = 1$
$\left(\dfrac{2}{3}\right)T - \left(\dfrac{1}{4}\right)T = 1$
$8T - 3T = 12$
$5T = 12$
$T = \dfrac{12}{5} \textbf{ hr}$

5. $\dfrac{2}{6} \cdot \dfrac{3}{6} = \dfrac{6}{36} = \dfrac{1}{6}$

6. Possible roots: $\pm\dfrac{1}{4}, \pm\dfrac{1}{2}, \pm\dfrac{3}{4}, \pm 1, \pm\dfrac{3}{2}, \pm 3$

$$\begin{array}{r|rrrr} -1 & 4 & -4 & -5 & 3 \\ & & -4 & 8 & -3 \\ \hline & 4 & -8 & 3 & 0 \end{array}$$

$4x^2 - 8x + 3 = 0$
$(2x - 1)(2x - 3) = 0$
$x = \dfrac{1}{2} \qquad\qquad x = \dfrac{3}{2}$
Roots $= \textbf{-1}, \dfrac{\textbf{1}}{\textbf{2}}, \dfrac{\textbf{3}}{\textbf{2}}$

7. Possible roots: $\pm\dfrac{1}{4}, \pm\dfrac{1}{2}, \pm\dfrac{3}{4}, \pm 1, \pm\dfrac{3}{2}, \pm 2, \pm 3, \pm 6$

$$\begin{array}{r|rrrr} -2 & 4 & 0 & -13 & 6 \\ & & -8 & 16 & -6 \\ \hline & 4 & -8 & 3 & 0 \end{array}$$

$4x^2 - 8x + 3 = 0$
$(2x - 1)(2x - 3)$
$x = \dfrac{1}{2} \qquad\qquad x = \dfrac{3}{2}$
Roots $= \textbf{-2}, \dfrac{\textbf{1}}{\textbf{2}}, \dfrac{\textbf{3}}{\textbf{2}}$

8. Asymptote: $x = 3$

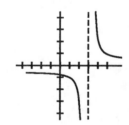

9. $y = \dfrac{-2(x + 3)}{(x + 3)(x + 2)}$
$y = \dfrac{-2}{x + 2}$
Asymptote: $x = -2$
Hole at $\begin{cases} x = -3 \\ y = 2 \end{cases}$

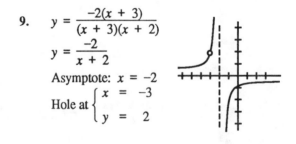

10.

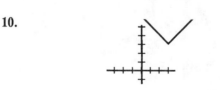

11. Asymptote: $x = 3$

12. $x = 2y - 4$
$2y = x + 4$
$y = \dfrac{1}{2}x + 2$

13. $y = 4x^3 - 4x^2 - 5x + 3$

x	y
-1	0
0	3
$\dfrac{1}{2}$	0
1	-2
$\dfrac{3}{2}$	0

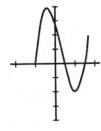

14. $x = 2 + \dfrac{2}{5}(-5 - 2)$
$= 2 - \dfrac{14}{5} = -\dfrac{4}{5}$

$y = 4 + \dfrac{2}{5}(2 - 4)$
$= 4 + \left(-\dfrac{4}{5}\right) = \dfrac{16}{5}$

$\left(-\dfrac{4}{5}, \dfrac{16}{5}\right)$

15. Refer to Solution Set 114, problem 7.

16. $(3 + x)3 = (2x - 4)(x - 1)$
$9 + 3x = 2x^2 - 2x - 4x + 4$
$2x^2 - 9x - 5 = 0$
$(2x + 1)(x - 5) = 0$
$x = 5$

17. Refer to Solution Set 114, problem 9.

18. Refer to Solution Set 76, problem 6.

19. Construction

20. Construction

21. Refer to Solution Set 88, problem 7.

22. Refer to Solution Set 88, problem 6.

23. $f(x) = \begin{cases} -1 & x < -3 \\ x - 1 & -3 \le x \le 1 \\ 1 & 1 < x \le 4 \\ 3 & x > 4 \end{cases}$

24. Base $= 5^2 = 25$
$V = \dfrac{1}{3}(25)(9) = \textbf{75 cm}^3$

25. (a) **Parabola**
(b) **Parabola**
(c) **Hyperbola**
(d) **Ellipse**
(e) **Circle**

26. $4(x^2 + 10x + 25) + 36(y^2 - 8y + 16)$
$= -532 + 100 + 576 = 144$
$\dfrac{(x + 5)^2}{36} + \dfrac{(y - 4)^2}{4} = 1$
Center: (-5, 4)
Major axis: 12
Minor axis: 4

27. $(-4 + 6i)^{1/3}$
$r = \sqrt{16 + 36} \approx 7.2$
$\theta = \tan^{-1}\left(-\dfrac{6}{4}\right) \approx 123.7°$
$(7.2 \text{ cis } 123.7°)^{1/3}$
First root $= \sqrt[3]{7.2} \text{ cis } \dfrac{123.7°}{3}$
$\approx \textbf{1.9 cis 41.2}°$
Angles differ by $\dfrac{360°}{3} = 120°$
1.9 cis 161.2°, 1.9 cis 281.2°

28. $\cos 2x + \sin 2x + 2\sin^2 x$
$= \cos^2 x - \sin^2 x + 2\sin x \cos x + 2\sin^2 x$
$= \sin^2 x + 2\sin x \cos x + \cos^2 x$
$= (\sin x + \cos x)^2$

29. $2\dfrac{\cos^2 x}{\sin^2 x} + \dfrac{3}{\sin x} = 0$
$2\cos^2 x + 3\sin x = 0$
$2(1 - \sin^2 x) + 3\sin x = 0$
$2 - 2\sin^2 x + 3\sin x = 0$
$2\sin^2 x - 3\sin x - 2 = 0$
$(2\sin x + 1)(\sin x - 2) = 0$
$\sin x = -\dfrac{1}{2} \qquad \sin x = 2$
$x = \textbf{210°, 330°} \qquad \emptyset$

30. $\dfrac{\log 10}{\log 7} = \dfrac{1}{\log 7}$

EP

107. For $k = 1$, we get $(3 \cdot 1 - 2)$

$= \dfrac{1(3 \cdot 1 - 1)}{2} \cdot (3 - 2) = \dfrac{3 - 1}{2}$

$\dfrac{k(3k - 1)}{2} + (3k + 1)$

$= \dfrac{k(3k - 1) + 2(3k + 1)}{2} = \dfrac{3k^2 + 5k + 2}{2}$

$= \dfrac{(k + 1)(3k + 2)}{2} = \dfrac{(k + 1)[3(k + 1) - 1]}{2}$

108. **Invalid**

PROBLEM SET 119

1. $500 = 800\, e^{2k}$
$0.625 = e^{2k}$
$e^{-0.47} = e^{2k}$
$k \approx -0.235$
$A_5 = 800\, e^{-0.235(5)} \approx \mathbf{247}$

2. $R_C T_C = 240$
$R_W T_W = 160$
$R_W = \dfrac{160}{T_W}$
$R_C = R_W + 20$
$T_C = T_W - 2$

$\Big(R_W + 20\Big)(T_W - 2) = 240$
$R_W T_W - 2R_W + 20T_W - 40 = 240$
$160 - 2R_W + 20T_W = 280$
$-2R_W + 20T_W = 120$
$R_W - 10T_W = -60$
$\dfrac{160}{T_W} - 10T_W = -60$
$160 - 10T_W^2 = -60T_W$
$10T_W^2 - 60T_W - 160 = 0$
$T_W^2 - 6T_W - 16 = 0$
$\Big(T_W - 8\Big)\Big(T_W + 2\Big) = 0$
$T_W = \mathbf{8}$
$T_C = 8 - 2 = \mathbf{6}$
$R_W = \dfrac{160}{8} = \mathbf{20}$
$R_C = 20 + 20 = \mathbf{40}$

3. A: $10N_R = 2N_B + 26$
$\qquad N_B = 5N_R - 13$

B: $N_B = N_R + 7$
$N_R + 7 = 5N_R - 13$
$4N_R = 20$

$N_R = \mathbf{5}$
$N_B = 5(5) - 13 = \mathbf{12}$

4. $\dfrac{26}{52} + \dfrac{4}{52} - \dfrac{2}{52} = \dfrac{28}{52} = \dfrac{7}{13}$

5.
$$\begin{array}{r|rrrr}
2 & 1 & -6 & 13 & -10 \\
  &   & 2 & -8 & 0 \\
\hline
  & 1 & -4 & 5 & 0
\end{array}$$
$x^2 - 4x + 5 = 0$
$x = \dfrac{4 \pm \sqrt{16 - 4(1)(5)}}{2(1)}$
$= \dfrac{4 \pm \sqrt{-4}}{2} = \dfrac{4 \pm 2i}{2} = \mathbf{2 \pm i}$

6.
$$\begin{array}{r|rrrr}
1 & 3 & -1 & 2 & -4 \\
  &   & 3 & 2 & 4 \\
\hline
  & 3 & 2 & 4 & 0
\end{array}$$
$3x^2 + 2x + 4 = 0$
$x = \dfrac{-2 \pm \sqrt{4 - 4(3)(4)}}{2(3)}$
$= \dfrac{-2 \pm \sqrt{-44}}{6} = \dfrac{-2 \pm 2\sqrt{11}}{6} = -\dfrac{1}{3} \pm \dfrac{\sqrt{11}}{3}\, i$

7. $x^4 - 2x^3 + 3x^2 + 4x - 7 = 0$
3 sign changes
1 or 3 positive roots

8. $f(-x) = 3x^4 + 4x^3 + 2x^2 - 5x - 2 = 0$
1 sign change
1 negative root

9. $6x^5 - 17x^4 - 3x^3 + 22x^2 - 7x + 20 = 0$
4 sign changes
0, 2, or 4 positive roots

10. $f(-x) = -2x^5 - 3x^4 + 5x^3 + 11x^2 + 4x + 5 = 0$
1 sign change
1 negative root

11.

```
4| 1   0   -21   19
       4   16   -20
   ─────────────────
     1   4   -5   -1
```

```
5| 1   0   -21   19
       5   25   20
   ─────────────────
     1   5   4   39
```

All positive; **5 is upper bound**

```
-4| 1    0   -21   19
        -4   16   20
   ──────────────────
     1   -4   -5   39
```

```
-5| 1    0   -21   19
        -5   25   -20
   ──────────────────
     1   -5   4   -1
```

Signs alternate; **−5 is lower bound**

12.

```
3| 1   -2   0   -17    5
        2   0    0   -24
   ─────────────────────
     1   1   3   -8   -19
```

```
4| 1   -2   0   -17    5
        4   8   32    60
   ─────────────────────
     1   2   8   15   65
```

All positive; **4 is upper bound**

```
0| 1   -2   0   -17   5
        0   0    0    0
   ────────────────────
     1   -2   0   -17   5
```

Signs alternate; **0 is lower bound**

13. Possible roots: $\pm 1, \pm 2$

```
1| 1   2   -1   -2
       1   3    2
   ────────────────
     1   3   2   0
```

$x^2 + 3x + 2 = 0$
$(x + 2)(x + 1) = 0$
$x = -1, -2$
Roots = **1, −1, −2**

14. Possible roots: $\pm 1, \pm 2, \pm 3, \pm 4, \pm 6, \pm 12$

```
3| 1   -3   4   -12
        3   0    12
   ─────────────────
     1   0   4    0
```

$x^2 + 4 = 0$
$x^2 = -4$
$x = \pm 2i$
Roots = **3, 2i, −2i**

15. Asymptote: $x = 4$

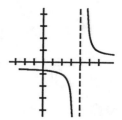

16.

17. Asymptote: $x = 2$

18. $x = 5y + 6$
$5y = x - 6$
$y = \dfrac{1}{5}x - \dfrac{6}{5}$

19. $x = 3 + \dfrac{1}{4}(-4 - 3) = 3 + \left(-\dfrac{7}{4}\right) = \dfrac{5}{4}$

$y = 5 + \dfrac{1}{4}(-3 - 5) = 5 + (-2) = 3$

$\left(\dfrac{5}{4}, 3\right)$

20. Base $= 7^2 = 49$
$V = \dfrac{1}{3}(49)(12) = $ **196 ft³**

21. $(-i)^{1/4}$
$r = \sqrt{0^2 + (-1)^2} = 1$
$\theta = 270°$

First root $= \sqrt[4]{1}\ \text{cis}\ \dfrac{270°}{4} = $ **1 cis 67.5°**

Angles differ by $\dfrac{360°}{4} = 90°$

1 cis 157.5°, 1 cis 247.5°, 1 cis 337.5°

22. $\dfrac{\log 72}{\log 6} \approx 2.387$

23. Refer to Solution Set 88, problem 7.

24. Refer to Solution Set 88, problem 6.

25. $4\dfrac{1}{2} + \dfrac{3}{5}\left(-10\dfrac{1}{5} - 4\dfrac{1}{2}\right)$

$= \dfrac{9}{2} + \dfrac{3}{5}\left(-\dfrac{51}{5} - \dfrac{9}{2}\right) = \dfrac{9}{2} + \dfrac{3}{5}\left(-\dfrac{102}{10} - \dfrac{45}{10}\right)$

$= \dfrac{9}{2} + \dfrac{3}{5}\left(-\dfrac{147}{10}\right) = \dfrac{9}{2} + \left(-\dfrac{147}{10}\right)$

$= \dfrac{225 - 441}{50} = -\dfrac{216}{50} = -\dfrac{108}{25}$